Philosophy in the Twentieth Century

Philosophy in the Twentieth Century

AN ANTHOLOGY

Volume Three

Edited and with Introductions
by

WILLIAM BARRETT
New York University

and

HENRY D. AIKEN
Harvard University

Random House : New York

First Trade Edition

 Published in New York by Random House, Inc. and simultaneously in Toronto, Canada, by Random House of Canada, Limited.
Library of Congress Catalog Card Number: 61–10672
Manufactured in the United States of America
by H. Wolff, New York

Contents

Volume One

3 : *The Fate of Philosophy in the Twentieth Century* HENRY D. AIKEN
19 : *The Twentieth Century in Its Philosophy* WILLIAM BARRETT

PART ONE

Pragmatism and America's Philosophical Coming of Age

47 : *Introduction* HENRY D. AIKEN

JOSIAH ROYCE

83 : *Reality and Idealism: The Inner World and Its Meaning*

CHARLES S. PEIRCE

105 : *How to Make Our Ideas Clear*
122 : *The Doctrine of Necessity*
136 : *What Pragmatism Is*

WILLIAM JAMES

152 : *The Sentiment of Rationality*
179 : *What Pragmatism Means*
193 : *Pragmatism's Conception of Truth*
207 : *Does 'Consciousness' Exist?*
222 : *A World of Pure Experience*
241 : *The Will To Believe*
259 : *The Varieties of Religious Experience: Conclusions and Postscript*

JOHN DEWEY

287 : *Some Historical Factors in Philosophical Reconstruction*

298 : *The Scientific Factor in Reconstruction of Philosophy*
309 : *Changed Conceptions of Experience and Reason*
321 : *Changed Conceptions of the Ideal and the Real*
334 : *Reconstruction in Moral Conceptions*
346 : *The Construction of Good*

GEORGE SANTAYANA

367 : *Dewey's Naturalistic Metaphysics*
381 : *There Is No First Principle of Criticism*
384 : *Dogma and Doubt*
387 : *Wayward Scepticism*
393 : *Doubts About Self-Consciousness*
397 : *Doubts About Change*
400 : *Ultimate Scepticism*
405 : *Nothing Given Exists*
410 : *Essence and Intuition*
415 : *Belief in Experience*
422 : *Belief in the Self*
425 : *The Cognitive Claims of Memory*
434 : *Knowledge Is Faith Mediated by Symbols*
445 : *Belief in Substance*
451 : *Hypostatic Ethics*

Volume Two

PART TWO

The Rise of Analytical Philosophy in England

463 : *Introduction* HENRY D. AIKEN

F. H. BRADLEY

497 : *The Absolute and Its Appearances*

G. E. MOORE

520 : *What Is Philosophy?*
543 : *The Refutation of Idealism*
561 : *A Defence of Common Sense*
584 : *Proof of the External World*
603 : *The Subject-Matter of Ethics*

BERTRAND RUSSELL

630 : *Logic as the Essence of Philosophy*
646 : *On Our Knowledge of the External World*
666 : *The World of Physics and the World of Sense*
683 : *On the Notion of Cause, with Applications to the Free-Will Problem*
703 : *A Free Man's Worship*

LUDWIG WITTGENSTEIN

710 : *The Blue Book*

J. WISDOM AND J. L. AUSTIN

774 : *A Symposium: Other Minds*

ALFRED NORTH WHITEHEAD

822 : *The Origins of Modern Science*
836 : *Mathematics as an Element in the History of Thought*
851 : *The Century of Genius*
865 : *Nature Alive*

Volume Three

PART THREE

Positivism

3 : *Introduction* WILLIAM BARRETT

MORITZ SCHLICK

23 : *Unanswerable Questions?*
28 : *Meaning and Verification*

A. J. AYER

52 : *The Elimination of Metaphysics*
63 : *The Function of Philosophy*
74 : *The* A Priori
87 : *Critique of Ethics and Theology*

W. V. QUINE

102 : *Two Dogmas of Empiricism*

PART FOUR

Phenomenology and Existentialism

125 : *Introduction* WILLIAM BARRETT

Germany

EDMUND HUSSERL

171 : *The Thesis of the Natural Standpoint and Its Suspension*

179 : *Consciousness and Natural Reality*

MARTIN HEIDEGGER

206 : *The Way Back into the Ground of Metaphysics*

219 : *The Fundamental Question of Metaphysics*

251 : *Plato's Doctrine of Truth*

270 : *Letter on Humanism*

France

HENRI BERGSON

303 : *An Introduction to Metaphysics*

331 : *Time in the History of Western Philosophy*

GABRIEL MARCEL

364 : *On the Ontological Mystery*

JEAN-PAUL SARTRE

387 : *Materialism and Revolution*

ALBERT CAMUS

430 : *Thought at the Meridian*

Volume Four

PART FIVE

Marxism and the Philosophy of History

453 : *Introduction* WILLIAM BARRETT

BENEDETTO CROCE

471 : *Art and Philosophy*

478 : *Ideal Genesis and Dissolution of the 'Philosophy of History'*

489 : *The Positivity of History*

496 : *Philosophy and Methodology*

V. I. LENIN

505 : *How Certain "Marxists" in 1908 and Certain Idealists in 1710 Refuted Materialism*

518 : *The Theory of Knowledge of Empirio-Criticism and of Dialectical Materialism*

561 : *On Dialectics*

KARL JASPERS

565 : *The Axial Period*

584 : *The Present Situation of the World*

597 : *The Unity of History*

PART SIX

Neo-Orthodoxy

617 : *Introduction* WILLIAM BARRETT

ETIENNE GILSON

629 : *The Spirit of Thomism*

PAUL TILLICH

652 : *Courage and Individualization*

668 : *Courage and Transcendence*

MARTIN BUBER

688 : *What Is Man?*

PART THREE

Positivism

Introduction

1.

Though positivism is not a philosophic creation of the twentieth century, it has nevertheless had such radical reformulation and elaboration in our period as to make it almost a transmutation of the original doctrine propounded by Auguste Comte (1798-1857) in the nineteenth century. Hence, some members of this school have preferred to call their doctrine logical empiricism—to indicate it is an empiricism grounded on logical analysis rather than upon historical generalization as in the case of Comte. Yet it is the name positivism that sticks, both in common usage and in ordinary philosophical reference; and historically there would seem to be good sense in this usage that links up this contemporary philosophy, no matter how more precisely and differently elaborated, with its nineteenth-century progenitor.

Both in its nineteenth-century and its contemporary version, positivism is a school formed on the Continent. Yet it is not at all typical of the traditional spirit of Continental philosophy, since its provenance is in so many ways British. In this book it follows naturally and logically after British analysis since its point of departure, philosophically speaking, was Bertrand Russell in his middle period. This was the Russell who had given up his earlier Platonic Realism and turned to the empiricism of David Hume; above all, the Russell who had co-authored the *Principia Mathematica* with Alfred North Whitehead, for mathematical logic was to play a leading role in the formulation of modern positivism. And Russell himself has perhaps made the most succinct and incisive summation in a single sentence of the total attitude of positivism:

> Whatever knowledge is attainable, must be attained by scientific methods; and what science cannot discover, mankind cannot know.

Moreover, the movement, once it had developed on the Continent, obtained in another Englishman, Professor A. J. Ayer, its most vigorous and popular spokesman. Thus as a sign of national traits and the role they play in philosophy, it is noteworthy that the only empiricist school that developed on the European Continent in this century was an offspring of British philosophy, the doughty and perpetual guardian of European empiricism.

The connecting link between Russell and the Continent in this case was Ludwig Wittgenstein, whose *Tractatus Logico-Philosophicus* appeared in 1922. For Wittgenstein himself, as has already been indicated in this book, the *Tractatus* was only a stage on his philosophic way, and he was to go on to develop and change his positions in most radical ways. Nevertheless the *Tractatus,* bold in its conception and dogmatic in tone, was to be the seminal influence upon a group of young and vigorous minds: Moritz Schlick, Rudolf Carnap, Otto Neurath. Associated with them were also Karl Popper, Hans Reichenbach, who was developing a parallel notion of "scientific philosophy" in Berlin; the physicist Philip Frank; and the mathematician Richard von Mises. The group around Carnap and Schlick became known as the "Vienna Circle." Wittgenstein himself never actually took part in the activities of this group, but his influence was dominant at the start.

There were two main points in the *Tractatus* that formed the point of departure for the philosophizing of this group:

(1.) *Logical Atomism.* The world, for Wittgenstein, was an assemblage of atomic facts. These facts were mirrored in language. Between fact and sentence there was a similarity of structure. (The true logical language, it was believed, was that of *Principia Mathematica,* and the structure of the world resembled the structure of the *Principia.*) These atomic facts, supposedly, would be reported in elementary sentences, called "protocol statements"; and such protocol statements—"Here now is a red patch"—would be the building bricks for all of science.

(2.) *The distinction between logical and empirical propositions.* Wittgenstein seemed to have at long last established the final and clear distinction between factual propositions and the propositions of mathematics and logic. The latter were tautologies, and hence said nothing about the world. This allowed positivists to escape from the ancient view of the semisacred character of mathematics as a body of eternal truths about eternal objects only imperfectly manifested in sensory experience. The whole of mathematics now was viewed as an elaborate systems of symbols for saying that A=A.

Actually, it was not Wittgenstein but Russell who first publicly proclaimed these principles of logical atomism in 1918. However, Russell gives full and candid acknowledgment that he had learned these views from his "pupil," Wittgenstein. The acknowledgment is touching not only as testimony of the free give-and-take of ideas between the two men that made it possible for the teacher in this case to be the learner; there is even a warmer human note in Russell's declaration of his intellectual debt, for at this time Russell did not know whether Wittgenstein, who had disappeared into the Austrian Army at the outbreak of war, was still alive. The later divergence of the two philosophers must be seen against this earlier and warmer glow of intellectual comradeship.

To be sure, these ideas had already been implicit in Russell's thinking; Wittgenstein was simply bolder and more extreme in pushing them to the limit. They were already implicit in the influence upon Russell of another thinker without whom any history of positivism would be incomplete: Ernst Mach (1838-1916), to whom Russell also acknowledges a considerable debt. Mach, a physicist, had ventured into philosophy primarily as a means of clarifying the concepts of physics itself. He viewed physical science as a system of conventions whose function was to be descriptive and predictive of sensory experience. The whole complex structure of science is thus merely a means of getting us from one sensory experience to another. Accordingly, the working concepts of physics—those that were not merely otiose—must be grounded in sensory experience; and Mach undertook the task of showing further that these concepts must in fact be grounded ultimately in elementary sensations. Where the concept was not thus grounded it was to be rejected as void, useless, a relic of mythology.

Aware of all these influences, and acting to consolidate them, the younger men on the Continent were now conscious of themselves as a distinct philosophical school and heirs of a considerable philosophic tradition. If they used the word "positivist" to characterize their own thought, they were very careful to distinguish themselves from the original founder of positivism, Auguste Comte. Comte had based his own positivism upon a grand and sweeping historical speculation: human history, he said, had passed through the successive stages of religion and metaphysics, and now, after the French Revolution, mankind had at last reached the age of science. In this last stage the theories of metaphysicians would simply become obsolete, like the myths of primitives at an earlier stage. Comte's philosophy was thus a philosophical expression of the sweeping rationalism that had found political and social expression in the French Revolution. Moreover, it reflected the historical optimism of the Enlightenment that reason in the form of "the positive sciences" had at last come into its own and that if the methods of these sciences were applied universally the superstitions of the past would disappear like the shadows of night before the advancing dawn. By contrast, contemporary positivists have engaged in no historical speculations whatever; their doctrine, they insist, is not based upon any generalization from history—which would in any case be improper evidence according to their own conception of philosophy—

but upon the inescapable consequences of the logical analysis of language. The events of the twentieth century hardly tempt one to base one's belief in reason upon the facts of history.

From the point of view of philosophical analysis rather than historical speculation, a truer ancestor of modern positivism than Auguste Comte in the nineteenth century is David Hume of the eighteenth century. Despite all the apparatus of modern mathematical logic that contemporary positivism has employed, the simple core of its philosophical position is already to be found in Hume. The two key points in the Humean philosophy that prefigure Positivism are:

> (1) The distinction between truths about the relations of ideas, as in logic and mathematics, and truths about matters of fact, as in the empirical sciences; and
> (2) The attempted reduction of all ideas to sensory experiences, which Hume called "impressions" and the moderns "sense-data."

These have been continuing and cardinal points of empiricist doctrine since Hume; and, quite properly, they are the two points on which Professor Quine, in his essay "Two Dogmas of Empiricism," asks for a revaluation of the Positivist position.

Hume used his distinction between the two kinds of statements—the formal statements of logic and mathematics and the empirical statements about matters of fact—as a means of attack upon the metaphysicians. There is his famous advice to the reader, applauded by all positivists, that any book that contains neither statements about relations of ideas, as in logic and mathematics, nor statements about matters of fact, as in the empirical sciences, but purports to carry statements of some other kind than either of these, should be committed to the flames. Yet Hume himself was not consistent throughout with this rigid division. It is not clear that Hume would subsume moral judgments under either of these two classes of statements; and it is not clear either, despite all the doubts he casts on rational theology, that he does not leave one argument for the existence of God as plausible. On this question of the intrinsic impossibility of rational theology, Kant provided a far more strict and consistent model for positivists than did Hume.

Hume's distinction between the two kinds of statements was taken over by Kant, who baptized them as analytic and synthetic propositions—the names under which they have been discussed ever since. An analytic proposition is one in which the predicate is already contained in the very concept of the subject—"A bachelor is an unmarried male," to use Professor Quine's delicate example. In a synthetic proposition, on the other hand, the predicate is not contained in the idea of the subject but does add something new to it—as, in elementary physics, the proposition "The distance traversed by a falling body is proportional to the square of the time." Quite clearly, synthetic propositions are those that genuinely add to our knowledge, since the predicate brings us new information about the subject. We could drone on an endless litany of those dull analytic propositions that logicians delight to use as examples—"A bald man is a man," "A rose is a rose," etc., etc.—and the dreary process would afford us not one whit more knowledge of the world. The synthetic propositions, on the contrary, are the real building bricks out of which the structure of genuine knowledge is made.

Now, Kant held that certain synthetic propositions are *a priori*—known certainly to be true apart from experience. Among these synthetic a priori propositions were the truths of mathematics, and certain propositions of mathematical physics. The famous example from mathematics that Kant gave was the proposition "$7 + 5 = 12$." This is synthetic, according to Kant, because the predicate does not merely repeat the subject but requires the synthesizing and constructive act of counting.

The positivists reject the position of Kant on this matter; and this rejection provides perhaps the simplest key to the whole philosophy of modern positivism. Moritz Schlick himself has said that the whole of Positivism could be summed up in one statement: There are no synthetic a priori truths. A proposition in which the predicate adds to our knowledge of the subject must be based upon experience; hence all valid propositions of this kind belong to the empirical sciences, and no proposition that has genuine content can go beyond the bounds of possible experience. What then about the propositions of mathematics? How are they to be regarded? It is here that the contribution of Wittgenstein became decisive for the positivists, since he had seemed to succeed at last in showing that all mathematical propositions could be regarded as tautologies, so many intricate ways of saying "$A = A$"; and as tautologies they said nothing about the world. They were truths that were simply consequent upon our decision to use symbols in a certain way. The *Principia Mathematica* of Russell and Whitehead had paved the way, it seemed, for this view of mathematics, and that is why its imposing achievement seemed to the positivists such a solid buttress for their own philosophic position. The *Principia,* for example, using an axiomatization of arithmetic worked out by the Italian mathematician Peano toward the end of the nineteenth century could easily reduce Kant's example,

$$7 + 5 = 12$$

to the tautology:

$$1+1+1+1+1+1+1+1+1+1+1+1=1+1+1+1+1+1+1+1+1+1+1+1,$$

where the bare identity says nothing, and consequently has no synthetic or constructive character.

Armed thus with what looked like an invincible simplicity and clarity, positivism entered the lists of twentieth-century philosophy. In fact, it was spoiling for battle since the very simplicity of its position was an onslaught upon traditional philosophy. (The reader will gather some impression of the revolutionary élan of the movement from the ebullient and sweeping tone of Professor A. J. Ayer's contribution.) For where the traditional philosopher, according to the positivist, claims to be speaking about Reality or the world, he would be talking about matters of fact, and questions of matters of fact can only be settled by the empirical sciences. The rejection of metaphysics, therefore, becomes automatic and thoroughgoing. It is not that the propositions of metaphysics about the ultimate nature of reality are false, or that they are unknowable to us in this life; but that they are in their very nature "meaningless"—incapable of being established as either true or false. There are no unknowable mysteries but only propositions illogically formed by theologians and metaphysicians. The formal statements in logic and mathematics have meaning because we have chosen to use symbols in a certain way; the propositions of empirical science have meaning because there is a determinate process by means of which we can arrive at some sensory verification or refutation of them. But no such path leads from the utterances of metaphysicians about the nature of the world to any definite sensory observations that confirm or falsify these utterances. In a properly constructed language—which would never be ordinary language with its slipshod looseness—the statements of metaphysicians could not even be made; and hence the error of their ways would be obvious to everybody.

If, then, philosophy in this day and age can no longer claim to talk about reality or the nature of the world, what is left for philosophers to do? The positivist's answer to this question too is in keeping with the radical simplicity of his approach: All that is left for the philosopher to "do" is the logical analysis of language. But this analysis, it must be emphasized, is quite different from the kind envisaged by the school of British analysts, especially as these latter have felt the influence of the later Wittgenstein. The analysis of language, the positivist holds, can only be pursued profitably from the point of view of a formally constructed language that achieves a scientific precision and clarity not possible in ordinary language. Hence, he is not concerned, like his British cousin, in hunting down the meanings of words through all the byways and thickets of ordinary usage. Ordinary language may be closer to the actual occasions of life; but as an analyst, however he may be as a human person, the positivist is on the side of science and precision over against the diffuseness of ordinary life. This fundamental difference of orientation on the matter of language has led to some bitter wrangling in recent years between positivists and the younger British analysts. The outcome of this wrangling, not now apparent, ought to be one of the interesting developments of philosophy in this century.

But if metaphysics is to be thrown out, there still remain other branches of traditional philosophy—Ethics and Aesthetics, notably—and the question arises as to what is to become of them. Here the radical simplifications of positivism encountered sore spots that have not yet been salved. What kind of statements, in fact, are moral and aesthetic judgments? Clearly, they are not analytic statements like those of logic and mathematics: they are not concerned simply with the logical consequences of certain symbols. But just as clearly, they are not to be taken as statements about matters of fact, even though when we say "That action is good" or "That painting is beautiful" we may appear to be saying something about an objective fact. The statement "That painting is red" may be confirmed by simple sensory observation and its truth be agreed upon by all normal observers; but no strictly comparable process of confirmation holds for the proposition "That painting is beautiful." What, then, is to be done with value statements, since they do not seem to fit into the neat dualistic scheme of analytic and synthetic established by positivism?

The answer of positivism was a simple and straightforward subjectivism. All value statements are emotive expressions: they do not state something about an object but express how we feel about it. They are not meaningless statements, but they are in no sense cognitive. They have, as it is sometimes put, emotive meaning but not cognitive meaning. For a variety of reasons, which we cannot go into here, the simple emotive theory of value judgments has had repeatedly to be tinkered with and made more complicated. Whether or not all these successive qualifications of the original simple theory have been entirely satisfactory, remains in doubt; but they are part of the vital development of positivism in the last decades. Once again, it is the old story of an originally simple theory encountering the stubborn variety of fact and having to become considerably more flexible.

2.

There were other basic matters on which positivism was to change its point of view during the 1930's. One of these is the second of the two principles of positivism already cited: all statements about physical objects, as well as all terms referring to physical objects, could be reduced respectively to statements and terms involving reference only to sense-data. This is the position commonly designated as phenomenalism.

In 1927 Rudolf Carnap[1] published *Der Logische Aufbau der Welt —The Logical Structure of the World,* a title which surely sounds strange

[1] We regret very much that Professor Carnap is not represented in this collection. He thought his earlier work not sufficiently representative of his present views. His later work seemed to us too specifically technical.

coming from the lips of a positivist since it seems to imply at least four metaphysical assertions: (a) that there is a world; (b) that it has a logical structure; (c) that it has only one logical structure; and (d) that this logical structure is the one being described in the book. Actually, the book was about none of these things, but was simply an attempt to work out a phenomenalistic language for science in the most rigorous way possible by using the logical apparatus of *Principia Mathematica.* The basic terms in this language would refer only to the data of sensory experience; all statements referring to physical objects were to be exhibited as statements referring to classes of sensory data. This table, for example, on which I am writing could be spoken of as the aggregate of all the sensory data my experience of it yields. Carnap was here trying to carry out in a rigorous manner the original proposals, left rather sketchy and unformalized, of Mach and Russell.

By the mid-1930's Carnap had abandoned this effort to establish a thoroughly phenomenalistic language and replaced it by a new doctrine that he called physicalism. Instead of insisting on the reduction of all physical entities to sense-data, Carnap now proposed that terms referring to the recognizable physical objects and qualities within our ordinary environment—chairs and tables and the rest—could be taken as basic and unreduced terms within a precise and strict scientific language. The reduction of such objects to complexes or bundles or classes of sense-data, out of a supposed requirement of greater rigor, was now deemed unnecessary.

One impetus toward this new position came from Otto Neurath, who had adopted the point of view of behaviorism in psychology. The insistence upon the privileged and prior status of a sense-data language seemed to Neurath to lay the positivists open to the dangers of extreme subjectivism or even solipsism. In the discussions of positivists in the early 1930's—particularly on the question of "protocol sentences"—these dangers looked very real. Protocol sentences purported to report elementary experiences of sense-data: "Here now a red patch"; and scientific theories were looked upon not as referring to a world beyond language (which would have committed them to a metaphysics of realism), but simply as an elaborate means of connecting one set of protocol sentences with another. The general picture this left was that of a thoroughly private mind recording its own private data in protocol sentences but with no common world of reference for those sentences, and in such a picture the traces of Cartesian solipsism were all too strongly persistent. Neurath called attention to the fact of intersubjectivity in the scientific enterprise: in an experimental situation scientists take for granted the existence of the minds of other scientists who are sharing that experiment with them, as well as of the existence of the physical objects that make up the experimental apparatus. Indeed, science itself is premised upon this intersubjectivity of minds, for true confirmation of a theory is what can be confirmed also by other scientists. Moreover, Neurath pointed out, the application of scientific method in psychology had long gone away from "introspective psychology." To the extent that psychology applies experimental method it operates by observing external behavior and physical actions, and therefore takes the existence of bodies as quite evident. It seeks to understand the mental from the physical, not the other way about; hence there should no longer be the old phenomenalistic prejudice in favor of a language that based itself upon mental events like sensations.

All of this was persuasive to Carnap, and by 1937 he had formulated a new language for science that took simple physical terms as basic.

This step taken by positivism resembles the development in British analytic philosophy from Russell's phenomenalism to G. E. Moore's defense of common sense. Against Russell, Moore argued that statements about the recognizable and obvious physical objects in ordinary experience were just as certain as statements about sense-data; hence there was no need for a Cartesian skepticism to cast doubt on the existence of those objects. Yet there is a profound difference between the way in which Moore took his position and the parallel procedure of the positivists; and this difference illumines a fundamental difference between the British school and the positivists in their very modes of philosophizing. For Moore the position is one based on elaborate philosophical argument; for Carnap it is a matter of practical decision about the form of language that would be most convenient for scientific purposes. Moore's argument is a piece of dialectic in the traditional philosophic sense, and one, moreover, of considerable historical importance since it reverses the prejudice of three centuries of Cartesianism. The gist of this argument rests upon the meanings words actually do have in ordinary usage, not upon the conveniences of a formally constructed language: for what Moore essentially argues is that there are no valid "reasons" for holding "doubtful" the proposition "Here is a table" in favor of the supposed higher certainty of "I see a brown patch" in any ordinary sense of "doubtful." And Moore's position on this point is part and parcel of a general metaphysical conviction of realism that has been with him from the start: viz., the belief that physical objects do have an existence independent of mind.

Carnap's position, on the contrary, claims to assert no metaphysical doctrine of realism at all. The positivist is concerned with codifying a formal language adequate for the purposes of science. In doing this he no longer seeks to legislate a priori for the scientist, shackling the latter with an impossibly cumbersome sense-data language; he follows the scientist rather than prescribes for him; observing the linguistic behavior that is acceptable among scientists themselves, he attempts merely to codify this usage. For the physicist in the laboratory words that name things—particularly the recognizable things that compose his experimental set-up—are taken as understandable without being reduced to complexes of words that would name only sense-data. "Here," says the physicist, "is a weight, here a balance, here another weight"; and if he were required, in the name of some supposed higher certainty, to transform these into statements only about complexes of sense-data, he would become entangled in such laborious complications of language that he would hardly have time to get his experiment under way. Hence, Carnap's argument runs, the philosopher cannot have any valid theoretical objection to taking thing-words as basic and unreduced terms in a language. Scientific usage is the norm and measure. It is as simple as that.

Almost simultaneously with this transition from a language based on sense-data to a language based on physical objects, positivism broadened the scope of its logical analysis of language from Syntax to Semantics. Syntax permitted one to talk only about the formal structure of language without reference to what the terms of the language designated; in Semantics one could also talk about the things that the language designated. As in the transition from a phenomenalistic to a physicalistic language, here too the positivist could now escape the danger of solipsism—this time a solipsism that would leave him locked up in language itself without a means of reference to the things of which language spoke.

The breakthrough here came in a revolutionary paper in 1935 by Alfred Tarski, "On the Concept of Truth in Formalized Languages." Tarski showed how the traditional paradoxes involving the notion of truth could be avoided, and therefore truth could be talked about meaningfully and consistently in connection with the formal languages of logic and mathematics. To do this it was necessary to speak of what a statement designated, for a statement could be described as true only if what it designated was the case in fact. Tarski showed how this could be done rigorously for formal languages, and Carnap, quick to see the usefulness of this new approach, launched the idea of a general semantics: a discipline that could correlate the expressions of a language with their designata.

Hitherto, in their Humean and phenomenalistic phase, the positivists had shunned the idea of truth like the plague, for it seemed to carry with it inevitably the taint of metaphysics. In the history of philosophy, truth had too often been written Truth, capitalized as something supernal and quite beyond empirical confirmation. One can sympathize with the positivist's fear of contamination here, but this rejection of the concept itself of truth left a gaping hole; for ordinary language speaks quite naturally and without strain about statements as true or false, and scientists too accept or reject theories as true or false. Now however, after Tarski, it suddenly became possible to speak of truth without nonsense and without contradiction. The narrower discipline of logical syntax could now be safely embedded within the broader discipline of semantics; names once again could designate individuals, sentences could designate propositions, and positivism itself moved into the much broader uplands of philosophy, but without falling into the traditional ditch of metaphysics.

3.

In these developments within contemporary positivism the pragmatic motivation is unmistakably clear; and their net effect is equally clear: toward a more flexible doctrine, more adequate to describe the scientific, if not the human, condition. Professor Quine seeks to push this flexibility of mind one step further by relativizing the very distinction between analytic and synthetic statements on which positivism has based itself; and thereby bridging the chasm between the formal and empirical sciences.

His proposal has not won universal assent from contemporary philosophers. On the contrary, it has provoked outcries and catcalls from outraged traditionalists. Whether or not its argument proves ultimately valid, it is included in this collection not only for its own intrinsic merits as a piece of philosophical analysis but because it singles out the two continuing theses that make up the tradition of positivism and points beyond these to a future situation toward which this philosophy has been developing over the last decades: toward a rapprochement with pragmatism.

Quine's attitude throughout is strictly pragmatic. All human knowledge—the total body of science—is a tool for coping with experience. If there is a conflict with experience, we may change anything within that total body of knowledge in order to restore congruence between it and the conflicting experience. Knowledge can be regarded as a country that touches experience at its borders, or to change Quine's metaphor slightly: if there is a border clash, we may change the local border patrol or the provincial government; or the central government itself may be replaced by a revolution. Thus in a conflict with experience we may revise the local scientific law, the more general law, or even the central laws of logic and mathematics. Thus a logic has been proposed for quantum physics that would omit the law of the excluded middle. For the traditional Platonist, for whom the laws of logic and mathematics are the fundamental forms of Reason itself beyond time and change, this suggestion is nothing short of *lèse-majesté*. But if we take logic as an organon, as the first logic of Aristotle was called, then we should not shrink from recognizing its instrumental role. Logic is a man-made tool, forged by man and to be recast by him as his scientific purposes require. Quine's position here, though it moves within a relatively narrow orbit, is in line with one major development of twentieth-century philosophy shared by many schools: the relativizing of traditional Reason by recognizing that the forms of reason are eventual and constructed, forged by man within his total and determinate historic situation.

Now, if analytic and synthetic propositions are in the same boat because both are revisable instruments in the service of human knowledge, why seek to establish an iron-clad dualism between them? Such is the gist of Quine's contention.

More specifically, his argument turns on the difficulty of establishing definite rules for analyticity. An analytic proposition has been defined as one in which the predicate is included in the concept of the subject. Thus in "All bachelors are unmarried males" the idea of "unmarried male" is included in the very idea of "bachelor." They are, in fact, synonyms. The idea of synonymity would seem to be a very simple one; but it turns out to be extremely difficult to determine any *definite* rules for establishing what words are truly synonyms.

What lies behind Quine's arguments here, though he does not bring it explicitly forward, is the famous proof of the incompleteness of mathematics by Kurt Goedel in 1933. Goedel's result, one of the most epoch-making in modern mathematics, has consequences for the philosophy of mathematics that are only beginning to be felt by philosophers. Whether right or wrong in his argument, Quine has enough intellectual imagination to be in the vanguard here.

Goedel proved that any mathematical system rich enough to contain elementary arithmetic must also contain unprovable statements. Hence, no automatic procedure can be found for deciding whether any given statement is true or false within the system. No axioms will suffice to generate all the true statements in the system, for whatever axioms be chosen, there will always be unprovable statements. This means the formalization of the system will be forever incomplete. Mathematics remains an open rather than a closed system. No mechanical computer, however intricate and huge, will ever be constructed capable of grinding out all the theorems of mathematics.

This changes considerably the perspective on the definition of mathematical tautology that Wittgenstein had given in the *Tractatus* and that seemed so philosophically decisive at the time to the positivists. Wittgenstein had defined "analytic proposition" or "tautology" for the very narrow and restricted language of the propositional calculus. This language is definite and complete. There exists a mechanical procedure —Wittgenstein's truth-table device—for determining automatically whether any proposition in the system is true or false. In such a language it is easy to specify the conditions that determine the analytic or tautologous character of a proposition. But the situation is very different when one goes over to a richer and an indefinite language. Here there is no fixed procedure for determining the analyticity of a statement, and consequently the meaning of "analytic" itself is much harder to determine. Hence the tautologous or "empty" character of mathematical truths cannot be proclaimed in any clear-cut fashion.

All of this may look very technical to the reader. It *is;* but that does not mean that it is without profound philosophical significance. From the very beginning of Western philosophy in Plato, mathematics has had very great influence on philosophic thought—an influence that continues through Descartes, Leibniz, and Bertrand Russell. As the most rigorous of sciences, mathematics has provided the very model of what rationality and rational thought are, and what is the sweep of reason's powers. In the Western tradition—the tradition of Plato—mathematics has always been given a chosen status over against empirical science: its objects occupied some higher realm of Being or its methods permitted a ground of absolute certainty denied to the empirical sciences. Quine holds that Goedel's discovery obliterates the absolute distinction between the formal and empirical sciences; without going this far, we can at least say that Goedel's results do encourage us to look on mathematics in a somewhat different light from the traditional Platonic one. For mathematics as an incomplete system now becomes the field of mathematical activity, open perpetually to mathematical creativity and construction, but also guaranteed by no rock-bottom proof of consistency, and hence in its very richness exposed to the hazards and risks of paradox. This is a very far cry from the magical mathematical world of Pythagoras and Plato.

At the moment the whole philosophy of mathematics is in a state of flux. Part of the reason for this is that the philosophers, who in this case are truly birds of Minerva flying after the event, have not yet caught up with the fundamental discoveries of the mathematicians themselves in the field of the foundations of mathematics. The simple-minded clarity of the Russellian epoch seems to be at an end. This means that the positivistic view of mathematics—based as it was on Russell through the intermediary of the early Wittgenstein—may have to be remolded and qualified considerably in the years to come.

4.

This is not the only area in which we ought to expect further development on the part of positivism. For despite the great steps it has taken in the last decades toward the broadening of its doctrine, positivism still relegates to large areas of experience the role of poorly treated step-children. Perhaps in indicating some of these areas of difficulty, we may be better able to place positivism in the broad spectrum of twentieth-century philosophy, see how it is related to other contemporary philosophic schools, and gauge what it appears to be as a spiritual manifestation of the life of this period.

Its nearest kindred are the schools of British analytic philosophy and of pragmatism. It is close to the first in its origin and its general method of attack upon philosophical questions. In its later developments it has come closer to pragmatism in emphasizing the role of practical convenience in the choice of language that the philosopher or the scientist may make. It differs from both in that its range of reference is much narrower. As opposed to the British analysts who follow the later Wittgenstein, the positivist prefers not to deal with ordinary language but with some rational reconstruction of this language. This is quite understandable in the interests of precision and science: ordinary language has the flexible and organic variety of life itself, and it is a devilish business to try to trace the meanings of words through all their ramifications in usage. But the preference for a formal language does have the disadvantage of leaving one unable to deal with large areas of experience where our language is not yet ripe for any significant attempt at formalization. These areas may eventually become ripe for such formalization; then again, they may not; in the meantime they would remain untended if we were unwilling to deal with them in terms of the ordinary language in which they are at present expressed. And as for the difference with pragmatism, the gulf here is quite immense when one considers the variety of modes of experience—aesthetic, historical, religious—dealt with by William James and John Dewey. Toward such areas of experience the positivists have so far given at best a mere sidelong glance, at worst a peremptory rejection that makes impossible any fruitful attempt at interpretation at all.

This restriction of subject matter would not be very significant if we were also sure that it was not the result of some undue restriction of point of view. After all, a philosopher may be permitted to restrict himself to whatever problems he chooses; we have to be generous enough to allow him time to get around eventually to the matters he has neglected. The question is whether the basic position of positivism will not make impossible any adequate treatment of these bypassed, or in some cases rejected, areas. In philosophical terms: Is not the positivistic understanding of what is "cognitive," and what not, constructed on a much too narrow model?

In the case of metaphysics first: here one of the most positive accomplishments of positivism in its anti-metaphysical belligerence has been to make metaphysicians more uneasily conscious of stricter demands for clarity. (Its rough and aggressive attitude of no-nonsense has pricked the balloon of a good deal of empty rhetoric on the part of some philosophers.) To be sure, positivism has not destroyed the hydra whose hundred heads still keep rising; metaphysics goes on, and there are still metaphysicians; but probably no metaphysician today can write with that same high free-wheeling exuberance that the reader will find in this volume in the contribution by the absolute idealist F. H. Bradley. The speculative philosopher nowadays is likely to concede that his propositions do not have the same cognitive status as those of the positive sciences. The positivists have made their point. But this point—that metaphysics cannot claim the same cognitive status as the positive sciences—had already been advanced by Kant; yet Kant left open the way to a more flexible interpretation of the nature of metaphysics when he proposed that metaphysical statements had, if not a constitutive, at least a regulative role in knowledge. That is, to put Kant's point in the words of Peirce, metaphysical beliefs can function as guiding principles that lead to new discoveries or new theories in the positive sciences. And in fact, as such suggestive stimulants to scientific creation, metaphysical beliefs have played a continuing role throughout the history of science. The positivist's retort is that this usefulness of metaphysical beliefs is "merely psychological." But is the "merely psychological" so unimportant a thing when it leads to scientific creation? Could metaphysical beliefs have led to scientific creation if they were entirely "meaningless"? One can concede cheerfully that metaphysical statements do not have the same cognitive status as the statements of the positive sciences, but this concession need not be taken as equivalent to the assertion that the former are "meaningless." This last word hardly has such a simple and narrow meaning in ordinary language. The positivist has merely prescribed by fiat a definition of "meaningless" as "not a statement in logic or the physical sciences"—which he is perfectly free to do except that in his attack upon metaphysics he has made use of all the scathing emotional connotations that the word "meaningless" has in ordinary language.

It was something of a concession, though a half-hearted one, to the varieties of the meaningful that led positivism to add the notion of "emotive meaning," though at a considerably lower level, to that of "cognitive meaning." Yet it is very questionable whether the introduction of this notion helps very much since it is not accompanied by any attempt to grasp phenomenologically the nature of emotion or feeling. It seems to be assumed by the positivists that we know very clearly what emotions and feelings are like, and that we do not have to focus any direct and candid gaze on them. Feelings, it appears, are some kind of subcutaneous twinges, throbs, or tremors that in some odd way lie on the other side of mind from intellect and reason, which are the truly cognitive faculties. Yet any direct experience of numerous modes of feeling suggests that we cannot so sharply separate feeling from the cognitive. Ordinary language contains plenty of uses where we speak of knowledge in connection with the presence of feeling and ignorance in connection with its absence. There are situations in life, not so uncommon as might be thought, where the sheer dawning of a feeling upon a person is, directly as such, the dawning of an insight. Now he knows what is involved in this human situation because he feels, while his earlier absence of feeling was ignorance. Feeling is not a blind stab or spasm of some psychic substance underlying mind, but a form of consciousness that, like every other mode of consciousness, has its own intentionality and revelation. William James made this point long ago in a modest, but very significant, essay, "On a Certain Blindness in Human Beings"—the blindness being an absence of insight engendered by an inability to feel.

Thus the emotive theory of value judgments might fare better if the positivists were to give themselves to some direct scrutiny of the emotions themselves instead of merely passing them over as something altogether obvious in their nature. Value statements for the positivist, as we have already indicated, are not statements about an objective property of an act or thing; and not even statements at all, but emotional exclamations. "Ugh," "Ah!" "Unh-unh," "Mnn-MNNH," or with subtler inflection, "Haouaaahhh!" or with the full orchestration of Joyce, "Gooblazegrukbrukarchkrasht!"—such might be the proper linguistic translations, the positivist suggests, of our more artificial and deceitful value statements. These exclamations are not meant as mere spoofing; on the contrary they convey rather more definitely than words the primitive level of consciousness assigned to feeling. Whether or not we accept the contention that statements about values are not statements about objective qualities of things or actions but about our own subjective attitude toward these things or actions, still most of us would like to think that our own moral development as civilized beings from the unfeeling savagery of childhood and adolescence to the responsibility of adulthood is also a development in *understanding*. As yet the emotive theory has no satisfactory account of the human fact of moral development—and thus it hardly does justice to the humanity itself of *homo sapiens*.

This dualism between "the emotive" and "the cognitive" becomes all the harder to maintain when we come to the fields of art and the humanities. Not only does all our ordinary talk about works of art abound in expressions with cognitive implications, but the whole language of literary criticism, with all the weight of its tradition, is so similarly stocked that we can hardly believe there is nothing behind this usage and that we can dismiss it out of hand. We say of a certain novelist that he is a good technician but that his *understanding* of life is narrow, that Shakespeare has a much more profound and various *knowledge* of people than Milton, that the *vision* of Racine is subtler than that of Corneille, etc., etc. All of these expressions are patently cognitive in reference, but none can be successfully explicated as a form of scientific knowledge. If art does not express any vision, then there is left to it only the power to incite feelings. But what then, as before, are feelings? Blind spasms of some psychic substance that remain outside the light and insight of consciousness? Significantly, the only contemporary literary critic of stature who has adopted positivism, I. A. Richards, has carried his philosophy around rather like a hobbling ball and chain than as a positive aid to his own critical explorations. In an earlier and more extreme phase, Richards promulgated a theory of poetry as essentially a form of emotional engineering. How the poet was to work upon our neural system without presenting some imaginative vision that was his understanding of life was a question left untouched. Richards, curiously enough, came back to the problem in his *Coleridge on the Imagination,* where he implicitly breaks with a too narrow positivism and accords the imagination a cognitive role as a distinct mode of vision.

And what when we move from the artist to the professor of art, and from there to the cognitive status of the humanities as a whole—the *Geisteswissenschaften,* as the Germans call them, the sciences of the spirit, or, more freely translated, the sciences of man? Must we, as the strict letter of positivism would have us do, deny knowledge to the professor of literature, of the history of art, and of history generally, except insofar as he merely presents and classifies *facts?* Is a great interpreter of Shakespeare—of whom we do say "He *knows* his Shakespeare"—merely he who is capable of producing laundry lists or other grubby factual data? It is odd that the positivist, who makes his home in the university as the organized center for the pursuit of knowledge, and who there rubs elbows and may in some cases be extremely friendly with his colleagues in the humanities, nevertheless in his philosophy harbors so limited a view of the varieties of knowledge that he would accord to these colleagues a very paltry place in the cognitive hierarchy. When we say of a great professor of Shakespeare, if we are lucky enough to find such, that "he really knows his Shakespeare," we do not mean that he is able to recite the text like a parrot or that his head is crammed full of facts about the poet and his times, but, quite beyond such factual lumber, that he is able in imagination to enter into the world of Shakespeare's plays; and this knowledge grasped by the imagination is a kind of knowledge that cannot be explicated on any strict model of the physical sciences. Works of art, in fact, are our chief means of knowing the past; and this fact leads us to ask whether the knowledge of history, which draws so much from works of the imagination, can be interpreted in any strict analogy to the knowledge provided by the physical sciences. (Indeed the whole problem of historical knowledge has been neglected by contemporary positivists.) So far as history unearths facts, it follows a method generally similar to that of the physical sciences; but where history is engaged in the labor of *interpretation*—whether of individual men or individual epochs of a civilization—it must draw upon other faculties of knowledge than those that are regnant in the physical sciences.

Nineteenth-century positivists did not neglect this problem of historical interpretation, and it might have profited their contemporary descendants to take note of past successes and failures in this field. Contemporary positivism, in one respect, has done well to maintain its distinctness from the doctrines of Comte and his followers, to insist that its own method, as a philosophic method, is more precisely and authentically based. But it has also suffered by failing to understand itself historically in the line of its continuity with the positivism of the past. For despite the divergences in method and premises there is certainly a continuity of spirit between the positivisms of the nineteenth and the twentieth centuries. Thus the nineteenth-century positivists frankly announced that they proposed to advance, as they put it, "the sciences of man in the manner of the natural sciences." Here the attitude of mind is clearly monistic and reductive. Despite contemporary positivism's rejection of any materialistic metaphysics, a basic prejudice in favor of the physical appears in the tendency to take the science of physics as the model of all knowledge.

On this point the positivistic attitude appears at present to be triumphant, at least here in the United States, in the so-called behavioral sciences. The sociologist and psychologist aspire to construct their sciences on the model of physics and therefore have a marked penchant for data that are "objective," quantitative, and physical. To be sure, this attitude is more often than not an unconscious and crude positivism, maintained by savants who have a marked distaste for philosophy but who, nevertheless, are likely to philosophize unconsciously all over the map. Indeed, the success of positivism in invading these fields would seem to indicate that it is not correct in its own estimate of the feeble power of philosophy as something that must follow, and never lead, the positive sciences. For here, quite clearly, in the behavioral sciences of man the philosophical prejudices of the scientist do dictate the lines along which he attempts to lay down his science. Simply as a philosophy, positivism has here supplied what Peirce would call "leading principles" for the sciences themselves.

In indicating these questions that make up the unfinished agenda of positivism, we may seem to have dealt unfairly with a philosophy that has expanded and developed remarkably in the last decades. A philosophy—and particularly a philosophy that believes in the method of piecemeal analysis—must begin with certain restricted problems to the neglect of others, and must be allowed time gradually to extend itself to encompass these latter problems. To be sure. But it is questionable whether positivism can go on to give an adequate account of these neglected areas—aesthetic, moral, and historical modes of experience—without transforming itself so completely and drastically that it would lose its own identity and become an entirely different philosophy.

There is one final point which I must not shrink from making—on which I have at once to acknowledge our greatest debt to and our greatest dissatisfaction with positivism—and this is the point of its accuracy as a spiritual expression of its time. There is no doubt that in its addiction to the physical sciences as the exemplary models of all knowledge it expresses the powerful penchant of our time to take physical facts as real above all else. This is, after all, the age of mathematical physics—an age launched philosophically three centuries ago by

Descartes that has come to a climax in our time with the discovery of nuclear power. In terms of the power it commands, one might very well say that physics almost has the right to set itself up as the model of all knowledge; but this rather peculiar intellectual version of might makes right leaves unanswered the question whether the sciences of man, which lag so disastrously behind the powers of destruction already contained in the physical sciences, can best be advanced by slavishly imitating the methods of the physical sciences. Is not the dualism between "the cognitive and the emotive"—with the disparagement of the latter that is necessarily entailed by this dualism, for if emotions provide no knowledge we would never learn anything at all by living—is not this dualism an expression of the fragmentation of modern man into two water-tight compartments that remain perpetually incommunicado with each other?

If these suspicions be true, they would not discredit positivism as a significant philosophical phenomenon. On the contrary, its great and real significance would be that its bold and drastic simplifications gave clear philosophical expression to certain fateful attitudes endemic to our time. The function of a philosophy is to reveal, and it may very well do this without leaving us very comfortable in the midst of its revelation. Nobody doubts that Descartes was a great philosopher though very few remain comfortable with the Cartesian dualism. Descartes' achievement was to give very sharp and clear formulation to attitudes already implicit within science and philosophy at his time. In its simplest bedrock terms, what the Cartesian dualism boils down to is a split between the world of science and the world of man. (This split, we suggest, is the hidden and real issue in the present quarrels between the positivists and the British analysts over the rival merits of formal and ordinary language.) The three centuries that followed Descartes have been saddled, disturbed, and embattled by this split; and at the present time it has become a fact for the political fate of mankind. This fissure, it seems to us, is still present in positivism, despite some of its radical recent changes.

W.B.

Moritz Schlick

UNANSWERABLE QUESTIONS?[1]

It is natural that mankind should take great pride in the steady advance of its knowledge. The joy we feel in the contemplation of scientific progress is fully justified. One problem after another is solved by science; and the success of the past gives us ample reason for our hope that this process will go on, perhaps even at a quicker pace. But will it, can it, go on indefinitely? It seems a little ridiculous to suppose that a day might come when all imaginable problems would be solved, so that there would be no questions left for which the human mind would crave an answer. We feel sure that our curiosity will never be completely satisfied and that the progress of knowledge will not come to a stop when it has reached its last goal.

It is commonly assumed that there are other imperative reasons why scientific advance cannot go on for ever. Most people believe in the existence of barriers that cannot be scaled by human reason and by human experience. The final and perhaps the most important truths are thought to be permanently hidden from our eyes; the key to the Riddle of the Universe is believed to be buried in depths the access to which is barred to all mortals by the very nature of the Universe. According to this common belief, there are many questions which we can formulate, and whose meaning we can grasp completely, though it is definitely impossible to know their answer which is beyond the natural and necessary boundary of all knowledge. In regard to these questions a final ignorabimus is pronounced. Nature, it is said, does not wish

[1] From: *Gesammelte Aufsätze,* Moritz Schlick, pp. 369-375. Gerold & Co., Vienna, 1938.

her deepest secrets to be revealed; God has set a limit of knowledge which shall not be passed by his creatures, and beyond which faith must take the place of curiosity.

It is easy to understand how such a view originated, but it is not so clear why it should be considered to be a particularly pious or reverent attitude. Why should Nature seem more wonderful to us if she cannot be known completely? Surely she does not wish to conceal anything on purpose, for she has no secrets, nothing to be ashamed of. On the contrary, the more we know of the world the more we shall marvel at it; and if we should know its ultimate principles and its most general laws, our feeling of wonder and reverence would pass all bounds. Nothing is gained by picturing God as jealously hiding from his creatures the innermost structure of his creation, indeed, a worthier conception of a Supreme Being should imply that no ultimate boundary should be set to the knowledge of beings to whom an infinite desire of knowledge has been given. The existence of an absolute ignorabimus would form an exceedingly vexing problem to a philosophical mind. It would be a great step forward in philosophy, if the burden of this bewildering problem could be thrown off.

This, one may argue, is evidently impossible, for without doubt there are unanswerable questions. It is very easy to ask questions the answers to which, we have the strongest reasons to believe, will never be known to any human being. What did Plato do at eight o'clock in the morning of his fiftieth birthday? How much did Homer weigh when he wrote the first line of the Iliad? Is there a piece of silver to be found on the other side of the moon, three inches long and shaped like a fish? Obviously, men will never know the answers to these questions, however hard they may try. But at the same time, we know that they would never try very hard. These problems, they will say, are of no importance, no philosopher would worry about them, and no historian or naturalist would care whether he knew the answers or not.

Here, then, we have certain questions whose insolubility does not trouble the philospher; and evidently there are reasons why it need not trouble him. This is important. We must be content to have insoluble questions. But what if all of them could be shown to be of such a kind as not to cause any really serious concern to the philosopher? In that case he would be relieved. Although there would be many things he could not know, the real burden of the ignorabimus would be lifted from his shoulders. At first sight there seems to be little hope for this as some of the most important issues of philosophy are generally held to belong to the class of insoluble problems. Let us consider this point carefully.

What do we mean when we call a question important? When do we hold it to be of interest to the philosopher? Broadly speaking, when it is a question of principle; one that refers to a general feature of the world, not a detail; one that concerns the structure of the world, a valid law, not a single unique fact. This distinction may be described as the difference between the real nature of the Universe and the accidental form in which this nature manifests itself.

Correspondingly, the reasons why a given problem is insoluble may be of two entirely different kinds. In the first place, the impossibility of answering a given question may be an impossibility in principle or, as we shall call it, a logical impossibility. In the second place, it may be due to accidental circumstances which do not affect the general laws, and in this case we shall speak of an empirical impossibility.

In the simple instances given above, it is clear that the impossibility of answering these questions is of the empirical kind. It is merely a matter of chance that neither Plato nor any of his friends took exact notes of his doings on his fiftieth birthday (or that such notes were lost if any were taken); and a similar remark applies to the questions concerning the weight of Homer and things on the other side of the moon. It is practically or technically impossible for human beings to reach the moon and go around it, and most probably such an exploration of our earth's satellite will never take place. But we cannot declare it impossible in principle. The moon happens to be very far off; it happens to turn always the same side towards the earth; it happens to possess no atmosphere in which human beings could breathe—but we can very easily imagine all these circumstances to be different. We are prevented from visiting the moon only by brute facts, by an unfortunate state of affairs, not by any principle by which certain things were deliberately withheld from our knowledge. Even if the impossibility of solving a certain question is due to a Law of Nature, we shall have to say that it is only empirical, not logical, provided we can indicate how the law would have to be changed in order to make the question answerable. After all, the existence of any Law of Nature must be considered as an empirical fact which might just as well be different. The scientist's whole interest is concentrated on the particular Laws of Nature; but the philosopher's general point of view must be independent of the validity of any particular one of them.

It is one of the most important contentions of the philosophy I am advocating that there are many questions which it is empirically impossible to answer, but not a single real question for which it would be logically impossible to find a solution. Since only the latter kind of impossibility would have that hopeless and fatal character which is implied by the ignorabimus and which could cause philosophers to speak of a "Riddle of the Universe" and to despair of such problems as the "cognition of things in themselves", and similar ones, it would seem that the acceptance of my opinion would bring the greatest relief to all those who have been unduly concerned about the essential incompetence of human knowledge in regard to the greatest issues. Nobody can reasonably complain about the empirical impossibility of knowing everything, for that would be equivalent to complaining that we cannot live at all times and be in all places simultaneously. Nobody wants to know all the facts, and it is not important to know them: the really essential principles of the universe reveal themselves at any time and any place. I do not suggest, of course, that they lie open at first glance, but they can always be discovered by the careful and penetrating methods of science.

How can I prove my point? What assures us that the impossibility of answering questions never belongs to the question as such, is never a matter of principle, but is always due to accidental empirical circumstances, which may some day change? There is no room here for a real proof;[2] but I can indicate in general how the result is obtained.

It is done by an analysis of the meaning of our questions. Evidently philosophical issues—and very often other problems too—are difficult to understand: we have to ask for an explanation of what is meant by them. How is such an explanation given? How do we indicate the meaning of a question?

A conscientious examination shows that all the various ways of explaining what is actually meant by a question are, ultimately, nothing but various descriptions of ways in which the answer to the question must be found. Every explanation or indication of the meaning of a question consists, in some way or other, of prescriptions for finding its answer. This principle has proved to be of fundamental importance for the method of science. For example, it led Einstein, as he himself admits, to the discovery of the Theory of Relativity. It may be empirically impossible to follow those prescriptions (like traveling around the moon), but it cannot be logically impossible. For what is logically impossible cannot even be described, i.e., it cannot be expressed by words or other means of communication.

The truth of this last statement is shown by an analysis of "description" and "expression" into which we cannot enter here. But taking it for granted, we see that no real question is in principle—i.e., logically—unanswerable. For the logical impossibility of solving a problem is equivalent to the impossibility of describing a method of finding its solution; and this, as we have stated, is equivalent to the impossibility of indicating the meaning of the problem. Thus a question which is unanswerable in principle can have no meaning, it can be no question at all: it is nothing but a nonsensical series of words with a question mark after them. As it is logically impossible to give an answer where there is no question, this cannot be a cause of wonder, dissatisfaction, or despair.

This conclusion can be made clearer by considering one or two examples. Our question as to the weight of Homer has meaning, of

[2] For a more complete account of the matter I may refer the English reader to two lectures which appeared in the *Publications in Philosophy,* edited by the College of the Pacific in 1932, and more especially to an article on "Meaning and Verification" in a forthcoming issue of the *American Philosophical Review.* [See p. 28 of this volume. Eds.]

course, because we can easily describe methods of weighing human bodies (even poets); in other words, the notion of weight is accurately defined. Probably Homer was never weighed, and it is empirically impossible to do it now, because his body no longer exists; but these accidental facts do not alter the sense of the question.

Or take the problem of survival after death. It is a meaningful question, because we can indicate ways in which it could be solved. One method of ascertaining one's own survival would simply consist in dying. It would also be possible to describe certain observations of scientific character that would lead us to accept a definite answer. That such observations could not be made thus far is an empirical fact which cannot entail a definite ignorabimus in regard to the problem.

Now consider the question: "What is the nature of time? What does it mean? What do the words "the nature of" stand for? The scientist might, perhaps, invent some kind of explanation, he might suggest some statements which he would regard as possible answers to the question; but his explanation could be nothing but the description of a method of discovering which of the suggested answers is the true one. In other words, by giving a meaning to the question he has at the same time made it logically answerable, although he may not be able to make it empirically soluble. Without such an explanation, however, the words "What is the nature of time?" are no question at all. If a philosopher confronts us with a series of words like this and neglects to explain the meaning, he cannot wonder if no answer is forthcoming. It is as if he had asked us: "How much does philosophy weigh?" in which case it is immediately seen that this is not a question at all, but mere nonsense. Questions like "Can we know the Absolute?" and innumerable similar ones must be dealt with in the same way as the "problem" concerning the nature of Time.

All great philosophical issues that have been discussed since the time of Parmenides to our present day are of one of two kinds; we can either give them a definite meaning by careful and accurate explanations and definitions, and then we are sure that they are soluble in principle, although they may give the scientist the greatest trouble and may even never be solved on account of unfavorable empirical circumstances, or we fail to give them any meaning, and then they are no questions at all. Neither case need cause uneasiness for the philosopher. His greatest troubles arose from a failure to distinguish between the two.

MEANING AND VERIFICATION[1]

1.

Philosophical questions, as compared with ordinary scientific problems, are always strangely paradoxical. But it seems to be an especially strange paradox that the question concerning the meaning of a proposition should constitute a serious philosophical difficulty. For is it not the very nature and purpose of every proposition to express its own meaning? In fact, when we are confronted with a proposition (in a language familiar to us) we usually know its meaning immediately. If we do not, we can have it explained to us, but the explanation will consist of a new proposition; and if the new one is capable of expressing the meaning, why should not the original one be capable of it? So that a snippy person when asked what he meant by a certain statement might be perfectly justified in saying, 'I meant exactly what I said!'.

It is logically legitimate and actually the normal way in ordinary life and even in science to answer a question concerning the meaning of a proposition by simply repeating it either more distinctly or in slightly different words. Under what circumstances, then, can there be any sense in asking for the meaning of a statement which is well before our eyes or ears?

Evidently the only possibility is that we have not understood it. And in this case what is actually before our eyes or ears is nothing but a series of words which we are unable to handle; we do not know how to use it, how to 'apply it to reality'. Such a series of words is for us simply a complex of signs 'without meaning', a mere sequel of sounds or a mere row of marks on paper, and we have no right to call it 'a proposition' at all; we may perhaps speak of it as 'a sentence'.

If we adopt this terminology we can now easily get rid of our para-

[1] From: *Gesammelte Aufsätze,* Moritz Schlick, pp. 338-367. Gerold & Co., Vienna, 1938.

dox by saying that we cannot inquire after the meaning of a proposition, but can ask about the meaning of a sentence, and that this amounts to asking, 'What proposition does the sentence stand for?'. And this question is answered either by a proposition in a language with which we are already perfectly familiar; or by indicating the logical rules which will make a proposition out of the sentence, i.e., will tell us exactly in what circumstances the sentence is to be used. These two methods do not actually differ in principle; both of them give meaning to the sentence (transform it into a proposition) by locating it, as it were, within the system of a definite language; the first method making use of a language which is already in our possession, the second one building it up for us. The first method represents the simplest kind of ordinary 'translation'; the second one affords a deeper insight into the nature of meaning, and will have to be used in order to overcome philosophical difficulties connected with the understanding of sentences.

The source of these difficulties is to be found in the fact that very often we do not know how to handle our own words; we speak or write without having first agreed upon a definite logical grammar which will constitute the signification of our terms. We commit the mistake of thinking that we know the meaning of a sentence (i.e., understand it as a proposition) if we are familiar with all the words occurring in it. But this is not sufficient. It will not lead to confusion or error as long as we remain in the domain of everyday life by which our words have been formed and to which they are adapted, but it will become fatal the moment we try to think about abstract problems by means of the same terms without carefully fixing their signification for the new purpose. For every word has a definite signification only within a definite context into which it has been fitted; in any other context it will have no meaning unless we provide new rules for the use of the word in the new case, and this may be done, at least in principle, quite arbitrarily.

Let us consider an example. If a friend should say to me, 'Take me to a country where the sky is three times as blue as in England!' I should not know how to fulfill his wish; his phrase would appear nonsensical to me, because the word 'blue' is used in a way which is not provided for by the rules of our language. The combination of a numeral and the name of a color does not occur in it; therefore my friend's sentence has no meaning, although its exterior linguistic form is that of a command or a wish. But he can, of course, give it a meaning. If I ask him, 'What do you mean by "three times as blue"?', he can arbitrarily indicate certain definite physical circumstances concerning the serenity of the sky which he wants his phrase to be the description of. And then, perhaps, I shall be able to follow his directions; his wish will have become meaningful for me.

Thus, whenever we ask about a sentence, 'What does it mean?', what we expect is instruction as to the circumstances in which the sentence is to be used; we want a description of the conditions under which the sentence will form a true proposition, and of those which will make it false. The meaning of a word or a combination of words is, in this way, determined by a set of rules which regulate their use and which, following Wittgenstein, we may call the rules of their grammar, taking this word in its widest sense.

(If the preceding remarks about meaning are as correct as I am convinced they are, this will, to a large measure, be due to conversations with Wittgenstein which have greatly influenced my own views about these matters. I can hardly exaggerate my indebtedness to this philosopher. I do not wish to impute to him any responsibility for the contents of this article, but I have reason to hope that he will agree with the main substance of it.)

Stating the meaning of a sentence amounts to stating the rules according to which the sentence is to be used, and this is the same as stating the way in which it can be verified (or falsified). The meaning of a proposition is the method of its verification.

The 'grammatical' rules will partly consist of ordinary definitions, i.e., explanations of words by means of other words, partly of what are called 'ostensive' definitions, i.e., explanations by means of a procedure which puts the words to actual use. The simplest form of an ostensive definition is a pointing gesture combined with the pronouncing of the word, as when we teach a child the signification of the sound 'blue' by showing a blue object. But in most cases the ostensive definition is of a more complicated form; we cannot point to an object corresponding to words like 'because', 'immediate', 'chance', 'again', etc. In these cases we require the presence of certain complex situations, and the meaning of the words is defined by the way we use them in these different situations.

It is clear that in order to understand a verbal definition we must know the signification of the explaining words beforehand, and that the only explanation which can work without any previous knowledge is the ostensive definition. We conclude that there is no way of understanding any meaning without ultimate reference to ostensive definitions, and this means, in an obvious sense, reference to 'experience' or 'possibility of verification'.

This is the situation, and nothing seems to me simpler or less questionable. It is this situation and nothing else that we describe when we affirm that the meaning of a proposition can be given only by giving the rule of its verification in experience. (The addition, 'in experience', is really superfluous, as no other kind of verification has been defined.)

This view has been called the "experimental theory of meaning"; but it certainly is no theory at all, for the term 'theory' is used for a set of hypotheses about a certain subject-matter, and there are no hypotheses involved in our view, which proposes to be nothing but a simple statement of the way in which meaning is actually assigned to propositions, both in everyday life and in science. There has never been any other way, and it would be a grave error to suppose that we believe we have discovered a new conception of meaning which is contrary to common opinion and which we want to introduce into philosophy. On the contrary, our conception is not only entirely in agreement with, but even derived from, common sense and scientific procedure. Although our criterion of meaning has always been employed in practice, it has very rarely been formulated in the past, and this is perhaps the only excuse for the attempts of so many philosophers to deny its feasibility.

The most famous case of an explicit formulation of our criterion is Einstein's answer to the question, What do we mean when we speak of two events at distant places happening simultaneously? This answer consisted in a description of an experimental method by which the simultaneity of such events was actually ascertained. Einstein's philosophical opponents maintained—and some of them still maintain—that they knew the meaning of the above question independently of any method of verification. All I am trying to do is to stick consistently to Einstein's position and to admit no exceptions from it. (Professor Bridgman's book on *The Logic of Modern Physics* is an admirable attempt to carry out this program for all concepts of physics.) I am not writing for those who think that Einstein's philosophical opponents were right.

2.

Professor C. I. Lewis, in a remarkable address on "Experience and Meaning" (published in this Review, March 1934), has justly stated that the view developed above (he speaks of it as the "empirical-meaning requirement") forms the basis of the whole philosophy of what has been called the "logical positivism of the Viennese Circle". He criticizes this basis as inadequate chiefly on the ground that its acceptance would impose certain limitations upon "significant philosophic discussion" which, at some points, would make such discussion altogether impossible and, at other points, restrict it to an intolerable extent.

Feeling responsible as I do for certain features of the Viennese philosophy (which I should prefer to call Consistent Empiricism), and being of the opinion that it really does not impose any restrictions upon significant philosophizing at all, I shall try to examine Professor Lewis's chief arguments and point out why I think that they do not endanger our position—at least as far as I can answer for it myself. All of my own arguments will be derived from the statements made in section 1.

Professor Lewis describes the empirical-meaning requirement as demanding "that any concept put forward or any proposition asserted shall have a definite denotation; that it shall be intelligible not only verbally and logically but in the further sense that one can specify those empirical items which would determine the applicability of the concept or constitute the verification of the proposition" (loc. cit. 125). Here it seems to me that there is no justification for the words "but in the further sense . . .", i.e., for the distinction of two (or three?) senses of intelligibility. The remarks in section 1 show that, according to our opinion, 'verbal and logical' understanding consists in knowing how the proposition in question could be verified. For, unless we mean by 'verbal understanding' that we know how the words are actually used, the term could hardly mean anything but a shadowy feeling of being acquainted with the words, and in a philosophical discussion it does not seem advisable to call such a feeling 'understanding'. Similarly, I should not advise that we speak of a sentence as being 'logically intelligible' when we just feel convinced that its exterior form is that of a proper proposition (if, e.g. it has the form, substantive—copula—adjective, and therefore appears to predicate a property of a thing). For it seems to me that by such a phrase we want to say much more, namely, that we are completely aware of the whole grammar of the sentence, i.e., that we know exactly the circumstances to which it is fitted. Thus knowledge of how a proposition is verified is not anything over and above its verbal and logical understanding, but is identical with it. It seems to me, therefore, that when we demand that a proposition be verifiable we are not adding a new requirement but are simply formulating the conditions which have actually always been acknowledged as necessary for meaning and intelligibility.

The mere statement that no sentence has meaning unless we are able to indicate a way of testing its truth or falsity is not very useful if we do not explain very carefully the signification of the phrases 'method of testing' and 'verifiability'. Professor Lewis is quite right when he asks for such an explanation. He himself suggests some ways in which it might be given, and I am glad to say that his suggestions appear to me to be in perfect agreement with my own views and those of my philosophical friends. It will be easy to show that there is no serious divergence between the point of view of the pragmatist as Professor Lewis conceives it and that of the Viennese Empiricist. And if in some special questions they arrive at different conclusions, it may be hoped that a careful examination will bridge the difference.

How do we define verifiability?

In the first place I should like to point out that when we say that "a proposition has meaning only if it is verifiable" we are not saying ". . . if it is verified". This simple remark does away with one of the chief objections; the "here and now predicament", as Professor Lewis calls it, does not exist any more. We fall into the snares of this predicament only if we regard verification itself as the criterion of meaning, instead of 'possibility of verification' (= verifiability); this would indeed lead to a "reduction to absurdity of meaning". Obviously the predicament arises through some fallacy by which these two notions are confounded. I do not know if Russell's statement, "Empirical knowledge is confined to what we actually observe" (quoted by Professor Lewis loc. cit. 130), must be interpreted as containing this fallacy, but it would certainly be worth while to discover its genesis.

Let us consider the following argument which Professor Lewis discusses (131), but which he does not want to impute to anyone:

> Suppose it maintained that no issue is meaningful unless it can be put to the test of decisive verification. And no verification can take place except in the immediately present experience of the subject. Then nothing can be meant except what is actually present in the experience in which that meaning is entertained.

This argument has the form of a conclusion drawn from two premisses. Let us for the moment assume the second premiss to be meaningful and true. You will observe that even then the conclusion does not follow. For the first premiss assures us that the issue has meaning if it can be verified; the verification does not have to take place, and therefore it is quite irrelevant whether it can take place in the future or in the present only. Apart from this, the second premiss is, of course, nonsensical; for what fact could possibly be described by the sentence 'verification can take place only in present experience'? Is not verifying an act or process like hearing or feeling bored? Might we not just as well say that I can hear or feel bored only in the present moment? And what could I mean by this? The particular nonsense involved in such phrases will become clearer when we speak of the 'egocentric predicament' later on; at present we are content to know that our empirical-meaning postulate has nothing whatever to do with the now-predicament. 'Verifiable' does not even mean 'verifiable here now'; much less does it mean 'being verified now'.

Perhaps it will be thought that the only way of making sure of the verifiability of a proposition would consist in its actual verification. But we shall soon see that this is not the case.

There seems to be a great temptation to connect meaning and the 'immediately given' in the wrong way; and some of the Viennese positivists may have yielded to this temptation, thereby getting dangerously near to the fallacy we have just been describing. Parts of Carnap's *Logischer Aufbau der Welt,* for instance, might be interpreted as implying that a proposition about future events did not really refer to the future at all but asserted only the present existence of certain expectations (and, similarly, speaking about the past would really mean speaking about present memories). But it is certain that the author of that book does not hold such a view now, and that it cannot be regarded as a teaching of the new positivism. On the contrary, we have pointed out from the beginning that our definition of meaning does not imply such absurd consequences, and when someone asked, "But how can you verify a proposition about a future event?", we replied, "Why, for instance, by waiting for it to happen! 'Waiting' is a perfectly legitimate method of verification".

Thus I think that everybody—including the Consistent Empiricist—agrees that it would be nonsense to say, 'We can mean nothing but the immediately given'. If in this sentence we replace the word 'mean' by the word 'know' we arrive at a statement similar to Bertrand Russell's mentioned above. The temptation to formulate phrases of this sort arises, I believe, from a certain ambiguity of the verb 'to know' which is the source of many metaphysical troubles and to which, therefore, I have often had to call attention on other occasions (see e.g. *Allgemeine Erkenntnislehre,* 2nd ed. 1925, § 12). In the first place the word may stand simply for 'being aware of a datum', i.e. for the mere presence of a feeling, a color, a sound, etc.; and if the word 'knowledge' is taken in this sense the assertion 'Empirical, knowledge is confined to what we actually observe' does not say anything at all, but is a mere tautology. (This case, I think, would correspond to what Professor Lewis calls "identity-theories" of the "knowledge-relation". Such theories, resting on a tautology of this kind, would be empty verbiage without significance.)

In the second place the word 'knowledge' may be used in one of the significant meanings which it has in science and ordinary life; and in this case Russell's assertion would obviously (as Professor Lewis remarked) be false. Russell himself, as is well known, distinguishes between 'knowledge by acquaintance' and 'knowledge by description', but perhaps it should be noted that this distinction does not entirely coincide with the one we have been insisting upon just now.

3.

Verifiability means possibility of verification. Professor Lewis justly remarks that to "omit all examination of the wide range of significance which could attach to 'possible verification', would be to leave the whole conception rather obscure" (loc. cit. 137). For our purpose it suffices to distinguish between two of the many ways in which the word 'possibility' is used. We shall call them 'empirical possibility' and 'logical possibility'. Professor Lewis describes two meanings of 'verifiability' which correspond exactly to this difference; he is fully aware of it, and there is hardly anything left for me to do but carefully to work out the distinction and show its bearing upon our issue.

I propose to call 'empirically possible' anything that does not contradict the laws of nature. This is, I think, the largest sense in which we may speak of empirical possibility; we do not restrict the term to happenings which are not only in accordance with the laws of nature but also with the actual state of the universe (where 'actual' might refer to the present moment of our own lives, or to the condition of human beings on this planet, and so forth). If we chose the latter definition (which seems to have been in Professor Lewis's mind when he spoke of "possible experience as conditioned by the actual", loc. cit. 141) we should not get the sharp boundaries we need for our present purpose. So 'empirical possibility' is to mean 'compatibility with natural laws'.

Now, since we cannot boast of a complete and sure knowledge of nature's laws, it is evident that we can never assert with certainty the empirical possibility of any fact, and here we may be permitted to speak of degrees of possibility. Is it possible for me to lift this book? Surely!—This table? I think so!—This billiard table? I don't think so! —This automobile? Certainly not!—It is clear that in these cases the answer is given by experience, as the result of experiments performed in the past. Any judgment about empirical possibility is based on experience and will often be rather uncertain; there will be no sharp boundary between possibility and impossibility.

Is the possibility of verification which we insist upon of this empirical sort? In that case there would be different degrees of verifiability, the question of meaning would be a matter of more or less, not a matter of yes or no. In many disputes concerning our issue it is the empirical possibility of verification which is discussed; the various examples of verifiability given by Professor Lewis, e.g., are instances of different empirical circumstances in which the verification is carried out or prevented from being carried out. Many of those who refuse to accept our criterion of meaning seem to imagine that the procedure of its application in a special case is somewhat like this: A proposition is presented to us ready made, and in order to discover its meaning we have to try various methods of verifying or falsifying it, and if one of these methods works we have found the meaning of the proposition; but if not, we say it has no meaning. If we really had to proceed in this way, it is clear that the determination of meaning would be entirely a matter of experience, and that in many cases no sharp and ultimate decision could be obtained. How could we ever know that we had tried long enough, if none of our methods were successful? Might not future efforts disclose a meaning which we were unable to find before?

This whole conception is, of course, entirely erroneous. It speaks of meaning as if it were a kind of entity inherent in a sentence and hidden in it like a nut in its shell, so that the philosopher would have to crack the shell or sentence in order to reveal the nut or meaning. We know from our considerations in section I that a proposition cannot be given 'ready made'; that meaning does not inhere in a sentence where it might be discovered, but that it must be bestowed upon it. And this is done by applying to the sentence the rules of the logical grammar of our language, as explained in section I. These rules are not facts of nature which could be 'discovered', but they are prescriptions stipulated by acts of definition. And these definitions have to be known to those who pronounce the sentence in question and to those who hear or read it. Otherwise they are not confronted with any proposition at all, and there is nothing they could try to verify, because you can't verify or falsify a mere row of words. You cannot even start verifying before you know the meaning, i.e., before you have established the possibility of verification.

In other words, the possibility of verification which is relevant to meaning cannot be of the empirical sort; it cannot be established post festum. You have to be sure of it before you can consider the empirical circumstances and investigate whether or no or under what conditions they will permit of verification. The empirical circumstances are all-important when you want to know if a proposition is true (which is the concern of the scientist), but they can have no influence on the meaning of the proposition (which is the concern of the philosopher). Professor Lewis has seen and expressed this very clearly (loc. cit. 142, first six lines), and our Vienna positivism, as far as I can answer for it, is in complete agreement with him on this point. It must be emphasized that when we speak of verifiability we mean logical possibility of verification, and nothing but this.

I call a fact or a process 'logically possible' if it can be described, i.e., if the sentence which is supposed to describe it obeys the rules of grammar we have stipulated for our language. (I am expressing myself rather incorrectly. A fact which could not be described would, of course, not be any fact at all; any fact is logically possible. But I think my meaning will be understood.) Take some examples. The sentences, 'My friend died the day after tomorrow'; 'The lady wore a dark red dress which was bright green'; 'The campanile is 100 feet and 150 feet high'; 'The child was naked, but wore a long white nightgown', obviously violate the rules which, in ordinary English, govern the use of the words occurring in the sentences. They do not describe any facts at all; they are meaningless, because they represent logical impossibilities.

It is of the greatest importance (not only for our present issue but for philosophical problems in general) to see that whenever we speak of logical impossibility we are referring to a discrepancy between the definitions of our terms and the way in which we use them. We must avoid the severe mistake committed by some of the former Empiricists like Mill and Spencer, who regarded logical principles (e.g. the Law of Contradiction) as laws of nature governing the psychological process of thinking. The nonsensical statements alluded to above do not correspond to thoughts which, by a sort of psychological experiment, we find ourselves unable to think; they do not correspond to any thoughts at all. When we hear the words, 'A tower which is both 100 feet and 150 feet high', the image of two towers of different heights may be in our mind, and we may find it psychologically (empirically) impossible to combine the two pictures into one image, but it is not this fact which is denoted by the words 'logical impossibility'. The height of a tower cannot be 100 feet and 150 feet at the same time; a child cannot be naked and dressed at the same time—not because we are unable to imagine it, but because our definitions of 'height', of the numerals, of the terms 'naked' and 'dressed', are not compatible with the particular combinations of those words in our examples. 'They are not compatible with such combinations' means that the rules of our language have not provided any use for such combinations; they do not describe any fact. We could change these rules, of course, and thereby arrange a meaning for the terms 'both red and green', 'both naked and dressed'; but if we decide to stick to the ordinary definitions (which reveal themselves in the way we actually use our words) we have decided to regard those combined terms as meaningless, i.e., not to use them as the description of any fact. Whatever fact we may or may not imagine, if the word 'naked' (or 'red') occurs in its description we have decided that the word 'dressed' (or 'green') cannot be put in its place in the same description. If we do not follow this rule it means that we want to introduce a new definition of the words, or that we don't mind using words without meaning and like to indulge in nonsense. (I am far from condemning this attitude under all circumstances; on certain occasions—as in *Alice in Wonderland*—it may be the only sensible attitude and far more delightful than any treatise on Logic. But in such a treatise we have a right to expect a different attitude.)

The result of our considerations is this: Verifiability, which is the sufficient and necessary condition of meaning, is a possibility of the logical order; it is created by constructing the sentence in accordance with the rules by which its terms are defined. The only case in which verification is (logically) impossible is the case where you have made it impossible by not setting any rules for its verification. Grammatical rules are not found anywhere in nature, but are made by man and are, in principle, arbitrary; so you cannot give meaning to a sentence by discovering a method of verifying it, but only by stipulating how it shall be done. Thus logical possibility or impossibility of verification is always selfimposed. If we utter a sentence without meaning it is always our own fault.

The tremendous philosophic importance of this last remark will be realized when we consider that what we said about the meaning of assertions applies also to the meaning of questions. There are, of course, many questions which can never be answered by human beings. But the impossibility of finding the answer may be of two different kinds. If it is merely empirical in the sense defined, if it is due to the chance circumstances to which our human existence is confined, there may be reason to lament our fate and the weakness of our physical and mental powers, but the problem could never be said to be absolutely insoluble and there would always be some hope, at least for future generations. For the empirical circumstances may alter, human facilities may develop, and even the laws of nature may change (perhaps even suddenly and in such a way that the universe would be thrown open to much more extended investigation). A problem of this kind might be called practically unanswerable or technically unanswerable, and might cause the scientist great trouble, but the philosopher, who is concerned with general principles only, would not feel terribly excited about it.

But what about those questions for which it is logically impossible to find an answer? Such problems would remain insoluble under all imaginable circumstances; they would confront us with a definite hopeless Ignorabimus; and it is of the greatest importance for the philosopher to know whether there are any such issues. Now it is easy to see from what has been said before that this calamity could happen only if the question itself had no meaning. It would not be a genuine question at all, but a mere row of words with a question-mark at the end. We must say that a question is meaningful, if we can understand it, i.e., if we are able to decide for any given proposition whether, if true, it would be an answer to our question. And if this is so, the actual decision could only be prevented by empirical circumstances, which means that it would not be logically impossible. Hence no meaningful problem can be insoluble in principle. If in any case we find an answer to be logically impossible we know that we really have not been asking anything, that what sounded like a question was actually a nonsensical combination of words. A genuine question is one for which an answer is logically possible. This is one of the most characteristic results of our empiricism. It means that in principle there are no limits to our knowledge. The boundaries which must be acknowledged are of an empirical nature and, therefore, never ultimate; they can be pushed back further and further; there is no unfathomable mystery in the world.

The dividing line between logical possibility and impossibility of verification is absolutely sharp and distinct; there is no gradual transition between meaning and nonsense. For either you have given the grammatical rules for verification, or you have not; *tertium non datur.*

Empirical possibility is determined by the laws of nature, but meaning and verifiability are entirely independent of them. Everything that I can describe or define is logically possible—and definitions are in no way bound up with natural laws. The proposition 'Rivers flow uphill' is meaningful, but happens to be false because the fact it describes is physically impossible. It will not deprive a proposition of its meaning if the conditions which I stipulate for its verification are incompatible with the laws of nature; I may prescribe conditions, for instance, which could be fulfilled only if the velocity of light were greater than it actually is, or if the Law of Conservation of Energy did not hold, and so forth.

An opponent of our view might find a dangerous paradox or even a contradiction in the preceding explanations, because on the one hand we insisted so strongly on what has been called the "empirical-meaning requirement", and on the other hand we assert most emphatically that meaning and verifiability do not depend on any empirical conditions whatever, but are determined by purely logical possibilities. The opponent will object: if meaning is a matter of experience, how can it be a matter of definition and logic?

In reality there is no contradiction or difficulty. The word 'experience' is ambiguous. Firstly, it may be a name for any so-called 'immediate data'—which is a comparatively modern use of the word—and secondly we can use it in the sense in which we speak e.g., of an 'experienced traveller', meaning a man who has not only seen a great deal but also knows how to profit from it for his actions. It is in this second sense (by the way, the sense the word has in Hume's and Kant's philosophy) that verifiability must be declared to be independent of experience. The possibility of verification does not rest on any 'experiential truth', on a law of nature or any other true general proposition, but is determined solely by our definitions, by the rules which have been fixed for our language, or which we can fix arbitrarily at any moment. All of these rules ultimately point to ostensive definitions, as we have explained, and through them verifiability is linked to experience in the first sense of the word. No rule of expression presupposes any law or regularity in the world (which is the condition of 'experience' as Hume and Kant use the word), but it does presuppose data and situations, to which names can be attached. The rules of language are rules of the application of language; so there must be something to which it can be applied. Expressibility and verifiability are one and the same thing. There is no antagonism between logic and experience. Not only can the logician be an empiricist at the same time; he must be one if he wants to understand what he himself is doing.

4.

Let us glance at some examples in order to illustrate the consequences of our attitude in regard to certain issues of traditional philosophy. Take the famous case of the reality of the other side of the moon (which is also one of Professor Lewis's examples). None of us, I think, would be willing to accept a view according to which it would be nonsense to speak of the averted face of our satellite. Can there be the slightest doubt that, according to our explanations, the conditions of meaning are amply satisfied in this case?

I think there can be no doubt. For the question, 'What is the other side of the moon like?', could be answered, for instance, by a description of what would be seen or touched by a person located somewhere behind the moon. The question whether it be physically possible for a human being—or indeed any other living being—to travel around the moon does not even have to be raised here; it is entirely irrelevant. Even if it could be shown that a journey to another celestial body were absolutely incompatible with the known laws of nature, a proposition about the other side of the moon would still be meaningful. Since our sentence speaks of certain places in space as being filled with matter (for that is what the words 'side of the moon' stand for), it will have meaning if we indicate under what circumstances a proposition of the form, 'this place is filled with matter', shall be called true or false. The concept 'physical substance at a certain place' is defined by our language in physics and geometry. Geometry itself is the grammar of our propositions about 'spatial' relations, and it is not very difficult to see how assertions about physical properties and spatial relations are connected with 'sense-data' by ostensive definitions. This connection, by the way, is not such as to entitle us to say that physical substance is 'a mere construction put upon sense-data', or that a physical body is 'a complex of sense-data'—unless we interpret these phrases as rather inadequate abbreviations of the assertion that all propositions containing the term 'physical body' require for their verification the presence of sense-data. And this is certainly an exceedingly trivial statement.

In the case of the moon we might perhaps say that the meaning-requirement is fulfilled if we are able to 'imagine' (picture mentally) situations which would verify our proposition. But if we should say in general that verifiability of an assertion implies possibility of 'imagining' the asserted fact, this would be true only in a restricted sense. It would not be true in so far as the possibility is of the empirical kind, i.e., implying specific human capacities. I do not think, for instance, that we can be accused of talking nonsense if we speak of a universe of ten dimensions, or of beings possessing sense-organs and having perceptions entirely different from ours; and yet it does not seem right to say that we are able to 'imagine' such beings and such perceptions, or a ten-dimensional world. But we must be able to say under what observable circumstances we should assert the existence of the beings or sense-organs just referred to. It is clear that I can speak meaningfully of the sound of a friend's voice without being able actually to recall it in my imagination.—This is not the place to discuss the logical grammar of the word 'to imagine'; these few remarks may caution us against accepting too readily a psychological explanation of verifiability.

We must not identify meaning with any of the psychological data which form the material of a mental sentence (or 'thought') in the same sense in which articulated sounds form the material of a spoken sentence, or black marks on paper the material of a written sentence. When you are doing a calculation in arithmetic it is quite irrelevant whether you have before your mind the images of black numbers or of red numbers, or no visual picture at all. And even if it were empirically impossible for you to do any calculation without imagining black numbers at the same time, the mental pictures of those black marks could, of course, in no way be considered as constituting the meaning, or part of the meaning, of the calculation.

Carnap is right in putting great stress upon the fact (always emphasized by the critics of 'psychologism') that the question of meaning has nothing to do with the psychological question as to the mental processes of which an act of thought may consist. But I am not sure that he has seen with equal clarity that reference to ostensive definitions (which we postulate for meaning) does not involve the error of a confusion of the two questions. In order to understand a sentence containing, e.g., the words 'red flag', it is indispensable that I should be able to indicate a situation where I could point to an object which I should call a 'flag', and whose color I could recognize as 'red' as distinguished from other colors. But in order to do this it is not necessary that I should actually call up the image of a red flag. It is of the utmost importance to see that these two things have nothing in common. At this moment I am trying in vain to imagine the shape of a capital G in German print; nevertheless I can speak about it without talking nonsense, and I know I should recognize it if I saw the letter. Imagining a red patch is utterly different from referring to an ostensive definition of 'red'. Verifiability has nothing to do with any images that may be associated with the words of the sentence in question.

No more difficulty than in the case of the other side of the moon will be found in discussing, as another significant example, the question of 'immortality', which Professor Lewis calls, and which is usually called, a metaphysical problem. I take it for granted that 'immortality' is not supposed to signify never-ending life (for that might possibly be meaningless on account of infinity being involved), but that we are concerned with the question of survival after 'death'. I think we may agree with Professor Lewis when he says about this hypothesis: "Our understanding of what would verify it has no lack of clarity." In fact, I can easily imagine e.g. witnessing the funeral of my own body and continuing to exist without a body, for nothing is easier than to describe a world which differs from our ordinary world only in the complete absence of all data which I would call parts of my own body.

We must conclude that immortality, in the sense defined, should not be regarded as a 'metaphysical problem', but is an empirical hypothesis, because it possesses logical verifiability. It could be verified by following the prescription: 'Wait until you die!' Professor Lewis seems to hold that this method is not satisfactory from the point of view of science. He says (143):

> The hypothesis of immortality is unverifiable in an obvious sense. . . . if it be maintained that only what is scientifically verifiable has

> meaning, then this conception is a case in point. It could hardly be verified by science; and there is no observation or experiment which science could make, the negative result of which would disprove it.

I fancy that in these sentences the private method of verification is rejected as being unscientific because it would apply only to the individual case of the experiencing person himself, whereas a scientific statement should be capable of a general proof, open to any careful observer. But I see no reason why even this should be declared to be impossible. On the contrary, it is easy to describe experiences such that the hypothesis of an invisible existence of human beings after their bodily death would be the most acceptable explanation of the phenomena observed. These phenomena, it is true, would have to be of a much more convincing nature than the ridiculous happenings alleged to have occurred in meetings of the occultists—but I think there cannot be the slightest doubt as to the possibility (in the logical sense) of phenomena which would form a scientific justification of the hypothesis of survival after death, and would permit an investigation by scientific methods of that form of life. To be sure, the hypothesis could never be established as absolutely true, but it shares this fate with all hypotheses. If it should be urged that the souls of the deceased might inhabit some supercelestial space where they would not be accessible to our perception, and that therefore the truth or falsity of the assertion could never be tested, the reply would be that if the words 'supercelestial space' are to have any meaning at all, that space must be defined in such a way that the impossibility of reaching it or of perceiving anything in it would be merely empirical, so that some means of overcoming the difficulties could at least be described, although it might be beyond human power to put them into use.

Thus our conclusion stands. The hypothesis of immortality is an empirical statement which owes its meaning to its verifiability, and it has no meaning beyond the possibility of verification. If it must be admitted that science could make no experiment the negative result of which would disprove it, this is true only in the same sense in which it is true for many other hypotheses of similar structure—especially those that have sprung up from other motives than the knowledge of a great many facts of experience which must be regarded as giving a high probability to the hypothesis.

The question about the 'existence of the external world' will be discussed in the next section.

5.

Let us now turn to a point of fundamental importance and the deepest philosophic interest. Professor Lewis refers to it as the "egocentric predicament", and he describes as one of the most characteristic features of logical positivism its attempt to take this predicament seriously. It seems to be formulated in the sentence (128), "Actually given experience is given in the first person", and its importance for the doctrine of logical positivism seems to be evident from the fact that Carnap, in his *Der Logische Aufbau der Welt,* states that the method of this book may be called "methodological solipsism". Professor Lewis thinks, rightly, that the egocentric or solipsistic principle is not implied by our general principle of verifiability, and so he regards it as a second principle which, together with that of verifiability, leads, in his opinion, to the main results of the Viennese philosophy.

If I may be permitted to make a few general remarks here I should like to say that one of the greatest advantages and attractions of true positivism seems to me to be the antisolipsistic attitude which characterizes it from the very beginning. There is as little danger of solipsism in it as in any 'realism', and it seems to me to be the chief point of difference between idealism and positivism that the latter keeps entirely clear of the egocentric predicament. I think it is the greatest misunderstanding of the positivist idea (often even committed by thinkers who called themselves positivists) to see in it a tendency towards solipsism or a kinship to subjective idealism. We may regard Vaihinger's *Philosophy of As If* as a typical example of this mistake (he calls his book a "System of Idealistic Positivism"), and perhaps the philosophy of Mach and Avenarius as one of the most consistent attempts to avoid it. It is rather unfortunate that Carnap has advocated what he calls "methodological solipsism", and that in his construction of all concepts out of elementary data the "eigenpsychische Gegenstände" (for-me entities) come first and form the basis for the construction of physical objects, which finally lead to the concept of other selves; but if there is any mistake here it is chiefly in the terminology, not in the thought. "Methodological solipsism" is not a kind of solipsism, but a method of building up concepts. And it must be borne in mind that the order of construction which Carnap recommends—beginning with "for-me entities"—is not asserted to be the only possible one. It would have been better to have chosen a different order, but in principle Carnap was well aware of the fact that original experience is "without a subject" (see Lewis loc. cit. 145).

The strongest emphasis should be laid on the fact that primitive experience is absolutely neutral or, as Wittgenstein has occasionally put it, that immediate data "have no owner". Since the genuine positivist denies (with Mach etc.) that original experience "has that quality or status, characteristic of all given experience, which is indicated by the adjective 'first person'" (loc. cit. 145), he cannot possibly take the 'egocentric predicament' seriously; for him this predicament does not exist. To see that primitive experience is not first-person experience seems to me to be one of the most important steps which philosophy must take towards the clarification of its deepest problems.

The unique position of the 'self' is not a basic property of all experience, but is itself a fact (among other facts) of experience. Idealism (as represented by Berkeley's "esse = percipi" or by Schopenhauer's "Die Welt ist meine Vorstellung") and other doctrines with egocentric tendencies commit the great error of mistaking the unique position of the ego, which is an empirical fact, for a logical, a priori truth, or, rather, substituting the one for the other. It is worth while to investigate this matter and analyse the sentence which seems to express the egocentric predicament. This will not be a digression, for without the clarification of this point it will be impossible to understand the basic position of our empiricism.

How does the idealist or the solipsist arrive at the statement that the world, as far as I know it, is 'my own idea', that ultimately I know nothing but the 'content of my own consciousness'?

Experience teaches that all immediate data depend in some way or other upon those data that constitute what I call 'my body'. All visual data disappear when the eyes of this body are closed; all sounds cease when its ears are stuffed up; and so on. This body is distinguished from the 'bodies of other beings' by the fact that it always appears in a peculiar perspective (its back or its eyes, for instance, never appear except in a looking glass); but this is not nearly so significant as the other fact that the quality of all data is conditioned by the state of the organs of this particular body. Obviously these two facts—and perhaps originally the first one—form the only reason why this body is called 'my' body. The possessive pronoun singles it out from among other bodies; it is an adjective which denotes the uniqueness described.

The fact that all data are dependent upon 'my' body (particularly those parts of it which are called 'sense-organs') induces us to form the concept of 'perception'. We do not find this concept in the language of unsophisticated, primitive people; they do not say, 'I perceive a tree', but simply, 'there is a tree'. 'Perception' implies the distinction between a subject which perceives and an object which is perceived. Originally the perceiver is the sense-organ or the body to which it belongs, but since the body itself—including the nervous system—is also one of the perceived things, the original view is soon 'corrected' by substituting for the perceiver a new subject, which is called 'ego' or 'mind' or 'consciousness'. It is usually thought of as somehow residing in the body, because the sense-organs are on the surface of the body. The mistake of locating consciousness or mind inside the body ('in the head'), which has been called "introjection" by R. Avenarius, is the main source of the difficulties of the so-called 'mind-body problem'. By avoiding the error of introjection we avoid at the same time the idealistic fallacy which leads to solipsism. It is easy to show that introjection is an error. When I see a green meadow the 'green' is declared to be a content of my consciousness, but it certainly is not inside my head. Inside my skull there is nothing but my brain; and if there should happen to be a green spot in my brain, it would obviously not be the green of the meadow, but the green of the brain.

But for our purpose it is not necessary to follow this train of thought; it is sufficient to restate the facts clearly.

It is a fact of experience that all data depend in some way or other upon the state of a certain body which has the peculiarity that its eyes and its back are never seen (except by means of a mirror). It is usually called 'my' body; but here, in order to avoid mistakes, I shall take the liberty of calling it the body 'M'. A particular case of the dependence just mentioned is expressed by the sentence, 'I do not perceive anything unless the sense-organs of the body M are affected'. Or, taking a still more special case, I may make the following statement:

'I feel pain only when the body M is hurt.' (P)

I shall refer to this statement as 'proposition P'.

Now let us consider another proposition (Q):

'I can feel only my pain.' (Q)

The sentence Q may be interpreted in various ways. Firstly, it may be regarded as equivalent to P, so that P and Q would just be two different ways of expressing one and the same empirical fact. The word 'can' occurring in Q would denote what we have called 'empirical possibility', and the words 'I' and 'my' would refer to the body M. It is of the utmost importance to realize that in this first interpretation Q is the description of a fact of experience, i.e., a fact which we could very well imagine to be different.

We could easily imagine (here I am closely following ideas expressed by Mr. Wittgenstein) that I experience a pain every time the body of my friend is hurt, that I am gay when his face bears a joyful expression, that I feel tired after he has taken a long walk, or even that I do not see anything when his eyes are closed, and so forth. Proposition Q (if interpreted as being equivalent to P) denies that these things ever happen; but if they did happen, Q would be falsified. Thus we indicate the meaning of Q (or P) by describing facts which make Q true, and other facts that would make it false. If facts of the latter kind occurred our world would be rather different from the one in which we are actually living; the properties of the 'data' would depend on other human bodies (or perhaps only one of them) as well as upon the body M.

This fictitious world may be empirically impossible, because incompatible with the actual laws of nature—though we cannot at all be sure of this—but it is logically possible, because we were able to give a description of it. Now let us for a moment suppose this fictitious world to be real. How would our language adapt itself to it? It might be done in two different ways which are of interest for our problem.

Proposition P would be false. As regards Q, there would be two possibilities. The first is to maintain that its meaning is still to be the same as that of P. In this case Q would be false and could be replaced by the true proposition,

'I can feel somebody else's pain as well as my own.' (R)

R would state the empirical fact (which for the moment we suppose to be true) that the datum 'pain' occurs not only when M is hurt, but also when some injury is inflicted upon some other body, say, the body 'O'.

If we express the supposed state of affairs by the proposition R, there will evidently be no temptation and no pretext to make any 'solipsistic' statement. My body—which in this case could mean nothing but 'body M'—would still be unique in that it would always appear in a particular perspective (with invisible back, etc.), but it would no longer be unique as being the only body upon whose state depended the properties of all other data. And it was only this latter characteristic which gave rise to the egocentric view. The philosophic doubt concerning the 'reality of the external world' arose from the consideration that I had no knowledge of that world except by perception, i.e., by means of the sensitive organs of my body. If this is no longer true, if the data depend also on other bodies O (which differ from M in certain empirical respects, but not in principle), then there will be no more justification in calling the data 'my own'; other individuals O will have the same right to be regarded as owners or proprietors of the data. The sceptic was afraid that other bodies O might be nothing but images owned by the 'mind' belonging to the body M, because everything seemed to depend on the state of the latter; but under the circumstances described there exists perfect symmetry between O and M; the egocentric predicament has disappeared.

You will perhaps call my attention to the fact that the circumstances we have been describing are fictitious, that they do not occur in our real world, so that in this world, unfortunately, the egocentric predicament holds its sway. I answer that I wish to base my argument only on the fact that the difference between the two words is merely empirical, i.e., proposition P just happens to be true in the actual world as far as our experience goes. It does not even seem to be incompatible with the known laws of nature; the probability which these laws give to the falsity of P is not zero.

Now if we still agree that proposition Q is to be regarded as identical with P (which means that 'my' is to be defined as referring to M), the word 'can' in Q will still indicate empirical possibility. Consequently, if a philosopher tried to use Q as the basis of a kind of solipsism, he would have to be prepared to see his whole construction falsified by some future experience. But this is exactly what the true solipsist refuses to do. He contends that no experience whatever could possibly contradict him, because it would always necessarily have the peculiar for-me character, which may be described by the 'egocentric predicament'. In other words, he is well aware that solipsism cannot be based on Q as long as Q is, by definition, nothing but another way of expressing P. As a matter of fact, the solipsist who makes the statement Q attaches a different meaning to the same words; he does not wish merely to assert P, but he intends to say something entirely different. The difference lies in the word 'my'. He does not want to define the personal pronoun by reference to the body M, but uses it in a much more general way. What meaning does he give to the sentence Q?

Let us examine this second interpretation which may be given to Q. The idealist or solipsist who says, 'I can feel only my own pain', or, more generally, 'I can be aware only of the data of my own consciousness', believes that he is uttering a necessary, self-evident truth which no possible experience can force him to sacrifice. He will have to admit the possibility of circumstances such as those we described for our fictitious world; but, he will say, even if I feel pain every time when another body O is hurt, I shall never say, 'I feel O's pain', but always, 'My pain is in O's body'.

We cannot declare this statement of the idealist to be false; it is just a different way of adapting our language to the imagined new circumstances, and the rules of language are, in principle, arbitrary. But, of course, some uses of our words may recommend themselves as practical and well adapted; others may be condemned as misleading. Let us examine the idealist's attitude from this point of view.

He rejects our proposition R and replaces it by the other one:

'I can feel pain in other bodies as well as in my own.' (S)

He wants to insist that any pain I feel must be called my pain, no matter where it is felt, and in order to assert this he says:

'I *can* feel only *my* pain.' (T)

Sentence T is, as far as the words are concerned, the same as Q. I have used slightly different signs by having the words 'can' and 'my' printed in italics, in order to indicate that, when used by the solipsist, these two words have a signification which is different from the signification they had in Q when we interpreted Q as meaning the same as P. In T 'my pain' no longer means 'pain in body M', because, according to the solipsist's explanation, 'my pain' may also be in another body O; so we must ask: what does the pronoun 'my' signify here?

It is easy to see that it does not signify anything; it is a superfluous word which may just as well be omitted. 'I feel pain' and 'I feel my pain' are, according to the solipsist's definition, to have identical meaning; the word 'my', therefore, has no function in the sentence. If he says, 'The pain which I feel is my pain', he is uttering a mere tautology, because he has declared that whatever the empirical circumstances may be, he will never allow the pronouns 'your' or 'his' to be used in connection with 'I feel pain', but always the pronoun 'my'. This stipulation, being independent of empirical facts, is a logical rule, and if it is followed, T becomes a tautology; the word 'can' in T (together with 'only') does not denote empirical impossibility, but logical impossibility. In other words it would not be false, it would be nonsense (grammatically forbidden) to say 'I can feel somebody else's pain'. A tautology, being the negation of nonsense, is itself devoid of meaning in the sense that it does not assert anything, but merely indicates a rule concerning the use of words.

We infer that T, which is the second interpretation of Q, adopted by the solipsist and forming the basis of his argument, is strictly meaningless. It does not say anything at all, does not express any interpretation of the world or view about the world; it just introduces a strange way of speaking, a clumsy kind of language, which attaches the index 'my' (or 'content of my consciousness') to everything without exception. Solipsism is nonsense, because its starting-point, the egocentric predicament, is meaningless.

The words 'I' and 'my', if we use them according to the solipsist's prescription, are absolutely empty, mere adornments of speech. There would be no difference of meaning between the three expressions, 'I feel my pain'; 'I feel pain'; and 'there is pain'. Lichtenberg, the wonderful eighteenth-century physicist and philosopher, declared that Descartes had no right to start his philosophy with the proposition 'I think', instead of saying 'it thinks'. Just as there would be no sense in speaking of a white horse unless it were logically possible that a horse might not be white, so no sentence containing the words 'I' or 'my' would be meaningful unless we could replace them by 'he' or 'his' without speaking nonsense. But such a substitution is impossible in a sentence that would seem to express the egocentric predicament or the solipsistic philosophy.

R and S are not different explanations or interpretations of a certain state of affairs which we have described, but simply verbally different formulations of this description. It is of fundamental importance to see that R and S are not two propositions, but one and the same proposition in two different languages. The solipsist, by rejecting the language of R and insisting upon the language of S, has adopted a terminology which makes Q tautological, transforms it into T. Thus he has made it impossible to verify or falsify his own statements; he himself has deprived them of meaning. By refusing to avail himself of the opportunities (which we showed him) to make the statement 'I can feel somebody else's pain' meaningful, he has at the same time lost the opportunity of giving meaning to the sentence 'I can feel only my own pain'.

The pronoun 'my' indicates possession; we cannot speak of the 'owner' of a pain—or any other datum—except in cases where the word 'my' can be used meaningfully, i.e., where by substituting 'his' or 'your' we would get the description of a possible state of affairs. This condition is fulfilled if 'my' is defined as referring to the body M, and it would also be fulfilled if I agree to call 'my body' any body in which I can feel pain. In our actual world these two definitions apply to one and the same body, but that is an empirical fact which might be different. If the two definitions did not coincide and if we adopted the second one we should need a new word to distinguish the body M from other bodies in which I might have sensations; the word 'my' would have meaning in a sentence of the form 'A is one of my bodies, but B is not', but it would be meaningless in the statement 'I can feel pain only in my bodies', for this would be a mere tautology.

The grammar of the word 'owner' is similar to that of the word 'my': it makes sense only where it is logically possible for a thing to change its owner, i.e., where the relation between the owner and the owned object is empirical, not logical ('external', not 'internal'). Thus one could say 'Body M is the owner of this pain' or 'that pain is owned by the bodies M and O'. The second proposition can, perhaps, never be truthfully asserted in our actual world (although I cannot see that it would be incompatible with the laws of nature), but both of them would make sense. Their meaning would be to express certain relations of dependence between the pain and the state of certain bodies, and the existence of such a relation could easily be tested.

The solipsist refuses to use the word 'owner' in this sensible way. He knows that many properties of the data do not depend at all upon any states of human bodies, viz., all those regularities of their behavior that can be expressed by 'physical laws'; he knows, therefore, that it would be wrong to say 'my body is the owner of everything', and so he speaks of a 'self', or 'ego', or 'consciousness', and declares this to be the owner of everything. (The idealist, by the way, makes the same mistake when he asserts that we know nothing but 'appearances'.) This is nonsense because the word 'owner', when used in this way, has lost its meaning. The solipsistic assertion cannot be verified or falsified, it will be true by definition, whatever the facts may be; it simply consists in the verbal prescription to add the phrase 'owned by Me' to the names of all objects, etc.

Thus we see that unless we choose to call our body the owner or bearer of the data—which seems to be a rather misleading expression—we have to say that the data have no owner or bearer. This neutrality of experience—as against the subjectivity claimed for it by the idealist—is one of the most fundamental points of true positivism. The sentence 'All experience is first-person experience' will either mean the simple empirical fact that all data are in certain respects dependent on the state of the nervous system of my body M, or it will be meaningless. Before this physiological fact is discovered, experience is not 'my' experience at all, it is self-sufficient and does not 'belong' to anybody. The proposition 'The ego is the centre of the world' may be regarded as an expression of the same fact, and has meaning only if it refers to the body. The concept of 'ego' is a construction put upon the same fact, and we could easily imagine a world in which this concept would not have been formed, where there would be no idea of an insurmountable barrier between what is inside the Me and what is outside of it. It would be a world in which occurrences like those corresponding to proposition R and similar ones were the rule, and in which the facts of 'memory' were not so pronounced as they are in our actual world. Under those circumstances we should not be tempted to fall into the 'egocentric predicament', but the sentence which tries to express such a predicament would be meaningless under any circumstances.

After our last remarks it will be easy to deal with the so-called problem concerning the existence of the external world. If, with Professor Lewis (143), we formulate the 'realistic' hypothesis by asserting, "If all minds should disappear from the universe, the stars would still go on in their courses", we must admit the impossibility of verifying it, but the impossibility is merely empirical. And the empirical circumstances are such that we have every reason to believe the hypothesis to be true. We are as sure of it as of the best founded physical laws that science has discovered.

As a matter of fact, we have already pointed out that there are certain regularities in the world which experience shows to be entirely independent of what happens to human beings on the earth. The laws of motion of the celestial bodies are formulated entirely without reference to any human bodies, and this is the reason why we are justified in maintaining that they will go on in their courses after mankind has vanished from the earth. Experience shows no connection between the two kinds of events. We observe that the course of the stars is no more changed by the death of human beings than, say, by the eruption of a volcano, or by a change of government in China. Why should we suppose that there would be any difference if all living beings on our planet, or indeed everywhere in the universe, were extinguished? There can be no doubt that on the strength of empirical evidence the existence of living beings is no necessary condition for the existence of the rest of the world.

The question 'Will the world go on existing after I am dead?' has no meaning unless it is interpreted as asking 'Does the existence of the stars etc. depend upon the life or death of a human being?', and this question is answered in the negative by experience. The mistake of the solipsist or idealist consists in rejecting this empirical interpretation and looking for some metaphysical issue behind it; but all their efforts to construct a new sense of the question end only in depriving it of its old one.

It will be noticed that I have taken the liberty of substituting the phrase 'if all living beings disappeared from the universe' for the phrase 'if all minds disappeared from the universe'. I hope it will not be thought that I have changed the meaning of the issue by this substitution. I have avoided the word 'mind' because I take it to signify the same as the words 'ego' or 'consciousness', which we have found to be so dark and dangerous. By living beings I meant beings capable of perception, and the concept of perception had been defined only by reference to living bodies, to physical organs. Thus I was justified in substituting 'death of living beings' for 'disappearance of minds'. But the arguments hold for any empirical definition one may choose to give for 'mind'. I need only point out that, according to experience, the motion of the stars etc. is quite independent of all 'mental' phenomena such as feeling joy or sorrow, meditating, dreaming, etc.; and we may infer that the course of the stars would not be affected if those phenomena should cease to exist.

But is it true that this inference could be verified by experience? Empirically it seems to be impossible, but we know that only logical possibility of verification is required. And verification without a 'mind' is logically possible on account of the 'neutral', impersonal character of experience on which we have insisted. Primitive experience, mere existence of ordered data, does not presuppose a 'subject', or 'ego', or 'Me', or 'mind'; it can take place without any of the facts which lead to the formation of those concepts; it is not an experience of anybody. It is not difficult to imagine a universe without plants and animals and human bodies (including the body M), and without the mental phenomena just referred to: it would certainly be a 'world without minds' (for what else could deserve this name?), but the laws of nature might be exactly the same as in our actual world. We could describe this universe in terms of our actual experience (we would only have to leave out all terms referring to human bodies and emotions); and that is sufficient to speak of it as a world of possible experience.

The last considerations may serve as an example of one of the main theses of true positivism: that the naïve representation of the world, as the man in the street sees it, is perfectly correct; and that the solution of the great philosophical issues consists in returning to this original world-view, after having shown that the troublesome problems arose only from an inadequate description of the world by means of a faulty language.

A. J. Ayer

THE ELIMINATION OF METAPHYSICS[1]

The traditional disputes of philosophers are, for the most part, as unwarranted as they are unfruitful. The surest way to end them is to establish beyond question what should be the purpose and method of a philosophical enquiry. And this is by no means so difficult a task as the history of philosophy would lead one to suppose. For if there are any questions which science leaves it to philosophy to answer, a straightforward process of elimination must lead to their discovery.

We may begin by criticising the metaphysical thesis that philosophy affords us knowledge of a reality transcending the world of science and common sense. Later on, when we come to define metaphysics and account for its existence, we shall find that it is possible to be a metaphysician without believing in a transcendent reality; for we shall see that many metaphysical utterances are due to the commission of logical errors, rather than to a conscious desire on the part of their authors to go beyond the limits of experience. But it is convenient for us to take the case of those who believe that it is possible to have knowledge of a transcendent reality as a starting-point for our discussion. The arguments which we use to refute them will subsequently be found to apply to the whole of metaphysics.

One way of attacking a metaphysician who claimed to have knowledge of a reality which transcended the phenomenal world would be to enquire from what premises his propositions were deduced. Must he not begin, as other men do, with the evidence of his senses? And if so, what valid process of reasoning can possibly lead him to the conception of a

[1] From: *Language, Truth and Logic,* A. J. Ayer, Ch. 1. Dover Publications, Inc., New York, and Victor Gollancz, Ltd., London. Reprinted by permission.

transcendent reality? Surely from empirical premises nothing whatsoever concerning the properties, or even the existence, of anything super-empirical can legitimately be inferred. But this objection would be met by a denial on the part of the metaphysician that his assertions were ultimately based on the evidence of his senses. He would say that he was endowed with a faculty of intellectual intuition which enabled him to know facts that could not be known through sense-experience. And even if it could be shown that he was relying on empirical premises, and that his venture into a non-empirical world was therefore logically unjustified, it would not follow that the assertions which he made concerning this non-empirical world could not be true. For the fact that a conclusion does not follow from its putative premise is not sufficient to show that it is false. Consequently one cannot overthrow a system of transcendent metaphysics merely by criticising the way in which it comes into being. What is required is rather a criticism of the nature of the actual statements which comprise it. And this is the line of argument which we shall, in fact, pursue. For we shall maintain that no statement which refers to a "reality" transcending the limits of all possible sense-experience can possibly have any literal significance; from which it must follow that the labours of those who have striven to describe such a reality have all been devoted to the production of nonsense.

It may be suggested that this is a proposition which has already been proved by Kant. But although Kant also condemned transcendent metaphysics, he did so on different grounds. For he said that the human understanding was so constituted that it lost itself in contradictions when it ventured out beyond the limits of possible experience and attempted to deal with things in themselves. And thus he made the impossibility of a transcendent metaphysic not, as we do, a matter of logic, but a matter of fact. He asserted, not that our minds could not conceivably have had the power of penetrating beyond the phenomenal world, but merely that they were in fact devoid of it. And this leads the critic to ask how, if it is possible to know only what lies within the bounds of sense-experience, the author can be justified in asserting that real things do exist beyond, and how he can tell what are the boundaries beyond which the human understanding may not venture, unless he succeeds in passing them himself. As Wittgenstein says, "in order to draw a limit to thinking, we should have to think both sides of this limit," [2] a truth to which Bradley gives a special twist in maintaining that the man who is ready to prove that metaphysics is impossible is a brother metaphysician with a rival theory of his own.[3]

Whatever force these objections may have against the Kantian doctrine, they have none whatsoever against the thesis that I am about to set forth. It cannot here be said that the author is himself over-

[2] *Tractatus Logico-Philosophicus,* Preface.

[3] Bradley, *Appearance and Reality,* 2nd ed., p. 1.

stepping the barrier he maintains to be impassable. For the fruitlessness of attempting to transcend the limits of possible sense-experience will be deduced, not from a psychological hypothesis concerning the actual constitution of the human mind, but from the rule which determines the literal significance of language. Our charge against the metaphysician is not that he attempts to employ the understanding in a field where it cannot profitably venture, but that he produces sentences which fail to conform to the conditions under which alone a sentence can be literally significant. Nor are we ourselves obliged to talk nonsense in order to show that all sentences of a certain type are necessarily devoid of literal significance. We need only formulate the criterion which enables us to test whether a sentence expresses a genuine proposition about a matter of fact, and then point out that the sentences under consideration fail to satisfy it. And this we shall now proceed to do. We shall first of all formulate the criterion in somewhat vague terms, and then give the explanations which are necessary to render it precise.

The criterion which we use to test the genuineness of apparent statements of fact is the criterion of verifiability. We say that a sentence is factually significant to any given person, if, and only if, he knows how to verify the proposition which it purports to express—that is, if he knows what observations would lead him, under certain conditions, to accept the proposition as being true, or reject it as being false. If, on the other hand, the putative proposition is of such a character that the assumption of its truth, or falsehood, is consistent with any assumption whatsoever concerning the nature of his future experience, then, as far as he is concerned, it is, if not a tautology, a mere pseudo-proposition. The sentence expressing it may be emotionally significant to him; but it is not literally significant. And with regard to questions the procedure is the same. We enquire in every case what observations would lead us to answer the question, one way or the other; and, if none can be discovered, we must conclude that the sentence under consideration does not, as far as we are concerned, express a genuine question, however strongly its grammatical appearance may suggest that it does.

As the adoption of this procedure is an essential factor in the argument of this book, it needs to be examined in detail.

In the first place, it is necessary to draw a distinction between practical verifiability, and verifiability in principle. Plainly we all understand, in many cases believe, propositions which we have not in fact taken steps to verify. Many of these are propositions which we could verify if we took enough trouble. But there remain a number of significant propositions, concerning matters of fact, which we could not verify even if we chose; simply because we lack the practical means of placing ourselves in the situation where the relevant observations could be made. A simple and familiar example of such a proposition is the proposition that there are mountains on the farther side of the moon.[4] No rocket has yet been invented which would enable me to go and look at the farther side of the moon, so that I am unable to decide the matter by actual observation. But I do know what observations would decide it for me, if, as is theoretically conceivable, I were once in a position to make them. And therefore I say that the proposition is verifiable in principle, if not in practice, and is accordingly significant. On the other hand, such a metaphysical pseudo-proposition as "the Absolute enters into, but is itself incapable of, evolution and progress,"[5] is not even in principle verifiable. For one cannot conceive of an observation which would enable one to determine whether the Absolute did, or did not, enter into evolution and progress. Of course it is possible that the author of such a remark is using English words in a way in which they are not commonly used by English-speaking people, and that he does, in fact, intend to assert something which could be empirically verified. But until he makes us understand how the proposition that he wishes to express would be verified, he fails to communicate anything to us. And if he admits, as I think the author of the remark in question would have admitted, that his words were not intended to express either a tautology or a proposition which was capable, at least in principle, of being verified, then it follows that he has made an utterance which has no literal significance even for himself.

A further distinction which we must make is the distinction between the "strong" and the "weak" sense of the term "verifiable." A proposition is said to be verifiable, in the strong sense of the term, if, and only if, its truth could be conclusively established in experience. But it is verifiable, in the weak sense, if it is possible for experience to render it probable. In which sense are we using the term when we say that a putative proposition is genuine only if it is verifiable?

It seems to me that if we adopt conclusive verifiability as our criterion of significance, as some positivists have proposed,[6] our argument will prove too much. Consider, for example, the case of general propositions of law—such propositions, namely, as "arsenic is poisonous"; "all men are mortal"; "a body tends to expand when it is heated." It is of the very nature of these propositions that their truth cannot be established with certainty by any finite series of observations. But if it is recognised that such general propositions of law are designed to cover an infinite number of cases, then it must be admitted that they cannot, even in principle, be verified conclusively. And then, if we adopt con-

[4] This example has been used by Professor Schlick to illustrate the same point.

[5] A remark taken at random from *Appearance and Reality*, by F. H. Bradley.

[6] e.g. M. Schlick, "Positivismus und Realismus," *Erkenntnis*, Vol. I, 1930. F. Waismann, "Logische Analyse des Warscheinlichkeitsbegriffs," *Erkenntnis*, Vol. I, 1930.

clusive verifiability as our criterion of significance, we are logically obliged to treat these general propositions of law in the same fashion as we treat the statements of the metaphysician.

In face of this difficulty, some positivists[7] have adopted the heroic course of saying that these general propositions are indeed pieces of nonsense, albeit an essentially important type of nonsense. But here the introduction of the term "important" is simply an attempt to hedge. It serves only to mark the authors' recognition that their view is somewhat too paradoxical, without in any way removing the paradox. Besides, the difficulty is not confined to the case of general propositions of law, though it is there revealed most plainly. It is hardly less obvious in the case of propositions about the remote past. For it must surely be admitted that, however strong the evidence in favour of historical statements may be, their truth can never become more than highly probable. And to maintain that they also constituted an important, or unimportant, type of nonsense would be unplausible, to say the very least. Indeed, it will be our contention that no proposition, other than a tautology, can possibly be anything more than a probable hypothesis. And if this is correct, the principle that a sentence can be factually significant only if it expresses what is conclusively verifiable is self-stultifying as a criterion of significance. For it leads to the conclusion that it is impossible to make a significant statement of fact at all.

Nor can we accept the suggestion that a sentence should be allowed to be factually significant if, and only if, it expresses something which is definitely confutable by experience.[8] Those who adopt this course assume that, although no finite series of observations is ever sufficient to establish the truth of a hypothesis beyond all possibility of doubt, there are crucial cases in which a single observation, or series of observations, can definitely confute it. But, as we shall show later on, this assumption is false. A hypothesis cannot be conclusively confuted any more than it can be conclusively verified. For when we take the occurrence of certain observations as proof that a given hypothesis is false, we presuppose the existence of certain conditions. And though, in any given case, it may be extremely improbable that this assumption is false, it is not logically impossible. We shall see that there need be no self-contradiction in holding that some of the relevant circumstances are other than we have taken them to be, and consequently that the hypothesis has not really broken down. And if it is not the case that any hypothesis can be definitely confuted, we cannot hold that the genuineness of a proposition depends on the possibility of its definite confutation.

Accordingly, we fall back on the weaker sense of verification. We say that the question that must be asked about any putative state-

[7] e.g. M. Schlick, "Die Kausalität in der gegenwärtigen Physik," *Naturwissenschaft,* Vol. 19, 1931.

[8] This has been proposed by Karl Popper in his *Logik der Forschung.*

ment of fact is not, Would any observations make its truth or falsehood logically certain? but simply, Would any observations be relevant to the determination of its truth or falsehood? And it is only if a negative answer is given to this second question that we conclude that the statement under consideration is nonsensical.

To make our position clearer, we may formulate it in another way. Let us call a proposition which records an actual or possible observation an experiential proposition. Then we may say that it is the mark of a genuine factual proposition, not that it should be equivalent to an experiential proposition, or any finite number of experiential propositions, but simply that some experiential propositions can be deduced from it in conjunction with certain other premises without being deducible from those other premises alone.[9]

This criterion seems liberal enough. In contrast to the principle of conclusive verifiability, it clearly does not deny significance to general propositions or to propositions about the past. Let us see what kinds of assertion it rules out.

A good example of the kind of utterance that is condemned by our criterion as being not even false but nonsensical would be the assertion that the world of sense-experience was altogether unreal. It must, of course, be admitted that our senses do sometimes deceive us. We may, as the result of having certain sensations, expect certain other sensations to be obtainable which are, in fact, not obtainable. But, in all such cases, it is further sense-experience that informs us of the mistakes that arise out of sense-experience. We say that the senses sometimes deceive us, just because the expectations to which our sense-experiences give rise do not always accord with what we subsequently experience. That is, we rely on our senses to substantiate or confute the judgements which are based on our sensations. And therefore the fact that our perceptual judgements are sometimes found to be erroneous has not the slightest tendency to show that the world of sense-experience is unreal. And, indeed, it is plain that no conceivable observation, or series of observations, could have any tendency to show that the world revealed to us by sense-experience was unreal. Consequently, anyone who condemns the sensible world as a world of mere appearance, as opposed to reality, is saying something which, according to our criterion of significance, is literally nonsensical.

An example of a controversy which the application of our criterion obliges us to condemn as fictitious is provided by those who dispute concerning the number of substances that there are in the world. For it is admitted both by monists, who maintain that reality is one substance, and by pluralists, who maintain that reality is many, that it is impossible to imagine any empirical situation which would be relevant

[9] This is an over-simplified statement, which is not literally correct. I give what I believe to be the correct formulation in the Introduction, p. 13.

to the solution of their dispute. But if we are told that no possible observation could give any probability either to the assertion that reality was one substance or to the assertion that it was many, then we must conclude that neither assertion is significant. We shall see later on[10] that there are genuine logical and empirical questions involved in the dispute between monists and pluralists. But the metaphysical question concerning "substance" is ruled out by our criterion as spurious.

A similar treatment must be accorded to the controversy between realists and idealists, in its metaphysical aspect. A simple illustration, which I have made use of in a similar argument elsewhere,[11] will help to demonstrate this. Let us suppose that a picture is discovered and the suggestion made that it was painted by Goya. There is a definite procedure for dealing with such a question. The experts examine the picture to see in what way it resembles the accredited works of Goya, and to see if it bears any marks which are characteristic of a forgery; they look up contemporary records for evidence of the existence of such a picture, and so on. In the end, they may still disagree, but each one knows what empirical evidence would go to confirm or discredit his opinion. Suppose, now, that these men have studied philosophy, and some of them proceed to maintain that this picture is a set of ideas in the perceiver's mind, or in God's mind, others that it is objectively real. What possible experience could any of them have which would be relevant to the solution of this dispute one way or the other? In the ordinary sense of the term "real," in which it is opposed to "illusory," the reality of the picture is not in doubt. The disputants have satisfied themselves that the picture is real, in this sense, by obtaining a correlated series of sensations of sight and sensations of touch. Is there any similar process by which they could discover whether the picture was real, in the sense in which the term "real" is opposed to "ideal"? Clearly there is none. But, if that is so, the problem is fictitious according to our criterion. This does not mean that the realist-idealist controversy may be dismissed without further ado. For it can legitimately be regarded as a dispute concerning the analysis of existential propositions, and so as involving a logical problem which, as we shall see, can be definitively solved.[12] What we have just shown is that the question at issue between idealists and realists becomes fictitious when, as is often the case, it is given a metaphysical interpretation.

There is no need for us to give further examples of the operation of our criterion of significance. For our object is merely to show that philosophy, as a genuine branch of knowledge, must be distinguished from metaphysics. We are not now concerned with the historical question how much of what has traditionally passed for philosophy is

[10] In [*Language, Truth and Logic*], Chapter VIII.
[11] Vide "Demonstration of the Impossibility of Metaphysics," *Mind,* 1934, p. 339.
[12] Vide [*Language, Truth and Logic*], Chapter VIII.

actually metaphysical. We shall, however, point out later on that the majority of the "great philosophers" of the past were not essentially metaphysicians, and thus reassure those who would otherwise be prevented from adopting our criterion by considerations of piety.

As to the validity of the verification principle, in the form in which we have stated it, a demonstration will be given in the course of this book. For it will be shown that all propositions which have factual content are empirical hypotheses; and that the function of an empirical hypothesis is to provide a rule for the anticipation of experience.[13] And this means that every empirical hypothesis must be relevant to some actual, or possible, experience, so that a statement which is not relevant to any experience is not an empirical hypothesis, and accordingly has no factual content. But this is precisely what the principle of verifiability asserts.

It should be mentioned here that the fact that the utterances of the metaphysician are nonsensical does not follow simply from the fact that they are devoid of factual content. It follows from that fact, together with the fact that they are not *a priori* propositions. And in assuming that they are not *a priori* propositions, we are once again anticipating the conclusions of a later chapter in this book.[14] For it will be shown there that *a priori* propositions, which have always been attractive to philosophers on account of their certainty, owe this certainty to the fact that they are tautologies. We may accordingly define a metaphysical sentence as a sentence which purports to express a genuine proposition, but does, in fact, express neither a tautology nor an empirical hypothesis. And as tautologies and empirical hypotheses form the entire class of significant propositions, we are justified in concluding that all metaphysical assertions are nonsensical. Our next task is to show how they come to be made.

The use of the term "substance," to which we have already referred, provides us with a good example of the way in which metaphysics mostly comes to be written. It happens to be the case that we cannot, in our language, refer to the sensible properties of a thing without introducing a word or phrase which appears to stand for the thing itself as opposed to anything which may be said about it. And, as a result of this, those who are infected by the primitive superstition that to every name a single real entity must correspond assume that it is necessary to distinguish logically between the thing itself and any, or all, of its sensible properties. And so they employ the term "substance" to refer to the thing itself. But from the fact that we happen to employ a single word to refer to a thing, and make that word the grammatical subject of the sentences in which we refer to the sensible appearances of the thing, it does not by any means follow that the thing itself is a "simple entity," or that it cannot be defined in terms of

13 Vide [*Language, Truth and Logic*], Chapter V.
14 Chapter IV. [This volume pp. 74-87].

the totality of its appearances. It is true that in talking of "its" appearances we appear to distinguish the thing from the appearances, but that is simply an accident of linguistic usage. Logical analysis shows that what makes these "appearances" the "appearances of" the same thing is not their relationship to an entity other than themselves, but their relationship to one another. The metaphysician fails to see this because he is misled by a superficial grammatical feature of his language.

A simpler and clearer instance of the way in which a consideration of grammar leads to metaphysics is the case of the metaphysical concept of Being. The origin of our temptation to raise questions about Being, which no conceivable experience would enable us to answer, lies in the fact that, in our language, sentences which express existential propositions and sentences which express attributive propositions may be of the same grammatical form. For instance, the sentences "Martyrs exist" and "Martyrs suffer" both consist of a noun followed by an intransitive verb, and the fact that they have grammatically the same appearance leads one to assume that they are of the same logical type. It is seen that in the proposition "Martyrs suffer," the members of a certain species are credited with a certain attribute, and it is sometimes assumed that the same thing is true of such a proposition as "Martyrs exist." If this were actually the case, it would, indeed, be as legitimate to speculate about the Being of martyrs as it is to speculate about their suffering. But, as Kant pointed out,[15] existence is not an attribute. For, when we ascribe an attribute to a thing, we covertly assert that it exists: so that if existence were itself an attribute, it would follow that all positive existential propositions were tautologies, and all negative existential propositions self-contradictory; and this is not the case.[16] So that those who raise questions about Being which are based on the assumption that existence is an attribute are guilty of following grammar beyond the boundaries of sense.

A similar mistake has been made in connection with such propositions as "Unicorns are fictitious." Here again the fact that there is a superficial grammatical resemblance between the English sentences "Dogs are faithful" and "Unicorns are fictitious," and between the corresponding sentences in other languages, creates the assumption that they are of the same logical type. Dogs must exist in order to have the property of being faithful, and so it is held that unless unicorns in some way existed they could not have the property of being fictitious. But, as it is plainly self-contradictory to say that fictitious objects exist, the device is adopted of saying that they are real in some non-empirical sense—that they have a mode of real being which is different

[15] Vide *The Critique of Pure Reason,* "Transcendental Dialectic," Book II, Chapter iii, section 4.

[16] This argument is well stated by John Wisdom, *Interpretation and Analysis,* pp. 62, 63.

from the mode of being of existent things. But since there is no way of testing whether an object is real in this sense, as there is for testing whether it is real in the ordinary sense, the assertion that fictitious objects have a special non-empirical mode of real being is devoid of all literal significance. It comes to be made as a result of the assumption that being fictitious is an attribute. And this is a fallacy of the same order as the fallacy of supposing that existence is an attribute, and it can be exposed in the same way.

In general, the postulation of real non-existent entities results from the superstition, just now referred to, that, to every word or phrase that can be the grammatical subject of a sentence, there must somewhere be a real entity corresponding. For as there is no place in the empirical world for many of these "entities," a special non-empirical world is invoked to house them. To this error must be attributed, not only the utterances of a Heidegger, who bases his metaphysics on the assumption that "Nothing" is a name which is used to denote something peculiarly mysterious,[17] but also the prevalence of such problems as those concerning the reality of propositions and universals whose senselessness, though less obvious, is no less complete.

These few examples afford a sufficient indication of the way in which most metaphysical assertions come to be formulated. They show how easy it is to write sentences which are literally nonsensical without seeing that they are nonsensical. And thus we see that the view that a number of the traditional "problems of philosophy" are metaphysical, and consequently fictitious, does not involve any incredible assumptions about the psychology of philosophers.

Among those who recognise that if philosophy is to be accounted a genuine branch of knowledge it must be defined in such a way as to distinguish it from metaphysics, it is fashionable to speak of the metaphysician as a kind of misplaced poet. As his statements have no literal meaning, they are not subject to any criteria of truth or falsehood: but they may still serve to express, or arouse, emotion, and thus be subject to ethical or æsthetic standards. And it is suggested that they may have considerable value, as means of moral inspiration, or even as works of art. In this way, an attempt is made to compensate the metaphysician for his extrusion from philosophy.[18]

I am afraid that this compensation is hardly in accordance with his deserts. The view that the metaphysician is to be reckoned among the poets appears to rest on the assumption that both talk nonsense. But this assumption is false. In the vast majority of cases the sentences

[17] Vide *Was ist Metaphysik,* by Heidegger: criticised by Rudolf Carnap in his "Überwindung der Metaphysik durch logische Analyse der Sprache," *Erkenntnis,* Vol. II, 1932.

[18] For a discussion of this point, see also C. A. Mace, "Representation and Expression," *Analysis,* Vol. I, No. 3; and "Metaphysics and Emotive Language," *Analysis,* Vol. II, Nos. 1 and 2.

which are produced by poets do have literal meaning. The difference between the man who uses language scientifically and the man who uses it emotively is not that the one produces sentences which are incapable of arousing emotion, and the other sentences which have no sense, but that the one is primarily concerned with the expression of true propositions, the other with the creation of a work of art. Thus, if a work of science contains true and important propositions, its value as a work of science will hardly be diminished by the fact that they are inelegantly expressed. And similarly, a work of art is not necessarily the worse for the fact that all the propositions comprising it are literally false. But to say that many literary works are largely composed of falsehoods, is not to say that they are composed of pseudo-propositions. It is, in fact, very rare for a literary artist to produce sentences which have no literal meaning. And where this does occur, the sentences are carefully chosen for their rhythm and balance. If the author writes nonsense, it is because he considers it most suitable for bringing about the effects for which his writing is designed.

The metaphysician, on the other hand, does not intend to write nonsense. He lapses into it through being deceived by grammar, or through committing errors of reasoning, such as that which leads to the view that the sensible world is unreal. But it is not the mark of a poet simply to make mistakes of this sort. There are some, indeed, who would see in the fact that the metaphysician's utterances are senseless a reason against the view that they have æsthetic value. And, without going so far as this, we may safely say that it does not constitute a reason for it.

It is true, however, that although the greater part of metaphysics is merely the embodiment of humdrum errors, there remain a number of metaphysical passages which are the work of genuine mystical feeling; and they may more plausibly be held to have moral or æsthetic value. But, as far as we are concerned, the distinction between the kind of metaphysics that is produced by a philosopher who has been duped by grammar, and the kind that is produced by a mystic who is trying to express the inexpressible, is of no great importance: what is important to us is to realise that even the utterances of the metaphysician who is attempting to expound a vision are literally senseless; so that henceforth we may pursue our philosophical researches with as little regard for them as for the more inglorious kind of metaphysics which comes from a failure to understand the workings of our language.

THE FUNCTION OF PHILOSOPHY[1]

Among the superstitions from which we are freed by the abandonment of metaphysics is the view that it is the business of the philosopher to construct a deductive system. In rejecting this view we are not, of course, suggesting that the philosopher can dispense with deductive reasoning. We are simply contesting his right to posit certain first principles, and then offer them with their consequences as a complete picture of reality. To discredit this procedure, one has only to show that there can be no first principles of the kind it requires.

As it is the function of these first principles to provide a certain basis for our knowledge, it is clear that they are not to be found among the so-called laws of nature. For we shall see that the "laws of nature," if they are not mere definitions, are simply hypotheses which may be confuted by experience. And, indeed, it has never been the practice of the system-builders in philosophy to choose inductive generalizations for their premises. Rightly regarding such generalizations as being merely probable, they subordinate them to principles which they believe to be logically certain.

This is illustrated most clearly in the system of Descartes. It is commonly said that Descartes attempted to derive all human knowledge from premises whose truth was intuitively certain: but this interpretation puts an undue stress on the element of psychology in his system. I think he realised well enough that a mere appeal to intuition was insufficient for his purpose, since men are not all equally credulous, and that what he was really trying to do was to base all our knowledge on propositions which it would be self-contradictory to deny. He thought he had found such a proposition in *"cogito,"* which must not here be understood in its ordinary sense of "I think," but rather as meaning "there is a thought now." In fact he was wrong, because *"non cogito"* would be self-contradictory only if it negated itself: and this no

[1] From: *Language, Truth and Logic,* A. J. Ayer, Ch. 2. Dover Publications, Inc., New York, and Victor Gollancz, Ltd., London. Reprinted by permission.

significant proposition can do. But even if it were true that such a proposition as "there is a thought now" was logically certain, it still would not serve Descartes' purpose. For if *"cogito"* is taken in this sense, his initial principle, *"cogito ergo sum,"* is false. "I exist" does not follow from "there is a thought now." The fact that a thought occurs at a given moment does not entail that any other thought has occurred at any other moment, still less that there had occurred a series of thoughts sufficient to constitute a single self. As Hume conclusively showed, no one event intrinsically points to any other. We infer the existence of events which we are not actually observing, with the help of general principles. But these principles must be obtained inductively. By mere deduction from what is immediately given we cannot advance a single step beyond. And, consequently, any attempt to base a deductive system on propositions which describe what is immediately given is bound to be a failure.

The only other course open to one who wished to deduce all our knowledge from "first principles," without indulging in metaphysics, would be to take for his premises a set of *a priori* truths. But, as we have already mentioned, and shall later show, an *a priori* truth is a tautology. And from a set of tautologies, taken by themselves, only further tautologies can be validly deduced. But it would be absurd to put forward a system of tautologies as constituting the whole truth about the universe. And thus we may conclude that it is not possible to deduce all our knowledge from "first principles"; so that those who hold that it is the function of philosophy to carry out such a deduction are denying its claim to be a genuine branch of knowledge.

The belief that it is the business of the philosopher to search for first principles is bound up with the familiar conception of philosophy as the study of reality as a whole. And this conception is one which it is difficult to criticize, because it is so vague. If it is taken to imply, as it sometimes is, that the philosopher somehow projects himself outside the world, and takes a bird's-eye view of it, then it is plainly a metaphysical conception. And it is also metaphysical to assert, as some do, that "reality as a whole" is somehow generically different from the reality which is investigated piecemeal by the special sciences. But if the assertion that philosophy studies reality as a whole is understood to imply merely that the philosopher is equally concerned with the content of every science, then we may accept it, not indeed as an adequate definition of philosophy, but as a truth about it. For we shall find, when we come to discuss the relationship of philosophy to science, that it is not, in principle, related to any one science more closely than to any other.

In saying that philosophy is concerned with each of the sciences, in a manner which we shall indicate[2] we mean also to rule out the sup-

[2] Vide [*Language, Truth and Logic*], Chapter III and Chapter VIII.

position that philosophy can be ranged alongside the existing sciences, as a special department of speculative knowledge. Those who make this supposition cherish the belief that there are some things in the world which are possible objects of speculative knowledge and yet lie beyond the scope of empirical science. But this belief is a delusion. There is no field of experience which cannot, in principle, be brought under some form of scientific law, and no type of speculative knowledge about the world which it is, in principle, beyond the power of science to give. We have already gone some way to substantiate this proposition by demolishing metaphysics; and we shall justify it to the full in the course of this book.

With this we complete the overthrow of speculative philosophy. We are now in a position to see that the function of philosophy is wholly critical. In what exactly does its critical activity consist?

One way of answering this question is to say that it is the philosopher's business to test the validity of our scientific hypotheses and everyday assumptions. But this view, though very widely held, is mistaken. If a man chooses to doubt the truth of all the propositions he ordinarily believes, it is not in the power of philosophy to reassure him. The most that philosophy can do, apart from seeing whether his beliefs are self-consistent, is to show what are the criteria which are used to determine the truth or falsehood of any given proposition: and then, when the sceptic realises that certain observations would verify his propositions, he may also realize that he could make those observations, and so consider his original beliefs to be justified. But in such a case one cannot say that it is philosophy which justifies his beliefs. Philosophy merely shows him that experience can justify them. We may look at the philosopher to show us what we accept as constituting sufficient evidence for the truth of any given empirical proposition. But whether the evidence is forthcoming or not is in every case a purely empirical question.

If anyone thinks that we are here taking too much for granted, let him refer to the chapter on "Truth and Probability," in which we discuss how the validity of synthetic propositions is determined. He will see there that the only sort of justification that is necessary or possible for self-consistent empirical propositions is empirical verification. And this applies just as much to the laws of science as to the maxims of common sense. Indeed there is no difference in kind between them. The superiority of the scientific hypothesis consists merely in its being more abstract, more precise, and more fruitful. And although scientific objects such as atoms and electrons seem to be fictitious in a way that chairs and tables are not, here, too, the distinction is only a distinction of degree. For both these kinds of objects are known only by their sensible manifestations and are definable in terms of them.

It is time, therefore, to abandon the superstition that natural science cannot be regarded as logically respectable until philosophers have solved the problem of induction. The problem of induction is, roughly speaking, the problem of finding a way to prove that certain empirical generalizations which are derived from past experience will hold good also in the future. There are only two ways of approaching this problem on the assumption that it is a genuine problem, and it is easy to see that neither of them can lead to its solution. One may attempt to deduce the proposition which one is required to prove either from a purely formal principle or from an empirical principle. In the former case one commits the error of supposing that from a tautology it is possible to deduce a proposition about a matter of fact; in the latter case one simply assumes what one is setting out to prove. For example, it is often said that we can justify induction by invoking the uniformity of nature, or by postulating a "principle of limited independent variety." [3] But, in fact, the principle of the uniformity of nature merely states, in a misleading fashion, the assumption that past experience is a reliable guide to the future; while the principle of limited independent variety pre-supposes it. And it is plain that any other empirical principle which was put forward as a justification of induction would beg the question in the same way. For the only grounds which one could have for believing such a principle would be inductive grounds.

Thus it appears that there is no possible way of solving the problem of induction, as it is ordinarily conceived. And this means that it is a fictitious problem, since all genuine problems are at least theoretically capable of being solved: and the credit of natural science is not impaired by the fact that some philosophers continue to be puzzled by it. Actually, we shall see that the only test to which a form of scientific procedure which satisfies the necessary condition of self-consistency is subject, is the test of its success in practice. We are entitled to have faith in our procedure just so long as it does the work which it is designed to do—that is, enables us to predict future experience, and so to control our environment. Of course, the fact that a certain form of procedure has always been successful in practice affords no logical guarantee that it will continue to be so. But then it is a mistake to demand a guarantee where it is logically impossible to obtain one. This does not mean that it is irrational to expect future experience to conform to the past. For when we come to define "rationality" we shall find that for us "being rational" entails being guided in a particular fashion by past experience.

The task of defining rationality is precisely the sort of task that it is the business of philosophy to undertake. But in achieving this it does not justify scientific procedure. What justifies scientific procedure, to the extent to which it is capable of being justified, is the success of the

[3] cf. J. M. Keynes, *A Treatise on Probability,* Part III.

predictions to which it gives rise: and this can be determined only in actual experience. By itself, the analysis of a synthetic principle tells us nothing whatsoever about its truth.

Unhappily, this fact is generally disregarded by philosophers who concern themselves with the so-called theory of knowledge. Thus it is common for writers on the subject of perception to assume that, unless one can give a satisfactory analysis of perceptual situations, one is not entitled to believe in the existence of material things. But this is a complete mistake. What gives one the right to believe in the existence of a certain material thing is simply the fact that one has certain sensations: for, whether one realises it or not, to say that the thing exists is equivalent to saying that such sensations are obtainable. It is the philosopher's business to give a correct definition of material things in terms of sensations. But his success or failure in this task has no bearing whatsoever on the validity of our perceptual judgements. That depends wholly on actual sense-experience.

It follows that the philosopher has no right to despise the beliefs of common sense. If he does so, he merely displays his ignorance of the true purpose of his enquiries. What he is entitled to despise is the unreflecting analysis of those beliefs, which takes the grammatical structure of the sentence as a trustworthy guide to its meaning. Thus, many of the mistakes made in connection with the problem of perception can be accounted for by the fact, already referred to in connection with the metaphysical notion of "substance," that it happens to be impossible in an ordinary European language to mention a thing without appearing to distinguish it generically from its qualities and states. But from the fact that the common-sense analysis of a proposition is mistaken it by no means follows that the proposition is not true. The philosopher may be able to show us that the propositions we believe are far more complex than we suppose; but it does not follow from this that we have no right to believe them.

It should now be sufficiently clear that if the philosopher is to uphold his claim to make a special contribution to the stock of our knowledge, he must not attempt to formulate speculative truths, or to look for first principles, or to make *a priori* judgements about the validity of our empirical beliefs. He must, in fact, confine himself to works of clarification and analysis of a sort which we shall presently describe.

In saying that the activity of philosophising is essentially analytic, we are not, of course, maintaining that all those who are commonly called philosophers have actually been engaged in carrying out analyses. On the contrary, we have been at pains to show that a great deal of what is commonly called philosophy is metaphysical in character. What we have been in search of, in enquiring into the function of philosophy, is a definition of philosophy which should accord to some extent with the practice of those who are commonly called philosophers, and at the same time be consistent with the common assumption that philosophy is a special branch of knowledge. It is because metaphysics fails to satisfy this second condition that we distinguish it from philosophy, in spite of the fact that it is commonly referred to as philosophy. And our justification for making this distinction is that it is necessitated by our original postulate that philosophy is a special branch of knowledge, and our demonstration that metaphysics is not.

Although this procedure is logically unassailable, it will perhaps be attacked on the ground that it is inexpedient. It will be said that the "history of philosophy" is, almost entirely, a history of metaphysics; and, consequently, that although there is no actual fallacy involved in our using the word "philosophy" in the sense in which philosophy is incompatible with metaphysics, it is dangerously misleading. For all our care in defining the term will not prevent people from confusing the activities which we call philosophical with the metaphysical activities of those whom they have been taught to regard as philosophers. And therefore it would surely be advisable for us to abandon the term "philosophy" altogether, as a name for a distinctive branch of knowledge, and invent some new description for the activity which we were minded to call the activity of philosophizing.

Our answer to this is that it is not the case that the "history of philosophy" is almost entirely a history of metaphysics. That it contains some metaphysics is undeniable. But I think it can be shown that the majority of those who are commonly supposed to have been great philosophers were primarily not metaphysicians but analysts. For example, I do not see how anyone who follows the account which we shall give of the nature of philosophical analysis and then turns to Locke's *Essay Concerning Human Understanding* can fail to conclude that it is essentially an analytic work. Locke is generally regarded as being one who, like G. E. Moore at the present time, puts forward a philosophy of common sense.[4] But he does not, any more than Moore, attempt to give an *a priori* justification of our common-sense beliefs. Rather does he appear to have seen that it was not his business as a philosopher to affirm or deny the validity of any empirical propositions, but only to analyse them. For he is content, in his own words, "to be employed as an under-labourer in clearing the ground a little, and removing some of the rubbish that lies in the way of knowledge"; and so devotes himself to the purely analytic tasks of defining knowledge, and classifying propositions, and displaying the nature of material things. And the small portion of his work which is not philosophical, in our sense, is not given over to metaphysics, but to psychology.

Nor is it fair to regard Berkeley as a metaphysician. For he did not, in fact, deny the reality of material things, as we are still too commonly told. What he denied was the adequacy of Locke's analysis

[4] Vide G. E. Moore, "A Defence of Common Sense," *Contemporary British Philosophy*, Vol. 11. [Vol. I of this work, pp. 561-584.]

of the notion of a material thing. He maintained that to say of various "ideas of sensation" that they belonged to a single material thing was not, as Locke thought, to say that they were related to a single unobservable underlying "somewhat," but rather that they stood in certain relations to one another. And in this he was right. Admittedly he made the mistake of supposing that what was immediately given in sensation was necessarily mental; and the use, by him and by Locke, of the word "idea" to denote an element in that which is sensibly given is objectionable, because it suggests this false view. Accordingly we replace the word "idea" in this usage by the neutral word "sense-content," which we shall use to refer to the immediate data not merely of "outer" but also of "introspective" sensation, and say that what Berkeley discovered was that material things must be definable in terms of sense-contents. We shall see, when we come finally to settle the conflict between idealism and realism, that his actual conception of the relationship between material things and sense-contents was not altogether accurate. It led him to some notoriously paradoxical conclusions, which a slight emendation will enable us to avoid. But the fact that he failed to give a completely correct account of the way in which material things are constituted out of sense-contents does not invalidate his contention that they are so constituted. On the contrary, we know that it must be possible to define material things in terms of sense-contents, because it is only by the occurrence of certain sense-contents that the existence of any material thing can ever be in the least degree verified. And thus we see that we have not to inquire whether a phenomenalist "theory of perception" or some other sort of theory is correct, but only what form of phenomenalist theory is correct. For the fact that all causal and representative theories of perception treat material things as if they were unobservable entities entitles us, as Berkeley saw, to rule them out *a piori*. The unfortunate thing is that, in spite of this, he found it necessary to postulate God as an unobservable cause of our "ideas"; and he must be criticised also for failing to see that the argument which he uses to dispose of Locke's analysis of a material thing is fatal to his own conception of the nature of the self, a point which was effectively seized upon by Hume.

Of Hume we may say not merely that he was not in practice a metaphysician, but that he explicitly rejected metaphysics. We find the strongest evidence of this in the passage with which he concludes his *Enquiry Concerning Human Understanding*. "If," he says, "we take in our hand any volume; of divinity, or school metaphysics, for instance; let us ask, Does it contain any abstract reasoning concerning quantity or number? No. Does it contain any experimental reasoning concerning matter of fact and existence? No. Commit it then to the flames. For it can contain nothing but sophistry and illusion." What is this but a rhetorical version of our own thesis that a sentence which does not express either a formally true proposition or an empirical hypothesis is devoid of literal significance? It is true that Hume does not, so far as I know, actually put forward any view concerning the nature of philosophical propositions themselves, but those of his works which are commonly accounted philosophical are, apart from certain passages which deal with questions of psychology, works of analysis. If this is not universally conceded, it is because his treatment of causation, which is the main feature of his philosophical work, is often misinterpreted. He has been accused of denying causation, whereas in fact he was concerned only with defining it. So far is he from asserting that no causal propositions are true that he is himself at pains to give rules for judging of the existence of causes and effects.[5] He realised well enough that the question whether a given causal proposition was true or false was not one that could be settled *a priori,* and accordingly confined himself to discussing the analytic question, What is it that we are asserting when we assert that one event is causally connected with another? And in answering this question he showed, I think conclusively, first that the relation of cause and effect was not logical in character, since any proposition asserting a causal connection could be denied without self-contradiction, secondly that causal laws were not analytically derived from experience, since they were not deducible from any finite number of experiential propositions, and, thirdly, that it was a mistake to analyse propositions asserting causal connections in terms of a relation of necessitation which held between particular events, since it was impossible to conceive of any observations which would have the slightest tendency to establish the existence of such a relation. He thus laid the way open for the view, which we adopt, that every assertion of a particular causal connection involves the assertion of a causal law, and that every general proposition of the form "C causes E" is equivalent to a proposition of the form "whenever C, then E," where the symbol "whenever" must be taken to refer, not to a finite number of actual instances of C, but to the infinite number of possible instances. He himself defines a cause as "an object, followed by another, and where all the objects similar to the first are followed by objects similar to the second," or, alternatively, as "an object followed by another, and whose appearance always conveys the thought to that other";[6] but neither of these definitions is acceptable as it stands. For, even if it is true that we should not, according to our standards of rationality, have good reason to believe that an event C was the cause of an event E unless we had observed a constant conjunction of events like C with events like E, still there is no self-contradiction involved in asserting the proposition "C is the cause of E" and at the same time denying that any events like C or like E ever have been observed; and this would be self-contradictory if the first of

[5] Vide *A Treatise of Human Nature,* Book I, Part III, section 15.
[6] *An Enquiry Concerning Human Understanding,* section 7.

the definitions quoted was correct. Nor is it inconceivable, as the second definition implies, that there should be causal laws which have never yet been thought of. But although we are obliged, for these reasons, to reject Hume's actual definitions of a cause, our view of the nature of causation remains substantially the same as his. And we agree with him that there can be no other justification for inductive reasoning than its success in practice, while insisting more strongly than he did that no better justification is required. For it is his failure to make this second point clear that has given his views the air of paradox which had caused them to be so much undervalued and misunderstood.

When we consider, also, that Hobbes and Bentham were chiefly occupied in giving definitions, and that the best part of John Stuart Mill's work consists in a development of the analyses carried out by Hume, we may fairly claim that in holding that the activity of philosophising is essentially analytic we are adopting a standpoint which has always been implicit in English empiricism. Not that the practice of philosophical analysis has been confined to members of this school. But it is with them that we have the closest historical affinity.

If I refrain from discussing these questions in detail, and make no attempt to furnish a complete list of all the "great philosophers" whose work is predominantly analytic—a list which would certainly include Plato and Aristotle and Kant—it is because the point to which this discussion is relevant is one of minor importance in our enquiry. We have been maintaining that much of "traditional philosophy" is genuinely philosophical, by our standards, in order to defend ourselves against the charge that our retention of the word "philosophy" is misleading. But even if it were the case that none of those who are commonly called philosophers had ever been engaged in what we call the activity of philosophising, it would not follow that our definition of philosophy was erroneous, given our initial postulates. We may admit that our retention of the word "philosophy" is causally dependent on our belief in the historical propositions set forth above. But the validity of these historical propositions has no logical bearing on the validity of our definition of philosophy, nor on the validity of the distinction between philosophy, in our sense, and metaphysics.

It is advisable to stress the point that philosophy, as we understand it, is wholly independent of metaphysics, inasmuch as the analytic method is commonly supposed by its critics to have a metaphysical basis. Being misled by the associations of the word "analysis," they assume that philosophical analysis is an activity of dissection; that it consists in "breaking up" objects into their constituent parts, until the whole universe is ultimately exhibited as an aggregate of "bare particulars," united by external relations. If this were really so, the most effective way of attacking the method would be to show that its basic presupposition was nonsensical. For to say that the universe was an aggregate of bare particulars would be as senseless as to say that it was

Fire or Water or Experience. It is plain that no possible observation would enable one to verify such an assertion. But, so far as I know, this line of criticism is in fact never adopted. The critics content themselves with pointing out that few, if any, of the complex objects in the world are simply the sum of their parts. They have a structure, an organic unity, which distinguishes them, as genuine wholes, from mere aggregates. But the analyst, so it is said, is obliged by his atomistic metaphysics to regard an object consisting of parts *a, b, c,* and *d* in a distinctive configuration as being simply $a+b+c+d$, and thus gives an entirely false account of its nature.

If we follow the Gestalt psychologists, who of all men talk most constantly about genuine wholes, in defining such a whole as one in which the properties of every part depend to some extent on its position in the whole, then we may accept it as an empirical fact that there exist genuine, or organic, wholes. And if the analytic method involved a denial of this fact, it would indeed be a faulty method. But, actually, the validity of the analytic method is not dependent on any empirical, much less any metaphysical, presupposition about the nature of things. For the philosopher, as an analyst, is not directly concerned with the physical properties of things. He is concerned only with the way in which we speak about them.

In other words, the propositions of philosophy are not factual, but linguistic in character—that is, they do not describe the behaviour of physical, or even mental, objects; they express definitions, or the formal consequences of definitions. Accordingly, we may say that philosophy is a department of logic. For we shall see that the characteristic mark of a purely logical enquiry is that it is concerned with the formal consequences of our definitions and not with questions of empirical fact.

It follows that philosophy does not in any way compete with science. The difference in type between philosophical and scientific propositions is such that they cannot conceivably contradict one another. And this makes it clear that the possibility of philosophical analysis is independent of any empirical assumptions. That it is independent of any metaphysical assumptions should be even more obvious still. For it is absurd to suppose that the provision of definitions, and the study of their formal consequences, involves the nonsensical assertion that the world is composed of bare particulars, or any other metaphysical dogma.

What has contributed as much as anything to the prevalent misunderstanding of the nature of philosophical analysis is the fact that propositions and questions which are really linguistic are often expressed in such a way that they appear to be factual.[7] A striking in-

[7] Carnap has stressed this point. Where we speak of "linguistic" propositions expressed in "factual" or "pseudo-factual" language he speaks of "Pseudo-Objekt-

stance of this is provided by the proposition that a material thing cannot be in two places at once. This looks like an empirical proposition, and is constantly invoked by those who desire to prove that it is possible for an empirical proposition to be logically certain. But a more critical inspection shows that it is not empirical at all, but linguistic. It simply records the fact that, as the result of certain verbal conventions, the proposition that two sense-contents occur in the same visual or tactual sensefield is incompatible with the proposition that they belong to the same material thing.[8] And this is indeed a necessary fact. But it has not the least tendency to show that we have certain knowledge about the empirical properties of objects. For it is necessary only because we happen to use the relevant words in a particular way. There is no logical reason why we should not so alter our definitions that the sentence "A thing cannot be in two places at once" comes to express a self-contradiction instead of a necessary truth.

Another good example of linguistically necessary proposition which appears to be a record of empirical fact is the proposition, "Relations are not particulars, but universals." One might suppose that this was a proposition of the same order as, "Armenians are not Mohammedans, but Christians": but one would be mistaken. For, whereas the latter proposition is an empirical hypothesis relating to the religious practices of a certain group of people, the former is not a proposition about "things" at all, but simply about words. It records the fact that relation-symbols belong by definition to the class of symbols for characters, and not to the class of symbols for things.

The assertion that relations are universals provokes the question, "What is a universal?"; and this question is not, as it has traditionally been regarded, a question about the character of certain real objects, but a request for a definition of a certain term. Philosophy, as it is written, is full of questions like this, which seem to be factual but are not. Thus, to ask what is the nature of a material object is to ask for a definition of "material object," and this, as we shall shortly see, is to ask how propositions about material objects are to be translated into propositions about sense-contents. Similarly, to ask what is a number is to ask some such question as whether it is possible to translate propositions about natural numbers into propositions about classes. And the same thing applies to all the other philosophical questions of the form, "What is an *x?*" or, "What is the nature of *x?*" They are all requests for definitions, and, as we shall see, for definitions of a peculiar sort.

Although it is misleading to write about linguistic questions in "factual" language, it is often convenient for the sake of brevity. And we shall not always avoid doing it ourselves. But it is important that no one

---

sätze" or "quasi-syntaktische Sätze" as being expressed in the "Inhaltliche," as opposed to the "Formale Redeweise." Vide *Logische Syntax der Sprache,* Part V.

[8] cf. my article "On Particulars and Universals," *Proceedings of the Aristotelian Society, 1933-4,* pp. 54, 55.

should be deceived by this practice into supposing that the philosopher is engaged on an empirical or metaphysical enquiry. We may speak loosely of him as analysing facts, or notions, or even things. But we must make it clear that these are simply ways of saying that he is concerned with the definition of the corresponding words.

THE *A PRIORI* [1]

The view of philosophy which we have adopted may, I think, fairly be described as a form of empiricism. For it is characteristic of an empiricist to eschew metaphysics, on the ground that every factual proposition must refer to sense-experience. And even if the conception of philosophizing as an activity of analysis is not to be discovered in the traditional theories of empiricists, we have seen that it is implicit in their practice. At the same time, it must be made clear that, in calling ourselves empiricists, we are not avowing a belief in any of the psychological doctrines which are commonly associated with empiricism. For, even if these doctrines were valid, their validity would be independent of the validity of any philosophical thesis. It could be established only by observation, and not by the purely logical considerations upon which our empiricism rests.

Having admitted that we are empiricists, we must now deal with the objection that is commonly brought against all forms of empiricism; the objection, namely, that it is impossible on empiricist principles to account for our knowledge of necessary truths. For, as Hume conclusively showed, no general proposition whose validity is subject to the test of actual experience can ever be logically certain. No matter how often it is verified in practice, there still remains the possibility that it will be confuted on some future occasion. The fact that a law has been substantiated in $n-1$ cases affords no logical guarantee that it

[1] From: *Language, Truth and Logic,* A. J. Ayer, Ch. 4. Dover Publications, Inc., New York, and Victor Gollancz, Ltd., London. Reprinted by permission.

will be substantiated in the *n*th case also, no matter how large we take *n* to be. And this means that no general proposition referring to a matter of fact can ever be shown to be necessarily and universally true. It can at best be a probable hypothesis. And this, we shall find, applies not only to general propositions, but to all propositions which have a factual content. They can none of them ever become logically certain. This conclusion, which we shall elaborate later on, is one which must be accepted by every consistent empiricist. It is often thought to involve him in complete scepticism; but this is not the case. For the fact that the validity of a proposition cannot be logically guaranteed in no way entails that it is irrational for us to believe it. On the contrary, what is irrational is to look for a guarantee where none can be forthcoming; to demand certainty where probability is all that is obtainable. We have already remarked upon this, in referring to the work of Hume. And we shall make the point clearer when we come to treat of probability, in explaining the use which we make of empirical propositions. We shall discover that there is nothing perverse or paradoxical about the view that all the "truths" of science and common sense are hypotheses; and consequently that the fact that it involves this view constitutes no objection to the empiricist thesis.

Where the empiricist does encounter difficulty is in connection with the truths of formal logic and mathematics. For whereas a scientific generalisation is readily admitted to be fallible, the truths of mathematics and logic appear to everyone to be necessary and certain. But if empiricism is correct no proposition which has a factual content can be necessary or certain. Accordingly the empiricist must deal with the truths of logic and mathematics in one of the two following ways: he must say either that they are not necessary truths, in which case he must account for the universal conviction that they are; or he must say that they have no factual content, and then he must explain how a proposition which is empty of all factual content can be true and useful and surprising.

If neither of these courses proves satisfactory, we shall be obliged to give way to rationalism. We shall be obliged to admit that there are some truths about the world which we can know independently of experience; that there are some properties which we can ascribe to all objects, even though we cannot conceivably observe that all objects have them. And we shall have to accept it as a mysterious inexplicable fact that our thought has this power to reveal to us authoritatively the nature of objects which we have never observed. Or else we must accept the Kantian explanation which, apart from the epistemological difficulties which we have already touched on, only pushes the mystery a stage further back.

It is clear that any such concession to rationalism would upset the main argument of this book. For the admission that there were some facts about the world which could be known independently of experience would be incompatible with our fundamental contention that a sentence says nothing unless it is empirically verifiable. And thus the whole force of our attack on metaphysics would be destroyed. It is vital, therefore, for us to be able to show that one or other of the empiricist accounts of the propositions of logic and mathematics is correct. If we are successful in this, we shall have destroyed the foundations of rationalism. For the fundamental tenet of rationalism is that thought is an independent source of knowledge, and is moreover a more trustworthy source of knowledge than experience; indeed some rationalists have gone so far as to say that thought is the only source of knowledge. And the ground for this view is simply that the only necessary truths about the world which are known to us are known through thought and not through experience. So that if we can show either that the truths in question are not necessary or that they are not "truths about the world," we shall be taking away the support on which rationalism rests. We shall be making good the empiricist contention that there are no "truths of reason" which refer to matters of fact.

The course of maintaining that the truths of logic and mathematics are not necessary or certain was adopted by Mill. He maintained that these propositions were inductive generalizations based on an extremely large number of instances. The fact that the number of supporting instances was so very large accounted, in his view, for our believing these generalizations to be necessarily and universally true. The evidence in their favour was so strong that it seemed incredible to us that a contrary instance should ever arise. Nevertheless it was in principle possible for such generalizations to be confuted. They were highly probable, but, being inductive generalizations, they were not certain. The difference between them and the hypotheses of natural science was a difference in degree and not in kind. Experience gave us very good reason to suppose that a "truth" of mathematics or logic was true universally; but we were not possessed of a guarantee. For these "truths" were only empirical hypotheses which had worked particularly well in the past; and, like all empirical hypotheses, they were theoretically fallible.

I do not think that this solution of the empiricist's difficulty with regard to the propositions of logic and mathematics is acceptable. In discussing it, it is necessary to make a distinction which is perhaps already enshrined in Kant's famous dictum that, although there can be no doubt that all our knowledge begins with experience, it does not follow that it all arises out of experience.[2] When we say that the truths of logic are known independently of experience, we are not of course saying that they are innate, in the sense that we are born knowing them. It is obvious that mathematics and logic have to be learned in

[2] *Critique of Pure Reason,* 2nd ed., Introduction, section i.

the same way as chemistry and history have to be learned. Nor are we denying that the first person to discover a given logical or mathematical truth was led to it by an inductive procedure. It is very probable, for example, that the principle of the syllogism was formulated not before but after the validity of syllogistic reasoning had been observed in a number of particular cases. What we are discussing, however, when we say that logical and mathematical truths are known independently of experience, is not a historical question concerning the way in which these truths were originally discovered, nor a psychological question concerning the way in which each of us comes to learn them, but an epistemological question. The contention of Mill's which we reject is that the propositions of logic and mathematics have the same status as empirical hypotheses; that their validity is determined in the same way. We maintain that they are independent of experience in the sense that they do not owe their validity to empirical verification. We may come to discover them through an inductive process; but once we have apprehended them we see that they are necessarily true, that they hold good for every conceivable instance. And this serves to distinguish them from empirical generalizations. For we know that a proposition whose validity depends upon experience cannot be seen to be necessarily and universally true.

In rejecting Mill's theory, we are obliged to be somewhat dogmatic. We can do no more than state the issue clearly and then trust that his contention will be seen to be discrepant with the relevant logical facts. The following considerations may serve to show that of the two ways of dealing with logic and mathematics which are open to the empiricist, the one which Mill adopted is not the one which is correct.

The best way to substantiate our assertion that the truths of formal logic and pure mathematics are necessarily true is to examine cases in which they might seem to be confuted. It might easily happen, for example, that when I came to count what I had taken to be five pairs of objects, I found that they amounted only to nine. And if I wished to mislead people I might say that on this occasion twice five was not ten. But in that case I should not be using the complex sign "$2 \times 5 = 10$" in the way in which it is ordinarily used. I should be taking it not as the expression of a purely mathematical proposition, but as the expression of an empirical generalization, to the effect that whenever I counted what appeared to me to be five pairs of objects I discovered that they were ten in number. This generalization may very well be false. But if it proved false in a given case, one would not say that the mathematical proposition "$2 \times 5 = 10$" had been confuted. One would say that I was wrong in supposing that there were five pairs of objects to start with, or that one of the objects had been taken away while I was counting, or that two of them had coalesced, or that I had counted wrongly. One would adopt as an explanation whatever empirical hypothesis fitted in best with the accredited facts. The one explanation which would in no circumstances be adopted is that ten is not always the product of two and five.

To take another example: if what appears to be a Euclidean triangle is found by measurement not to have angles totalling 180 degrees, we do not say that we have met with an instance which invalidates the mathematical proposition that the sum of the three angles of a Euclidean triangle is 180 degrees. We say that we have measured wrongly, or, more probably, that the triangle we have been measuring is not Euclidean. And this is our procedure in every case in which a mathematical truth might appear to be confuted. We always preserve its validity by adopting some other explanation of the occurrence.

The same thing applies to the principles of formal logic. We may take an example relating to the so-called law of excluded middle, which states that a proposition must be either true or false, or, in other words, that it is impossible that a proposition and its contradictory should neither of them be true. One might suppose that a proposition of the form "*x* has stopped doing *y*" would in certain cases constitute an exception to this law. For instance, if my friend has never yet written to me, it seems fair to say that it is neither true nor false that he has stopped writing to me. But in fact one would refuse to accept such an instance as an invalidation of the law of excluded middle. One would point out that the proposition "My friend has stopped writing to me" is not a simple proposition, but the conjunction of the two propositions "My friend wrote to me in the past" and "My friend does not write to me now": and, furthermore, that the proposition "My friend has not stopped writing to me" is not, as it appears to be, contradictory to "My friend has stopped writing to me," but only contrary to it. For it means "My friend wrote to me in the past, and he still writes to me." When, therefore, we say that such a proposition as "My friend has stopped writing to me" is sometimes neither true nor false, we are speaking inaccurately. For we seem to be saying that neither it nor its contradictory is true. Whereas what we mean, or anyhow should mean, is that neither it nor its apparent contradictory is true. And its apparent contradictory is really only its contrary. Thus we preserve the law of excluded middle by showing that the negating of a sentence does not always yield the contradictory of the proposition originally expressed.

There is no need to give further examples. Whatever instance we care to take, we shall always find that the situations in which a logical or mathematical principle might appear to be confuted are accounted for in such a way as to leave the principle unassailed. And this indicates that Mill was wrong in supposing that a situation could arise which would overthrow a mathematical truth. The principles of logic and mathematics are true universally simply because we never allow them to be anything else. And the reason for this is that we cannot abandon them without contradicting ourselves, without sinning against the rules which govern the use of language, and so making our utterances self-stultifying. In other words, the truths of logic and mathematics are analytic propositions or tautologies. In saying this we are making what will be held to be an extremely controversial statement, and we must now proceed to make its implications clear.

The most familiar definition of an analytic proposition, or judgement, as he called it, is that given by Kant. He said [3] that an analytic judgement was one in which the predicate B belonged to the subject A as something which was covertly contained in the concept of A. He contrasted analytic with synthetic judgements, in which the predicate B lay outside the subject A, although it did stand in connection with it. Analytic judgements, he explains, "add nothing through the predicate to the concept of the subject, but merely break it up into those constituent concepts that have all along been thought in it, although confusedly." Synthetic judgements, on the other hand, "add to the concept of the subject a predicate which has not been in any wise thought in it, and which no analysis could possibly extract from it." Kant gives "all bodies are extended" as an example of an analytic judgement, on the ground that the required predicate can be extracted from the concept of "body," "in accordance with the principle of contradiction"; as an example of a synthetic judgement, he gives "all bodies are heavy." He refers also to "$7 + 5 = 12$" as a synthetic judgement, on the ground that the concept of twelve is by no means already thought in merely thinking the union of seven and five. And he appears to regard this as tantamount to saying that the judgement does not rest on the principle of contradiction alone. He holds, also, that through analytic judgements our knowledge is not extended as it is through synthetic judgements. For in analytic judgements "the concept which I already have is merely set forth and made intelligible to me."

I think that this is a fair summary of Kant's account of the distinction between analytic and synthetic propositions, but I do not think that it succeeds in making the distinction clear. For even if we pass over the difficulties which arise out of the use of the vague term "concept," and the unwarranted assumption that every judgement, as well as every German or English sentence, can be said to have a subject and a predicate, there remains still this crucial defect. Kant does not give one straightforward criterion for distinguishing between analytic and synthetic propositions; he gives two distinct criteria, which are by no means equivalent. Thus his ground for holding that the proposition "$7 + 5 = 12$" is synthetic is, as we have seen, that the subjective intension of "$7 + 5$" does not comprise the subjective intension of "12"; whereas his ground for holding that "all bodies are extended" is an analytic proposition is that it rests on the principle of contradiction alone. That is, he employs a psychological criterion in the first of these

[3] *Critique of Pure Reason,* 2nd ed., Introduction, sections iv and v.

examples, and a logical criterion in the second, and takes their equivalence for granted. But, in fact, a proposition which is synthetic according to the former criterion may very well be analytic according to the latter. For, as we have already pointed out, it is possible for symbols to be synonymous without having the same intensional meaning for anyone: and accordingly from the fact that one can think of the sum of seven and five without necessarily thinking of twelve, it by no means follows that the proposition "$7 + 5 = 12$" can be denied without self-contradiction. From the rest of his argument, it is clear that it is this logical proposition, and not any psychological proposition, that Kant is really anxious to establish. His use of the psychological criterion leads him to think that he has established it, when he has not.

I think that we can preserve the logical import of Kant's distinction between analytic and synthetic propositions, while avoiding the confusions which mar his actual account of it, if we say that a proposition is analytic when its validity depends solely on the definitions of the symbols it contains, and synthetic when its validity is determined by the facts of experience. Thus, the proposition "There are ants which have established a system of slavery" is a synthetic proposition. For we cannot tell whether it is true or false merely by considering the definitions of the symbols which constitute it. We have to resort to actual observation of the behaviour of ants. On the other hand, the proposition "Either some ants are parasitic or none are" is an analytic proposition. For one need not resort to observation to discover that there either are or are not ants which are parasitic. If one knows what is the function of the words "either," "or," and "not," then one can see that any proposition of the form "Either *p* is true or *p* is not true" is valid, independently of experience. Accordingly, all such propositions are analytic.

It is to be noticed that the proposition "Either some ants are parasitic or none are" provides no information whatsoever about the behaviour of ants, or, indeed, about any matter of fact. And this applies to all analytic propositions. They none of them provide any information about any matter of fact. In other words, they are entirely devoid of factual content. And it is for this reason that no experience can confute them.

When we say that analytic propositions are devoid of factual content, and consequently that they say nothing, we are not suggesting that they are senseless in the way that metaphysical utterances are senseless. For, although they give us no information about any empirical situation, they do enlighten us by illustrating the way in which we use certain symbols. Thus if I say, "Nothing can be coloured in different ways at the same time with respect to the same part of itself," I am not saying anything about the properties of any actual thing; but I am not talking nonsense. I am expressing an analytic proposition, which records our determination to call a colour expanse which differs in quality from a neighbouring colour expanse a different part of a given thing. In other words, I am simply calling attention to the implications of a certain linguistic usage. Similarly, in saying that if all Bretons are Frenchmen, and all Frenchmen Europeans, then all Bretons are Europeans, I am not describing any matter of fact. But I am showing that in the statement that all Bretons are Frenchmen, and all Frenchmen Europeans, the further statement that all Bretons are Europeans is implicitly contained. And I am thereby indicating the convention which governs our usage of the words "if" and "all."

We see, then, that there is a sense in which analytic propositions do give us new knowledge. They call attention to linguistic usages, of which we might otherwise not be conscious, and they reveal unsuspected implications in our assertions and beliefs. But we can see also that there is a sense in which they may be said to add nothing to our knowledge. For they tell us only what we may be said to know already. Thus, if I know that the existence of May Queens is a relic of tree-worship, and I discover that May Queens still exist in England, I can employ the tautology "If p implies q, and p is true, q is true" to show that there still exists a relic of tree-worship in England. But in saying that there are still May Queens in England, and that the existence of May Queens is a relic of tree-worship, I have already asserted the existence in England of a relic of tree-worship. The use of the tautology does, indeed, enable me to make this concealed assertion explicit. But it does not provide me with any new knowledge, in the sense in which empirical evidence that the election of May Queens had been forbidden by law would provide me with new knowledge. If one had to set forth all the information one possessed, with regard to matters of fact, one would not write down any analytic propositions. But one would make use of analytic propositions in compiling one's encyclopædia, and would thus come to include propositions which one would otherwise have overlooked. And, besides enabling one to make one's list of information complete, the formulation of analytic propositions would enable one to make sure that the synthetic propositions of which the list was composed formed a self-consistent system. By showing which ways of combining propositions resulted in contradictions, they would prevent one from including incompatible propositions and so making the list self-stultifying. But in so far as we had actually used such words as "all" and "or" and "not" without falling into self-contradiction, we might be said already to know what was revealed in the formulation of analytic propositions illustrating the rules which govern our usage of these logical particles. So that here again we are justified in saying that analytic propositions do not increase our knowledge.

The analytic character of the truths of formal logic was obscured in the traditional logic through its being insufficiently formalized. For in speaking always of judgements, instead of propositions, and introducing irrelevant psychological questions, the traditional logic gave the impression of being concerned in some specially intimate way with the workings of thought. What it was actually concerned with was the formal relationship of classes, as is shown by the fact that all its principles of inference are subsumed in the Boolean class-calculus, which is subsumed in its turn in the propositional calculus of Russell and Whitehead.[4] Their system, expounded in *Principia Mathematica,* makes it clear that formal logic is not concerned with the properties of men's minds, much less with the properties of material objects, but simply with the possibility of combining propositions by means of logical particles into analytic propositions, and with studying the formal relationship of these analytic propositions, in virtue of which one is deducible from another. Their procedure is to exhibit the propositions of formal logic as a deductive system, based on five primitive propositions, subsequently reduced in number to one. Hereby the distinction between logical truths and principles of inference, which was maintained in the Aristotelian logic, very properly disappears. Every principle of inference is put forward as a logical truth and every logical truth can serve as a principle of inference. The three Aristotelian "laws of thought," the law of identity, the law of excluded middle, and the law of non-contradiction, are incorporated in the system, but they are not considered more important than the other analytic propositions. They are not reckoned among the premises of the system. And the system of Russell and Whitehead itself is probably only one among many possible logics, each of which is composed of tautologies as interesting to the logician as the arbitrarily selected Aristotelian "laws of thought." [5]

A point which is not sufficiently brought out by Russell, if indeed it is recognised by him at all, is that every logical proposition is valid in its own right. Its validity does not depend on its being incorporated in a system, and deduced from certain propositions which are taken as self-evident. The construction of systems of logic is useful as a means of discovering and certifying analytic propositions, but it is not in principle essential even for this purpose. For it is possible to conceive of a symbolism in which every analytic proposition could be seen to be analytic in virtue of its form alone.

The fact that the validity of an analytic proposition in no way depends on its being deducible from other analytic propositions is our justification for disregarding the question whether the propositions of mathematics are reducible to propositions of formal logic, in the way that Russell supposed.[6] For even if it is the case that the definition of a cardinal number as a class of classes similar to a given class is circular,

[4] Vide Karl Menger, "Die Neue Logik," *Krise und Neuaufbau in den Exakten Wissenschaften,* pp. 94-6; and Lewis and Langford, *Symbolic Logic,* Chapter v.
[5] Vide Lewis and Langford, *Symbolic Logic,* Chapter vii, for an elaboration of this point.
[6] Vide *Introduction to Mathematical Philosophy,* Chapter ii.

and it is not possible to reduce mathematical notions to purely logical notions, it will still remain true that the propositions of mathematics are analytic propositions. They will form a special class of analytic propositions, containing special terms, but they will be none the less analytic for that. For the criterion of an analytic proposition is that its validity should follow simply from the definition of the terms contained in it, and this condition is fulfilled by the propositions of pure mathematics.

The mathematical propositions which one might most pardonably suppose to be synthetic are the propositions of geometry. For it is natural for us to think, as Kant thought, that geometry is the study of the properties of physical space, and consequently that its propositions have factual content. And if we believe this, and also recognise that the truths of geometry are necessary and certain, then we may be inclined to accept Kant's hypothesis that space is the form of intuition of our outer sense, a form imposed by us on the matter of sensation, as the only possible explanation of our *a priori* knowledge of these synthetic propositions. But while the view that pure geometry is concerned with physical space was plausible enough in Kant's day, when the geometry of Euclid was the only geometry known, the subsequent invention of non-Euclidean geometries has shown it to be mistaken. We see now that the axioms of a geometry are simply definitions, and that the theorems of a geometry are simply the logical consequences of these definitions.[7] A geometry is not in itself about physical space; in itself it cannot be said to be "about" anything. But we can use a geometry to reason about physical space. That is to say, once we have given the axioms a physical interpretation, we can proceed to apply the theorems to the objects which satisfy the axioms. Whether a geometry can be applied to the actual physical world or not, is an empirical question which falls outside the scope of the geometry itself. There is no sense, therefore, in asking which of the various geometries known to us are false and which are true. In so far as they are all free from contradiction, they are all true. What one can ask is which of them is the most useful on any given occasion, which of them can be applied most easily and most fruitfully to an actual empirical situation. But the proposition which states that a certain application of a geometry is possible is not itself a proposition of that geometry. All that the geometry itself tells us is that if anything can be brought under the definitions, it will also satisfy the theorems. It is therefore a purely logical system, and its propositions are purely analytic propositions.

It might be objected that the use made of diagrams in geometrical treatises shows that geometrical reasoning is not purely abstract and logical, but depends on our intuition of the properties of figures. In fact, however, the use of diagrams is not essential to completely rigorous geometry. The diagrams are introduced as an aid to our reason. They

[7] Cf. H. Poincaré, *La Science et l'Hypothèse,* Part II, Chapter iii.

provide us with a particular application of the geometry, and so assist us to perceive the more general truth that the axioms of the geometry involve certain consequences. But the fact that most of us need the help of an example to make us aware of those consequences does not show that the relation between them and the axioms is not a purely logical relation. It shows merely that our intellects are unequal to the task of carrying out very abstract processes of reasoning without the assistance of intuition. In other words, it has no bearing on the nature of geometrical propositions, but is simply an empirical fact about ourselves. Moreover, the appeal to intuition, though generally of psychological value, is also a source of danger to the geometer. He is tempted to make assumptions which are accidentally true of the particular figure he is taking as an illustration, but do not follow from his axioms. It has, indeed, been shown that Euclid himself was guilty of this, and consequently that the presence of the figure is essential to some of his proofs.[8] This shows that his system is not, as he presents it, completely rigorous, although of course it can be made so. It does not show that the presence of the figure is essential to a truly rigorous geometrical proof. To suppose that it did would be to take as a necessary feature of all geometries what is really only an incidental defect in one particular geometrical system.

We conclude, then, that the propositions of pure geometry are analytic. And this leads us to reject Kant's hypothesis that geometry deals with the form of intuition of our outer sense. For the ground for this hypothesis was that it alone explained how the propositions of geometry could be both true *a priori* and synthetic: and we have seen that they are not synthetic. Similarly our view that the propositions of arithmetic are not synthetic but analytic leads us to reject the Kantian hypothesis[9] that arithmetic is concerned with our pure intuition of time, the form of our inner sense. And thus we are able to dismiss Kant's transcendental æsthetic without having to bring forward the epistemological difficulties which it is commonly said to involve. For the only argument which can be brought in favour of Kant's theory is that it alone explains certain "facts." And now we have found that the "facts" which it purports to explain are not facts at all. For while it is true that we have *a priori* knowledge of necessary propositions, it is not true, as Kant supposed, that any of these necessary propositions are synthetic. They are without exception analytic propositions, or, in other words, tautologies.

We have already explained how it is that these analytic propositions are necessary and certain. We saw that the reason why they cannot be confuted in experience is that they do not make any assertion about the empirical world. They simply record our determination to use

[8] Cf. M. Black, *The Nature of Mathematics,* p. 154.

[9] This hypothesis is not mentioned in the *Critique of Pure Reason,* but was maintained by Kant at an earlier date.

words in a certain fashion. We cannot deny them without infringing the conventions which are presupposed by our very denial, and so falling into self-contradiction. And this is the sole ground of their necessity. As Wittgenstein puts it, our justification for holding that the world could not conceivably disobey the laws of logic is simply that we could not say of an unlogical world how it would look.[10] And just as the validity of an analytic proposition is independent of the nature of the external world; so is it independent of the nature of our minds. It is perfectly conceivable that we should have employed different linguistic conventions from whose which we actually do employ. But whatever these conventions might be, the tautologies in which we recorded them would always be necessary. For any denial of them would be self-stultifying.

We see, then, that there is nothing mysterious about the apodeictic certainty of logic and mathematics. Our knowledge that no observation can ever confute the proposition "7 + 5 = 12" depends simply on the fact that the symbolic expression "7 + 5" is synonymous with "12," just as our knowledge that every oculist is an eye-doctor depends on the fact that the symbol "eye-doctor" is synonymous with "oculist." And the same explanation holds good for every other *a priori* truth.

What is mysterious at first sight is that these tautologies should on occasion be so surprising, that there should be in mathematics and logic the possibility of invention and discovery. As Poincaré says: "If all the assertions which mathematics puts forward can be derived from one another by formal logic, mathematics cannot amount to anything more than an immense tautology. Logical inference can teach us nothing essentially new, and if everything is to proceed from the principle of identity, everything must be reducible to it. But can we really allow that these theorems which fill so many books serve no other purpose than to say in a roundabout fashion 'A = A'?" [11] Poincaré finds this incredible. His own theory is that the sense of invention and discovery in mathematics belongs to it in virtue of mathematical induction, the principle that what is true for the number 1, and true for $n + 1$ when it is true for n,[12] is true for all numbers. And he claims that this is a synthetic *a priori* principle. It is, in fact, *a priori,* but it is not synthetic. It is a defining principle of the natural numbers, serving to distinguish them from such numbers as the infinite cardinal numbers, to which it cannot be applied.[13] Moreover, we must remember that discoveries can be made, not only in arithmetic, but also in geometry and formal logic, where no use is made of mathematical induction. So that even if Poincaré were right about mathematical induction, he

10 *Tractatus Logico-Philosophicus,* 3:031.

11 *La Science et l'Hypothèse,* Part I, Chapter i.

12 This was wrongly stated in previous editions as "true for n when it is true for $n + 1$."

13 Cf. B. Russell's *Introduction to Mathematical Philosophy,* Chapter iii, p. 27.

would not have provided a satisfactory explanation of the paradox that a mere body of tautologies can be so interesting and so surprising.

The true explanation is very simple. The power of logic and mathematics to surprise us depends, like their usefulness, on the limitations of our reason. A being whose intellect was infinitely powerful would take no interest in logic and mathematics.[14] For he would be able to see at a glance everything that his definitions implied, and, accordingly, could never learn anything from logical inference which he was not fully conscious of already. But our intellects are not of this order. It is only a minute proportion of the consequences of our definitions that we are able to detect at a glance. Even so simple a tautology as "91 × 79 = 7189" is beyond the scope of our immediate apprehension. To assure ourselves that "7189" is synonymous with "91 × 79" we have to resort to calculation, which is simply a process of tautological transformation—that is, a process by which we change the form of expressions without altering their significance. The multiplication tables are rules for carrying out this process in arithmetic, just as the laws of logic are rules for the tautological transformation of sentences expressed in logical symbolism or in ordinary language. As the process of calculation is carried out more or less mechanically, it is easy for us to make a slip and so unwittingly contradict ourselves. And this accounts for the existence of logical and mathematical "falsehoods," which otherwise might appear paradoxical. Clearly the risk of error in logical reasoning is proportionate to the length and the complexity of the process of calculation. And in the same way, the more complex an analytic proposition is, the more chance it has of interesting and surprising us.

It is easy to see that the danger of error in logical reasoning can be minimized by the introduction of symbolic devices, which enable us to express highly complex tautologies in a conveniently simple form. And this gives us an opportunity for the exercise of invention in the pursuit of logical enquiries. For a well-chosen definition will call our attention to analytic truths, which would otherwise have escaped us. And the framing of definitions which are useful and fruitful may well be regarded as a creative act.

Having thus shown that there is no inexplicable paradox involved in the view that the truths of logic and mathematics are all of them analytic, we may safely adopt it as the only satisfactory explanation of their *a priori* necessity. And in adopting it we vindicate the empiricist claim that there can be no *a priori* knowledge of reality. For we show that the truths of pure reason, the propositions which we know to be valid independently of all experience, are so only in virtue of their lack of factual content. To say that a proposition is true *a priori* is to say that it is a tautology. And tautologies, though they may serve to

[14] Cf. Hans Hahn, "Logik, Mathematik und Naturerkennen," *Einheitswissenschaft,* Heft II, p. 18. "Ein allwissendes Wesen braucht keine Logik und keine Mathematik."

guide us in our empirical search for knowledge, do not in themselves contain any information about any matter of fact.

CRITIQUE OF ETHICS AND THEOLOGY[1]

There is still one objection to be met before we can claim to have justified our view that all synthetic propositions are empirical hypotheses. This objection is based on the common supposition that our speculative knowledge is of two distinct kinds—that which relates to questions of empirical fact, and that which relates to questions of value. It will be said that "statements of value" are genuine synthetic propositions, but that they cannot with any show of justice be represented as hypotheses, which are used to predict the course of our sensations; and, accordingly, that the existence of ethics and æsthetics as branches of speculative knowledge presents an insuperable objection to our radical empiricist thesis.

In face of this objection, it is our business to give an account of "judgements of value" which is both satisfactory in itself and consistent with our general empiricist principles. We shall set ourselves to show that in so far as statements of value are significant, they are ordinary "scientific" statements; and that in so far as they are not scientific, they are not in the literal sense significant, but are simply expressions of emotion which can be neither true nor false. In maintaining this view, we may confine ourselves for the present to the case of ethical statements. What is said about them will be found to apply, *mutatis mutandis,* to the case of æsthetic statements also.[2]

The ordinary system of ethics, as elaborated in the works of ethical philosophers, is very far from being a homogeneous whole. Not only is it apt to contain pieces of metaphysics, and analyses of non-ethical

[1] From: *Language, Truth and Logic,* A. J. Ayer, Ch. 6. Dover Publications, Inc., New York, and Victor Gollancz, Ltd., London. Reprinted by permission.

[2] The argument that follows should be read in conjunction with the Introduction, pp. 20-2 [of *Language, Truth and Logic*].

concepts: its actual ethical contents are themselves of very different kinds. We may divide them, indeed, into four main classes. There are, first of all, propositions which express definitions of ethical terms, or judgements about the legitimacy or possibility of certain definitions. Secondly, there are propositions describing the phenomena of moral experience, and their causes. Thirdly, there are exhortations to moral virtue. And, lastly, there are actual ethical judgements. It is unfortunately the case that the distinction between these four classes, plain as it is, is commonly ignored by ethical philosophers; with the result that it is often very difficult to tell from their works what it is that they are seeking to discover or prove.

In fact, it is easy to see that only the first of our four classes, namely that which comprises the propositions relating to the definitions of ethical terms, can be said to constitute ethical philosophy. The propositions which describe the phenomena of moral experience, and their causes, must be assigned to the science of psychology, or sociology. The exhortations to moral virtue are not propositions at all, but ejaculations or commands which are designed to provoke the reader to action of a certain sort. Accordingly, they do not belong to any branch of philosophy or science. As for the expressions of ethical judgements, we have not yet determined how they should be classified. But inasmuch as they are certainly neither definitions nor comments upon definitions, nor quotations, we may say decisively that they do not belong to ethical philosophy. A strictly philosophical treatise on ethics should therefore make no ethical pronouncements. But it should, by giving an analysis of ethical terms, show what is the category to which all such pronouncements belong. And this is what we are now about to do.

A question which is often discussed by ethical philosophers is whether it is possible to find definitions which would reduce all ethical terms to one or two fundamental terms. But this question, though it undeniably belongs to ethical philosophy, is not relevant to our present enquiry. We are not now concerned to discover which term, within the sphere of ethical terms, is to be taken as fundamental; whether, for example, "good" can be defined in terms of "right," or "right" in terms of "good," or both in terms of "value." What we are interested in is the possibility of reducing the whole sphere of ethical terms to non-ethical terms. We are enquiring whether statements of ethical value can be translated into statements of empirical fact.

That they can be so translated is the contention of those ethical philosophers who are commonly called subjectivists, and of those who are known as utilitarians. For the utilitarian defines the rightness of actions, and the goodness of ends, in terms of the pleasure, or happiness, or satisfaction, to which they give rise; the subjectivist, in terms of the feelings of approval which a certain person, or group of people, has towards them. Each of these types of definition makes moral judgements into a sub-class of psychological or sociological judgements; and for this reason they are very attractive to us. For, if either was correct, it would follow that ethical assertions were not generically different from the factual assertions which are ordinarily contrasted with them; and the account which we have already given of empirical hypotheses would apply to them also.

Nevertheless we shall not adopt either a subjectivist or a utilitarian analysis of ethical terms. We reject the subjectivist view that to call an action right, or a thing good, is to say that it is generally approved of, because it is not self-contradictory to assert that some actions which are generally approved of are not right, or that some things which are generally approved of are not good. And we reject the alternative subjectivist view that a man who asserts that a certain action is right, or that a certain thing is good, is saying that he himself approves of it, on the ground that a man who confessed that he sometimes approved of what was bad or wrong would not be contradicting himself. And a similar argument is fatal to utilitarianism. We cannot agree that to call an action right is to say that of all the actions possible in the circumstances it would cause, or be likely to cause, the greatest happiness, or the greatest balance of pleasure over pain, or the greatest balance of satisfied over unsatisfied desire, because we find that it is not self-contradictory to say that it is sometimes wrong to perform the action which would actually or probably cause the greatest happiness, or the greatest balance of pleasure over pain, or of satisfied over unsatisfied desire. And since it is not self-contradictory to say that some pleasant things are not good, or that some bad things are desired, it cannot be the case that the sentence "*x* is good" is equivalent to "*x* is pleasant," or to "*x* is desired." And to every other variant of utilitarianism with which I am acquainted the same objection can be made. And therefore we should, I think, conclude that the validity of ethical judgements is not determined by the felicific tendencies of actions, any more than by the nature of people's feelings; but that it must be regarded as "absolute" or "intrinsic," and not empirically calculable.

If we say this, we are not, of course, denying that it is possible to invent a language in which all ethical symbols are definable in non-ethical terms, or even that it is desirable to invent such a language and adopt it in place of our own; what we are denying is that the suggested reduction of ethical to non-ethical statements is consistent with the conventions of our actual language. That is, we reject utilitarianism and subjectivism, not as proposals to replace our existing ethical notions by new ones, but as analyses of our existing ethical notions. Our contention is simply that, in our language, sentences which contain normative ethical symbols are not equivalent to sentences which express psychological propositions, or indeed empirical propositions of any kind.

It is advisable here to make it plain that it is only normative ethical symbols, and not descriptive ethical symbols, that are held by us to be indefinable in factual terms. There is a danger of confusing these two types of symbols, because they are commonly constituted by signs of the same sensible form. Thus a complex sign of the form "*x* is wrong" may constitute a sentence which expresses a moral judgement concerning a certain type of conduct, or it may constitute a sentence which states that a certain type of conduct is repugnant to the moral sense of a particular society. In the latter case, the symbol "wrong" is a descriptive ethical symbol, and the sentence in which it occurs expresses an ordinary sociological proposition; in the former case, the symbol "wrong" is a normative ethical symbol, and the sentence in which it occurs does not, we maintain, express an empirical proposition at all. It is only with normative ethics that we are at present concerned; so that whenever ethical symbols are used in the course of this argument without qualification, they are always to be interpreted as symbols of the normative type.

In admitting that normative ethical concepts are irreducible to empirical concepts, we seem to be leaving the way clear for the "absolutist" view of ethics—that is, the view that statements of value are not controlled by observation, as ordinary empirical propositions are, but only by a mysterious "intellectual intuition." A feature of this theory, which is seldom recognized by its advocates, is that it makes statements of value unverifiable. For it is notorious that what seems intuitively certain to one person may seem doubtful, or even false, to another. So that unless it is possible to provide some criterion by which one may decide between conflicting intuitions, a mere appeal to intuition is worthless as a test of a proposition's validity. But in the case of moral judgements, no such criterion can be given. Some moralists claim to settle the matter by saying that they "know" that their own moral judgements are correct. But such an assertion is of purely psychological interest, and has not the slightest tendency to prove the validity of any moral judgement. For dissentient moralists may equally well "know" that their ethical views are correct. And, as far as subjective certainty goes, there will be nothing to choose between them. When such differences of opinion arise in connection with an ordinary empirical proposition, one may attempt to resolve them by referring to, or actually carrying out, some relevant empirical test. But with regard to ethical statements, there is, on the "absolutist" or "intuitionist" theory, no relevant empirical test. We are therefore justified in saying that on this theory ethical statements are held to be unverifiable. They are, of course, also held to be genuine synthetic propositions.

Considering the use which we have made of the principle that a synthetic proposition is significant only if it is empirically verifiable, it is clear that the acceptance of an "absolutist" theory of ethics would undermine the whole of our main argument. And as we have already rejected the "naturalistic" theories which are commonly supposed to provide the only alternative to "absolutism" in ethics, we seem to have reached a difficult position. We shall meet the difficulty by showing that the correct treatment of ethical statements is afforded by a third theory, which is wholly compatible with our radical empiricism.

We begin by admitting that the fundamental ethical concepts are unanalysable, inasmuch as there is no criterion by which one can test the validity of the judgements in which they occur. So far we are in agreement with the absolutists. But, unlike the absolutists, we are able to give an explanation of this fact about ethical concepts. We say that the reason why they are unanalysable is that they are mere pseudo-concepts. The presence of an ethical symbol in a proposition adds nothing to its factual content. Thus if I say to someone, "You acted wrongly in stealing that money," I am not stating anything more than if I had simply said, "You stole that money." In adding that this action is wrong I am not making any further statement about it. I am simply evincing my moral disapproval of it. It is as if I had said, "You stole that money," in a peculiar tone of horror, or written it with the addition of some special exclamation marks. The tone, or the exclamation marks, adds nothing to the literal meaning of the sentence. It merely serves to show that the expression of it is attended by certain feelings in the speaker.

If now I generalise my previous statement and say, "Stealing money is wrong," I produce a sentence which has no factural meaning—that is, expresses no proposition which can be either true or false. It is as if I had written "Stealing money!!"—where the shape and thickness of the exclamation marks show, by a suitable convention, that a special sort of moral disapproval is the feeling which is being expressed. It is clear that there is nothing said here which can be true or false. Another man may disagree with me about the wrongness of stealing, in the sense that he may not have the same feelings about stealing as I have, and he may quarrel with me on account of my moral sentiments. But he cannot, strictly speaking, contradict me. For in saying that a certain type of action is right or wrong, I am not making any factual statement, not even a statement about my own state of mind. I am merely expressing certain moral sentiments. And the man who is ostensibly contradicting me is merely expressing his moral sentiments. So that there is plainly no sense in asking which of us is in the right. For neither of us is asserting a genuine proposition.

What we have just been saying about the symbol "wrong" applies to all normative ethical symbols. Sometimes they occur in sentences which record ordinary empirical facts besides expressing ethical feeling about those facts: sometimes they occur in sentences which simply express ethical feeling about a certain type of action, or situation, without making any statement of fact. But in every case in which one would commonly be said to be making an ethical judgement, the function of the relevant ethical word is purely "emotive." It is used to express feeling about certain objects, but not to make any assertion about them.

It is worth mentioning that ethical terms do not serve only to express feeling. They are calculated also to arouse feeling, and so to stimulate action. Indeed some of them are used in such a way as to give the sentences in which they occur the effect of commands. Thus the sentence "It is your duty to tell the truth" may be regarded both as the expression of a certain sort of ethical feeling about truthfulness and as the expression of the command "Tell the truth." The sentence "You ought to tell the truth" also involves the command "Tell the truth," but here the tone of the command is less emphatic. In the sentence "It is good to tell the truth" the command has become little more than a suggestion. And thus the "meaning" of the word "good," in its ethical usage, is differentiated from that of the word "duty" or the word "ought." In fact we may define the meaning of the various ethical words in terms both of the different feelings they are ordinarily taken to express, and also the different responses which they are calculated to provoke.

We can now see why it is impossible to find a criterion for determining the validity of ethical judgements. It is not because they have an "absolute" validity which is mysteriously independent of ordinary sense-experience, but because they have no objective validity whatsoever. If a sentence makes no statement at all, there is obviously no sense in asking whether what it says is true or false. And we have seen that sentences which simply express moral judgements do not say anything. They are pure expressions of feeling and as such do not come under the category of truth and falsehood. They are unverifiable for the same reason as a cry of pain or a word of command is unverifiable—because they do not express genuine propositions.

Thus, although our theory of ethics might fairly be said to be radically subjectivist, it differs in a very important respect from the orthodox subjectivist theory. For the orthodox subjectivist does not deny, as we do, that the sentences of a moralizer express genuine propositions. All he denies is that they express propositions of a unique non-empirical character. His own view is that they express propositions about the speaker's feelings. If this were so, ethical judgements clearly would be capable of being true or false. They would be true if the speaker had the relevant feelings, and false if he had not. And this is a matter which is, in principle, empirically verifiable. Furthermore they could be significantly contradicted. For if I say, "Tolerance is a virtue," and someone answers, "You don't approve of it," he would, on the ordinary subjectivist theory, be contradicting me. On our theory, he would not be contradicting me, because, in saying that tolerance was a virtue, I should not be making any statement about my own feelings or about anything else. I should simply be evincing my feelings, which is not at all the same thing as saying that I have them.

The distinction between the expression of feeling and the assertion of feeling is complicated by the fact that the assertion that one has a certain feeling often accompanies the expression of that feeling, and is then, indeed, a factor in the expression of that feeling. Thus I may simultaneously express boredom and say that I am bored, and in that case my utterance of the words, "I am bored," is one of the circumstances which make it true to say that I am expressing or evincing boredom. But I can express boredom without actually saying that I am bored. I can express it by my tone and gestures, while making a statement about something wholly unconnected with it, or by an ejaculation, or without uttering any words at all. So that even if the assertion that one has a certain feeling always involves the expression of that feeling, the expression of a feeling assuredly does not always involve the assertion that one has it. And this is the important point to grasp in considering the distinction between our theory and the ordinary subjectivist theory. For whereas the subjectivist holds that ethical statements actually assert the existence of certain feelings, we hold that ethical statements are expressions and excitants of feeling which do not necessarily involve any assertions.

We have already remarked that the main objection to the ordinary subjectivist theory is that the validity of ethical judgements is not determined by the nature of their author's feelings. And this is an objection which our theory escapes. For it does not imply that the existence of any feelings is a necessary and sufficient condition of the validity of an ethical judgement. It implies, on the contrary, that ethical judgements have no validity.

There is, however, a celebrated argument against subjectivist theories which our theory does not escape. It has been pointed out by Moore that if ethical statements were simply statements about the speaker's feelings, it would be impossible to argue about questions of value.[3] To take a typical example: if a man said that thrift was a virtue, and another replied that it was a vice, they would not, on this theory, be disputing with one another. One would be saying that he approved of thrift, and the other that *he* didn't; and there is no reason why both these statements should not be true. Now Moore held it to be obvious that we do dispute about questions of value, and accordingly concluded that the particular form of subjectivism which he was discussing was false.

It is plain that the conclusion that it is impossible to dispute about questions of value follows from our theory also. For as we hold that such sentences as "Thrift is a virtue" and "Thrift is a vice" do not express propositions at all, we clearly cannot hold that they express incompatible propositions. We must therefore admit that if Moore's argument really refutes the ordinary subjectivist theory, it also refutes ours. But, in fact, we deny that it does refute even the ordinary subjectivist theory. For we hold that one really never does dispute about questions of value.

[3] Cf. *Philosophical Studies,* "The Nature of Moral Philosophy."

This may seem, at first sight, to be a very paradoxical assertion. For we certainly do engage in disputes which are ordinarily regarded as disputes about questions of value. But, in all such cases, we find, if we consider the matter closely, that the dispute is not really about a question of value, but about a question of fact. When someone disagrees with us about the moral value of a certain action or type of action, we do admittedly resort to argument in order to win him over to our way of thinking. But we do not attempt to show by our arguments that he has the "wrong" ethical feeling towards a situation whose nature he has correctly apprehended. What we attempt to show is that he is mistaken about the facts of the case. We argue that he has misconceived the agent's motive: or that he has misjudged the effects of the action, or its probable effects in view of the agent's knowledge; or that he has failed to take into account the special circumstances in which the agent was placed. Or else we employ more general arguments about the effects which actions of a certain type tend to produce, or the qualities which are usually manifested in their performance. We do this in the hope that we have only to get our opponent to agree with us about the nature of the empirical facts for him to adopt the same moral attitude towards them as we do. And as the people with whom we argue have generally received the same moral education as ourselves, and live in the same social order, our expectation is usually justified. But if our opponent happens to have undergone a different process of moral "conditioning" from ourselves, so that, even when he acknowledges all the facts, he still disagrees with us about the moral value of the actions under discussion, then we abandon the attempt to convince him by argument. We say that it is impossible to argue with him because he has a distorted or undeveloped moral sense; which signifies merely that he employs a different set of values from our own. We feel that our own system of values is superior, and therefore speak in such derogatory terms of his. But we cannot bring forward any arguments to show that our system is superior. For our judgement that it is so is itself a judgement of value, and accordingly outside the scope of argument. It is because argument fails us when we come to deal with pure questions of value, as distinct from questions of fact, that we finally resort to mere abuse.

In short, we find that argument is possible on moral questions only if some system of values is presupposed. If our opponent concurs with us in expressing moral disapproval of all actions of a given type *t,* then we may get him to condemn a particular action A, by bringing forward arguments to show that A is of type *t.* For the question whether A does or does not belong to that type is a plain question of fact. Given that a man has certain moral principles, we argue that he must, in order to be consistent, react morally to certain things in a certain way. What we do not and cannot argue about is the validity of these moral principles. We merely praise or condemn them in the light of our own feelings.

If anyone doubts the accuracy of this account of moral disputes, let him try to construct even an imaginary argument on a question of value which does not reduce itself to an argument about a question of logic or about an empirical matter of fact. I am confident that he will not succeed in producing a single example. And if that is the case, he must allow that its involving the impossibility of purely ethical arguments is not, as Moore thought, a ground of objection to our theory, but rather a point in favour of it.

Having upheld our theory against the only criticism which appeared to threaten it, we may now use it to define the nature of all ethical enquiries. We find that ethical philosophy consists simply in saying that ethical concepts are pseudo-concepts and therefore unanalysable. The further task of describing the different feelings that the different ethical terms are used to express, and the different reactions that they customarily provoke, is a task for the psychologist. There cannot be such a thing as ethical science, if by ethical science one means the elaboration of a "true" system of morals. For we have seen that, as ethical judgements are mere expressions of feeling, there can be no way of determining the validity of any ethical system, and, indeed, no sense in asking whether any such system is true. All that one may legitimately enquire in this connection is, What are the moral habits of a given person or group of people, and what causes them to have precisely those habits and feelings? And this enquiry falls wholly within the scope of the existing social sciences.

It appears, then, that ethics, as a branch of knowledge, is nothing more than a department of psychology and sociology. And in case anyone thinks that we are overlooking the existence of casuistry, we may remark that casuistry is not a science, but is a purely analytical investigation of the structure of a given moral system. In other words, it is an exercise in formal logic.

When one comes to pursue the psychological enquiries which constitute ethical science, one is immediately enabled to account for the Kantian and Hedonistic theories of morals. For one finds that one of the chief causes of moral behaviour is fear, both conscious and unconscious, of a god's displeasure, and fear of the enmity of society. And this, indeed, is the reason why moral precepts present themselves to some people as "categorical" commands. And one finds, also, that the moral code of a society is partly determined by the beliefs of that society concerning the conditions of its own happiness—or, in other words, that a society tends to encourage or discourage a given type of conduct by the use of moral sanctions according as it appears to promote or detract from the contentment of the society as a whole. And this is the reason why altruism is recommended in most moral codes and egotism condemned. It is from the observation of this connection between morality and happiness that hedonistic or eudæmonistic theories of morals ultimately spring, just as the moral theory of Kant is based on the fact, previously explained, that moral precepts have for some people the force of inexorable commands. As each of these theories ignores the fact which lies at the root of the other, both may be criticized as being one-sided; but this is not the main objection to either of them. Their essential defect is that they treat propositions which refer to the causes and attributes of our ethical feelings as if they were definitions of ethical concepts. And thus they fail to recognise that ethical concepts are pseudo-concepts and consequently indefinable.

As we have already said, our conclusions about the nature of ethics apply to æsthetics also. Æsthetic terms are used in exactly the same way as ethical terms. Such æsthetic words as "beautiful" and "hideous" are employed, as ethical words are employed, not to make statements of fact, but simply to express certain feelings and evoke a certain response. It follows, as in ethics, that there is no sense in attributing objective validity to æsthetic judgements, and no possibility of arguing about questions of value in æsthetics, but only about questions of fact. A scientific treatment of æsthetics would show us what in general were the causes of æsthetic feeling, why various societies produced and admired the works of art they did, why taste varies as it does within a given society, and so forth. And these are ordinary psychological or sociological questions. They have, of course, little or nothing to do with æsthetic criticism as we understand it. But that is because the purpose of æsthetic criticism is not so much to give knowledge as to communicate emotion. The critic, by calling attention to certain features of the work under review, and expressing his own feelings about them, endeavours to make us share his attitude towards the work as a whole. The only relevant propositions that he formulates are propositions describing the nature of the work. And these are plain records of fact. We conclude, therefore, that there is nothing in æsthetics, any more than there is in ethics, to justify the view that it embodies a unique type of knowledge.

It should now be clear that the only information which we can legitimately derive from the study of our æsthetic and moral experiences is information about our own mental and physical make-up. We take note of these experiences as providing data for our psychological and sociological generalisations. And this is the only way in which they serve to increase our knowledge. It follows that any attempt to make our use of ethical and æsthetic concepts the basis of a metaphysical theory concerning the existence of a world of values, as distinct from the world of facts, involves a false analysis of these concepts. Our own analysis has shown that the phenomena of moral experience cannot fairly be used to support any rationalist or metaphysical doctrine whatsoever. In particular, they cannot, as Kant hoped, be used to establish the existence of a transcendent god.

This mention of God brings us to the question of the possibility of religious knowledge. We shall see that this possibility has already been ruled out by our treatment of metaphysics. But, as this is a point of considerable interest, we may be permitted to discuss it at some length.

It is now generally admitted, at any rate by philosophers, that the existence of a being having the attributes which define the god of any non-animistic religion cannot be demonstratively proved. To see that this is so, we have only to ask ourselves what are the premises from which the existence of such a god could be deduced. If the conclusion that a god exists is to be demonstratively certain, then these premises must be certain; for, as the conclusion of a deductive argument is already contained in the premises, any uncertainty there may be about the truth of the premises is necessarily shared by it. But we know that no empirical proposition can ever be anything more than probable. It is only *a priori* propositions that are logically certain. But we cannot deduce the existence of a god from an *a priori* proposition. For we know that the reason why *a priori* propositions are certain is that they are tautologies. And from a set of tautologies nothing but a further tautology can be validly deduced. It follows that there is no possibility of demonstrating the existence of a god.

What is not so generally recognised is that there can be no way of proving that the existence of a god, such as the God of Christianity, is even probable. Yet this also is easily shown. For if the existence of such a god were probable, then the proposition that he existed would be an empirical hypothesis. And in that case it would be possible to deduce from it, and other empirical hypotheses, certain experiential propositions which were not deducible from those other hypotheses alone. But in fact this is not possible. It is sometimes claimed, indeed, that the existence of a certain sort of regularity in nature constitutes sufficient evidence for the existence of a god. But if the sentence "God exists" entails no more than that certain types of phenomena occur in certain sequences, then to assert the existence of a god will be simply equivalent to asserting that there is the requisite regularity in nature; and no religious man would admit that this was all he intended to assert in asserting the existence of a god. He would say that in talking about God, he was talking about a transcendent being who might be known through certain empirical manifestations, but certainly could not be defined in terms of those manifestations. But in that case the term "god" is a metaphysical term. And if "god" is a metaphysical term, then it cannot be even probable that a god exists. For to say that "God exists" is to make a metaphysical utterance which cannot be either true or false. And by the same criterion, no sentence which purports to describe the nature of a transcendent god can possess any literal significance.

It is important not to confuse this view of religious assertions with the view that is adopted by atheists, or agnostics.[4] For it is characteristic of an agnostic to hold that the existence of a god is a possibility in

[4] This point was suggested to me by Professor H. H. Price.

which there is no good reason either to believe or disbelieve; and it is characteristic of an atheist to hold that it is at least probable that no god exists. And our view that all utterances about the nature of God are nonsensical, so far from being identical with, or even lending any support to, either of these familiar contentions, is actually incompatible with them. For if the assertion that there is a god is nonsensical, then the atheist's assertion that there is no god is equally nonsensical, since it is only a significant proposition that can be significantly contradicted. As for the agnostic, although he refrains from saying either that there is or that there is not a god, he does not deny that the question whether a transcendent god exists is a genuine question. He does not deny that the two sentences "There is a transcendent god" and "There is no transcendent god" express propositions one of which is actually true and the other false. All he says is that we have no means of telling which of them is true, and therefore ought not to commit ourselves to either. But we have seen that the sentences in question do not express propositions at all. And this means that agnosticism also is ruled out.

Thus we offer the theist the same comfort as we gave to the moralist. His assertions cannot possibly be valid, but they cannot be invalid either. As he says nothing at all about the world, he cannot justly be accused of saying anything false, or anything for which he has insufficient grounds. It is only when the theist claims that in asserting the existence of a transcendent god he is expressing a genuine proposition that we are entitled to disagree with him.

It is to be remarked that in cases where deities are identified with natural objects, assertions concerning them may be allowed to be significant. If, for example, a man tells me that the occurrence of thunder is alone both necessary and sufficient to establish the truth of the proposition that Jehovah is angry, I may conclude that, in his usage of words, the sentence "Jehovah is angry" is equivalent to "It is thundering." But in sophisticated religions, though they may be to some extent based on men's awe of natural process which they cannot sufficiently understand, the "person" who is supposed to control the empirical world is not himself located in it; he is held to be superior to the empirical world, and so outside it; and he is endowed with super-empirical attributes. But the notion of a person whose essential attributes are nonempirical is not an intelligible notion at all. We may have a word which is used as if it named this "person," but, unless the sentences in which it occurs express propositions which are empirically verifiable, it cannot be said to symbolize anything. And this is the case with regard to the word "god," in the usage in which it is intended to refer to a transcendent object. The mere existence of the noun is enough to foster the illusion that there is a real, or at any rate a possible entity corresponding to it. It is only when we enquire what God's attributes are that we discover that "God," in this usage, is not a genuine name.

It is common to find belief in a transcendent god conjoined with belief in an after-life. But, in the form which it usually takes, the content of this belief is not a genuine hypothesis. To say that men do not ever die, or that the state of death is merely a state of prolonged insensibility, is indeed to express a significant proposition, though all the available evidence goes to show that it is false. But to say that there is something imperceptible inside a man, which is his soul or his real self, and that it goes on living after he is dead, is to make a metaphysical assertion which has no more factual content than the assertion that there is a transcendent god.

It is worth mentioning that, according to the account which we have given of religious assertions, there is no logical ground for antagonism between religion and natural science. As far as the question of truth or falsehood is concerned, there is no opposition between the natural scientist and the theist who believes in a transcendent god. For since the religious utterances of the theist are not genuine propositions at all, they cannot stand in any logical relation to the propositions of science. Such antagonism as there is between religion and science appears to consist in the fact that science takes away one of the motives which make men religious. For it is acknowledged that one of the ultimate sources of religious feeling lies in the inability of men to determine their own destiny; and science tends to destroy the feeling of awe with which men regard an alien world, by making them believe that they can understand and anticipate the course of natural phenomena, and even to some extent control it. The fact that it has recently become fashionable for physicists themselves to be sympathetic towards religion is a point in favour of this hypothesis. For this sympathy towards religion marks the physicists' own lack of confidence in the validity of their hypotheses, which is a reaction on their part from the anti-religious dogmatism of nineteenth-century scientists, and a natural outcome of the crisis through which physics has just passed.

It is not within the scope of this enquiry to enter more deeply into the causes of religious feeling, or to discuss the probability of the continuance of religious belief. We are concerned only to answer those questions which arise out of our discussion of the possibility of religious knowledge. The point which we wish to establish is that there cannot be any transcendent truths of religion. For the sentences which the theist uses to express such "truths" are not literally significant.

An interesting feature of this conclusion is that it accords with what many theists are accustomed to say themselves. For we are often told that the nature of God is a mystery which transcends the human understanding. But to say that something transcends the human understanding is to say that it is unintelligible. And what is unintelligible cannot significantly be described. Again, we are told that God is not an object of reason but an object of faith. This may be nothing more than an admission that the existence of God must be taken on trust, since it cannot be proved. But it may also be an assertion that God is the object of a purely mystical intuition, and cannot therefore be defined in terms which are intelligible to the reason. And I think there are many theists who would assert this. But if one allows that it is impossible to define God in intelligible terms, then one is allowing that it is impossible for a sentence both to be significant and to be about God. If a mystic admits that the object of his vision is something which cannot be described, then he must also admit that he is bound to talk nonsense when he describes it.

For his part, the mystic may protest that his intuition does reveal truths to him, even though he cannot explain to others what these truths are; and that we who do not possess this faculty of intuition can have no ground for denying that it is a cognitive faculty. For we can hardly maintain *a priori* that there are no ways of discovering true propositions except those which we ourselves employ. The answer is that we set no limit to the number of ways in which one may come to formulate a true proposition. We do not in any way deny that a synthetic truth may be discovered by purely intuitive methods as well as by the rational method of induction. But we do say that every synthetic proposition, however it may have been arrived at, must be subject to the test of actual experience. We do not deny *a priori* that the mystic is able to discover truths by his own special methods. We wait to hear what are the propositions which embody his discoveries, in order to see whether they are verified or confuted by our empirical observations. But the mystic, so far from producing propositions which are empirically verified, is unable to produce any intelligible propositions at all. And therefore we say that his intuition has not revealed to him any facts. It is no use his saying that he has apprehended facts but is unable to express them. For we know that if he really had acquired any information, he would be able to express it. He would be able to indicate in some way or other how the genuineness of his discovery might be empirically determined. The fact that he cannot reveal what he "knows," or even himself devise an empirical test to validate his "knowledge," shows that his state of mystical intuition is not a genuinely cognitive state. So that in describing his vision the mystic does not give us any information about the external world; he merely gives us indirect information about the condition of his own mind.

These considerations dispose of the argument from religious experience, which many philosophers still regard as a valid argument in favour of the existence of a god. They say that it is logically possible for men to be immediately acquainted with God, as they are immediately acquainted with a sense-content, and that there is no reason why one should be prepared to believe a man when he says that he is seeing a yellow patch, and refuse to believe him when he says that he is seeing God. The answer to this is that if the man who asserts that he is seeing God is merely asserting that he is experiencing a peculiar kind of sense-content, then we do not for a moment deny that his assertion may be true. But, ordinarily, the man who says that he is seeing God is saying not merely that he is experiencing a religious emotion, but also that there exists a transcendent being who is the object of this emotion; just as the man who says that he sees a yellow patch is ordinarily saying not merely that his visual sense-field contains a yellow sense-content, but also that there exists a yellow object to which the sense-content belongs. And it is not irrational to be prepared to believe a man when he asserts the existence of a yellow object, and to refuse to believe him when he asserts the existnce of a transcendent god. For whereas the sentence "There exists here a yellow-coloured material thing" expresses a genuine synthetic proposition which could be empirically verified, the sentence "There exists a transcendent god" has, as we have seen, no literal significance.

We conclude, therefore, that the argument from religious experience is altogether fallacious. The fact that people have religious experiences is interesting from the psychological point of view, but it does not in any way imply that there is such a thing as religious knowledge, any more than our having moral experiences implies that there is such a thing as moral knowledge. The theist, like the moralist, may believe that his experiences are cognitive experiences, but, unless he can formulate his "knowledge" in propositions that are empirically verifiable, we may be sure that he is deceiving himself. It follows that those philosophers who fill their books with assertions that they intuitively "know" this or that moral or religious "truth" are merely providing material for the psycho-analyst. For no act of intuition can be said to reveal a truth about any matter of fact unless it issues in verifiable propositions. And all such propositions are to be incorporated in the system of empirical propositions which constitutes science.

W. V. Quine

TWO DOGMAS OF EMPIRICISM[1]

Modern empiricism has been conditioned in large part by two dogmas. One is a belief in some fundamental cleavage between truths which are *analytic,* or grounded in meanings independently of matters of fact, and truths which are *synthetic,* or grounded in fact. The other dogma is *reductionism:* the belief that each meaningful statement is equivalent to some logical construct upon terms which refer to immediate experience. Both dogmas, I shall argue, are ill-founded. One effect of abandoning them is, as we shall see, a blurring of the supposed boundary between speculative metaphysics and natural science. Another effect is a shift toward pragmatism.

1. *Background for analyticity*

Kant's cleavage between analytic and synthetic truths was foreshadowed in Hume's distinction between relations of ideas and matters of fact, and in Leibniz's distinction between truths of reason and truths of fact. Leibniz spoke of the truths of reason as true in all possible worlds. Picturesqueness aside, this is to say that the truths of reason are those which could not possibly be false. In the same vein we hear analytic statements defined as statements whose denials are self-contradictory. But this definition has small explanatory value; for the notion of self-contradictoriness, in the quite broad sense needed for this definition of

[1] From: *From a Logical Point of View,* W. V. Quine, Ch. 2. Harvard University Press, Cambridge, Mass. Copyright 1953 by the President and Fellows of Harvard College. By permission.

analyticity, stands in exactly the same need of clarification as does the notion of analyticity itself. The two notions are the two sides of a single dubious coin.

Kant conceived of an analytic statement as one that attributes to its subject no more than is already conceptually contained in the subject. This formulation has two shortcomings: it limits itself to statements of subject-predicate form, and it appeals to a notion of containment which is left at a metaphorical level. But Kant's intent, evident more from the use he makes of the notion of analyticity than from his definition of it, can be restated thus: a statement is analytic when it is true by virtue of meanings and independently of fact. Pursuing this line, let us examine the concept of *meaning* which is presupposed.

Meaning, let us remember, is not to be identified with naming.[2] Frege's example of 'Evening Star' and 'Morning Star', and Russell's of 'Scott' and 'the author of *Waverley*', illustrate that terms can name the same thing but differ in meaning. The distinction between meaning and naming is no less important at the level of abstract terms. The terms '9' and 'the number of the planets' name one and the same abstract entity but presumably must be regarded as unlike in meaning; for astronomical observation was needed, and not mere reflection on meanings, to determine the sameness of the entity in question.

The above examples consist of singular terms, concrete and abstract. With general terms, or predicates, the situation is somewhat different but parallel. Whereas a singular term purports to name an entity, abstract or concrete, a general term does not; but a general term is *true* of an entity, or of each of many, or of none.[3] The class of all entities of which a general term is true is called the *extension* of the term. Now paralleling the contrast between the meaning of a singular term and the entity named, we must distinguish equally between the meaning of a general term and its extension. The general terms 'creature with a heart' and 'creature with kidneys', for example, are perhaps alike in extension but unlike in meaning.

Confusion of meaning with extension, in the case of general terms, is less common than confusion of meaning with naming in the case of singular terms. It is indeed a commonplace in philosophy to oppose intension (or meaning) to extension, or, in a variant vocabulary, connotation to denotation.

The Aristotelian notion of essence was the forerunner, no doubt, of the modern notion of intension or meaning. For Aristotle it was essential in men to be rational, accidental to be two-legged. But there is an important difference between this attitude and the doctrine of meaning. From the latter point of view it may indeed be conceded (if only for the sake of argument) that rationality is involved in the meaning of the word 'man' while two-leggedness is not; but two-leggedness may

[2] See [*From a Logical Point of View*], p. 9.
[3] See [*From a Logical Point of View*], p. 10 and pp. 107-115.

at the same time be viewed as involved in the meaning of 'biped' while rationality is not. Thus from the point of view of the doctrine of meaning it makes no sense to say of the actual individual, who is at once a man and a biped, that his rationality is essential and his two-leggedness accidental or vice versa. Things had essences, for Aristotle, but only linguistic forms have meanings. Meaning is what essence becomes when it is divorced from the object of reference and wedded to the word.

For the theory of meaning a conspicuous question is the nature of its objects: what sort of things are meanings? A felt need for meant entities may derive from an earlier failure to appreciate that meaning and reference are distinct. Once the theory of meaning is sharply separated from the theory of reference, it is a short step to recognizing as the primary business of the theory of meaning simply the synonymy of linguistic forms and the analyticity of statements; meanings themselves, as obscure intermediary entities, may well be abandoned.[4]

The problem of analyticity then confronts us anew. Statements which are analytic by general philosophical acclaim are not, indeed, far to seek. They fall into two classes. Those of the first class, which may be called *logically true,* are typified by:

(1) No unmarried man is married.

The relevant feature of this example is that it not merely is true as it stands, but remains true under any and all reinterpretations of 'man' and 'married'. If we suppose a prior inventory of *logical* particles, comprising 'no', 'un-', 'not', 'if', 'then', 'and', etc., then in general a logical truth is a statement which is true and remains true under all reinterpretations of its components other than the logical particles.

But there is also a second class of analytic statements, typified by:

(2) No bachelor is married.

The characteristic of such a statement is that it can be turned into a logical truth by putting synonyms for synonyms; thus (2) can be turned into (1) by putting 'unmarried man' for its synonym 'bachelor'. We still lack a proper characterization of this second class of analytic statements, and therewith of analyticity generally, inasmuch as we have had in the above description to lean on a notion of "synonymy" which is no less in need of clarification than analyticity itself.

In recent years Carnap has tended to explain analyticity by appeal to what he calls state-descriptions.[5] A state-description is any exhaustive assignment of truth values to the atomic, or noncompound, statements of the language. All other statements of the language are, Carnap assumes, built up of their component clauses by means of the familiar logical devices, in such a way that the truth value of any complex state-

[4] See [*From a Logical Point of View*], pp. 11f and pp. 48f.
[5] Rudolph Carnap, *Meaning and Necessity,* pp. 9ff. [4].

ment is fixed for each state-description by specifiable logical laws. A statement is then explained as analytic when it comes out true under every state description. This account is an adaptation of Leibniz's "true in all possible worlds." But note that this version of analyticity serves its purpose only if the atomic statements of the language are, unlike 'John is a bachelor' and 'John is married', mutually independent. Otherwise there would be a state-description which assigned truth to 'John is a bachelor' and to 'John is married', and consequently 'No bachelors are married' would turn out synthetic rather than analytic under the proposed criterion. Thus the criterion of analyticity in terms of state-descriptions serves only for languages devoid of extra-logical synonym-pairs, such as 'bachelor' and 'unmarried man'—synonym-pairs of the type which give rise to the "second class" of analytic statements. The criterion in terms of state-descriptions is a reconstruction at best of logical truth, not of analyticity.

I do not mean to suggest that Carnap is under any illusions on this point. His simplified model language with its state-descriptions is aimed primarily not at the general problem of analyticity but at another purpose, the clarification of probability and induction. Our problem, however, is analyticity; and here the major difficulty lies not in the first class of analytic statements, the logical truths, but rather in the second class, which depends on the notion of synonymy.

2. *Definition*

There are those who find it soothing to say that the analytic statements of the second class reduce to those of the first class, the logical truths, by *definition;* 'bachelor', for example, is *defined* as 'unmarried man'. But how do we find that 'bachelor' is defined as 'unmarried man'? Who defined it thus, and when? Are we to appeal to the nearest dictionary, and accept the lexicographer's formulation as law? Clearly this would be to put the cart before the horse. The lexicographer is an empirical scientist, whose business is the recording of antecedent facts; and if he glosses 'bachelor' as 'unmarried man' it is because of his belief that there is a relation of synonymy between those forms, implicit in general or preferred usage prior to his own work. The notion of synonymy presupposed here has still to be clarified, presumably in terms relating to linguistic behavior. Certainly the "definition" which is the lexicographer's report of an observed synonymy cannot be taken as the ground of the synonymy.

Definition is not, indeed, an activity exclusively of philologists. Philosophers and scientists frequently have occasion to "define" a recondite term by paraphrasing it into terms of a more familiar vocabulary. But ordinarily such a definition, like the philologist's, is pure lexicography, affirming a relation of synonymy antecedent to the exposition in hand.

Just what it means to affirm synonymy, just what the interconnections may be which are necessary and sufficient in order that two linguistic forms be properly describable as synonymous, is far from clear; but, whatever these interconnections may be, ordinarily they are grounded in usage. Definitions reporting selected instances of synonymy come then as reports upon usage.

There is also, however, a variant type of definitional activity which does not limit itself to the reporting of preëxisting synonymies. I have in mind what Carnap calls *explication*—an activity to which philosophers are given, and scientists also in their more philosophical moments. In explication the purpose is not merely to paraphrase the definiendum into an outright synonym, but actually to improve upon the definiendum by refining or supplementing its meaning. But even explication, though not merely reporting a preëxisting synonymy between definiendum and definiens, does rest nevertheless on *other* preëxisting synonymies. The matter may be viewed as follows. Any word worth explicating has some contexts which, as wholes, are clear and precise enough to be useful; and the purpose of explication is to preserve the usage of these favored contexts while sharpening the usage of other contexts. In order that a given definition be suitable for purposes of explication, therefore, what is required is not that the definiendum in its antecedent usage be synonymous with the definiens, but just that each of these favored contexts of the definiendum, taken as a whole in its antecedent usage, be synonymous with the corresponding context of the definiens.

Two alternative definientia may be equally appropriate for the purposes of a given task of explication and yet not be synonymous with each other; for they may serve interchangeably within the favored contexts but diverge elsewhere. By cleaving to one of these definientia rather than the other, a definition of explicative kind generates, by fiat, a relation of synonymy between definiendum and definiens which did not hold before. But such a definition still owes its explicative function, as seen, to preëxisting synonymies.

There does, however, remain still an extreme sort of definition which does not hark back to prior synonymies at all: namely, the explicitly conventional introduction of novel notations for purposes of sheer abbreviation. Here the definiendum becomes synonymous with the definiens simply because it has been created expressly for the purpose of being synonymous with the definiens. Here we have a really transparent case of synonymy created by definition; would that all species of synonymy were as intelligible. For the rest, definition rests on synonymy rather than explaining it.

The word 'definition' has come to have a dangerously reassuring sound, owing no doubt to its frequent occurrence in logical and mathematical writings. We shall do well to digress now into a brief appraisal of the role of definition in formal work.

In logical and mathematical systems either of two mutually antagonistic types of economy may be striven for, and each has its peculiar practical utility. On the one hand we may seek economy of practical expression—ease and brevity in the statement of multifarious relations. This sort of economy calls usually for distinctive concise notations for a wealth of concepts. Second, however, and oppositely, we may seek economy in grammar and vocabulary; we may try to find a minimum of basic concepts such that, once a distinctive notation has been appropriated to each of them, it becomes possible to express any desired further concept by mere combination and iteration of our basic notations. This second sort of economy is impractical in one way, since a poverty in basic idioms tends to a necessary lengthening of discourse. But it is practical in another way: it greatly simplifies theoretical discourse *about* the language, through minimizing the terms and the forms of construction wherein the language consists.

Both sorts of economy, though prima facie incompatible, are valuable in their separate ways. The custom has consequently arisen of combining both sorts of economy by forging in effect two languages, the one a part of the other. The inclusive language, though redundant in grammar and vocabulary, is economical in message lengths, while the part, called primitive notation, is economical in grammar and vocabulary. Whole and part are correlated by rules of translation whereby each idiom not in primitive notation is equated to some complex built up of primitive notation. These rules of translation are the so-called *definitions* which appear in formalized systems. They are best viewed not as adjuncts to one language but as correlations between two languages, the one a part of the other.

But these correlations are not arbitrary. They are supposed to show how the primitive notations can accomplish all purposes, save brevity and convenience, of the redundant language. Hence the definiendum and its definiens may be expected, in each case, to be related in one or another of the three ways lately noted. The definiens may be a faithful paraphrase of the definiendum into the narrower notation, preserving a direct synonymy[6] as of antecedent usage; or the definiens may, in the spirit of explication, improve upon the antecedent usage of the definiendum; or finally, the definiendum may be a newly created notation, newly endowed with meaning here and now.

In formal and informal work alike, thus, we find that definition—except in the extreme case of the explicitly conventional introduction of new notations—hinges on prior relations of synonymy. Recognizing then that the notion of definition does not hold the key to synonymy and analyticity, let us look further into synonymy and say no more of definition.

[6] According to an important variant sense of 'definition', the relation preserved may be the weaker relation of mere agreement in reference; see [*From a Logical Point of View*], p. 132. But definition in this sense is better ignored in the present connection, being irrelevant to the question of synonymy.

3. *Interchangeability*

A natural suggestion, deserving close examination, is that the synonymy of two linguistic forms consists simply in their interchangeability in all contexts without change of truth value—interchangeability, in Leibniz's phrase, *salva veritate*.[7] Note that synonyms so conceived need not even be free from vagueness, as long as the vaguenesses match.

But it is not quite true that the synonyms 'bachelor' and 'unmarried man' are everywhere interchangeable *salva veritate*. Truths which become false under substitution of 'unmarried man' for 'bachelor' are easily constructed with the help of 'bachelor of arts' or 'bachelor's buttons'; also with the help of quotation, thus:

'Bachelor' has less than ten letters.

Such counterinstances can, however, perhaps be set aside by treating the phrases 'bachelor of arts' and 'bachelor's buttons' and the quotation ' 'bachelor' ' each as a single indivisible word and then stipulating that the interchangeability *salva veritate* which is to be the touchstone of synonymy is not supposed to apply to fragmentary occurrences inside of a word. This account of synonymy, supposing it acceptable on other counts, has indeed the drawback of appealing to a prior conception of "word" which can be counted on to present difficulties of formulation in its turn. Nevertheless some progress might be claimed in having reduced the problem of synonymy to a problem of wordhood. Let us pursue this line a bit, taking "word" for granted.

The question remains whether interchangeability *salva veritate* (apart from occurrences within words) is a strong enough condition for synonymy, or whether, on the contrary, some heteronymous expressions might be thus interchangeable. Now let us be clear that we are not concerned here with synonymy in the sense of complete identity in psychological associations or poetic quality; indeed no two expressions are synonymous in such a sense. We are concerned only with what may be called *cognitive* synonymy. Just what this is cannot be said without successfully finishing the present study; but we know something about it from the need which arose for it in connection with analyticity in §1. The sort of synonymy needed there was merely such that any analytic statement could be turned into a logical truth by putting synonyms for synonyms. Turning the tables and assuming analyticity, indeed, we could explain cognitive synonymy of terms as follows (keeping to the familiar example): to say that 'bachelor' and 'unmarried man' are cognitively synonymous is to say no more nor less than that the statement:

7 Cf. C. I. Lewis, *A Survey of Symbolic Logic,* p. 373.

(3) All and only bachelors are unmarried men

is analytic.[8]

What we need is an account of cognitive synonymy not presupposing analyticity—if we are to explain analyticity conversely with help of cognitive synonymy as undertaken in §1. And indeed such an independent account of cognitive synonymy is at present up for consideration, namely, interchangeability *salva veritate* everywhere except within words. The question before us, to resume the thread at last, is whether such interchangeability is a sufficient condition for cognitive synonymy. We can quickly assure ourselves that it is, by examples of the following sort. The statement:

(4) Necessarily all and only bachelors are bachelors

is evidently true, even supposing 'necessarily' so narrowly construed as to be truly applicable only to analytic statements. Then, if 'bachelor' and 'unmarried man' are interchangeable *salva veritate,* the result:

(5) Necessarily all and only bachelors are unmarried men

of putting 'unmarried man' for an occurrence of 'bachelor' in (4) must, like (4), be true. But to say that (5) is true is to say that (3) is analytic, and hence that 'bachelor' and 'unmarried man' are cognitively synonymous.

Let us see what there is about the above argument that gives it its air of hocus-pocus. The condition of interchangeability *salva veritate* varies in its force with variations in the richness of the language at hand. The above argument supposes we are working with a language rich enough to contain the adverb 'necessarily', this adverb being so construed as to yield truth when and only when applied to an analytic statement. But can we condone a language which contains such an adverb? Does the adverb really make sense? To suppose that it does is to suppose that we have already made satisfactory sense of 'analytic'. Then what are we so hard at work on right now?

Our argument is not flatly circular, but something like it. It has the form, figuratively speaking, of a closed curve in space.

Interchangeability *salva veritate* is meaningless until relativized to a language whose extent is specified in relevant respects. Suppose now we consider a language containing just the following materials. There is an indefinitely large stock of one-place predicates (for example, '*F*' where '*Fx*' means that x is a man) and many-place predicates (for example, '*G*' where '*Gxy*' means that x loves y), mostly having to do

[8] This is cognitive synonymy in a primary, broad sense. Carnap (*Meaning and Necessity*, pp. 56ff) and Lewis (*An Analysis of Knowledge and Valuation*, pp. 83ff) have suggested how, once this notion is at hand, a narrower sense of cognitive synonymy which is preferable for some purposes can in turn be derived. But this special ramification of concept-building lies aside from the present purposes and must not be confused with the broad sort of cognitive synonymy here concerned.

with extralogical subject matter. The rest of the language is logical. The atomic sentences consist each of a predicate followed by one or more variables '*x*', '*y*', etc.; and the complex sentences are built up of the atomic ones by truth functions ('not', 'and', 'or', etc.) and quantification.[9] In effect such a language enjoys the benefits also of descriptions and indeed singular terms generally, these being contextually definable in known ways.[10] Even abstract singular terms naming classes, classes of classes, etc., are contextually definable in case the assumed stock of predicates includes the two-place predicate of class membership.[11] Such a language can be adequate to classical mathematics and indeed to scientific discourse generally, except in so far as the latter involves debatable devices such as contrary-to-fact conditionals or modal adverbs like 'necessarily'.[12] Now a language of this type is extensional, in this sense: any two predicates which agree extensionally (that is, are true of the same objects) are interchangeable *salva veritate.*[13]

In an extensional language, therefore, interchangeability *salva veritate* is no assurance of cognitive synonymy of the desired type. That 'bachelor' and 'unmarried man' are interchangeable *salva veritate* in an extensional language assures us of no more than that (3) is true. There is no assurance here that the extensional agreement of 'bachelor' and 'unmarried man' rests on meaning rather than merely on accidental matters of fact, as does the extensional agreement of 'creature with a heart' and 'creature with kidneys'.

For most purposes extensional agreement is the nearest approximation to synonymy we need care about. But the fact remains that extensional agreement falls far short of cognitive synonymy of the type required for explaining analyticity in the manner of §1. The type of cognitive synonymy required there is such as to equate the synonymy of 'bachelor' and 'unmarried man' with the analyticity of (3), not merely with the truth of (3).

So we must recognize that interchangeability *salva veritate,* if construed in relation to an extensional language, is not a sufficient condition of cognitive synonymy in the sense needed for deriving analyticity in the manner of §1. If a language contains an intensional adverb 'necessarily' in the sense lately noted, or other particles to the same effect, then interchangeability *salva veritate* in such a language does afford a sufficient condition of cognitive synonymy; but such a language is intelligible only in so far as the notion of analyticity is already understood in advance.

[9] Pp. 81ff [of *From a Logical Point of View*], contain a description of just such a language, except that there happens there to be just one predicate, the two-place predicate '∊'.
[10] See [*From a Logical Point of View*], pp. 5-8; also pp. 85f, 166f.
[11] See [*From a Logical Point of View*], p. 87.
[12] On such devices see also Essay VIII.
[13] This is the substance of W. V. Quine, *Mathematical Logic,* *121.

The effort to explain cognitive synonymy first, for the sake of deriving analyticity from it afterward as in §1, is perhaps the wrong approach. Instead we might try explaining analyticity somehow without appeal to cognitive synonymy. Afterward we could doubtless derive cognitive synonymy from analyticity satisfactorily enough if desired. We have seen that cognitive synonymy of 'bachelor' and 'unmarried man' can be explained as analyticity of (3). The same explanation works for any pair of one-place predicates, of course, and it can be extended in obvious fashion to many-place predicates. Other syntactical categories can also be accommodated in fairly parallel fashion. Singular terms may be said to be cognitively synonymous when the statement of identity formed by putting '=' between them is analytic. Statements may be said simply to be cognitively synonymous when their biconditional (the result of joining them by 'if and only if') is analytic.[14] If we care to lump all categories into a single formulation, at the expense of assuming again the notion of "word" which was appealed to early in this section, we can describe any two linguistic forms as cognitively synonymous when the two forms are interchangeable (apart from occurrences within "words") *salva* (no longer *veritate* but) *analyticitate*. Certain technical questions arise, indeed, over cases of ambiguity or homonymy; let us not pause for them, however, for we are already digressing. Let us rather turn our backs on the problem of synonymy and address ourselves anew to that of analyticity.

4. *Semantical rules*

Analyticity at first seemed most naturally definable by appeal to a realm of meanings. On refinement, the appeal to meanings gave way to an appeal to synonymy or definition. But definition turned out to be a will-o'-the-wisp, and synonymy turned out to be best understood only by dint of a prior appeal to analyticity itself. So we are back at the problem of analyticity.

I do not know whether the statement 'Everything green is extended' is analytic. Now does my indecision over this example really betray an incomplete understanding, an incomplete grasp of the "meanings", of 'green' and 'extended'? I think not. The trouble is not with 'green' or 'extended', but with 'analytic'.

It is often hinted that the difficulty in separating analytic statements from synthetic ones in ordinary language is due to the vagueness of ordinary language and that the distinction is clear when we have a precise artificial language with explicit "semantical rules." This, however, as I shall now attempt to show, is a confusion.

The notion of analyticity about which we are worrying is a pur-

[14] The 'if and only if' itself is intended in the truth functional sense. See Carnap, *Meaning and Necessity*, p. 14.

ported relation between statements and languages: a statement *S* is said to be *analytic for* a language *L,* and the problem is to make sense of this relation generally, that is, for variable '*S*' and '*L*'. The gravity of this problem is not perceptibly less for artificial languages than for natural ones. The problem of making sense of the idiom '*S* is analytic for *L*', with variable '*S*' and '*L*', retains its stubbornness even if we limit the range of the variable '*L*' to artificial languages. Let me now try to make this point evident.

For artificial languages and semantical rules we look naturally to the writings of Carnap. His semantical rules take various forms, and to make my point I shall have to distinguish certain of the forms. Let us suppose, to begin with, an artificial language L_0 whose semantical rules have the form explicitly of a specification, by recursion or otherwise, of all the analytic statements of L_0. The rules tell us that such and such statements, and only those, are the analytic statements of L_0. Now here the difficulty is simply that the rules contain the word 'analytic', which we do not understand! We understand what expressions the rules attribute analyticity to, but we do not understand what the rules attribute to those expressions. In short, before we can understand a rule which begins 'A statement *S* is analytic for language L_0 if and only if . . .', we must understand the general relative term 'analytic for'; we must understand '*S* is analytic for *L*' where '*S*' and '*L*' are variables.

Alternatively we may, indeed, view the so-called rule as a conventional definition of a new simple symbol 'analytic-for-L_0', which might better be written untendentiously as '*K*' so as not to seem to throw light on the interesting word 'analytic'. Obviously any number of classes *K, M, N,* etc. of statements of L_0 can be specified for various purposes or for no purpose; what does it mean to say that *K,* as against *M, N,* etc., is the class of the "analytic" statements of L_0?

By saying what statements are analytic for L_0 we explain 'analytic-for-L_0' but not 'analytic', not 'analytic for'. We do not begin to explain the idiom '*S* is analytic for *L*' with variable '*S*' and '*L*', even if we are content to limit the range of '*L*' to the realm of artificial languages.

Actually we do know enough about the intended significance of 'analytic' to know that analytic statements are supposed to be true. Let us then turn to a second form of semantical rule, which says not that such and such statements are analytic but simply that such and such statements are included among the truths. Such a rule is not subject to the criticism of containing the un-understood word 'analytic'; and we may grant for the sake of argument that there is no difficulty over the broader term 'true'. A semantical rule of this second type, a rule of truth, is not supposed to specify all the truths of the language; it merely stipulates, recursively or otherwise, a certain multitude of statements which, along with others unspecified, are to count as true. Such a rule may be conceded to be quite clear. Derivatively, afterward, analyticity can be demarcated thus: a statement is analytic if it is (not merely true but) true according to the semantical rule.

Still there is really no progress. Instead of appealing to an unexplained word 'analytic', we are now appealing to an unexplained phrase 'semantical rule'. Not every true statement which says that the statements of some class are true can count as a semantical rule—otherwise *all* truths would be "analytic" in the sense of being true according to semantical rules. Semantical rules are distinguishable, apparently, only by the fact of appearing on a page under the heading 'Semantical Rules'; and this heading is itself then meaningless.

We can say indeed that a statement is *analytic-for-*L_0 if and only if it is true according to such and such specifically appended "semantical rules," but then we find ourselves back at essentially the same case which was originally discussed: 'S is analytic-for-L_0 if and only if. . . .' Once we seek to explain 'S is analytic for L' generally for variable 'L' (even allowing limitation of 'L' to artificial languages), the explanation 'true according to the semantical rules of L' is unavailing; for the relative term 'semantical rule of' is as much in need of clarification, at least, as 'analytic for'.

It may be instructive to compare the notion of semantical rule with that of postulate. Relative to a given set of postulates, it is easy to say what a postulate is: it is a member of the set. Relative to a given set of semantical rules, it is equally easy to say what a semantical rule is. But given simply a notation, mathematical or otherwise, and indeed as thoroughly understood a notation as you please in point of the translations or truth conditions of its statements, who can say which of its true statements rank as postulates? Obviously the question is meaningless—as meaningless as asking which points in Ohio are starting points. Any finite (or effectively specifiable infinite) selection of statements (preferably true ones, perhaps) is as much *a* set of postulates as any other. The word 'postulate' is significant only relative to an act of inquiry; we apply the word to a set of statements just in so far as we happen, for the year or the moment, to be thinking of those statements in relation to the statements which can be reached from them by some set of transformations to which we have seen fit to direct our attention. Now the notion of semantical rule is as sensible and meaningful as that of postulate, if conceived in a similarly relative spirit—relative, this time, to one or another particular enterprise of schooling unconversant persons in sufficient conditions for truth of statements of some natural or artificial language L. But from this point of view no one signalization of a subclass of the truths of L is intrinsically more a semantical rule than another; and, if 'analytic' means 'true by semantical rules', no one truth of L is analytic to the exclusion of another.[15]

[15] The foregoing paragraph was not part of the present essay as originally published. It was prompted by R. M. Martin, "On Analytic," Philosophical Studies 3, as was the end of Essay VII.

It might conceivably be protested that an artificial language L (unlike a natural one) is a language in the ordinary sense *plus* a set of explicit semantical rules—the whole constituting, let us say, an ordered pair; and that the semantical rules of L then are specifiable simply as the second component of the pair L. But, by the same token and more simply, we might construe an artificial language L outright as an ordered pair whose second component is the class of its analytic statements; and then the analytic statements of L become specifiable simply as the statements in the second component of L. Or better still, we might just stop tugging at our bootstraps altogether.

Not all the explanations of analyticity known to Carnap and his readers have been covered explicitly in the above considerations, but the extension to other forms is not hard to see. Just one additional factor should be mentioned which sometimes enters: sometimes the semantical rules are in effect rules of translation into ordinary language, in which case the analytic statements of the artificial language are in effect recognized as such from the analyticity of their specified translations in ordinary language. Here certainly there can be no thought of an illumination of the problem of analyticity from the side of the artificial language.

From the point of view of the problem of analyticity the notion of an artificial language with semantical rules is a *feu follet par excellence.* Semantical rules determining the analytic statements of an artificial language are of interest only in so far as we already understand the notion of analyticity; they are of no help in gaining this understanding.

Appeal to hypothetical languages of an artificially simple kind could conceivably be useful in clarifying analyticity, if the mental or behavioral or cultural factors relevant to analyticity—whatever they may be —were somehow sketched into the simplified model. But a model which takes analyticity merely as an irreducible character is unlikely to throw light on the problem of explicating analyticity.

It is obvious that truth in general depends on both language and extralinguistic fact. The statement 'Brutus killed Caesar' would be false if the world had been different in certain ways, but it would also be false if the word 'killed' happened rather to have the sense of 'begat'. Thus one is tempted to suppose in general that the truth of a statement is somehow analyzable into a linguistic component and a factual component. Given this supposition, it next seems reasonable that in some statements the factual component should be null; and these are the analytic statements. But, for all its a priori reasonableness, a boundary between analytic and synthetic statements simply has not been drawn. That there is such a distinction to be drawn at all is an unempirical dogma of empiricists, a metaphysical article of faith.

5. *The verification theory and reductionism*

In the course of these somber reflections we have taken a dim view first of the notion of meaning, then of the notion of cognitive synonymy, and finally of the notion of analyticity. But what, it may be asked, of the verification theory of meaning? This phrase has established itself so firmly as a catchword of empiricism that we should be very unscientific indeed not to look beneath it for a possible key to the problem of meaning and the associated problems.

The verification theory of meaning, which has been conspicuous in the literature from Peirce onward, is that the meaning of a statement is the method of empirically confirming or infirming it. An analytic statement is that limiting case which is confirmed no matter what.

As urged in §1, we can as well pass over the question of meanings as entities and move straight to sameness of meaning, or synonymy. Then what the verification theory says is that statements are synonymous if and only if they are alike in point of method of empirical confirmation or infirmation.

This is an account of cognitive synonymy not of linguistic forms generally, but of statements.[16] However, from the concept of synonymy of statements we could derive the concept of synonymy for other linguistic forms, by considerations somewhat similar to those at the end of §3. Assuming the notion of "word," indeed, we could explain any two forms as synonymous when the putting of the one form for an occurrence of the other in any statement (apart from occurrences within "words") yields a synonymous statement. Finally, given the concept of synonymy thus for linguistic forms generally, we could define analyticity in terms of synonymy and logical truth as in §1. For that matter, we could define analyticity more simply in terms of just synonymy of statements together with logical truth; it is not necessary to appeal to synonymy of linguistic forms other than statements. For a statement may be described as analytic simply when it is synonymous with a logically true statement.

So, if the verification theory can be accepted as an adequate account of statement synonymy, the notion of analyticity is saved after all. However, let us reflect. Statement synonymy is said to be likeness of method of empirical confirmation or infirmation. Just what are these methods which are to be compared for likeness? What, in other words,

[16] The doctrine can indeed be formulated with terms rather than statements as the units. Thus Lewis describes the meaning of a term as *"a criterion in mind,* by reference to which one is able to apply or refuse to apply the expression in question in the case of presented, or imagined, things or situations" (*An Analysis of Knowledge and Valuation,* p. 133).—For an instructive account of the vicissitudes of the verification theory of meaning, centered however on the question of meaning*fulness* rather than synonymy and analyticity, see C. G. Hempel, "Problems and Changes in Empiricist Criterion of Meaning," Revue Internationale de philosophie.

is the nature of the relation between a statement and the experiences which contribute to or detract from its confirmation?

The most naïve view of the relation is that it is one of direct report. This is *radical reductionism.* Every meaningful statement is held to be translatable into a statement (true or false) about immediate experience. Radical reductionism, in one form or another, well antedates the verification theory of meaning explicitly so called. Thus Locke and Hume held that every idea must either originate directly in sense experience or else be compounded of ideas thus originating; and taking a hint from Tooke we might rephrase this doctrine in semantical jargon by saying that a term, to be significant at all, must be either a name of a sense datum or a compound of such names or an abbreviation of such a compound. So stated, the doctrine remains ambiguous as between sense data as sensory events and sense data as sensory qualities; and it remains vague as to the admissible ways of compounding. Moreover, the doctrine is unnecessarily and intolerably restrictive in the term-by-term critique which it imposes. More reasonably, and without yet exceeding the limits of what I have called radical reductionism, we may take full statements as our significant units—thus demanding that our statements as wholes be translatable into sense-datum language, but not that they be translatable term by term.

This emendation would unquestionably have been welcome to Locke and Hume and Tooke, but historically it had to await an important reorientation in semantics—the reorientation whereby the primary vehicle of meaning came to be seen no longer in the term but in the statement. This reorientation, explicit in Frege ([1], §60), underlies Russell's concept of incomplete symbols defined in use; [17] also it is implicit in the verification theory of meaning, since the objects of verification are statements.

Radical reductionism, conceived now with statements as units, set itself the task of specifying a sense-datum language and showing how to translate the rest of significant discourse, statement by statement, into it. Carnap embarked on this project in the *Aufbau.*

The language which Carnap adopted as his starting point was not a sense-datum language in the narrowest conceivable sense, for it included also the notations of logic, up through higher set theory. In effect it included the whole language of pure mathematics. The ontology implicit in it (that is, the range of values of its variables) embraced not only sensory events but classes, classes of classes, and so on. Empiricists there are who would boggle at such prodigality. Carnap's starting point is very parsimonious, however, in its extralogical or sensory part. In a series of constructions in which he exploits the resources of modern logic with much ingenuity, Carnap succeeds in defining a wide array

[17] See [*From a Logical Point of View*], p. 6.

of important additional sensory concepts which, but for his constructions, one would not have dreamed were definable on so slender a basis. He was the first empiricist who, not content with asserting the reducibility of science to terms of immediate experience, took serious steps toward carrying out the reduction.

If Carnap's starting point is satisfactory, still his constructions were, as he himself stressed, only a fragment of the full program. The construction of even the simplest statements about the physical world was left in a sketchy state. Carnap's suggestions on this subject were, despite their sketchiness, very suggestive. He explained spatio-temporal point-instants as quadruples of real numbers and envisaged assignment of sense qualities to point-instants according to certain canons. Roughly summarized, the plan was that qualities should be assigned to point-instants in such a way as to achieve the laziest world compatible with our experience. The principle of least action was to be our guide in constructing a world from experience.

Carnap did not seem to recognize, however, that his treatment of physical objects fell short of reduction not merely through sketchiness, but in principle. Statements of the form 'Quality *q* is at point-instant *x;y;z;t*' were, according to his canons, to be apportioned truth values in such a way as to maximize and minimize certain over-all features, and with growth of experience the truth values were to be progressively revised in the same spirit. I think this is a good schematization (deliberately oversimplified, to be sure) of what science really does; but it provides no indication, not even the sketchiest, of how a statement of the form 'Quality *q* is at *x;y;z;t*' could ever be translated into Carnap's initial language of sense data and logic. The connective 'is at' remains an added undefined connective; the canons counsel us in its use but not in its elimination.

Carnap seems to have appreciated this point afterward; for in his later writings he abandoned all notion of the translatability of statements about the physical world into statements about immediate experience. Reductionism in its radical form has long since ceased to figure in Carnap's philosophy.

But the dogma of reductionism has, in a subtler and more tenuous form, continued to influence the thought of empiricists. The notion lingers that to each statement, or each synthetic statement, there is associated a unique range of possible sensory events such that the occurrence of any of them would add to the likelihood of truth of the statement, and that there is associated also another unique range of possible sensory events whose occurrence would detract from that likelihood. This notion is of course implicit in the verification theory of meaning.

The dogma of reductionism survives in the supposition that each statement, taken in isolation from its fellows, can admit of confirmation or infirmation at all. My countersuggestion, issuing essentially from Carnap's doctrine of the physical world in the *Aufbau,* is that our statements about the external world face the tribunal of sense experience not individually but only as a corporate body.[18]

The dogma of reductionism, even in its attenuated form, is intimately connected with the other dogma—that there is a cleavage between the analytic and the synthetic. We have found ourselves led, indeed, from the latter problem to the former through the verification theory of meaning. More directly, the one dogma clearly supports the other in this way: as long as it is taken to be significant in general to speak of the confirmation and infirmation of a statement, it seems significant to speak also of a limiting kind of statement which is vacuously confirmed, *ipso facto,* come what may; and such a statement is analytic.

The two dogmas are, indeed, at root identical. We lately reflected that in general the truth of statements does obviously depend both upon language and upon extralinguistic fact; and we noted that this obvious circumstance carries in its train, not logically but all too naturally, a feeling that the truth of a statement is somehow analyzable into a linguistic component and a factual component. The factual component must, if we are empiricists, boil down to a range of confirmatory experiences. In the extreme case where the linguistic component is all that matters, a true statement is analytic. But I hope we are now impressed with how stubbornly the distinction between analytic and synthetic has resisted any straightforward drawing. I am impressed also, apart from prefabricated examples of black and white balls in an urn, with how baffling the problem has always been of arriving at any explicit theory of the empirical confirmation of a synthetic statement. My present suggestion is that it is nonsense, and the root of much nonsense, to speak of a linguistic component and a factual component in the truth of any individual statement. Taken collectively, science has its double dependence upon language and experience; but this duality is not significantly traceable into the statements of science taken one by one.

The idea of defining a symbol in use was, as remarked, an advance over the impossible term-by-term empiricism of Locke and Hume. The statement, rather than the term, came with Frege to be recognized as the unit accountable to an empiricist critique. But what I am now urging is that even in taking the statement as unit we have drawn our grid too finely. The unit of empirical significance is the whole of science.

6. *Empiricism without the dogmas*

The totality of our so-called knowledge or beliefs, from the most casual matters of geography and history to the profoundest laws of atomic

18 This doctrine was well argued by Pierre Duhem in *La Theorie physique, son objet et sa structure,* pp. 303-328. Or see Armand Lowinger, *The Methodology of Pierre Duhem,* pp. 132-140.

physics or even of pure mathematics and logic, is a man-made fabric which impinges on experience only along the edges. Or, to change the figure, total science is like a field of force whose boundary conditions are experience. A conflict with experience at the periphery occasions readjustments in the interior of the field. Truth values have to be redistributed over some of our statements. Reëvaluation of some statements entails reëvaluation of others, because of their logical interconnections —the logical laws being in turn simply certain further statements of the system, certain further elements of the field. Having reëvaluated one statement we must reëvaluate some others, which may be statements logically connected with the first or may be the statements of logical connections themselves. But the total field is so underdetermined by its boundary conditions, experience, that there is much latitude of choice as to what statements to reëvaluate in the light of any single contrary experience. No particular experiences are linked with any particular statements in the interior of the field, except indirectly through considerations of equilibrium affecting the field as a whole.

If this view is right, it is misleading to speak of the empirical content of an individual statement—especially if it is a statement at all remote from the experiential periphery of the field. Furthermore it becomes folly to seek a boundary between synthetic statements, which hold contingently on experience, and analytic statements, which hold come what may. Any statement can be held true come what may, if we make drastic enough adjustments elsewhere in the system. Even a statement very close to the periphery can be held true in the face of recalcitrant experience by pleading hallucination or by amending certain statements of the kind called logical laws. Conversely, by the same token, no statement is immune to revision. Revision even of the logical law of the excluded middle has been proposed as a means of simplifying quantum mechanics; and what difference is there in principle between such a shift and the shift whereby Kepler superseded Ptolemy, or Einstein Newton, or Darwin Aristotle?

For vividness I have been speaking in terms of varying distances from a sensory periphery. Let me try now to clarify this notion without metaphor. Certain statements, though *about* physical objects and not sense experience, seem peculiarly germane to sense experience—and in a selective way: some statements to some experiences, others to others. Such statements, especially germane to particular experiences, I picture as near the periphery. But in this relation of "germaneness" I envisage nothing more than a loose association reflecting the relative likelihood, in practice, of our choosing one statement rather than another for revision in the event of recalcitrant experience. For example, we can imagine recalcitrant experiences to which we would surely be inclined to accommodate our system by reëvaluating just the statement that there are brick houses on Elm Street, together with related statements on the same topic. We can imagine other recalcitrant experiences to which we would be inclined to accommodate our system by reëvaluating just the statement that there are no centaurs, along with kindred statements. A recalcitrant experience can, I have urged, be accommodated by any of various alternative reëvaluations in various alternative quarters of the total system; but, in the cases which we are now imagining, our natural tendency to disturb the total system as little as possible would lead us to focus our revisions upon these specific statements concerning brick houses or centuars. These statements are felt, therefore, to have a sharper empirical reference than highly theoretical statements of physics or logic or ontology. The latter statements may be thought of as relatively centrally located within the total network, meaning merely that little preferential connection with any particular sense data obtrudes itself.

As an empiricist I continue to think of the conceptual scheme of science as a tool, ultimately, for predicting future experience in the light of past experience. Physical objects are conceptually imported into the situation as convenient intermediaries—not by definition in terms of experience, but simply as irreducible posits[19] comparable, espistemologically, to the gods of Homer. For my part I do, qua lay physicist, believe in physical objects and not in Homer's gods; and I consider it a scientific error to believe otherwise. But in point of epistemological footing the physical objects and the gods differ only in degree and not in kind. Both sorts of entities enter our conception only as cultural posits. The myth of physical objects is epistemologically superior to most in that it has proved more efficacious than other myths as a device for working a manageable structure into the flux of experience.

Positing does not stop with macroscopic physical objects. Objects at the atomic level are posited to make the laws of macroscopic objects, and ultimately the laws of experience, simpler and more manageable; and we need not expect or demand full definition of atomic and subatomic entities in terms of macroscopic ones, any more than definition of macroscopic things in terms of sense data. Science is a continuation of common sense, and it continues the common-sense expedient of swelling ontology to simplify theory.

Physical objects, small and large, are not the only posits. Forces are another example; and indeed we are told nowadays that the boundary between energy and matter is obsolete. Moreover, the abstract entities which are the substance of mathematics—ultimately classes and classes of classes and so on up—are another posit in the same spirit. Epistemologically these are myths on the same footing with physical objects and gods, neither better nor worse except for differences in the degree to which they expedite our dealings with sense experiences.

The over-all algebra of rational and irrational numbers is underdetermined by the algebra of rational numbers, but is smoother and more

[19] Cf. [*From a Logical Point of View*], pp. 17f.

convenient; and it includes the algebra of rational numbers as a jagged or gerrymandered part.[20] Total science, mathematical and natural and human, is similarly but more extremely underdetermined by experience. The edge of the system must be kept squared with experience; the rest, with all its elaborate myths or fictions, has as its objective the simplicity of laws.

Ontological questions, under this view, are on a par with questions of natural science.[21] Consider the question whether to countenance classes as entities. This, as I have argued elsewhere,[22] is the question whether to quantify with respect to variables which take classes as values. Now Carnap [6] has maintained that this is a question not of matters of fact but of choosing a convenient language form, a convenient conceptual scheme or framework for science. With this I agree, but only on the proviso that the same be conceded regarding scientific hypotheses generally. Carnap ([6], p. 32n) has recognized that he is able to preserve a double standard for ontological questions and scientific hypotheses only by assuming an absolute distinction between the analytic and the synthetic; and I need not say again that this is a distinction which I reject.[23]

The issue over there being classes seems more a question of convenient conceptual scheme; the issue over there being centaurs, or brick houses on Elm Street, seems more a question of fact. But I have been urging that this difference is only one of degree, and that it turns upon our vaguely pragmatic inclination to adjust one strand of the fabric of science rather than another in accommodating some particular recalcitrant experience. Conservatism figures in such choices, and so does the quest for simplicity.

Carnap, Lewis, and others take a pragmatic stand on the question of choosing between language forms, scientific frameworks; but their pragmatism leaves off at the imagined boundary between the analytic and the synthetic. In repudiating such a boundary I espouse a more thorough pragmatism. Each man is given a scientic heritage plus a continuing barrage of sensory stimulation; and the considerations which guide him in warping his scientific heritage to fit his continuing sensory promptings are, where rational, pragmatic.

[20] Cf. [*From a Logical Point of View*], p. 18.

[21] "L'ontologie fait corps avec la science elle-même et ne peut en être separée." Emile Meyerson, *Identité et Realité,* p. 439.

[22] [*From a Logical Point of View*], pp. 12f, pp. 102ff.

[23] For an effective expression of further misgivings over this distinction, see White, "The Analytic and Synthetic: an Untenable Dualism" in Sidney Hook (ed.), *John Dewey: Philosopher of Science and Freedom.*

PART FOUR

Phenomenology and Existentialism

Introduction

1. *"To the things themselves!"*

With this section we cross the English channel to settle down on the European continent. And though this formidable body of water does not divide mankind into two different races, as some doughty Britishers seem to think, still a very marked shift in the philosophic climate and temper will meet us. If we whose language is English and whose modes of thought may in some matters be attuned too closely to our own language are to adjust to this change of climate, then we have to make a brave effort toward sympathy and flexibility of mind. Frenchmen and Germans do not philosophize like the British or the Americans; and in resigning ourselves to this fact that must seem melancholy to some Anglo-American philosophers, we might remember the wise and witty words of Winston Churchill spoken in the House of Commons during a debate in 1942 over some curious behavior of the French that seemed incomprehensible to some members of Parliament: "God, in His wisdom," said Mr. Churchill, "has not seen fit to create all men in the image of Englishmen." This warning from a great Englishman ought to be a word to the wise to some English philosophers whose insular ferocity prevents them from comprehending any philosophy that speaks a different language from their own. This book has been organized on thematic, not geographic, lines; yet it is remarkable how the two converge, and how distinctly and strongly the national character registers itself in philosophy. It would seem very much to be the case that man does not think alone, not even the philosopher; but that his thought, however solitary and rarefied it may appear in its more complex cerebrations, does take root in the soil of his culture and his group. This century has expended an extraordinary energy upon the question of language; and perhaps here at our very doorstep, in this variety of national styles in philosophizing, we have proof once again that man exists in language. It would seem as if the specific genius of a language sounded the key in which the philosopher was to speak.

Of course, this philosophic distance of England from the Continent is not something new with our century. From the beginning of the modern period in philosophy, from the seventeenth century onwards, England and the Continent—allowing for certain powerful and focal occasions of cross-fertilization—have gone their separate ways in philosophy, England as the traditional home of empiricism, the continent of rationalism. If we invoke the names of Descartes, Spinoza, and Leibniz, on the one hand, and, on the other, of Locke, Berkeley, and Hume, we have some measure of the persistence with which the philosophers of the Continent had stressed the certainty and power of Reason, while the English had insisted that Reason, whatever its scope or certainty, has to base every one of its ideas upon sensory experience. The remarkable thing in our period is that the cleavage between English and Continental philosophy, though quite as marked as in previous centuries, acquires a very different sense: now it is from the Continent that one hears the boldest questionings of reason, and the urgent pleading that reason, if it is to become once more the rule of our troubled time, must be refashioned upon some new and more radical bases.

Why this switch should have taken place, we cannot know with any great certainty; it is always difficult to attribute *the* basic causes for any cultural change. Yet it does not seem unreasonable to expect, since all things human have a tendency to pass into their opposite, that the Continent, which at the beginning of the modern period had produced the strongest affirmations of reason, should toward the culmination of this very same historical period produce the most radical doubts and questionings of reason. The English were not called to question reason since they had never been so passionately infatuated with it. The great political genius of the English has been based always upon their ability to muddle through, upon their sense that no human situation can be comprehended in a neat formula, and their tact in never setting a clear and distinct concept over concrete precedent. The Englishman, at least the average Englishman, is suspicious of the Continental, particularly the Frenchman, because the latter is too rational. Granted this base in the national character, with its stubborn conviction that life is not a matter of clear and distinct ideas, the British philosopher can afford to indulge himself in the trappings of logic, dialectically paring away at his fingernails, while the Continental philosopher seems to be speaking in some more literary, imaginative, or generally less logical mode. Moreover, the extraordinary stability of political institutions in England, as compared with the Continent, has provided both the social context and the accompanying frame of mind that do not require that the English philosopher question "things in their totality." In their darkest hour in World War II, when the whole outward structure of their world seemed ready to collapse under the German onslaught, the English responded with a brave and tinny little popular song, "There'll always be an England"—symbol of faith that the real and total context of their life, whatever might happen, could not be radically transformed. English philosophers do philosophy as if there would always be an England, while the Germans, by contrast, appear to philosophize as if Germany had not yet been, perhaps never would be, born.

The great initiator of the critique of reason on the Continent was, of course, Immanuel Kant. The Kantian critical philosophy, it is commonly said, brings together the two different streams of influence of Continental rationalism and British empiricism. This description is correct enough as a convenient and approximate label, but it is incorrect if taken to suggest that the Kantian philosophy is a building in which these two separate wings of rationalism and empiricism have been mechanically annexed to each other; nor does this description indicate the area of Kant's thought that was to bear such immense and varied fruit among the questioners of reason who were to follow him on the Continent. To be sure, his connection with the empirical line of philosophy is clear enough: in his insistence, which in fact was much more rigorous than Hume's, that no cognitively valid concept can ever go beyond the limits of possible experience, he can be taken as the father of positivism; he can also be taken as the father of pragmatism for insisting that a concept is but a synthesis of actual and possible sense-data—which Charles Peirce translated into the proposal that every idea is but a design of action. It is in a very different sense that he is the father of the philosophical tendencies that we shall encounter in this section. For Kant, unlike so many philosophers of the empirical turn of mind, in rejecting the cognitive claims of metaphysics and theology, did not propose to banish them from the human scene as wayward and "meaningless" forms of self-indulgence; on the contrary, the religious and moral dimensions of the human personality, which traditionally had invoked realities transcendent of sensory or scientific experience, were to be preserved and given their own specific rationale, which was to be distinct from that of scientific reason. The sources of validity in these spheres were to be the moral will and faith, which provided different data from those of scientific observation and reasoning. Here Kant planted the seeds of a very different kind of critique of reason from that propounded by simple empiricism or by positivism. Since there were faculties within the human personality that had their own compelling validity distinct from that of reason in its strictly scientific employment, why could not these faculties themselves take a critical look at reason? Here we pass from the critique of reason as reason's own interrogation of itself to a critique from a point of view outside reason. Simply as a matter of sober scientific responsibility, reason is called, as Kant put it, to be the keeper of its own house; but how if there is a house next door with very different rules and procedures that has an equal right to a voice within the human community? Accordingly, the way was thrown open to philosophers to take the leap beyond reason in order to see how reason might look from the outside—that is, from the point of view of some other power of vision granted to the human animal. This venture need not at all be a leap into unreason: the philosopher may grant to reason the right to be the keeper of the rules in its own house, and he may not in the least wish to undo those rules; but he may also wish to take a look from the house across the street. Thus neither Bergson, with his proposed leap into intuition, nor Heidegger, who proposes that traditional reason must be superseded by a more fundamental mode of thinking in which the thinker stands in closer proximity to Being, can properly be described as "irrationalists." What such philosophers are proposing is in effect a new interpretation of reason and its operations; and this project, however much it may differ from him, is in the line of the fundamental undertaking launched by the Kantian critique. Even Husserl, the arch-rationalist, cannot escape this challenge of the Kantian inheritance, for his very assertion that the task of our time is the "reconstitution of reason" implies that the traditional view of reason has to be reinterpreted, and indeed on the basis of new and radical method in philosophy that will reveal new data within experience.

The dominant figure in German philosophy in the first quarter of the century is Edmund Husserl (1859-1938) just as clearly as his pupil and one-time disciple Martin Heidegger (1889-   ) is dominant in the second quarter of the century. There are, of course, other significant figures active in Germany, particularly in the first twenty-five years of the century, but these two together, Husserl and Heidegger, indicate the main themes and directions of German philosophy. In France our simplification of matters is made easier since there the figure of Henri Bergson (1859-1941) almost exclusively dominates the scene in the opening years of the century. It is not until the 1930's and 1940's that the younger men, existentialists like Gabriel Marcel, Jean-Paul Sartre, Maurice Merleau-Ponty, emerge into prominence. And while there is some degree of artificiality in treating Germany and France here as a unit, nevertheless we shall see that in these figures the Continent still preserves its philosophical identity vis-à-vis America and England, for among those figures there are not only parallel and independent directions of thought but also strong cross-influences.

Husserl—to begin with the man who proposed to launch a new and bold program for the whole of twentieth-century philosophy—strikes us now in historical retrospect as a strangely paradoxical figure. A German Jew, he was a product of the most cultivated of European minorities—a minority that had assimilated itself to the ideals of German culture but was to suffer so cruelly at the hands of its adopted nation. And Husserl himself, who spoke always with the voice of the Good European profoundly concerned with the destiny of European civilization, was to experience persecution by the Nazis during the last years of his life. A less cruelly paradoxical fate, though paradoxical it is, was to attend his thought: he proposed a new philosophical discipline of phenomenology as a more accurate and modern version of Cartesianism, yet the characteristics of consciousness that this method unveiled were to take philosophy radically beyond Cartesianism; and indeed, the phenomenological method, in the hands of Husserl's follower Heidegger, was to take twentieth-century philosophy in one bold leap beyond any vestiges of Cartesianism. Finally, Husserl, trained as a mathematician, was by temperament a thorough-going rationalist, yet in his final phase he was to urge that man, as a problematic being, must even call in question his own existence as a "rational" being; and it is from this motive that Husserl urged a reconstitution, or redefinition, of human reason as the primary philosophical task of our epoch. Needless to say, these paradoxical qualities of Husserl—whether they be due to historical fate or to the development of his own thought—do not diminish his stature but enrich the complexity and significance of his thought as one of the major philosophers of the century.

The point of Husserl's phenomenology can best be seen in relation to the situation of German philosophy toward the end of the nineteenth century. Unlike the prevailing climates in America and England, the dominance of absolute idealism in the form of Hegelianism had diminished in Germany. Hegel had been like a tidal wave washing everything before him, but this wave, having been felt first at home in Germany, had washed out into the ocean to touch other shores. To be sure, there was not a field of philosophic thought in Germany that had not felt the impact of Hegel from top to bottom; but this influence had been digested, and philosophers turned to the more cautious critical idealism of Kant rather than the absolutism of Hegel. The prevailing atmosphere was that of Neo-Kantianism in a variety of shades and colors. But here again, as in England, the watchword for the development of twentieth-century philosophy is a revolt against idealism in the name of realism, and the philosopher who plays the role parallel to that of G. E. Moore is Franz Brentano (1838-1917), who was eventually to become a powerful influence upon Husserl himself.

While Moore had been pushed into his brand of realism through a rootedness in common sense and a power of dialectic, at once literal-minded and lucid, Brentano, on the other hand, was led to similar realistic convictions through the historical influences of Aristotle and Scholastic philosophy. A Catholic who had been thoroughly trained in

Aristotle and the medieval Aristotelians, Brentano found it altogether congenial to his own intellectual temperament to adopt the straightforward and simple realistic attitude of Pre-Kantian philosophy. For Aristotle, be it remembered, any other point of view contrary to realism does not even arise: the object of knowledge is what it is independently of the act of knowledge. Knowledge is always knowledge *of* an object, and this object is not altered by entering into the intellectual ken of the knower. Knowledge is a relation between the mind and the known object, but while the first term of this relation, the mind, is qualified by the relation, the second term, the known object, is not at all altered by this relation. The mind does not construct objects, as in Kant, but is a transparency that receives the forms that are materialized in things outside the mind. Aristotle here is the voice of a kind of luminous common sense that dominated the minds of men for centuries until with Descartes the subjectivistic complexities of modern thought broke through the "naïve" objectivity of medieval philosophy. Brentano sought to revive this classical and medieval point of view, insisting that while an idea may be "in the mind," the object that the idea *intends* may be quite independent of mind.

In launching this revolt against idealism, Brentano was quite a few years ahead of the parallel efforts of Moore and Russell in England; and it may be worthwhile to observe in passing that the influence of Brentano, through his pupil Alexius Meinong, was acknowledged by Russell himself in his attempt to develop his own brand of realism in the earlier years of this century.

Yet this realism of Brentano, so straightforward and classical in form, was not wholly acceptable to Husserl, whose thinking remained too strongly attached to Kantianism, particularly to the Kantian insistence that the startling point of philosophy must be the pure (or transcendental) subjectivity of consciousness. As Husserl saw it, the situation in philosophy at which the nineteenth century had finally arrived was just this impasse between realism and idealism. Both sides seemed to have compelling reasons on their side; the idealist in his insistence that we never get beyond mind, since every object known to exist is known through consciousness; the realist urging the conviction of common sense that we are creatures of a world that quite clearly exists independently of human consciousness. And so the tennis ball of dialectic can be bounced back and forth across the net, and the game goes on indefinitely and fruitlessly. Husserl felt that what was needed was a "third way" out of this impasse between realism and idealism. This "third way" was to be the discipline of phenomenology, which would be a rigorous and purely descriptive study of what was given us in experience without making any metaphysical postulate in the fashion of realism or idealism. Such metaphysical speculations, as Husserl put it, were to be "bracketed"—that is, simply set aside, though not declared meaningless, as by the positivists. Instead of metaphysical speculation, and the incessant and fruitless dialectic that ensues from such speculation, let the philosopher turn "to the things themselves" to see what it is that is really given in experience when we scrutinize it without any obscuring and empty preconceptions. Philosophy was to become descriptive rather than dialectical—a difference which, incidentally, separates German and British philosophy throughout this century.

Husserl's call "To the things themselves!" was to become a rallying cry for a whole generation of youthful philosophers in Germany. As Husserl conceived it, phenomenology was to become a very arduous and elaborate discipline requiring the collaboration of many minds. His *Ideas* (the full title of the book is *Ideas toward a Pure Phenomenology*) was published in 1913, and by this time Husserl had begun to gather his disciples and collaborators around him. The results of their research into pure experience were to be published in an extraordinary series of *Yearbooks for Phenomenology*. Among the contributors to this series were Moritz Geiger, Oskar Becker, A. Pfander, A. Reinoch; but the most famous of the group were Max Scheler, brilliant and volatile philosopher of many periods and convictions, and of course Heidegger, who was eventually to give phenomenology itself a new direction.

The call to joint effort and collaboration in philosophy is always a noble one, yet there is something plainly paradoxical about this group of dedicated phenomenologists. The point of departure for phenomenology, as Husserl conceived it, was the "bracketing" of the world: the common-sense belief in a world of objects existing independently and externally to consciousness as well as the belief in the existence of other minds independently and equally conscious as one's own private mind, were to be suspended; the phenomenologist was to concern himself with the pure data open and accessible to consciousness. The point of departure, in short, was the pure privacy of the Cartesian consciousness. And Husserl himself in a rather late work, *Cartesian Meditations* (1929), acknowledges Descartes as the prototype of his own, and indeed of all truly philosophical reflection. To be sure, the suspension of beliefs in an external world and in other minds had a different goal in Descartes than in Husserl: for Descartes the eventual aim of his philosophical reflection was to provide a basis of certainty for the "new science" of mathematical physics; for Husserl it was to reach some fuller and more adequate description of experience that would get beyond some of the empty abstractions which blocked the progress of philosophy. But there is another considerable difference between the two: Descartes performed his solitary journey into the wasteland of the Systemic Doubt alone and without disciples, while Husserl gathered together a body of collaborators. There is something plainly paradoxical in calling together a group of men and saying: "Gentlemen, we are going to suspend the belief in external objects and in one another's minds. This will free us for the description of the pure structures of experience as these manifest themselves within consciousness. We will all adopt the point of view of the pure privacy of mind and—the result of this joint effort will be most fruitful!"

The point of this paradox was not lost upon Heidegger. Quite clearly, the project of detaching oneself from the world is a definite project to accomplish certain goals within the world. This is as true of Descartes as it is of Husserl. Indeed, Descartes so surrounds his journey into the solitude of consciousness with the shrewd practical cautions of a seventeenth-century French Catholic that we cannot read his *Discourse on Method* without smiling at the worldliness of this mind that proposes to forsake the world. And so it must always be: the project to detach oneself from the world is significant—and Descartes' Systematic Doubt and Husserl's "bracketing" of the world, however paradoxical, are among the really significant ventures in the history of philosophy—only when it is a highly meaningful project within the world. Heidegger's conclusion from this is to posit as the essential trait of man that he is a Being-in-the-world, a creature enmeshed in the cares of time and history and essentially involved in the destinies of other people existing with him in a common world. The enterprises of Descartes and of Husserl are significant because they are launched at a very definite point in the history of science and philosophy, and therefore at a very definite epoch in the history of the human race, upon this planet. Thus, once we grasp the *context* within which the privacy of the Cartesian consciousness is postulated, we recognize that postulate for the purely practical fiction that it is.

But apart from this paradox involved in the call to collaborative effort, the positive developments within Husserl's phenomenology were to lead far beyond the traditional Cartesian simplifications on the nature of consciousness.

Husserl had borrowed from Brentano the idea that consciousness was essentially "intentional"—that is, that it is always consciousness *of* something, that it always *intends* or points toward some object. But he was to develop this doctrine of intentionality far beyond the point where Brentano left it. As a Catholic, Brentano still held to the traditional view of the soul as a substance. Though ideas clearly intended, or pointed to, things outside the mind, they inhered in the mind in the fashion in which attributes generally inhere in substances—as, for example, the brown color "exists in" this table. Here Brentano follows the tradition established by Aristotle: in his *Categories* Aristotle makes it quite clear that from the point of view of logic an idea "is present in the mind" in the same logical sense in which the color white is present in a body. Notice that this lumping together of ideas existing in the mind with attributes existing in substances is done by Aristotle in a treatise on logic, and particularly a treatise dealing with the logical use of words. Perhaps the greatest misunderstandings of consciousness have come from this tendency to understand it by the words and logic appropriate to things. Here, plainly, there is need for the phenomenological eye to get beyond words "to the things themselves," and to see consciousness for what it is rather than as it is distorted by the categories derived from words. Certainly, however an idea may exist in the mind, it hardly does so, except for the sheer accident of human grammar, in any way comparable to the way in which a quality exists in a material substance.

Once Husserl had taken over the idea of the intentionality of consciousness he did not restrict its application to the limited and ready-made states of consciousness that usually occupy philosophers. Consciousness is essentially consciousness *of;* and this must be taken to apply to absolutely every state of consciousnes, however fleeting, formless, or obscure. It is just as true of a dull inchoate pain, an indefinable and nameless joy, the twilight states of consciousness, as it is true of the more clear-cut states of consciousnes that possess a prepared label for their objects. Every, absolutely every, state of consciousness has its own intentional correlate, and is what it is only through that correlate. Of Husserl we might say, parodying the words of the Roman poet Terence, that nothing conscious was alien to him. His phenomenological eye discloses an immense realm of consciousness, as richly abundant in flora and fauna as a tropical region, in place of the tidy and compartmentalized objects of mind to which philosophers have too often restricted themselves.

The result of following through on this intentionality of consciousness is to change radically the way of regarding consciousness. Instead of its being some kind of substance, or thing, in which ideas exist, it becomes a vast *field* of intentional relations. On this point Husserl should be compared with William James in the latter's essay "Does Consciousness Exist?" published in 1904. James had answered the question of his title in the negative; but then had gone on to explain that he did not mean to deny that consciousness existed as essentially *relational*, he meant only to deny that it existed as something substantial, as a thing. Neither Husserl nor James directly influenced the other; their developments here are parallel but independent; and this striking similarity in the direction of thought seems evidence once again for the old Hegelian hypothesis of a *Zeitgeist,* a spirit of the time that leads men's minds in the same direction.

Turning "to the things themselves"—to the data of consciousness instead of to the words with which we chatter about these data—we find that some of the most common words become questionable. Where ordinary language for the ordinary user seems clear and simple, it suddenly becomes obscure and puzzling. The phrase "in the mind" is itself a prime example. We commonly say that ideas or thoughts are in the mind. We mean by this that they are subjective occurrences; they do not exist out there in the world with physical objects. The separation between subjective and objective, mental and physical, seems so neat and clear in these common modes of speech. Now, the range of the conscious includes moods and emotions. What would seem more subjective, more "in the mind" rather than in things outside, than a dim and fleeting mood? A dull malaise of mind, for example, for which I can find no clearly named object, certainly has to be called a subjective mood, something in my mind and not an object in the world. However, when the phenomenological eye is turned upon this mood, it does not find it as a special datum within consciousness; this mood is present everywhere, coloring the whole world as it is given to me, penetrating the squalor and formlessness of objects as they loom around me, present in their dirt and drabness, enclosing me in the enclosure of this room. Or let us take, to vary the key, a mood of quiet and nameless joy. Here again, we speak correctly in the mode of ordinary language when we say that this is a subjective occurrence that exists only in my mind. But if I try to penetrate this joy, to find its "intentional correlate," I find nothing like a datum that I can plainly label as mental. This joy is there shining through the world that momentarily surrounds me, attuning it, in the dull shine of rain in the street, the red houses grown slightly dusky in the twilight, the placid smoke settling from chimneys through the wet air. This apparently merely subjective mood is not given to me as in my mind but in the world; to be sure, not as a distinct object within that world, but as the tonality, or form, in which that world is now manifest. Consciousness is not so much "mental" as, to use Husserl's phrase, *"weltlich,"* worldly. That is to say, when we gaze directly at the contents of consciousness, far from finding ourselves in any specifically mental realm, we are more and more immersed in the world.

This emphasis upon the idea of "world" as an inexpugnable component of the given, became one of the main emphases of Husserl in his last phase; and it is this particular emphasis of his phenomenology that was to lead to the existentialism of Heidegger, and, following him in turn, of Sartre. In his *Being and Time,* published in 1927, Heidegger acknowledges his great debt to the unpublished writings of Husserl. Husserl had been elaborating in great detail the idea of the *"Lebenswelt"* (lived world) as the structuring context within which all experience took place. The Cartesian ego, solitary and worldless, is replaced by the human person whose real experience is always within the world. Husserl had indeed traveled a long way from his Cartesian starting point. In *Being and Time* Heidegger was to discard the Cartesian premise altogether, even as a mere starting device, and turn from the notion of consciousness itself to that of Being. Since one finds no strictly mental contents within consciousness (that is, contents that belong to a specific realm distinct from the world) but only the world and the objects within the world, why make even consciousness itself—much less a Cartesian consciousness—the starting point of philosophy? Accordingly, Heidegger pushed further a phenomenological analysis of moods like dread, fear, guilt, and boredom, not as merely mental figments, but as modes of man's Being-in-the-world.

Since so much of twentieth-century philosophy has been concerned with the attempt to escape the heritage of Descartes, it may be worthwhile to try to sum up the progress in the view of consciousness from Descartes through Husserl to Heidegger. Admittedly, a picture simplifies an idea, and it may sometimes be allowed to oversimplify it, usually when we attempt to carry the picture too far and too literally; but for the purposes of clarification it is also true in the old phrase, that one picture is worth a thousand words.

For Descartes imagine the mind as a sphere hermetically sealed to the world without. This sphere is imposed tangentially upon another sphere, the body, with which it has some unknowable relation. The first sphere is a mental substance, the second a material substance. The two seem to have causal relations with each other, but the manner in which they can possibly interact is not knowable to us. Ideas in the mind are attributes inhering in a mental substance. There is no intrinsic characteristic of these ideas that makes them essentially refer to a world beyond mind. On the contrary, the correspondence of these ideas with realities outside the mind is guaranteed, according to Descartes, only by the hypothesis of an omnipotent and benevolent God who has fashioned our mind to represent the realities outside of mind. In short, consciousness is essentially substantial, not referential.

With Husserl the walls of this sphere have become transparent and porous, penetrated everywhere by the arrows of intentionality. An idea is always an idea *of* something, and hence its very nature is to point beyond itself. Consciousness always and essentially transcends itself—that is, points beyond itself to the objects of consciousness. This transcendence of itself by consciousness is not given us by some fact external to consciousness, as, for example, by a God who would guarantee that our mind corresponds with things; no, it is given us in the very experience of consciousness, indeed as the central characteristic of consciousness itself. (This notion of transcendence was to be taken up and developed further in the varying existential philosophies of Heidegger, Jaspers, and Sartre.)

With Heidegger the walls of the sphere have disappeared altogether. We are not creatures enclosed in consciousness as in a sphere and gazing out through windows of this sphere on a world outside; on the contrary, as Heidegger puts it, man is already out-of-doors in the open air of the world. Husserl's doctrine of the essential self-transcendence of consciousness leads to Heidegger's interpretation of human existence in terms of the basic etymology of the word: to ek-sist means to stand out beyond oneself. As a creature open to the future and enmeshed in the world and its cares, man always and essentially stands beyond himself. (Phenomenology has here developed to the point where it can retrieve the hidden and primitive meanings of the words of Indo-European speech.) Instead of a sphere of consciousness, no matter how enriched by all the innumerable flora and fauna of intentional correlates, you have here, with Heidegger, a field or region of Being which, though it may be forgotten by man, inescapably encompasses man and within which his own human projects alone define what he is.

It may be that the future will judge that it is Heidegger, rather than Husserl, who really enters upon a new terrain for philosophy. But it was Husserl who opened the door for him; and the dedication of *Being and Time* to Edmund Husserl, more than an expression of reverence and affection on the part of pupil toward master, is also a frank confession of Heidegger's intellectual debt to his teacher.

Husserl, as we have seen, attempted to launch a new and special kind of philosophical discipline. Yet, distinct as it is, Husserl's philosophy does seem to fit in with the general pattern of philosophical development within this century. This development, as we encounter it again and again within this book, is a turning away from idealism. To be sure, the paths which philosophers travel away from the once secure and shining citadel of idealism are very different from each other: in America it is pragmatism, in England analytic philosophy, in Germany (and eventually in France too) phenomenology and existentialism. Is there any positive tendency that unifies all these philosophic schools beside the merely negative fact that they are all departing from idealism? One has a certain caution at imposing an arbitrary pattern from above, but it does seem that, underneath the surface of all this variety, there is a common impulse working and that this common tendency is a rather revealing sign of the mind of the twentieth century, so far as this mind has succeeded in working out its own identity. Since the flight from absolute idealism is an abandonment of the dazzling and sweeping claims of speculative metaphysics, the new philosophies must take upon themselves a vow of modesty. Philosophy is to become more piecemeal, exploratory, tentative, even fragmentary; it will be less sweeping in its claims but will claim to be more concrete—though, to be sure, in the varying modes in which each of these schools understands concreteness. William James described—the description is repeated approvingly by Whitehead for his own philosophy—the goal of his own pragmatism as a movement of thought "towards concreteness and adequacy." This search for concreteness and adequacy is manifest everywhere in contemporary philosophy. John Dewey's tentative, groping, and often awkward search for a reconstruction of philosophy is an effort to bring philosophic concepts, hitherto remote and aristocratic, more closely in line with the humble and practical actualities of life in a democratic society. And though different in temper and tone, and even more different in its method of attack upon problems, recent British philosophy has sought to plant its feet more firmly in the usages of ordinary language that are tied in with the situations of daily life. And as for phenomenology itself, we have already seen that Husserl's cry "To the things themselves!" was a summons towards a more concrete and adequate description of experience that, to his mind, had become covered over by the preconceptions and standardized abstractions mechanically taken over from the philosophic tradition. Philosophy in this century had been very much of a search for new beginnings; no wonder that it has sometimes had the bewildered look of a man digging himself out of the ruins of the past.

There is one very glaring, but deliberate, omission from the above list, and that is the name of Henri Bergson, who belongs, if any philosopher does, among the searchers for the concrete in this century. The omission was intended to call special attention to Bergson. This special attention is required not only to establish a distinct link in our argument in this section; it is required also out of our desire to do simple justice to Bergson's fallen reputation; and such justice must be done if we are to keep a proper perspective upon the developments in contemporary philosophy. The fact is that Bergson's fame, at least outside of France, has probably sunk to its lowest point, especially among the professional philosophers in this country. Part of the reason for this may be the compensatory swing of the pendulum from the great fame which Bergson once enjoyed because he wrote well and was read by a wide audience. Part of the reason may be disparaging essays by Russell and Santayana, which to some minds may have seemed to despatch Bergson once and for all. On the other side of the ledger, we ought to remember the glowing admiration expressed by James and Whitehead, and the considerable debt owed to Bergson's evolutionary views by John Dewey. James's admiration almost passed to the point of adulation, for in Bergson he seemed to read a more incisive statement of his own views that life as lived is more rich and abundant than its pale replica in the static concepts of classical rationalism. Whitehead derived from Bergson his emphasis upon the reality of time and process as the radical creation of novelty. Dewey owed to Bergson the doctrine of the essentially practical nature of the intellect as an instrument in the evolutionary struggle. Perhaps these thinkers might have traveled the paths they did without Bergson, but the powerful example of Bergson was there before them to add impetus to their own exertions. In view of this considerable influence, Bergson is hardly a philosopher to be brushed aside with a deprecatory shrug. Perhaps the time has come for a reëvaluation that will avoid the excess of acclaim at the high peak of his fame or the present low-water mark of disparagement. In any case, it is certainly time that he was reread.

A new reading of Bergson may be possible to us now after the advent of existentialism. Bergson is quite properly placed in this section of our volume for two very good, and connected reasons: he did in fact make use of the phenomenological method before Husserl although he did not coin the name; and his insistence on the reality of time opened the way to existentialism. These two achievements—quite apart from his influence upon the three great American philosophers (Whitehead was an American citizen before he died)—are in themselves sufficient to establish Bergson as a very important link in the development of twentieth-century philosophy.

Husserl, we recall, had launched his phenomenological program as a "third way" between the Scylla and Charybdis of idealism and realism. As early as 1897 Bergson expressed the same need of a fresh and more concrete attack upon philosophical problems: in the opening pages of *Matter and Memory,* published that year, he insisted that in the study of the data of consciousness it was necessary to get to a point of view beyond both idealism and realism that would be more concrete than either. If one places oneself within experience as it is directly given to us on a prephilosophical level, idealism and realism undoubtedly express aspects of this experience, but both are abstractions that do not succeed in embracing ordinary experience for what it is. Experience is both realistic (of objects) and idealistic (of a subjective consciousness); and it is neither, for it is also the immediate unity that embraces and transcends these opposite poles. Bergson's criticism of other philosophies always turns on the point that they are one-sided abstractions that fail to do justice to the concreteness of experience as it actually unfolds within the stream of life.

This was the typically Bergsonian method that sprang full-born into the world with his first book, *Time and Free Will* (1889). The French title of this work—*Essai sur les données immédiates de la conscience,* "essay on the immediate data of consciousness"—indicates quite clearly that Bergson aims to get close to the given in experience; and in this effort, of course, he anticipates Husserl by a good number of years. Nearly all of the Bergsonian themes appear in this first work. The conceptual intelligence, according to Bergson, tends to distort reality by setting its own static concepts in place of the concrete flux of experience. The intellect has an inherent tendency to externalize, and therefore to spatialize all phenomena since spatial entities are the most readily apprehended as clear and distinct ideas. Time and duration are two such misunderstood realities. Bergson gives special point to this contention by an analysis of the traditional philosophic problem of free will. Both the philosophers who argue for, as well as those who argue against free will, have not caught the free act in its concreteness. If we consider an individual case of a free act as it actually unfolds—say, the expressive activity of an artist in its creative flow—then this act is at once bound and free; bound, because the work of art that issues from these creative moments has about it the accent of inevitability; free, because the artist has liberated himself at such moments from external and internal impediments to his liberty of expression. Thus the doctrines of determinism, as well as of free will, are one-sided abstractions that convey only one aspect of the creative process. We are both free and determined, and neither free nor determined—at least in the manner in which traditional philosophy has rigged these artificial abstractions. For Bergson we might say, echoing the famous phrase of Kierkegaard, that the logical intellect is an either-or affair; but the realities of process and change are both-and, and, perhaps even more accurately, neither-nor: that is, they escape the artificial opposites erected by the intelligence.

This direction of Bergson's thought that runs parallel to Husserl's suggests at once that it is useful to distinguish in Bergson the descriptive from the speculative thinker, the phenomenologist from the metaphysician. And this distinction in turn may enable us to do more justice to Bergson's celebrated doctrine of intuition. Probably this emphasis upon intuition has been the one doctrine that has done most damage to Bergson's reputation in the eyes of Anglo-American philosophers. The word "intuition" has so many malign connotations in ordinary life, associated as it is with the preternatural and the arcane, with fortune-tellers and seers, that we can hardly be surprised that philosophers have shrunk from it with fear and trembling. The philosopher earns his daily bread from the conceptual intellect, and he is naturally suspicious of anything that would question or limit the adequacy of this organ. Of course, he can train this specialized organ to the point where his intuition dwindles and almost disappears, so that he comes at last to believe that no such thing exists. But if we think of Bergson now from the phenomenological side—as a philosopher seeking to isolate and describe the various modes of experience—then we need not reject a priori the idea of intuition. As it operates in the affairs of daily life, or in the varieties of aesthetic experience, intuition is a perfectly natural, normal, and indeed indispensable function. There is nothing occult or preternatural about it any more than in the operation of any other modes of consciousness. To be sure, it is very different from the conceptual intellect, and there are very different laws by which it operates. If you doubt this, try sometime to explain a work of art to a friend trained more in logic than aesthetics, and consider if in the struggle of this heavily freighted mind to get around the aesthetic datum, the conceptual intellect does not somewhat resemble a hippopotamus struggling to pick up a pea. The varieties of experience are what they are, and to record them is merely to be faithful to fact, not to engage in any piece of speculative metaphysics.

Bergson, of course, did go further. He was not content merely to isolate intuition as it operates naturally amid the particular contingencies of daily life, and as it functions as the indispensable organ in the creation and enjoyment of works of art; he went on to take the metaphysical leap and make a number of speculations about the source and ultimate scope of intuition. Instead of being one among many instruments of consciousness, intuition became for Bergson the central one by means of which we can hear the secret beating of the heart of things. In his *Creative Evolution* (1907), more distinctly a product of Bergson the speculative metaphysician, he advances the hypothesis that intuition is an evolutionary outgrowth of instinct and, like the latter, remains closer to reality than the abstract intellect. How fruitful his speculative hypotheses may prove, time alone will tell. In the meantime, however, Bergson's rank as a philosopher need not be taken to ride exclusively on the success or failure of such hypotheses. Speculative metaphysics is now out of favor in all but a very few quarters; pending its revival or its ultimate obsolescence, we can still urge the importance of Bergson the phenomenologist, the intellectual intuitive whom William James celebrated for his marvelous sensitivity to the concreteness of experience.

The central point in the Bergsonian philosophy is the doctrine of the absolute reality of time. In this he belongs with the pragmatists and existentialists in their common revolt against absolute idealism, which held that time is only an appearance and not an ultimate reality. But Bergson, who was extremely well grounded in the history of philosophy, perceived that this insistence upon the reality of time was a revolt not only against absolute idealism but against the whole Platonizing tendency that lurked in the very core of Western philosophy. Philosophers in the tradition of classical rationalism, with a few great exceptions, have tended to accord to time a secondary and derivative status in relation to the timeless and eternal. In Plato's words, time is the moving image of eternity—that is to say, time is an imperfect copy of eternity and derives its being therefrom. On the face of it, it is an altogether extraordinary fact about the history of philosophy that philosophers have tended so often and so strongly to relegate time to the realm of unreality; and for ordinary men who feel the pinch and push of time so urgently in their lives, this fact might suggest that philosophy itself had lost some contact with life. For Bergson it led to the suspicion that the conceptual intellect has an essential tendency to spatialize and detemporalize events. As a young student of philosophy, he had become convinced of the reality of time, and the problem consequently presented itself: What could have led philosophers so persistently astray that they should have relegated time to the limbo of the unreal? Bergson's answer was that the intellect itself in so far as it seeks essences that remain identical with themselves (in Plato's language the essence is *to auto kath'auto,* that which remains the same in relation to itself—in short, that which never changes) becomes hypnotized by these essences and takes them as the real and unchanging reality.

The history of Western philosophy, therefore, is for Bergson essentially a development of Platonism. His brilliant sketch of this history, taken from the final section of *Creative Evolution,* should be compared with Heidegger's essay on *Plato's Doctrine of Truth.* Both see an essentially Platonizing tendency dominant in Western philosophy, though they characterize the source of this tendency differently. (The same point, incidentally, is also made by Whitehead, though in a mood much more favorable to Plato, when he remarks that twenty-five hundred years of Western philosophy are but a series of footnotes to Plato.) Bergson sees this Platonism as the substitution by the intellect of its own static concepts for the ceaselessly changing flow of reality. For Heidegger the fundamental step that launches Western philosophy on its long journey into our present "night of the world" is a shift in the meaning of truth within Plato's thought: truth becomes located in the intellect as the correctness of its concepts in measuring the real, while the more primordial meaning of truth as the unhiddenness of Being becomes lost. Yet, according to Heidegger, this latter meaning of truth is presupposed in the view of truth as the correspondence between mind and things; for we could never compare our mental judgment with the thing which it purports to judge unless both mind and thing were manifest together within a common context, the open field of Being which embraces both subject and object. Whatever their difference here, Bergson and Heidegger are both agreed that it is the dominance of the conceptual intellect—or at least a certain version of this intellect—that explains the main lines taken by Western philosophy.

Bergson's doctrine of the reality of time became thus an insistence that philosophers must recognize the difference between reality as it is lived and reality as it is conceptualized by the intellect. Now this insistence is one of the cardinal points in existentialism, and here Bergson may be considered not only to anticipate the existentialists but already to be walking upon their terrain.

2. *"What is existentialism?"*

No school of philosophy in recent decades has attracted quite so much popular attention as existentialism. The reasons for this popular curiosity have not always been of the most valid kind, philosophically speaking; yet in a time when philosophy in its pursuit of trivial and technical matters had seemed to be relegated to the academic cloister, and a narrow place within that cloister to boot, any outburst of popular curiosity and interest in a philosophical school might very well be accounted a desirable thing. A great deal of this popular interest arose because the first news about existentialism came to us in this country from the French, who have a distinct talent for the colorful launching of programs, whether in art or thought. French existentialism became a kind of Bohemian ferment in Paris in the years immediately following the Second World War, and it was even associated with certain bistros, and in its younger devotees with certain styles of hairdo and dress. Moreover, it was a literary as well as a philosophical movement, and its leaders—Jean-Paul Sartre and Albert Camus—were brilliant and engaging writers. All this made news; and the result was that thousands of Americans who had perhaps never bothered about philosophy before were walking about with the question on their lips, "What *is* existentialism?"

The effect of all this agitation and excitement upon the academic philosophers was quite the opposite. Die-hard academicians saw in this excitement one more indication that existentialism was not really a philosophy, and that the existentialists themselves were sensation-mongers who dealt with such unappetizing subjects as the lonely self, anxiety, and death.

Yet in the course of the last decade the situation has changed on both accounts. As a popular cult, existentialism no longer generates any news or excitement, while as a subject for serious study it has already entered the academy, where couurses are taught in it and students research it for Ph.D.'s.

There are many reasons for this change in attitude. For one thing, we have just learned here that in Europe for more than the past twenty years a well-developed movement in existential psychoanalysis has been going on; and, further, that this movement, far from being the creation of Bohemian intellectuals, is headed by practicing psychiatrists, directors of hospitals, sanatoria and mental clinics. When healers of the mind have to go to a new philosophy for help in understanding human psychology, we, too, begin to feel that we may have more to learn from this philosophy than we might have supposed.

Another reason for this new and more serious interest is the continuing and mounting influence of modern art and literature. As we reflect more and more upon the strange and powerful art of the first fifty years of this century—upon the disturbing world of a Kafka or Joyce or the early Faulkner, or upon the baffling image, or lack of image, of man in modern painting and sculpture; as we search for ourselves and our time in all this art, we begin to find our life today riddled with more questions than we had suspected. And we also see that existentialism is the one philosophy of this period that has raised the themes that have obsessed modern art to the level of explicit intellectual questioning.

The immense vogue of such popular works of social analysis as Riesman's *The Lonely Crowd* and W. H. Whyte's *The Organization Man* has led people to reflect uneasily about what is taking place in modern society. These books have one central theme: that modern mass society, while it raises the material level of all, tends to swallow up the individual in its intricate machinery. Modern society becomes a kind of bureaucratically organized flight from the Self; a flight into which everybody can easily drift. These criticisms, however, do not originate with our own social analysts; more than a century ago Kierkegaard inveighed against the depersonalizing forces of modern society far more powerfully than do Riesman and Whyte. The same line of criticism has been developed with great subtlety by Ortega y Gasset, Jaspers, Marcel and Buber. Present-day sociologists have provided some admirable documentation of the way in which these depersonalizing forces work, but they have hardly attacked the philosophical root of the matter. For this we have to go to the existentialists themselves.

Finally, a simpler and more direct reason for this keener interest in existentialism is the increasing number of translations of the existentialist writings. As we get more English versions of the books of Martin Buber, Gabriel Marcel, Martin Heidegger, Karl Jaspers, José Ortega y Gasset, the name of Jean-Paul Sartre no longer pre-empts the field; and we see that existentialism is a basic movement among European thinkers, one that is neither peripheral nor faddist but central to our time. It becomes apparent that the body of the existentialist writings constitutes a commentary upon the human situation as rich and profound as any produced in our century, and that it would be folly for Americans to ignore it.

What, then, is existentialism?

The question is relatively easy to answer; for the irony here is that, despite its portentous label, this philosophy derives from concrete and everyday human experience rather than from any abstract or specialized areas of knowledge. Existentialism is a philosophy that confronts the human situation *in its totality* to ask what the basic conditions of human existence are and how man can establish his own meaning out of these conditions. Its method is to begin with this human existence as a fact without any ready-made preconceptions about the *essence* of man. There is no prefabricated human nature that freezes human possibilities into a preordained mold; on the contrary, man exists first and makes himself what he is out of the conditions into which he is thrown. "Existence precedes essence," as the formula puts it.

Here philosophy itself—no longer a mere game for technicians or an obsolete discipline superseded by science—becomes a fundamental dimension of human existence. For man is the one animal who not only can, but must ask himself what his life means. We are all philosophers in this sense whenever we reach a point in life where total reflection upon ourselves is called for. Most of the time we try to avoid such occasions for total reflection by temporary expedients: we plug leaks in the ship without bothering to ask where it is heading. But if the problem is fundamental, expedients do not serve and we are faced with such questions as: What am I ultimately interested in? What is the point of it all? What meaning does my life have?

With these questions we become actively engaged with the problems of philosophy. The existential philosopher spends a lifetime asking these questions that assail the ordinary man only in unusual or extreme moments. One of the achievements of existential philosophers is that they have restored to the philosophical profession the true meaning of the latter word: a full-time vocation to which a man feels summoned or called. If the old saying that "Philosophy bakes no bread" has its point, it is also true that in the end we do not bake bread or in fact do anything else without a philosophy.

So much by way of a schematic answer to the question what existentialism is. But existentialism itself is opposed to schematic and abstract answers about human facts, which are always concrete, individual, situated in a definite place and time. Man is a historical being—that is his uniqueness among all other animals—and he can never be understood apart from his history. This is true of existential philosophy itself as a historical human fact. To understand it concretely we have to see where its roots lie in the history of modern thought and what urgencies of the modern spirit drive it onward.

The existential philosophers themselves have taught us to reread in a new and more profound way the whole history of modern thought. By showing us philosophy as an essentially human enterprise they have enabled us to see the whole history of philosophy for the momentous human drama it really is. Most of us tend to think of the history of philosophy as a succession of contradicting opinions held by rival philosophers or rival schools decade after decade or century after century. The dramatic parts of human history seem to be wars and battles, or great political decisions that change the external patterns of our lives. But for the existentialist the history of philosophy is one of the most dramatic and fateful chapters in human history; the great philosophers, far from being mere airy speculators, are in fact the real prophets. Their thinking illuminates the problems that mankind as a whole, in its external and social history, will have to live out for generations.

Our modern epoch in philosophy—and with it our whole modern world—begins with the great French philosopher René Descartes. Descartes, who was also a mathematician and a physicist, wanted his philosophy to establish a basis for the then "new science" of mathematical physics. For this, the first step needed was to establish the solid objectivity of the world of physical things, and particularly those aspects of things that are quantitative and measurable and so can be expressed in mathematical laws. Hence Descartes declared that matter was essentially extension: that is, the real properties of any physical object are the quantitative ones. What about the qualities of things? They are declared to be merely subjective effects in the human mind. Here the world of the new science is no longer the ordinary human world in which we live. This qualitative world of our everyday life, with all the color, warmth and vibrancy of its texture, is thrust out of the real world and relegated to the human mind as a kind of shadowy specter. Such is the famous Cartesian dualism: the world of matter (objects) is split off from the human mind (subject). More significantly, it splits the human and the scientific worlds.

Today, we are still experiencing the consequences of this dualism. Descartes is a founder and a prophet of the historical era in which mathematical physics comes more and more to dominate the whole of human life. Today, when we tremble before the possibilities of atomic bombs and missiles, when the mathematical physicists and technicians are more important instruments of power than any military general, we need hardly be told that this Cartesian era of mathematical physics approaches its violent climax. But also, with all the human turmoil of our period, with its political unrest and individual rootlessness, we are aware of the skeleton that lurks in the Cartesian closet: our power to deal with the world of matter has multiplied out of all proportion to our wisdom in coping with the problems of our human and spiritual world.

Descartes could bear the consequences of his philosophy because in the rest of his person he was still a Catholic of the Middle Ages. Descartes the thinker was one thing; Descartes the man something else; although in Descartes' philosophy there was no place for the two to meet, in his life—for very practical human purposes—he had established a concordat between them by remaining a faithful son of the church. When he discovered analytic geometry, he promptly made a pilgrimage of gratitude to the shrine of the Virgin of Loretto. So too in his philosophy: however much the prophet of the new science, he still retained the medieval conviction that human reason has its own luminous and direct access to the transcendent reality of God. So long as Descartes could prove to his own satisfaction that God exists, this omnipotent and benevolent God could heal the breach between man's physical and spiritual being.

But this comforting assurance of the Middle Ages receded more and more as "the new science" of Descartes and Newton made astounding progress through the next century. The trouble—and it is a trouble at the heart of our whole modern epoch—comes to the surface again with Immanuel Kant. Writing at the end of the great century of rationalism in 1781 in his *Critique of Pure Reason,* Kant showed that the transcendent ideals of our traditionally Christian civilization—God, the human soul and its possible immortality, the freedom of man as a spiritual person—could not be known by human reason. Like everything human, reason has its history; and here, in the course of its evolution, it had at last become strictly scientific reason. Insofar as reason sought to be scientific and exact it had to exclude all references to the ultimate things that man had lived by in his ethical and spiritual life.

Had Kant been merely what is now called a "scientific philosopher," like the modern positivists, he would at this point simply have thrown out God and the human soul as "meaningless" and gone off in search of new values. Since he retained the vestiges of a pious Protestant upbringing, however, he chose to live by the values of traditional Christianity. Hence he went on to write a *Critique of Practical Reason* in which he argued that, though science could never deal with these ultimate things, man in the seriousness of his ethical striving is called upon to live as if he had an immortal soul, and as if there were a God who providentially guided the destinies of the world. Kant held that in our inner conscience we touch a reality more absolute than anything in science.

The human, or existential, import of Kant's whole philosophy comes then to this: what Kant, the man, lived by as an ethical and spiritual person, Kant, the scientific thinker, could not even bring into thought. The split between the scientific and the human world with which Descartes launched our modern epoch has here become more sharply drawn. Kant, like Descartes before him, had that naïveté which sometimes accompanies great genius, and hardly anticipated the explosive effects of his philosophy. When his first *Critique* dropped like a bombshell on intellectual Germany, Kant himself was most astonished that his contemporaries were shocked.

The idealist philosophers after Kant felt that he had dug a chasm between two parts of the human personality, and by one means or another they sought to restore the spiritual wholeness or integrity of man. One of the greatest of these was Hegel, whose means of restoring the wholeness of man was an imperialism of reason so audacious that it eventually brought existentialism into being as a necessary corrective. If there are ethical and spiritual realities that concern us ultimately as human beings, Hegel argued, then these must be accessible to reason. Reason takes in all areas of human experience; nothing can be denied to it. In making reason all-inclusive, however, Hegel also made it omnivorous: wishing to give it wings to soar, he also gave it the devouring beak of a vulture. Everything vital and individual is swallowed up in the maw of the Hegelian system. In Hegel's thought, religion—even a religion like Christianity in which the central faith revolves around the unique and unreasonable moment in history when God became man in order to save the human race—becomes merely a crude approximation, by parable and myth, of the absolute truth that reason can spin out of its own ideas.

Enter now existentialism. The moment was perfectly timed in this great human drama of western thought—for the situation was ripe for revolt. The revolt came in the persons of Sören Kierkegaard and Friedrich Nietzsche, who are now accepted as the founding fathers of existential philosophy. Neither was an academic philosopher, though Nietzsche had earlier been a professor of classical philology; and perhaps just because they were outsiders to academic philosophy, they had sharper eyes for the real human root of the trouble. Sometimes an outsider coming into a family can see more clearly the source of its dissensions than can those blinded by their intramural quarrels.

Kierkegaard put an end to the totalitarian claims for reason made by philosophers like Hegel. If religion could be reduced to reason, said Kierkegaard, there would be no need for religion—least of all a religion like Christianity whose central belief in the God-Man is altogether paradoxical to reason. As a believing Christian, Kierkegaard insisted on the necessity of faith as a vital act beyond reason. But beyond this message as a Christian apologist, Kierkegaard brought to the attention of philosophers—and more recently to psychologists—the fact that human existence can never be totally enclosed in any system. To exist as an individual is to strive, change, develop, stand open to the future, be incomplete—while a system by its very nature is closed, complete, static, dead. The philosopher or scientist who thinks he can freeze our human existence into a system does so by substituting a pallid and abstract concept for the living and concrete reality. Life is lived forward and understood backward, says Kierkegaard. If we were ever to understand it completely, we would have to be already dead, without a future and with no untried and novel possibilities before us.

In one sense Kierkegaard returns us to the situation of Kant before Hegel: he gives a more urgent and powerful expression to the Kantian view that each of us, as individuals, touches reality inwardly in our moments of serious moral decision rather than in the detached speculations of reason. In another sense, however, Kierkegaard destroys the makeshift supports of Kantian ethics by calling attention to the fact that the values Kant espouses—and espouses in spite of scientific reason—live or die with the Christian faith. These values are not rooted in the eternal nature of the human conscience, but historically and existentially derive from the Christian religion; and the central crisis of the modern period is that this religion now stands on trial. Kant's values cannot be kept alive by mere rational reflection on the so-called "postulates of practical reason"; in the end they can be kept alive only by the energy of faith.

Nietzsche starts from this same historical insight, but attacks Kant from just the opposite direction. If, says Nietzsche, the development of human reason along the line of science has brought us to the point in human history where scientific reason rules out those transcendent ideals—God, the immortal soul, our essential freedom as moral agents—that Christians have lived by for centuries, then why persist in Kant's blind old prejudice for these concepts? Why not throw them on the dust heap of history? Besides, is not Christianity already dead or at least dying in our time when, though some people may give it lip service, it no longer rules the total life of man as it did in the earlier ages of faith?

Had Nietzsche stopped here, he would have been merely one among many nineteenth-century atheists; more brilliant and incisive in his language than the others, but hardly a founder of existential philosophy. Nietzsche was, however, a man of great imagination and perhaps even greater religious yearning. He could see that the abolishing of the transcendent world in which the human spirit had hitherto sought its home would not solve all problems, as some of the rationalists of his century thought, but would only bring into desperate relief the pathos of our human situation. For when God is at last dead for man, when the last gleam of light is extinguished and only the impenetrable darkness of a universe that exists for no purpose surrounds us, then at last man knows he is alone in a world where he has to create his own values. The disappearance of religion would be the greatest challenge in human history—perhaps the ultimate challenge—for man would then be fully and dreadfully responsible to himself and for himself. Moreover, the natural sciences that helped bring about this situation could not help here, for they can never explain to man what he really is. Man steps beyond the world of natural objects in the very act of asking what this world means, what he himself means, and in seeking to create this meaning for himself. The natural sciences are tools that man can use in the service of his own values, but these sciences will never create a guiding ideal for human life.

This slow, unfolding development of modern philosophy is like a great symphony which Descartes opens with the leading theme, andante; other philosophers enrich with variations and counterthemes, allegro; and Kierkegaard and Nietzsche bring to a furious and boiling presto. It might be tempting to hope that the existential philosophers of the twentieth century have at last brought us the grand finale; but unlike a symphony, the process of human thought admits no finale so long as man continues to be man, a being perpetually open to the future. The existentialists of this century are the heirs of Kierkegaard and Nietzsche, and their task has been, first, to save the great revolt of these two giants from being buried under the apathy of academic philosophers; and secondly and more importantly, to enrich and carry on the line of thought initiated in that revolt.

The very richness and diversity of existential thought in this century makes it difficult to fashion any easy summary of its conclusions. How sum up the philosophies of such men as Karl Jaspers and Martin Heidegger of Germany, Gabriel Marcel and Jean-Paul Sartre of France, Unamuno and Ortega y Gasset of Spain? Or the thought of such existential theologians as Nikolai Berdyaev and Paul Tillich? These men have different problems, attack the problems by different methods, and on a number of points are in disagreement. Hence some critics have declared that existentialism is not a unified movement at all, with the implication that it may not even be a definite philosophy. On the contrary, a movement is alive and vital only when it is able to generate differences among its followers; when everybody agrees, we may be sure that it has declined into the stereotyped rigidity of death. Moreover, despite the differences among existentialists, there is a common core to their thinking. Let us try now to see what some of the main points of this common core are.

If the modern era began with the way of thinking launched by Descartes, then we must, to save ourselves, recast our fundamental way of thinking. The world Descartes portrays—of material objects stripped of all qualities, extended in mathematical space of three dimensions, and with only quantitative and measurable properties—is not the world in which we live as human beings but a high-level abstraction from the world that surrounds and involves us, exalts or enchants or terrifies us. We live in the human world, not in the world of science. And it is from the context of this human world that all the abstractions of science ultimately derive their meaning.

So, too, those fateful abstractions, the body and the mind. Man is not basically a body to which a mind is annexed in some incomprehensible way. Man is first and foremost a concrete involvement or enmeshment with the world, and within this concreteness of his being we distinguish the opposed poles of body and mind. We do not first exist inside our bodies and then proceed to infer a world existing beyond ourselves; on the contrary, in the very act of existing we are beyond ourselves and within the world. The verb "ex-ist" means, etymologically, to stand outside or beyond oneself. It is this self-transcendence that makes man what he is and distinguishes him from all the other animals whose existence does not reach backward and forward in time and history, and which remain rooted in space to their own natural habitat.

Because he is this perpetually self-transcending animal, man cannot be understood in his totality by the natural sciences—physics, chemistry, biology, or purely behaviorist psychology—as materialists have held. Man has expressed the truth of his existence in art and religion as well as in science; we would get less than the truth about human life if we left out any of these expressions of truth. One great achievement of existential philosophy has been a new interpretation of the idea of truth in order to point out that there are different kinds of truth, where a rigid scientific rationalism had postulated but one kind: objective scientific truth.

Kierkegaard introduced this difference by his analysis of religious truth. The truth with which religion is ultimately concerned, said Kierkegaard, has nothing to do with questions of rational proof. We do not exclaim, "There is a genuinely religious person!" when we happen to encounter a man who is an expert in all the subtle dialectic of theology. If we have ever encountered a genuinely spiritual person, we know that the heart of the matter lies elsewhere: in the being of the total person, not in the cerebrations of reason. Religious truth is realized actively and inwardly in the life of the individual man; it is not something embodied in a system of concepts, like science. Hence the fact that seemed so catastrophic to Kant—that the existence of God could not be proved rationally—is perfectly acceptable. For God is never real in our lives when He is considered a mere object of scientific proof or disproof.

Similarly, Heidegger has elucidated the unique kind of truth found in art. Truth is that peculiar relation of man to the object in which he lets the object be seen for what it is. Science is truth in this sense, but so too is art, though its way of letting the thing be seen is distinctly different from that of science. What kind of truth would we have about the long life of man upon this planet without those great works of art that have appeared in the tortuous course of human history? Here existentialism, a new philosophy, goes back to a tradition before Plato, who on purely intellectualist grounds condemned all art as illusion. The older tradition among the Greeks was that their great poets were seers who voiced the hidden wisdom of the race. The Greek people of that earlier age were wiser than Plato.

Because it denies the restrictions of scientific rationalism, existentialism sometimes has been labeled a form of irrationalism. This accusation is both glib and ungrounded. We do not cast all doubt upon an instrument by pointing out its functional limitations. A crowbar is not a key, and even if we wanted to pick the lock, we should do better with a hairpin. In making this observation we can hardly be called guilty of anticrowbarism.

Scientific reason is abstract and universal; life as we live it is individual and concrete. There are bridges between the two, but the former can never claim to supersede the latter without doing violence to it. You may use the crowbar to batter down the door, but then you will have to stand the expense of having the door repaired. We smile at the absurdity of the remark by the French mathematician Laplace after he had witnessed, without being moved, a performance of Racine's *Phèdre:* "What does it prove?" The mind of this great mathematician was geared to only one kind of truth. In considering Laplace's question absurd we are only using plain human judgment, not espousing a philosophic system of irrationalism. When scientific rationalists raise the facile cry of "irrationalism," they are exposing their own mental blind spots. The danger to our civilization is that as this rigid rationalism attempts to embrace all areas of life we will not only profit from its vision but also be the victim of its blindness.

Reason, after all, is *human* reason and we should expect it, like everything human, to have its limitations. There is no positive without a correlated negative. Being always involves non-Being. As reason becomes more abstract, it seems to soar beyond the human conditions from which it took its initial leap; but it has perpetually to return to the solid earth of our human condition for refueling. What we need is neither a blind exaltation nor an empty rejection of reason, but a new concept of what Ortega y Gasset calls "vital reason"—a reason rooted in the fundamental conditions of human existence. The man who exists and the man who thinks is in the end (as in the beginning) one and the same; and if as thinker he chooses to forget that he is a man, he will end, as Kierkegaard pointed out in rebutting Hegel, by becoming humanly absurd.

One final and central point common to the existentialists is their emphasis upon time and history as fundamental dimensions of human existence. Among all the animals man stands in a unique relation to time because he stands open to a future in which the present conditions of life can be transformed. Standing open to this future, he orders his present and connects it with his past. Hence our lives become meaningful to the degree that we bind together tomorrow, today and yesterday in an active whole. Time is thus the fundamental condition of our human existence; without time there would be no human meaning. But time, real time, is never the abstract "once upon a time" of the fairy story; it is always time here and now, urgent and pressing upon us. We are temporal beings not because we reckon with abstract mathematical time sequences, but because we experience time in the historical pressure of our generation with its challenging and fateful tasks.

What these tasks of the second half of our century may be in the great world beyond philosophy, we cannot pretend to say. But even here philosophy is not without some indication. Strictly within confines of the philosophical enterprise itself, a good many philosophers have felt that the historical task of philosophy has been to escape the trammels of Cartesian thinking. And Descartes, as we have seen, is the prophet of the Age of Mathematical Physics that is now upon us. The existentialists ask for a new philosophical anthropology, a more complete and integral philosophical understanding of man. Thus what this philosophy suggests to mankind generally as the historical task it has to confront in the second half of this century is nothing less than to face without evasion this question: Are we, at long last, to decide whether the coming epoch shall be the Age of Man or the Age of Mathematical Physics?

3. *The case of Heidegger*

There are several good reasons why Heidegger should be singled out for special comment in this section, and these reasons are also such as to justify speaking of him as a case, though nothing pejorative or clinical is intended by this word. Somebody is a case when there is some special problem about him—a problem which may make him more difficult or significant or both; and in this century which has dared to regard itself as the most problematic in history, there is perhaps no philosopher who is more problematic and paradoxical than Heidegger. His relation to other existentialist philosophers is just such an instance of this paradoxical character: "I am not an existentialist," Heidegger himself has said, and there can be no doubt that if one interprets existentialism in a certain fashion, this statement is not willful paradox but literal truth. Yet there is the fact of his enormous influence upon other existentialists; and, even more, the fact that the historical judgment of existentialism as a philosophy—whether, that is, it brings forth something really new in the history of philosophy—will probably ride on the case of Heidegger. A good deal of the content of existentialism has been Socratic in nature: a summons or an appeal to awaken man to his own human and self-conscious humanity amid the extraordinary historical pressures now exerted in the opposite direction. Such an "appeal" is not the primary purpose of Heidegger as a thinker. And in this respect his philosophy is very different from that of Karl Jaspers, who is generally looked upon as the cofounder, with Heidegger, of contemporary existentialism. Heidegger claims to bring a new point of view *within philosophy* itself, not a new note of human warning that sounds outside academic philosophy; and therefore it would be with him that the more strictly philosophical content of existentialism is to be measured.

Then again, there is the matter of Heidegger's famous "obscurity," which would seem to require that special comment be made upon him. A great deal of this "obscurity" is a matter of translation, and disappears when Heidegger is read in German. To be sure, his German is at times a very highly individualized vehicle of expression: Heidegger does coin his own terms when he has to, and usually these are coinings that stick very close to the etymological roots of German. Heidegger thinks very much within the matrix of the German language, and his expression hugs the particularity of this language to its bosom. All of this makes for difficulty in translation; and indeed accounts in part (the other part is the laziness and lack of interest of publishers) for the fact that not much of Heidegger has yet appeared in English. Obscurity, however, has always been taken as a kind of hallmark of the German philosopher, especially in comparison with his English cousin; and if we compare Heidegger with two classical German philosophers, like Kant or Hegel, his sentences are remarkably compact and incisive, his expression notably terse. Very often, in reading Hegel, we get the feeling, while lost in the almost interminable labyrinths of his sentences, that the philosopher is deliberately willing to be obscure. One never gets this impression from Heidegger: he is struggling to communicate, and his command of his own means of communication is powerful and impressive. The difficulty comes, rather, from the obscurity of the matters with which Heidegger is grappling.

That there are obscure matters at all in our experience is a contention that rubs against the prejudice of some positivistic philosophers that whatever cannot be said clearly and distinctly cannot be said at all and the effort to say it can only result in "meaningless" verbalism. Every philosopher, in this view, ought to be able to express himself with the simple-minded clarity of, say, Bertrand Russell. And if the philosopher does not do this, it is a clear sign of intellectual incompetence. All this, of course, is oversimplified psychologizing. A philosopher may be quite capable of mastering one or another of the clear and distinct dialects of philosophy and of bouncing the ball of dialectic deftly back and forth across the net; but he may be drawn by other subject matters into following a quite different path in philosophy. From the point of view of a philosopher like Heidegger there are parts of our experience that ordinary language finds itself hard put to express, if it can express these matters at all; indeed, this ordinary language seems to have been formed out of a kind of conspiracy to cover over or forget these parts of experience altogether. This conviction immediately places somebody like Heidegger at a disadvantage in the market place of opinion vis-à-vis the English philosopher of ordinary language who is quite satisfied that the language of the ordinary man can say whatever philosophy has to say. It is a disadvantage that gives Heidegger a very bad press within the academic world of Anglo-American philosophers. In the final reckoning, however, this is a disadvantage that he may be able to survive. But before that reckoning can fairly be made, there will have to much more labor of assimilation of Heidegger by American and British philosophers. And this need, once again, is such as to justify our singling out Heidegger as a special case, or problem, requiring special comment.

Heidegger, we have said, is a special case even among the existentialist philosophers; and before we proceed, it is necessary to make clear precisely what this difference consists in.

So far the attempts in this country to make existentialism known have centered rather on the sensational and dramatic character of some of its principal themes. Consequently, it has been considered as an expression more of human pathos than of rigorous thinking; and its contributions, when admitted, have been seen as a needed corrective to an excessive rationalism rather than a necessity of thought itself. For the philosopher in this country existentialism has sounded like a voice crying from the wilderness outside philosophy proper rather than one speaking strictly and soberly within philosophy itself about traditional and specifically philosophical problems.

No doubt, there is a basis for this prevailing view of existentialism in the one side of its tradition that goes from Pascal through Kierkegaard. For the man passionately concerned with his own individual salvation—which as human beings we all ought to be, however we interpret salvation—certain disputes of philosophers may provoke him at moments to echo what Pascal said of the whole of philosophy: that it was not worth half an hour's time. In the depths of despair, the grip of anxiety, or the mere ordinary struggle for a decent human happiness, there are bound to be moments when the purely theoretical attitude is not possible for us; indeed seems like a travesty of our own individual existence. As sober professional men, however, philosophers are expected to keep such moments to themselves. Great and wayward geniuses like Kierkegaard or Nietzsche may exploit their own sufferings for the illumination of the rest of the tribe. The rest of us had better keep such experiences strictly extracurricular: we are expected to solve our problems in life and not to drag them into our professional job of philosophy. That there is another side of existentialism which has something to say to philosophers as thinkers, and not merely as human beings, will be part of what I intend to suggest as the distinctive contribution of Heidegger.

These two sides of the existentialist tradition have produced two different concepts of existence itself. The clearest and sharpest expression of these is to be found, I believe, in Kierkegaard and Heidegger. It should be made clear at this point that the word "concept" is philosophically neutral here. I could just as well speak of two different approaches to existence, or use any other philosophically uncharged word. My discussion here, in short, has nothing to do with that famous problem raised by Kant as to whether existence is a genuine concept or not. Whatever decision one might make on this Kantian question, it would still be possible to approach the question of existence from two diametrically opposed directions as Kierkegaard and Heidegger do.

For Kierkegaard existence is the sheer factual existence of the individual. Hence, it is something that I have primarily to live rather than transmute into philosophic concepts. Indeed, just because it is something that I live and have to live, it can never be completely expressed by any concept. This is the point of Kierkegaard's famous polemic against Hegel in the *Concluding Unscientific Postscript:* that thought and existence can never fully coincide; or, to put it in more traditional language, that the individual can never be exhausted by any concept or set of concepts.

But this traditional point, which goes as far back as Aristotle, if expressed as a general truth for all individual beings, would exceed the scope of Kierkegaard's intention, since he is restricting his point to apply only to the subjective existence of the human person. This human existence, as our own personal and actual existence, is encountered, according to Kierkegaard, in the situation of serious ethical choice. So long as we remain pure aesthetes in detached contemplation of artistic or intellectual spectacles, we may forget our own actual situation for the delightful world of possibilities. Here Kierkegaard distinguishes very sharply his own thought from that of the speculative philosopher: for the latter, consumed by the sheer desire to know, the universal as essence and therefore possibility takes precedence over the actual individual; while for the actually existing individual, in the crisis of moral choice, there is no escape from his actual situation into a world of pure possibilities, and therefore actuality ranks as more real than possibility.

Here again Kierkegaard is giving new and subjective expression to a thoroughly traditional point, which is expressed in the scholastic axiom, *"Actus melius ac prius est quam potentia,"* "Actuality is better and prior to potentiality." That is, possibility is always grounded on the actual constitution of an actual entity. The traditional character of Kierkegaard's position, where it can be boiled down to something like ordinary ontology, has prompted Heidegger to say that Kierkegaard was a great religious writer but no "thinker"—in the sense, for example, that Heidegger, as a thinker, is concerned with recasting the very meaning of Being—and that Kierkegaard's ontology does not go beyond his reading of Trendelenberg's commentary upon Aristotle. Since Kierkegaard made no claims as an ontologist or philosopher, it is not likely that he would disagree with this judgment of himself. His treatment of existence, it must be pointed out, is nowhere concerned with the philosophical problem of transcendence that has plagued philosophers throughout the period of modern philosophy since Descartes and that is such a central concern to Heidegger himself.

In his *Sein und Zeit* (*Being and Time*), Heidegger attempts, as it is commonly said, to describe the general structures of human existence. Thus it would seem that the difference between his understanding of existence and Kierkegaard's is merely that between the universal and the particular. But this does not encompass the whole matter: Kierkegaard deals with existence as an "ontic" fact, while Heidegger's investigation is "ontological." This barbarous jargon has now to be explained.

The distinction between ontic and ontological in Heidegger has to be explained by the parallel distinction in Kant between an empirical and a transcendental inquiry. (This strict relation of Heidegger's thinking to Kant has usually been overlooked because of the sensational character of some of the matters he discusses, but this relation to Kant is central to his thought in the period of *Being and Time*.) An empirical inquiry, for Kant, is concerned with examining individual facts in order to discover what laws regulate these facts; a transcendental inquiry is concerned with the conditions that make possible our experience of these facts. As an illustration consider Kant's view of space and time as fundamental forms of perception. An empirical scientific investigation of perception would deal with individual facts of perception, the relations among these, and the possible empirical laws that might serve to generalize these facts. But these individual facts presuppose space and time as the field, region, or context within which they occur. Thus one use of a transcendental inquiry, as Kant understood it, was to insist against the atomism of the British tradition that space cannot be constructed as an aggregate or set of sense-data—colored patches, for example—since it is possible for me to see a colored patch only within spatial context; and therefore space is presupposed as the condition for my seeing any colored patch whatsoever. In the same way time cannot be built up as an aggregate of instants—nor even from an aggregate of finite chunks of duration, as Whitehead attempts—since to perceive this moment now as present I have to perceive it as the juncture between past and future; and thus the whole temporal spread is presupposed as the context within which the "now" is experienced. The guiding principle of the Kantian transcendental inquiry is always contextual and holistic.

In the same way, Heidegger's description of existence, since it is "ontological" rather than "ontic," is concerned with the a priori conditions that make certain individual modes of existence, as ontic facts, possible.

So far, then, we have got the following as the two chief points of difference:

(1) For Heidegger the question of existence is primarily connected with the philosophical problem of transcendence, not with the urgent concern of the individual for ethico-religious salvation. To exist is to ek-sist—i.e., stand beyond oneself within a world. World must be given with man as the a priori horizon within which any individual facts at all can become the objects of his care.

(2) Heidegger is concerned with the possibilities that constitute the actual existence of man. Change Kant's subjectivistic language about the conditions under which experience is possible—and Heidegger has declared that his thought is against every form of subjectivism—and we get here a radical ontological doctrine that actuality is constituted by potentiality. Heidegger announces his point in explicit opposition to Kierkegaard: "Possibility is higher than actuality."

Each of these two points must now be examined more carefully.

Let us take the second point first.

Since Heidegger is attempting "ontological" and not "ontic" descriptions of human existence, some of the words he is using—like death, care, anxiety, guilt—have a different sense for him than in ordinary usage. Take death, for example: as an ontic fact, it is the usual thing noticed in an obituary—the actual event of a man's decease. As an ontological characteristic of existence, on the other hand, death is the possibility not to be—a possibility that continues with me so long as I live. Thus it seems to me no refutation of Heidegger's view that some individuals appear to feel no anxiety at the approach of death, and that a Kamikaze pilot, for example, could speak of his death with the expectant ecstasy of watching the cherry blossoms fall. (A more admirable human example would be the aged André Gide in the last pages of his journal writing about the autumn leaves and the exhilaration with which he accepted the necessity of death.) Any such individual decision about one's attitude toward death is an ontic fact, and as such can occur only in the given context of death as an ontological possibility. Only a being, that is, whose being is disclosed to himself as capable also of not being—only such a being can make a decision as to what attitude he will maintain toward the event that finally actualizes this possibility.

This seems perfectly obvious, but perhaps also perfectly nugatory. Of course the axe cuts only if it can cut, it will be argued, but this is not to say very much if anything; and furthermore we know that the axe can cut because we see that it actually cuts. This is the kind of argument, by the way, that the American neorealists directed against the whole Kantian Copernican revolution in philosophy; and it is not surprising that it should turn up in somewhat changed form against Kant's heir, Heidegger. But potentiality and actuality are one thing for *objects* like axes and quite a different thing for beings, like man, to whom their own possibilities are disclosed. Thus in the case of death, for example: if my own possibility not to be is disclosed to me, this possibility becomes an actual constituent of my existence.

Such a fact leads us to recast the whole traditional distinction of potentiality and actuality as it stems from Aristotle. Aristotle's view is formed for a world of *objects*—for the primary substances, with their attributes and relations, as the residual supposita of Being. Thus if a primary substance has a potentiality, it is because of some actual characteristic or arrangement of its matter. Opium has a dormitive power because of its *actual* chemical composition, which acts upon the bloodstream and the nervous system in a certain way. This is the sense of the traditional axiom, "Actuality is prior to potentiality." Potentialities, in short, are never—directly and as such—actual characteristics of actual entities; they are only secondarily such—if, for example, the actual entity is brought into contact with another entity on which, because of its actual character, it will act in a certain fashion. In our modern parlance: potentialities are all disposition predicates; to say "That glass is breakable" means that if such and such is done to it, then it will actually break. Ultimately, however, we believe that the disposition predicate "breakable" holds true of glass because of its *actual* molecular structure.

In the modern period this Aristotelian doctrine is continued unchanged in Locke, except that it is now elaborated within a thoroughly Newtonian climate. All potentialities (including the secondary qualities) are to be derived from the mass, arrangement, and momentum of material particles. We need not call attention here to all the impossible puzzles to which this scheme of thought has led over the last three centuries. A revolt against this scheme is the motive behind the metaphysics of Whitehead, which on certain points, as we shall indicate in a moment, runs parallel—in its aims at any rate—with the ontology of Heidegger.

The Aristotelian distinction, like all of traditional metaphysics, as Heidegger has repeatedly insisted, was formed for a world of objects. The meaning of Being is interpreted in terms of the ultimate supposita of the primary substances. To that question, as Aristotle puts it, asked today as of old and eternally to be asked, What is it to be?, the Aristotelian answer has at least the virtue of simplicity and clarity: "To be" is defined disjunctively; "To be" is to be a primary substance or a quality of a primary substance or a relation between two primary substances or an action of primary substance or a passion, etc. etc. etc. The resultant picture is bits of matter filling space, with various qualities pinned on their surface—a scheme of thought that Whitehead has labeled the "Fallacy of Simple Location." Among other things, this scheme cannot give any adequate interpretation of the fact of human *transcendence*.

With this fact of transcendence we come back to the first of the two distinguishing features we remarked on above in Heidegger's concept of existence. But this point was already implicit in our discussion of possibility and actuality; for it is only because he is a being actually constituted by possibilities that man, as Heidegger puts it, is *a creature of distance*. Because a future possibility is disclosed to me now as something-that-I-can-be, this something-that-I-can-be already qualifies my being now. Because my actual being is constituted by possibilities, I am already beyond myself. It would be the fallacy of simple location to think of existence as a subcutaneous fact or process.

Transcendence, in short, must be taken as a primary and underived fact of existence. Exist is to ek-sist. Since the seventeenth century every attempt to derive transcendence from *consciousness*—either as a projection or an inference of consciousness—has foundered, and in the end only succeeded in leaving consciousness an utterly private and incomprehensible fact within a universe of alien objects. This transcendence is as directly given as the physical objects, chairs and tables, of our acquaintance; indeed it is the condition without which such objects could not be given. But this transcendence is not to be confused with the ontic fact—as discussed by Kierkegaard and later by Jaspers—of my individual struggle to surpass myself in the constant human effort toward self-development. Transcendence here is simply the name for that structured complex of possibilities that constitute the being of that actual entity we call man.

In the foregoing I have attempted merely to present, not to judge between, two different points of view toward existence. Since these two points of view are adopted for very different purposes, and in answer to very different questions, obviously they need not be taken to contradict each other. Many critics—Martin Buber is one—have expressed the uneasy feeling that Heidegger's description of the human being (the *Dasein*) leaves out something essential, that it does not give us the actual existing individual, the man of flesh and blood. To this charge the answer must be that of course it does not give us the actually existing individual, for this is no more a part of its intention than it was Kant's to give us the actually existing subject in his *Critique of Pure Reason.* In stressing this parallel with Kant, I have meant to indicate that Heidegger's project takes place strictly within philosophy, that it is addressed to certain traditional and strictly philosophical problems, and that it does not at all attempt to be religious or moral exhortation, or to perpetuate the figure of Socrates in an appeal to know and realize ourselves.

Whether or not the Heideggerian approach does indeed illumine the philosophical matters it is addressed to, remains to be seen. In the meantime, however, it may be useful to keep these two different concepts of existence clear since contemporary existentialist philosophers themselves often blur them. Only Heidegger, I believe, sticks consistently to his own point of view. Though Jaspers does describe certain general structures of transcendence, in the end he is a Kierkegaardian who conceives philosophy fundamentally as a summons to an authentic life. Sartre is another mixed case, though the mixture starts from the opposite end of the spectrum: he appears to proceed on a purely phenomenological terrain, but the note of moral exhortation takes over —as perhaps is inevitable in a man who plays the role of leader of his generation. Hence, inevitably, he comes to diverge from Heidegger on the crucial issue of act and possibility, and makes doing prior to being. A life, says Sartre, is nothing but the totality of its acts. No doubt, from the point of view of the moral judge examining the individual life as already finished, with all its excuses and evasions swept away, this is true. But it is true on the ontic level, where as an individual I cannot take credit for the possible things that I have not done or be censured for the possible sins I have not committed. On the ontological level, however, where we are concerned not with the moral value of the individual but with the Being of an existent open and enmeshed with the future, an individual action is possible only within a field of possibility. On this level Being is prior to doing; and the will to action can carve out a meaningful action only within a field or region of beings that it has first chosen to let be what they are.

The new and bold attack upon the age-old problem of Being was announced by Heidegger in 1927 in his *Being and Time.* This book had an explosive effect upon the philosophic community in Germany, and with good reason. Perhaps never before in the history of philosophy had the picture of man as a radically finite and time-bound creature been drawn so graphically and powerfully as in this book. Heidegger's theory of time might be expressed indirectly through this simple truism: Man is the being who makes clocks. That is, he makes an instrument to count time in order to measure and regulate his own human projects. The connection of this with pragmatism should be obvious. But Heidegger adds a further ontological dimension to his analysis: in order for man to invent an instrument like a clock and to measure time by it, his own being must be essentially temporal. Future-present-past must be given as a field of possibilities that constitute his being, and as a field within which he can count actual moments of time. To say "*Now* it is one o'clock" is meaningful only if the now is grasped as the present juncture between past and future; and hence the whole temporal spread of future-present-past must be given in experience as the a priori ground for clocking off time as a sequence of moments. To exist is to ek-sist, to stand beyond oneself temporally as well as spatially. Man's being is not given as an existence at a point-instant but as a temporal spread. That man is essentially a temporal being means that he is essentially transcendence; and he is a transcendence before he is an isolated body or an isolated mind.

Heidegger's description of human experience in *Being and Time* has been characterized as pragmatism with a sense of inwardness. This is a suggestive comparison as far as it goes, but it would lead to misunderstanding if it were taken to mean that Heidegger merely annexes some very "subjective" categories to his description of man as a creature of action who essentially determines his own being by his chosen projects. The extraordinary accomplishment of *Being and Time* is that it describes man without the subjective-objective split. On the one hand, the being of man is not described as the being of a *thing;* on the other hand, this being is not at all rendered as some purely subjective flux of experience. It is in just this respect—that Heidegger has described man as a creature of inwardness but at the same time enmeshed in the world and time—that he has seemed to existential psychoanalysts like Ludwig Binswanger to offer new basic principles for psychology.

Nearly all Heidegger's basic themes are contained, at least in germ, in his *Being and Time*. Nevertheless, he is not really, as some critics think, a man of this one book; and he was to go on to develop his position quite radically from it. This later phase of Heidegger is even less known than the earlier one; and for this reason, as well as because this last phase seems to indicate an amazing turn-about within German philosophy itself, we have to try to indicate briefly where Heidegger's final reflections take him.

In 1929, two years after *Being and Time,* Heidegger published the first of his many controversial studies in the history of philosophy: *Kant and the Problem of Metaphysics*. The usual charge made against Heidegger's historical interpretations is that, in seeking to read between the lines for what the philosopher has left unsaid, he really reads his own doctrine into the philosopher. Heidegger himself is very aware of the risks he is taking in his own kind of historical interpretation: it would be easier in fact to do simple philological studies in exhuming a thinker's ideas as if they were a skeleton to be restored with accurate objectivity than to attempt to maintain a dialogue with the philosopher, who in fact may be dead but whose ideas are not. The risks of such a dialogue are always great; yet there is no other way by which the history of philosophy can be rescued from the graveyard of historical documentation and become a living thing that perpetually renews itself from within.

Moreover, however daring Heidegger's historical interpretations may be, they are always anchored on some simple and central point; however far he may push them, they do not start from anything farfetched in its initial premises. This is very much the case with his study of Kant. Heidegger's interpretation revolves around the problem, central to the *Critique of Pure Reason,* of the "transcendental deduction of the categories." What Kant was concerned with in this portion of his *Critique* was to show that the basic forms of thought, the categories of the understanding, must apply necessarily to any future experience. With the details of this Kantian problem we need not be concerned here, except to observe that Kant makes the deduction turn on the essentially temporal nature of consciousness. For Kant, be it remembered, a concept is a synthesis of actual and possible perceptions. My concept of this table, for example, is a synthesis of all the sense-data I have had from it as well as of the data I would have if I were to walk about it and see it from different angles, lean forward to touch it, crawl under its legs, etc. etc. All this is what it means to say, "Here is a table." Charles Peirce drew from Kant here the basic principle of pragmatism: namely, that an idea is a design for action. That is, if the idea synthesizes actual and possible data it has an intrinsic reference to the future: if I say "Here is a table," I mean among other things that if I were to walk around the table and look I would see it from the other side. Thus every idea has meaning in relation to some future possible action or actions of mine. Heidegger isolates this same Kantian emphasis upon the basic temporality of consciousness, but gives it a further twist from that of Peirce. Man can have concepts only insofar as they are related to the future—that is, only insofar as he is an essentially temporal being open to the future. The possibility that there can be meaning at all is grounded on the fact of temporality—on the fact that man is a being who can bind together past, present, and future!

How revolutionary this conclusion is may be gathered from our previous remarks about the persistent tendency within the history of philosophy for philosophers to take the eternal or timeless as more real than the temporal. However, even when they speak of the eternal or timeless, Heidegger holds, they must do so in terms that are borrowed from the temporal, for all thinking, like Being itself, is circumscribed by the horizon of the temporal.

Kant's *Critique* thus becomes for Heidegger not so much a treatise in the theory of knowledge as a revelation of the temporal being of man; and, since man is essentially temporal insofar as he is finite, a study in human finitude. No doubt, this looks very much like pushing Kant in the direction of Heidegger, and reading the *Critique* as if it were merely anticipating the line of thought developed in *Being and Time.* But it may be questioned whether a philosopher reading another philosopher, from the time Aristotle interpreted or misinterpreted the Pre-Socratics, has not always done something like this. In any case, the ultimate value of Heidegger's interpretation hinges on whether it turns the eyes of the mind to perceive new depths within the Kantian philosophy; and this, not even its critics seem to doubt.

It is in this same year, 1929, that the real turning point in Heidegger's development is marked by the publication of another essay, *Vom Wesen des Grundes* (On the Nature of Ground, or Cause). This is one of Heidegger's most pregnant and incisive essays; and one, incidentally, that seems to have been most influential upon his French follower, Sartre. Though its doctrine is pretty well anchored in *Being and Time,* it rings much more as a summons to action than the earlier work. The picture that emerges from this essay is of man as a being who seeks to ground his own existence, and in seeking this ground must create and found his world. Man looks very much here like the master of Being, lord of the planet, the creature who subdues and dominates nature. Though the name of Nietzsche is not invoked, the temper of thought is very much Nietzschean, and the shadow of Nietzsche seems to be present over the whole of the essay.

To be sure, this emphasis was present already in *Being and Time,* particularly in the later sections where Heidegger spoke of the way in which man seeks his own human authenticity by seeking to ground his own existence. On the other hand, there was the opposite emphasis upon man as the being who, among all other animals, stands in the peculiar situation of being open to the truth of Being. The book, indeed, is perfectly ambivalent between these two emphases, and Heidegger could have gone in one or the other opposite directions in his subsequent thinking: either he could become a voluntarist, a philosopher of the will to action, in the manner of Nietzsche (and, we may add, of Sartre too); or he could turn away from the will to action to insist upon the need of man's becoming receptive and open to the Being that encompasses him. The question, quite simply, is whether being is prior to doing, or the reverse. From *Vom Wesen des Grundes* it looks very much as if Heidegger were on his way toward making doing prior to being, and thus launching another of those thoroughly modern and activistic philosophies of which Nietzsche is the most extreme and brilliant exponent. In fact, however, it was just the opposite path that Heidegger was to take.

Though the change does not become fully elaborated until years later, it begins in the 1930's with his studies of the poet Hölderlin. What part the experience of Nazism had in this development cannot be said with any degree of certainty, yet it does not seem at all implausible to associate his philosophical change with the brief period of his entanglement with the Nazi party. This episode in Heidegger's career will probably always be a mark against him as a man, yet it has been made perhaps too much so in the eyes of the world. The full facts have not been presented, and it is to be hoped that Dr. Hannah Arendt, who has access to them, will someday do so. Heidegger did not cover himself with glory, to say the least, though he behaved better than most German professors, who were not at all deprived of their chairs when the Allies took over after the end of the War. Heidegger had made the mistake, apparently, of being too vocal about his sympathies in the early days of the movement. What might be said most charitably of him at this point is that he was politically naïve and out of German nationalist feeling felt that he heard in Nazism a resolute call to action on the part of the German nation. As the 1930's went on, however, and he severed his ties more and more with the Nazis, he began to speak more strongly against the will to action that is central in so much modern philosophy: the crowning error, for Heidegger now, is to locate the essence of man in his becoming the master of this planet. His political disillusionment and his philosophical change do not seem here to be unconnected. In any case, it is not without significance that Heidegger, perhaps the last of that odd breed, the German philosopher, should have become entangled in the fate of his nation, with which German philosophy has always been strangely and paradoxically bound.

His studies of Hölderlin were not undertaken solely out of Heidegger's growing conviction, as a philosopher concerned with the problem of language, that poetry was the essential form of speech. His tie to Hölderlin is closer than this. Hölderlin, like Heidegger, is the enraptured Hellenist who turns his eyes back to the sunlit age of the Greeks and speaks of the modern age as "the night of the world" from which all the gods have departed. Hölderlin here is the most extreme and the most visionary of the romantic poets, all of whom were possessed by the uneasy dread that in the modern age man had come to sever himself so drastically from nature that some new and uncanny fate would fall upon him. In English poetry this uneasiness, which is something new in the history of poetry, begins with Blake and Wordsworth. It becomes a clamor of warning voices among some of our greatest contemporary poets: for Yeats this is the time of the dark of the moon, of empty objectivity and bloody violence; for Eliot (before his conversion at least, and perhaps after it too) ours is the wasteland in which the saving waters no longer flow; for Rilke (on whom Heidegger has written a perceptive study) this is the time when the lost angelic voices are no longer heard; for Robert Graves, we have lost all contact with the great Goddess, and we are "no longer at home with the lady of the house"—we are no longer at home in nature. This testimony of the poets is so extraordinary that we can hardly afford to brush it aside lightly; and a society that does so has already lost all contact with its poets and thereby confirms their prophecy. Heidegger is the thinker of what these poets seek to poetize. As the poets, from romanticism onward, warn against the severance of man from nature, Heidegger seeks to warn us of a severance of thinking from Being; and this not merely as a severance of man's instincts from the way of nature, but also as something that takes place in the very mode of his thinking.

Heidegger's interpretations of Hölderlin have thus to be seen in the context of a general interpretation of history that is also one of the remarkable products of this last phase of his thought. This view of history is very bold and sweeping, yet in a fashion typical of Heidegger it starts from a very simple and banal observation of the present. This observation is that the characteristic of the modern age in comparison with past ages is the extraordinary development of technology that has made possible the organization of men into mass societies and secured the domination by man of the whole planet. So far, nothing very new about this. But Heidegger pushes this point in a very simple-minded and persistent way: If technology is now the dominant thing in man's life, how did this become possible? Through modern science. And where did modern science begin? In the seventeenth century, when for the sake of precision and measurement men began to apply mathematics to natural phenomena. The concurrent philosophic expression of this is the Cartesian philosophy of clear and distinct ideas. But it is quite obvious that the development of science in the seventeenth century could not have taken place without the knowledge of Greek science that had been rediscovered by the Renaissance. Our steps from the present backward lead us thus to Greek science.

But Greek science is, in its turn, the offspring of Greek philosophy, for it is out of the speculations of the Greek philosophers that science is born. The seed then of what the world is today and of what we ourselves are lies in the step taken by the Greek thinkers to detach beings as beings, objects as objects, from the environing presence of Being, and so to make possible eventually the thematic elaboration of these objects in science.

With this objectification of nature—that is, the detachment of objects as objects from the environing ground of Being—the age of metaphysics begins. This age culminates 2500 years later in modern science, where the objectification of nature is almost complete. Its final philosophic utterance is in Nietzsche's doctrine of the will to power: for here, in Nietzsche, is the extreme expression of man's drive to tear himself loose from nature and manipulate it in the interests of his own power. The process that begins with the earliest Greek philosopher, Anaximander, culminates in Nietzsche; and with a very neat, perhaps too neat, stroke of symmetry Heidegger speaks of the age from Anaximander to Nietzsche as a single unit. This age of metaphysics is now finished, says Heidegger, not in the sense the positivists would aver that metaphysics itself has become "meaningless"; on the contrary, the positivists themselves are unconscious dupes of metaphysics since they are completely captured by its spirit of objectification; no, this age is finished because it has, after Nietzsche, no further fundamental possibilities open to it. The step taken by the Greeks to distinguish clear and distinct objects was the great historical step taken by no other people (the Greeks alone among ancient people created science); but in this great step forward the sheer *presence* of Being as the environing context from which all objects are detached was lost and forgotten. Poets remind us of this presence. But if there is to be genuine renewal in the perspectives of civilization, there must be a new kind of thinking (of which Heidegger would be the groping forerunner) that would seek to make us stand once again in the sheer *presence* of that which is.

All of this historical framework has to be kept in mind in reading Heidegger's brief essay *Plato's Doctrine of Truth.* Plato, according to Heidegger, shifts the meaning of truth from a characteristic of Being—namely the open-ness or unhiddenness of Being (the Greek word we translate as "truth," *aletheia,* means literally "unhiddenness")—to a characteristic of mental concepts: their correctness or precision. Hence the Idea becomes for Plato the real reality. But Idea, in Greek, has its root in the verb for seeing: an Idea is always thus a human perspective. Thus the consequence of Plato's shift in the meaning of truth is to turn from Being itself in order to confer preëminent reality upon our own human and mental perspectives upon Being. It is a first step in that long journey that is Western philosophy toward the severance of man from Being. With this little change in words Plato has launched Western history toward the age of cerebration and computing machines.

This may look altogether pat to some readers. It would look less so, however, if all the connecting links were put in, and if Heidegger were to expound his point about Platonism in a broader and less microscopic way. He chooses instead to burrow in the words of the Greek text, and to unfold his point from those words like a man unwrapping tiny nuggets. But to each writer must be granted his own mode of exposition, as to each thinker his own mode of attack; and for Heidegger it is a consecrated task to dig back to the original thinking of the Greeks as it is caught in the web of the Greek language.

The Letter on Humanism has also to be read within the context of Heidegger's historical vision. It is easy to misunderstand Heidegger here as anti-humanist (perhaps in the sense of anti-humane) because he does not see humanism as the essential message for our time. But this would be an entirely superficial and frivolous reading. Heidegger's point of view is historical, and philosophy, in view of the essential temporality of man, must always take the historical point of view: Humanism was a great historical effort on the part of the Greeks, and it was necessary at that turning point of time to rescue man from his immersion in nature and to define the strictly human as distinct from the animal. The great artistic expressions of humanism are those beautiful and idealized forms of man created by the classic Greek sculptors. If the modern sculptor cannot create such idealized human forms, it is not because he is anti-human or anti-humane; another vision claims him, such as the need to reintegrate man into nature, so that some of Henry Moore's carvings, for example, exhibit the human body as a rock eroded by the sea and cast upon the shore from the waves. Man needs to preserve the inherited values of his humanity; but humanism as a doctrine is incomplete for an age when the human is threatening to overpower nature and in the wake of the population explosion some decades from now all mankind will live in housing developments from pole to pole, and the face of nature will be obscured except for some solitary lawn or tree here and there in the immense arid waste of billions and billions of humans.

Jean-Paul Sartre had proclaimed existentialism to the French as "a new humanism," and Heidegger's letter indicates how sharply the thought of these two "existentialists" diverges. Sartre has never been able to think outside the context of strictly humanistic claims and projects, and his thought is truly a form of humanism from beginning to end, though to some traditionalists a very disturbing humanism indeed. He has taken over the early Heidegger (and at that only in parts), but he is altogether untouched by the later Heidegger. How far this later Heidegger has changed from the earlier may be seen from the title of one of his most recent books: *Gelassenheit,* Abandonment (1959). Man here is no longer seen as the creature who—in the words of Francis Bacon at the very beginning of our modern epoch—seeks to put nature to the rack in order to compel from her an answer to his needs, but rather the being who can surrender to Being as the poet abandons himself to the sheer presence (Being) of the woods in which he walks.

We said earlier that this development within Heidegger's thinking marks a turn-about within German philosophy, and this revolution may be all the more remarkable in that Heidegger gives every sign of being the last German philosopher of the old high prophetic breed. The egotism of German philosophy has been the constant point of complaint by non-German critics—notably by Santayana, Dewey, and Croce, among the more important philosophers of our period. No doubt these criticisms were somewhat inflamed by the passions of war, but that does not mean that their essential contention, at least in regard to the spirit of German philosophy if not its direct relation to the enormities of German political behavior in this century, is not correct. The correlation between German philosophy and the politics of Germany is not an empty one, but it has been much oversimplified, though this is not the place to correct that simplification by further qualification. The criticism by Santayana and Dewey is valid as a description of German philosophy: this philosophy has tended, at least in philosophers like Fichte and Hegel, toward an extreme subjectivism, a belief that the ego or the self can somehow spin the world out of its own depths. The result is that it sees man and nature in an improper perspective, and man, placed too much in the foreground, elbows nature out of place. (We may observe by the way, and not without irony, that this is exactly the criticism that Santayana directs against Dewey's pragmatism.) For Mediterranean temperaments like Santayana and Croce, the Teutonic temperament is soaring and sublime, but too possessed by its own arrogance and hubris of spirit. The central hero of Germanic culture is Faust, who in the second part of Goethe's drama is represented as engaged in a demoniacal and never-ending struggle to conquer nature. The result of inflating the individual will over nature, so now the political side of the criticism runs, is that one ends by inflating oneself and one's nation (as an extension of oneself) over others, and so is driven to run amok politically.

Waiving the question of how just all these indictments are, we can, however, observe that if they are true in good part, or even in any part, then it is altogether fitting and proper historically, and perhaps is even an omen of some kind, that it should be a German philosopher in this century who most conspicuously reverses these philosophic tendencies. If German philosophy has been egotistic, then it is significant that Heidegger, a German, should announce that his philosophy is "against every form of subjectivism"; if German philosophy has projected the human will above nature, it is now Heidegger who calls for a surrender of man to Being; and, finally, if this philosophy has been guilty of hubris of spirit, then quite properly it should be a German philosopher who makes the most profound confession of humility for the claims of philosophy, telling us that "thought must descend again into the poverty of its materials." May it not be that here, within philosophy itself, a light breaks through on that enigma known as The German Problem, which has troubled the conscience of Europe for so long?

"Thought must descend once again into the poverty of its materials." It is well to conclude with this remarkable statement of Heidegger for it brings us back to the spirit of Husserl's cry, with which we began this section: "To the things themselves!" It is in a sense the same summons. But Heidegger's statement is the expression of thought that has traveled a very far piece from the original cry of Husserl. Heidegger's words sound in the domain of thought what in the domain of art has become the spiritual struggle of the modern artist: to descend into the poverty of his materials. This is the struggle of the sculptor to know the sheer feel of stone, steel, wire, board; of the painter to see once again texture, color, planes; of the musician to hear sounds and rhythms that had been covered over by the harmonic superstructures of tonal music; of the writer to descend from rhetoric and rediscover the word. That Heidegger's thought, keeping the laws within its own house, has nevertheless moved parallel to the direction of modern art, suggests that it comes out of the same secret depths and answers the same secret needs as does this art. If this be so, this thought, however groping and tentative in its results, would be one of the really authentic manifestations of this time.

Postscript

This introduction has to forego any lengthy comment on the existentialists Gabriel Marcel and Jean-Paul Sartre. Enough has been said about existentialism generally to establish an interpretative context for these philosophers. Moreover, the selections from Marcel and Sartre explain themselves in a way that Heidegger's do not. Not to have given special comment on Heidegger would have left the reader puzzled and wondering; to give the same extended comment to all existentialists would swell this part of the book out of all proper proportions.

Yet though Marcel and Sartre can be passed by for any lengthy comment, one brief and final word ought to be said about the essay of *Albert Camus* that concludes this group of selections. Camus was one of the nobler voices of our generation, and his untimely death in an automobile accident a few years back has left Europe without one of its few significant intellectual spokesmen. It is quite proper too that this section on existentialism should end on the note of a thoroughly human voice addressing itself to its fellow humans in the midst of our troubled and confused time.

Camus was not a professional philosopher, but his philosophical instincts were nonetheless shrewd and perceptive. This is not to say that he was a philosophical illiterate either. On the contrary, Camus had been trained in philosophy and was at the point of taking his degree and becoming a teacher of philosophy when events pulled him aside into the life of politics, the theatre, and literature. Reviewing *The Myth of Sisyphus* (1942), Sartre found occasion to sneer a little at Camus' lack of understanding of the existentialist philosophers. This may be true in some technical matters, but it is hardly true of Camus' fundamental insight into these philosophers; I venture to think, for example, that *The Myth of Sisyphus* betrays a more sensitive feeling for the meaning of Heidegger than Sartre himself, for all his formidable powers of dialectic, was able to extract from the German philosopher. But the question of Camus' technical equipment as a philosopher is not the issue here: this book is concerned with the philosophies of the twentieth century, but in being concerned with them it has found itself repeatedly involved in the historical reality of this century itself; and Camus was a writer singularly equipped by temperament and experience to address himself to this reality.

He was a spokesman for that generation in Europe that had grown up with the Terror—compounded of the various but not unrelated terrors of depression, war, totalitarianism—only to be delivered at the end of the Second World War not into a genuine and saving peace but into the paralyzing stalemate of the Cold War. Camus's central point in *The Rebel* (of which "Thought at the Meridian" is the final chapter) is simply the plea for an end to the terror; and in its simplicity and eloquence this plea was possibly the most hopeful and moving message of the post-war years.

Nor was this plea any mere piece of topical journalism. Camus had buttressed his moving exhortation by a long intellectual and historical analysis. He saw that this Time of the Terror, our own period, was not simply an accidental historical episode fallen upon us from the skies, but that it had long been prepared for intellectually by the ideologies of the late eighteenth and nineteenth centuries. The West had been running toward intellectual excess, toward a fanatical arrogance of mind, long before these tendencies exploded in the violence of wars, concentration camps, and executioners. What Camus wishes to affirm against the dehumanizing tendencies of ideologies is a renewed sense of the human, which means a renewal of the classical sense of moderation and limits that is to be found in the Greek poets if not in Plato. His final hero from Greek mythology is Ulysses, prudent, reasonable, tenacious, and above all the most *human* of all the warriors who went to Troy.

His message is thus very much in the main stream of existentialist thought. There is a direct line from Kierkegaard's protests in the nineteenth century against the arrogant and totalitarian rationalism of Hegel to Camus' attack upon any ideological fanaticism that would make life itself subservient to the Idea. In his play *State of Siege* the actor representing The Plague (which in the modern world, according to Camus, is no longer the Black Death of the Middle Ages but the totalitarian organization of life) announces to the people whom he has just subjected that henceforth even their deaths will be logical and statistical: "I have suppressed these mental luxuries of sentiment, emotion, and personal honor and put logic in their stead, for I can't bear untidiness and irrationality." If these words, pointing as they do to a very real menace in modern life, strike a note of gloom that is all too commonly associated with existentialist writers, we have to set beside them the final cry of *The Rebel,* which rings with hope and exultation.

W.B.

Edmund Husserl

THE THESIS OF THE NATURAL STANDPOINT AND ITS SUSPENSION[1]

27. *The world of the natural standpoint: I and my world about me*

Our first outlook upon life is that of natural human beings, imaging, judging, feeling, willing, *"from the natural standpoint"*. Let us make clear to ourselves what this means in the form of simple meditations which we can best carry on in the first person.

I am aware of a world, spread out in space endlessly, and in time becoming and become, without end. I am aware of it, that means, first of all, I discover it immediately, intuitively, I experience it. Through sight, touch, hearing, etc., in the different ways of sensory perception, corporeal things somehow spatially distributed are *for me simply there,* in verbal or figurative sense "present", whether or not I pay them special attention by busying myself with them, considering, thinking, feeling, willing. Animal beings also, perhaps men, are immediately there for me; I look up, I see them, I hear them coming towards me, I grasp them by the hand; speaking with them, I understand immediately what they are sensing and thinking, the feelings that stir them, what they wish or will. They too are present as realities in my field of intuition, even when I pay them no attention. But it is not necessary that they and other objects likewise should be present precisely in my *field of perception.* For me real objects are there, definite, more or less familiar,

[1] From: *Ideas,* Edmund Husserl, Ch. 1. Reprinted by permission of The Macmillan Company, New York, and George Allen & Unwin, Ltd., London. 1931.

agreeing with what is actually perceived without being themselves perceived or even intuitively present. I can let my attention wander from the writing-table I have just seen and observed, through the unseen portions of the room behind my back to the verandah, into the garden, to the children in the summer-house, and so forth, to all the objects concerning which I precisely "know" that they are there and yonder in my immediate co-perceived surroundings—a knowledge which has nothing of conceptual thinking in it, and first changes into clear intuiting with the bestowing of attention, and even then only partially and for the most part very imperfectly.

But not even with the added reach of this intuitively clear or dark, distinct or indistinct *co-present* margin, which forms a continuous ring around the actual field of perception, does that world exhaust itself which in every waking moment is in some conscious measure "present" before me. It reaches rather in a fixed order of being into the limitless beyond. What is actually perceived, and what is more or less clearly co-present and determinate (to some extent at least), is partly pervaded, partly girt about with a *dimly apprehended depth or fringe of indeterminate reality*. I can pierce it with rays from the illuminating focus of attention with varying success. Determining representations, dim at first, then livelier, fetch me something out, a chain of such recollections takes shape, the circle of determinacy extends ever farther, and eventually so far that the connexion with the actual field of perception as the *immediate* environment is established. But in general the issue is a different one: an empty mist of dim indeterminacy gets studded over with intuitive possibilities or presumptions, and only the "form" of the world as "world" is foretokened. Moreover, the zone of indeterminacy is infinite. The misty horizon that can never be completely outlined remains necessarily there.

As it is with the world in its ordered being as a spatial present—the aspect I have so far been considering—so likewise is it with the world in respect to its *ordered being in the succession of time*. This world now present to me, and in every waking 'now' obviously so, has its temporal horizon, infinite in both directions, its known and unknown, its intimately alive and its unalive past and future. Moving freely within the moment of experience which brings what is present into my intuitional grasp, I can follow up these connexions of the reality which immediately surrounds me. I can shift my standpoint in space and time, look this way and that, turn temporally forwards and backwards; I can provide for myself constantly new and more or less clear and meaningful perceptions and representations, and images also more or less clear, in which I make intuitable to myself whatever can possibly exist really or supposedly in the steadfast order of space and time.

In this way, when consciously awake, I find myself at all times, and without my ever being able to change this, set in relation to a world which, through its constant changes, remains one and ever the same. It is continually "present" for me, and I myself am a member of it. Therefore this world is not there for me as a mere *world of facts and affairs*, but, with the same immediacy, as a *world of values*, a *world of goods*, a *practical world*. Without further effort on my part I find the things before me furnished not only with the qualities that befit their positive nature, but with value-characters such as beautiful or ugly, agreeable or disagreeable, pleasant or unpleasant, and so forth. Things in their immediacy stand there as objects to be used, the "table" with its "books", the "glass to drink from", the "vase", the "piano", and so forth. These values and practicalities, they too belong to *the constitution of the "actually present" objects as such*, irrespective of my turning or not turning to consider them or indeed any other objects. The same considerations apply of course just as well to the men and beasts in my surroundings as to "mere things". They are my "friends" or my "foes", my "servants" or "superiors", "strangers" or "relatives", and so forth.

28. *The "cogito". My natural world-about-me and the ideal worlds-about-me*

It is then to this world, *the world in which I find myself and which is also my world-about-me*, that the complex forms of my manifold and shifting *spontaneities* of consciousness stand related: observing in the interests of research the bringing of meaning into conceptual form through description; comparing and distinguishing, collecting and counting, presupposing and inferring, the theorizing activity of consciousness, in short, in its different forms and stages. Related to it likewise are the diverse acts and states of sentiment and will: approval and disapproval, joy and sorrow, desire and aversion, hope and fear, decision and action. All these, together with the sheer acts of the Ego, in which I become acquainted with the world as *immediately* given me, through spontaneous tendencies to turn towards it and to grasp it, are included under the one Cartesian expression: *Cogito*. In the natural urge of life I live continually in *this fundamental form of all "wakeful" living*, whether in addition I do or do not assert the *cogito*, and whether I am or am not "reflectively" concerned with the Ego and the *cogitare*. If I am so concerned, a new *cogito* has become livingly active, which for its part is not reflected upon, and so not objective for me.

I am present to myself continually as someone who perceives, represents, thinks, feels, desires, and so forth; and *for the most part* herein I find myself related in present experience to the fact-world which is constantly about me. But I am not always so related, not every *cogito* in which I live has for its *cogitatum* things, men, objects or contents of one kind or another. Perhaps I am busied with pure numbers and the laws they symbolize: nothing of this sort is present in the world about me, this world of "real fact". And yet the world of numbers also is there for me, as the field of objects with which I am arithmetically busied; while I am thus occupied some numbers or constructions of a numerical kind will be at the focus of vision, girt by an arithmetical horizon partly defined, partly not; but obviously this being-there-for-me, like the being there at all, is something very different from this. *The arithmetical world is there for me only when and so long as I occupy the arithmetical standpoint.* But the *natural* world, the world in the ordinary sense of the word, is *constantly there for me,* so long as I live naturally and look in its direction. I am then at the *"natural standpoint"*, which is just another way of stating the same thing. And there is no need to modify these conclusions when I proceed to appropriate to myself the arithmetical world, and other similar "worlds", by adopting the corresponding standpoint. The natural world *still remains "present"*, I am at the natural standpoint after as well as before, and in this respect *undisturbed by the adoption of new standpoints.* If my *cogito* is active *only* in the worlds proper to the new standpoints, the natural world remains unconsidered; it is now the background for my consciousness as act, but it is *not the encircling sphere within which an arithmetical world finds its true and proper place.* The two worlds are present together but *disconnected,* apart, that is, from their relation to the Ego, in virtue of which I can freely direct my glance or my acts to the one or to the other.

29. *The "other" ego-subject and the intersubjective natural world-about-me*

Whatever holds good for me personally, also holds good, as I know, for all other men whom I find present in my world-about-me. Experiencing them as men, I understand and take them as Ego-subjects, units like myself, and related to their natural surroundings. But this in such wise that I apprehend the world-about-them and the world-about-me objectively as one and the same world, which differs in each case only through affecting consciousness differently. Each has his place whence he sees the things that are present, and each enjoys accordingly different appearances of the things. For each, again, the fields of perception and memory actually present are different, quite apart from the fact that even that which is here intersubjectively known in common is known in different ways, is differently apprehended, shows different grades of clearness, and so forth. Despite all this, we come to understandings with our neighbours, and set up in common an objective spatio-temporal fact-world as *the world about us that is there for us all, and to which we ourselves none the less belong.*

30. *The general thesis of the natural standpoint*

That which we have submitted towards the characterization of what is given to us from the natural standpoint, and thereby of the natural standpoint itself, was a piece of pure description *prior to all "theory"*. In these studies we stand bodily aloof from all theories, and by 'theories' we here mean anticipatory ideas of every kind. Only as facts of our environment, not as agencies for uniting facts validly together, do theories concern us at all. But we do not set ourselves the task of continuing the pure description and raising it to a systematically inclusive and exhaustive characterization of the data, in their full length and breadth, discoverable from the natural standpoint (or from any standpoint, we might add, that can be knit up with the same in a common consent). A task such as this can and must—as scientific—be undertaken, and it is one of extraordinary importance, although so far scarcely noticed. Here it is not ours to attempt. For us who are striving towards the entrance-gate of phenomenology all the necessary work in this direction has already been carried out; the few features pertaining to the natural standpoint which we need are of a quite general character, and have already figured in our descriptions, and been sufficiently *and fully clarified.* We even made a special point of securing this full measure of clearness.

We emphasize a most important point once again in the sentences that follow: I find continually present and standing over against me the one spatio-temporal fact-world to which I myself belong, as do all other men found in it and related in the same way to it. This "fact-world", as the word already tells us, I find to *be out there,* and also *take it just as it gives itself to me as something that exists out there.* All doubting and rejecting of the data of the natural world leaves standing the *general thesis of the natural standpoint.* "The" world is as fact-world always there; at the most it is at odd points "other" than I supposed, this or that under such names as "illusion", "hallucination", and the like, must be struck *out of it,* so to speak; but the "it" remains ever, in the sense of the general thesis, a world that has its being out there. To know it more comprehensively, more trustworthily, more perfectly than the naïve lore of experience is able to do, and to solve all the problems of scientific knowledge which offer themselves upon its ground, that is the goal of the *sciences of the natural standpoint.*

31. *Radical alteration of the natural thesis "disconnexion", "bracketing"*

Instead now of remaining at this standpoint, we propose to alter it radically. Our aim must be to convince ourselves of the possibility of this alteration on grounds of principle.

The General Thesis according to which the real world about me is at all times known not merely in a general way as something apprehended, but as a fact-world *that has its being out there,* does *not* consist of course *in an act proper,* in an articulated judgment *about* existence. It is and remains something all the time the standpoint is adopted, that is, it endures persistently during the whole course of our life of natural endeavour. What has been at any time perceived clearly, or obscurely made present, in short everything out of the world of nature known through experience and prior to any thinking, bears in its totality and in all its articulated sections the character "present" "out there", a character which can function essentially as the ground of support for an explicit (predicative) existential judgment which is in agreement with the character it is grounded upon. If we express that same judgment, we know quite well that in so doing we have simply put into the form of a statement and grasped as a predication what already lay somehow in the original experience, or lay there as the character of something "present to one's hand".

We can treat the potential and unexpressed thesis exactly as we do the thesis of the explicit judgment. A procedure of this sort, *possible at any time,* is, for instance, *the attempt to doubt everything* which *Descartes,* with an entirely different end in view, with the purpose of setting up an absolutely indubitable sphere of Being, undertook to carry through. We link on here, but add directly and emphatically that this attempt to doubt everything should serve us *only as a device of method,* helping us to stress certain points which by its means, as though secluded in its essence, must be brought clearly to light.

The attempt to doubt everything has its place in the realm of our *perfect freedom.* We can *attempt to doubt* anything and everything, however convinced we may be concerning what we doubt, even though the evidence which seals our assurance is completely adequate.

Let us consider what is essentially involved in an act of this kind. He who attempts to doubt is attempting to doubt "Being" of some form or other, or it may be Being expanded into such predicative forms as "It is", "It is this or thus", and the like. The attempt does not affect the form of Being itself. He who doubts, for instance, whether an object, whose Being he does not doubt, is constituted in such and such a way, doubts *the way it is constituted.* We can obviously transfer this way of speaking from the doubting to the *attempt* at doubting. It is clear that we cannot doubt the Being of anything, and in the same act of consciousness (under the unifying form of simultaneity) bring what is substantive to this Being under the terms of the Natural Thesis, and so confer upon it the character of "being actually there" (*vorhanden*). Or to put the same in another way: we cannot at once doubt and hold for certain one and the same quality of Being. It is likewise clear that the *attempt* to doubt any object of awareness in respect of its *being actually there necessarily conditions a certain suspension* (*Aufhebung*) *of the thesis;* and it is precisely this that interests us. It is not a transformation of the thesis into its antithesis, of positive into negative; it is also not a transformation into presumption, suggestion, indecision, doubt (in one or another sense of the word); such shifting indeed is not at our free pleasure. *Rather is it something quite unique. We do not abandon the thesis we have adopted, we make no change in our conviction,* which remains in itself what it is so long as we do not introduce new motives of judgment, which we precisely refrain from doing. And yet the thesis undergoes a modification—whilst remaining in itself what it is, *we set it as it were "out of action", we "disconnect it", "bracket it".* It still remains there like the bracketed in the bracket, like the disconnected outside the connexional system. We can also say: The thesis is experience as lived (*Erlebnis*), *but we make "no use" of it,* and by that, of course, we do not indicate privation (as when we say of the ignorant that he makes no use of a certain thesis); in this case rather, as with all parallel expressions, we are dealing with indicators that point to a definite but *unique form of consciousness,* which clamps on to the original simple thesis (whether it actually or even predicatively *posits* existence or not), and transvalues it in a quite peculiar way. *This transvaluing is a concern of our full freedom, and is opposed to all cognitive attitudes* that would set themselves up as co-ordinate with *the thesis,* and yet within the unity of "simultaneity" remain incompatible with it, as indeed it is in general with all attitudes whatsoever in the strict sense of the word.

In *the attempt to doubt* applied to a thesis which, as we presuppose, is certain and tenaciously held, the "disconnexion" takes place in and with a modification of the antithesis, namely, with the *"supposition"* (*Ansetzung*) *of Non-Being,* which is thus the partial basis of the attempt to doubt. With Descartes this is so markedly the case that one can say that his universal attempt at doubt is just an attempt at universal denial. We disregard this possibility here, we are not interested in every analytic component of the attempt to doubt, nor therefore in its exact and completely sufficing analysis. *We extract only the phenomenon of "bracketing" or "disconnecting",* which is obviously not limited to that of the attempt to doubt, although it can be detached from it with special ease, but can appear *in other contexts also,* and with no less ease *independently.* In relation to *every* thesis and wholly uncoerced we can use this *peculiar ἐποχή, a certain refraining from judgment which is compatible with the unshaken and unshakable because self-evidencing conviction of Truth.* The thesis is "put out of action", bracketed, it passes off into the modified status of a "bracketed thesis", and the judgment *simpliciter* into *"bracketed judgment".*

Naturally one should not simply identify this consciousness with that of "mere supposal", that nymphs, for instance, are dancing in a ring; for thereby *no disconnecting* of a living conviction that goes on living takes place, although from another side the close relation of the two forms of consciousness lies clear. Again, we are not concerned here with supposal in the sense of *"assuming"* or *taking for granted,* which in the equivocal speech of current usage may also be expressed in the words: "I suppose (I make the assumption) that it is so and so."

Let us add further that nothing hinders us *from speaking of bracketing correlatively* also, in respect of *an objectivity to be posited,* whatever be the region or category to which it belongs. What is meant in this case is that *every thesis related to this objectivity* must be *disconnected* and changed into its bracketed counterpart. On closer view, moreover, the 'bracketing' image is from the outset better suited to the sphere of the object, just as the expression 'to put out of action' better suits the sphere of the Act or of Consciousness.

32. *The phenomenological ἐποχή*

We can now let the universal ἐποχή in the sharply defined and novel sense we have given to it step into the place of the Cartesian attempt at universal doubt. But on good grounds we *limit* the universality of this ἐποχή. For were it as inclusive as it is in general capable of being, then since every thesis and every judgment can be modified freely to any extent, and every objectivity that we can judge or criticize can be bracketed, no field would be left over for unmodified judgments, to say nothing of a science. But our design is just to discover a new scientific domain, such as might be won precisely *through the method of bracketing,* though only through a definitely limited form of it.

The limiting consideration can be indicated in a word.

We put out of action the general thesis which belongs to the essence of the natural standpoint, we place in brackets whatever it includes respecting the nature of Being: *this entire natural world therefore* which is continually "there for us", "present to our hand", and will ever remain there, is a "fact-world" of which we continue to be conscious, even though it pleases us to put it in brackets.

If I do this, as I am fully free to do, I do *not* then *deny* this "world", as though I were a sophist, *I do not doubt that it is there* as though I were a sceptic; but I use the "phenomenological" ἐποχή, which *completely bars* me *from using any judgment that concerns spatio-temporal existence* (*Dasein*).

Thus *all sciences which relate to this natural world,* though they stand never so firm to me, though they fill me with wondering admiration, though I am far from any thought of objecting to them in the least degree, *I disconnect them* all, *I make absolutely no use of their standards, I do not appropriate a single one of the propositions that enter into their systems, even though their evidential value is perfect, I take none of them, no one of them serves me for a foundation*—so long, that is, as it is understood, in the way these sciences themselves understand it, as a truth *concerning the realities* of this world. *I may accept it only after I have placed it in the bracket.* That means: only in the modified consciousness of the judgment as it appears in disconnexion, and *not as it figures within the science as its proposition, a proposition which claims to be valid and whose validity I recognize and make use of.*

The ἐποχή here in question will not be confused with that which positivism demands, and against which, as we were compelled to admit, it is itself an offender. We are not concerned at present with removing the preconceptions which trouble the pure positivity (*Sachlichkeit*) of research, with the constituting of a science "free from theory" and "free from metaphysics" by bringing all the grounding back to the immediate data, nor with the means of reaching such ends, concerning whose value there is indeed no question. What *we* demand lies along another line. The whole world as placed within the nature-setting and presented in experience as real, taken completely "free from all theory", just as it is in reality experienced, and made clearly manifest in and through the linkings of our experiences, has now no validity for us, it must be set in brackets, untested indeed but also uncontested. Similarly all theories and sciences, positivistic or otherwise, which relate to this world, however good they may be, succumb to the same fate.

CONSCIOUSNESS AND NATURAL REALITY[1]

33. *Intimation concerning "pure" or "transcendental consciousness" as phenomenological residuum*

We have learnt to understand the meaning of the phenomenological ἐποχή, but we are still quite in the dark as to its serviceability. In the first place it is not clear to what extent the limitation of the total field of the ἐποχή, as discussed in the previous pages, involves a real narrowing of its general scope. *For what can remain over when the whole world is bracketed, including ourselves and all our thinking* (*cogitare*)?

[1] From: *Ideas,* Edmund Husserl, Ch. 2. Reprinted by permission of The Macmillan Company, New York, and George Allen & Unwin, Ltd., London. 1931.

Since the reader already knows that the interest which governs these 'Meditations' concerns a new eidetic science, he will indeed at first expect the world as fact to succumb to the disconnexion, but not *the world as Eidos,* nor any other sphere of Essential Being. The disconnecting of the world does not as a matter of fact mean the disconnecting of the number series, for instance, and the arithmetic relative to it.

However, we do not take this path, nor does our goal lie in its direction. That goal we could also refer to as *the winning of a new region of Being, the distinctive character of which has not yet been defined,* a region of *individual* Being, like every genuine region. We must leave the sequel to teach us what that more precisely means.

We proceed in the first instance by showing up simply and directly what we see; and since the Being to be thus shown up is neither more nor less than that which we refer to on essential grounds as "pure experiences (*Erlebnisse*)", "pure consciousness" with its pure "correlates of consciousness", and on the other side its "pure Ego", we observe that it is from *the* Ego, *the* consciousness, *the* experience as given to us from the natural standpoint, that we take our start.

I, the real human being, am a real object like others in the natural world. I carry out *cogitationes,* "acts of consciousness" in both a narrower and a wider sense, and these acts, as belonging to this human subject, are events of the same natural world. And all my remaining experiences (*Erlebnisse*) likewise, out of whose changing stream the specific acts of the Ego shine forth in so distinctive a way, glide into one another, enter into combinations, and are being incessantly modified. Now in its *widest connotation* the expression *"consciousness"* (then indeed less suited for its purpose) includes *all* experiences (*Erlebnisse*), and entrenched in the natural standpoint as we are even in our scientific thinking, grounded there in habits that are most firmly established since they have never misled us, we take all these data of psychological reflexion as real world-events, as the experiences (*Erlebnisse*) of animal beings. So natural is it to us to see them only in this light that, though acquainted already with the possibility of a change of standpoint, and on the search for the new domain of objects, we fail to notice that it is from out these centres of experience (*Erlebnisse*) themselves that through the adoption of the new standpoint the new domain emerges. Connected with this is the fact that instead of keeping our eyes turned towards these centres of experience, we turned them away and sought the new objects in the ontological realms of arithmetic, geometry, and the like, whereby indeed nothing truly new was to be won.

Thus we fix our eyes steadily upon the sphere of Consciousness and study what it is that we find immanent in *it.* At first, without having yet carried out the phenomenological suspensions of the element of judgment, we subject this sphere of Consciousness in its essential nature to a systematic though in no sense exhaustive analysis. What we lack above all is a certain general insight into the essence of *consciousness in general,* and quite specially also of consciousness, so far as in and through its essential Being, the "natural" fact-world comes to be known. In these studies we go so far as is needed to furnish the full insight at which we have been aiming, to wit, *that Consciousness in itself has a being of its own which in its absolute uniqueness of nature remains unaffected by the phenomenological disconnexion.* It therefore remains over as a *"phenomenological residuum"*, as a region of Being which is in principle unique, and can become in fact the field of a new science—the science of Phenomenology.

Through this insight the "phenomenological" ἐποχή will for the first time deserve its name; to exercise it in full consciousness of its import will turn out to be the necessary operation which *renders "pure" consciousness accessible to us, and subsequently the whole phenomenological region.* And thus we shall be able to understand why this region and the new science attached to it was fated to remain unknown. From the natural standpoint nothing can be seen except the natural world. So long as the possibility of the phenomenological standpoint was not grasped, and the method of relating the objectivities which emerge therewith to a primordial form of apprehension had not been devised, the phenomenological world must needs have remained unknown, and indeed barely divined at all.

We would add yet the following to our terminology: Important motives which have their ground in epistemological requirements justify us in referring to "pure" consciousness, of which much is yet to be said, also as *transcendental consciousness,* and the operation through which it is acquired as *transcendental* ἐποχή. On grounds of method this operation will split up into different steps of "disconnexion" or "bracketing", and thus our method will assume the character of a graded reduction. For this reason we propose to speak, and even preponderatingly, of *phenomenological reductions* (though, in respect of their unity as a whole, we would speak in unitary form of *the* phenomenological reduction). From the epistemological viewpoint we would also speak of transcendental reductions. Moreover, these and *all* our terms must be understood exclusively in accordance with the sense which *our* presentations indicate for them, but not in any other one which history or the terminological habits of the reader may favour.

34. *The essence of consciousness as theme of inquiry*

We start with a series of observations within which we are not troubled with any phenomenological ἐποχή. We are directed to an "outer world", and, without forsaking the natural standpoint, reflect psychologically on our Ego and its experience (*Erleben*). We busy ourselves, precisely as we would have done if we had never heard of the new viewpoint, with *the essential nature of "the consciousness of some-*

thing", following, for instance, our consciousness of the existence of material things, living bodies and men, or that of technical and literary works, and so forth. We adhere to our general principle that each individual event has its essence that can be grasped in its eidetic purity, and in this purity must belong to a field available to eidetic inquiry. In accordance herewith the universal fact of nature conveyed by the words "I am", "I think", "I have a world over against me", and the like, has also its essential content, and it is on this exclusively that we now intend to concentrate. Thus we rehearse to ourselves by way of illustration certain conscious experiences chosen at random, and in their individuality just as they are in their natural setting as real facts of human life, and we make these present to ourselves through memory or in the free play of fancy. On the ground of illustrations such as these, which we assume to be presented with perfect clearness, we grasp and fix in adequate ideation the pure essences that interest us. The individual facts, the fact-character of the natural world in general, thereby escapes our theoretical scrutiny—as in all cases where our inquiry is purely eidetic.

We limit still further the theme of our inquiry. Its title ran: Consciousness, or more distinctly *Conscious experience* (*Erlebnis*) *in general,* to be taken in an extremely wide sense, about whose exact definition we are fortunately not concerned. Exact definitions do not lie at the threshold of analysis of the kind we are here making, but are a later result involving great labour. As starting-point we take consciousness in a pregnant sense which suggests itself at once, most simply indicated through the Cartesian *cogito,* "I think". As is known, Descartes understood this in a sense so wide as to include every case of "I perceive, I remember, I fancy, I judge, feel, desire, will", and all experiences of the Ego that in any way resemble the foregoing, in all the countless fluctuations in their special patterns. The Ego itself to which they are all related, or which in very differing ways "lives in" them, active, passive, spontaneous, in receptive or any other "attitude", and indeed the Ego in any and every sense, we leave at first out of consideration. We shall be concerned with it later, and fundamentally. For the present there is sufficient other material to serve as support for our analysis and grasp of the essential. And we shall find ourselves forthwith referred thereby to enveloping connexions of experience which compel us to widen our conception of a conscious experience beyond this circle of specific *cogitationes.*

We shall consider conscious experiences *in the concrete fullness and entirety* with which they figure in their concrete context—the *stream of experience*—and to which they are closely attached through their own proper essence. It then becomes evident that every experience in the stream which our reflexion can lay hold on has *its own essence open to intuition,* a "content" which can be considered in its *singularity in and for itself*. We shall be concerned to grasp this individual content of the *cogitatio* in its *pure* singularity, and to describe it in its general features, excluding everything which is not to be found in the *cogitatio* as it is in itself. We must likewise describe the *unity of consciousness* which is demanded *by the intrinsic nature of the cogitationes,* and so necessarily demanded that they could not be without this unity.

35. *The cogito as "act". The modal form of marginal actuality*

Let us start with an example. In front of me, in the dim light, lies this white paper. I see it, touch it. This perceptual seeing and touching of the paper as the full concrete experience *of* the paper that lies here as given in truth precisely with these qualities, precisely with this relative lack of clearness, with this imperfect definition, appearing to me from this particular angle—is a *cogitatio,* a conscious experience. The paper itself with its objective qualities, its extension in space, its objective position in regard to that spatial thing I call my body, is not *cogitatio,* but *cogitatum,* not perceptual experience, but something perceived. Now that which is perceived can itself very well be a conscious experience; but it is evident that an object such as a material thing, this paper, for instance, as given in perceptual experience, is in principle other than an experience, a being of a completely different kind.

Before pursuing this point farther, let us amplify the illustration. In perception properly so-called, as an explicit awareness (*Gewahren*), I am turned towards the object, to the paper, for instance, I apprehend it as being this here and now. The apprehension is a singling out, every perceived object having a background in experience. Around and about the paper lie books, pencils, ink-well, and so forth, and these in a certain sense are also "perceived", perceptually there, in the "field of intuition"; but whilst I was turned towards the paper there was no turning in their direction, nor any apprehending of them, not even in a secondary sense. They appeared and yet were not singled out, were not posited on their own account. Every perception of a thing has such a zone of *background intuitions* (or background awarenesses, if "intuiting" already includes the state of being turned towards), and this also is a *"conscious experience",* or more briefly a "consciousness *of"* all indeed that in point of fact lies in the co-perceived objective "background". We are not talking here of course of that which is to be found as an "objective" element in the objective space to which the background in question may belong, of all the things and thing-like events which a valid and progressive experience may establish there. What we say applies exclusively to that zone of consciousness which belongs to the model essence of a perception as "being turned towards an object", and further to that which belongs to the proper essence of this zone itself. But it is here implied that certain modifications of the original experience are possible, which we refer to as a free turning of the "look"—not precisely nor merely of the physical but of the *"men-*

tal look"—from the paper at first *descried* to objects which had already appeared before, of which we had been "implicitly" aware, and whereof *subsequent* to the directing of one's look thither we are explicitly aware, perceiving them "attentively", or "noticing them near by".

We are aware of things not only in perception, but also consciously in recollections, in representations similar to recollections, and also in the free play of fancy; and this in "clear intuition" it may be, or without noticeable perceptibility after the manner of "dim" presentations; they float past us in different "characterizations" as real, possible, fancied, and so forth. All that we have stated concerning perceptual experiences holds good, obviously, of these other experiences, essentially different as they are. We shall not think of confusing the *objects of which we are aware* under these forms of consciousness (the fancy-shaped nymphs, for instance) with the conscious experiences themselves which are a consciousness *of* them. Then, again, we know that it is the essence of all such experiences—taking the same, as always, in their concrete fullness—to show that remarkable modification which transfers consciousness in the *mode of actual orientation* to consciousness in *the mode of non-actuality* and conversely. At the one time the experience is, so to speak, *"explicitly"* aware of its objective content, at the other implicitly and merely *potentially*. The objective factor, whether in perception, memory, or fancy, may already be appearing to us, but *our mental gaze is not yet "directed" towards it,* not even in a secondary sense, to say nothing of being "busied" with it in some special way.

Similar remarks apply to all and any of the *cogitationes* in the sense illustrated by Descartes' use of the term, to all experiences of thought, feeling and will, except that, as will be emphasized (in the next paragraph), the "directedness towards", the "being turned towards", which is the distinctive mark of focal actuality, does not coincide, as in the favourite because simplest examples of sensory presentations, with singling out and noting the objects we are aware of. It is also obviously true of all such experiences that the focal is girt about with a "zone" of the marginal; *the stream of experience can never consist wholly of focal actualities.* These indeed determine, in a very general sense which must be extended beyond the circle of our illustrations, and through the contrast with marginal actualities already drawn, the *pregnant* meaning of the expression "cogito", "I have *consciousness* of something", "I perform an *act* of consciousness". In order to keep this well-established concept purely separate, we propose to reserve for it exclusively the Cartesian expressions *cogito* and *cogitationes,* unless through some addition, such as "marginal" or the like, we expressly indicate the modified use we are making of the term.

We can define a *"wakeful" Ego* as one that within its stream of experience is continually conscious in the specific form of the *cogito;* which, of course, does not mean that it can and does bring these experiences persistently or in general to predicative expression. Ego-subjects include animals. But, according to what we have said above, it belongs to the essence of the stream of experience of a wakeful Self that the continuously prolonged chain of *cogitationes* is constantly enveloped in a medium of dormant actuality (*Inaktualität*), which is ever prepared to pass off into the wakeful mode (*Aktualität*), as conversely the wakeful into the dormant.

36. *Intentional experience. Experience in general*

However drastic the change which the experiences of a wakeful Consciousness undergo in their transition into the dormant state, the experiences as modified share the essential nature of the original experiences in an important respect. It belongs as a general feature to the essence of every actual *cogito* to be a consciousness *of* something. But according to what we have already said, the *modified cogitatio is likewise and in its own way Consciousness,* and *of the same* something as with the corresponding unmodified consciousness. Thus the essential property of Consciousness in its general form is preserved in the modification. All experiences which have these essential properties in common are also called *"intentional experiences"* (acts in the *very wide sense* of the *Logical Studies*); in so far as they are a consciousness of something they are said to be *"intentionally related"* to this something.

We must, however, be quite clear on this point that *there is no question here of a relation between a psychological event—called experience (Erlebnis)—and some other real existence (Dasein)—called Object*—or of a *psychological connexion* obtaining between the one and the other *in objective reality*. On the contrary, we are concerned with experiences in their essential purity, with *pure essences,* and with that which is *involved in* the essence *"a priori," in unconditioned necessity*.

That an experience is the consciousness of something: a fiction, for instance, the fiction of this or that centaur; a perception, the perception of its "real" object; a judgment, the judgment concerning its subject-matter, and so forth, this does not relate to the experimental fact as lived within the world, more specifically within some given psychological context, but to the pure essence grasped ideationally as pure idea. In the very essence of an experience lies determined not only *that,* but also *whereof* it is a consciousness, and in what determinate or indeterminate sense it is this. So too in the essence of consciousness as dormant lies included the variety of wakeful *cogitationes,* into which it can be differentiated through the modification we have already referred to as "the noticing of what was previously unnoticed".

Under *experiences* in the *widest sense* we understand whatever is to be found in the stream of experience, not only therefore intentional experiences, *cogitationes* actual and potential taken in their full concreteness, but all the real (*reellen*) phases to be found in this stream and in its concrete sections.

For it is easily seen that *not every real phase* of the concrete unity of an intentional experience has itself the *basic character of intentionality,* the property of being a "consciousness of something". This is the case, for instance, with all *sensory data,* which play so great a part in the perceptive intuitions of things. In the experience of the perception of this white paper, more closely in those components of it related to the paper's quality of whiteness, we discover through properly directed noticing the sensory datum "white". This "whiteness" is something that belongs inseparably to the essence of the concrete perception, as a real (*reelles*) concrete constitutive portion of it. As the content which presents the whiteness of the paper as it appears to us it is the *bearer of* an intentionality, but not itself a consciousness of something. The same holds good of other data of experience, of the so-called *sensory feelings,* for instance. We shall be speaking of these at greater length in a later context.

37. *The "directedness" of the pure ego in the cogito, and the noticing that apprehends*

Though we are unable at this point to proceed farther with our descriptive analysis of intentional experiences in their essential nature, we would single out certain aspects as noteworthy in relation to further developments. If an intentional experience is actual, carried out, that is, after the manner of the *cogito,* the subject "directs" itself within it towards the intentional object. To the *cogito* itself belongs an immanent "glancing-towards" the object, a directedness which from another side springs forth from the "Ego", which can therefore never be absent. This glancing of the Ego towards something is in harmony with the act involved, perceptive in perception, fanciful in fancy, approving in approval, volitional in will, and so forth. This means, therefore, that this having in one's glance, in one's mental eye, which belongs to the *essence* of the *cogito,* to the act as such, is not in itself in turn a proper act, and in particular should not be confused with a perceiving (in however wide a sense this term be used), or with any other types of act related to perceptions. It should be noticed that *intentional* object of a consciousness (understood as the latter's full correlate) is by no means to be identified with *apprehended* object. We are accustomed without further thought to include the being apprehended in the concept of the object (of that generally which stands over against the subject), since in so far as we think of it and say something *about* it, we have made it into an object in the sense of something apprehended. In the widest sense of the word, apprehending an object (*Erfas-*

sen) coincides with mindfully heeding it (*achten*), and noting its nature (*bemerken*), whether attentively as a special case, or cursorily, provided at least that these expressions are used in their customary sense. *This heeding or apprehending is not to be identified with the modus of "cogito" in general,* that of actuality, but seen more closely, with a *special act-modus* which every consciousness or every act which does not yet possess it can assume. Should it do this, its intentional object is not only known in a general way and brought within the directed glance of the mind, but is an apprehended and noted object. A turning towards a Thing, to be sure, cannot take place otherwise than in the way of apprehension, and the same holds good of all *objectivities that are "plainly presentable":* here a turning towards (be it even in fancy) is *eo ipso* an "apprehending" and a "heeding". But in the act of valuation we are turned towards values, in acts of joy to the enjoyed, in acts of love to the beloved, in acting to the action, and *without* apprehending all this. The intentional object rather, that which is valued, enjoyed, beloved, hoped as such, the action as action, first becomes an apprehended object through a distinctively *"objectifying" turn of thought.* If one is turned towards some matter absorbed in appreciation, the apprehension of the matter is no doubt included in the total attitude; but it is not the *mere* matter in general, but the matter *valued* or the *value* which is (and the point will concern us more in detail later on) *the complete intentional correlate of the act of valuation.* Thus *"to be turned in appreciation* towards some matter" does not already imply *"having"* the value *"for object"* in the special sense of object apprehended, as indeed we must have the object if we are to predicate anything of it; and similarly in regard to all logical acts which are related to it.

Thus in acts like those of appreciation we have an *intentional object in a double sense:* we must distinguish between the *"subject matter" pure and simple* and the *full intentional object,* and corresponding to this, a *double intentio,* a twofold directedness. If we are directed towards some matter in an act of appreciation, the direction towards the matter in question is a noting and apprehending of it; but we are "directed"—only not in an apprehending way—also to the value. Not merely the *representing of the matter* in question, but also the *appreciating* which includes this representing, has the modus of actuality.

But we must hasten to add that it is only in respect of simple acts of valuation that the matter stands so simply. In general, acts of sentiment and will are consolidated upon a higher level, and the intentional objectivity also differentiates itself accordingly: there is also a complicating of the ways in which the objects included in the unitary total objectivity come under the directed mental glance. But in any case the following main propositions hold good:—

In every act some mode of heeding (Achtsamkeit) holds sway. But wherever it is not the plain consciousness of a subject-matter, wherever some further "attitude towards" the subject-matter is grounded in such consciousness, *subject-matter and full intentional object* ("subject-matter" and "value", for instance), likewise *heeding the object and mentally scrutinizing it, separate out the one from the other.* But at the same time the possibility of a modification remains an essential property of these grounded acts, a modification whereby their full intentional objects become noticed, and in this sense *"represented"* objects, which now, from their side, become capable of serving as bases for explanations, relations, conceptual renderings, and predications. Thanks to this objectification we find facing us in the natural setting, and therefore *as members of the natural world,* not natural things merely, but values and practical objects of every kind, cities, streets with street-lighting arrangements, dwellings, furniture, works of art, books, tools, and so forth.

38. *Reflexions on acts. Immanent and transcendent perceptions*

We add the following: Living in the *cogito* we have not got the *cogitatio* consciously before us as intentional object; but it can at any time become this: to its essence belongs in principle the possibility of a *"reflexive" directing of the mental glance* towards itself naturally in the form of a new *cogitatio* and by way of a simple apprehension. In other words, every *cogitatio* can become the object of a so-called "inner perception", and eventually the object of a *reflexive* valuation, an approval or disapproval, and so forth. The same holds good in correspondingly modified ways, not only of real acts in the sense of acts of perception (*Aktimpressionen*), but also of acts of which we are aware "in" fancy, "in" memory, or "in" empathy, when we understand and re-live the acts of others. We can reflect "in" *memory, empathy,* and so forth, and in these various possible modifications make the acts we are "therein" aware of into objects of our apprehending and of the attitude-expressing acts which are grounded in the apprehension.

We connect with the foregoing the distinction between *transcendent* and *immanent* perceptions and acts generally. We avoid talking about inner and outer perception as there are serious objections to this way of speaking. We give the following explanations:—

Under *acts immanently directed,* or, to put it more generally, under *intentional experiences immanently related,* we include those acts which are *essentially* so constituted *that their intentional objects, when these exist at all, belong to the same stream of experience as themselves.* We have an instance of this wherever an act is related to an act (a *cogitatio* to a *cogitatio*) of the same Ego, or likewise an act to a given sensible affect of the same Ego, and so forth. Consciousness and its object build up an individual unity purely set up through experiences.

Intentional experiences for which this does *not* hold good are *tran-*

scendentally directed, as, for instance, all acts directed towards essences, or towards the intentional experiences of other Egos with other experience-streams; likewise all acts directed upon things, upon realities generally, as we have still to show.

In the case of an immanently directed, or, more briefly, *immanent* (the so-called "inner") *perception, perception and perceived essentially* constitute *an unmediated unity, that of a single concrete cogitatio.* The perceiving here so conceals its object in itself that it can be separated from it only through abstraction, and as something *essentially incapable of subsisting alone.* If the perceived is an intentional experience, as when we reflect upon some still lively conviction (expressed, it may be, in the form: I am convinced that—) we have a nexus of two intentional experiences, of which at least the superimposed one is dependent, and, moreover, not merely grounded in the deeper-lying, but at the same time intentionally directed towards it.

This type of *real* (*reellen*) *"self-containedness"* (in strictness a similitude only) is a *distinctive characteristic of immanent perception and of the mental attitudes founded upon it;* it is lacking in most of the other cases of immanent relationship between intentional experiences, as, for instance, in the remembering of remembering. The remembered remembering of yesterday does not belong to the present remembering as a real constituent of its concrete unity. The present remembering could still retain its *own* full essential nature, even though yesterday's in truth never took place, whilst the latter, on the other hand, *assuming that* it really happened, belongs necessarily with it to one and the same unbroken stream of experience, which through manifold concrete experiences mediates continuously between the two. In this respect transcendent perceptions and the other transcendently related intentional experiences are clearly ordered very differently. The perception of a thing not only does not contain in itself, in its real (*reellen*) constitution, the thing itself, it is also without *any essential unity with it,* its existence naturally presupposed. *A unity determined purely by the proper essence of the experiences themselves can be only the unity of the stream of experience,* or, which is the same thing, it is only with experiences that an experience can be bound into one whole of which the essence in its totality envelops these experiences' own essences and is grounded within them. This proposition will become still clearer in the sequel and its great significance will become apparent.

39. *Consciousness and natural reality. The view of the "man in the street"*

All the essential characteristics of experience and consciousness which we have reached are for us necessary steps towards the attainment of the end which is unceasingly drawing us on, the discovery, namely, of the essence of that *"pure" consciousness* which is to fix the limits of the phenomenological field. Our inquiries were eidetic; but the individual instances of the essences we have referred to as experience, stream of experience, "consciousness" in all its senses, belonged as real events to the natural world. To that extent we have not abandoned the ground of the natural standpoint. Individual consciousness is interwoven with the *natural world* in a *twofold* way: it is some *man's* consciousness, or that of some *man* or *beast,* and in a large number at least of its particularizations it is a consciousness of this world. *In respect now of this intimate attachment with the real world, what is meant by saying that consciousness has an essence "of its own",* that with other consciousness it constitutes a self-contained *connexion determined purely through this, its own essence,* the connexion, namely, of the stream of consciousness? Moreover, since we can interpret consciousness in the widest sense to cover eventually whatever the concept of experience includes, the question concerns the experience-stream's own essential nature and that of all its components. To what extent, in the first place, must the *material world* be fundamentally different in kind, *excluded from the experience's own essential nature?* And if it is this, if over against all consciousness and the essential being proper to it, it is that which is *"foreign"* and *"other",* how can consciousness be *interwoven* with it, and consequently with the whole world that is alien to consciousness? For it is easy to convince oneself that the material world is not just any portion of the natural world, but its fundamental stratum to which all other real being is *essentially* related. It still fails to include the souls of men and animals; and the new factor which these introduce is first and foremost their "experiencing" together with their conscious relationship to the world surrounding them. *But here consciousness and thinghood form a connected whole,* connected within the particular psychological unities which we call *animalia,* and in the last resort within the *real unity of the world as a whole.* Can the unity of a whole be other than made one through the essential proper nature of its parts, which must therefore have some *community of essence* instead of a fundamental heterogeneity?

To be clear, let us seek out the ultimate sources whence the general thesis of the world which I adopt when taking up the natural standpoint draws its nourishment, thereby enabling me as a conscious being to discover over against me an existing world of things, to ascribe to myself in this world a body, and to find for myself within this world a proper place. This ultimate source is obviously *sensory experience.* For our purpose, however, it is sufficient to consider *sensory perception,* which in a certain proper sense plays among experiencing acts the part of an original experience, whence all other experiencing acts draw a chief part of their power to serve as a ground. Every perceiving consciousness has this peculiarity, that it is the consciousness of *the em-*

bodied (*leibhaftigen*) *self-presence of an individual object,* which on its own side and in a pure logical sense of the term is an individual or some logico-categorical modification of the same.[2] In our own instance, that of sensory perception, or, in distincter terms, perception of a world of things, the logical individual is the Thing; and it is sufficient for us to treat the perception of things as representing all other perceptions (of properties, processes, and the like).

The natural wakeful life of our Ego is a continuous perceiving, actual or potential. The world of things and our body within it are continuously present to our perception. How then does and can *Consciousness itself* separate out as a *concrete thing in itself,* from that within it, of which we are conscious, namely, the *perceived being, "standing over against"* consciousness *"in and for itself"?*

I meditate first as would the man "in the street". I see and grasp the thing itself in its bodily reality. It is true that I sometimes deceive myself, and not only in respect of the perceived constitution of the thing, but also in respect of its being there at all. I am subject to an illusion or hallucination. The perception is not then "genuine". But if it is, if, that is, we can "confirm" its presence in the actual context of experience, eventually with the help of correct empirical thinking, then the perceived thing *is real* and itself really given, and that bodily in perception. Here perceiving considered simply as consciousness, and apart from the body and the bodily organs, appears as something in itself essenceless, an empty looking of an empty "Ego" towards the object itself which comes into contact with it in some astonishing way.

40. *"Primary" and "secondary" qualities. The bodily given thing "mere appearance" of the "physically true"*

If as a "man in the street" misled by sensibility I have indulged the inclination to spin out such thoughts as these, now, as "a man of science", I call to mind the familiar distinction between *secondary* and *primary* qualities, according to which the specific qualities of sense should be "merely subjective" and only the geometrico-physical qualities "objective". The colour and sound of a thing, its smell, its taste, and so forth, though they appear to cleave to the thing "bodily" as though belonging to its essence, are not themselves and as they appear to be, real, but mere "signs" of certain primary qualities. But if I recall familiar theories of Physics, I see at once that the meaning of such much-beloved propositions can hardly be the one which the words warrant: as though really only the "specific" sensory qualities of the perceived thing were mere appearance; which would come to saying that the "primary" qualities which remain after the *subtraction* of these same sensory

[2] Cf. [*Ideas*], §15, p. 75 et seq.

qualities belonged to the same thing as it objectively and truly is, together with other such qualities which did not show forth as appearance. So understood, the old Berkeleian objection would hold good, namely, that extension, this essential nucleus of corporeality and all primary qualities, is unthinkable apart from the secondary qualities. Rather *the whole essential content of the perceived thing,* all that is present in the body, with all its qualities and all that can ever be perceived, *is "mere appearance",* and the *"true thing" is that of physical science.* When the latter defines the given thing exclusively through concepts such as atoms, ions, energies, and so forth, and in every case as space-filling processes whose sole *characteristica* are mathematical expressions, its reference is to *something that transcends the whole content of the thing as present to us in bodily form.* It cannot therefore mean even the thing as lying in natural sensible space; in other words, its physical space cannot be the space of the world of bodily perception: otherwise it would also fall under the Berkeleian objection.

The *"true Being"* would therefore be entirely and *fundamentally something that is defined otherwise than as that which is given in perception as corporeal reality,* which is given exclusively through its sensory determinations, among which must also be reckoned the sensori-spatial. *The thing as strictly experienced gives the mere "this", an empty X which becomes the bearer of mathematical determinations, and of the corresponding mathematical formulæ,* and exists not in perceptual space, but in an *"objective space",* of which the former is the mere "symbol", *a Euclidean manifold of three dimensions that can be only symbolically represented.*

Let us then accept this. Let that which is given bodily in any perception be, as is taught there, "mere appearance", in principle "merely subjective", and yet no empty illusion. Yet that which is given in perception serves in the rigorous method of natural science for the valid determination, open to anyone to carry out and to verify through his own insight of that transcendent being whose "symbol" it is. The sensory content of that which is given in perception itself continues indeed to be reckoned as other than the true thing as it is in itself, but the *substratum,* the bearer (the empty X) of the perceived determinations still continues to count as that which is determined through exact method in the form of physical predicates. *All physical knowledge serves accordingly, and in the reverse sense, as an indicator of the course of possible experiences with the sensory things found in them and the occurrences in which they figure.* Thus it helps us to find our way about in the world of actual experience in which we all live and act.

41. *The real nature of perception and its transcendent object*

All this being presupposed, *what is it, we ask, that belongs to the concrete real nature (reellen Bestande) of the perception itself, as cogitatio?* Not the physical thing, as is obvious: radically transcendent as it is, transcendent over against the whole "world of appearance". But *even the latter,* though we refer to it habitually as "merely subjective", does not belong in all its detail of things and events to the real nature of perception, but is opposed to it as "transcendent". Let us consider this more closely. We have indeed already spoken of the transcendence of the thing, but only in passing. It concerns us now to win a deeper insight into *the relation of the transcendent to the Consciousness* that knows it, and to see how this mutual connexion, which has its own riddles, is to be understood.

We shut off the whole of physics and the whole domain of theoretical thought. We remain within the framework of plain intuition and the syntheses that belong to it, including perception. It is then evident that intuition and the intuited, perception and the thing perceived, though essentially related to each other, are in principle and of necessity *not really (reell) and essentially one and united.*

We start by taking an example. Keeping this table steadily in view as I go round it, changing my position in space all the time, I have continually the consciousness of the bodily presence out there of this one and self-same table, which in itself remains unchanged throughout. But the perception of the table is one that changes continuously, it is a continuum of changing perceptions. I close my eyes. My other senses are inactive in relation to the table. I have now no perception of it. I open my eyes, and the perception returns. The perception? Let us be more accurate. Under no circumstances does it return to me individually the same. Only the table is the same, known as identical through the synthetic consciousness which connects the new perception with the recollection. The perceived thing can be, without being perceived, without my being aware of it even as potential only (in the way of inactuality, as previously[3] described), and perhaps without itself changing at all. But the perception itself is what it is within the steady flow of consciousness, and is itself constantly in flux; the perceptual now is ever passing over into the adjacent consciousness of the just-past, a new now simultaneously gleams forth, and so on. The perceived thing in general, and all its parts, aspects, and phases, whether the quality be primary or secondary, are necessarily transcendent to the perception, and on the same grounds everywhere. The colour of the thing seen is not in principle a real phase of the consciousness of colour; it appears, but even while it is appearing the appearance can and *must*

[3] Cf. [*supra*], §35, esp. p. 184 [this volume].

be continually changing, as experience shows. The *same* colour appears "in" continuous varying patterns of *perspective colour-variations.* Similarly for every sensory quality and likewise for every spatial shape! One and the same shape (given *as* bodily the same) appears continuously ever again "in another way", in ever-differing perspective variations of shape. That is a necessary state of things, and it has obviously a more general bearing. For it is only in the interests of simplicity that we have illustrated our point by reference to a thing that appears unchanged in perception. The transfer to changes of any other sort is a perfectly simple proceeding.

An empirical consciousness of a self-same thing that looks "all-round" its object, and in so doing is continually confirming the unity of its own nature, essentially and necessarily possesses a manifold system of continuous patterns of appearances and perspective variations, in and through which all objective phases of the bodily self-given which appear in perception manifest themselves perspectively in definite continua. Every determinate feature has *its own* system of perspective variations; and for each of these features, as for the thing as a whole, the following holds good, namely, that it remains one and the same for the consciousness that in grasping it unites recollection and fresh perception synthetically together, despite interruption in the continuity of the course of actual perception.

We now see also what it is that really and indubitably belongs to the real nature of the concrete intentional experiences which we refer to here as perceptions of things. Whilst the thing is the intentional unity, that which we are conscious of as one and self-identical within the continuously ordered flow of perceptual patterns as they pass off the one into the other, these patterns themselves have always their *definite descriptive nature* (*Bestand*), which is *essentially* correlated with that unity. To every phase of perception there necessarily belongs, for instance, a definite content in the way of perspective variations of colour, shape, and so forth. They are counted among the *"sensory data"*, data of a particular region with determinate divisions, which within every such division gather together into concrete unities of experience *sui generis* (*sensory "fields"*); which, further, in ways we cannot here describe more closely, are ensouled within the concrete unity of perception through *"apprehensions"*, and, in this ensouling, exercise the *"exhibitive* (*darstellende*) *function"*, or in unison with it constitute that which we call the "appearing of" colour, shape, and so forth. This, after interweaving itself with still further features, constitutes the real nature (*Bestand*) of perception, which is the consciousness of one identical thing derived through the confluence into one *unity of apprehension,* a confluence grounded in the *essential Being* of the apprehensions unified, and again through the possibility, grounded in the very *essence* of different unities of this kind, of *syntheses of identification.*

We must keep this point clearly before our eyes, that the sensory data which exercise the function of presenting colour, smoothness, shape, and so forth perspectively (the function of "exhibiting"), differ wholly and in principle from colour, smoothness, shape *simpliciter,* in short, from all the generic aspect which *a thing* can show. *The perspective variation* (*the "Abschattung"*), *though verbally similar to the perspected variable* (*the "Abgeschattetes"*), *differs from it generically and in principle.* The perspective variation is an experience. But experience is possible only as experience, and not as something spatial. The perspected variable, however, is in principle possible only as spatial (it is indeed spatial in its essence), but not possible as experience. In particular it is also nonsense to take the perspective shape-variation (that of a triangle, for instance) for something spatial and capable of being in space, and whoever does this is confusing it with the perspected variable, the shape that manifests itself through the appearances. How further we are to separate with systematic thoroughness the different real (*reellen*) phases of the perception as *cogitatio* (as contrasted with the phases of the *cogitatum* which transcends it), and to characterize them in accordance with their natural divisions, very difficult to trace, in part, that is a theme for inquiries on a large scale.

42. *Being as consciousness and being as reality. Intrinsic difference between the modes of tuition*

The studies we have just completed left us with the transcendence of the thing over against the perception of it, and as a further consequence, over against every consciousness generally which refers to the thing; not merely in the sense that the thing as a real (*reelles*) constituent part of consciousness is as a matter of fact not to be found—the whole situation rather concerns eidetic insight: in *absolutely unconditioned* generality or necessity, a thing cannot be given as really immanent in any possible perception or, generally, in any possible consciousness. Thus a basic and essential difference arises between *Being as Experience* and *Being as Thing.* In principle it is a property of the regional essence experience (more specifically of the regional subdivision *cogitatio*), that it is perceivable through immanent perception, but it is of the essence of a spatial thing that this is not possible. When, as a deeper analysis teaches, it belongs to the essence of every thing-giving intuition that in unity with the given thing other data analogous to things can be apprehended through looking in the appropriate direction, detachable strata, and stages in the make-up of what appears as a thing—*"visual illusions",* for instance, in their various specifications—precisely the same holds good for them too: they are in principle transcendent entities.

Before pursuing somewhat farther this opposition between immanence and transcendence, we insert the following remark: Apart from perception, we find a variety of intentional experiences which essentially exclude the real immanence of their intentional objects, whatever for the rest the nature of these objects may be. This holds, for instance, of every representative activity: of every recollection, of the apprehension through empathy of the consciousness of others, and so forth. Naturally we should not confuse this transcendence with that which is here concerning us. The inability to be perceived immanently, and therefore, generally, to find a place in the system of experience belongs in essence and "in principle" [4] altogether to the thing as such, to every reality in that genuine sense which we have still to fix and make clear. Thus the Thing itself, *simpliciter,* we call transcendent. In so doing we give voice to the most fundamental and pivotal difference between ways of being, that between *Consciousness* and *Reality*.

This opposition between immanence and transcendence, as our exposition has further brought out, is accompanied by a *fundamental difference in the mode of being given.* Immanent and transcendent perception do not only differ generally in this, that the intentional object which has its lodgment in the character of the bodily self is in the one case really immanent in the perceiving, but not so in the other case; they differ much more through a mode of being given which embodies the difference in its essential form, and conveys it *mutatis mutandis* into all the representational modifications of perception, and into the correlated intuitions of memory and fancy. We perceive the Thing through the "perspective" manifestations of all its determinate qualities which in any given case are "real", and strictly "fall" within the perception. *An experience has no perspectives* (*Ein Erlebnis schattet sich nicht ab*). It is not an accidental caprice of the Thing nor an accident of "our human constitution" that "our" perception can reach the things themselves only and merely through their perspective modifications. On the contrary, it is evident, and it follows from the essential nature of spatial thing-hood (and in the widest sense inclusive of "visual illusions") that Being of this species can, in principle, be given in perceptions only by way of perspective manifestation; and it follows likewise from the essential nature of *cogitationes,* of experiences in general, that they exclude these perspective shadings; or, otherwise stated, when referring to that which has being in this region, anything of the nature of "appearing", or self-revealing through perspective variations, has simply no meaning. Where there is no Being in space, it is senseless to speak of seeing from different standpoints with a changing orientation, and under the different aspects thereby opened up, or through varying appearances and perspective shadings; on the

[4] We use the term "in principle" (*prinzipiell*) here, as in this work generally, in a rigorous sense, with reference to the highest and therefore most radical generalities or necessities of an essential character.

other hand, it is an essential necessity to be apprehended as such with apodeictic insight that spatial Being in general can be perceived by any Ego actual or possible only when presented in the way described. It can "appear" only with a certain "orientation", which necessarily carries with it sketched out in advance the system of arrangements which makes fresh orientations possible, each of which again corresponds to a certain "way of appearing", which we perhaps express as a being presented from this or that "aspect", and so forth. If we take the reference to ways of appearing to apply to ways of *experiencing* (it can also, as is clear from the description we have just given, bear a correlative ontic meaning), it comes to saying this, that it belongs to the essential nature of certain peculiarly constructed *types of experience,* or, more specifically, peculiarly constructed concrete perceptions, that the intentional element in them is known as a spatial thing; and that the ideal possibility of passing over into determinate, ordered, continuous perceptual patterns, which can always be continued, and are therefore never exhausted, belongs to their very essence. It lies then in the essential structure of these pattern-groups that they establish the unity of a *singly intentional* consciousness: the consciousness of a *single* perceptual thing appearing with ever-increasing completeness, from endlessly new points of view, and with ever-richer determinations. On the other hand, a spatial thing is no other than an intentional unity, which, in principle, can be given only as the unity of such ways of appearing.

43. *Light on a fundamental error*

It is thus a fundamental error to suppose that perception (and every other type of the intuition of things, each after its own manner) fails to come into contact with the thing itself. We are told that the thing in itself and in its itselfness is not given to us; that what every existent (*Seienden*) in principle possesses is the possibility of seeing things as they plainly are, and, more specifically, of perceiving them in an adequate perception which gives us the bodily self *without any mediation through "appearances"*. God, the Subject of absolutely perfect knowledge, and therefore also of every possible adequate perception, naturally possesses what to us finite beings is denied, the perception of things in themselves.

But this view is nonsensical. It implies that there is no *essential difference* between transcendent and immanent, that in the postulated divine intuition a spatial thing is a real (*reelles*) constituent, and indeed an experience itself, a constituent of the stream of the divine consciousness and the divine experience. The thought that the transcendence of the thing is that of an *image* or *sign* has proved misleading here. The image-theory is often zealously attacked and a sign-theory substituted for it. But the one and the other alike are not only incorrect but nonsensical. The spatial thing which we see is, despite all its transcendence, perceived, we are consciously aware of it as given in its *embodied form*. We are not given an image or a sign *in its place*. We must not substitute the consciousness of a sign or an image for a perception.

Between *perception* on the one hand and, on the other, *the presentation of a symbol in the form of an image or meaning* there is an unbridgeable and essential difference. With these types of presentation we intuit something, in the consciousness that it copies something else or indicates its meaning; and though we already have the one in the field of intuition, we are not directed towards it, but through the medium of a secondary apprehension are directed towards the other, that which is copied or indicated. There is nothing of all this in perception, as little as in plain recollection or fancy.

Through acts of immediate intuition we intuit a "self". No apprehensions at a higher level are built up on the basis of these apprehending acts of intuition; nothing is therefore known *for which* the intuited might serve as a "sign" or "image". And for this reason, therefore, it is said to be immediately intuited as "self". The same, in perception, is still uniquely characterized as "bodily" as contrasted with the modified character of "hovering before the mind", or being "presented to it" in memory or free fancy.[5] We collapse into nonsense when, as is ordinarily done, we completely mix up these modes of presentation with their essentially different constructions, and correlatively the data correspondingly presented: thus plain presentation with symbolic interpretation (whether on the basis of image or sign) and downright plain perception with both of these. The perception of things does not present something that is not present as though it were a recollection or a fancy; it presents and apprehends a Self in its bodily presence. It does this in accordance with the apprehended object's *own meaning,* and to suppose that it acts otherwise is just to run counter to its own proper sense. Moreover, if it is a question, as it is here, of the perception of things, its essential nature is to be a perception that works through perspectives; and correlatively it belongs to the meaning of its intentional object of the thing *as* given within it, to be perceivable, in principle, only through perceptions of such a kind, perceptions that imply perspectives.

[5] In my lectures delivered at Göttingen (and indeed since the summer term of 1904) I have substituted an improved version of the inadequate exposition which I gave in the *Logical Studies* (an exposition still influenced overmuch by the views of the dominant Psychology) dealing with the relations between these simple intuitions and those that are grounded in them, and have made detailed communications covering the researches that are leading me forward, and in the interval, moreover, have been influencing literary thought both in point of terminology and of literary substance. In the coming volumes of the *Fahrbuch* I hope to publish these and other studies which have for long been utilized in lectures.

44. *The merely phenomenal being of the transcendent, the absolute being of the immanent*

A certain *inadequacy* belongs, further, to the perception of things, and that too is an essential necessity. In principle a thing can be given only "in one of its aspects", and that not only means incompletely, in some sense or other imperfectly, but precisely that which presentation through perspectives prescribes. A thing is necessarily given in mere *"modes of appearing"*, and the necessary factors in this case are *a nucleus of what is "really presented"*, an outlying zone of apprehension consisting of *marginal "co-data" of an accessory kind* (*uneigentlicher*), and a more or less vague *indeterminacy*. And the meaning of this indeterminacy is once again foreshadowed by the general meaning of the thing perceived as such, or by the general and essential nature of this type of perception which we call thing-perception. The indeterminacy necessarily means the *determinability of a rigorously prescribed mode* (*Stils*). It *points forward to* possible patterns of perception, which, continually passing off into one another, coalesce in the unity of a single perception in which the continuously enduring thing in every new series of perspectives reveals ever again new "aspects" (or retraces the old). Meanwhile the subsidiary co-apprehended phases of the thing come gradually into the focus of real presentation as real data, the indeterminacies define themselves more clearly to turn at length into clear data themselves; contrariwise, what is clear passes back into the unclear, the presented into the non-presented, and so forth. *To remain for ever incomplete after this fashion is an ineradicable essential of the correlation Thing and Thing-perception.* If the meaning of Thing gets determined through what is given in Thing-perception (and what else could determine the meaning?), it must require such incompleteness, and we are referred of necessity to unified and continuous series of possible perceptions which, developed from any one of these, stretch out in an infinite number of directions in *systematic strictly ordered ways,* in each direction endlessly, and always dominated throughout by some unity of meaning. In principle a margin of determinable indeterminacy always remains over, however far we go along our empirical way, and however extended the continua of actual perceptions of the same thing which we may have treasured. No God can alter this is any way, any more than He can the equation $1 + 2 = 3$, or the stability of any other essential truth.

On broad lines we can always see that transcendent Being in general, whatever its genus may be, when understood as Being *for* an Ego, can become a datum only in a way analogous to that in which a thing is given, thus only through appearances. Otherwise it would really be a Being which could also become immanent; whereas what is immanently perceivable is this and *nothing more.* Only when we fall into the confusions we have indicated above, and have now cleared up, can we hold it possible that one and the same could at one time be given through appearance, in the form of transcendent perception, and at another through immanent perception.

Still, let us first develop from the other side also the specific contrast between Thing and Experience (*Erlebnis*). *Experience,* we said, does not present itself. This implies that the perception of experience is plain insight into something which in *perception is given* (or to be given) *as "absolute",* and not as an identity uniting modes of appearance through perspective continua. All that we have stated concerning the givenness of things here loses its meaning, and we must bring this home to ourselves in detail with full clearness. The experience of a feeling has no perspectives. If I look upon it, I have before me an absolute; it has no aspects which might present themselves now in this way, and now in that. In thought I can think truly or falsely about it, but that which is there at the focus of mental vision is there absolutely with its qualities, its intensity, and so forth. Contrariwise, the tone of a violin with its objective identity is given through perspectives, it has its changing forms of appearance. They differ according as I approach the violin or recede from it, according as I am in the concert hall itself or listen through its closed doors, and so forth. No way of appearing claims to rank as giving its data absolutely, although a certain type, appearing as normal within the compass of my practical interests, has a certain advantage; in the concert hall, at the "right" spot, I hear the tone "itself" as it "really" sounds. So likewise we say of everything in its visual relations that it has a normal appearance; we say of the colour, the form, and the thing as a whole which we see in ordinary daylight, and normally oriented in regard to us, so the thing really looks, that is its real colour, and the like. But that points only to *a kind of secondary objectification* within the compass of the total objectification of the thing, as we can easily convince ourselves. It is indeed clear that, if we were to hold fast to the "normal" form of appearance as the one and only form, and cut away all other varieties of appearance and the essential connexions with them, no vestige of the meaning of the givenness of the thing would be left over.

We therefore maintain: whereas it is an essential mark of what is given through appearances that no one of these gives the matter in question in an "absolute" form instead of presenting just one side of it, it is an essential mark of what is immanently given precisely to give an absolute that simply cannot exhibit aspects and vary them perspectively. It is also indeed self-evident that the perspectively varying sensory contents themselves, which, as real (*reell*), belong to our experience of the perception of the thing, function, no doubt, for something other as perspective variations, but are not themselves manifested in turn through perspective variation.

We must note the following distinction also: Even an experience

(*Erlebnis*) is not, and never is, perceived in its completeness, it cannot be grasped adequately in its full unity. It is essentially something that flows, and starting from the present moment we can swim after it, our gaze reflectively turned towards it, whilst the stretches we leave in our wake are lost to our perception. Only in the form of retention or in the form of retrospective remembrance have we any consciousness of what has immediately flowed past us. And in the last resort the whole stream of my experience is a unity of experience, of which it is in principle impossible "swimming with it" to obtain a complete perceptual grasp. But *this* incompleteness or "imperfection" which belongs to the essence of our perception of experience is fundamentally other than that which is of the essence of "transcendent" perception, perception through a presentation that varies perspectively through such a thing as appearance.

All the ways of being given, and the differences between these which we find in the sphere of perception, reappear, in modified form, in the *modifications connected with reproduction*. The presentings of things are set out through presentations whereby the perspective variations themselves, the apprehensions, and thus the pehnomena in their entirety and *through and through*, are modified *in reproduction*. We have also reproductions of experiences and acts of reproductive intuition in the manner of presentation and of reflexion in presentation. Here naturally there is no hint of reproduced perspective variations.

We now add the following case of contrast: It is of the essence of presentations to show gradual differences of relative clearness or dimness. Obviously also this difference in degree of perfection has nothing to do with that which relates to the conditions under which perspectively varying appearances are given to us. A presentation that is more or less clear does not in its graded changes of clearness pass through changes of perspective in the same sense as that which has shaped our own terminology, when we say that a spatial configuration, every quality that clothes it, and so the whole "appearing thing as such", changes perspectively in manifold ways, whether the presentation is clear or obscure. The reproduced presentation of a thing has its different possibilities of graded clearness, and this indeed for every form of perspective variation. As one sees, the question concerns differences in different dimensions. It is also obvious that the differences which we make in the sphere of perception itself under the headings clear and unclear, distinct and indistinct vision, show indeed a certain analogy with the differences in clearness just referred to, so far, that is, as we are concerned in either case with gradual increases and decreases in the fullness with which the presented material is given, but that even these differences belong to different dimensions.

45. *Unperceived experience, unperceived reality*

If we live ourselves into these positions, we shall understand also the following essential difference in the way in which experiences (*Erlebnisse*) and things stand to one another in respect of their perceivability.

It is a mark of the type of Being peculiar to experience that perceptual insight can direct its immediate, unobstructed gaze upon every real experience, and so enter into the life of a primordial presence. This insight operates as a "reflexion", and it has this remarkable peculiarity that that which is thus apprehended through perception is, in principle, characterized as something which not only is and endures within the gaze of perception, but *already was before* this gaze was directed to it. "All experiences are conscious experiences": this tells us specifically with respect to intentional experiences that they are not only the consciousness of something, and as such present not merely when they are objects of a reflective consciousness, but that when unreflected on they are already there as a "background", and therefore in principle, and at first in an analogical sense, *available for perception,* like unnoticed things in our external field of vision. These can be available only in so far as they are already, as unnoticed, objects of consciousness in a certain sense, and that means, in their case, when they appear. *Not all* things fulfil this condition: the field of view of my attention which includes all that appears is not endless. On the other hand, unreflective experience must also fulfil certain conditions of preparedness, although in a quite different way more in conformity with its own nature. It cannot "appear". It fulfils these conditions none the less at all times through the mere manner of its existence, and indeed for that same Ego to which it belongs whose pure personal gaze on occasion lives "in" it. It is only because reflexion and experience have the *essential* peculiarities which are here only hinted at that we can know anything about experiences that we do not reflect on, and therefore also about the reflexions themslves. And it goes without saying that the modifications of experiences in reproduction (and retention) run, *mutatis mutandis,* on similar lines.

Let us carry the contrast farther. We see that *it is the intrinsic nature of an experience to be perceivable through reflexion.* Things also are *perceivable,* on principle, and in perception they are apprehended as things of the world that surround me. Also they belong to this world without being perceived, they are thus *there for the Ego even then.* Still, in general, not so that a glance noting their presence could be sent in their direction! The background area, taken as the field of sheer noticeability, includes indeed only a small portion of the world that surrounds me. The statement "It is there" means rather that from actual perceptions and their background of real appearances *possible* series of perceptions lead up under *motives* that are constant and continuous and girt about (as unnoticed backgrounds) with ever-changing fields of things; and so further till we reach those systems of perceptions in which the Thing in question appears and is apprehended. In principle we make no essential alteration here when in the place of a single Ego we consider a plurality of Egos. Only through the relation of a possible reciprocity of understanding can I identify the world of my experience with that of others, and at the same time enrich it through the overflowings of their experience. A transcendence which dispensed with the aforesaid systematically motived connexion with my existing sphere of actual perception would be a completely groundless assumption; a transcendence which dispensed with the same, *on principle,* would be *nonsense.* The presence of what is actually not perceived in the world of things is then of this type, and is essentially different from that mode of Being of which we are intrinsically sensible, the Being of our own inward experiences.

46. *Indubitability of immanent, dubitability of transcendent perception*

From all this important consequences follow. Every immanent perception necessarily guarantees the existence (*Existenz*) of its object. If reflective apprehension is directed to my experience, I apprehend an absolute Self whose existence (*Dasein*) is, in principle, undeniable, that is, the insight that it does not exist is, in principle, impossible; it would be nonsense to maintain the possibility of an experience *given in such a way not* truly existing. The stream of experience which is mine, that, namely, of the one who is thinking, may be to ever so great an extent uncomprehended, unknown in its past and future reaches, yet as soon as I glance towards the flowing life and into the real present it flows through, and in so doing grasp myself as the pure subject of this life (what that means will expressly concern us at a later stage), I say forthwith and because I must: *I am,* this life is, I live: *cogito.*

To every stream of experience, and to every Ego as such, there belongs, in principle, the possibility of securing this self-evidence: each of us bears in himself the warrant of his absolute existence (*Daseins* as a fundamental possibility. But is it not conceivable, one might ask, that an Ego might have only fancies in its stream of experience, that the latter might consist of nothing beyond fictive intuitions? Such an Ego would thus discover only fictive *cogitationes;* its reflexions, by the very nature of this experiential medium, would be exclusively reflexions within the imagination. But that is obvious nonsense. That which floats before the mind may be a mere fiction; the floating itself, the fiction-producing consciousness, is not itself imagined, and the possibility of a perceiving reflexion which lays hold on absolute existence belongs to its essence as it does to every experience. No nonsense lies in the possibility that all alien consciousness which I posit in the experience of empathy does not exist. But *my* empathy and my consciousness in general is given in a primordial and absolute sense, not only essentially but existentially. This privileged position holds only for oneself and for the stream of experience to which the self is related; here only is there, and must there be, anything of the nature of immanent perception.

In contrast to this, it is, as we know, an essential feature of the thing-world that no perception, however perfect it may be, gives us anything absolute within its domain; and with this the following is essentially connected, namely, that every experience (*Erfahrung*), however far it extends, leaves open the possibility that what is given, despite the persistent consciousness of its bodily self-presence, does *not* exist. It is an essentially valid law that *existence in the form of a thing is never demanded as necessary by virtue of its givenness,* but in a certain way is always *contingent.* That means: It can always happen that the further course of experience will compel us to abandon what has already been set down and justified *in the light of empirical canons of rightness.* It was, so we afterwards say, mere illusion, hallucination, merely a coherent dream, and the like. Moreover, in this sphere of given data the open possibility remains of changes in apprehension, the turning of an appearance over into one which cannot unite with it harmoniously, and therewith an influence of later empirical positions on earlier ones whereby the intentional objects of these earlier positings suffer, so to speak, a posthumous reconstruction—eventualities which in the sphere of subject-experience (*Erlebnis*) are essentially excluded. In the absolute sphere, opposition, illusion, and being-otherwise have no place. It is a sphere of the absolutely established (*absoluter Position*).

In every way, then, it is clear that everything which is there for me in the world of things is on grounds of principle *only a presumptive reality;* that *I myself,* on the contrary, for whom it is there (excluding that which is imputed to the thing-world "by me"), I myself or my experience in its actuality am *absolute* Reality (*Wirklichkeit*), given through a positing that is unconditioned and simply indissoluble.

The thesis of my pure Ego and its personal life, which is "necessary" and plainly indubitable, thus stands opposed to the thesis of the world which is "contingent". All corporeally given thing-like entities can also not be, no corporeally given experiencing can also not be: that is the essential law, which defines this necessity and that contingency.

Obviously then the ontic necessity of the actual present experiencing is no pure essential necessity, that is, no pure eidetic specification of an essential law; it is the necessity of a fact (*Faktum*), and called 'necessity' because an essential law is involved in the fact, and here indeed in its existence as such. The ideal possibility of a reflexion which has the essential character of a self-evident unshakeable *existential* thesis has its ground in the essential nature of a pure Ego *in general* and of an experiencing *in general.*[6]

The reflexions in which we have been indulging also make it clear that no proofs drawn from the empirical consideration of the world can be conceived which could assure us with absolute certainty of the world's existence. The world is not doubtful in the sense that there are rational grounds which might be pitted against the tremendous force of unanimous experiences, but in the sense that a doubt is *thinkable,* and this is so because the possibility of non-Being is in principle never excluded. Every empirical power, be it ever so great, can be gradually outweighed and overcome. Nothing is thereby altered in the absolute Being of experiences, indeed these remain presupposed in all this all the time.

With this conclusion our study has reached its climax. We have won the knowledge we needed. In the essential connexions it has revealed to us already involved the most important of the premises on which depend those inferences we would draw concerning the detachability in principle of the whole natural world from the domain of consciousness, the sphere in which experiences have their being; inferences in which, as we can readily convince ourselves, a central, though not fully developed, thought of the quite otherwise oriented meditations of Descartes comes at last to its own. To reach our final goal we shall need indeed to add in the sequel a few supplementary discussions, which for the rest will not trouble us too much. Meanwhile let us draw our conclusions provisionally within a compass of limited bearing.

[6] Cf. on this point the Third Study of the Second Book in the new edition of the *Logical Studies.*

Martin Heidegger

THE WAY BACK INTO THE GROUND OF METAPHYSICS[1]

[*Preface:* Martin Heidegger was born in 1889. His major work, *Sein und Zeit,* appeared in 1927, and the many later printings retain the pagination of the original edition which is also cited in the following essay. Heidegger sometimes cites it as "S. u. Z." (equivalent to *B. & T.,* for *Being and Time*), even as Kant's *Kritik der reinen Vernunft* is often cited as "K. d. r. V."

In 1929 Heidegger published a seventeen-page lecture, *What is Metaphysics?* to which a nine-page postscript was added in 1943. Both have appeared in English, together with three other short pieces and editorial material almost twice the length of the texts (400 pp. in all), under the title *Existence and Being.* In 1949, Heidegger added a fifteen-page introduction to the fifth printing of his lecture. This introduction is a self-contained essay with a title of its own, and Heidegger attaches the utmost importance to it. He himself selected it for inclusion in the present volume.

The essay, not previously available in English, was translated for this purpose, and Heidegger answered questions, orally and in writing, about the translation of key terms and particularly difficult passages. My rendering of *Sein* as *Being,* of *Seiendes* as *beings,* of *vorstellender Denken* as *representational thinking,* and of *andenkendes Denken* as *a*

[1] From: *Existentialism from Dostoevsky to Sartre,* edited by Walter Kaufmann, Ch. 8. (This essay was translated by Walter Kaufmann.)

thinking that recalls, to give only a few examples, has his full approval; but he has not gone over the entire text.

Every attempt was made to make the English version smooth and yet faithful, and the reader should keep in mind that Heidegger's difficulty is almost legendary, and that like Aristotle and Hegel before him, and like Faulkner in our time, he often deliberately defies the idiomatic vernacular, although at other times he appeals to it. Moreover, the "weight" of a word is scarcely less important to him than its meaning. The reader who is not put off by what at first seems strange but reads the essay through should, even at first reading, understand a good deal.]

Descartes, writing to Picot, who translated the *Principia Philosophiae* into French, observed: "Thus the whole of philosophy is like a tree: the roots are metaphysics, the trunk is physics, and the branches that issue from the trunk are all the other sciences . . ." (*Opp. ed. Ad. et Ta.* IX, 14.)

Sticking to this image, we ask: In what soil do the roots of the tree of philosophy have their hold? Out of what ground do the roots—and through them the whole tree—receive their nourishing juices and strength? What element, concealed in the ground, enters and lives in the roots that support and nourish the tree? What is the basis and element of metaphysics? What is metaphysics, viewed from its ground? What is metaphysics itself, at bottom?

Metaphysics thinks about beings as beings. Wherever the question is asked what beings are, beings as such are in sight. Metaphysical representation owes this sight to the light of Being. The light itself, i.e., that which such thinking experiences as light, does not come within the range of metaphysical thinking; for metaphysics always represents beings only as beings. Within this perspective, metaphysical thinking does, of course, inquire about the being which is the source and originator of this light. But the light itself is considered sufficiently illuminated as soon as we recognize that we look through it whenever we look at beings.

In whatever manner beings are interpreted—whether as spirit, after the fashion of spiritualism; or as matter and force, after the fashion of materialism; or as becoming and life, or idea, will, substance, subject, or *energeia;* or as the eternal recurrence of the same events—every time, beings as beings appear in the light of Being. Wherever metaphysics represents beings, Being has entered into the light. Being has arrived in a state of unconcealedness (Αλήθεια). But whether and how Being itself involves such unconcealedness, whether and how it manifests itself in, and as, metaphysics, remains obscure. Being in its revelatory essence, i.e. in its truth, is not recalled. Nevertheless, when metaphysics gives answers to its question concerning beings as such, metaphysics speaks out of the unnoticed revealedness of Being. The truth of Being may thus be called the ground in which metaphysics, as the root of the tree of philosophy, is kept and from which it is nourished.

Because metaphysics inquires about beings as beings, it remains concerned with beings and does not devote itself to Being as Being. As the root of the tree, it sends all nourishment and all strength into the trunk and its branches. The root branches out in the soil to enable the tree to grow out of the ground and thus to leave it. The tree of philosophy grows out of the soil in which metaphysics is rooted. The ground is the element in which the root of the tree lives, but the growth of the tree is never able to absorb this soil in such a way that it disappears in the tree as part of the tree. Instead, the roots, down to the subtlest tendrils, lose themselves in the soil. The ground is ground for the roots, and in the ground the roots forget themselves for the sake of the tree. The roots still belong to the tree even when they abandon themselves, after a fashion, to the element of the soil. They squander themselves and their element on the tree. As roots, they do not devote themselves to the soil—at least not as if it were their life to grow only into this element and to spread out in it. Presumably, the element would not be the same element either if the roots did not live in it.

Metaphysics, insofar as it always represents only beings as beings, does not recall Being itself. Philosophy does not concentrate on its ground. It always leaves its ground—leaves it by means of metaphysics. And yet it never escapes its ground.

Insofar as a thinker sets out to experience the ground of metaphysics, insofar as the attempts to recall the truth of Being itself instead of merely representing beings as beings, his thinking has in a sense left metaphysics. From the point of view of metaphysics, such thinking goes back into the ground of metaphysics. But what still appears as ground from this point of view is presumably something else, once it is experienced in its own terms—something as yet unsaid, according to which the essence of metaphysics, too, is something else and not metaphysics.

Such thinking, which recalls the truth of Being, is no longer satisfied with mere metaphysics, to be sure; but it does not oppose and think against metaphysics either. To return to our image, it does not tear up the root of philosophy. It tills the ground and plows the soil for this root. Metaphysics remains the basis of philosophy. The basis of thinking, however, it does not reach. When we think of the truth of Being, metaphysics is overcome. We can no longer accept the claim of metaphysics that it takes care of the fundamental involvement in "Being" and that it decisively determines all relations to beings as such. But this "overcoming of metaphysics" does not abolish metaphysics. As long as man remains the *animal rationale* he is also the *animal meta-*

physicum. As long as man understands himself as the rational animal, metaphysics belongs, as Kant said, to the nature of man. But if our thinking should succeed in its efforts to go back into the ground of metaphysics, it might well help to bring about a change in human nature, accompanied by a transformation of metaphysics.

If, as we unfold the question concerning the truth of Being, we speak of overcoming metaphysics, this means: recalling Being itself. Such recalling goes beyond the tradition of forgetting the ground of the root of philosophy. The thinking attempted in *Being and Time* (1927) sets out on the way to prepare an overcoming of metaphysics, so understood. That, however, which prompts such thinking can only be that which is to be recalled. That Being itself and how Being itself concerns our thinking does not depend upon our thinking alone. That Being itself, and the manner in which Being itself, strikes a man's thinking, that rouses his thinking and stirs it to rise from Being itself to respond and correspond to Being as such.

Why, however, should such an overcoming of metaphysics be necessary? Is the point merely to underpin that discipline of philosophy which was the root hitherto, or to supplant it with a yet more basic discipline? Is it a question of changing the philosophic system of instruction? No. Or are we trying to go back into the ground of metaphysics in order to uncover a hitherto overlooked presupposition of philosophy, and thereby to show that philosophy does not yet stand on an unshakable foundation and therefore cannot yet be the absolute science? No.

It is something else that is at stake with the arrival of the truth of Being or its failure to arrive: it is neither the state of philosophy nor philosophy itself alone, but rather the proximity or remoteness of that from which philosophy, insofar as it means the representation of beings as such, receives its nature and its necessity. What is to be decided is nothing less than this: can Being itself, out of its own unique truth, bring about its involvement in human nature; or shall metaphysics, which turns its back to its ground, prevent further that the involvement of Being in man may generate a radiance out of the very essence of this involvement itself—a radiance which might lead man to belong to Being?

In its answers to the question concerning beings as such, metaphysics operates with a prior conception of Being. It speaks of Being necessarily and hence continually. But metaphysics does not induce Being itself to speak, for metaphysics does not recall Being in its truth, nor does it recall truth as unconcealedness, nor does it recall the nature of unconcealedness. To metaphysics the nature of truth always appears only in the derivative form of the truth of knowledge and the truth of propositions which formulate our knowledge. Unconcealedness, however, might be prior to all truth in the sense of *veritas.* Ἀλήθεια might be the word that offers a hitherto unnoticed hint concerning the nature of *esse* which has not yet been recalled. If this should be so, then the representational thinking of metaphysics could certainly never reach this nature of truth, however zealously it might devote itself to historical studies of pre-Socratic philosophy; for what is at stake here is not some renaissance of pre-Socratic thinking: any such attempt would be vain and absurd. What is wanted is rather some regard for the arrival of the hitherto unexpressed nature of unconcealedness, for it is in this form that Being has announced itself. Meanwhile the truth of Being has remained concealed from metaphysics during its long history from Anaximander to Nietzsche. Why does metaphysics not recall it? Is the failure to recall it merely a function of some kinds of metaphysical thinking? Or is it an essential feature of the fate of metaphysics that its own ground eludes it because in the rise of unconcealedness its very core, namely concealedness, stays away in favor of the unconcealed which appears in the form of beings?

Metaphysics, however, speaks continually and in the most various ways of Being. Metaphysics gives, and seems to confirm, the appearance that it asks and answers the question concerning Being. In fact, metaphysics never answers the question concerning the truth of Being, for it never asks this question. Metaphysics does not ask this question because it thinks of Being only by representing beings as beings. It means all beings as a whole, although it speaks of Being. It refers to Being and means beings as beings. From its beginning to its completion, the propositions of metaphysics have been strangely involved in a persistent confusion of beings and Being. This confusion, to be sure, must be considered an event and not a mere mistake. It cannot by any means be charged to a mere negligence of thought or a carelessness of expression. Owing to this persistent confusion, the claim that metaphysics poses the question of Being lands us in utter error.

Due to the manner in which it thinks of beings, metaphysics almost seems to be, without knowing it, the barrier which keeps man from the original involvement of Being in human nature.

What if the absence of this involvement and the oblivion of this absence determined the entire modern age? What if the absence of Being abandoned man more and more exclusively to beings, leaving him forsaken and far from any involvement of Being in his nature, while this forsakenness itself remained veiled? What if this were the case—and had been the case for a long time now? What if there were signs that this oblivion will become still more decisive in the future?

Would there still be occasion for a thoughtful person to give himself arrogant airs in view of this fateful withdrawal with which Being presents us? Would there still be occasion, if this should be our situation, to deceive ourselves with pleasant phantasms and to indulge, of all things, in an artificially induced elation? If the oblivion of Being which has been described here should be real, would there not be occasion enough for a thinker who recalls Being to experience a genuine horror?

What more can his thinking do than to endure in dread this fateful withdrawal while first of all facing up to the oblivion of Being? But how could thought achieve this as long as its fatefully granted dread seems to it no more than a mood of depression? What does such dread, which is fated by Being, have to do with psychology or psychoanalysis?

Suppose that the overcoming of metaphysics involved the endeavor to commence with a regard for the oblivion of Being—the attempt to learn to develop such a regard, in order to experience this oblivion and to absorb this experience into the involvement of Being in man, and to preserve it there: then, in the distress of the oblivion of Being, the question "What is metaphysics?" might well become the most necessary necessity for thought.

Thus everything depends on this: that our thinking should become more thoughtful in its season. This is achieved when our thinking, instead of implementing a higher degree of exertion, is directed toward a different point of origin. The thinking which is posited by beings as such, and therefore representational and illuminating in that way, must be supplanted by a different kind of thinking which is brought to pass by Being itself and, therefore, responsive to Being.

All attempts are futile which seek to make representational thinking which remains metaphysical, and only metaphysical, effective and useful for immediate action in everyday public life. The more thoughtful our thinking becomes and the more adequate it is to the involvement of Being in it, the purer our thinking will stand *eo ipso* in the one action appropriate to it: recalling what is meant for it and thus, in a sense, what is already meant.

But who still recalls what is meant? One makes inventions. To lead our thinking on the way on which it may find the involvement of the truth of Being in human nature, to open up a path for our thinking on which it may recall Being itself in its truth—to do that the thinking attempted in *Being and Time* is "on its way." On this way—that is, in the service of the question concerning the truth of Being—it becomes necessary to stop and think about human nature; for the experience of the oblivion of Being, which is not specifically mentioned because it still had to be demonstrated, involves the crucial conjecture that in view of the unconcealedness of Being the involvement of Being in human nature is an essential feature of Being. But how could this conjecture, which is experienced here, become an explicit question before every attempt had been made to liberate the determination of human nature from the concept of subjectivity and from the concept of the *animal rationale?* To characterize with a single term both the involvement of Being in human nature and the essential relation of man to the openness ("there") of Being as such, the name of "being there [*Dasein*]" was chosen for that sphere of being in which man stands as man. This term was employed, even though in metaphysics it is used interchangeably with *existentia,* actuality, reality, and objectivity, and although this metaphysical usage is further supported by the common [German] expression *"menschliches Dasein."* Any attempt, therefore, to re-think *Being and Time* is thwarted as long as one is satisfied with the observation that, in this study, the term "being there" is used in place of "consciousness." As if this were simply a matter of using different words! As if it were not the one and only thing at stake here: namely, to get men to think about the involvement of Being in human nature and thus, from our point of view, to present first of all an experience of human nature which may prove sufficient to direct our inquiry. The term "being there" neither takes the place of the term "consciousness" nor does the "object" designated as "being there" take the place of what we think of when we speak of "consciousness." "Being there" names that which should first of all be experienced, and subsequently thought of, as a place—namely, the location of the truth of Being.

What the term "being there" means throughout the treatise on *Being and Time* is indicated immediately (page 42) by its introductory key sentence: *"The 'essence' of being there lies in its existence."* [*Das "Wesen" des Daseins liegt in seiner Existenz.*]

To be sure, in the language of metaphysics the word "existence" is a synonym of "being there": both refer to the reality of anything at all that is real, from God to a grain of sand. As long, therefore, as the quoted sentence is understood only superficially, the difficulty is merely transferred from one word to another, from "being there" to "existence." In *B.&T.* the term "existence" is used exclusively for the being of man. Once "existence" is understood rightly, the "essence" of being there can be recalled: in its openness, Being itself manifests and conceals itself, yields itself and withdraws; at the same time, this truth of Being does not exhaust itself in being there, nor can it by any means simply be identified with it after the fashion of the metaphysical proposition: all objectivity is as such also subjectivity.

What does "existence" mean in *B.&T.?* The word designates a mode of Being; specifically, the Being of those beings who stand open for the openness of Being in which they stand, by standing it. This "standing it," this enduring, is experienced under the name of "care." The ecstatic essence of being there is approached by way of care, and, conversely, care is experienced adequately only in its ecstatic essence. "Standing it," experienced in this manner, is the essence of the *ekstasis* which must be grasped by thought. The ecstatic essence of existence is therefore still understood inadequately as long as one thinks of it as merely "standing out," while interpreting the "out" as meaning "away from" the inside of an immanence of consciousness and spirit. For in this manner, existence would still be understood in terms of "subjectivity" and "substance"; while, in fact, the "out" ought to be understood in terms of the openness of Being itself. The *stasis* of the ecstatic consists—strange as it may sound—in standing in the "out" and "there" of unconcealedness in which Being itself is present. What is meant by "existence" in the context of an inquiry that is prompted by, and directed toward, the truth of Being, can be most beautifully designated by the word "instancy [*Inständigkeit*]." We must think at the same time, however, of standing in the openness of Being, of enduring and outstanding this standing-in (care), and of out-braving the utmost (being toward death); for it is only together that they constitute the full essence of existence.

The being that exists is man. Man alone exists. Rocks are, but they do not exist. Trees are, but they do not exist. Horses are, but they do not exist. Angels are, but they do not exist. God is, but he does not exist. The proposition "man alone exists" does not mean by any means that man alone is a real being while all other beings are unreal and mere appearances or human ideas. The proposition "man exists" means: man is that being whose Being is distinguished by the open-standing standing-in in the unconcealedness of Being, from Being, in Being. The existential nature of man is the reason why man can represent beings as such, and why he can be conscious of them. All consciousness presupposes ecstatically understood existence as the *essentia* of man—*essentia* meaning that as which man is present insofar as he is man. But consciousness does not itself create the openness of beings, nor is it consciousness that makes it possible for man to stand open for beings. Whither and whence and in what free dimension could the intentionality of consciousness move, if instancy were not the essence of man in the first instance? What else could be the meaning—if anybody has ever seriously thought about this—of the word *sein* in the [German] words *Bewusstsein* ["consciousness"; literally: "being conscious"] and *Selbstbewusstsein* ["self-consciousness"] if it did not designate the existential nature of that which is in the mode of existence? To be a self is admittedly one feature of the nature of that being which exists; but existence does not consist in being a self, nor can it be defined in such terms. We are faced with the fact that metaphysical thinking understands man's selfhood in terms of substance or—and at bottom this amounts to the same—in terms of the subject. It is for this reason that the first way which leads away from metaphysics to the ecstatic existential nature of man must lead through the metaphysical conception of human selfhood (*B.&T.*, §§63 and 64).

The question concerning existence, however, is always subservient to that question which is nothing less than the only question of thought. This question, yet to be unfolded, concerns the truth of Being as the concealed ground of all metaphysics. For this reason the treatise which sought to point the way back into the ground of metaphysics did not bear the title "Existence and Time," nor "Consciousness and Time," but *Being and Time*. Nor can this title be understood as if it were parallel to the customary juxtapositions of Being and Becoming, Being and Seeming, Being and Thinking, or Being and Ought. For in all these cases Being is limited, as if Becoming, Seeming, Thinking, and Ought did not belong to Being, although it is obvious that they are not nothing and thus belong to Being. In *Being and Time,* Being is not something other than Time: "Time" is called the first name of the truth of Being, and this truth is the presence of Being and thus Being itself. But why "Time" and "Being"?

By recalling the beginnings of history when Being unveiled itself in the thinking of the Greeks, it can be shown that the Greeks from the very beginning experienced the Being of beings as the presence of the present. When we translate εἶναι as "being," our translation is linguistically correct. Yet we merely substitute one set of sounds for another. As soon as we examine ourselves it becomes obvious that we neither think εἶναι, as it were, in Greek nor have in mind a correspondingly clear and univocal concept when we speak of "being." What, then, are we saying when instead of εἶναι we say "being," and instead of "being," εἶναι and *esse?* We are saying nothing. The Greek, Latin, and German word all remain equally obtuse. As long as we adhere to the customary usage we merely betray ourselves as the pacemakers of the greatest thoughtlessness which has ever gained currency in human thought and which has remained dominant until this moment. This εἶναι, however, means: to be present [*anwesen;* this verb form, in place of the idiomatic *"anwesend sein,"* is Heidegger's neology]. The true being of this being present [*das Wesen dieses Anwesens*] is deeply concealed in the earliest names of Being. But for us εἶναι and οὐσία as παρῖ and ἀπουσία means this first of all: in being present there moves, unrecognized and concealed, present time and duration—in one word, Time. Being as such is thus unconcealed owing to Time. Thus Time points to unconcealedness, i.e., the truth of Being. But the Time of which we should think here is not experienced through the changeful career of beings. Time is evidently of an altogether different nature which neither has been recalled by way of the time concept of metaphysics nor ever can be recalled in this way. Thus Time becomes the first name, which is yet to be heeded, of the truth of Being, which is yet to be experienced.

A concealed hint of Time speaks not only out of the earliest metaphysical names of Being but also out of its last name, which is "the eternal recurrence of the same events." Through the entire epoch of metaphysics, Time is decisively present in the history of Being, without being recognized or thought about. To this Time, space is neither co-ordinated nor merely subordinated.

Suppose one attempts to make a transition from the representation of beings as such to recalling the truth of Being: such an attempt, which starts from this representation, must still represent, in a certain sense, the truth of Being, too; and any such representation must of necessity be heterogeneous and ultimately, insofar as it is a representation, inadequate for that which is to be thought. This relation, which comes out of metaphysics and tries to enter into the involvement of the truth of Being in human nature, is called understanding. But here understanding is viewed, at the same time, from the point of view of the unconcealedness of Being. Understanding is a pro-ject thrust forth and ecstatic, which means that it stands in the sphere of the open. The sphere which opens up as we project, in order that something (Being in this case) may prove itself as something (in this case, Being as itself in its unconcealedness), is called the sense. (Cf. *B.&T.*, p. 151) "The sense of Being" and "the truth of Being" mean the same.

Let us suppose that Time belongs to the truth of Being in a way that is still concealed: then every project that holds open the truth of Being, representing a way of understanding Being, must look out into Time as the horizon of any possible understanding of Being. (Cf. *B.&T.*, §§31-34 and 68.)

The preface to *Being and Time,* on the first page of the treatise, ends with these sentences: "To furnish a concrete elaboration of the question concerning the sense of 'Being' is the intention of the following treatise. The interpretation of Time as the horizon of every possible attempt to understand Being is its provisional goal."

All philosophy has fallen into the oblivion of Being which has, at the same time, become and remained the fateful demand on thought in *B.&T.;* and philosophy could hardly have given a clearer demonstration of the power of this oblivion of Being than it has furnished us by the somnambulistic assurance with which it has passed by the real and only question of *B.&T*. What is at stake here is, therefore, not a series of misunderstandings of a book but our abandonment by Being.

Metaphysics states what beings are as beings. It offers a λόγος (statement) about the ὄντα (beings). The later title "ontology" characterizes its nature, provided, of course, that we understand it in accordance with its true significance and not through its narrow scholastic meaning. Metaphysics moves in the sphere of the ὄν ᾗ ὄν: it deals with beings as beings. In this manner, metaphysics always represents beings as such in their totality; it deals with the beingness of beings (the οὐσία of the ὄν). But metaphysics represents the beingness of beings [*die Seiendheit des Seienden*] in a twofold manner: in the first place, the totality of beings as such with an eye to their most universal traits (ὄν καθόλου, κοινόν;) but at the same time also the totality of beings as such in the sense of the highest and therefore divine being (ὄν καθόλου, ἀκρότατον, θεῖον). In the metaphysics of Aristotle, the unconcealedness of beings as such has specifically developed in this twofold manner. (Cf. Met. Γ, E, K.)

Because metaphysics represents beings as beings, it is, two-in-one, the truth of beings in their universality and in the highest being. According to its nature, it is at the same time ontology in the narrower sense and theology. This ontotheological nature of philosophy proper (πρώτη φιλοσοφία) is, no doubt, due to the way in which the ὄν opens up in it, namely as ὄν. Thus the theological character of ontology is not merely due to the fact that Greek metaphysics was later taken up and transformed by the ecclesiastic theology of Christianity. Rather it is due to the manner in which beings as beings have from the very beginning disconcealed themselves. It was this unconcealedness of beings that provided the possibility for Christian theology to take possession of Greek philosophy—whether for better or for worse may be decided by the theologians, on the basis of their experience of what is Christian; only they should keep in mind what is written in the First Epistle of Paul the Apostle to the Corinthians: "οὐχὶ ἐμώρανεν ὁ θεός τὴν σοφίαν τοῦ κόσμου; Has not God let the wisdom of this world become foolishness?" (I Cor. 1:20) The σοφία τοῦ κόσμου [wisdom of this world], however, is that which, according to 1:22, the Ἕλληνες ζητοῦσιν, the Greeks seek. Aristotle even calls the πρώτη φιλοσοφία (philosophy proper) quite specifically ζητουμένη—what is sought. Will Christian theology make up its mind one day to take seriously the word of the apostle and thus also the conception of philosophy as foolishness?

As the truth of beings as such, metaphysics has a twofold character. The reason for this twofoldness, however, let alone its origin, remains unknown to metaphysics; and this is no accident, nor due to mere neglect. Metaphysics has this twofold character because it is what it is: the representation of beings as beings. Metaphysics has no choice. Being metaphysics, it is by its very nature excluded from the experience of Being; for it always represents beings (ὄν) only with an eye to what of Being has already manifested itself as beings (η ὄν). But metaphysics never pays attention to what has concealed itself in this very ὄν insofar as it became unconcealed.

Thus the time came when it became necessary to make a fresh attempt to grasp by thought what precisely is said when we speak of ὄν or use the word "being" [*seiend*]. Accordingly, the question concerning the ὄν was reintroduced into human thinking. (Cf. *B.&T.*, Preface.) But this reintroduction is no mere repetition of the Platonic-Aristotelian question; instead it asks about that which conceals itself in the ὄν.

Metaphysics is founded upon that which conceals itself here as long as metaphysics studies the ὄν ᾗ ὄν. The attempt to inquire back into what conceals itself here seeks, from the point of view of metaphysics, the fundament of ontology. Therefore this attempt is called, in *Being and Time* (page 13) "fundamental ontology" [*Fundamentalontologie*]. Yet this title, like any title, is soon seen to be inappropriate. From the point of view of metaphysics, to be sure, it says something that is correct; but precisely for that reason it is misleading, for what matters is success in the transition from metaphysics to recalling the truth of Being. As long as this thinking calls itself "fundamental ontology" it blocks and obscures its own way with this title. For what the title "fundamental ontology" suggests is, of course, that the attempt to recall the truth of Being—and not, like all ontology, the truth of beings—is itself (seeing that it is called "fundamental ontology") still a kind of ontology. In fact, the attempt to recall the truth of Being sets out on the way back into the ground of metaphysics, and with its first step it immediately leaves the realm of all ontology. On the other hand, every philosophy which revolves around an indirect or direct conception of "transcendence" remains of necessity essentially an ontology, whether it achieves a new foundation of ontology or whether it assures us that it repudiates ontology as a conceptual freezing of experience.

Coming from the ancient custom of representing beings as such, the very thinking that attempted to recall the truth of Being became entangled in these customary conceptions. Under these circumstances it would seem that both for a preliminary orientation and in order to prepare the transition from representational thinking to a new kind of thinking that recalls [*das andenkende Denken*], nothing could be more necessary than the question: What is metaphysics?

The unfolding of this question in the following lecture culminates in another question. This is called the basic question of metaphysics: Why is there any being at all and not rather Nothing? Meanwhile [since this lecture was first published in 1929], to be sure, people have talked back and forth a great deal about dread and the Nothing, both of which are spoken of in this lecture. But one has never yet deigned to ask oneself why a lecture which moves from thinking of the truth of Being to the Nothing, and then tries from there to think into the nature of metaphysics, should claim that this question is the basic question of metaphysics. How can an attentive reader help feeling on the tip of his tongue an objection which is far more weighty than all protests against dread and the Nothing? The final question provokes the objection that an inquiry which attempts to recall Being by way of the Nothing returns in the end to a question concerning beings. On top of that, the question even proceeds in the customary manner of metaphysics by beginning with a causal "Why?" To this extent, then, the attempt to recall Being is repudiated in favor of representational knowledge of beings on the basis of beings. And to make matters still worse, the final question is obviously the question which the metaphysician Leibniz posed in his *Principes de la nature et de la grace: "Pourquoi il y a plutot quelque chose que rien?"* (Opp. ed. Gerh. tom. VI, 602.n. 7).

Does the lecture, then fall short of its intention? After all, this would be quite possible in view of the difficulty of effecting a transition from metaphysics to another kind of thinking. Does the lecture end up by asking Leibniz' metaphysical question about the supreme cause of all things that have being? Why, then, is Leibniz' name not mentioned, as decency would seem to require?

Or is the question asked in an altogether different sense? If it does not concern itself with beings and inquire about their first cause among all beings, then the question must begin from that which is not a being. And this is precisely what the question names, and it capitalizes the word: the Nothing. This is the sole topic of the lecture. The demand seems obvious that the end of the lecture should be thought through, for once, in its own perspective which determines the whole lecture. What has been called the basic question of metaphysics would then have to be understood and asked in terms of fundamental ontology as the question that comes out of the ground of metaphysics and as the question about this ground.

But if we grant this lecture that in the end it thinks in the direction of its own distinctive concern, how are we to understand this question?

The question is: Why is there any being at all and not rather Nothing? Suppose that we do not remain within metaphysics to ask metaphysically in the customary manner; suppose we recall the truth of Being out of the nature and the truth of metaphysics; then this might be asked as well: How did it come about that beings take precedence everywhere and lay claim to every "is" while that which is not a being is understood as Nothing, though it is Being itself, and remains forgotten? How did it come about that with Being It really is nothing and that the Nothing really is not? Is it perhaps from this that the as yet unshaken presumption has entered into all metaphysics that "Being" may simply be taken for granted and that Nothing is therefore made more easily than beings? That is indeed the situation regarding Being and Nothing. If it were different, then Leibniz could not have said in the same place by way of an explanation: *"Car le rien est plus simple et plus facile que quelque chose* [For the nothing is simpler and easier than any thing]."

What is more enigmatic: that beings are, or that Being is? Or does even this reflection fail to bring us close to that enigma which has occurred with the Being of beings?

Whatever the answer may be, the time should have ripened meanwhile for thinking through the lecture "What is Metaphysics?" which has been subjected to so many attacks, from its end, for once—from *its* end and not from an imaginary end.

THE FUNDAMENTAL QUESTION OF METAPHYSICS[1]

Why are there essents[2] rather than nothing? That is the question. Clearly it is no ordinary question. "Why are there essents, why is there anything at all, rather than nothing?"—obviously this is the first of all questions, though not in a chronological sense. Individuals and peoples ask a good many questions in the course of their historical passage through time. They examine, explore, and test a good many things before they run into the question "Why are there essents rather than nothing?" Many men never encounter this question, if by encounter we mean not merely to hear and read about it as an interrogative formulation but to ask the question, that is, to bring it about, to raise it, to feel its inevitability.

And yet each of us is grazed at least once, perhaps more than once, by the hidden power of this question, even if he is not aware of what is happening to him. The question looms in moments of great despair, when things tend to lose all their weight and all meaning becomes obscured. Perhaps it will strike but once like a muffled bell that rings into our life and gradually dies away. It is present in moments of rejoicing, when all the things around us are transfigured and seem to be there for the first time, as if it might be easier to think they are not than to understand that they are and are as they are. The question is upon us in boredom, when we are equally removed from despair and joy, and everything about us seems so hopelessly commonplace that we no longer care whether anything is or is not—and with this the question "Why are there essents rather than nothing?" is evoked in a particular form.

But this question may be asked expressly, or, unrecognized as a question, it may merely pass through our lives like a brief gust of wind;

[1] From: *An Introduction to Metaphysics,* Martin Heidegger, Ch. 1. Yale University Press, Inc., New Haven, 1959.

[2] "Essents" = "existents," "things that are."

it may press hard upon us, or, under one pretext or another, we may thrust it away from us and silence it. In any case it is never the question that we ask first in point of time.

But it is the first question in another sense—in regard to rank. This may be clarified in three ways. The question "Why are there essents rather than nothing?" is first in rank for us first because it is the most far reaching, second because it is the deepest, and finally because it is the most fundamental of all questions.

It is the widest of all questions. It confines itself to no particular essent of whatever kind. The question takes in everything, and this means not only everything that is present in the broadest sense but also everything that ever was or will be. The range of this question finds its limit only in nothing, in that which simply is not and never was. Everything that is not nothing is covered by this question, and ultimately even nothing itself; not because it is *something,* since after all we speak of it, but because it *is* nothing. Our question reaches out so far that we can never go further. We do not inquire into this and that, or into each essent in turn, but from the very outset into the essent as a whole, or, as we say for reasons to be discussed below: into the essent as such in its entirety.

This broadest of questions is also the deepest: Why are there essents . . . ? Why, that is to say, on what ground? from what source does the essent derive? on what ground does it stand? The question is not concerned with particulars, with what essents are and of what nature at any time, here and there, with how they can be changed, what they can be used for, and so on. The question aims at the ground of what is insofar as it is. To seek the ground is to try to get to the bottom; what is put in question is thus related to the ground. However, since the question is a question, it remains to be seen whether the grounds arrived at is really a ground, that is, whether it provides a foundation; whether it is a primal ground <Ur-grund>; or whether it fails to provide a foundation and is an abyss <Ab-grund>; or whether the ground is neither one nor the other but presents only a perhaps necessary appearance of foundation—in other words, it is a non-ground <Ungrund>. Be that as it may, the ground in question must account for the being of the essent as such. This question "why" does not look for causes that are of the same kind and on the same level as the essent itself. This "why" does not move on any one plane but penetrates to the "underlying" <"zu-grunde" liegend> realms and indeed to the very last of them, to the limit; turning away from the surface, from all shallowness, it strives toward the depths; this broadest of all questions is also the deepest.

Finally, this broadest and deepest question is also the most fundamental. What do we mean by this? If we take the question in its full scope, namely the essent as such in its entirety, it readily follows that in asking this question we keep our distance from every particular and individual essent, from every this and that. For we mean the essent as a whole, without any special preference. Still, it is noteworthy that in this questioning *one* kind of essent persists in coming to the fore, namely the men who ask the question. But the question should not concern itself with any particular essent. In the spirit of its unrestricted scope, all essents are of equal value. An elephant in an Indian jungle "is" just as much as some chemical combustion process at work on the planet Mars, and so on.

Accordingly, if our question "Why are there essents rather than nothing?" is taken it its fullest sense, we must avoid singling out any special, particular essent, including man. For what indeed is man? Consider the earth within the endless darkness of space in the universe. By way of comparison it is a tiny grain of sand; between it and the next grain of its own size there extends a mile or more of emptiness; on the surface of this grain of sand there lives a crawling, bewildered swarm of supposedly intelligent animals, who for a moment have discovered knowledge.[3] And what is the temporal extension of a human life amid all the millions of years? Scarcely a move of the second hand, a breath. Within the essent as a whole there is no legitimate ground for singling out this essent which is called mankind and to which we ourselves happen to belong.

But whenever the essent as a whole enters into this question, a privileged, unique relation arises between it and the act of questioning. For through this questioning the essent as a whole is for the first time opened up *as such* with a view to its possible ground, and in the act of questioning it is kept open. In relation to the essent as such in its entirety the asking of the question is not just any occurrence within the realm of the essent, like the falling of raindrops for example. The question "why" may be said to confront the essent as a whole, to break out of it, though never completely. But that is exactly why the act of questioning is privileged. Because it confronts the essent as a whole, but does not break loose from it, the content of the question reacts upon the questioning itself. Why the why? What is the ground of this question "why" which presumes to ask after the ground of the essent as a whole? Is the ground asked for in *this* why not merely a foreground —which would imply that the sought-for ground is again an essent? Does not the "first" question nevertheless come first in view of the intrinsic rank of the question of being and its modulations?

To be sure, the things in the world, the essents, are in no way affected by our asking of the question "Why are there essents rather than nothing?" Whether we ask it or not, the planets move in their orbits, the sap of life flows through plant and animal.

But *if* this question is asked and if the act of questioning is really carried out, the content and the object of the question react inevitably

[3] Cf. Nietzsche, *Über Wahreit und Lüge im aussermoralischen Sinne.* 1873 *Nachlass.*

on the act of questioning. Accordingly this questioning is not just any occurrence but a privileged happening that we call an *event*.

This question and all the questions immediately rooted in it, the questions in which this one question unfolds—this question "why" is incommensurable with any other. It encounters the search for its own why. At first sight the question "Why the why?" looks like a frivolous repetition ad infinitum of the same interrogative formulation, like an empty and unwarranted brooding over words. Yes, beyond a doubt, that is how it looks. The question is only whether we wish to be taken in by this superficial look and so regard the whole matter as settled, or whether we are capable of finding a significant event in this recoil of the question "why" upon itself.

But if we decline to be taken in by surface appearances we shall see that this question "why," this question as to the essents as such in its entirety, goes beyond any mere playing with words, provided we possess sufficient intellectual energy to make the question actually recoil into its "why"—for it will not do so of its own accord. In so doing we find out that this privileged question "why" has its ground in a leap through which man thrusts away all the previous security, whether real or imagined, of his life. The question is asked only in this leap; it *is* the leap; without it there is no asking. What "leap" means here will be elucidated later. Our questioning is not yet the leap; for this it must undergo a transformation; it still stands perplexed in the face of the essent. Here it may suffice to say that the leap in this questioning opens up its own source—with this leap the question arrives at its own ground. We call such a leap, which opens up its own source, the original source or origin <Ur-sprung>, the findings of one's own ground. It is because the question "Why are there essents rather than nothing?" breaks open the ground for all authentic questions and is thus at the origin <Ur-sprung> of them all that we must recognize it as the most fundamental of all questions.

It is the most fundamental of questions because it is the broadest and deepest, and conversely.

In this threefold sense the question is the first in rank—first, that is, in the order of questioning within the domain which this first question opens, defining its scope and thus founding it. Our question is the *question* of all authentic questions, i.e. of all self-questioning questions, and whether consciously or not it is necessarily implicit in every question. No questioning and accordingly no single scientific "problem" can be fully intelligible if it does not include, i.e. ask, the question of all questions. Let us be clear about this from the start: it can never be objectively determined whether anyone, whether we, really ask this question, that is whether we make the leap, or never get beyond a verbal formula. In a historical setting that does not recognize questioning as a fundamental human force, the question immediately loses its rank.

Anyone for whom the Bible is divine revelation and truth has the answer to the question "Why are there essents rather than nothing?" even before it is asked: everything that is, except God himself, has been created by Him. God himself, the increate creator, "is." One who holds to such faith can in a way participate in the asking of our question, but he cannot really question without ceasing to be a believer and taking all the consequences of such a step. He will only be able to act "as if" . . . On the other hand a faith that does not perpetually expose itself to the possibility of unfaith is no faith but merely a convenience: the believer simply makes up his mind to adhere to the trational doctrine. This is neither faith nor questioning, but the indifference of those who can busy themselves with everything, sometimes even displaying a keen interest in faith as well as questioning.

What we have said about security in faith as one position in regard to the truth does not imply that the biblical "In the beginning God created heaven and earth" is an answer to our question. Quite aside from whether these words from the Bible are true or false for faith, they can supply no answer to our question because they are in no way related to it. Indeed, they cannot even be brought into relation with our question. From the standpoint of faith our question is "foolishness."

Philosophy is this very foolishness. A "Christian philosophy" is a round square and a misunderstanding. There is, to be sure, a thinking and questioning elaboration of the world of Christian experience, i.e. of faith. That is theology. Only epochs which no longer fully believe in the true greatness of the task of theology arrive at the disastrous notion that philosophy can help to provide a refurbished theology if not a substitute for theology, which will satisfy the needs and tastes of the time. For the original Christian faith philosophy is foolishness. To philosophize is to ask "Why are there essents rather than nothing?" Really to ask the question signifies: a daring attempt to fathom this unfathomable question by disclosing what it summons us to ask, to push our questioning to the very end. Where such an attempt occurs there is philosophy.

It would not serve our purpose to begin our discussion with a detailed report on philosophy. But there are a few things that all must know who wish to concern themselves with philosophy. They can be briefly stated.

All essential philosophical questioning is necessarily untimely. This is so because philosophy is always projected far in advance of its time, or because it connects the present with its antecedent, with what *initially* was. Philosophy always remains a knowledge which not only cannot be adjusted to a given epoch but on the contrary imposes its measure upon its epoch.

Philosophy is essentially untimely because it is one of those few things that can never find an immediate echo in the present. When such an echo seems to occur, when a philosophy becomes fashionable, either it is no real philosophy or it has been misinterpreted and misused for ephemeral and extraneous purposes.

Accordingly, philosophy cannot be directly learned like manual and technical skills; it cannot be directly applied, or judged by its usefulness in the manner of economic or other professional knowledge.

But what is useless can still be a force, perhaps the only real force. What has no immediate echo in everyday life can be intimately bound up with a nation's profound historical development, and can even anticipate it. What is untimely will have its own times. This is true of philosophy. Consequently there is no way of determining once and for all what the task of philosophy is, and accordingly what must be expected of it. Every stage and every beginning of its development bears within it its own law. All that can be said is what philosophy cannot be and cannot accomplish.

A question has been stated: "Why are there essents rather than nothing?" We have claimed first place for this question and explained in what sense it is regarded as first.

We have not even begun to ask the question itself, but have digressed into a discussion about it. Such a digression is indispensable. For this question has nothing in common with our habitual concerns. There is no way of familiarizing ourselves with this question by a gradual transition from the things to which we are accustomed. Hence it must, as it were, be singled out in advance, presented. Yet in introducing the question and speaking of it, we must not postpone, let alone forget, the questioning itself.

Here then let us conclude our preliminary remarks.

Every essential form of spiritual life is marked by ambiguity. The less commensurate it is with other forms, the more it is misinterpreted.

Philosophy is one of the few autonomous creative possibilities and at times necessities of man's historical being-there.[4] The current misinterpretations of philosophy, all of which have some truth about them, are legion. Here we shall mention only two, which are important because of the light they throw on the present and future situation of philosophy. The first misinterpretation asks too much of philosophy. The second distorts its function.

Roughly speaking, philosophy always aims at the first and last grounds of the essent, with particular emphasis on man himself and on

[4] The word "Dasein" is ordinarily translated as "existence." It is used in "normal," popular discourse. But Heidegger breaks it into its components "Da," "there" and "Sein," "being," and puts his own definition on it. In general he means man's conscious, historical existence in the world, which is always projected into a there beyond its here. The German word "Dasein" has often been carried over into translations; the English strikes me as preferable. For further remarks on "being-there" see the bracketed passage on p. 236. R.M.

the meaning and goals of human being-there. This might suggest that philosophy can and must provide a foundation on which a nation will build its historical life and culture. But this is beyond the power of philosophy. As a rule such excessive demands take the form of a belittling of philosophy. It is said, for example: Because metaphysics did nothing to pave the way for the revolution it should be rejected. This is no cleverer than saying that because the carpenter's bench is useless for flying it should be abolished. Philosophy can never *directly* supply the energies and create the opportunities and methods that bring about a historical change; for one thing, because philosophy is always the concern of the few. Which few? The creators, those who initiate profound transformations. It spreads only indirectly, by devious paths that can never be laid out in advance, until at last, at some future date, it sinks to the level of a commonplace; but by then it has long been forgotten as original philosophy.

What philosophy essentially can and must be is this: a thinking that breaks the paths and opens the perspectives of the knowledge that sets the norms and hierarchies, of the knowledge in which and by which a people fulfills itself historically and culturally, the knowledge that kindles and necessitates all inquiries and thereby threatens all values.

The second misinterpretation involves a distortion of the function of philosophy. Even if philosophy can provide no foundation for a culture, the argument goes, it is nevertheless a cultural force, whether because it gives us an over-all, systematic view of what is, supplying a useful chart by which we may find our way amid the various possible things and realms of things, or because it relieves the sciences of their work by reflecting on their premises, basic concepts, and principles. Philosophy is expected to promote and even to accelerate—to make easier as it were—the practical and technical business of culture.

But—it is in the very nature of philosophy never to make things easier but only more difficult. And this not merely because its language strikes the everyday understanding as strange if not insane. Rather, it is the authentic function of philosophy to challenge historical being-there and hence, in the last analysis, being pure and simple. It restores to things, to the essents, their weight (being). How so? Because the challenge is one of the essential prerequisites for the birth of all greatness, and in speaking of greatness we are referring primarily to the works and destinies of nations. We can speak of historical destiny only where an authentic knowledge of things dominates man's being-there. And it is philosophy that opens up the paths and perspectives of such knowledge.

The misinterpretations with which philosophy is perpetually beset are promoted most of all by people of our kind, that is, by professors of philosophy. It is our customary business—which may be said to be justified and even useful—to transmit a certain knowledge of the philosophy of the past, as part of a general education. Many people suppose that this is philosophy itself, whereas at best it is the technique of philosophy.

In correcting these two misinterpretations I cannot hope to give you at one stroke a clear conception of philosophy. But I do hope that you will be on your guard when the most current judgments and even supposed observations assail you unawares. Such judgments are often disarming, precisely because they seem so natural. You hear remarks such as "Philosophy leads to nothing," "You can't do anything with philosophy," and readily imagine that they confirm an experience of your own. There is no denying the soundness of these two phrases, particularly common among scientists and teachers of science. Any attempt to refute them by proving that after all it does "lead to something" merely strengthens the prevailing misinterpretation to the effect that the everyday standards by which we judge bicycles or sulphur baths are applicable to philosophy.

It is absolutely correct and proper to say that "You can't do anything with philosophy." It is only wrong to suppose that this is the last word on philosophy. For the rejoinder imposes itself: granted that *we* cannot do anything with philosophy, might not philosophy, if we concern ourselves with it, do something *with us?* So much for what philosophy is not.

At the outset we stated a question: "Why are there essents rather than nothing?" We have maintained that to ask this question is to philosophize. When in our thinking we open our minds to this question, we first of all cease to dwell in any of the familiar realms. We set aside everything that is on the order of the day. Our question goes beyond the familiar and the things that have their place in everyday life. Nietzsche once said (*Werke, 7,* 269): "A philosopher is a man who never ceases to experience, see, hear, suspect, hope, and dream extraordinary things . . ."

To philosophize is to inquire into the *extra*-ordinary. But because, as we have just suggested, this questioning recoils upon itself, not only what is asked after is extraordinary but also the asking itself. In other words: this questioning does not lie along the way so that we bump into it one day unexpectedly. Nor is it part of everyday life: there is no requirement or regulation that forces us into it; it gratifies no urgent or prevailing need. The questioning itself is "out of order." It is entirely voluntary, based wholly and uniquely on the mystery of freedom, on what we have called the leap. The same Nietzsche said: "Philosophy . . . is a voluntary living amid ice and mountain heights" (*Werke, 15,* 2). To philosophize, we may now say, is an extra-ordinary inquiry into the extra-ordinary.

In the age of the earliest and crucial unfolding of Western philosophy among the Greeks, who first raised the authentic question of the essent as such in its entirety, the essent was called *physis.* This basic Greek word for the essent is customarily translated as "nature." This derives from the Latin translation, *natura,* which properly means "to be born," "birth." But with this Latin translation the original meaning of the Greek word *physis* is thrust aside, the actual philosophical force of the Greek word is destroyed. This is true not only of the Latin translation of *this* word but of all other Roman translations of the Greek philosophical language. What happened in this translation from the Greek into the Latin is not accidental and harmless; it marks the first stage in the process by which we cut ourselves off and alienated ourselves from the original essence of Greek philosophy. The Roman translation was later taken over by Christianity and the Christian Middle Ages. And the Christian Middle Ages were prolonged in modern philosophy, which, moving in the conceptual world of the Middle Ages, coined those representations and terms by means of which we still try to understand the beginnings of Western philosophy. These beginnings are regarded as something that present-day philosophers have supposedly transcended and long since left behind them.

But now let us skip over this whole process of deformation and decay and attempt to regain the unimpaired strength of language and words; for words and language are not wrappings in which things are packed for the commerce of those who write and speak. It is in words and language that things first come into being and are. For this reason the misuse of language in idle talk, in slogans and phrases, destroys our authentic relation to things. What does the word *physis* denote? It denotes self-blossoming emergence (e.g. the blossoming of a rose), opening up, unfolding, that which manifests itself in such unfolding and perseveres and endures in it; in short, the realm of things that emerge and linger on. According to the dictionary *phyein* means to grow or make to grow. But what does growing mean? Does it imply only to increase quantitatively, to become more and larger?

Physis as emergence can be observed everywhere, e.g. in celestial phenomena (the rising of the sun), in the rolling of the sea, in the growth of plants, in the coming forth of man and animal from the womb. But *physis,* the realm of that which arises, is not synonymous with these phenomena, which today we regard as part of "nature." This opening up and inward-jutting-beyond-itself <in-sich-aus-sich-hinausstehen> must not be taken as a process among other processes that we observe in the realm of the essent. *Physis* is being itself, by virtue of which essents become and remain observable.

The Greeks did not learn what *physis* is through natural phenomena, but the other way around: it was through a fundamental poetic and intellectual experience of being that they discovered what they had to call *physis*. It was this discovery that enabled them to gain a glimpse into nature in the restricted sense. Hence *physis* originally encompassed heaven as well as earth, the stone as well as the plant, the animal as well as man, and it encompassed human history as a work of men and the gods; and ultimately and first of all, it meant the gods themselves as subordinated to destiny. *Physis* means the power that emerges and the enduring realm under its sway. This power of emerging and enduring includes "becoming" as well as "being" in the restricted sense of inert duration. *Physis* is the process of a-rising, of emerging from the hidden, whereby the hidden is first made to stand.

But if, as is usually done, *physis* is taken not in the original sense of the power to emerge and endure, but in the later and present signification of nature; and if moreover the motion of material things, of the atoms and electrons, of what modern physics investigates as *physis,* is taken to be the fundamental manifestation of nature, then the first philosophy of the Greeks becomes a nature philosophy, in which all things are held to be of a material nature. In this case the beginning of Greek philosophy, as is perfectly proper for a beginning according to the common-sense view, gives the impression of what we, once again in Latin, designate as primitive. Thus the Greeks become essentially a higher type of Hottentot, whom modern science has left far behind. Disregarding the lesser absurdities involved in this view of the beginning of Western philosophy as something primitive, we need only say this: those who put forward such an interpretation forget that what is under discussion is philosophy, one of man's few great achievements. But what is great can only begin great. Its beginning is in fact the greatest thing of all. A small beginning belongs only to the small, whose dubious greatness it is to diminish all things; small are the beginnings of decay, though it may later become great in the sense of the enormity of total annihilation.

The great begins great, maintains itself only through the free recurrence of greatness within it, and if it is great ends also in greatness. So it is with the philosophy of the Greeks. It ended in greatness with Aristotle. Only prosaic common sense and the little man imagine that the great must endure forever, and equate this duration with eternity.

The Greeks called the essent as a whole *physis.* But it should be said in passing that even within Greek philosophy a narrowing of the word set in forthwith, although the original meaning did not vanish from the experience, knowledge, and orientation of Greek philosophy. Knowledge of its original meaning still lives on in Aristotle, when he speaks of the grounds of the essent as such (see *Metaphysics,* I, 1003 a 27).

But this narrowing of *physis* in the direction of "physics" did not occur in the way that we imagine today. We oppose the psychic, the animated, the living, to the "physical." But for the Greeks all this belonged to *physis* and continued to do so even after Aristotle. They contrasted it with what they called *thesis,* thesis, ordinance, or *nomos,* law, rule in the sense of *ethos.* This, however, denotes not mere norms but mores, based on freely accepted obligations and traditions; it is that which concerns free behavior and attitudes, the shaping of man's historical being, the *ethos* which under the influence of morality was later degraded to the ethical.

The meaning of *physis* is further restricted by contrast with *technē*—which denotes neither art nor technology but a knowledge, the ability to plan and organize freely, to master institutions (cf. Plato's *Phaedrus*). *Technē* is creating, building in the sense of a deliberate pro-ducing. (It would require a special study to explain what is essentially the same in *physis* and *technē*.) The physical was opposed to the historical, a domain which for the Greeks was part of the originally broader concept of *physis*. But this has nothing whatever to do with a naturalistic interpretation of history. The realm of being as such and as a whole is *physis*—i.e. its essence and character are defined as that which emerges and endures. It is experienced primarily through what in a way imposes itself most immediately on our attention, and this was the later, narrower sense of *physis: ta physei onta, ta physika,* nature. If the question concerning *physis* in general was asked at all, i.e. if it was asked: What is the realm of being as such? it was primarily *ta physei onta* that gave the point of departure. Yet from the very outset the question could not dwell in this or that realm of nature, inanimate bodies, plants, animals, but had to reach out beyond *ta physika.*

In Greek, "beyond something" is expressed by the word *meta.* Philosophical inquiry into the realm of being as such is *meta ta physika;* this inquiry goes beyond the essent, it is metaphysics. Here it is not important to follow the genesis and history of this term in detail.

Accordingly, the question to which we have given first rank, "Why are there essents rather than nothing?" is the fundamental question of metaphysics. Metaphysics is a name for the pivotal point and core of all philosophy.

[In this introduction our treatment of the entire subject has been intentionally superficial and hence essentially vague. According to our explanation of the word *physis,* it signifies the being of the essent. If the questioning is *peri physeōs,* if it concerns the being of the essent, then the discussion has gone beyond *physis,* beyond "physics" in the ancient sense, and essentially beyond *ta physika,* beyond essents, and deals with being. From the very first "physics" has determined the essence and history of metaphysics. Even in the doctrines of being as pure act (Thomas Aquinas), as absolute concept (Hegel), as eternal recurrence of the identical will to power (Nietzsche), metaphysics has remained unalterably "physics."

But the inquiry into being as such is of a different nature and origin.

Within the purview of metaphysics and thinking on its level, we can, to be sure, consider the question about being as such as merely a mechanical repetition of the question about the essent as such. In this case the question about being as such is just another transcendental question, though one of a higher order. But this reinterpretation of the question about being as such bars the road to its appropriate unfolding.

However, this new interpretation comes readily to mind; it is bound to suggest itself, particularly as we have spoken in *Sein und Zeit* of a "transcendental horizon." But the "transcendental" there intended is not that of the subjective consciousness; rather, it defines itself in terms of the existential-ecstatic temporality of human being-there. Yet the reinterpretation of the question of being as such tends to take the same form as the question of the essent as such, chiefly because the essential origin of the question of the existent as such and with it the essence of metaphysics remain obscure. And this draws all questions that are in any way concerned with being into the indeterminate.

In the present attempt at an "introduction to metaphysics" I shall keep this confused state of affairs in mind.

In the current interpretation the "question of being" signifies the inquiry into the essent as such (metaphysics). But from the standpoint of *Sein und Zeit,* the "question of being" means the inquiry into being as such. This signification of the title is also the appropriate one from the standpoint of the subject matter and of linguistics; for the "question of being" in the sense of the metaphysical question regarding the essent as such does *not inquire* thematically into being. In this way of asking, being remains forgotten.

But just as ambiguous as the "question of being" referred to in the title is what is said about "forgetfulness of being." It is pointed out—quite correctly—that metaphysics inquires into the being of the essent and that it is therefore an obvious absurdity to impute a forgetfulness of being to metaphysics.

But if we consider the question of being in the sense of an inquiry into being as such, it becomes clear to anyone who follows our thinking that being *as such* is precisely hidden from metaphysics, and remains forgotten—and so radically that the forgetfulness of being, which itself falls into forgetfulness, is the unknown but enduring impetus to metaphysical questioning.

If for the treatment of the "question of being" in the indeterminate sense we choose the name "metaphysics," then the title of the present work is ambiguous. For at first sight the questioning seems to remain within the sphere of the essent as such, yet at the very first sentence it strives to depart from this sphere in order to consider and inquire into another realm. Actually the title of the work is deliberately ambiguous.

The fundamental question of this work is of a different kind from the leading question of metaphysics. Taking what was said in *Sein und Zeit* (pp. 21 f. and 37 f.) as a starting point, we inquired into the *"disclosure of being."* "Disclosure of being" means the unlocking of what forgetfulness of being closes and hides. And it is through this questioning that a light first falls on the *essence* of metaphysics that had hitherto also been hidden.]

"Introduction to metaphysics" means accordingly: an introduction to the asking of the fundamental question. But questions and particularly fundamental questions do not just occur like stones and water. Questions are not found ready-made like shoes and clothes and books. Questions *are,* and are only as they are actually asked. A leading into the asking of the fundamental questions is consequently not a going to something that lies and stands somewhere; no, this leading-to must first awaken and create the questioning. The leading is itself a questioning advance, a preliminary questioning. It is a leading for which in the very nature of things there can be no following. When we hear of disciples, "followers," as in a school of philosophy for example, it means that the nature of questioning is misunderstood. Such schools can exist only in the domain of scientific and technical work. Here everything has its definite hierarchical order. This work is also an indispensable part of philosophy and has today been lost. But the best technical ability can never replace the actual power of seeing and inquiring and speaking.

"Why are there essents rather than nothing?" That is the question. To state the interrogative sentence, even in a tone of questioning, is not yet to question. To repeat the interrogative sentence several times in succession does not necessarily breathe life into the questioning; on the contrary, saying the sentence over and over may well dull the questioning.

But even though the interrogative sentence is not the question and not the questioning, it must not be taken as a mere linguistic form of communication, as though, for example, the interrogative sentence were only a statement "about" a question. When I say to you "Why are there essents rather than nothing?" the purpose of my speaking and questioning is not to communicate to you the fact that a process of questioning is now at work within me. The spoken interrogative sentence can of course be interpreted in this way, but this means precisely that the questioning has not been heard. In this case you do not join me in questioning, nor do you question yourself. No sign of a questioning attitude or state of mind is awakened. Such a state of mind consists in a *willing* to know. Willing—that is no mere wishing or striving. Those who wish to know also seem to question; but they do not go beyond the stating of the question; they stop precisely where the question begins. To question is to will to know. He who wills, he who puts his whole existence into a will, *is* resolved. Resolve does not shift about; it does not shirk, but acts from out of the moment and never stops. Re-solve is no mere decision to act, but the crucial beginning of action that anticipates and reaches through all action. To will is to be resolved. [The essence of willing is here carried back to determination

<Ent-schlossenheit, unclosedness>. But the essence of resolve lies in the opening, the coming-out-of-cover <Ent-borgenheit> of human being-there into the clearing of being, and not in a storing up of energy for "action." See *Sein und Zeit,* §44 and §60. But its relation to being is one of letting-be. The idea that all willing should be grounded in letting-be offends the understanding. See my lecture *Vom Wesen der Wahrheit,* 1930.]

But to know means: to be able to stand in the truth. Truth is the manifestness of the essent. To know is accordingly the ability to stand <stehen> in the manifestness of the essent, to endure <bestehen> it. Merely to have information, however abundant, is not to know. Even if curricula and examination requirements concentrate this information into what is of the greatest practical importance, it still does not amount to knowledge. Even if this information, pruned down to the most indispensable needs, is "close to life," its possession is not knowledge. The man who possesses such information and has learned a few practical tricks, will still be perplexed in the presence of real reality, which is always different from what the philistine means by down-to-earth; he will always be a bungler. Why? Because he has no knowledge, for to know means *to be able to learn.*

In the common-sense view, to be sure, knowledge belongs to the man who has no further need to learn because he has finished learning. No, only that man is knowing who understands that he must keep learning over and over again and who above all, on the basis of this understanding, has attained to the point where he is always *able to learn.* This is much more difficult than to possess information.

Ability to learn presupposes ability to inquire. Inquiry is the willing-to-know analyzed above: the resolve to be able to stand in the openness of the essent. Since we are concerned with the asking of the question that is first in rank, clearly the willing as well as the knowing is of a very special kind. So much the less will the interrogative sentence, even if it is uttered in an authentically questioning tone and even if the listener joins in the questioning, exhaustively reproduce the question. The questioning, which indeed is sounded in the interrogative sentence but which is still enclosed, wrapped up in the words, remains to be unwrapped. The questioning attitude must clarify and secure itself in this process, it must be consolidated by training.

Our next task lies in the development of the question "Why are there essents rather than nothing?" In what direction can it be asked? First of all the question is accessible in the interrogative sentence, which gives a kind of approximation of it. Hence its linguistic formulation must be correspondingly broad and loose. Let us consider our sentence in this respect. "Why are there essents rather than nothing?" The sentence has a caesura. "Why are there essents?" With these words the question is actually asked. The formulation of the question includes: 1) a definite indication of what is put into question, of what is *questioned;* 2) an indication of what the question is about, of what is asked. For it is clearly indicated what the question is about, namely the essent. What is asked after, that which is asked, is the why, i.e. the ground. What follows in the interrogative sentence, "rather than nothing," is only an appendage, which may be said to turn up of its own accord if for purposes of introduction we permit ourselves to speak loosely, a turn of phrase that says nothing further about the question or the object of questioning, an ornamental flourish. Actually the question is far more unambiguous and definite without such an appendage, which springs only from the prolixity of loose discourse. "Why are there essents?" The addition "rather than nothing" is dropped not only because we are striving for a strict formulation of the question but even more because it says nothing. For why should we go on to ask about nothing? Nothing is simply nothing. Here there is nothing more to inquire about. And above all, in talking about nothing or nothingness, we are not making the slightest advance toward the knowledge of the essent.

He who speaks of nothing does not know what he is doing. In speaking of nothing he makes it into a something. In speaking he speaks against what he intended. He contradicts himself. But discourse that contradicts itself offends against the fundamental rule of discourse (*logos*), against "logic." To speak of nothing is illogical. He who speaks and thinks illogically is unscientific. But he who goes so far as to speak of nothing in the realm of philosophy, where logic has its very home, exposes himself most particularly to the accusation of offending against the fundamental rule of all thinking. Such a speaking about nothing consists entirely of meaningless propositions. Moreover: he who takes the nothing seriously is allying himself with nothingness. He is patently promoting the spirit of negation and serving the cause of disintegration. Not only is speaking of nothing utterly repellent to thought; it also undermines all culture and all faith. What disregards the fundamental law of thought and also destroys faith and the will to build is pure nihilism.

On the basis of such considerations we shall do well, in our interrogative sentence, to cross out the superfluous words "rather than nothing" and limit the sentence to the simple and strict form: "Why are there essents?"

To this there would be no objection if . . . if in formulating our question, if altogether, in the asking of this question, we were as free as it may have seemed to us up to this point. But in asking this question we stand in a tradition. For philosophy has always, from time immemorial, asked about the ground of what is. With this question it began and with this question it will end, provided that it ends in greatness and not in an impotent decline. Ever since the question about the essent began, the question about the nonessent, about nothing, has gone side by side with it. And not only outwardly, in the manner of a by-product. Rather, the question about nothing has been asked with the same breadth, depth, and originality as the question about the essent. The manner of asking about nothing may be regarded as a gauge and hallmark for the manner of asking about the essent.

If we bear this in mind, the interrogative sentence uttered in the beginning, "Why are there essents rather than nothing?" seems to express the question about the essent far more adequately than the abbreviated version. It is not looseness of speech or prolixity that leads us to mention nothing. Nor is it an invention of ours; no, it is only strict observance of the original tradition regarding the meaning of the fundamental question.

Still, this speaking of nothing remains in general repellent to thought and in particular demoralizing. But what if both our concern for the fundamental rules of thought and our fear of nihilism, which both seem to counsel against speaking of nothing, should be based on a misunderstanding? And this indeed is the case. True, this misunderstanding is not accidental. It is rooted in long years of failure to understand the question about the essent. And this failure to understand arises from an increasingly hardened forgetfulness of being.

For it cannot be decided out of hand whether logic and its fundamental rules can, altogether, provide a standard for dealing with the question about the essent as such. It might be the other way around. Perhaps the whole body of logic as it is known to us, perhaps all the logic that we treat as a gift from heaven, is grounded in a very definite answer to the question about the essent; perhaps, in consequence, all thinking which solely follows the laws of thought prescribed by traditional logic is incapable from the very start of even understanding the question about the essent by its own resources, let alone actually unfolding the question and guiding it toward an answer. Actually it is only an appearance of strict, scientific method when we invoke the principle of contradiction and logic in general, in order to prove that all thinking and speaking about nothing are contradictory and therefore meaningless. In such a contention "logic" is regarded as a court of justice, established for all eternity, whose rights as first and last authority no rational man will impugn. Anyone who speaks against logic is therefore tacitly or explicitly accused of irresponsibility. And the mere accusation is taken as a proof and an argument relieving one of the need for any further, genuine reflection.

It is perfectly true that we cannot talk about nothing, as though it were a thing like the rain outside or a mountain or any object whatsoever. In principle, nothingness remains inaccessible to science. The man who wishes truly to speak about nothing must of necessity become unscientific. But this is a misfortune only so long as one supposes that scientific thinking is the only authentic rigorous thought, and that it alone can and must be made into the standard of philosophical thinking. But the reverse is true. All scientific thought is merely a derived form of philosophical thinking, which proceeded to freeze into its scientific cast. Philosophy never arises out of science or through science and it can never be accorded equal rank with the sciences. No, it is prior in rank, and not only "logically" or in a table representing the system of the sciences. Philosophy stands in a totally different realm and order. Only poetry stands in the same order as philosophy and its thinking, though poetry and thought are not the same thing. To speak of nothing will always remain a horror and an absurdity for science. But aside from the philosopher, the poet can do so—and not because, as common sense supposes, poetry is without strict rules, but because the spirit of poetry (only authentic and great poetry is meant) is essentially superior to the spirit that prevails in all mere science. By virtue of this superiority the poet always speaks as though the essent were being expressed and invoked for the first time. Poetry, like the thinking of the philosopher, has always so much world space to spare that in it each thing—a tree, a mountain, a house, the cry of a bird—loses all indifference and commonplaceness.

Authentic speaking about nothing always remains extraordinary. It cannot be vulgarized. It dissolves if it is placed in the cheap acid of a merely logical intelligence. Consequently true discourse about nothing can never be immediate like the description of a picture for example. Here I should like to cite a passage from one of Knut Hamsun's last works, *The Road Leads On.* The work forms a whole with *Vagabonds* and *August.* It describes the last years and end of this August, who embodies the uprooted modern man who can do everything equally well yet who cannot lose his ties with the extraordinary, because even in his weakness and despair he remains authentic and superior. In his last days August is alone in the high mountains. And the poet says: "Here he sits between his ears and all he hears is emptiness. An amusing conception, indeed. On the sea there were both motion and sound, something for the ear to feed upon, a chorus of waters. Here nothingness meets nothingness and the result is zero, not even a hole. Enough to make one shake one's head, utterly at a loss." [5]

We see that there is something very interesting about nothing. Let us then go back to our interrogative sentence; let us ask it through, and see whether this "rather than nothing" is merely a meaningless appendage or whether it does not have an essential meaning even in our provisional statement of the question.

Let us begin with the abbreviated, seemingly simpler, and ostensibly stricter form of the question: "Why are there essents?" When we inquire in this way, we start from the essent. The essent *is.* It is given, it confronts us; accordingly, it is to be found at any time, and it is, in certain realms, known to us. Now this essent, from which we start, is immediately questioned as to its ground. The questioning advances im-

[5] Knut Hamsun, *The Road Leads On* (Coward-McCann, 1934), p. 508. Trans. Eugene Gay-Tifft.

mediately toward a ground. Such a method is only an extension and enlargement, so to speak, of a method practiced in everyday life. Somewhere in the vineyard, for example, the vine-disease occurs; something incontestably present. We ask: where does it come from, where and what is the reason for it, the ground? Similarly the essent as a whole is present. We ask: where and what is the ground? This manner of questioning is represented in the simple formula: Why are there essents? Where and what is their ground? Tacitly we are asking after another and higher kind of essent. But here the question is not by any means concerned with the essent as such and as a whole.

But if we put the question in the form of our original interrogative sentence: "Why are there essents rather than nothing?" this addition prevents us in our questioning from beginning directly with an unquestionably given essent and, having scarcely begun, from continuing on to another expected essent as a ground. Instead this essent, through questioning, is held out into the possibility of nonbeing. Thereby the why takes on a very different power and penetration. Why is the essent torn away from the possibility of nonbeing? Why does it not simply keep falling back into nonbeing? Now the essent is no longer that which just happens to be present; it begins to waver and oscillate, regardless of whether or not we recognize the essent in all certainty, regardless of whether or not we apprehend it in its full scope. Henceforth the essent as such oscillates, insofar as we draw it into the question. The swing of the pendulum extends to the extreme and sharpest contrary possibility, to nonbeing and nothingness. And the search for the why undergoes a parallel change. It does not aim simply at providing an also present ground and explanation for what is present; now a ground is sought which will explain the emergence of the essent as an overcoming of nothingness. The ground that is now asked after is the ground of the decision for the essent over against nothingness, or more precisely, the ground for the oscillation of the essent, which sustains and unbinds us, half being, half not being, which is also why we can belong entirely to no thing, not even to ourselves; yet being-there <Dasein> is in every case mine.

[The qualification "in every case mine" means that being-there is allotted to me in order that my self should be being-there. But being-there signifies: care of the ecstatically manifested being of the essent as such, not only of human being. Being-there is "in every case mine"; this means neither "posited through me" nor "apportioned to an individual ego." Being-there is *itself* by virtue of its essential relation to being in general. That is the meaning of the sentence that occurs frequently in *Sein und Zeit:* Being-there implies awareness of being.]

It is already becoming clearer that this "rather than nothing" is no superfluous appendage to the real question, but is an essential component of the whole interrogative sentence, which as a whole states an entirely different question from that intended in the question "Why are there essents?" With our question we place ourselves in the essent in such a way that it loses its self-evident character *as the essent.* The essent begins to waver between the broadest and most drastic extremes: "either essents—or nothing"—and thereby the questioning itself loses all solid foundation. Our questioning being-there is suspended, and in this suspense is nevertheless self-sustained.

But the essent is not changed by our questioning. It remains what it is and as it is. Our questioning is after all only a psycho-spiritual process in us which, whatever course it may take, cannot in any way affect the essent itself. True, the essent remains as it is manifested to us. But it cannot slough off the problematic fact that it might also *not* be what it is and as it is. We do not experience this possibility as something that we add to the essent by thinking; rather, the essent itself elicits this possibility, and in this possibility reveals itself. Our questioning only opens up the horizon, in order that the essent may dawn in such questionableness.

We still know far too little about the process of such questioning, and what we do know is far too crude. In this questioning we seem to belong entirely to ourselves. Yet it is this questioning that moves us into the open, provided that in questioning it transform itself (which all true questioning does), and cast a new space over everything and into everything.

The main thing is not to let ourselves be led astray by overhasty theories, but to experience things as they are on the basis of the first thing that comes to hand. This piece of chalk has extension; it is a relatively solid, grayish white thing with a definite shape, and apart from all that, it is a thing to write with. This particular thing has the attribute of lying here; but just as surely, it has the attribute of potentially not lying here and not being so large. The possibility of being guided along the blackboard and of being used up is not something that we add to the thing by thought. Itself, as this essent, is in this possibility; otherwise it would not be chalk as a writing material. Correspondingly, every essent has in it this potentiality in a different way. This potentiality belongs to the chalk. It has in itself a definite aptitude for a definite use. True, we are accustomed and inclined, in seeking this potentiality in the chalk, to say that we cannot see or touch it. But that is a prejudice, the elimination of which is part of the unfolding of our question. For the present our question is only to open up the essent in its wavering between nonbeing and being. Insofar as the essent resists the extreme possibility of nonbeing, it stands in being, but it has never caught up with or overcome the possibility of nonbeing.

We suddenly find ourselves speaking of the nonbeing and being of the essent, without saying how this being or nonbeing is related to the essent. Are the two terms the same? The essent and its being? What, for example, is "the essent" in this piece of chalk? The very question is ambiguous, because the word "the essent" can be understood in two respects, like the Greek *to on.* The essent means first *that* which is at any time, in particular this grayish white, so-and-so-shaped, light, brittle mass. But "the essent" also means that which "brings it about," so to speak, that this thing is an essent rather than a nonessent, that which constitutes its being if it *is.* In accordance with this twofold meaning of the word "the essent," the Greek *to on* often has the second significance, not the essent itself, not that which is, but "is-ness," essentness, being. Over against this, "the essent" in the first sense signifies all or particular essent things themselves, in respect to themselves and not to their is-ness, their *ousia.*

The first meaning of *to on* refers to *ta onta* (entia), the second to *to einai* (esse). We have listed what the essent is in the piece of chalk. This was relatively easy to do. It was also easy to see that the object named can also *not* be, that this chalk need ultimately not be here and not be. What then is being in distinction to what can stand in being or fall back into nonbeing—what is being in distinction to the essent? Is it the same as the essent? We ask the question once again. But in the foregoing we did not list being; we listed only material mass, grayish-white light, so-and-so-shaped, brittle. But where is the being situated? It must belong to the chalk, for this chalk *is.*

We encounter the essent everywhere; it sustains and drives us, enchants and fills us, elevates and disappoints us; but with all this, where is, and wherein consists, the being of the essent? One might reply: this distinction between the essent and its being may occasionally have an importance from the standpoint of language and even of meaning; this distinction can be effected in mere thought, i.e. in ideas and opinions, but is it certain that anything essent in the essent corresponds to the distinction? And even this merely cogitated distinction is questionable; for it remains unclear *what* is to be thought under the name of "being." Meanwhile it suffices to know the essent and secure our mastery over it. To go further and introduce being as distinct from it is artificial and leads to nothing.

We have already said a certain amount about this frequent question: What comes of such distinctions? Here we are going to concentrate on our undertaking. We ask: "Why are there essents rather than nothing?" And in this question we seemingly stick to the essent and avoid all empty brooding about being. But what really are we asking? Why the essent as such is. We are asking for the ground of the essent: that it is and is what it is, and that there is not rather nothing. Fundamentally we are asking about being. But how? We are asking about the being of the essent. We are questioning the essent in regard to its being.

But if we persevere in our questioning we shall actually be questioning forward, asking about being in respect to its ground, even if this question remains undeveloped and it remains undecided whether being itself is not in itself a ground and a sufficient ground. If we regard this question of being as the first question in order of rank, should we ask it without knowing how it stands with being and how being stands in its distinction to the essent? How shall we inquire into, not to say find, the ground for the being of the essent, if we have not adequately considered and understood being itself? This undertaking would be just as hopeless as if someone were to try to bring out the cause and ground of a fire, and yet claim that he need not worry about the actual course of the fire or examine the scene of it.

Thus it transpires that the question "Why are there essents rather than nothing?" compels us to ask the preliminary question: "How does it stand with being?"

Here we are asking about something which we barely grasp, which is scarcely more than the sound of a word for us, and which puts us in danger of serving a mere word idol when we proceed with our questioning. Hence it is all the more indispensable that we make it clear from the very outset how it stands at present with being and with our understanding of being. And in this connection the main thing is to impress it on our experience that we cannot immediately grasp the being of the essent itself, either through the essent or in the essent—or anywhere else.

A few examples may be helpful. Over there, across the street, stands the high school building. An essent. We can look over the building from all sides, we can go in and explore it from cellar to attic, and note everything we encounter in that building: corridors, staircases, schoolrooms, and their equipment. Everywhere we find essents and we even find them in a very definite arrangement. Now where is the being of this high school? For after all it *is*. The building *is*. If anything belongs to this essent, it is its being; yet we do not find the being inside it.

Nor does the being consist in the fact that we look at the essent. The building stands there even if we do not look at it. We can find it only because it already *is*. Moreover, this building's being does not by any means seem to be the same for everyone. For us, who look at it or ride by, it is different than for the pupils who sit in it; not because they see it only from within but because for them this building really is what it is and as it is. You can, as it were, smell the being of this building in your nostrils. The smell communicates the being of this essent far more immediately and truly than any description or inspection could ever do. But on the other hand the building's being is not based on this odor that is somewhere in the air.

How does it stand with being? Can you see being? We see essents; this chalk for example. But do we see being as we see color and light and shade? Or do we hear, smell, taste, feel being? We hear the motorcycle racing through the street. We hear the grouse gliding through the forest. But actually we hear only the whirring of the motor, the sound the grouse makes. As a matter of fact it is difficult to describe even the pure sound, and we do not ordinarily do so, because it is *not* what we commonly hear. [From the standpoint of sheer sound] we always hear *more*. We hear the flying bird, even though strictly speaking we should say: a grouse is nothing audible, it is no manner of tone that fits into a scale. And so it is with the other senses. We touch velvet, silk; we see them directly as this and that kind of essent, the one different from the other. Wherein lies and wherein consists being?

But we must take a wider look around us and consider the lesser and greater circle within which we spend our days and hours, wittingly and unwittingly, a circle whose limits shift continuously and which is suddenly broken through.

A heavy storm coming up in the mountains "is," or what here amounts to the same thing, "was" during the night. Wherein consists its being?

A distant mountain range under a broad sky . . . It "is." Wherein consists the being? When and to whom does it reveal itself? To the traveler who enjoys the landscape, or to the peasant who makes his living in it and from it, or to the meteorologist who is preparing a weather report? Who of these apprehends being? All and none. Or is what these men apprehend of the mountain range under the great sky only certain aspects of it, not the mountain range itself as it "is" as such, not that wherein its actual being consists? Who may be expected to apprehend this being? Or is it a non-sense, contrary to the sense of being, to inquire after what is in itself, behind those aspects? Does the being lie in the aspects?

The door of an early romanesque church is an essent. How and to whom is its being revealed? To the connoisseur of art, who examines it and photographs it on an excursion, or to the abbot who on a holiday passes through this door with his monks, or to the children who play in its shadow on a summer's day? How does it stand with the being of this essent?

A state—*is*. By virtue of the fact that the state police arrest a suspect, or that so-and-so-many typewriters are clattering in a government building, taking down the words of ministers and state secretaries? Or "is" the state in a conversation between the chancellor and the British foreign minister? The state *is*. But where is being situated? Is it situated anywhere at all?

A painting by Van Gogh. A pair of rough peasant shoes, nothing else. Actually the painting represents nothing. But as to what *is* in that picture, you are immediately alone with it as though you yourself were making your way wearily homeward with your hoe on an evening in late fall after the last potato fires have died down. What *is* here? The canvas? The brush strokes? The spots of color?

What in all these things we have just mentioned is the being of the essent? We run (or stand) around in the world with our silly subtleties and conceit. But where in all this is being?

All the things we have named *are* and yet—when we wish to apprehend being, it is always as though we were reaching into the void. The being after which we inquire is almost like nothing, and yet we have always rejected the contention that the essent in its entirety *is not.*

But being remains unfindable, almost like nothing, or ultimately *quite* so. Then, in the end, the word "being" is no more than an empty word. It means nothing real, tangible, material. Its meaning is an unreal vapor. Thus in the last analysis Nietzsche was perfectly right in calling such "highest concepts" as being "the last cloudy streak of evaporating reality." Who would want to chase after such a vapor, when the very term is merely a name for a great fallacy! "Nothing indeed has exercised a more simple power of persuasion hitherto than the error of Being . . ."[6]

"Being"—a vapor and a fallacy? What Nietzsche says here of being is no random remark thrown out in the frenzy of preparation for his central, never finished work. No, this was his guiding view of being from the earliest days of his philosophical effort. It is the fundamental support and determinant of his philosophy. Yet even now this philosophy holds its ground against all the crude importunities of the scribblers who cluster round him more numerous with each passing day. And so far there seems to be no end in sight to this abuse of Nietzsche's work. In speaking here of Nietzsche, we mean to have nothing to do with all that—or with blind hero worship for that matter. The task in hand is too crucial and at the same time too sobering. It consists first of all, if we are to gain a true grasp of Nietzsche, in bringing his accomplishment to a full unfolding. Being a vapor, a fallacy? If this were so, the only possible consequence would be to abandon the question "Why are there essents as such and as a whole, rather than nothing?" For what good is the question if what it inquires into is only a vapor and a fallacy?

Does Nietzsche speak the truth? Or was he himself only the last victim of a long process of error and neglect, but as such the unrecognized witness to a new necessity?

Is it the fault of being that it is so involved? is it the fault of the word that it remains so empty? or are we to blame that with all our effort, with all our chasing after the essent, we have fallen out of being? And should we not say that the fault did not begin with us, or with our immediate or more remote ancestors, but lies in something that runs through Western history from the very beginning, a happening which the eyes of all the historians in the world will never perceive, but which nevertheless happens, which happened in the past and will happen in the future? What if it were possible that man, that nations in their greatest movements and traditions, are linked to being and yet had long fallen out of being, without knowing it, and that this was the most

[6] *The Twilight of Idols,* Nietzsche's Complete Works, Edinburgh and London. *16* (1911), 19, 22.

powerful and most central cause of their decline? (See *Sein und Zeit,* §38, in particular pp. 179 f.)

We do not ask these questions incidentally, and still less do they spring from any particular outlook or state of mind; no, they are questions to which we are driven by that preliminary question which sprang necessarily from our main question "How does it stand with being?" —a sober question perhaps, but assuredly a very useless one. And yet a *question, the* question: is "being" a mere word and its meaning a vapor or is it the spiritual destiny of the Western world?

This Europe, in its ruinous blindness forever on the point of cutting its own throat, lies today in a great pincers, squeezed between Russia on one side and America on the other. From a metaphysical point of view, Russia and America are the same; the same dreary technological frenzy, the same unrestricted organization of the average man. At a time when the farthermost corner of the globe has been conquered by technology and opened to economic exploitation; when any incident whatever, regardless of where or when it occurs, can be communicated to the rest of the world at any desired speed; when the assassination of a king in France and a symphony concert in Tokyo can be "experienced" simultaneously; when time has ceased to be anything other than velocity, instantaneousness, and simultaneity, and time as history has vanished from the lives of all peoples; when a boxer is regarded as a nation's great man; when mass meetings attended by millions are looked on as a triumph—then, yes then, through all this turmoil a question still haunts us like a specter: What for?—Whither?—And what then?

The spiritual decline of the earth is so far advanced that the nations are in danger of losing the last bit of spiritual energy that makes it possible to see the decline (taken in relation to the history of "being"), and to appraise it as such. This simple observation has nothing to do with *Kulturpessimismus,* and of course it has nothing to do with any sort of optimism either; for the darkening of the world, the flight of the gods, the destruction of the earth, the transformation of men into a mass, the hatred and suspicion of everything free and creative, have assumed such proportions throughout the earth that such childish categories as pessimism and optimism have long since become absurd.

We are caught in a pincers. Situated in the center, our nation incurs the severest pressure. It is the nation with the most neighbors and hence the most endangered. With all this, it is the most metaphysical of nations. We are certain of this vocation, but our people will only be able to wrest a destiny from it if *within itself* it creates a resonance, a possibility of resonance for this vocation, and takes a creative view of its tradition. All this implies that this nation, as a historical nation, must move itself and thereby the history of the West beyond the center of their future "happening" and into the primordial realm of the powers of being. If the great decision regarding Europe is not to bring annihilation, that decision must be made in terms of new spiritual energies unfolding historically from out of the center.

To ask "How does it stand with being?" means nothing less than to recapture, to repeat <wieder-holen>, the beginning of our historical-spiritual existence, in order to transform it into a new beginning. This is possible. It is indeed the crucial form of history, because it begins in the fundamental event. But we do not repeat a beginning by reducing it to something past and now known, which need merely be imitated; no, the beginning must be begun again, more radically, with all the strangeness, darkness, insecurity that attend a true beginning. Repetition as we understand it is anything but an improved continuation with the old methods of what has been up to now.

The question "How is it with being?" is included as a preliminary question in our central question "Why are there essents rather than nothing?" If we now begin to look into that which is questioned in our preliminary question, namely being, the full truth of Nietzsche's dictum is at once apparent. For if we look closely, what more is "being" to us than a mere word, an indeterminate meaning, intangible as a vapor? Nietzsche's judgment, to be sure, was meant in a purely disparaging sense. For him "being" is a delusion that should never have come about. Is "being," then, indeterminate, vague as a vapor? It is indeed. But we do not mean to sidestep this fact. On the contrary, we must see how much of a fact it is if we are to perceive its full implication.

Our questioning brings us into the landscape we must inhabit as a basic prerequisite, if we are to win back our roots in history. We shall have to ask why this fact, that for us "being" is no more than a word and a vapor, should have arisen precisely today, or whether and why it has existed for a long time. We must learn to see that this fact is not as harmless as it seems at first sight. For ultimately what matters is not that the word "being" remains a mere sound and its meaning a vapor, but that we have fallen away from what this word says and for the moment cannot find our way back; that it is for this and no other reason that the word "being" no longer applies to anything, that everything, if we merely take hold of it, dissolves like a tatter of cloud in the sunlight. Because this is so—that is why we ask about being. And we *ask* because we know that truths have never fallen into any nation's lap. The fact that people still cannot and do not wish to understand this question, even if it is asked in a still more fundamental form, deprives the question of none of its cogency.

Of course we can, seemingly with great astuteness and perspicacity, revive the old familiar argument to the effect that "being" is the most universal of concepts, that it covers anything and everything, even the nothing which also, in the sense that it is thought or spoken, "is" something. Beyond the domain of this most universal concept "being," there is, in the strictest sense of the word, nothing more, on the basis of which being itself could be more closely determined. The concept of being is an ultimate. Moreover, there is a law of logic that says: the more comprehensive a concept is—and what could be more comprehensive than the concept of "being"?—the more indeterminate and empty is its content.

For every normally thinking man—and we all should like to be normal men—this reasoning is immediately and wholly convincing. But the question now arises: does the designation of being as the most universal concept strike the essence of being, or is it not from the very outset such a misinterpretation that all questioning becomes hopeless? This then is the question: can being be regarded only as the most universal concept which inevitably occurs in all special concepts, or is being of an entirely different essence, and hence anything but an object of "ontology," provided we take this word in its traditional sense?

The word "ontology" was first coined in the seventeenth century. It marks the development of the traditional doctrine of the essent into a discipline of philosophy and a branch of the philosophical system. But the traditional doctrine was an academic classification and ordering of what for Plato and Aristotle and again for Kant was a question, though no longer to be sure a primordial one. And it is in this sense that the word "ontology" is used today. Under this title each school of philosophy has set up and described a branch within its system. But we can also take the word "ontology" in the "broadest sense," "without reference to ontological directions and tendencies" (cf. *Sein und Zeit*, p. 11 top). In this case "ontology" signifies the endeavor to make being manifest itself, and to do so by way of the question "how does it stand with being?" (and not only with the essent as such). But since thus far this question has not even been heard, let alone echoed; since it has been expressly rejected by the various schools of academic philosophy, which strive for an "ontology" in the traditional sense, it may be preferable to dispense in the future with the terms "ontology" and "ontological." Two modes of questioning which, as we now see clearly, are worlds apart, should not bear the same name.

We ask the questions "How does it stand with being?" "What is the meaning of being?" *not* in order to set up an ontology on the traditional style, much less to criticize the past mistakes of ontology. We are concerned with something totally different: to restore man's historical being-there—and that always includes our own future being-there in the totality of the history allotted to us—to the domain of being, which it was originally incumbent on man to open up for himself. All this, to be sure, in the limits within which philosophy can accomplish anything.

Out of the fundamental question of metaphysics, "Why are there essents rather than nothing?" we have separated the preliminary question, "How does it stand with being?" The relation between the two questions requires clarification, for it is of a special kind. Ordinarily a preliminary question is dealt with before and outside the main question, though in reference to it. But, in principle, philosophical questions are never dealt with as though we might some day cast them aside. Here the preliminary question is not by any means outside of the main question; rather, it is the flame which burns as it were in the asking of the fundamental question; it is the flaming center of all questioning. That is to say: it is crucial for the first asking of the fundamental question that in asking its *preliminary* question we derive the decisive fundamental attitude that is here essential. That is why we have related the question of being to the destiny of Europe, where the destiny of the earth is being decided—while our own historic being-there proves to be the center for Europe itself.

The question is:

Is being a mere word and its meaning a vapor, or does what is designated by the word "being" hold within it the historical destiny of the West?

To many ears the question may sound violent and exaggerated: for one might in a pinch suppose that a discussion of the question of being might be related in some very remote and indirect way to the decisive historical question of the earth, but assuredly not that the basic position and attitude of our questioning might be directly determined by the history of the human spirit on earth. And yet this relationship exists. Since our purpose is to set in motion the asking of the preliminary question, we must now show that, and to what extent, the asking of this question is an immediate and fundamental factor in the crucial historical question. For this demonstration it is necessary to anticipate an essential insight in the form of an assertion.

We maintain that this preliminary question and with it the fundamental question of metaphysics are historical questions through and through. But do not metaphysics and philosophy thereby become a historical science? Historical science after all investigates the temporal, while philosophy investigates the timeless. Philosophy is historical only insofar as it—like every work of the spirit—realizes itself in time. But in this sense the designation of metaphysical questioning as historical cannot characterize metaphysics, but merely expresses something obvious. Accordingly, the assertion is either meaningless and superfluous or else impossible, because it creates an amalgam of two fundamentally different kinds of science: philosophy and historical science.

In answer to this it must be said:

1. Metaphysics and philosophy are not sciences at all, and the fact that their questioning is basically historical cannot make them so.

2. Historical science does not determine a fundamental relation to history, but always presupposes such a relation. It is only for this reason that historical science can distort men's relation to history, which itself is always historical; or misinterpret it and degrade it to a mere knowledge of antiquities; or else deal with crucial fields in the light of this

once established relation to history, and so produce cogent history. A historical relation between our historical being-there and history may become an object of knowledge and mark an advanced state of knowledge; but it need not. Moreover, all relations to history cannot be scientifically objectified and given a place in science, and it is precisely the essential ones that cannot. Historical science can never produce the historical relation to history. It can only illuminate a relation once supplied, ground it in knowledge, which is indeed an absolute necessity for the historical being-there of a wise people, and not either an "advantage" or a "disadvantage." Because it is only in philosophy —*as distinguished from all science*—that essential relations to the realm of what is take shape, this relation *can,* indeed *must,* for us today be a fundamentally historical one.

But for an understanding of our assertion that the "metaphysical" asking of the preliminary question is historical through and through, it is above all necessary to consider this: for us history is not synonymous with the past; for the past is precisely what is no longer happening. And much less is history the merely contemporary, which never happens but merely "passes," comes and goes by. History as happening is an acting and being acted upon which pass through the *present,* which are determined from out of the future, and which take over the past. It is precisely the present that vanishes in happening.

Our asking of the fundamental question of metaphysics is historical because it opens up the process of human being-there in its essential relations—i.e. its relations to the essent as such and as a whole—opens it up to unasked possibilities, futures, and at the same time binds it back to its past beginning, so sharpening it and giving it weight in its present. In this questioning our being-there is summoned to its history in the full sense of the word, called to history and to a decision in history. And this not after the fact, in the sense that we draw ethical, ideological lessons from it. No, the basic attitude of the questioning is in itself historical; it stands and maintains itself in happening, in giving out of happening for the sake of happening.

But we have not yet come to the essential reason why this inherently historical asking of the question about being is actually an integral part of history on earth. We have said that the world is darkening. The essential episodes of this darkening are: the flight of the gods, the destruction of the earth, the standardization of man, the pre-eminence of the mediocre.

What do we mean by world when we speak of a darkening of the world? World is always world of the *spirit.* The animal has no world nor any environment <Umwelt>. Darkening of the world means emasculation of the spirit, the disintegration, wasting away, repression, and misinterpretation of the spirit. We shall attempt to explain the emasculation of the spirit in one respect, that of misinterpretation. We have said: Europe lies in a pincers between Russia and America, which are metaphysically the same, namely in regard to their world character and their relation to the spirit. What makes the situation of Europe all the more catastrophic is that this enfeeblement of the spirit originated in Europe itself and—though prepared by earlier factors—was definitively determined by its own spiritual situation in the first half of the nineteenth century. It was then that occurred what is popularly and succinctly called the "collapse of German idealism." This formula is a kind of shield behind which the already dawning spiritlessness, the dissolution of the spiritual energies, the rejection of all original inquiry into grounds and men's bond with the grounds, are hidden and masked. It was not German idealism that collapsed; rather, the age was no longer strong enough to stand up to the greatness, breadth, and originality of that spiritual world, i.e. truly to realize it, for to realize a philosophy means something very different from applying theorems and insights. The lives of men began to slide into a world which lacked that depth from out of which the essential always comes to man and comes back to man, so compelling him to become superior and making him act in conformity to a rank. All things sank to the same level, a surface resembling a blind mirror that no longer reflects, that casts nothing back. The prevailing dimension became that of extension and number. Intelligence no longer meant a wealth of talent, lavishly spent, and the command of energies, but only what could be learned by everyone, the practice of a routine, always associated with a certain amount of sweat and a certain amount of show. In America and in Russia this development grew into a boundless etcetera of indifference and always-the-sameness—so much so that the quantity took on a quality of its own. Since then the domination in those countries of a cross section of the indifferent mass has become something more than a dreary accident. It has become an active onslaught that destroys all rank and every world-creating impulse of the spirit, and calls it a lie. This is the onslaught of what we call the demonic (in the sense of destructive evil). There are many indications of the emergence of this demonism, identical with the increasing helplessness and uncertainty of Europe against it and within itself. One of these signs is the emasculation of the spirit through misinterpretation; we are still in the midst of this process. This misinterpretation of the spirit may be described briefly in four aspects.

1. The crux of the matter is the reinterpretation of the spirit as *intelligence,* or mere cleverness in examining and calculating given things and the possibility of changing them and complementing them to make new things. This cleverness is a matter of mere talent and practice and mass division of labor. The cleverness itself is subject to the possibility of organization, which is never true of the spirit. The attitude of the *littérateur* and esthete is merely a late consequence and variation of the spirit falsified into intelligence. Mere intelligence is a semblance of spirit, masking its absence.

2. The spirit falsified into intelligence thus falls to the level of a tool in the service of others, a tool the manipulation of which can be taught and learned. Whether this use of intelligence relates to the regulation and domination of the material conditions of production (as in Marxism) or in general to the intelligent ordering and explanation of everything that is present and already posited at any time (as in positivism), or whether it is applied to the organization and regulation of a nation's vital resources and race—in any case the spirit as intelligence becomes the impotent superstructure of something else, which, because it is without spirit or even opposed to the spirit, is taken for the actual reality. If the spirit is taken as intelligence, as is done in the most extreme form of Marxism, then it is perfectly correct to say, in defense against it, that in the order of the effective forces of human being-there, the spirit, i.e. intelligence, must always be ranked below healthy physical activity and character. But this order becomes false once we understand the true essence of the spirit. For all true power and beauty of the body, all sureness and boldness in combat, all authenticity and inventiveness of the understanding, are grounded in the spirit and rise or fall only through the power or impotence of the spirit. The spirit is the sustaining, dominating principle, the first and the last, not merely an indispensable third factor.

3. As soon as the misinterpretation sets in that degrades the spirit to a tool, the energies of the spiritual process, poetry and art, statesmanship and religion, become subject to *conscious* cultivation and planning. They are split into branches. The spiritual world becomes culture and the individual strives to perfect himself in the creation and preservation of this culture. These branches become fields of free endeavor, which sets its own standards and barely manages to live up to them. These standards of production and consumption are called values. The cultural values preserve their meaning only by restricting themselves to an autonomous field: poetry for the sake of poetry, art for the sake of art, science for the sake of science.

Let us consider the example of science, which is of particular concern to us here at the university. The state of science since the turn of the century—it has remained unchanged despite a certain amount of house cleaning—is easy to see. Though today two seemingly different conceptions of science seem to combat one another—science as technical, practical, professional knowledge and science as cultural value per se—both are moving along the same downgrade of misinterpretation and emasculation of the spirit. They differ only in this: in the present situation the technical, practical conception of science as specialization can at least lay claim to frank and clear consistency, while the reactionary interpretation of science as a cultural value, now making its reappearance, seeks to conceal the impotence of the spirit behind an unconscious lie. The confusion of spiritlessness can even go so far as to lead the upholders of the technical, practical view of science to profess their belief in science as a cultural value; then the two understand each other perfectly in the same spiritlessness. We may choose to call the institution where the specialized sciences are grouped together for purposes of teaching and research a university, but this is no more than a name; the "university" has ceased to be a fundamental force for unity and responsibility. What I said here in 1929, in my inaugural address, is still true of the German university: "The scientific fields are still far apart. Their subjects are treated in fundamentally different ways. Today this hodgepodge of disciplines is held together only by the technical organization of the universities and faculties and preserves what meaning it has only through the practical aims of the different branches. The sciences have lost their roots in their essential ground." (*Was ist Metaphysik?* 1929, p. 8.) Science today in all its branches is a technical, practical business of gaining and transmitting information. An awakening of the spirit cannot take its departure from such science. It is itself in need of an awakening.

4. The last misinterpretation of the spirit is based on the abovementioned falsifications which represent the spirit as intelligence, and intelligence as a serviceable tool which, along with its product, is situated in the realm of culture. In the end the spirit as utilitarian intelligence and the spirit as culture become holiday ornaments cultivated along with many other things. They are brought out and exhibited as a proof that there is *no* intention to combat culture or favor barbarism. In the beginning Russian Communism took a purely negative attitude but soon went over to propagandist tactics of this kind.

In opposition to this multiple misinterpretation of the spirit, we define the essence of the spirit briefly as follows (I shall quote from the address I delivered on the occasion of my appointment as rector, because of its succinct formulation: "Spirit is neither empty cleverness nor the irresponsible play of the wit, nor the boundless work of dismemberment carried on by the practical intelligence; much less is it world-reason; no, spirit is a fundamental, knowing resolve toward the essence of being." (*Rektoratsrede,* p. 13.) Spirit is the mobilization of the powers of the essent as such and as a whole. Where spirit prevails, the essent as such becomes always and at all times more essent. Thus the inquiry into the essent as such and as a whole, the asking of the question of being, is one of the essential and fundamental conditions for an awakening of the spirit and hence for an original world of historical being-there. It is indispensable if the peril of world darkening is to be forestalled and if our nation in the center of the Western world is to take on its historical mission. Here we can explain only in these broad outlines why the asking of the question of being is in itself through and through historical, and why, accordingly, our question as to whether being will remain a mere vapor for us or become the destiny of the West is anything but an exaggeration and a rhetorical figure.

But if our question about being has this essential and decisive character, we must above all take an absolutely serious view of *the fact* that gives the question its immediate necessity, the fact that for us being has become little more than a mere word and its meaning an evanescent vapor. This is not the kind of fact which merely confronts us as something alien and other, which we need merely note as an occurrence. It is a fact in which we stand. It is a state of our being-there. And by state, of course, I do not mean a quality that can be demonstrated only psychologically. Here state means our entire constitution, the way in which we ourselves are constituted in regard to being. Here we are not concerned with psychology but with our history in an essential respect. When we call it a "fact" that being for us is a mere word and vapor, we are speaking very provisionally. We are merely holding fast, establishing something which has not yet been thought through, for which we still have no locus, even if it looks as though this something were an occurrence among us, here and now, or "in" us, as we like to say.

One would like to integrate the individual fact that for us being remains no more than an empty word and an evanescent vapor with the more general fact that many words, and precisely the essential ones, are in the same situation; that the language in general is worn out and used up—an indispensable but masterless means of communication that may be used as one pleases, as indifferent as a means of public transport, as a street car which everyone rides in. Everyone speaks and writes away in the language, without hindrance and above all *without danger*. That is certainly true. And only a very few are capable of thinking through the full implications of this misrelation and unrelation of present-day being-there to language.

But the emptiness of the word "being," the total disappearance of its appellative force, is not merely a particular instance of the general exhaustion of language; rather, the destroyed relation to being as such is the actual reason for the general misrelation to language.

The organizations for the purification of the language and defense against its progressive barbarization are deserving of respect. But such efforts merely demonstrate all the more clearly that we no longer know what is at stake in language. Because the destiny of language is grounded in a nation's *relation* to *being,* the question of being will involve us deeply in the question of language. It is more than an outward accident that now, as we prepare to set forth, in all its implication, the fact of the evaporation of being, we find ourselves compelled to take linguistic considerations as our starting point.

PLATO'S DOCTRINE OF TRUTH[1]

(TRANSLATED BY JOHN BARLOW)

The knowledge of the sciences is usually expressed in propositions which are then set before man as comprehensible results for him to put to use. The "doctrine" of a thinker is that which is left unsaid in what he says, to which man is exposed in order to expend himself upon it.

In order to learn and henceforth know what a thinker has left unsaid, whatever it may be, it is necessary to consider what he has said. To meet this challenge correctly we would have to discuss all of Plato's "dialogues" thoroughly and in their context. Since this is impossible, another way will have to lead to what is left unsaid in Plato's thought.

What remains unsaid in Plato is a shift in the definition of the essence of truth. An exposition of the "allegory of the cave" would make it clear that this shift takes place, what this shift consists in, and what this change of the essence of truth is the basis for.

The seventh book of the "dialogue" on the essence of the πόλις begins with the presentation of the "allegory of the cave" (*Republic* VII, 514a, 2—517a, 7). The "allegory" tells a story. The tale unfolds in the dialogue between Socrates and Glaucon. While Socrates presents the story, Glaucon shows the astonishment of one awakening. The parentheses in the following translation[2] indicate where it has interpretively gone beyond the Greek text.

"Imagine the condition of men living in a sort of cavernous chamber underground, with an entrance open to the light and a long passage all down the cave. Here they have been from childhood, chained by the leg

[1] *Platons Lehre von der Wahrheit. Mit einen Brief uber den "Humanismus,"* pp. 5-52. A. Francke, Bern, 1947.

[2] The translation is for the most part that of Francis MacDonald Cornford, revised in places to coincide with Heidegger's own translation.

and also by the neck, so that they cannot move and can see only what is in front of them, because the chains will not let them turn their heads. At some distance higher up is the light of a fire burning behind them; and between the fire and the prisoners (therefore behind them) is a track with a parapet built along it, like the screen at a puppetshow, which hides the performers while they show their puppets over the top. —I see, said he.—

"Now behind this parapet imagine persons carrying along various artificial objects, including figures of men and animals in wood or stone or other materials, which project over the parapet. Naturally, some of these persons will be talking, others silent.

"—It is a strange image, he said, and a strange sort of prisoners. —Like ourselves, I replied; for in the first place prisoners so confined would have seen nothing of themselves or of one another, except the shadows (constantly) thrown by the fire-light on the wall of the cave facing them, would they?

"—Not if all their lives they had been prevented from moving their heads.—

"—And they would have seen as little of the objects carried past. —Of course.—

"—Now, if they could talk to one another about what they caught sight of, don't you think they would consider what they saw were beings (that which is)? —Necessarily.—

"And suppose their prison had an echo from the wall facing them (upon which alone they constantly gaze)? When one of the people crossing behind them spoke, they could only suppose that the sound came from the shadow passing before their eyes. —No doubt.—In every way, then, men so chained would recognize as the unhidden nothing but the shadows of those artificial objects. —Inevitably.—

"Now consider what would happen if their release from the chains and the healing of their lack of insight should come about in this way. Suppose one of them set free and forced suddenly to stand up, turn his head around, and walk with eyes lifted to the light; all these movements would (always) be painful, and he would be too dazzled to make out the objects whose shadows he had been used to see. (If all this should happen to him), what do you think he would say, if someone told him that what he had formerly seen was (only) nothingness, but now, since he is somewhat nearer to beings and turned towards things that are being more, he was getting a more correct view? Suppose further that he were shown the various objects being carried by and were made to say, in reply to questions, what each of them was. Would he not be perplexed and believe what he formerly saw (with his own eyes) to be more unhidden than the objects now shown to him (by another)? —Most certainly, he said.—

"And if he were forced to look at the fire-light itself, would not his eyes ache, so that he would try to escape and turn back to the things which he could see distinctly, convinced that they really were clearer than these other objects now being shown to him? —Yes.—

"And suppose someone were to drag him away forcibly up the steep and rugged ascent and not let him go until he had hauled him out into the sunlight, would he not suffer pain and vexation at such treatment, and, when he had come out into the light, find his eyes so full of its radiance that he could not see anything of what he was now told was the unhidden?

"—Certainly he would not see much of them.—

"He would need, then, to grow accustomed before he could see things in that upper world (outside of the cave in the light of the sun). (With such an orientation) it would at first be easiest to make out shadows, and then the aspect of men and things reflected in water, and later on the things themselves (beings instead of the diminishing reflections). After that, it would be easier to watch the heavenly bodies and the sky itself by night, looking at the light of the moon and stars rather than the sun and the sun's light in the day-time. —Yes, surely.—

"Last of all, he would be able to look at the sun itself and contemplate its nature, not as it appears when reflected in water or any alien medium, but as it is in itself in its own domain. —No doubt.—

"And now he would begin to draw the conclusion that it is the sun that produces the seasons and the course of the year and controls everything in the (currently) visible region (of sunlight), and moreover is in a way the cause of all that he and his companions (who are remaining down in the cave) used to see.

"—Clearly, he said, he would turn to this (to the sun and to whatever is in its light) after he had gone over all that (which is only reflection and shadow).—

"Then if he called to mind his fellow prisoners and what passed for wisdom in his former dwelling-place, he would surely think himself happy in the change and be sorry for them. They may have had a practice of honoring and commending one another, with prizes for the man who had the keenest eye for the passing shadows and the best memory for the order in which they followed or accompanied one another, so that he could make a good guess as to which was going to come next. Would our released prisoner be likely to covet those prizes or to envy the men exalted to honor and power in the cave? Would he not feel like Homer's Achilles, that he would far sooner 'be on earth as a hired servant in the house of a landless man' or endure anything rather than go back to his old beliefs and live in the old way?

"—Yes, he would prefer any fate to such a life.—

"Now imagine what would happen if he went down again to take his former seat in the cave. Coming suddenly out of the sunlight, his eyes would be filled with darkness. He might be required once more to deliver his opinion on those shadows, in competition with the prisoners who had never been released, while his eyesight was still dim and unsteady; and it might take some time to become used to the darkness. They would laugh at him and say that he had gone up only to come back with his sight ruined; it was worth no one's while even to attempt the ascent. If they could lay hands on the man who was trying to set them free and lead them up, they would kill him.—

"—Yes, they would.—"

What does this story mean? Plato gives the answer himself, for he immediately follows the story with its interpretation (517a, 8—518d, 7).

The cavernous chamber is the "image" for τὴν . . . δι' ὄψεως φαινομένην ἕδραν "the realm where we abide and which (in everyday life) is revealed to us through the sense of sight." The fire in the cave, which burns above the cave-dwellers, is the "image" for the sun. The vault of the cave represents the firmament. Under this vault, assigned to the earth and bound to it, men are living. Whatever goes on around them and concerns them there, is, to them, "the real," i.e. beings (that which is). In this cavernous chamber they feel "in the world" and "at home" and find here what they can depend upon.

The things mentioned in the "allegory," which are visible outside the cave, are, on the other hand, the image for what the real reality of beings consists in. This is, according to Plato, that through which beings display themselves in their "outward appearance" (*Aussehen*). Plato does not take this "outward appearance" as a mere "aspect." "Outward appearance" even has for him something of an extrusion through which each thing "presents" itself. Situated in their "outward appearance," beings themselves display themselves. In Greek "outward appearance" is εἶδος or ἰδέα. The things lying in the daylight outside the cave, where everything is in plain sight, clarify the "ideas" in the "allegory." According to Plato, if man did not have these ideas before his gaze as the respective "outward appearance" of things, living creatures, men, numbers, and the gods, then he would never be able to perceive this or that particular thing as a house, as a tree, or as a god. Man usually believes he sees just exactly this house and that tree and therefore everything that is. For the most part, man never suspects that everything holding value for him in all its familiarity as the "real" is always seen only in the light of "ideas." That which is supposed to be alone and really real, the immediately visible, audible, comprehensible, and calculable, still steadily remains, according to Plato, only the silhouette projected by the ideas, and consequently a shadow. This "reality," the nearest even if it is shadowy, keeps man in its grasp day in and day out. He lives in a prison and leaves all "ideas" behind him. And just because he does not recognize this prison for what it is, he considers this commonplace region under the firmament to be the area in which the free unfolding of experience and judgment is possible, the area which alone gives the measure to all things and relationships and the rule for their direction and organization.

Now, if man, considered in terms of the "allegory," is suddenly to look from within the cave at the fire in back, whose light projects the silhouette of things moving back and forth, then he immediately senses that this strange inversion of his viewpoint is at once a disturbance of his conventional attitude and his everyday opinion. Already the mere demand of such an astonishing orientation, which should be accepted inside the cave as well, is rejected; for there, in the cave, one is in full and unequivocal possession of the real. The man of the cave, so obsessed with his own "opinion," cannot even surmise the possibility that what he considers real is only real in a shadowy sense. How is he even to know about shadows, if he will recognize neither the fire in the cave nor its light, since this fire is still only an "artifact" and therefore has to be familiar to man. On the other hand the sunlight outside the cave is not at all manufactured by man. In its brightness things that have grown and are present immediately manifest themselves without needing to be represented by projecting a silhouette. These self-manifesting things are, in the "allegory," the "image" for the "ideas." The sun in the "allegory" is still looked upon as the "image" for that which makes all ideas visible. It is the "image" for the Idea of all ideas. This is, according to Plato, *ἡτοῦ ἀγαθοῦ ἰδέα,* which is translated "literally" and therefore quite incorrectly as "the Idea of the Good."

So far we have only enumerated the allegorical correspondences between the shadows and the real experienced day after day, between the light of the fire in the cave and the brightness in which the nearest and most commonly "real" is found, between the things outside the cave and the ideas, between the sun and the Highest Idea; but these correspondences do not exhaust the content of the "allegory." To be sure, its real significance is not yet grasped at all. For the "allegory" tells a story of incidents and does not just report on the abodes and situations of man inside or outside the cave. But the incidents that are reported are the transitions from the cave out into the light of day and back again from the latter into the cave.

What occurs during these transitions? What makes these occurrences possible? What gives them their necessity? What is it about these transitions that matters?

The transitions from the cave into the light of day and from there back into the cave always demand a reorientation of the eyes from the darkness to the light and from the light to the darkness. Because of the opposite bases of sight, the eyes are confused every time: *διτταὶ καὶ ἀπὸ διττῶν γίγνονται ἐπιταράξεις ὄμμασιν* (518a, 2). "There are two ways the eyes get confused and two reasons for this confusion."

This means: a man can either be transported from an ignorance he hardly notices to a state where beings more essentially emerge, in which case he has not grown in the vicinity of the essential; or a man can fall from a position of an essential knowing and be confined in a region under the power of ordinary reality without still being able to recognize what is usual and used here as the real.

And just as one's own eye must reorient itself slowly and steadily, whether to the brightness or to the darkness, so also must the soul, with patience and with a relevant series of steps, get used to being in the realm of the beings to which it is exposed. Such a process of orientation still demands that the soul on the whole, in the basic direction of its striving, be turned around in relation to everything in front of it, just as the eye too can only then look about correctly and in every direction when the body on the whole has previously occupied the corresponding position.

But why must one get used to dwelling in each successive region so slowly and steadily? Because the inversion concerns the Being of man and therefore takes place in the basis of his nature or essence. This means that the position taken as a standard, which is supposed to originate through an inversion, must be developed from a relation already within human nature into a firm attitude. This orienting and reorienting of human nature into the realm respectively designated for it is the essence of what Plato calls παιδεία. The word cannot be translated. According to Plato's essential definition παιδεία means the περιαγωγὴ ὅλης τῆς ψυχῆς, that which leads to turning the whole man around in his nature or essence. παιδεία is therefore essentially a transition, indeed a transition from ἀπαιδευσία into παιδεία. According to the character of this transition παιδεία constantly stays related to ἀπαιδευσία. The German *Bildung* [a word commonly used in everyday speech for "education"] is the most sufficient word for παιδεία, even if it is not the most complete. We certainly have to give the word back the strength of its original meaning and forget the misinterpretation it fell into during the later nineteenth century. "Education" (*Bildung*) implies two things: it means first of all forming in the sense of developing and molding a character. This "forming" however "forms" (molds) at the same time through its preconceived adaptation to a standard aspect which is therefore called the prototype. Education (*Bildung*) is above all molding and giving direction by means of a form. The essence opposite to παιδεία is ἀπαιδευσία, being uneducated (*Bildungslosigkeit*). In it there is neither the awakening of a development of a fundamental orientation nor the establishing of a standard prototype.

The significant force of the "allegory of the cave" is concentrated in making the essence of παιδεία visible and knowable in whatever is evident in the story told. At the same time Plato cautiously wants to show that the essence of παιδεία is not in pouring mere knowledge into the contrary, where there is pure education the soul itself is seized and transformed as a whole, while at the same time man is transplanted to the region of his essence and oriented to it. The sentence with which Plato introduces the "allegory of the cave" at the beginning of Book

VII makes it clear enough that here the essence of παιδεία is supposed to be put into form: Μετὰ ταῦτα δή, εἶπον, ἀπείκασον τοιούτῳ πάθει τὴν ἡμετέραν φύσιν παιδείας τε πέρι καὶ ἀπαιδευσίας. "Next, said I, here is a parable to give us an aspect (of the essence) of education as well as of the lack of it, which fundamentally concerns our Being as men."

According to Plato's unmistakable assertion the "allegory of the cave" illustrates the essence of education. On the other hand the exposition of the "allegory" we are now attempting is supposed to point out the Platonic "doctrine" of truth. Is not then too much of an alien burden being placed on the "allegory"? Our exposition threatens to degenerate into a violent reinterpretation. This may seem to be the case until our insight has convinced itself that what underlies Plato's thinking is a change in the essence of truth, which becomes the hidden law of what he says as a thinker. In accordance with the future needs of this exposition, the "allegory" illustrates not only the essence of education, but at the same time it opens up a glimpse into a change in the essence of "truth." However, if the "allegory" can show both, is it not so that an essential relation must then prevail between "education" and "truth"? There is, in fact, this relation. And it is found in the fact that the essence of truth and the manner of its change first made "education" in its fundamental structure possible.

But what links "education" and "truth" together into an original and essential unity?

παιδεία means the inversion of the whole man in the sense of uprooting him from the region in which he encounters merely immediate things and transplanting him to another realm where beings themselves make their appearance. This transplanting is only possible if everything commonly known to man up to this time and the way it was known become different. That which is persistently unhidden to man and the manner of this unhiddenness has to change. Unhiddenness in Greek is ἀλήθεια, which word is translated as "truth." And for a long time "truth" has meant, for the Western mind, the agreement of the mental concept (or representation) with the thing: *adaequatio intellectus et rei.*

If however we are still not content with the mere "literal" translation of the words παιδεία and ἀλήθεια, and if we seek rather to think as the Greeks thought about the real essence indicated by these words, then "education" and "truth" crystallize into an essential unity. If we are to take the real meaning of ἀλήθεια seriously, then we must raise the question: where did Plato proceed from to define the essence of unhiddenness? The answer to this question is seen when we refer to the real content of the "allegory of the cave." This answer shows that the "allegory" deals with the essence of truth as well as how it deals with it.

The unhidden and its unhiddenness refer persistently to what is always openly present in the region in which man abides. But now the "allegory" tells a story about the transitions from one abode to another. From there this story is organized into a series of four different abodes, each with its characteristic stage. The variations of the abodes and stages of the transitions are based on the difference of what persists in being standardly ἀληθές, the kind of "truth" that prevails every time. Therefore, ἀληθές, the unhidden, must one way or another be considered and named at every stage.

At the first stage men live chained in the cave and are encompassed in whatever they immediately encounter. The description of this abode winds up with the emphatic sentence: παντάπασι δὴ . . . οἱ τοιοῦτοι οὐκ ἂν ἄλλο τι νομίζοιεν τὸ ἀληθὲς ἢ τὰς τῶν σκευαστῶν σκιάς (515c, 1-2). "In every way, then, men so chained would recognize as the unhidden nothing but the shadows of those artificial objects."

The chains are taken off at the second stage. The prisoners are now certainly free, but they still remain confined in the cave. Here they can now turn around towards all sides. It is even possible for them now to see those very things which were previously carried by behind them. Having previously looked only at the shadows, they come μᾶλλόν τι ἐγγυτέρω τοῦ ὄντος (515d, 2) "somewhat nearer to beings." The things themselves offer their outward appearance in a certain manner, specifically in the light of the artificial fire in the cave, and are no longer hidden by means of projected silhouettes. If only shadows are encountered, one's gaze is held captive and these shadows move thus in front of the things themselves. But if one's sight is released from being captive to shadows, then the man so freed acquires the possibility of coming into the sphere of what is known as ἀληθέστερα (515d, 6) "more unhidden." And still it has to be said of one so freed: ἡγεῖσθαι τὰ τότε ὁρώμενα ἀληθέστερα ἢ τὰ νῦν δεικνύμενα (Ib.). "He will consider (without further ado) what he previously saw (the shadows) to be more unhidden than what is now shown him (especially by others)."

Why? The firelight, to which the eye is not accustomed, blinds him who has just been set free. The dazzling light hinders him from seeing the fire itself and from perceiving how its radiance shines upon things and causes them to make their appearance. Thus blinded one cannot even comprehend that what was formerly seen was only a silhouette of the things projected by the light of just this fire. To be sure one who has just been set free now sees other things than shadows, but still only in a single confusion. Compared with this, the shadows, perceived in the reflection of the unknown and unseen fire, emerge in sharp outlines. What thus appears as the perpetuation of the shadows must therefore be the "more unhidden" to one who has just been set free, because it is visible without confusion. And so, at the end of the description of the second stage the word ἀληθές comes up again, this time in the comparative ἀληθέστερα, the "more unhidden." The more real "truth" presents itself in the shadows. For even the man freed from his chains still evaluates himself in his application of the "true," because for him the presupposition of the "value," freedom, is missing. To be sure the removal of the chains brings a liberation; but the mere act of shedding one's bonds is not yet real freedom.

This is first attained at the third stage. Here one who has just been freed from his chains is at the same time transplanted into the world outside of the cave, "into the open." There everything lies openly manifest all day long. The aspect of the individual things no longer makes its appearance now in the artificial and confusing light of the fire inside the cave. The things themselves stand there in the starkness and the urgency of their own outward appearance. The open air, into which the freed man has now been transplanted, does not indicate the unlimited quality of a mere distance, but the limiting clasp of the brightness which radiates in the light of the simultaneously discovered sun. The aspects of the individual things themselves, the *εἴδη* (ideas) constitute the essence in whose light each individual being emerges as one thing and another, in which emergence the phenomenal first becomes unhidden and accessible.

On the other hand the stage of the abode just reached defines itself according to what is here, in a standard and real sense, the unhidden. Therefore even at the beginning of the third stage the discussion is immediately concerned with *τῶν νῦν λεγομένων ἀληθῶν* (516a, 3), "with what are now called the unhidden." This state of the unhidden is *ἀληθέστερον*, even more unhidden than the artificially illuminated things inside the cave in their distinction from the shadows. The unhidden now attained is the most unhidden of all: *τὰ ἀληθέστατα*. To be sure Plato does not use this designation in this place, rather he calls *τὸ ἀληθέστατον* the most unhidden in the corresponding and equally essential discussion at the beginning of Book VI of the *Republic*. Here (484c, 5 sq.) are mentioned *οἱ . . . εἰς τὸ ἀληθέστατον ἀποβλέποντες* "those who always look towards the most unhidden." The most unhidden emerges in what is always being. Without such an emergence of the What (i.e. of the ideas), each specific and separate thing, and therefore generally everything, remains hidden. "The most unhidden" is so named because it makes its appearance first of all in everything phenomenal and makes the phenomenal accessible.

If however it is difficult, inside the cave, to shift one's gaze away from the shadows to the firelight and to the things emerging therein, then getting free in the open demands by far the greatest patience and effort. Liberation does not take place in the mere act of getting free from the chains and does not consist merely in being untrammeled, but begins first as the steady orienting of oneself so that one's gaze is made fast to the firm limits of the things standing fast in their outward appearance. Actual liberation lies in the steadiness with which one turns towards what manifests itself in its outward appearance and is in this manifesting the most unhidden. Freedom subsists only as this sort of turning-towards. The essence of *παιδεία* fulfills this as an inversion. The consummation of the essence of "education" can therefore take place only in the realm and at the root of the most unhidden, i.e. the ἀληθέστατον, i.e. the most true, i.e. the really true. The essence of "education" is founded in the essence of "truth."

Because παιδεία still has its essence in the περιαγωγὴ ὅλης τῆς ψυχῆς, it constantly remains, as such a turning around, the overcoming of ἀπαιδευσία. παιδεία contains in itself its own essential reflexive relationship to being uneducated (*Bildungslosigkeit*). And if the "allegory of the cave," according to Plato's own interpretation, is supposed to make the essence of παιδεία clear, this essential aspect, the constant overcoming of being uneducated, must be made visible. Therefore the narrative in the story does not end, as one likes to believe, with the description of the highest stage one attains in his ascent from the cave. On the contrary, the narrative of the freed man's return to those still enchained in the cave also belongs to the "allegory." Now the freed man is supposed to lead these men away from what is unhidden to them, and out of the cave to what is most unhidden. But this liberator cannot find his way around in the cave any more. He comes into the danger of succumbing to the overpowering force of what is standard truth there, i.e., to the demand ordinary "reality" makes to be the only reality. The liberator is threatened with the possibility of being killed, a possibility which became a reality in the fate of Plato's "teacher" Socrates.

The return into the cave and the fight within the cave between the liberator and the prisoners opposing all liberation forms its own fourth stage of the "allegory," the one in which the "allegory" is completed. In this section of the narrative the word ἀληθές is, to be sure, no longer used. Nevertheless the unhidden must be dealt with at this stage, for it defines a region of the cave which has been sought out anew. But is it not at the first stage that the standardly "unhidden," the shadows, is named? Certainly. Essentially, it is not only that the unhidden, in any kind of way, makes what shines (*das Scheinende*) accessible and leaves it open in its appearing, but that the unhidden steadily overcomes a hiddenness of the hidden. The unhidden must be torn away from a hiddenness, in a certain sense it must be stolen from such. Since for the Greeks at first hiddenness reigns throughout the essence of Being as a quality that hides itself and thereby defines even beings in their presence and accessibility ("truth"), the word the Greeks used for what the Romans called "veritas" and we call "truth" is distinguished by the α-privative (ἀ-λήθεια). At first truth meant what was wrested from a hiddenness. Truth then is just such a perpetual wrenching-away in this manner of uncovering. Consequently there can be different kinds of hiddenness: enclosing, hoarding, disguising, covering-up, veiling, dissimulation. Because the most extremely unhidden must, according to Plato's "allegory," be wrested from a base and stubborn concealment, even the removal from the cave out into the open of the light of day is therefore a fight for life and death. The fourth stage of the "allegory" gives its own hint that "privation," the constantly wresting extortion of the unhidden, belongs to the essence of truth. As each of the three preceding stages of the "allegory of the cave," it therefore deals with *ἀλήθεια*.

Therefore this "allegory" can only be, for the most part, an "allegory" built on the aspect of the cave, because it is also defined in advance by what is to the Greeks the self-evident and fundamental experience of *ἀλήθεια*, the unhiddenness of beings. For what is the subterranean cave other than something also quite overt in itself, but which remains at the same time sealed over and enclosed by the surrounding walls of the earth in spite of its entrance. The enclosure of the cave, open in itself, and what it surrounds and thus hides, indicate together an outer part, the unhidden, which by day extends in the light. What in Greek was at first thought to be the essence of truth in the sense of *ἀλήθεια*, unhiddenness in relation to the hidden (the pretended and the disguised), only this has an essential relation to the image of the cave underground. Where the truth is of another essence and is not unhiddenness or at least where unhiddenness is not a component of this definition, an "allegory of the cave" has no basis from which it can be clarified.

But still, even if *ἀλήθεια* in the "allegory of the cave" may be specifically experienced and named at emphatic points, another essence of truth besides unhiddenness forces its way into the foreground. In saying this it is also granted that unhiddenness still retains its own place in the background.

The representation of the "allegory" and Plato's own interpretation take the subterranean cave and its externality almost self-evidently as the realm in whose sphere the proceedings reported are enacted. Nevertheless the narrated transitions and the ascent from the region of artificial firelight into the brightness of the sunlight as well as the descent from the source of all light back into the dark of the cave are also essential. In the "allegory of the cave" the force of the clarification does not spring from the image of being enclosed in a subterranean vault and imprisoned in this enclosing, it does not even spring from the aspect of the openness outside of the cave. The image-making interpretative force of the "allegory" is gathered together for Plato rather in the role of the fire, the firelight and the shadows, the brightness of the day, the sunlight, and the sun. Everything depends upon the shining of the phenomenal and the possibility of its visibleness. To be sure unhiddenness is named in its various stages, but one can only consider it in the way it makes the phenomenal accessible in its outward appearance (*εἶδος*) and the way it makes this emerging (*ἰδέα*) visible. Consciousness, properly speaking, has to do with the way outward appearance manifests itself and is preserved in the brightness of its steady appearance. Through this one can view whatever each being is present as. Consciousness, properly speaking, applies to the *ἰδέα*. The "idea" is the outward appearance which gives a perspective upon what is present. The *ἰδέα* is pure shining in the sense of the phrase "the sun shines." The "idea" does not just let something else (behind it) "make an appearance," it itself is what appears, and it depends upon itself alone for its appearing. The ἰδέα is the apparent. The essence of the idea lies in the qualities of being apparent and visible. The idea achieves presence, namely the presence of every being as what it is. Each being is continuously present in the What of beings. Presence however is really the essence of Being. Being, then, for Plato, has its real essence in its What. Even more recent terminology betrays the conviction that the true *esse* is the *quidditas* or the *essentia* and not the *existentia*. What the idea brings into sight and offers to be seen is, for the glance directed upon it, the thing unhidden making its appearance as what it is. And so the unhidden is conceived primarily and solely as what is perceived in the act of perceiving the ἰδέα as what is known (γιγνωσκόμενον) in the act of knowing (γιγνώσκειν). Only in this shift do νοεῖν and νοῦς (perception) preserve, according to Plato, their essential relation to the "idea." The adjustment involved in thus directing oneself to the ideas defines the essence of perception and consequently the essence of "reason."

"Unhiddenness" means here the unhidden as it can steadily be approached through the apparentness (*Scheinsamkeit*) of the idea. But in so far as this approach is necessarily carried out through a "seeing," unhiddenness is hitched to the "relation" to seeing, and is "relative" to this. This brings up the question developed towards the end of Book VI of the *Republic:* How do the seen and seeing become what they are in their relationship? In what does the span between them both consist? What yoke (ζυγόν 508a, 1) holds them both together? The answer, to demonstrate which the "allegory of the cave" is presented, is stated with an image: The sun, as the source of light, gives "visibleness" to what has been sighted. But seeing sees the visible only in so far as the eye is ἡλιοειδές, "sunlike," while it has the ability of belonging to the nature of the sun's essence, i.e. to its shining. The eye itself "gleams" and submits to this shining, and can therefore receive and apprehend the phenomenal. As a matter of fact this image indicates a connection which Plato expresses (*Republic* VI, 508e, 1 sq.) as follows: τοῦτο τοίνυν τὸ τὴν ἀλήθειαν παρέχον τοῖς γιγνωσκομένοις καὶ τῷ γιγνώσκοντι τὴν δύναμιν ἀποδιδὸν τὴν τοῦ ἀγαθοῦ ἰδέαν φάθι εἶναι. "This, then, which gives unhiddenness to what is known and the ability (to know) to him who knows, this, I say, is the Idea of the Good."

The "allegory" calls the sun the image for the Idea of the Good. In what does the essence of this Idea consist? As ἰδέα the Good is something that shines. As this it is the sight-giving, thus something sighted and therefore knowable, and, to be sure, ἐν τῷ γνωστῷ τελευταία ἡ τοῦ ἀγαθοῦ ἰδέα καὶ μόγις ὁρᾶσθαι (517b, 8). "In the realm of the knowable the Idea of the Good is the last thing to become visible and the most difficult thing to be seen."

τὸ ἀγαθόν is translated with the expression "the Good," which seems easy to understand. For the most part such a term makes one think of the "morally good," so called because it is suitable to the moral law. This interpretation is not consistent with Greek thinking, although Plato's exposition of ἀγαθόν as idea becomes [later] an excuse for thinking of "the Good" in "moral" terms and eventually mistaking it as a "value." The concept of value as an inner consequence of the modern comprehension of "truth," a concept which came into fashion in the nineteenth century, is the most recent and at the same time the weakest offspring of ἀγαθόν. In so far as "the value" and the exposition resting on "values" support Nietzsche's metaphysics—and this in the absolute form of a "transvaluation of all 'values' "—Nietzsche too is bound within the history of Western metaphysics as the unfettered Platonist, since to him all wisdom starts from the metaphysical origin of "value." Since he grasps "value" as the condition "life itself" sets for the possibility of "life," Nietzsche has adhered to the essence of ἀγαθόν with less prejudice than those who chase after the groundless chimaera of "intrinsic values."

If the essence of "Idea" is still thought of in the modern sense as *perceptio* ("subjective representation"), then in the "Idea of the Good" a value can be found that can exist anywhere in itself so that there is moreover still another "idea." This "idea" must of course be the highest since everything depends upon its occurrence in the "Good" (in the well-being of a welfare or in the organization of an order). Within the sphere of this sort of modern thinking it is certainly impossible to conceive of any more of the original essence of Plato's ἰδέα τοῦ ἀγαθοῦ.

As the Greeks thought of it, τὸ ἀγαθόν means that which is of use to something and which makes something useful. Every ἰδέα, the outward appearance of something, directs the sight to every being as what it is. The "ideas," therefore, as the Greeks thought, make it useful that something can make an appearance as what it is and can therefore be present in its permanence. The ideas are the beings of everything that is. What makes every idea useful to an idea is, Platonically expressed, the Idea of all ideas and, consists therefore in making it possible for everything present to make its appearance in all its visibility (*Sichtsamkeit*). The essence of every idea lies after all in making anything possible and useful for the shining which preserves a sight of its outward appearance. Therefore the Idea of ideas is simply that which makes something useful, τὸ ἀγαθόν. This induces everything apparent to shine and is therefore itself the really phenomenal, that which is most apparent in its shining. Therefore Plato also calls ἀγαθόν (518c, 9) τοῦ ὄντος τὸ φανότατον, "the most phenomenal (most apparent) of beings."

For modern opinion "the Idea of the Good" is an expression all too liable to lead one astray; but it is the name for that specified idea which, as the Idea of Ideas, remains for everything that which makes it useful. This idea, which alone can be called "the Good," remains ἰδέα τελευταία because the essence of the Idea is fulfilled in it, that is, it begins to be an essence, so that only out of it springs even the possibility of all other ideas. The Good can be called the "Highest Idea" in a double sense: it is the highest in the rank of possibility, and the glance up towards it is the steepest and therefore the most laborious. In spite of the labor involved in really comprehending the Idea, which, as the Greeks thought, must mean, in consequence of the essence of the Idea, "the Good"—the Idea is in a certain sense permanently kept in view wherever any sort of being emerges at all. Even here, where only the still-hidden shadows are sighted in their essence, a firelight must still shine, even if this light is not grasped specifically and experienced as a product given by the fire, even if here above all it still remains unrecognized that this fire is only a descendant (*ἔκγονον* VI, 507a, 3) of the sun. Inside of the cave the sun remains invisible and yet the shadows live on its light. The fire in the cave however, which makes the perception of the shadows possible—a perception which does not know itself in its own essence—is the image for the unknown basis of that realization of beings, which certainly means what is but does not know it as such. Still, the sun presents through its shining not only brightness and therefore visibleness and therefore "unhiddenness" to everything phenomenal. Its shining also radiates heat and through its glow makes it possible for everything "originating" to arise in the visible aspect of its duration (509b).

But if the sun itself is looked at (*ὀφθεῖσα δὲ*) specifically, without speaking metaphorically, the Highest Idea is for once caught sight of, and then *συλλογιστέα εἶναι ὡς ἄρα πᾶσι πάντων αὕτη ὀρθῶν τε καὶ καλῶν αἰτία* (517c), "then we cannot help but gather (from the Highest Idea) that this is for all men the first cause of everything right (in its attitude) as well as of everything beautiful," that is, the first cause of what is shown to the attitude so that it induces the shining of its outward appearance to manifest itself. For all "things" and their "thingness" the Highest Idea is the origin, i.e. the first cause. "The Good" preserves the manifestation of outward appearance, wherein what is present as what it is has its duration. Through this preservation beings are held together in Being and "delivered."

From the essence of the Highest Idea it follows for every circumspect glance busy looking around, *ὅτι δεῖ ταύτην ἰδεῖν τὸν μέλλοντα ἐμφρόνως πράξειν ἢ ἰδίᾳ ἢ δημοσίᾳ* (517c, 4/5), "that whoever cares to act with insight, either in private or in public, he must have this (the idea which is called the possibility of the essence of the Idea of the Good) before his eyes." Whoever is supposed to act in a world defined through "the Idea"—and wants to—needs before everything else the glimpse of the Idea. And the essence of *παιδεία* also consists in making men free and secure for the clear permanence of the essential glimpse. Because the "allegory of the cave," according to Plato's own interpretation, is now supposed to bring the essence of *παιδεία* into an intuitively clear form, it must therefore also tell about the ascent to where the Highest Idea is sighted.

But doesn't the "allegory of the cave" deal specifically with ἀλήθεια? Certainly not. And nevertheless the fact is: this "allegory" contains Plato's "doctrine" of truth. For it is based on the unstated occurrence whereby the ἰδέα became the master of ἀλήθεια. The "allegory" gives an image of what Plato says about the ἰδέα τοῦ ἀγαθοῦ: αὐτὴ κυρία ἀλήθειαν καὶ νοῦν παρασχομένη (517c, 4), "it is itself master, dispensing both unhiddenness (to what emerges) and the ability to perceive (the unhidden)." ἀλήθεια comes under the yoke of the ἰδέα. When Plato says that the ἰδέα is the master permitting unhiddenness, he banishes to something left unsaid the fact that henceforth the essence of truth does not unfold out of its own essential fullness as the essence of unhiddenness, but shifts its abode to the essence of the ἰδέα. The essence of truth relinquishes the basic feature of unhiddenness.

If, in every attitude towards beings there is, we are concerned with the ἰδεῖν of ἰδέα, with catching sight of "outward appearance," then every effort must be gathered into the possibility of such a "seeing." For that, the right glance is necessary. No doubt one who has been set free inside the cave, once he turns himself from the shadows to the things, directs his glance to such things that are "being more" than the mere shadows: πρὸς μᾶλλον ὄντα τετραμμένος ὀρθότερον βλέποι (515d, 3/4), "turned towards things that are being more, he can have a more correct glance." The transition from one situation into another consists in making one's glance more correct. Everything depends on the ὀρθότης, the correctness of the glance. Through this correctness, seeing and recognizing become something right, so that it (this correctness) can eventually be directed straight ahead to the Highest Idea and made fast in this "straightening-out." In this directing of itself, perceiving is compared to what is supposed to be sighted. That is the "outward appearance" of beings. In consequence of this assimilation of perceiving as an ἰδεῖν into an ἰδέα, an ὁμοίωσις subsists, an agreement between recognizing and the thing itself. And so, before ἀλήθεια a change in the essence of truth springs forth out of the front rank of the ἰδέα and the ἰδεῖν. Truth becomes ὀρθότης, correctness of the ability to perceive and to declare something.

In this change of the essence of truth a shift of the place of truth takes place at the same time. As unhiddenness truth is still a basic feature of beings themselves. But as correctness of "looking" truth becomes the label of the human attitude towards beings.

In a certain manner Plato still has to adhere to "truth" as a characteristic of beings, because beings, as what are present in appearing, have Being, and this brings unhiddenness along with it. But at the same time the inquiry into unhiddenness is shifted to the way outward appearance manifests itself and with that to the associated ability to see: to what is right and the correctness of seeing. Therefore there is necessarily an ambiguity in Plato's doctrine. Just this attests to the change in the essence of truth which has been unexpressed so far but is now about to be stated. The ambiguity is clearly obvious in the fact that ἀλήθεια is mentioned and treated while at the same time ὀρθότης is meant and set as a standard—and all in the same train of thought.

The ambiguity of the definition of the essence of truth can be gathered from the only sentence of the section which contains Plato's own interpretation of the "allegory of the cave" (517b, 7—c, 5). The leading thought is that the Highest Idea puts the yoke between recognizing and what is recognized. This relationship however is grasped in a twofold manner. First of all, as a standard, Plato says: let ἡ τοῦ ἀγαθοῦ ἰδέα be πάντων ὀρθῶν τε καὶ καλῶν αἰτία, "the first cause (i.e. the possibility of essence) of all that is correct as well as all that is beautiful." But then he says that the Idea of the Good ought to be κυρία ἀλήθειαν καὶ νοῦν παρασχομένη "master dispensing both unhiddenness and perceiving." These two expressions are not parallel, and ἀλήθεια does not correspond to ὀρθά (the correct), nor νοῦς (perceiving) to καλά (the beautiful). It is rather that the correspondence criss-crosses. Correct perceiving corresponds to ὀρθά, the correct and its correctness, and the unhidden corresponds to the beautiful; for the essence of the beautiful lies in being ἐκφανέσταον (Cf. *Phaedrus*), which, shining out of itself the most and with the most purity, gives the outward appearance and is therefore unhidden. Both sentences tell of the precedence of the Idea of the Good as the possibility of correctly recognizing something and the possibility of what is recognized becoming unhidden. Here truth is both unhiddenness and correctness, even though unhiddenness is still under the yoke of the ἰδέα. The same ambiguity of the definition of the essence of truth prevails in Aristotle. In the final chapter of the Book IX of his *Metaphysics* (*Met.*, θ, 10, 1051a, 34 sqq.), where Aristotelian thinking about the Being of beings reaches its peak, unhiddenness is the basic feature of beings holding sway over everything. But at the same time Aristotle can say: οὐ γάρ ἐστι τὸ ψεῦδος καὶ τὸ ἀληθὲς ἐν τοῖς πράγμασιν . . . ἀλλ'ἐν διανοίᾳ (*Met.* E, 4, 1027b, 25 sq.). "The false and the true are not in the act (itself) . . . but in the understanding."

Where the understanding makes an assertion in order to pass judgment is the place of truth and falsehood and their difference. The assertion is true in so far as it is compared to the circumstances and is therefore ὁμοίωσις (likeness). This essential definition of truth contains no further reference to ἀλήθεια in the sense of unhiddenness; but ἀλήθεια is turned around and thought of as the opposite of ψεῦδος, i.e., of the false in the sense of the incorrect, while truth is thought of as correctness. From now on the mold of the essence of truth becomes, as the correctness of representing through an assertion, the standard for all of Western thinking. As evidence of this it will be sufficient to quote propositions which are characteristic of the perpetual molding of the essence of truth in the principal ages of metaphysics.

A statement of St. Thomas Aquinas holds true for Medieval Scholasticism: *Veritas proprie invenitur in intellectu humano vel divino* (*Quaes-*

tiones de veritate; qu. I art. 4, resp.), "truth is really met with in the human or in the divine understanding." It has its essential place in the understanding. Here truth is no longer *ἀλήθεια*, but *ὁμοίωσις* (*adequatio*).

At the beginning of modern times Descartes sharpens the above quotation by saying: *veritatem proprie vel falsitatem non nisi in solo intellectu esse posse* (*Regulae ad directionem ingenii,* Reg. VII, Opp. X, 396). "Truth or falsehood in the real sense cannot be anywhere else except in the understanding alone."

And in the age in which the fulfillment of modern times commences Nietzsche sharpens the above statement even more: *"Truth is th kind of error* without which a definite kind of living species would not be able to live. The value for *life* decides in the end." (Notation made in 1885, *Der Wille zur Macht,* n. 493). If truth according to Nietzsche is a kind of error, then its essence lies in a manner of thinking which always and necessarily falsifies the real in so far as every act of representation causes the unexposed "becoming" to be still and sets up something that does not correspond (i.e. something incorrect) with what has thus been established in contradistinction to the fluent "becoming," thereby establishing something erroneous as the alledgedly real.

In Nietzsche's defining of truth is incorrectness of thinking there lies the concession to thinking of the traditional essence of truth as the correctness of making an assertion (λόγος). Nietzsche's concept of truth is an example of the last reflection of the extreme consequence of that changing of truth from the unhiddenness of beings to the correctness of the glance. The change itself takes place in the definition of the Being of beings (i.e., according to the Greeks, the presence of what is present) as *ἰδέα*.

In consequence of this exposition of beings, presence is no longer, as it was in the beginning of Western thinking, the rise of the hidden into unhiddenness, so that even this, as uncovering, makes up the basic feature of presence. Plato understands presence (*οὐσία*) as *ἰδέα*. This presence is nevertheless not under the control of unhiddenness because, serving the unhidden, it induces the latter to appear. On the contrary shining (emergence) inversely defines what, within its essence and in the only relationship back to itself, can still be called unhiddenness. The *ἰδέα* is not a foreground of *ἀλήθεια* in its presentation, but the basis for making it possible. But even so the *ἰδέα* still claims something of the original but unknown essence of *ἀλήθεια*.

Truth no longer is, as unhiddenness, the basic feature of Being itself, but it is, in consequence of having become correctness by being yoked under the Idea, from this time forth the label of the recognizing of beings.

Since then there has been a striving for "truth" in the sense of correctness of looking and the position of the glance. Since then the decisive thing in all basic positions taken to beings has been the acquisition of the right way of looking at the Idea. Consciousness of *παιδεία* and the change of the essence of ἀλήθεια belong together and belong in the same story of the transition from abode to abode as presented through the allegory of the cave.

The difference of both abodes inside and outside the cave is a distinction of σοφία. This word generally means the ability to know one's way about in something, to be well-acquainted with something. But in a more real sense σοφία means the ability to know ones way about in what is present as the unhidden and permanent as the present. Knowing one's way about is not identical with the mere possession of knowledge. It means keeping in an abode that first has its support in the permanent everywhere.

The standard for knowing one's way about down below in the cave, ἡ ἐκεῖ σοφία (516c, 5) is surpassed by another σοφία. This is nothing but catching sight of the Being of beings in the "ideas." Contrary to the former σοφία in the cave, this σοφία is distinguished through the desire to acquire, beyond what is most nearly present, support in its own emerging permanence. This σοφία is in itself a preference and friendship (φιλία) for the "ideas" which dispense the unhidden. σοφία outside the cave is φιλοσοφία. The language of the Greeks already knew this word before Plato's time and used it generally to designate their preference for knowing their way about correctly. Through Plato the word is first claimed as a name for knowing one's way about among beings in such a manner as to simultaneously define the Being of beings as Idea. Since Plato, thinking about the Being of beings becomes—"philosophy," because it is the gazing up to the "ideas." From this time on the "philosophy" that begins first with Plato has the characteristic of what later on is called "metaphysics." Plato himself makes the basic form of metaphysics clear in the story which tells the allegory of the cave. Even the word "metaphysics" is already being molded in Plato's representation. In the place where (516) he demonstrates the orientation of the glance to the ideas, Plato says that thinking goes μετ' ἐκεῖνα "over" the former, that which is only experienced as shadowy and copied, out εἰς ταῦτα, "away to" the latter, namely to the "ideas." They are the supersensuous, sighted in the nonsensuous glance. They are the Being of beings which cannot be grasped with the tools of the body. And in the realm of the supersensuous the highest is permanence and appearing of all beings. Because this "idea" is in such a way the first cause for everything, it is also "the idea" which is called "the Good." This highest and primary first cause is called the divine by that idea which as the Idea of all ideas remains the first cause for the Plato, corresponding to Aristotle's τὸ θεῖον. Since the exposition of Being as ἰδέα, thinking about the Being of beings has become metaphysical, and metaphysics has become theological. Theology means here the exposition of the "first cause" of beings as God and the misplacing of Being into this first cause, which contains Being in itself and discharges it from itself because it is the most being of beings.

The same exposition of Being as ἰδέα, which owes its precedence to a change in the essence of ἀλήθεια, demands that a label of the glance be placed upon the ideas. The role of παιδεία, of the "education" of man, corresponds to this label. Concern for human Being and for the position of man in the midst of beings dominates throughout metaphysics.

The beginning of metaphysics in Plato's thinking is at the same time the beginning of "Humanism." This word ought to be thought of essentially here and therefore in its broadest meaning. Hereafter then "Humanism" means the process bound up with the beginning, unfolding, and end of metaphysics so that man, after various considerations, but always knowingly, moves into a position in the midst of beings without becoming the highest being. "Man" means here sometimes a race of man or mankind, sometimes the individual or a community, sometimes the people or a group of people. When "man" is defined in such a context within the realm of a firmly made, metaphysical, basic structure of beings, it is always valid to induce him, the *animal rationale,* to set free his potentialities and come into the certainty of his definition and into the assurance of his "life." This happens as molding of his "moral" conduct, as salvation of his immortal soul, as unfolding of his creative powers, as development of his reason, as cultivation of his personality, as awkening of common sense, as training of his body, or as an appropriate coupling of some or all of these "humanities." In every case, man is one way or another encircled metaphysically. With the fulfillment of metaphysics even "Humanism" (or to put it "in Greek": anthropology) comes to extreme and unconditional "positions."

Plato's thinking follows the change of the essence of truth, which change becomes the story of metaphysics and which has begun its unconditional fulfillment in Nietzsche's thinking. Plato's doctrine of "truth" is therefore not something of the past. It is historically "present," but not as a historically recollected "consequence" of a piece of didacticism, not even as revival, not even as imitation of antiquity, not even as mere preservation of the traditional. That change of the essence of truth is present as the slowly confirmed and still uncontested basic reality, a reality reigning through everything, the basic reality of the history of the world rolling on and on into its most modern modernity.

Whatever is ventured with historical man follows as a consequence of a decision about the essence of truth [viz., unhiddenness] which has previously fallen, being unable to stand by itself in the presence of man. This decision excludes whatever in the light of the established essence of truth is sought and adhered to as something true and also thrown away and passed over as something untrue.

The story told in the allegory of the cave gives the aspect of what is now and always will be what really happens in the history of the humanity molded in the West: man thinks in terms of the fact that the essence of truth is the correctness of the representing of all beings according to "ideas" and esteems everything real according to "values." The decisive point is not which ideas and which values are set, but that the real is expounded according to "ideas" at all, that the "world" is weighed according to "values" at all.

Meanwhile the original essence of truth has been remembered. Unhiddenness reveals itself to this rememberance as the basic feature of beings themselves. Remembrance of the original essence of truth still has to thing of this essence more originally. It can therefore never assume unhiddenness in Plato's sense alone, that is in yoking it under the ἰδέα. Unhiddenness grasped Platonically remains clasped in its relationship to sighting, perceiving, thinking and stating. To pursue this relationship means to give up the essence of unhiddenness. No attempt to found the essence of unhiddenness in "reason," in "spirit," in "thinking," in the "logos," in any kind of "subjectivity" can even deliver the essence of unhiddenness. For that which is to be founded, the essence of unhiddenness itself, cannot be inquired into with sufficient success through such attempts. The most they can accomplish is only a steady "explanation" of an essential consequence of the ungrasped essence of unhiddenness.

Before this, there is a need of evaluating the "positive" in the "privative" essence of ἀλήθεια. Before this, such a positive thing has to be experienced as the basic feature of Being itself. First the need must force itself into our consciousness to question not only beings, but at some time, Being as well. Because this need is a task before us, the original essence of truth still rests therefore in its hidden beginning.

LETTER ON HUMANISM[1]

(TRANSLATED BY EDGAR LOHNER)

Our thinking about the essence of action is still far from resolute enough. Action is known only as the bringing about of an effect; it is assessed by its utility. But the essence of action is fulfillment. To fulfill is to unfold something in the fullness of its essence, to usher it forward into that fullness: *producere*. Hence only that can be truly

[1] *Platons Lehre von der Wahrheit. Mit einen Brief uber den "Humanismus,"* pp. 53-119. A. Francke, Bern, 1947.

fulfilled which is already in existence. Yet that which, above all, "is," is Being. Thought brings to fulfillment the relation of Being to the essence of man, it does not make or produce this relation. Thought merely offers it to Being as that which has been delivered to itself by Being. This offering consists in this: that in thought Being is taken up in language. Language is the house of Being. In its home man dwells. Whoever thinks or creates in words is a guardian of this dwelling. As guardian, he brings to fulfillment the unhiddenness of Being insofar as he, by his speaking, takes up this unhiddenness in language and preserves it in language. Thought does not become action because an effect issues from it, or because it is applied. Thought acts in that it thinks. This is presumably the simplest and, at the same time, the highest form of action: it concerns man's relation to what is. All effecting, in the end, rests upon Being, is bent upon what is. Thought, on the other hand, lets itself be called into service by Being in order to speak the truth of Being. It is thought which accomplishes this letting be (*Lassen*). Thought is *l'engagement par l'Etre pour l'Etre*. I do not know if it is linguistically possible to express both (*"par"* et *"pour"*) as one, i.e. by *penser, c'est l'engagement de l'Etre*. Here the possessive form *"de l' . . ."* is meant simultaneously to express the genitive as *genitivus subiectivus* and *obiectivus*. In this, "subject" and "object" are inadequate terms of the metaphysics which, in the form of Western "logic" and "grammar," early took possession of the interpretation of language. Today we can but begin to surmise what lies hidden in this process. The freeing of language from grammar, and placing it in a more original and essential framework, is reserved for thought and poetry. Thought is not merely *l'engagement dans l'action* for and by "what is" in the sense of the actual and present situation. Thought is *l'engagement* by and for the truth of Being. Its history is never past, it is always imminent. The history of Being sustains and determines every *condition et situation humaine*. In order that we may first learn how to perceive the aforesaid essence of thinking in its pure form—and that means to fulfill it as well—we must free ourselves from the technical interpretation of thought. Its beginnings reach back to Plato and Aristotle. With them thought is valued as *τέχνη*, the procedure of reflection in the service of doing and making. The reflection here is already seen from the viewpoint of *πρᾶξις* and *ποίησις*. Hence thought, when taken by itself, is not "practical." The characterization of thought as *θεωρία* and the determination of cognition as "theoretical" behavior occur already within the "technical" interpretation of thought. They constitute a reactive attempt of saving for thought an independence in the face of doing and acting. Ever since, "philosophy" has faced the constant distress of justifying its existence against "science." It believes it accomplishes this most securely by elevating itself to the rank of science. Yet this effort is the surrender of the essence of thought. Philosophy is haunted by the fear of losing prestige and validity, unless it becomes science. It is considered a failure equated with unscientific rigor. Being as the element of thought has been abandoned in the technical interpretation of thought. "Logic," since sophistry and Plato, is the initial sanction of this interpretation. Thought is judged by a measure inadequate to it. This judgment is like the procedure of trying to evaluate the nature and the capability of a fish by how long it is able to live on dry land. Too long, all too long, thought has been lying on dry land. Can the effort to bring thought back to its element be called "irrationalism" now?

The questions your letter raises would undoubtedly be more easily clarified in personal conversation. In writing thought tends to lose its flexibility. Above all, however, it can hardly preserve the multidimensional quality peculiar to its realm. Strictness of thought consists, in contradistinction to science, not merely in the artificial, i.e. the technico-theoretical exactitude of terms. It rests on the fact that speaking remains purely in the element of Being and lets the simplicity of the manifold dimensions of Being rule. But the written, on the other hand, offers the salutary compulsion toward thought-out composition of the spoken word. Today I should like to select only one of your questions, the discussion of which may cast light on the others too.

You ask: *Comment dedonner un sens au mot "Humanisme"?* This question is asked with the intention of retaining the word "humanism." I wonder if it is necessary. Or is the harm wrought by all such terms not obvious enough yet? Of course, for some time now, "isms" have been suspect. But the market of public opinion always demands new ones. Again and again this demand is readily answered. And terms like "logic," "ethics," "physics" occur only when original thinking has stopped. The Greeks, in their great age, did their thinking without such terms. They did not even call it "philosophy." Thinking ceases when it withdraws from its element. The element is that by means of which thinking can be thinking. It is the element which is potent, which is potency.[2] It concerns itself with thought and so brings thought into its essence. Thought is, more simply, thought of Being. The genitive has two meanings. Thought is of Being, insofar as thought, eventuated by Being, belongs to Being. Thought is at the same time thought of Being insofar as thought listens to, heeds, Being. Listening to and belonging to Being, thought constitutes what it is in its essential origin. Thought is—this means, Being has always, in the manner of destiny, concerned itself about its essence, embraced it. To concern oneself

[2] This and the following passage depends essentially on a play on words though it is not just that. The verb "vermögen" means "to be able to," "to have the power to do . . ." The noun "Vermögen" means "potency," also "wealth," "resources," "means." "Vermögend" means accordingly "potent" and also "propertied." The play lies in this that, without the prefix "ver" there is a word "mögen" meaning "to like." "Mögen" is then used here in a fusion of the two strains of meaning, potency and liking.

about a "thing" or a "person" means, to love, to like him or it. Such "liking," understood in a more original way, means: to confer essence. Such "liking origin" is the proper nature of potency (*Vermögen*), which not only can perform this or that, but which can let something be what it is as it stems from its true origin. It is the potency of this loving on the "strength of which something is in fact capable of being." This potency is the truly "possible," that whose essence rests on "Mögen." Being is capable of thought. The one makes the other possible. Being as the element is the "quiet power" of the loving potency, i.e. of the possible. Our words "possible" and "possibility," however, are, under the domination of "logic" and "metaphysics," taken only in contrast to "actuality," i.e. they are conceived with reference to a determined—viz. the metaphysical—interpretation of Being as *actus* and *potentia* the distinction of which is identified with that of *existentia* and *essentia.* When I speak of the "quiet power of the possible," I do not mean the possible of a merely represented *possibilitas,* nor the *potentia* as *essentia* of an *actus* of the *existentia,* but Being itself, which in its loving potency commands thought and thus also the essence of man, which means in turn his relationship to Being. To command something is to sustain it in its essence, to retain it in its element.

When thought comes to an end of withdrawing from its element, it replaces the loss by making its validity felt as τέχνη, as an educational instrument and therefore as a scholarly matter and later as a cultural matter. Philosophy gradually becomes a technique of explanation drawn from ultimate causes. One no longer thinks, but one occupies oneself with "philosophy." In competition such occupations publicly present themselves as "isms" and try to outdo each other. The domination achieved through such terminology does not just happen. It rests, especially in modern times, on the peculiar dictatorship of the public. So-called private existence does not mean yet, however, essentially and freely being human. It merely adheres obstinately to a negation of the public. It remains an offshoot dependent on the public and nourishes itself on its mere retreat from the public. So it is witness, against its own will, of its subjection to the public. The public itself, however, is the metaphysically conditioned—as it is derived from the domination of subjectivity—establishment and authorization of the overtness of the existent in the absolute objectivization of everything. Therefore, language falls into the service of arranging the lines of communication, on which objectification as the uniform accessibility of everything for everybody expands, disregarding all limits. So language comes under the dictatorship of the public. This public predetermines what is intelligible and what must be rejected as unintelligible. What has been said in *Sein und Zeit* (1927), §§ 27 and 35, about the word *"man"* (the impersonal one) is not simply meant to furnish, in passing, a contribution to sociology. In the same way the word *man* does not simply mean the counterpart—in an ethical existential way—to a person's self-Being. What has been said contains rather an indication—thought of from the question of the truth of Being—of the original pertinence of the word Being. This relationship remains concealed under the domination of subjectivity, which is represented as the public. When, however, the truth of Being has become memorable to thought, then reflection on the essence of language must obtain a new rank. It can no longer be mere philosophy of language. And for just this reason *Sein und Zeit* (§34) contains an indication of the essential dimension of language and broaches the simple question of what mode of Being the language as language from time to time is in. The ubiquitous and fast-spreading impoverishment of language does not gnaw only at aesthetic and moral responsibility in all use of language. It rises from an endangering of man's essence. A merely cultured use of language still does not demonstrate that we have as yet escaped this essential danger. Today it may rather signify that we have not yet seen the danger and cannot see it, because we have never exposed ourselves to its gaze. The decadence of language, quite recently considered though very late, is, however, not the cause but rather a consequence of the process that language under the domination of the modern metaphysics of subjectivity almost always falls out of its element. Language still denies us its essence: that it is the house of the truth of Being. Language, moreover, leaves itself to our mere willing and cultivating as an instrument of domination over beings. This itself appears as the actual in the concatenation of cause and effect. Calculating and acting we encounter beings as the actual, but also scientifically and in philosophizing with explanations and arguments. To these also belongs the assurance that something is inexplicable. Through such assertions we believe we confront the mystery. As if it were taken for granted that the truth of Being could be set up over causes and basic explanations or, what is the same, over their incomprehensibility.

If man, however, is once again to find himself in the nearness of Being, he must first learn to exist in the nameless. He must recognize the seduction of the public, as well as the impotence of the private. Man must, before he speaks, let himself first be claimed again by Being at the risk of having under this claim little or almost nothing to say. Only in this way will the preciousness of its essence be returned to the word, and to man the dwelling where he can live in the truth of Being.

But is there not now in this claim upon man, is there not in the attempt to make man ready for this claim, an effort in behalf of man? Where else does "Care" (*Sorge*) go, if not in the direction of bringing man back to his essence again? What else does this mean, but that man (*homo*) should become human (*humanus*)? Thus *humanitas* remains the concern of such thought; for this is humanism: to reflect and to care that man be human and not un-human, "inhuman", i.e.

outside of his essence. Yet, of what does the humanity of man consist? It rests in his essence.

But whence and how is the essence of man determined? Marx demands that the "human man" be known and acknowledged. He finds this man in society. The "social" man is for him the "natural" man. In "society" the "nature" of man, which means all of his "natural needs" (food, clothing, reproduction, economic sufficiency), is equally secured. The Christian sees the humanity of man, the *humanitas* of the *homo,* as the delimitation of *deitas.* He is, in the history of Grace, man as the "child of God," who hears in Christ the claim of the Father and accepts it. Man is not of this world, insofar as the "world," theoretically and Platonically understood, is nothing but a transitory passage into the other world.

Expressly in its own name, *humanitas* is first considered and striven for at the time of the Roman republic. The *homo humanus* is opposed to the *homo barbarus.* The *homo humanus* is here the Roman who exalts and ennobles the Roman *virtus* by the "incorporation" of the *paideia,* taken over from the Greeks. The Greeks are the Greeks of Hellenism, whose culture was taught in the philosophical schools. It is the *eruditio et institutio in bonas artes. Paideia* so understood, is translated by *humanitas.* The authentic *romanitas* of the *homo humanus* consists of such *humanitas.* In Rome we encounter the first humanism. It, thus, remains in its essence a specific Roman phenomenon, born of the encounter between the Roman and Hellenistic cultures. The so-called Renaissance of the fourteenth and fifteenth centuries in Italy is a *renascentia romanitatis.* Since the *romanitas* is what matters, all we are concerned with is *humanitas* and for that reason, the Greek *paideia.* The Greek world, however, is always seen in its late form and this, in turn, is seen as Roman. In addition the *homo romanus* of the Renaissance is seen in opposition to the *homo barbarus.* But the inhuman is now the pretended barbarism of the Gothic scholasticism of the Middle Ages. To humanism, historically understood, therefore, always belongs a *studium humanitatis,* which reaches back to antiquity and so always also becomes a revival of the Greek world. This is shown in our humanism of eighteenth century, which is sustained by Winckelmann, Goethe, and Schiller. Hölderlin, however, does not belong to "humanism" and thinks of the destiny of the essence of man in a more original way than this "humanism" is capable of doing.

But when one understands by humanism, in general, the effort of man to become free for his humanity and to find therein his dignity rather than some conceptual understanding of the "freedom" and the "nature" of man, the humanism is in each instance different. Likewise its modes of realization differ. Marx's humanism requires no return to antiquity, nor does the humanism which Sartre conceives existentialism to be. In this broad sense Christianity is also a humanism, insofar as, according to its doctrine, everything comes down to the salvation of the soul (*salus aeterna*) of man and the history of mankind appears in the frame of the history of salvation. However different these kinds of humanism may be, in regard to their aims and basis, in regard to the ways and means of their respective realizations, in regard to the form of their doctrine, all of them coincide in that the *humanitas* of the homo humanus is determined from the view of an already-established interpretation of nature, of history, of world, of the basis of the world (*Weltgrund*), i.e. of beings in their totality.

Every humanism is either founded in a metaphysics or is converted into the basis for a metaphysics. Every determination of the essence of man that presupposes the interpretation of beings without asking the question of the truth of Being, be it wittingly or not, is metaphysical. Therefore, and precisely in view of the way in which the essence of man is determined, the characteristic of all metaphysics shows itself in the fact that it is "humanistic." For this reason every humanism remains metaphysical. Humanism not only does not ask, in determining the humanity of man, for the relation of Being to the essence of man, but humanism even impedes this question, since, by virtue of its derivation from metaphysics it neither knows nor understands it. Inversely, the necessary and the proper way of asking the question of the truth of Being, in metaphysics but forgotten by it, can only come to light, if amidst the domination of metaphysics the question is asked: "What is metaphysics?" First of all each question of "Being," even that of the truth of Being, must be presented as a "metaphysical" question.

The first humanism, the Roman, and all the humanisms that have since appeared, presupposes as self-evident the most general "essence" of man. Man is considered as the *animal rationale*. This determination is not only the Latin translation of the Greek ζῷον λόγον ἔχον but a metaphysical interpretation. This essential determination of man is not wrong, but it is conditioned by metaphysics. Its essential extraction and not merely its limit has, however, become questionable in *Sein und Zeit*. This questionableness is first of all given to thought as what has to be thought, but not in such a way as to be devoured by an empty skepticism.

Certainly metaphysics posits beings in their Being and so thinks of the Being of beings. But it does not discriminate between the two (cf. "Vom Wesen des Grundes" 1929, p. 8; *Kant und das Problem der Metaphysik* 1929, p. 225; *Sein und Zeit*, p. 230). Metaphysics does not ask for the truth of Being itself. Nor does it ever ask, therefore, in what way the essence of man belongs to the truth of Being. This question metaphysics has not only not asked up to now, but this question cannot be treated by metaphysics as metaphysics. Being still waits for Itself to become memorable to man. However one may —in regard to the determination of the essence of man—determine the *ratio* of the animal and the reason of the living being, whether as "capacity for principles," or as "capacity for categories," or otherwise, everywhere and always the essence of reason is based upon the fact that for each perceiving of beings in their Being, Being itself is discovered and realized in its truth. In the same way, an interpretation of "life" is given in the term "animal," ζῷον, which necessarily rests on an interpretation of beings as ζωή and φύσις, within which what is living appears. Besides this, however, the question finally remains whether, originating and predetermining everything, the essence of man lies in the dimension of the *animalitas*. Are we on the right track at all to reach the essence of man, if and as long as we delimit man as a living-being amongst others, against plant, animal and God? One can so proceed, one can in such a way put man within beings as a being amongst others. Thereby one will always be able to assert what is correct about man. But one must also be clear in this regard that by this man remains cast off in the essential realm of *animalitas,* even when one does not put him on the same level as the animal, but attributes a specific difference to him. In principle one always thinks of the *homo animalis,* even when one puts *anima* as *animus sive mens* and later as subject, as person, as spirit. To put it so is the way of metaphysics. But by this the essence of man is too lightly considered and is not thought of in the light of its source, that essential source which always remains for historical humanity the essential future. Metaphysics thinks of man as arising from *animalitas* and does not think of him as pointing toward *humanitas.*

Metaphysics shuts itself off from the simple essential certitude that man is essentially only in his essence, in which he is claimed by Being. Only from this claim "has" he found wherein his essence dwells. Only from this dwelling "has" he "language" as the home which preserves the ecstatic for his essence. The standing in the clearing of Being I call the ex-sistence of man. Only man has this way to be. Ex-sistence, so understood, is not only the basis of the possibility of reason, *ratio,* but ex-sistence is that, wherein the essence of man preserves the source that determines him.

Ex-sistence can only be said of the essence of man, i.e. only of the human way "to be"; for only man, as far as we know, is admitted into the destiny of ex-sistence. Thus ex-sistence can never be thought of as a specific way, amongst other ways, of a living being, so long as man is destined to think of the essence of his Being and not merely to report theories of nature and history about his composition and activity. Thus all that we attribute to man as *animalitas* in comparing him to the "animal" is grounded in the essence of ex-sistence. The body of man is something essentially different from the animal organism. The error of biologism has not yet been overcome by the fact that one affixes the soul to corporeal man and the mind to the soul and the existential to the mind, and more strongly than ever before preaches the appreciation of the mind, in order that everything may then fall back into the experience of life, with the admonitory assurance that thought will destroy by its rigid concepts the stream of life and the thought of Being will deform existence. That physiology and physiological chemistry can scientifically examine man as an organism, does not prove that in this "organic" disposition, i.e. in the body scientifically explained, the essence of man rests. This has as little value as the opinion that the essence of nature is contained in atomic energy. It may very well be that nature hides its essence in that aspect of which human technology has taken possession. As little as the essence of man consists of being an animal organism, so little can this insufficient determination of the essence of man be eliminated and compensated for by the fact that man is equipped with an immortal soul or with the capability of reason or with the character of a person. Each time the essence is overlooked and, no doubt, on the basis of the same metaphysical design.

All that man is, i.e. in the traditional language of metaphysics the "essence" of man, rests in his ex-sistence. But ex-sistence, so thought of, is not identical with the traditional concept of *existentia,* which signifies actuality in contrast to essentia as possibility. In *Sein und Zeit* (p. 42) is the sentence, italicized: "The "essence" of being-there (*Dasein*) lies in its existence." Here, however, this is not a matter of opposing *existentia* and *essentia,* because these two metaphysical determinations of Being have not yet been placed in question, let alone their relationship. The sentence contains even less a general statement about "being-there," insofar as this term (brought into usage in the eighteenth century for the word "object") is to express the metaphysical concept of the actuality of the actual. The sentence says rather: man is essentially such that he is "Here" (*Da*), i.e. within the clearing of Being. This "Being" of the Here, and only this, has the basic trait of ex-sistence: i.e. it stands outside itself within the truth of Being. The ecstatic essence of man rests in the ex-sistence that remains different from the metaphysically conceived *existentia.* Medieval philosophy conceived this *existentia* as *actualitas.* Kant presents *existentia* as actuality in the sense of the objectivity of experience. Hegel determines *existentia* as the self-knowing idea of the absolute subjectivity. Nietzsche understands *existentia* as the eternal return of the same. Whether, however, through *existentia,* in its various interpretations as actuality, different only at first glance, the Being of the stone, or even life as the Being of plants and animals, has been sufficiently thought about, remains an open question here. In each case animals are as they are, without their standing—from their Being as such—in the truth of Being and preserving in such standing what is essentially their Being. Presumably, animals are the most difficult of all entities for us to think of, because we are, on the one hand, most akin to them and, on the other hand, they are, at the same time separated from our ex-sistential essence by an abyss. And against this it might seem that the essence of the divine is much nearer us than the strangeness of animals, nearer in an essential distance, which as distance is much more familiar to our existential essence than the barely conceivable abysmal corporeal kinship to the animal. Such reflections cast a strange light on the current and therefore still premature designation of man as an *animal rationale*. Because plants and animals, although bound to their environment, are never freely placed in the clearing of Being—and only this clearing is "world"—they have no language. But it is not because they are without language that they find themselves hanging worldless in their environment. Yet in the word "environment" is concentrated all the enigma of the animal. Language is in its essence not utterance of an organism nor is it expression of an animal. Thus it is never thought of with exactness in its symbolical or semantic character. Language is the clearing-and-concealing advent of Being itself.

Ex-sistence, ecstatically thought of, does not coincide with *existentia* either in regard to content or form. Ex-sistence means substantially the emerging into the truth of Being. *Existentia* (existence) means, however, *actualitas,* actuality in contrast to mere possibility as idea. Ex-sistence states the characteristic of man as he is in the destiny of truth. *Existentia* remains the name for the actualization of something-that-is, as an instance of its idea. The phrase, "man exists," does not answer the question of whether there are actually men or not; it answers the question of the "essence" of man. We usually put this question in an equally unsuitable way, whether we ask what man is or who he is. For, in the Who or What we are already on the lookout for something like a person or an object. Yet the personal, no less than the objective, misses and obstructs at the same time all that is essentially ex-sistence in its historical Being. Therefore, the quoted phrase in *Sein und Zeit* (p. 52) deliberately puts the word "essence" in quotation marks. This indicates that the "essence" is not now determined either from the *esse essentiae* or from the *esse existentiae,* but from the ec-static nature of "being-there." Insofar as he ex-sists, man endures the "being-there" by taking the There as the clearing of Being within his "care." The *Dasein* itself, however, is essentially the "thrown" (*geworfene*). It is essentially in the cast (*Wurf*) of Being, a destiny that destines, projects a destiny.

It would undoubtedly be the greatest error, if one were to explain the existent essence of man, as though it were the secularized translation of a thought about man by Christian theology via God (*Deus est suum esse*); for ex-sistence is neither the actualization of an essence, nor does ex-sistence itself realize and constitute the essential. If one understands the "project" (*Entwurf*), alluded to in *Sein und Zeit* as a representative concept [an idea in the mind of an agent] then one considers it as an act of subjectivity and does not think of it as one should within the realm of the "existential analysis" of the "Being-in-the-world" (*In-der-Welt-Seins*), i.e. as the ecstatic relation to the clearing of Being. The necessary and sufficiently verified comprehension of this other way of thought—the thought that abandons subjectivity—is, however, made more difficult by the fact that at the publication of *Sein und Zeit* the third section of the first part, i.e. "Time and Being," was suppressed (cf. *Sein und Zeit,* p. 39). Here the whole thing is reversed. The section in question was suppressed because the thinking failed to find language adequate to this reversal and did not succeed through the aid of the language of metaphysics. The lecture "On the Essence of Truth," which was composed and delivered in 1930, but was first printed in 1943, gives some insight into the thought of the reversal from "Being and Time" to "Time and Being". This reversal is not a change from the standpoint of *Sein und Zeit,* but in it the intended thought for the first time attains the place of the dimension from which "Being and Time" is experienced; and, indeed, experienced from the basic experience of Being.

Sartre formulates, on the other hand, the basic principle of existentialism as this: existence precedes essence, whereby he understands *existentia* and *essentia* in the sense of metaphysics, which since Plato has said *essentia* precedes *existentia.* Sartre reverses this phrasing. But the reversal of a metaphysical phrase remains a metaphysical phrase. As such it remains with metaphysics in the oblivion of the truth of Being. For though philosophy may determine the relationship between *essentia* and *existentia* in the sense of the controversy of the Middle Ages or in the sense of Leibniz or others, one must first of all ask, through what destiny of Being this difference in Being as *esse essentiae* and *esse existentiae* precedes thought. It remains to be considered why this question about the destiny of Being has never been asked and why it could never be thought. Or isn't this a sign of the oblivion of Being that there is this difference between *essentia* and *existentia?* We may suppose that this destiny does not lie in a mere neglect by human thought, let alone in an inferior capacity of earlier western thought. The difference—hidden in its essential source—between *essentia* (essentiality) and *existentia* (actuality) dominates the destiny of Western history and of all the history determined by Europe.

Sartre's key phrase on the superiority of *existentia* over *essentia* undoubtedly justifies the name "existentialism" as a suitable title for this philosophy. But the key phrase of "existentialism" has not the least thing in common with the same phrase in *Sein und Zeit;* apart from the fact that in *Sein und Zeit* a phrase about the relationship between *essentia* and *existentia* cannot yet be expressed, for there we are concerned with settling something preliminary. This, as can be seen from what has been said, is done there rather clumsily. What is yet to be said today might, perhaps, become an impulse to guide the essence of man to attend in thought to the dimension of the truth of Being, which pervades it. Yet even this can only happen for the dignity of Being and for the benefit of *Dasein* which man endures in existing; not for the sake of man, but that through his works civilization and culture may be vindicated.

In order that we today, however, may arrive at the dimension of the truth of Being, we have first of all to make clear how Being concerns man and how it claims him. Such an essential experience happens to us when it dawns upon us that man is, as long as he exists. Let us say this first in the language of tradition, which says: the ex-sistence of man is his substance. For this reason in *Sein und Zeit* the following phrase often recurs: "the 'substance' of man is existence" (p. 117, 212, 314). But "substance" is already understood according to the history of Being, the blanket translation of *οὐσία*, a word which designates the presence of one present and at the same time very often signifies with a mysterious ambiguity what is present (*das Anwesende*). If we think of the metaphysical term "substance" in this sense, which in *Sein und Zeit* is already suggested because of the "phenomenological destruction" realized there (cf. p. 25), then the phrase "the 'substance' of man is ex-istence" does not say anything other than that the way in which man is essentially in his own essence moving toward Being, is that he stands outside himself within the truth of Being. Through this essential determination of man the humanistic interpretations of man as *animal rationale,* as "person," or as an intellectual, spiritual, corporeal, being, are not declared wrong, nor rejected. The only thought is rather that the highest humanistic determinations of the essence of man do not yet come to know the authentic dignity of man. In this the thinking in *Sein und Zeit* runs counter to humanism. But this opposition does not mean that such thinking would make common cause with the opposite of the human and espouse the inhuman, defend inhumanity and degrade the dignity of man. Humanism is opposed because it does not set the *humanitas* of man high enough. However, the essential dignity of man does not lie in the fact that he is as the "subject" of beings, their substance, so that as the despot of Being he may let the character of beings dissolve into an "objectivity" that is much too loudly praised.

Man is rather "cast" by Being itself into the truth of Being, in order that he, ex-sisting thus, may guard the truth of Being; in order that in the light of Being, beings as beings may appear as what it is. Whether and how it appears, whether and how God and the gods, history and nature, enter, presenting and absenting themselves in the clearing of Being, is not determined by man. The advent of beings rests in the destiny of Being. For man, however, the question remains whether he finds what is appropriate to his essence to correspond to his destiny; according to this, as an ex-sisting person, he has to guard the truth of Being. Man is the guardian of Being. The thinking in *Sein und Zeit* proceeds towards this, when ecstatic existence only is experienced as "care" (cf. § 44a, p. 226 ff.).

Yet Being—what is Being? It is Itself. Future thought must learn to experience and to express this. "Being" is neither God nor the basis of the world. Being is further from all that is being and yet closer to man than every being, be it a rock, an animal, a work of art, a machine, be it an angel or God. Being is the closest. Yet its closeness remains farthest from man. Man first clings always and only to beings. But when thought represents beings as beings it no doubt refers to Being. Yet, in fact, it always thinks only of beings as such and never of Being as such. The "question of Being" always remains the question of beings. The question of Being still does not get at what this captious term means: the question seeking for Being. Philosophy, even when critical, as in Descartes and Kant, always follows the procedure of metaphysical representation. It thinks from beings to beings with a glance in passing at Being. For the light of Being already implies each departure from beings and each return to them.

Metaphysics, however, knows the clearing of Being as the looking toward what is present in its appearance (ἰδέα), or critically as what is seen of the external aspect of the categorical representation from the side of subjectivity. This means: the truth of Being as the clearing itself remains concealed from metaphysics. This concealment, however, is not a defect of metaphysics, but the treasure of its own richness, which is withheld and yet held up to it. The clearing itself, however, is Being. Within the destiny of Being the clearing grants a view to metaphysics, a view from which all that is present is attained by man as he presents himself to it, so that man himself can only attain Being (θιγεῖν, Aristotle, Met. Theta 1O) through intellection (νοεῖν). The outward view only draws upon itself. Man yields to this, when intellection has become the projection in the *perceptio* of the *res cogitans* taken as the *subiectum* of the *certitudo*.

Or to proceed in more straightforward fashion perhaps: What relation has Being to ex-sistence? Being itself is the relationship, insofar as It retains and reunites ex-sistence in its existential (i.e. ecstatic) essence—as the place of the truth of Being amidst the beings. Since man as an existing one comes to stand in this relationship which Being itself professes to be, insofar as he, man, ecstatically stands (*aussteht*) it, i.e. insofar as he, caring, takes over, he fails to recognize at first the closest and clings to the next closest. He even believes that this is the closest. Yet closer than the closest and at the same time, for ordinary thought, farther than his farthest is closeness itself: the truth of Being.

The oblivion of the truth of Being under the impact of beings, which is not considered in its essence, is the sense of "decadence" in *Sein und Zeit*. This word does not signify the fall of man, understood as in a "moral philosophy" that has been secularized; this word states an essential relationship between man and Being within the relation of Being to man's essence. In view of this, the terms "authenticity" and "un-authenticity" (*Eigentlichkeit und Uneigentlichkeit*) do not signify a moral-existential or an "anthropological" distinction, but the "ecstatic" relation of man's essence to the truth of Being, which is still to be realized and up to now has remained concealed from philosophy. But this relation, such as it is, does not derive from ex-sistence, but the essence of ex-sistence derives existential-ecstatically from the essence of the truth of Being.

The unique thought that *Sein und Zeit* attempts to express, wants to achieve, is something simple. As such, Being remains mysterious, the plain closeness of an unobtrusive rule. This closeness is essentially language itself. Yet the language is not merely language, insofar as we imagine it at the most as the unity of sound-form (script), melody and rhythm and meaning. We think of sound-form and script as the body of the word; of melody and rhythm as the soul and of meaning as the mind of language. We generally think of language as corresponding to the essence of man, insofar as this essence is represented as *animal rationale,* i.e. as the unity of body-soul-mind. But as in the *humanitas* of the *homo animalis* ex-sistence remains concealed and through this the relation of the truth of Being to man, so does the metaphysical-animal interpretation of language conceal its essence from the point of view of the history of Being. According to this, language is the house of Being, owned and pervaded by Being. Therefore, the point is to think of the essence of language in its correspondence to Being and, what is more, as this very correspondence, i.e., the dwelling of man's essence.

Man, however, is not only a living being, who besides other faculties possesses language. Language is rather the house of Being, wherein living, man ex-sists, while he, guarding it, belongs to the truth of Being.

Thus, what matters in the determination of the humanity of man as ex-sistence is not that man is the essential, but that Being is the essential as the dimension of the ecstatic of ex-sistence. This, however, is not the spatial dimension. All that is spatial and all time-space is essentially dimensional, which is what Being itself is.

Thought heeds these simple relationships. It seeks the appropriate word for them amidst the traditional language and grammar of metaphysics. Can such thought, if terminology is important at all, still be denominated as humanism? Certainly not, insofar as humanism thinks metaphysically. Certainly not, when it is existentialism and bears out the idea expressed by Sartre: *précisement nous sommes sur un plan où il y a seulement des hommes* (*L'Existentialisme est un humanisme,* p. 36). Instead of this, if we think as in *Sein und Zeit,* we should say: *précisement nous sommes sur un plan où il y a principialement l'Être.* But whence does *le plan* come and what is it? *L'Être et le plan* are the same. In *Sein und Zeit* (p. 212) it is said intentionally and cautiously: *il y a l'Etre:* "it gives" (there is) Being. The *il y a* translates the "it gives" inexactly. For the "it," which here "gives," is Being itself. The "gives" names, however, the essence of Being; the giving itself and the imparting of its truth. The giving itself into the open with this self, is Being itself.

At the same time "it gives" is used in order to avoid at once the locution: "Being is;" for usually the "is" is said of what-is. This we call the being. Being "is", however, precisely not "the being." Were the "is" said without closer interpretation of Being, then Being would all too easily be repersented as a "being" in the manner of the known being, which as cause effects and as effect is effectuated. Nevertheless, Parmenides had already said in the early days of thought: ἔστιν γὰρ εἶναι, "Being is." In this utterance the original mystery of all thought is concealed. Perhaps this "is" is not and could only be appropriately said of Being, so that no being ever properly "is." But because thought should first manage to express Being in its truth, instead of explaining it as a trait of the being, it must be open to the attention of thought whether and how Being is.

The ἔστιν γὰρ εἶναι of Parmenides has as yet been given no thought. From this we can realize the state of progress in philosophy. If it considers its essence, it never progresses at all. It marks time by continually thinking the same thing. The progressing, i.e., away from this spot, is an error that follows thought as the shadow it casts. Since Being is as yet unthought of, it is said of Being in *Sein und Zeit,* "it gives." Yet one cannot speculate directly and without help upon this *il y a.* The "it gives" rules as the destiny of Being. Its history finds expression in the words of the essential thinkers. So the thought that thinks of the truth of Being thinks historically. There is no "systematic" thinking, nor is there a history of past opinions as illustration. Nor is there even, as Hegel believed, a systematics, which could deduce from the laws of its thought a law of history and at the same time reduce it to the system. There is, it was originally believed, the history of Being, to which thought belongs as the remembrance of this history, realized by itself. This remembrance is to be distinguished essentially from the posterior representation of history in the sense of the past passing. History does not at first occur as occurrence. And it is not the passing. The occurrence of history lives as the destiny of the truth of Being, and derives from it (cf. The essay on Hölderlin's Hymn *"Wie wenn am Feiertage,"* 1941, p. 31). Being comes to destiny, as It, Being, gives itself. This, however, means from the point of view of destiny that it gives itself and negates itself at the same time. Nonetheless, Hegel's determination of history as the development of the "mind" is not wrong. Nor is it neither partly right, nor partly wrong. It is as true as metaphysics is, which through Hegel for the first time absolutely expresses its essence systematically. Absolute metaphysics belongs with its inversions via Marx and Nietzsche to the history of the truth of Being. Whatever stems from it cannot be affected or done away with by refutation. It can only be appraised, as its truth is reintegrated more incipiently into Being itself and removed from the sphere of mere human opinion.

To refute everything in the field of essential thought is ridiculous. A quarrel amongst thinkers is a "lovers' quarrel" for the thing itself. It helps them mutually in their belonging to that one and the same sphere, in which they find what is appropriate in the destiny of Being.

Granted that man is capable of thinking of the truth of Being in the future, he will think from his ex-sistence. Ex-sisting, he stands in the destiny of Being. The ex-sistence of man as ex-sistence is historical, but not primarily for that reason, or simply for that reason, because many a thing may occur with man and human affairs in the course of time. Because it is important to think of the ex-sistence of *Da-sein,* it is quite essential to the thinking in *Sein und Zeit* that the historicity of *Dasein* be grasped.

But is it not said in *Sein und Zeit* (p. 212), where the "it gives" finds expression that "only as long as Dasein is, is there Being?" Indeed, it is. This means that only as long as the clearing of Being is realized, is Being itself conveyed to man. That the "Da" (Here), however, the clearing of Being itself, is realized, is the destination of Being itself. This is the destiny of the clearing. The sentence, however, does not mean that the Dasein of man in the traditional sense of *existentia,* understood more recently as the actuality of the *ego cogito,* would be the existent through which alone Being is created. The sentence does not say that Being is a product of man. The introduction to *Sein und Zeit* (p. 38) states simply and clearly and even in italics that "Being is the *transcendens* as such." Just as the openness of spatial nearness surpasses everything near and far, so Being is essentially broader than all the beings, because it is the clearing itself. Thus, in accordance with the next inevitable attack of the still dominant metaphysics, Being will be thought of as deriving from beings. Only from such an outlook does Being show itself in such a surpassing.

The preliminary definition of "Being as the *transcendens* as such" expresses simply the way in which the essence of Being has so far been cleared for man. This retrospective definition of the essence of Being out of the clearing of beings is and remains indispensable for further thinking of the question of the truth of Being. So thought attests to its historical essence. It is far from the pretension of wishing to begin from the beginning and to declare all previous philosophy wrong. Whether, however, the definition of Being as the simple *transcendens* yet expresses the simple essence of the truth of Being, this and this alone is the immediate question for the thinking that tries to think of the truth of Being. For this reason you find (on page 230) that only from "meaning", that is from the truth of Being, can one understand how Being is. Being clears itself for man in ecstatic projection. But this projection does not create Being.

Moreover, the projection is essentially a matter of being cast. What projects in the project is not man, but Being itself, which destines man to the ex-sistence which is the essence of *Dasein.* This destiny is realized as the clearing of Being. The clearing imparts the closeness to Being. In this closeness, in the clearing of the *"Da"* (Here), man dwells as one ex-sisting, without being capable now of properly experiencing and taking over this dwelling. The closeness of Being, which is the *"Da"* of *Dasein,* is thought of (from the point of view of *Sein und Zeit*) in my essay on Hölderlin's elegy *"Heimkunft"* (1943) as the "Homeland" (*Heimat*), as understood by the poet from the experience of the oblivion of Being. The word is here thought of in an essential sense, neither patriotic, nor nationalistic, but according to the history of Being. The essence of the homeland, however, is at the same time expressed with the intention of thinking of the homelessness of modern man as seen from the essence of the history of Being. The last one to experience this homelessness was Nietzsche. He was incapable of finding any other way out of metaphysics than by the reversal of metaphysics. This, however, is the height of being lost. Hölderlin, in contrast, when he writes *"Heimkunft"* is concerned that his "countrymen" find their essential home. He by no means seeks this in an egoism of his people. He sees it rather in their belonging to the destiny of the Western World. But even the Western world is not thought of regionally as the Occident in contrast to the Orient, nor merely as Europe, but in the frame of world history from the closeness to its origin. We have hardly begun to think of the mysterious relations to the East, which find expression in Hölderlin's poetry (cf. *"Der Ister"* as well as *"Die Wanderung,"* 3rd. stanza and ff.). The "German" is not said to the world so that the world may be healed thanks to the German essence, but it is said to the Germans so that they from their fateful membership amongst the nations may become with them world-historical (cf. Hölderlin's poem *"Andenken," Tübinger Gedenkschrift,* 1943, v. 322). The homeland of this historical dwelling is the closeness to Being.

In this closeness the decision, if any, is reached as to whether and how God and the gods deny themselves and the night remains, whether and how the day of the Holy dawns, whether and how in the rise of the Holy an appearance of God and the gods can start anew. The Holy, however, which is only the essential space of divinity, for its part yields; but the dimension for the gods and God only comes into appearance when, first and after a long preparation, Being itself has been cleared and been experienced in its truth. Only in this way does the overcoming of homelessness start from Being, where not only man, but the essence of man, wanders about.

Homelessness, so understood, lies in beings' abandonment of Being. It is the sign of the oblivion of Being. Consequently, the truth of Being remains unthought of. The oblivion of Being is indirectly evidenced in the fact that man only considers and cultivates beings. Since he cannot help having a conception of Being it is explained as the "most general" and for that reason as what embraces beings; or as the universe of an infinite being or as the handiwork of a finite subject. At the same time "Being" stands of old for "beings" and vice-versa, both are tossed about in a strange and still thoughtless confusion.

Being as the destiny that destines truth remains concealed. But the world's destiny is proclaimed in poetry without its becoming apparent at once as the history of Being. Hölderlin's world-historical thought, which finds expression in the poem *"Andenken,"* is therefore essentially much more original and so much more appropriate to the future than the mere cosmopolitanism of Goethe. For the same reason Hölderlin's relation to the Greek world is an essentially different thing from humanism. Therefore, young Germans who knew of Hölderlin have thought and lived (in the face of death) other than what publicity proclaimed as the German attitude.

Homelessness becomes a world destiny. It is, therefore, necessary to think of this destiny from the point of view of the history of Being. What Marx, deriving from Hegel, recognized in an essential and significant sense as the alienation of man, reaches roots back into the homelessness of modern man. This is evoked—from the destiny of Being—in the form of metaphysics, strengthened by it and at the same time covered by it in its character as homelessness. Because Marx, in discovering this alienation, reaches into an essential dimension of history, the Marxist view of history excells all other history. Because, however, neither Husserl nor, as far as I can see, Sartre recognizes the essentially historical character of Being, neither phenomenology nor existentialism can penetrate that dimension within which alone a productive discussion with Marxism is possible.

For this it is necessary to liberate oneself from the naive conceptions of materialism and from the cheap, supposedly effective, refutations of it. The essence of materialism does not consist of the assertion that everything is merely matter, but rather of a metaphysical determination, according to which everything being appears as the material of labor. The modern metaphysical essence of labor is anticipated in Hegel's *Phenomenology of the Spirit* as the self-establishing process of unconditional production; i.e., the objectivization of the actual through man experienced as subjectivity. The essence of materialism is concealed in the essence of technics, about which, indeed, a great deal is written, but little is thought. Technics in its essence is a destiny (in the history of Being) of the truth of Being resting in oblivion. It not only goes back in its name to the Greek τέχνη, but it historically stems from τέχνη as a way of the ἀληθεύειν, i.e. the making open of beings. As a form of truth technics is grounded in the history of metaphysics. This is itself an exceptional phase of the history of Being. One can take various positions in regard to the theories (and arguments) of communism, but from the point of view of the history of Being, it is indisputable that in it an elementary experience has been made manifest of what is world-historical. He who takes "communism" only as a "party" or as *"Weltanschauung,"* is thinking just as narrowly as those who by the term "Americanism" mean—and what is more in a depreciatory way—a particular mode of life. The danger into which Europe up to now has been more and more clearly pushed, probably consists of the fact that its thought, which was once its greatness, lags behind the destiny that opens for the world, a destiny which undoubtedly in the basic traits of its essential origin remains European in its determination. No metaphysics, be it idealistic, materialistic, or Christian, considering its essence and not its sporadic efforts, can, to develop itself overtake this destiny, i.e. reach it by thought and bring together what, in a complete sense of Being, now is.

In view of the essential homelessness of man the thought of the history of Being demonstrates the future destiny of man in that he investigates the truth of Being and sets out toward its discovery. Each nationalism is metaphysically an anthropologism and as such subjectivism. Nationalism is not overcome by mere internationalism, but only expanded and elevated to a system. Nationalism is far from being annulled by it or brought to *humanitas,* as individualism is by historical collectivism. This is the subjectivity of man in totality. He realizes its absolute self-assertion. This cannot be canceled. It cannot even be sufficiently experienced by one-sided thinking that tries to mediate. Everywhere man, thrust out from the truth of Being, runs around in a circle as the *animal rationale.*

The essence of man, however, consists of being more than mere man, insofar as this mere man is represented as a rational animal. "More" must not be understood here in an additive sense, as if the traditional definition of man were to remain as the basic definition, in order to undergo an expansion through an addition of the existential. The "more" means: more original and, therefore, in essence more essential. But here the mysterious is manifest: man is in his thrownness (*Geworfenheit*). This means that man is as the ex-sisting counter-throw (*Gegenwurf*) of Being even more than the *animal rationale,* insofar as he is less related to the man who is conceived from subjectivity. Man is not the master of beings. Man is the shepherd of Being. In this "less" man does not suffer any loss, but gains, because he comes into the truth of Being. He gains the essential poverty of the shepherd whose dignity rests in the fact that he was called by Being itself into the trueness of his truth. This call comes as the throw, from which stems the thrownness of the *Da-sein.* Man is in his essence (from the point of view of the history of Being) that being whose Being as ex-sistence consists of dwelling in the nearness of Being. Man is the neighbor of Being.

But no doubt, you have wanted to reply for some time now, does not such thinking think precisely of the *humanitas* of the *homo humanus?* Does it not think of this *humanitas* in such a decisive meaning as no metaphysics has thought or even can think of it? Is not this "humanism" in an extreme sense? Certainly. It is the humanism that thinks of the humanity of man from the nearness to Being. But it is at the same time the humanism for which not man, but the historical essence of man in his derivation from the truth of Being, is playing. But does not the ex-sistence of man then stand and fall in this game at the same time? Indeed, it does.

In *Sein und Zeit* (p. 38) it is said that all questioning of philosophy "strikes back into existence." But existence is here not the actuality of the *ego cogito*. Nor is it the actuality of subjects that act with and for each other and in this way come into their own. "Ex-sistence" is basically different from all *existentia* and "existence," the ec-static dwelling in the nearness of Being. It is the guardianship, i.e. the concern of Being. Since in this thinking something simple is to be thought, it is very difficult to represent it by traditional philosophy. Yet the difficulty does not consist of indulging in a particular profundity and of forming complex conceptions, but it conceals itself in stepping back and letting thought take up a skilful inquiry and abandon the trained opinions of philosophy.

It is everywhere believed that the effort in *Sein und Zeit* has ended up a blind alley. We won't discuss this opinion here. The thought, which in the above mentioned essay attempted a few steps, has not yet passed beyond *Sein und Zeit*. But perhaps it has in the meantime come a little bit more into its own. As long as philosophy, however, occupies itself only with constantly obstructing possibilities, with engaging in matters of thought—i.e. the truth of Being—, so long is it perfectly secure from the danger of ever breaking down at the hardness of its matter. So the "philosophizing" about the failure is separated by an abyss from a failing thought. If a man should be fortunate in this, no misfortunes would occur. For him it would be the only gift that thought could receive from Being.

Yet this too is important: the matter of thinking is not reached by talking about "the truth of Being" and of "the history of Being". Everything depends upon bringing into language the truth of Being and letting thought penetrate this language. Perhaps then language requires far less precipitate utterance than correct silence. Yet who amongst us today would like to imagine that his attempts at thought were at home on the path of silence? If it goes far enough, our thought might perhaps point to the truth of Being and to it as what is to be thought. In this way it would be more than anything else removed from mere suspicion and opinion and be alloted to the already rare handiwork of script. The matters, in which something is, even if they are not determined for eternity, come in due time.

Whether the realm of the truth of Being is a blind alley or whether it is the free dimension in which freedom saves its essence, each one may judge for himself after having tried to go his appointed way or blaze a better; that is, one in more accord with the question. On the next to the last page of *Sein und Zeit* (p. 437) are the words "the *dispute* in regard to the interpretation of Being (i.e. not of the existent, nor of the Being of man) cannot be straightened out, *because it has not even been begun.* And in the end one cannot 'pick a quarrel,' for the beginning of a dispute requires some equipment. Only towards that is the investigation aimed." These words retain their validity even after two decades. Let us also in the coming days be voyagers to the neighborhood of Being. The question which you put helps to clarify the way.

You ask: *Comment redonner un sens au mot "Humanisme"?* "How can one restore meaning to the word humanism?" Your question not only presupposes that you want to retain the word "humanism," but it also contains the admission that the word has lost its meaning.

It has lost it through the realization that the essence of humanism is metaphysical and this now means that metaphysics not only does not ask the question of the truth of Being, but even abstracts asking it, insofar as metaphysics persists in its oblivion of Being. The thought, however, that leads to this realization of the questionable essence of humanism has at the same time brought us to think of the essence of man more originally. In view of this more essential *humanitas* of the *homo humanus,* the possibility follows of restoring to the word humanism an historical meaning that is older than what "history" considers the oldest. This restoration is not to be understood as though the word humanism were without meaning at all and a mere *flatus vocis.* The *"humanum"* in the word points to the *humanitas,* the essence of man. The "ism" indicates that the essence of man would like to be understood essentially. The word "humanism" has this meaning as a word. This requires first that we experience the essence of man more originally; and then show in what degree this essence becomes in its own way a destiny. The essence of man rests in ex-sistence. This essence desires from Being itself, insofar as Being raises man as the ex-sisting one for the guardianship of the truth of Being. "Humanism" means now, should we decide to retain the word: the essence of man is essential for the truth of Being, and apart from this truth of Being man himself does not matter. So we think of a "humanism" of a strange sort. The word offers a term which is a *lucus a non lucendo.*

Should one still call "humanism" this view which speaks out against all earlier humanism, but which does not at all advocate the in-human? And this only in order to swim perhaps in the dominant currents, which are stifled in a metaphysical subjectivism and find themselves drowned in the oblivion of Being? Or should thought, resisting the word "humanism," make an effort to become more attentive to the *humanitas* of the *homo humanus* and what grounds this *humanitas?* So, if the world-historical moment has not already gone that far itself, a reflection might be awakened that would not only think of man, but of the "nature" of man, and even more than this of his nature, the original dimension in which the essence of man, determined as coming from Being itself, is at home. But perhaps we should rather suffer for a while the inevitable misinterpretations to which the way of thought that centers on Being and time has so far been exposed and let them gradually be worn out? These misinterpretations are the natural reinterpretations of what people had read or rather, what they later thought they had read, but which, in fact, was preconception. They all show the same structure and the same basis.

Because "humanism" is argued against, one fears a defense of the inhuman and a glorification of barbaric cruelty. For what is more "logical" than that for one who negates humanism only the affirmation of inhumanity can remain?

Because "logic" is argued against, one believes that we renounce the rigor of thinking and in its place enthrone the despotism of instincts and emotions, and so proclaim "irrationalism" as the truth. For what is more "logical" than that one who argues against the logical defends the a-logical?

Because "values" are argued against, one is shocked by a philosophy that allegedly dares to neglect the highest goods of humankind. For what is more "logical" than that thinking which negates values must necessarily declare everything valueless?

Because it is said that the Being of man consists of "Being-in-the-World" (*In-der-Welt-sein*), one considers man to have been degraded to the level of a mere this-worldly being, and that philosophy thereby sinks into positivism. For what is more "logical" than that one who maintains the worldliness of man only admits the this-worldly, thereby negating the other-worldly and renouncing all "transcendency"?

Because reference is made to Nietzsche's expression of "God's death", one declares such a procedure to be atheism. For what is more "logical" than that one who has experienced "God's death" is a godless person?

Because in all that has been said I have argued everywhere against what mankind values as high and holy, this philosophy therefore teaches an irresponsible and destructive "nihilism." For what is more "logical" than that one who negates everywhere what is truly being, places himself on the side of the non-being and with that advocates mere nothingness as the meaning of reality?

What is happening here? One hears talk of "humanism," of "logic," of "values," of "world," of "God." One hears talk of an opposition to these. One knows and takes these things as positive. What is expressed against them, one immediately takes as their negation and thus "negative" in a sense of the destructive. This is a question of what, in a certain part of *Sein und Zeit,* we called "the phenomenological destruction." One believes that with the help of logic and *ratio* [Reason] that all that is not positive is negative and so would reject reason; and therefore, deserves to be branded as an infamy. One is so full of "logic", that everything which is repugnant to the usual somnolence of opinion is immediately charged to a censurable contrariness. One casts all that does not remain in the well-known beloved positive into the prearranged pit of bare negation that negates everything and therefore ends in nothingness and so achieves nihilism. In this logical way one lets everything succumb to a nihilism that one has fabricated with the help of logic.

But is it certain that the apparition that thought brings up against common opinion necessarily points to mere negation and to the negative? This occurs only when (but then so inevitably and so definitively, that is, without a free view of other directions) one fixes beforehand what is meant by "the positive" and from this decides absolutely and negatively against the sphere of possible oppositions to it. Such a procedure hides the refusal to expose to scrutiny the preconceived "positive," together with the black and white opposition, in which it believes that it has preserved itself. Through the constant appeal to logic one produces the illusion that one has yielded to thought, while one has abjured it.

That the opposition to "humanism" by no means implies the defence of the inhuman, but opens other prospectives must have become clearer to some extent now.

"Logic" understands thought as the representation of beings in their Being, and this Being as producing this representation as a universal concept. But how is it with the consideration of Being itself, i.e., with thought that thinks of the truth of Being? Such thought reaches the original essence of the λόγος, which in Plato and Aristotle, the founder of "logic," had already been dead and buried. To think "counter to logic" does not mean to stick up for the illogical, but only means to think the *logos,* and its essence as it appeared in the early days of thought; i.e. to make an effort first of all to prepare such an act of re-flecting (*Nach-denkens*). Of what use are all such prolix systems of logic to us, when even without knowing what they are doing they immediately avoid the task of asking after the essence of the λόγος? If one wanted to retaliate with objections, which is frankly fruitless, then one could more rightly say that irrationalism, as a renunciation of *ratio,* rules as unrecognized and undisputed master of that "logic" which believes it can avoid a consideration of the *logos* and of the essence of *ratio,* which is founded on the *logos.*

The thinking that runs counter to "values" does not state that all that one declares "values"—"culture," "art," "science," "human dignity," "world," and "God"—is worthless. One should rather come to understand that it is exactly through the characterization of something as "value," that it loses its dignity. This is to say that through the estimation of something as a value, one accepts what is evaluated only as a mere object for the appreciation of man. But what a thing is in its Being is not exhausted by its being an object, much less when the objectivity has the character of value. All valuing, even when it values positively, subjectivises the thing. It does not let beings be, but makes them valuable as the object of its action. The extravagant effort to demonstrate the objectivity of values does not know what it is doing. When one proclaims "God" as altogether "the highest value," this is a degradation of the essence of God. Thinking in values here and in general is the greatest blasphemy that can be thought of in the face of Being. To think counter to values, therefore, does not mean to beat the drum for the worthlessness and nullity of the existent, but means to bring—against the subjectivization of the existent as mere object—the clearing of the truth of Being before thought.

To refer to "Being-in-the-World" as the basic trait of the *humanitas* of the *homo humanus* is not to claim that man is simply a secular being, in the Christian sense, and so turned away from God and devoid of "transcendency." What is meant by this last word might be more clearly called: the Transcendent. The Transcendent is the super-sensual being. This is valued as the supreme being in the sense of the first cause of every being. God is thought of as this first cause. "World," however, does not in any way signify, in the term "Being-in-the-World," the earthly being in contrast to the heavenly, nor does it mean the "secular" in contrast to the "spiritual." "World" does not signify in this determination a being at all and no realm of beings, but the openness of Being. Man is and is man insofar as he is the existing. He stands exposed to the openness of Being, an openness which is Being itself, that has projected the essence of man into "care." So thrown, man stands "in" the openness of Being. "World" is the clearing of Being, wherein man stands out from his thrown essence. "Being-in-the-World" names the essence of ex-sistence in relation to the cleared dimension out of which the "ex" of the ex-sistence essentially arises. Thought of from the point of view of ex-sistence, "world" is in a way transcendence within and for existence. Man is never this-worldly and of the world as a "subject," whether this "subject" be understood as "I" or as "We." He is also not essentially a subject who is also always in reference to an object, so that his essence lies in the subject-object relation. Man is rather in his essence ex-sistent in the openness of Being; this Open only clears the "between," within which the "relation" between subject and object can "be."

The statement that the essence of man rests in Being-in-the-world contains no resolution about whether man is in the theological-metaphysical sense a mere this-worldly creature or an other-worldly one.

Therefore, with the existential determination of the essence of man nothing has yet been decided about the "existence" or "non-existence" of God, not about the possibility or impossibility of God. It is thus not only precipitate but erroneous to assert that the interpretation of the essence of man in its relation to the truth of Being is atheism. This arbitrary classification, besides everything else, lacks carefulness in reading. One ignores the fact that since 1929 the following statement could be found in the work *Vom Wesen des Grundes* (p. 28, fn. 1): "Through the ontological interpretation of *Dasein* as Being-in-the-World, there is neither a positive nor a negative resolution of a possible Being-towards-God. However, through the elucidation of the transcendency there is first obtained *an adequate concept of Dasein,* in consideration of which one may now ask what exactly is, ontologically, the relationship between God and *Dasein.*" Now when this observation, too, is, as usual, taken too narrowly, one is likely to say that this philosophy makes no decision either for or against the existence of God. It remains indifferent. Thus, the religious question does not concern it. Such "indifferentism" must surely turn into nihilism.

But does the quoted remark really teach indifferentism? Why, then, are some words, and not others, printed in italics in the footnotes? Only to indicate, surely, that thought that thinks from the question of the truth of Being questions more originally than metaphysics can. Only from the truth of Being can the essence of the holy be thought. Only from the essence of the holy can the essence of divinity be thought. Only in the light of the essence of divinity can it be thought and said what the word "God" is to signify. Or must we not first be able to understand and hear these words carefully if we as men, i.e., as exsisting beings, are to have the privilege of experiencing a relation of God to man? How, then, is the man of the present epoch even to be able to ask seriously and firmly whether God approaches or withdraws when man omits the primary step of thinking deeply in the one dimension where this question can be asked: that is, the dimension of the holy, which, even as dimension, remains closed unless the openness of Being is cleared and in its clearing is close to man. Perhaps the distinction of this age consists in the fact that the dimension of grace has been closed. Perhaps this is its unique dis-grace.

But with this indication, which points to the truth of Being as what-has-to-be-thought, this thought would in no way wish to have declared itself for theism. It can no more be theistic than it can be atheistic. This, however, is not because of any indifferent attitude but out of respect for the limits which have been set upon thought as thought, and precisely through which it is understood as that which has-to-be-thought, through the truth of Being. In so far as thought does not exceed the limits of its task, at the moment of present world destiny it gives man an indication of the original dimension of his historical abode. In so far as thought expresses in this way the truth of Being, it has entrusted itself to what is more essential than all values and all beings. Thought does not overcome metaphysics by surpassing and cancelling it in some direction or other and ascending even higher: it descends into the nearness of the nearest. The descent, especially where man has ascended too far into subjectivity, is more difficult and more dangerous than the ascent. The descent leads to the poverty of the ex-sistence of the *homo homanus*. In ex-sistence, the sphere of the *homo animalis* of metaphysics is abandoned. The domination of this sphere is the indirect and very old reason for the delusion and arbitrariness of what is denominated as biologism, but also for what is known as pragmatism. To think of the truth of Being means at the same time to think of the *humanitas* of the *homo humanus*. What is at stake is *humanitas,* in the service of the truth of Being but without humanism in the metaphysical sense.

But if the thought of Being is so essentially focussed on humanitas, must ontology then not be completed by "ethics"? Is not that effort essential which you express in the sentence, *"Ce que je cherche à faire, depuis longtemps déjà, c'est préciser le rapport de l'ontologie avec une éthique possible"?*

Shortly after *Sein und Zeit* appeared, a young friend asked me, "When are you going to write an ethics?" Where the essence of man is thought of so essentially, i.e., only from the question of the truth of Being, but without raising man to the center of beings, there the desire must arise for personally relevant directives and rules that tell how man, having gathered from his exsistence experience for Being is to live "fatefully." The wish for an ethics needs to be fulfilled, all the more urgently, because the overt no less than the concealed, perplexity of man increases to immeasurable dimensions. Every care must be given to ties to ethics, in an age of technology when the individual, subject to the nature of a mass society, can be brought to a dependable steadfastness only by means of ordering and gathering his plans and actions as a whole in a way that corresponds to a technological age.

Who can ignore this crisis? Should we not preserve and secure the ties we now have, even if they only hold human beings together precariously and in mere immediacy? Certainly. But does this crisis ever absolve thought of the responsibility of thinking of that which primarily remains to-be-thought and, as Being, remains the guarantee and truth prior to every being? Can thought continue to retreat from the thought of Being after this has lain so long hidden in oblivion and at the same time announces itself at this very moment of world history through the uprooting of every being?

Before we attempt to determine more precisely the relationship between "ontology" and "ethics," we must ask what "ontology" and "ethics" themselves are. It is necessary to consider whether what can be designated by these terms still remains adequate and close to what has been assigned to thought, which as thought has to think before all else of the truth of Being.

Should, however, "ontology" as well as "ethics" and all thinking in disciplines become untenable and our thinking thereby become more disciplined, what happens then to the question of the relationship between these two disciplines of philosophy?

Ethics appeared for the first time, along with logic and physics in the school of Plato. These disciplines were born at a time that converted thought into "philosophy," but philosophy into *episteme* (science) and science itself into a matter for schools and school administrations. In passing through philosophy, so understood, science was born and thought [*Denken*] vanished. Thinkers up to then had known neither a "logic," nor an "ethics," nor a "physics." Yet their thinking is neither illogical nor immoral. But their conception of *physis* had a profundity and breadth which all the later "physics" was never again able to attain. The tragedies of Sophocles, if such a comparison can be made at all, hold the ethics more originally concealed in their telling than Aristotle's lecture on "ethics." A saying of Heraclitus that only consists of three words says something so simple that from it the essence of the *ethos* immediately comes to light.

The saying of Heraclitus goes (fragment 119): ἦθος ἀνθρώπῳ δαίμων. This is usually translated as: "A man's character is his daimon." This translation is modern but not Greek thinking. ἦθος means abode, place of dwelling. The word designates the open sphere in which man dwells. The openness of his abode allows that to appear which approaches toward the essence of man and so arriving abides near him. The abode of man contains and maintains the advent of that to which man in essence belongs. This, according to Heraclitus' saying, is δαίμων, God. The fragment says: Man, insofar as he is man, dwells in the nearness of God. A story that Aristotle relates (de part. anim. A 5, 645 a 17) coincides with this saying of Heraclitus. It runs:

"An anecdote tells of an explanation that Heraclitus is said to have given strangers who wanted to approach him. Upon approaching they found him warming himself at a stove. They stopped surprised and all the more so because as they hesitated he encouraged them and bade them come in with the words: 'For here too there are Gods present.'

The story speaks for itself, yet some aspects should be stressed.

The group of unknown visitors in its inquisitive curiosity about the thinker is disappointed and puzzled at first by his abode. It believes that it must find the thinker in conditions which, contrary to man's usual way of living, show everywhere traits of the exceptional and the rare, and, therefore, the sensational. The group hopes to find through its visit with the thinker things which, at least for a time, will provide material for entertaining small talk. The strangers who wish to visit the thinker hope to see him perhaps precisely at the moment when, sunk in profound meditation, he is thinking. The visitors wish to experience this, not in order to be affected by his thinking, but merely so that they will be able to say that they have seen and heard one who is reputed to be a thinker.

Instead, the inquisitive ones find Heraclitus at a stove. This is a pretty ordinary and insignificant place. True enough, bread is baked there. But Heraclitus is not even busy with baking at the stove. He is there only to warm himself, and so he betrays the whole poverty of his life at this spot which is in itself prosaic. The glimpse of a freezing thinker offers little of interest. And so the inquisitive ones at this disappointing sight immediately lose their desire to come any closer. What are they to do there? This ordinary dull event of someone cold and standing by the stove one can find any time in his own home. Then, why look up a thinker? The visitors are about to leave again. Heraclitus reads the disappointed curiosity in their faces. He realizes that with the crowd the mere absence of an expected sensation is enough to make those who have just come leave. Therefore, he heartens them. He especially urges them to enter with the words εἶναι γὰρ καὶ ἐνταῦθα θέους. "There are Gods present even here."

This statement puts the abode (ἦθος) of the thinker and his doing in a different light. Whether the visitors have understood the statement immediately or at all and then seen everything in this different light, the story does not tell. But that the story was told and transmitted to us today, is due to the fact that what it reports is of the bearing of this thinker and characterizes it. και ἐνταῦθα. "Even here," at the baking oven, at this common place, where all things and every condition, each act and thought, are familiar and current, i.e., securer, "even there" in the sphere of the secure εἶναι θεούς, it is so "that even there there are gods present."

ἦθος ἀνθρώπῳ δαίμων as Heraclitus says: "The (secure) abode for man is the open quality of the presence (*Anwesung*) of God (of the, insecure, the strange) (*des Un-geheuren*).

If now, in accord with the basic meaning of the word ἦθος, ethics dwells in the abode of man, then that thought which thinks the truth of Being as the original element of man as exsisting is already in itself at the source of ethics. But then this kind of thinking is not ethics, either, because it is ontology. For ontology always thinks only the being (ὄν) in its Being. As long as the truth of Being, however, is not thought, all ontology remains without its base. Hence the thought, which with *Sein und Zeit* tried to think forward into the truth of Being, called itself fundamental ontology. It attempts to go back to the basic essence, from which the thought of the truth of Being derives. The formulation of different questions removes this thinking from the "ontology" of metaphysics (including that of Kant). The reason, however, why "ontology," be it transcendental or precritical, is not subject to criticism is not that it thinks the Being of beings and thereby forces Being into a concept, but that it does not think the truth of Being and so fails to realize the fact that there is a mode of thinking more rigorous than the conceptual. Thinking which tries to think forward into the truth of Being in the struggle of the first breakthrough expresses only a small part of this entirely different dimension. And the latter is further distorted in that it no longer retains the essential health of phenomenological vision and has not yet abandoned its inadequate pretensions toward "science" and "research." In order to make this attempt of thinking recognizable and understandable within philosophy, it was possible at first to speak only within the horizon of the existing philosophy and within the usage of the terms familiar to it.

In the meantime I have come to be convinced that even these terms must immediately and inevitably lead astray. For the terms and their corresponding conceptual language were not rethought by the readers from the thing which had-to-be-thought first; instead, this thing was imagined through terms maintained in their usual signification. Thinking that seeks for the truth of Being and thereby determines the essential abode of man from Being is neither ethics nor ontology. Therefore, the question of the relationship of the two to each other has no longer any basis in this sphere. Nevertheless your question, if it be thought more originally, continues to make sense and be of essential importance.

One must, of course, ask: If thought, considering the truth of Being, determines the essence of the *humanitas* as ex-sistence from its pertinence to Being, does this thought only remain a theoretical imagining of Being and of man, or is it possible to extract from knowledge directives for action and put them to use for life?

The answer is that such thinking is neither theoretical nor practical. It occurs before such a differentiation. This thinking is, insofar as it is, the recollection of Being and nothing else. Belonging to Being, because it is thrown by being into the trueness of its truth and claims for it, it thinks Being. Such thinking results in nothing. It has no effect. It suffices its own essence, in that it is. But it is, in that it expresses its matter. At each epoch of history one thing only is inportant to it: that it be in accord with its matter. Its material relevance is essentially superior to the validity of science, because it is freer. For it lets Being—be.

Thinking works at building the house of Being; in which house Being joins and as such the joining of Being enjoins that man, according to destiny, dwell in the truth of Being. This dwelling is the essence of "Being-in-the-world" (cf. *Sein und Zeit*). The reference there to the "in-Being" (*In-Sein*) as "dwelling" is no etymological game. The reference in the essay of 1936 to Hölderlin's phrase, "Laboring, yet poetically man dwells on this earth" is no mere gilding of a thought that abandoning science, takes refuge in poetry. To talk of the house of Being is not to transfer the image of "house" to Being, but from the materially understood essence of Being we shall some day be more easily able to think what "house" and "dwelling" are.

Nonetheless, thought never creates the house of Being, Thought accompanies historical existence, i.e., the *humanitas* of the *homo humanus,* to the domain where grace arises.

With grace, evil appears in the clearing of Being. The essence of evil does not consist in pure wickedness of human action, but in the malice of anger. Both grace and anger can, however, essentially only be in Being, insofar as Being itself is what is disputed. In it is hidden the essential source of nihilation (*das Nichten*). What nihilates, is manifest as the nothing-like (*das Nichthafte*). This can be approached in the "No." The "Not" does not arise from the Nay-saying of negation. Each "No" which is not misinterpreted as a self-willed insistence on the positing power of subjectivity (but remains letting-be of ex-sistence) answers the claim of the manifest nihilation. Every "No" is only the affirmation of the "Not." Every affirmation rests in recognition This lets that towards which it goes approach it. It is believed that nihilation cannot be found anywhere in beings themselves. This is true as long as one seeks for nihilation as something that is being, as an existing quality of the existent. But that is not the place to seek for nihilation. Being is no existing quality which characterizes the being. Nevertheless, Being is being more than any actual being. Because nihilation is essentially in Being itself, we can never become aware of it as something that is being in the existent. But this impossibility does not prove that the source of the Not is from Nay-saying. This proof only seems conclusive if one posits the existent as the object of subjectivity. From this alternative it then follows that each Not, since it never appears as something objective, must inevitably be the product of a subjective act. Whether, however, the Nay-saying constitutes the Not as something merely thought, or whether the nihilation only demands the "No" as what-is-to-be-said in the letting-be of beings, certainly can never be distinguished from the subjective reflection of thinking, which has already been posited as subjectivity. In such a reflection, the dimension for the formulation of the questions adequate to the matter has not yet been reached. It remains to be asked, granted that thought belongs to ex-sistence, whether all "Yes" and "No" is not already existent in the truth of Being. If so, then "Yes" and "No" are already in themselves bound to Being. As bondsmen, they can never first posit that to which they themselves belong.

Nihilation is essentially in Being itself and by no means in the *Dasein* of man, insofar as this is thought as subjectivity of the *ego cogito*. The Dasein by no means nihilates, insofar as man as subject performs the nihilation in the sense of rejection, but the Da-sein nihilates, insofar as, as essence, wherein man ex-sists, it itself belongs to the essence of Being. Being nihilates—as Being, Therefore, in the absolute idealism of Hegel and Schelling, the Not appears as the negativity of the negative in the essence of Being. This, however, is thought there in the essence of absolute actuality as the unconditioned will, which wills itself and, indeed, as the will of knowledge and love. In this will, Being is still concealed as the will to power. Why, however, the negativity of the absolute subjectivity is the "dialectical" and why, through the dialectic, the nihilation is discovered, but at the same time is concealed in its essence cannot here be discussed.

The nihilating (*das Nichtende*) in Being is the essence of what I call the Nothing. Because it thinks Being, thought thinks the Nothing.

Only Being lends to grace the ascent to graciousness and to anger the push toward disgrace.

Only so far as man, ex-sisting in the truth of Being, belongs to it, can the assigning of all the directions which must become for man law and rule, come from Being itself. The verb "assign" in Greek is νέμειν. The νόμος is not only law, but more originally the assigning concealed in the destiny of Being. Only this is capable of ordering man in Being. Only such ordering is capable of bearing up and binding. Otherwise, all law remains but the handiwork of human reason. More essential than any establishment of rule is the abode in the truth of Being. Only this abode yields the experience of the tenable (*das Haltbare*). The hold (*Halt*) for all behavior (*Verhalten*) is given by the truth of Being. "Hold" in our language means "shelter." Being is the shelter that in view of its own truth shelters man in his ex-sisting essence in such a way that it lodges ex-sistence in language. Thus language is at once the house of Being and the dwelling of human beings. Only because language is the dwelling of the essence of man, can the historical ways of mankind and men not be at home in their language, so that for them it becomes the shell of their machinations.

In what relationship now does the thought of Being stand to theoretical and practical behavior? It is superior to all contemplation, because it cares for the light in which only a seeing as theory can abide and move. Thought attends to the clearing of Being by putting its speaking of Being into language as the dwelling of existence. Thus thought is an action. But an action that is superior at the same time to all practice. Thinking surpasses doing and producing, not through the magnitude of its performance, nor through the consequences of its activity, but through the humbleness of the achievement that it accomplishes without result.

Thinking, as you know, brings into language in its saying only the unspoken word of Being.

The expression used here, "to bring into language," is now to be taken quite literally. Being, clearing itself, comes into language. It is always on its way towards it. As it arrives, it in its turn brings ex-sisting thought to language in its telling, which is thus elevated into the clearing of Being. Only thus, language *is* in its mysterious and yet humanly pervasive way. Insofar as language, thus brought fully into its essence, is historical, Being is preserved in remembering. Ex-sistence inhabits as it thinks the house of Being. In all this, it is as if nothing had happened at all through the utterance of thought.

But we have just seen an example of this insignificant act of thinking. For while we specifically think the expression "to bring to language," which was given to language, only this and nothing else, and while we retain in the observance of speaking what we have thought as something that always has-to-be-thought in the future, we have ourselves brought something essential of Being into language.

The strange thing in this thought of Being is its simplicity. This is precisely what keeps us from it. For we seek for the thought that in the name of "philosophy" has its world-historical prestige in the form of the unusual, which is only accessible to the initiate. At the same time we represent thought to ourselves in the manner of scientific knowledge and research. We measure the act against the impressive and successful achievements of practice. But the act of thinking is neither theoretical nor practical, nor is it the coupling together of both ways or behavior.

Through its simple essence the thought of Being is disguised for us. But when we become friends with the unusualness of the simple, another affliction befalls us at once. The suspicion arises that this thought of Being may lapse into the arbitrary; for it cannot cling to beings. From whence does thought derive its rule? What is the law of its action?

Here the third question of your letter must be heard: *Comment sauver l'élément d'aventure que comporte toute recherche sans faire de la philosophie une simple aventurière?* I shall mention poetry only in passing at this point. It confronts the same question in the same way as thought. But Aristotle's point in his *Poetics,* scarcely considered today, is still of value—that the making of poetry is truer than the exploration of beings.

But thought is *une aventure* not only as seeking and asking into the realm of the unthought. Thought, in its essence as thought of Being, is claimed by it. Thought is related to Being as the arriving (*l'avenant*). Thought is as thought in the advent of Being, is bound to Being as arrival. Being has already destined itself to thought. Being *is* as the destiny of thought. The destiny, however, is in itself historical. Its history has already arrived at language in the speaking of thinkers.

To express over and over again the advent of Being, permanent and in its permanence waiting for man, is the only matter for thought. That is why the essential thinkers always say the same thing. But that does not mean: the like. Yet they say this only to the one who undertakes to follow their thought. While thought, remembering historically, attends to the destiny of Being, it has already bound itself to what is according to destiny. To escape into the like is not dangerous. To venture into discord in order to say the same thing, that is the danger. Ambiguity and mere quibbling threaten.

That the speaking of Being can become the destiny of truth is the first law of thought and not the rules of logic, which can become rules only through the law of Being. To attend to the destiny of the thinking-speaking does not only include our recollecting each time *what* is to be said about Being and *how* it is to be said. It remains equally essential to consider *whether* that which has-to-be-thought may be said, to what extent, at what moment in the history of Being, in what dialogue with it, and with what claim. That threefold thing, mentioned in a previous letter, is determined in the interdependence of its parts by the law of the destiny or historical thought of Being: the rigor of reflection, the carefulness of speaking, the economy of the word.

It is about time to get rid of the habit of overestimating philosophy and thereby asking too much of it. It is necessary in the present plight of the world that there be less philosophy, but more attention to thought; less literature, but more cultivation of the letter.

Future thought is no longer philosophy, because it thinks more originally than metaphysics. But neither can future thought, as Hegel demanded, lay aside the name "love of wisdom" and become wisdom itself in the form of absolute knowledge. Thought is on its descent to the poverty of its provisional essence. Thought gathers language in simple speech. Language is thus the language of Being, as the clouds are the clouds of the sky. Thought by its speaking traces insignificant furrows in language. They seem even more insignificant than the furrows the peasant with deliberate steps traces in the field.

Henri Bergson

AN INTRODUCTION TO METAPHYSICS[1]

If we compare the various ways of defining metaphysics and of conceiving the absolute, we shall find, despite apparent discrepancies, that philosophers agree in making a deep distinction between two ways of knowing a thing. The first implies going all around it, the second entering into it. The first depends on the viewpoint chosen and the symbols employed, while the second is taken from no viewpoint and rests on no symbol. Of the first kind of knowledge we shall say that it stops at the *relative;* of the second that, wherever possible, it attains the *absolute.*

Take, for example, the movement of an object in space. I perceive it differently according to the point of view from which I look at it, whether from that of mobility or of immobility. I express it differently, furthermore as I relate it to the system of axes or reference points, that is to say, according to the symbols by which I translate it. And I call it *relative* for this double reason: in either case, I place myself outside the object itself. When I speak of an absolute movement, it means that I attribute to the mobile an inner being and, as it were, states of soul; it also means that I am in harmony with these states and enter into them by an effort of imagination. Therefore, according to whether the object is mobile or immobile, whether it adopts one movement or another, I shall not have the same feeling about it. And what I feel will depend neither on the point of view I adopt toward the object, since I am in the object itself, nor on the symbols by which I translate it, since I have renounced all translation in order to possess the origi-

[1] From: *The Creative Mind,* Henri Bergson, Ch. 6. The Philosophical Library, New York, 1946.

nal. In short, the movement will not be grasped from without and, as it were, from where I am, but from within, inside it, in what it is in itself. I shall have hold of an absolute.

Or again, take a character whose adventures make up the subject of a novel. The novelist may multiply traits of character, make his hero speak and act as much as he likes: all this has not the same value as the simple and indivisible feeling I should experience if I were to coincide for a single moment with the personage himself. The actions, gestures and words would then appear to flow naturally, as though from their source. They would no longer be accidents making up the idea I had of the character, constantly enriching this idea without ever succeeding in completing it. The character would be given to me all at once in its entirety, and the thousand and one incidents which make it manifest, instead of adding to the idea and enriching it, would, on the contrary, seem to me to fall away from it without in any way exhausting or impoverishing its essence. I get a different point of view regarding the person with every added detail I am given. All the traits which describe it to me, yet which can only enable me to know it by comparisons with persons or things I already know, are signs by which it is more or less symbolically expressed. Symbols and points of view then place me outside it; they give me only what it has in common with others and what does not belong properly to it. But what is properly itself, what constitutes its essence, cannot be perceived from without, being internal by definition, nor be expressed by symbols, being incommensurable with everything else. Description, history and analysis in this case leave me in the relative. Only by coinciding with the person itself would I possess the absolute.

It is in this sense, and in this sense alone, that *absolute* is synonymous with *perfection*. Though all the photographs of a city taken from all possible points of view indefinitely complete one another, they will never equal in value that dimensional object, the city along whose streets one walks. All the translations of a poem in all possible languages may add nuance to nuance and, by a kind of mutual retouching, by correcting one another, may give an increasingly faithful picture of the poem they translate, yet they will never give the inner meaning of the original. A representation taken from a certain point of view, a translation made with certain symbols still remain imperfect in comparison with the object whose picture has been taken or which the symbols seek to express. But the absolute is perfect in that it is perfectly what it is.

It is probably for the same reason that the *absolute* and the *infinite* are often taken as identical. If I wish to explain to someone who does not know Greek the simple impression that a line of Homer leaves upon me, I shall give the translation of the line, then comment on my translation, then I shall develop my commentary, and from explanation to explanation I shall get closer to what I wish to express; but I shall never quite reach it. When you lift your arm you accomplish a movement the simple perception of which you have inwardly; but outwardly, for me, the person who sees it, your arm passes through one point, then through another, and between these two points there will be still other points, so that if I begin to count them, the operation will continue indefinitely. Seen from within, an absolute is then a simple thing; but considered from without, that is to say relative to something else, it becomes, with relation to those signs which express it, the piece of gold for which one can never make up the change. Now what lends itself at the same time to an indivisible apprehension and to an inexhaustible enumeration is, by definition, an infinite.

It follows that an absolute can only be given in an *intuition,* while all the rest has to do with *analysis.* We call intuition here the *sympathy* by which one is transported into the interior of an object in order to coincide with what there is unique and consequently inexpressible in it. Analysis, on the contrary, is the operation which reduces the object to elements already known, that is, common to that object and to others. Analyzing then consists in expressing a thing in terms of what is not it. All analysis is thus a translation, a development into symbols, a representation taken from successive points of view from which are noted a corresponding number of contacts between the new object under consideration and others believed to be already known. In its eternally unsatisfied desire to embrace the object around which it is condemned to turn, analysis multiplies endlessly the points of view in order to complete the ever incomplete representation, varies interminably the symbols with the hope of perfecting the always imperfect translation. It is analysis ad infinitum. But intuition, if it is possible, is a simple act.

This being granted, it would be easy to see that for positive science analysis is its habitual function. It works above all with symbols. Even the most concrete of the sciences of nature, the sciences of life, confine themselves to the visible form of living beings, their organs, their anatomical elements. They compare these forms with one another, reduce the more complex to the more simple, in fact they study the functioning of life in what is, so to speak, its visual symbol. If there exists a means of possessing a reality absolutely, instead of knowing it relatively, of placing oneself within it instead of adopting points of view toward it, of having the intuition of it instead of making the analysis of it, in short, of grasping it over and above all expression, translation or symbolical representation, metaphysics is that very means. *Metaphysics is therefore the science which claims to dispense with symbols.*

There is at least one reality which we all seize from within, by intuition and not by simple analysis. It is our own person in its flowing through time, the self which endures. With no other thing can we sympathize intellectually, or if you like, spiritually. But one thing is sure: we sympathize with ourselves.

When, with the inner regard of my consciousness, I examine my person in its passivity, like some superficial encrustment, first I perceive all the perceptions which come to it from the material world. These perceptions are clear-cut, distinct, juxtaposed or mutually juxtaposable; they seek to group themselves into objects. Next I perceive memories more or less adherent to these perceptions and which serve to interpret them; these memories are, so to speak, as if detached from the depth of my person and drawn to the periphery by perceptions resembling them; they are fastened on me without being absolutely myself. And finally, I become aware of tendencies, motor habits, a crowd of virtual actions more or less solidly bound to those perceptions and these memories. All these elements with their well-defined forms appear to me to be all the more distinct from myself the more they are distinct from one another. Turned outwards from within, together they constitute the surface of a sphere which tends to expand and lose itself in the external world. But if I pull myself in from the periphery toward the centre, if I seek deep down within me what is the most uniformly, the most constantly and durably myself, I find something altogether different.

What I find beneath these clear-cut crystals and this superficial congelation is a continuity of flow comparable to no other flowing I have ever seen. It is a succession of states each one of which announces what follows and contains what precedes. Strictly speaking they do not constitute multiple states until I have already got beyond them, and turn around to observe their trail. While I was experiencing them they were so solidly organized, so profoundly animated with a common life, that I could never have said where any one of them finished or the next one began. In reality, none of them do begin or end; they all dove-tail into one another.

It is, if you like, the unrolling of a spool, for there is no living being who does not feel himself coming little by little to the end of his span; and living consists in growing old. But it is just as much a continual winding, like that of thread into a ball, for our past follows us, becoming larger and larger with the present it picks up on its way; and consciousness means memory.

To tell the truth, it is neither a winding nor an unwinding, for these two images evoke the representation of lines or surfaces whose parts are homogeneous to and superposable on one another. Now, no two moments are identical in a conscious being. Take for example the simplest feeling, suppose it to be constant, absorb the whole personality in it: the consciousness which will accompany this feeling will not be able to remain identical with itself for two consecutive moments, since the following moment always contains, over and above the preceding one, the memory the latter has left it. A consciousness which had two identical moments would be a consciousness without memory. It would therefore die and be re-born continually. How otherwise can unconsciousness be described?

We must therefore evoke a spectrum of a thousand shades, with imperceptible gradations leading from one shade to another. A current of feeling running through the spectrum, becoming tinted with each of these shades in turn, woud suffer gradual changes, each of which would announce the following and sum up within itself the preceding ones. Even then the successive shades of the spectrum will always remain external to each other. They are juxtaposed. They occupy space. On the contrary, what is pure duration excludes all ideas of juxtaposition, reciprocal exteriority and extension.

Instead, let us imagine an infinitely small piece of elastic, contracted, if that were possible, to a mathematical point. Let us draw it out gradually in such a way as to bring out of the point a line which will grow progressively longer. Let us fix our attention not on the line as line, but on the action which traces it. Let us consider that this action, in spite of its duration, is indivisible if one supposes that it goes on without stopping; that, if we intercalate a stop in it, we make two actions of it instead of one and that each of these actions will then be the indivisible of which we speak; that it is not the moving act itself which is never indivisible, but the motionless line it lays down beneath it like a track in space. Let us take our mind off the space subtending the movement and concentrate solely on the movement itself, on the act of tension or extension, in short, on pure mobility. This time we shall have a more exact image of our development in duration.

And yet that image will still be incomplete, and all comparison furthermore will be inadequate, because the unrolling of our duration in certain aspects resembles the unity of a movement which progresses, in others, a multiplicity of states spreading out, and because no metaphor can express one of the two aspects without sacrificing the other. If I evoke a spectrum of a thousand shades, I have before me a complete thing, whereas duration is the state of completing itself. If I think of an elastic being stretched, of a spring being wound or unwound, I forget the wealth of coloring characteristic of duration as something lived and see only the simple movement by which consciousness goes from one shade to the other. The inner life is all that at once, variety of qualities, continuity of progress, unity of direction. It cannot be represented by images.

But still less could it be represented by *concepts,* that is, by abstract ideas, whether general or simple. Doubtless no image will quite answer to the original feeling I have of the flowing of myself. But neither is it necessary for me to try to express it. To him who is not capable of giving himself the intuition of the duration constitutive of his being, nothing will ever give it, neither concepts nor images. In this regard, the philosopher's sole aim should be to start up a certain effort which the utilitarian habits of mind of everyday life tend, in most men, to discourage. Now the image has at least the advantage of keeping us in the concrete. No image will replace the intuition of duration, but many different images, taken from quite different orders of things, will be able, through the convergence of their action, to direct the consciousness to the precise point where there is a certain intuition to seize on. By choosing images as dissimilar as possible, any one of them will be prevented from usurping the place of the intuition it is instructed to call forth, since it would then be driven out immediately by its rivals. By seeing that in spite of their differences in aspect they all demand of our mind the same kind of attention and, as it were, the same degree of tension, one will gradually accustom the consciousness to a particular and definitely determined disposition, precisely the one it will have to adopt in order to appear unveiled to itself. But even then the consciousness must acquiesce in this effort; for we shall have shown it nothing. We shall simply have placed it in the attitude it must take to produce the desired effort and, by itself, to arrive at the intuition. On the other hand the disadvantage of too simple concepts is that they are really symbols which take the place of the object they symbolize and which do not demand any effort on our part. Upon close examination one would see that each of them retains of the object only what is common to that object and to others. Each of them is seen to express, even more than does the image, a *comparison* between the object and those objects resembling it. But as the comparison has brought out a resemblance, and as the resemblance is a property of the object, and as a property seems very much as though it were a *part* of the object possessing it, we are easily persuaded that by juxtaposing concepts to concepts we shall recompose the whole of the object with its parts and obtain from it, so to speak, an intellectual equivalent. We shall in this way think we are forming a faithful representation of duration by lining up the concepts of unity, multiplicity, continuity, finite or infinite divisibility, etc. That is precisely the illusion. And that, also, is the danger. In so far as abstract ideas can render service to analysis, that is, to a scientific study of the object in its relations with all others, to that very extent are they incapable of replacing intuition, that is to say, the metaphysical investigation of the object in what essentially belongs to it. On the one hand, indeed, these concepts placed end to end will never give us anything more than an artificial recomposition of the object of which they can symbolize only certain general and, as it were, impersonal aspects: therefore it is vain to believe that through them one can grasp a reality when all they present is its shadow. But on the other hand, alongside the illusion, there is also a very grave danger. For the concept generalizes at the same time that it abstracts. The concept can symbolize a particular property only by making it common to an infinity of things. Therefore it always more or less distorts this property by the extension it gives to it. A property put back into the metaphysical object to which it belongs coincides with the object, at least moulds itself on it, adopting the same contours. Extracted from the metaphysical object and represented in a concept, it extends itself indefinitely, surpassing the object since it must henceforth contain it along with others. The various concepts we form of the properties of a thing are so many much larger circles drawn round it, not one of which fits it exactly. And yet, in the thing itself, the properties coincided with it and therefore with each other. We have no alternative then but to resort to some artifice in order to re-establish the coincidence. We shall take any one of these concepts and with it try to rejoin the others. But the junction will be brought about in a different way, depending upon the concept we start from. According to whether we start, for example, from unity or from multiplicity, we shall form a different conception of the multiple unity of duration. Everything will depend on the weight we assign to this or that concept, and this weight will always be arbitrary, since the concept, extracted from the object, has no weight, being nothing more than the shadow of a body. Thus a multiplicity of different *systems* will arise, as many systems as there are external viewpoints on the reality one is examining or as there are larger circles in which to enclose it. The simple concepts, therefore, not only have the disadvantage of dividing the concrete unity of the object into so many symbolical expressions; they also divide philosophy into distinct schools, each of which reserves its place, chooses its chips, and begins with the others a game that will never end. Either metaphysics is only this game of ideas, or else, if it is a serious occupation of the mind, it must transcend concepts to arrive at intuition. To be sure, concepts are indispensable to it, for all the other sciences ordinarily work with concepts, and metaphysics cannot get along without the other sciences. But it is strictly itself only when it goes beyond the concept, or at least when it frees itself of the inflexible and ready-made concepts and creates others very different from those we usually handle, I mean flexible, mobile, almost fluid representations, always ready to mould themselves on the fleeting forms of intuition. I shall come back to this important point a little later. It is enough for us to have shown that our duration can be presented to us directly in an intuition, that it can be suggested indirectly to us by images, but that it cannot—if we give to the word *concept* its proper meaning—be enclosed in a conceptual representation.

Let us for an instant try to break it up into parts. We must add that the terms of these parts, instead of being distinguished like those of any multiplicity, encroach upon one another; that we can, no doubt, by an effort of imagination, solidify this duration once it has passed by, divide it into pieces set side by side and count all the pieces; but that this operation is achieved on the fixed memory of the duration, on the immobile track the mobility of the duration leaves behind it, not on the duration itself. Let us therefore admit that, if there is a multiplicity here, this multiplicity resembles no other. Shall we say then that this duration has unity? Undoubtedly a continuity of elements prolonged into one another partakes of unity as much as it does of multiplicity, but this moving, changing, colored and living unity scarcely resembles the abstract unity, empty and motionless, which the concept of pure unity circumscribes. Are we to conclude from this that duration must be defined by both unity and multiplicity at the same time? But curiously enough, no matter how I manipulate the two concepts, apportion them, combine them in various ways, practice on them the most delicate operations of mental chemistry, I shall never obtain anything which resembles the simple intuition I have of duration; instead of which, if I place myself back in duration by an effort of intuition, I perceive immediately how it is unity, multiplicity and many other things besides. These various concepts were therefore just so many external points of view on duration. Neither separated nor re-united have they made us penetrate duration itself.

We penetrate it, nevertheless, and the only way possible is by an intuition. In this sense, an absolute internal knowledge of the duration of the self by the self is possible. But if metaphysics demands and can obtain here an intuition, science has no less need of an analysis. And it is because of a confusion between the roles of analysis and intuition that the dissensions between schools of thought and the conflicts between systems will arise.

Psychology, in fact, like the other sciences, proceeds by analysis. It resolves the self, first given to it in the form of a simple intuition, into sensations, feelings, images, etc. which it studies separately. It therefore substitutes for the self a series of elements which are the psychological facts. But these *elements,* are they *parts?* That is the whole question, and it is because we have evaded it that we have often stated in insoluble terms the problem of the human personality.

It is undeniable that any psychological state, by the sole fact that it belongs to a person, reflects the whole of a personality. There is no feeling, no matter how simple, which does not virtually contain the past and present of the being which experiences it, which can be separated from it and constitute a "state," other than by an effort of abstraction or analysis. But it is no less undeniable that without this effort of abstraction or analysis there would be no possible development of psychological science. Now, of what does the operation consist by which the psychologist detaches a psychological state in order to set it up as a more or less independent entity? He begins by disregarding the person's special coloration, which can be expressed only in common and known terms. He then strives to isolate, in the person thus already simplified, this or that aspect which lends itself to an interesting study. If, for example, it is a question of inclination, he will leave out of account the inexpressible shading which colors it and which brings it about that my inclination is not yours; he will then fix his attention on the movement by which our personality tends towards a certain object; he will isolate this attitude, and it is this special aspect of the person, this point of view on the mobility of the inner life, this "schema" of the concrete inclination which he will set up as an independent fact. In this there is a work analogous to that of an artist who, on a visit to Paris, would, for example, make a sketch of a tower of Notre Dame. The tower is an inseparable part of the edifice, which is no less inseparably a part of the soil, the surroundings, the whole of Paris, etc. He must begin by detaching it; he will focus only on a certain aspect of the whole, and that aspect is this tower of Notre Dame. Now the tower is in reality constituted of stones whose particular grouping is what gives it its form; but the sketcher is not interested in the stones, he only notices the silhouette of the tower. He substitutes for the real and internal organization of the thing an external and schematic reconstitution. So that his design corresponds, in short, to a certain point of view of the object and to the choice of a certain mode of representation. Now the same holds for the operation by which the psychologist extracts a psychological state from the whole person. This isolated psychological state is scarcely more than a sketch, the beginning of an artificial recomposition; it is the whole envisaged under a certain elementary aspect in which one has become especially interested and which one has taken care to note. It is not a part, but an element. It has not been obtained by fragmentation, but by analysis.

Now at the bottom of all the sketches made in Paris the stranger will probably write "Paris" by way of reminder. And as he has really seen Paris, he will be able, by descending from the original intuition of the whole, to place his sketches in it and thus arrange them in relation to one another. But there is no way of performing the opposite operation; even with an infinity of sketches as exact as you like, even with the word "Paris" to indicate that they must bear close connection, it is impossible to travel back to an intuition one has not had, and gain the impression of Paris if one has never seen Paris. The point is that we are not dealing here with parts of the whole, but with *notes* taken on the thing as a whole. To choose a more striking example, where the notation is more completely symbolical, let us suppose someone puts before me, all jumbled together, the letters which go to make up a poem, without my knowing which poem it is. If the letters were *parts* of the poem, I could attempt to reconstruct it with them by trying various possible arrangements, as a child does with the pieces of a jigsaw puzzle. But I shall not for an instant think of attempting it, because the letters are not *component parts,* but *partial expressions,* which is quite another thing. That is why, if I know the poem, I put each one of the letters in its proper place and link them together without difficulty in one continuous chain, while the reverse operation is impossible. Even when I take it into my head to try that reverse operation, even when I place the letters end to end, I begin by imagining a plausible meaning:

I thus give myself an intuition, and it is from the intuition that I try to fall back on the elementary symbols which would re-create its expression. The very notion of reconstructing the thing by carrying out operations on symbolical elements alone implies such an absurdity that it would never occur to anyone if it were realized that he was not dealing with fragments of the thing, but in some sort with fragments of symbol.

That, however, is what philosophers undertake to do when they seek to recompose the person with psychological states, whether they confine themselves to these states or whether they add a thread for the purpose of tying the states to one another. Empiricists and rationalists alike are in this case dupes of the same illusion. Both take the *partial notions* for *real parts,* thus confusing the point of view of analysis and that of intuition, science and metaphysics.

The empiricists are right in saying that psychological analysis does not uncover in the person anything more than psychological states. And such is in fact the function, such is the very definition of analysis. The psychologist has nothing else to do but analyze the person, that is, take note of the states: at most he will place the rubric "Ego" on these states in saying that they are "states of ego," just as the sketcher writes the word "Paris" on each of his sketches. Within the sphere in which the psychologist places himself and where he should place himself, the "Ego" is only a sign by which one recalls the primitive intuition (a very vague one at that) which furnished psychology with its object: it is only a word, and the great mistake is to think that one could, by staying in the same sphere, find a thing behind the word. That has been the mistake of those philosophers who have not been able to resign themselves to being simply psychologists in psychology, Taine and Stuart Mill, for example. Psychologists by the method they apply, they have remained metaphysicians by the object they have in view. Looking for an intuition, through a strange inconsistency they seek to get this intuition from its very negation, analysis. They are seeking the self (le moi), and claim to find it in the psychological states, even though it has been possible to obtain that diversity of psychological states only by transporting oneself outside of the self and taking a series of sketches of the person, a series of notes, of more or less schematic and symbolic representations. And so although they place states side by side with states, multiply their contacts, explore their intervening spaces, the self always escapes them, so that in the end they see nothing more in it than an empty phantom. One might just as well deny that the *Iliad* has a meaning, on the plea that one has looked in vain for this meaning in the spaces between the letters which go to make it up.

Philosophical empiricism, then, is here born of a confusion between the point of view of intuition and that of analysis. It consists in seeking the original in the translation where it naturally cannot be, and in denying the original on the plea that ones does not find it in the translation. It necessarily ends in negations; but looking at it more closely, one perceives that these negations signify simply that analysis is not intuition, and this is self-evident. From the original and furthermore vague intuition which furnishes science with its object, science passes immediately to analysis, which multiplies indefinitely the points of view of that object. It is quickly persuaded that, by putting all the points of view together, it could reconstitute the object. Is it any wonder that, like the child who seeks to make a solid plaything of the shadows silhouetted along the wall, it too sees the object fleeing before it?

But rationalism is the dupe of the same illusion. It starts from the confusion empiricism made, and remains as powerless to reach the personality. Like empiricism, it takes the psychological states to be so many *fragments,* detached from an ego which supposedly holds them together. Like empiricism, it tries to bind these fragments to one another in order to reconstitute the unity of the person. Like empiricism, in short, it sees the unity of the person elude its grasp like a phantom each time it tries to lay hold of it. But while empiricism, tired of the struggle, in the end declares that there is nothing else than the multiplicity of psychological states, rationalism persists in affirming the unity of the person. It is true that, seeking this unity in the psychological states themselves, yet being obliged to put to the account of psychological states all the qualities or determinations it finds by analysis (since analysis, by definition, always ends in states, it is true that it has nothing left for the unity of the person but something purely negative, the absence of all determination. The psychological states having necessarily taken and kept for themselves in this analysis all that gives the slightest appearance of materiality, the "unity of the self" can be nothing more than a form without matter. It will be the absolute indeterminate and the absolute void. To the detached psychological states, to those shadows of the self the totality of which was, for the empiricists, the equivalent of the person, rationalism, to reconstitute the personality, adds something still more unreal, the vacuum in which these shadows move, one might say, the *locus* of the shadows. How could that "form," which is really formless, characterize a living, acting, concrete personality and distinguish Peter from Paul? Is it surprising that the philosophers who have isolated this "form" of the personality then find it powerless to determine a person, and that they are led by degrees to make of their empty Ego a bottomless receptacle which no more belongs to Paul than to Peter, and in which there will be place, as one sees fit, for the whole of humanity, or for God, or for existence in general? I see here between empiricism and rationalism this sole difference, that the first, seeking the unity of the self in the interstices, so to speak, of psychological states, is led to fill up these crannies with other states, and so on indefinitely, so that the self, confined in an interval which is continually contracting, tends towards Zero the further one pushes analysis;

while rationalism, making the self the place where the states are lodged, is in the presence of an empty space that one has no more reason to limit here rather than there, which goes beyond each one of the succeeding limits we undertake to assign to it, which goes on expanding and tends to be lost, not in Zero this time, but in the Infinite.

Considerably less than is supposed, therefore, is the distance between a so-called "empiricism" like Taine's and the most transcendent speculations of certain German Pantheists. The method is analogous in the two cases: it consists in reasoning on the *elements* of the translation as though they were parts of the original. But a true empiricism is the one which purposes to keep as close to the original itself as possible, to probe more deeply into its life, and by a kind of spiritual *auscultation,* to feel its soul palpitate; and this true empiricism is the real metaphysics. The work is one of extreme difficulty, because not one of the ready-made conceptions that thought uses for its daily operations can be of any use here. Nothing is easier than to say that the ego is multiplicity, or that it is unity, or that it is the synthesis of both! Here unity and multiplicity are representations one need not cut according to the object, that one finds already made and that one has only to choose from the pile,—ready-made garments which will suit Peter as well as Paul because they do not show off the figure of either of them. But an empiricism worthy of the name, an empiricism which works only according to measure, sees itself obliged to make an absolutely new effort for each new object it studies. It cuts for the object a concept appropriate to the object alone, a concept one can barely say is still a concept, since it applies only to that one thing. This empiricism does not proceed by combining ideas one already finds in stock, unity and multiplicity, for example; but the representation to which it leads us is, on the contrary, a simple, unique representation; and once it is formed one readily understands why it can be put into the frames unity, multiplicity, etc., all of which are much larger than itself. Finally, philosophy thus defined does not consist in choosing between concepts and taking sides with one school, but in seeking a unique intuition from which one can just as easily come down again to the various concepts, because one has placed oneself above the divisions of the schools.

That the personality has unity is certain; but such an affirmation does not teach me anything about the extraordinary nature of this unity which is the person. That our self is multiple I further agree, but there is in it a multiplicity which, it must be recognized, has nothing in common with any other. What really matters to philosophy is to know *what* unity, *what* multiplicity, what reality superior to the abstract one and the abstract multiple is the multiple unity of the person. And it will know this only if it once again grasps the simple intuition of the self by the self. Then, according to the slope it chooses to come down from the summit, it will arrive at unity or multiplicity or any one of the concepts by which we try to define the moving life of the person.

But no mixing of these concepts among themselves, I repeat, would give anything resembling the person which endures.

If you put a solid cone before me, I see without difficulty how it narrows toward the peak and tends to become a mathematical point, how it also grows larger at its base into an indefinitely increasing circle. But neither the point nor the circle nor the juxtaposition of the two on a plane will give me the slightest idea of a cone. It is the same for the multiplicity and unity of the psychological life; the same for the Zero and the Infinite towards which empiricism and rationalism direct the personality.

These concepts, as we shall show elsewhere, ordinarily go by pairs and represent the two opposites. There is scarcely any concrete reality upon which one cannot take two opposing views at the same time and which is consequently not subsumed under the two antagonistic concepts. Hence a thesis and an antithesis that it would be vain for us to try logically to reconcile, for the simple reason that never, with concepts or points of view, will you make a thing. But from the object, seized by intuition, one passes without difficulty in a good many cases to the two contrary concepts, and because thesis and antithesis are seen to emerge from the reality, one grasps at the same time how this thesis and antithesis are opposed and how they are reconciled.

It is true that in order to do that one must institute a reversal of the habitual work of the intelligence. To think consists ordinarily in going from concepts to things, and not from things to concepts. To know a reality in the ordinary meaning of the word "to know," is to take ready-made concepts, apportion them, and combine them until one obtains a practical equivalent of the real. But it must not be forgotten that the normal work of the intelligence is far from being a disinterested work. We do not, in general, aim at knowing for the sake of knowing, but at knowing in order to take a stand, gain a profit, in fact to satisfy an interest. We try to find out up to what point the object to be known is *this* or *that,* into what known genus it fits, what kind of action, step or attitude it should suggest to us. These various possible actions and attitudes are so many *conceptual directions* of our thought, determined once and for all; nothing remains but for us to follow them; precisely in that consists the application of concepts to things. To try a concept on an object is to ask of the object what we have to do with it, what it can do for us. To label an object with a concept is to tell in precise terms the kind of action or attitude the object is to suggest to us. All knowledge properly so-called is, therefore, turned in a certain direction or taken from a certain point of view. It is true that our interest is often complex. And that is why we sometimes manage to turn our knowledge of the same object in several successive directions and to cause view-points concerning it to vary. This is what, in the ordinary meaning of these terms, a "wide" and "comprehensive" knowledge of the object consists in: the object, then, is led back, not to a unique concept, but to several concepts in which it is deemed to "participate." How it is to participate in all these concepts at once is a question of no practical importance and one that need not be asked. It is, therefore, natural and legitimate that we proceed by juxtaposition and apportioning of concepts in every-day life: no philosophical difficulties will be born of this since, by tacit consent, we shall abstain from philosophizing. But to transfer this *modus operandi* to philosophy, to go—here again—from concepts to the thing, to employ for the disinterested knowledge of an object one now aims at attaining in itself, a manner of knowing inspired by a definite interest and consisting by definition in a view taken of the object externally, is to turn one's back on the goal at which one was aiming; it is to condemn philosophy to an eternal friction between the schools and set up a contradiction in the very heart of the object and the method. Either there is no philosophy possible and all knowledge of things is a practical knowledge turned to the profit to be gained from them, or philosophizing consists in placing oneself within the object itself by an effort of intuition.

But in order to comprehend the nature of this intuition, to determine precisely where intuition ends and analysis begins, we must return to what was said above concerning the flow of duration.

It is to be observed that the concepts of schemas, to which analysis leads, have the essential characteristic of being immobile while under consideration. I have isolated from the whole of the inner life that psychological entity which I call a simple sensation. So long as I study it I suppose it to remain what it is. If I were to find some change in it, I should say that it was not a single sensation, but several successive sensations; and it is to each one of the succeeding sensations that I should then transfer the immutability at first attributed to the whole sensation. In any case I shall, by carrying analysis far enough, be able to arrive at elements I shall hold to be immovable. It is there, and there only, that I shall find the solid base of operations which science needs for its proper development.

There is no mood, however, no matter how simple, which does not change at every instant, since there is no consciousness without memory, no continuation of a state without the addition, to the present feeling, of the memory of past moments. That is what duration consists of. Inner duration is the continuous life of a memory which prolongs the past into the present, whether the present distinctly contains the ever-growing image of the past, or whether, by its continual changing of quality, it attests rather the increasingly heavy burden dragged along behind one the older one grows. Without that survival of the past in the present there would be no duration but only instantaneity.

It is true that if I am criticized for abstracting the psychological state from duration by the mere fact of analyzing it, I shall defend myself against the charge by saying that each of these elementary psychological states to which my analysis leads is a state which still occupies time. "My analysis," I shall say, "easily resolves the inner life into states each of which is homogeneous to itself; only, since the homogeneity spreads out over a definite number of minutes or seconds, the elementary psychological state does not cease to have duration, though it does not change."

But who does not see that the definite number of minutes and seconds I attribute to the elementary psychological state, has no more than the value of an indication meant to remind me that the psychological state, supposedly homogeneous, is in reality a state which changes and endures? The state, taken in itself, is a perpetual becoming. I have extracted from this becoming a certain mean of quality which I have supposed invariable: I have thus constituted a state which is stable, and by that very fact, schematic. Again, I have extracted becoming in general, the becoming that would no more be the becoming of this than of that, and this is what I have called the *time* this state occupies. Were I to examine it closely, I should see that this abstract time is as immobile for me as the state I localize in it, that it could flow only by a continual changing of quality and that, if it is without quality, a simple theatre of change, it thus becomes an immobile milieu. I should see that the hypothesis of this homogeneous time is simply meant to facilitate the comparison between the various concrete durations, to permit us to count simultaneities and to measure one flowing of duration in relation to another. And finally, I should understand that in fastening to the representation of an elementary psychological state the indication of a definite number of minutes and seconds, I am merely recalling that the state has been detached from an ego which endures, and demarcating the place where it would have to be set in motion again in order to bring it, from the simple schema it has become, back to the concrete form it had at first. But I forget all that, having no use for it in analysis.

That is to say, analysis operates on immobility, while intuition is located in mobility or, what amounts to the same thing, in duration. That is the very clear line of demarcation between intuition and analysis. One recognizes the real, the actual, the concrete, by the fact that it is variability itself. One recognizes the element by the fact that it is invariable. And it is invariable by definition, being a schema, a simplified reconstruction, often a mere symbol, in any case, a view taken of the reality that flows.

But the mistake is to believe that with these schemas one could recompose the real. It cannot be too often repeated: from intuition one can pass on to analysis, but not from analysis to intuition.

With variability I shall make as many variations, as many qualities or modifications as I like because they are so many immobile views taken by analysis of the mobility given to intuition. But these modifications placed end to end will not produce anything resembling variability, because they were not parts of it but elements which is quite another thing.

Let us consider, for example, the variability nearest to homogeneity, movement in space. For the whole length of this movement I can imagine possible halts: they are what I call the positions of the mobile or the points through which the mobile passes. But with the positions, were they infinite in number, I shall not make movement. They are not parts of the movement; they are so many views taken of it; they are, we say, only halt suppositions. Never is the mobile really in any of these points; the most one can say is that it passes through them. But the passing, which is a movement, has nothing in common with a halt, which is immobility. A movement could not alight on an immobility for it would then coincide with it, which would be contradictory. The points are not *in* the movement as parts, nor even *under* the movement as places of the mobile. They are simply projected by us beneath the movement like so many places where, if it should stop, would be a mobile which by hypothesis does not stop. They are not, therefore, properly speaking, positions, but suppositions, views or mental viewpoints. How, with these points of view, could one construct a thing?

That, nevertheless, is what we try to do every time we reason about movement and also about time for which movement serves as representation. By an illusion deeply rooted in our mind, and because we cannot keep from considering analysis as equivalent to intuition, we begin by distinguishing, for the whole length of the movement, a certain number of possible halts or points which, willy-nilly, we make parts of the movement. Faced with our inability to recompose movement with these points we intercalate other points, in the belief that we are thus keeping closer to what mobility there is in movement. Then, as the mobility still escapes us, we substitute for a finite and definite number of points a number "infinitely increasing,"—trying thus, but vainly, through the movement of our thought, which indefinitely pursues the addition of points to points, to counterfeit the real and undivided movement of the mobile. Finally, we say that movement is made up of points, but that it comprises in addition the obscure, mysterious passing from one position to the next. As though the obscurity did not come wholly from the fact that we have assumed immobility to be clearer than mobility, the halt to precede movement! As though the mystery was not due to the fact that we claim to go from halts to movement by way of composition which is impossible, whereas we pass easily from movement to slowing down and to immobility! You have sought the meaning of a poem in the form of the letters which make it up, you have thought that in considering an increasing number of letters you would finally embrace the constantly fleeting meaning, and as a last resource, seeing that it was no use to seek a part of the meaning in each letter, you have assumed that between each letter and the one following was lodged the missing fragment of the mysterious meaning! But the letters, once more, are not parts of the thing, they are the elements of the symbol. The positions of the mobile are not parts of the movement: they are points of the space which is thought to subtend the movement. This empty and immobile space, simply *con*ceived, never *per*ceived, has exactly the value of a symbol. By manipulating symbols, how are you going to manufacture reality?

But in this case the symbol meets the demands of our most inveterate habits of thought. We install ourselves ordinarily in immobility, where we find a basis for practice, and with it we claim to recompose mobility. We obtain thus only a clumsy imitation, a counterfeit of real movement, but this imitation is of much greater use to us in life than the intuition of the thing itself would be. Now our mind has an irresistible tendency to consider the idea it most frequently uses to be the clearest. That is why immobility seems clearer to it than mobility, the halt preceding movement.

This explains the difficulties raised by the problem of movement from earliest antiquity. They are due to the fact that we claim to go from space to movement, from the trajectory to the flight, from immobile positions to mobility, and pass from one to the other by way of composition. But it is movement which precedes immobility, and between positions and a displacement there is not the relation of parts to the whole, but that of the diversity of possible viewpoints to the real indivisibility of the object.

Many other problems are born of the same illusion. What the immobile points are to the movement of a mobile, so are the concepts of various qualities to the qualitative change of an object. The different concepts into which a variation is resolved are therefore so many stable visions of the instability of the real. And to think an object, in the usual sense of the word "think," is to take one or several of these immobile views of its mobility. It is, in short, to ask oneself from time to time just where it is, in order to know what to do with it. Nothing is more legitimate than this method of procedure, as long as it is only a question of practical knowledge of reality. Knowledge, in so far as it is directed toward the practical, has only to enumerate the possible principal attitudes of the thing in relation to us, as also our best possible attitudes in respect to it. That is the ordinary role of ready-made concepts, those stations with which we mark out the passage of the becoming. But to desire, with them, to penetrate to the innermost nature of things, is to apply to the mobility of the real a method designed to give of it immobile points of view. It is to forget that if metaphysics is possible, it can only be an effort to re-ascend the slope natural to the work of thought, to place oneself immediately, through a dilation of the mind, in the thing one is studying, in short, to go from reality to concepts and not from concepts to reality. Is it surprising that philosophers so often see the object they claim to embrace recede from them, like children trying to catch smoke by closing their fists? A good many quarrels are thus perpetuated between the schools, in which each one accuses the others of having let the real escape them.

But if metaphysics is to proceed by intuition, if intuition has as its object the mobility of duration, and if duration is psychological in essence, are we not going to shut the philosopher up in exclusive self-contemplation? Will not philosophy consist simply in watching oneself live, "as a dozing shepherd watches the running water?" To speak in this fashion would be to return to the error I have not ceased to emphasize from the very beginning of this study. It would be to fail to recognize the particular nature of duration and at the same time the essentially active character of metaphysical intuition. It would be to fail to see that only the method of which we are speaking allows one to pass beyond idealism as well as realism, to affirm the existence of objects both inferior and superior to us, though nevertheless in a certain sense inferior to us, to make them coexistent without difficulty, and progressively to dispel the obscurities that analysis accumulates around great problems. Without taking up the study of these different points here, let us confine ourselves to showing how the intuition we are discussing is not a single act but an indefinite series of acts, all doubtless of the same genus but each one of a very particular species, and how this variety of acts corresponds to the degrees of being.

If I try to *analyze* duration, that is, to resolve it into ready-made concepts, I am certainly obliged by the very nature of the concept and the analysis, to take two opposing views of *duration in general,* views with which I shall then claim to recompose it. This combination can present neither a diversity of degrees nor a variety of forms: it is or it is not. I shall say, for example, that there is, on the one hand, a *multiplicity* of successive states of consciousness and, on the other hand, a *unity* which binds them together. Duration will be the "synthesis" of this unity and multiplicity, but how this mysterious operation can admit of shades or degrees—I repeat—is not quite clear. In this hypothesis there is, there can only be, a single duration, that in which our consciousness habitually operates. To make certain of what we mean, if we take duration under the simple aspect of a movement being accomplished in space and if we try to reduce to concepts movement considered as representative of time, we shall have on the one hand any desired number of points of the trajectory, and on the other hand an abstract unity joining them, like a thread holding together the beads of a necklace. Between this abstract multiplicity and this abstract unity their combination, once assumed to be possible, is some strange thing in which we shall find no more shadings than the addition of given numbers in arithmetic would allow. But if, instead of claiming to analyze duration (that is, in reality, to make a synthesis of it with concepts), one first installs oneself in it by an effort of intuition, one has the feeling of a certain well-defined *tension,* whose very definiteness seems like a choice between an infinity of possible durations. This being so one perceives any number of durations, all very different from one another, even though each one of them, reduced to concepts, that is to say, considered externally from two opposite points of view, is always brought back to the indefinable combination of the multiple and the one.

Let us express the same idea more precisely. If I consider duration as a multiplicity of moments bound to one another by a unity which runs through them like a thread, these moments, no matter how short the chosen duration, are unlimited in number. I can imagine them as close together as I like; there will always be, between these mathematical points, other mathematical points, and so on, ad infinitum. Considered from the standpoint of multiplicity, duration will therefore disappear in a dust of moments not one of which has duration, each one being instantaneous. If on the other hand I consider the unity binding the moments together, it is evident that it cannot have duration either since, by hypothesis, everything that is changing and really durable in duration has been put to the account of the multiplicity of the moments. This unity, as I examine its essence, will then appear to me as an immobile substratum of the moving reality, like some intemporal essence of time: that is what I shall call eternity,—the eternity of death, since it is nothing else than movement emptied of the mobility which made up its life. Examining closely the opinions of the schools antagonistic to the subject of duration, one would see that they differ simply in attributing to one or the other of these two concepts a capital importance. Certain of them are drawn to the point of view of the multiple; they set up as concrete reality the distinct moments of a time which they have, so to speak, pulverized; they consider as being far more artificial the unity which makes a powder of these grains. The others, on the contrary, set up the unity of duration as concrete reality. They place themselves in the eternal. But as their eternity nevertheless remains abstract, being empty, as it is the eternity of a concept which by hypothesis excludes the opposite concept, one cannot see how this eternity could allow an indefinite multiplicity of moments to co-exist with it. In the first hypothesis one has a world suspended in mid-air which would have to end and begin again by itself each instant. In the second, one has an infinitely abstract eternity of which one can say that it is especially difficult to understand why it does not remain enveloped in itself and how it allows things to co-exist with it. But in either case, and no matter which one of the two metaphysics is chosen, time appears from the psychological point of view as a mixture of two abstractions neither one of which admits of either degrees or shadings. In either system, there is only a single duration which carries everything along with it, a river without bottom and without banks and flowing without assignable force in a direction one cannot define. Even then it is a river and the river flows only because reality obtains this sacrifice from the two doctrines, taking advantage of an inadvertence in their logic. As soon as they regain possession of themselves, they congeal this flowing either into an immense solid sheet, or into an infinity of crystallized needles, but always in a *thing* which necessarily participates in the immobility of a *point of view*.

It is altogether different if one places oneself directly, by an effort of intuition, in the concrete flowing of duration. To be sure, we shall find no logical reason for positing multiple and diverse durations. Strictly speaking, there might exist no other duration than our own, as there might be no other color in the world than orange, for example. But just as a consciousness of color, which would harmonize inwardly with orange instead of perceiving it outwardly, would feel itself caught between red and yellow, would perhaps even have, beneath the latter color, a presentiment of a whole spectrum in which is naturally prolonged the continuity which goes from red to yellow, so the intuition of our duration, far from leaving us suspended in the void as pure analysis would do, puts us in contact with a whole continuity of durations which we should try to follow either downwardly or upwardly: in both cases we can dilate ourselves indefinitely by a more and more vigorous effort, in both cases transcend ourselves. In the first case, we advance toward a duration more and more scattered, whose palpitations, more rapid than ours, dividing our simple sensation, dilute its quality into quantity: at the limit would be the pure homogeneous, the pure *repetition* by which we shall define materiality. In advancing in the other direction, we go toward a duration which stretches, tightens, and becomes more and more intensified: at the limit would be eternity. This time not only conceptual eternity, which is an eternity of death, but an eternity of life. It would be a living and consequently still moving eternity where our own duration would find itself like the vibrations in light, and which would be the concretion of all duration as materiality is its dispersion. Between these two extreme limits moves intuition, and this movement is metaphysics itself.

We cannot stop here to outline the various stages of this movement. But after having presented a general view of the method and made a first application of it, it will perhaps be not without point to formulate in as precise terms as possible the principles upon which it rests. Of the propositions I am about to set forth, most have received in the present work a beginning of proof. I hope to demonstrate them more completely when we attack other problems.

I. *There is an external reality which is given immediately to our mind.* Common sense is right on this point against the idealism and realism of the philosophers.

II. This reality is mobility. There do not exist *things* made, but only things in the making, not *states* that remain fixed, but only states in process of change. Rest is never anything but apparent, or rather, relative. The consciousness we have of our own person in its continual flowing, introduces us to the interior of a reality on whose model we must imagine the others. *All reality is, therefore, tendency, if we agree to call tendency a nascent change of direction.*

III. Our mind, which seeks solid bases of operation, (*point d'aperçu*) has as its principal function, in the ordinary course of life, to imagine *states* and *things.* Now and then it takes quasi-instantaneous views of the undivided mobility of the real. It thus obtains *sensations* and *ideas.* By that means it substitutes for the continuous the discontinuous, for mobility stability, for the tendency in process of change it substitutes fixed points which mark a direction of change and tendency. This substitution is necessary to common sense, to language, to practical life, and even, to a certain extent which we shall try to determine, to positive science. *Our intelligence, when it follows its natural inclination, proceeds by solid perceptions on the one hand, and by stable conceptions on the other.* It starts from the immobile and conceives and expresses movement only in terms of immobility. It places itself in ready-made concepts and tries to catch in them, as in a net, something of the passing reality. It does not do so in order to obtain an internal and metaphysical knowledge of the real. It is simply to make use of them, each concept (like each sensation) being a *practical question* which our activity asks of reality and to which reality will answer, as is proper in things, by a yes or a no. But in so doing it allows what is the very essence of the real to escape.

IV. The difficulties inherent in metaphysics, the antinomies it raises, the contradictions into which it falls, the division into opposing schools and the irreducible oppositions between systems, are due in large part to the fact that we apply to the disinterested knowledge of the real the procedures we use currently with practical utility as the aim. They are due principally to the fact that we place ourselves in the immobile to watch for the moving reality as it passes instead of putting ourselves back into the moving reality to traverse with it the immobile positions. They come from the fact that we claim to reconstitute reality, which is tendency and consequently mobility, with the percepts and concepts which have as their function to immobilize it. One will never create mobility with halts, however numerous: if one begins with mobility, one can draw from it through thought as many halts as one wishes. In other words, *it is understood that fixed concepts can be extracted by our thought from the mobile reality; but there is no means whatever of reconstituting with the fixity of concepts the mobility of the real.* Dogmatism, as the constructor of systems, has nevertheless always attempted this reconstitution.

V. It was bound to fail. This is the impotence, and this alone, pointed out by the skeptical, idealistic and critical doctrines, all those doctrines, in fact, which question our mind's ability to attain the absolute. But it does not follow from the fact that we fail to reconstitute living reality with concepts that are rigid and ready-made, that we could not grasp it in any other manner. *The demonstrations which have been given of the relativity of our knowledge are therefore tainted with an original vice: they assume, like the dogmatism they attack, that all knowledge must necessarily start from rigidly defined concepts in order to grasp by their means the flowing reality.*

VI. But the truth is that our mind is able to follow the reverse procedure. It can be installed in the mobile reality, adopt its ceaselessly changing direction, in short, grasp it intuitively. But to do that, it must do itself violence, reverse the direction of the operation by which it ordinarily thinks, continually upsetting its categories, or rather, recasting them. In so doing it will arrive at fluid concepts, capable of following reality in all its windings and of adopting the very movement of the inner life of things. Only in that way will a progressive philosophy be constituted, freed from the disputes which arise between the schools, capable of resolving problems naturally because it will be rid of the artificial terms chosen in stating them. *To philosophize means to reverse the normal direction of the workings of thought.*

VII. This reversal has never been practised in a methodical manner; but a careful study of the history of human thought would show that to it we owe the greatest accomplishments in the sciences, as well as whatever living quality there is in metaphysics. The most powerful method of investigation known to the mind, infinitesimal calculus, was born of that very reversal. Modern mathematics is precisely an effort to substitute for the *ready-made* what is in process of *becoming,* to follow the growth of magnitudes, to seize movement no longer from outside and in its manifest result, but from within and in its tendency towards change, in short, to adopt the mobile continuity of the pattern of things. It is true that it contents itself with the pattern, being but the science of magnitudes. It is also true that it has been able to realize these marvellous applications only through the invention of certain symbols, and that, if the intuition we have just mentioned is at the origin of the invention, it is the symbol alone which intervenes in the application. But metaphysics, which does not aim at any application, can and for the most part ought to abstain from converting intuition into symbol. Exempt from the obligation of arriving at results useful from a practical standpoint, it will indefinitely enlarge the domain of its investigations. What it will have lost with regard to science, in utility and occurrence, it will regain in scope and range. If mathematics is only the science of magnitudes, if mathematical procedures only apply to quantities, it must not be forgotten that quantity is always nascent quality: it is, one might say, its limiting case. It is therefore natural that metaphysics should adopt the generative idea of our mathematics in order to extend it to all qualities, that is, to reality in general. In so doing, it will in no way proceed to universal mathematics, that chimera of modern philosophy. Quite the contrary, as it makes more headway, it will meet with objects less and less translatable into symbols. But it will at least have begun by making contact with the continuity and mobility of the real exactly where this contact happens to be the most utilisable. It will have looked at itself in a mirror which sends back an image of itself no doubt very reduced, but also very luminous. It will have seen with a superior clarity what mathematical procedures borrow from concrete reality, and it will continue in the direction of concrete reality, not of mathematical methods. Let us say, then, with all due qualifications to what might seem either too modest or too ambitious in this formula, that *one of the objects of metaphysics is to operate differentiations and qualitative integrations.*

VIII. What has caused this object to be lost sight of, and misled science itself about the origin of certain methods it employs, is that intuition once grasped must find a mode of expression and application which conforms to our habits of thought and which furnishes us, in well-defined concepts, the solid basis (*point d'aper çu*) we so greatly need. That is the condition of what we call strictness, precision, and indefinite extension of a general method to particular cases. Now this extension and this work of logical perfectioning can be carried on for centuries, while the generative act of the method lasts only an instant. That is why we so often take the logical apparatus of science for science itself, forgetting the intuition from which the rest was able to ensue.

All that has been said by the philosophers and by scientists themselves about the "relativity" of scientific knowledge is due to forgetting this intuition. *Relative is symbolic knowledge through pre-existing concepts, which goes from the fixed to the moving, but not so intuitive knowledge which establishes itself in the moving reality and adopts the life itself of things.* This intuition attains the absolute.

Science and metaphysics then meet in intuition. A truly intuitive philosophy would realize the union so greatly desired, of metaphysics and science. At the same time that it constituted metaphysics in positive science,—I mean progressive and indefinitely perfectible,—it would lead the positive sciences, properly speaking, to become conscious of their true bearing, which is often very superior to what they suppose. It would put more of science into metaphysics and more of metaphysics into science. Its result would be to re-establish the continuity between the intuitions which the various positive sciences have obtained at intervals in the course of their history, and which they have obtained only by strokes of genius.

IX. That there are not two different ways of knowing things thoroughly, that the various sciences have their roots in metaphysics, is what the philosophers of antiquity, in general, believed. Not in that lay their error. It consisted in adopting the belief so natural to the human mind, that a variation can only express and develop invariabilities. The result of this was that Action was a weakened Contemplation, duration a false, deceptive and mobile image of immobile eternity, the Soul a fall of the Idea. The whole of that philosophy which begins with Plato and ends with Plotinus is the development of a principle that we should formulate thus: "There is more in the immutable than in the moving, and one passes from the stable to the unstable by a simple diminution." Now the contrary is the truth.

Modern science dates from the day when mobility was set up as an independent reality. It dates from the day when Galileo, rolling a ball down an inclined plane, made the firm resolution to study this movement from high to low for itself, in itself, instead of seeking its principle in the concepts of the *high* and the *low,* two immobilities by which Aristotle thought he sufficiently explained its mobility. And that is not an isolated fact in the history of science. I take the view that several of the great discoveries, of those at least which have transformed the positive sciences or created new ones, have been so many soundings made in pure duration. The more living was the reality touched, the more profound had been the sounding.

But the sounding made on the sea floor brings up a fluid mass which the sun very quickly dries into solid and discontinuous grains of sand. And the intuition of duration, when exposed to the rays of the understanding, also quickly congeals into fixed, distinct and immobile concepts. In the living mobility of things, the understanding undertakes to mark out real or virtual stations, it notes arrivals and departures; that is all that is important to the thought of man in its natural exercise. But philosophy should be an effort to go beyond the human state.

On the concepts with which they have blazed the trail of intuition scholars have preferred to fix their glance. The more they considered these residua which have reached the state of symbols, the more they attributed to all science a symbolic character. And the more they believed in the symbolic character of science, the more they effected it and emphasized it. It was not long before they noticed no difference, in positive science, between the data of immediate intuition and the immense work of analysis that the understanding pursues around intuition. Thus they prepared the way for a doctrine which affirms the relativity of all our forms of knowledge.

But metaphysics has also worked toward that.

Why did the masters of modern philosophy, who were renovators of science in addition to being metaphysicians, not have the feeling of the mobile continuity of the real? Why did they not place themselves in what we call concrete duration? They did so more than they thought, and much more than they said they did. If any attempt is made to connect by continuous links the intuitions around which systems are organized, one finds, along with several other convergent or divergent lines, a well-determined direction of thought and feeling. What is this latent thought? How is this feeling to be expressed? To borrow once more the language of the Platonists, and stripping the words of their psychological meaning, by calling Idea a certain *assurance of easy intelligibility* and Soul a certain *preoccupation* with life, we shall say that an invisible current makes modern philosophy tend to lift the Soul above the Idea. In this, as in modern science and even more so, it tends to move in the opposite direction from ancient thought.

But this metaphysics, like this science, has deployed around its inner life a rich tissue of symbols, occasionally forgetting that if science needs symbols in its analytical development, the principal justification for metaphysics is a break with symbols. Here again the understanding has pursued its work of fixing, dividing, reconstructing. True, it has pursued it under a somewhat different form. Without emphasizing a point I propose to develop elsewhere, let me confine myself to saying that the understanding, whose role is to operate on stable elements, can seek stability either in *relations* or in *things*. In so far as it works on relational concepts, it ends in *scientific* symbolism. In so far as it operates on concepts of things, it ends in *metaphysical* symbolism. But in either case the arrangement comes from it. It would willingly believe itself independent. Rather than recognizing at once what it owes to the deep intuition of reality, it is exposed to what is only seen in all its work, to an artificial arrangement of symbols. With the result that if one keeps to the letter of what metaphysicians and scholars say, as well as to the content of what they do, one might believe that the first have dug a deep tunnel under reality, while the others have thrown over it an elegant bridge, but that the moving river of things passes between these two works of art without touching them.

One of the principal tricks of Kantian criticism consisted in taking the metaphysician and the scholar at their word, in pushing metaphysics and science to the utmost possible limit of symbolism, where, in any case, they lead of their own accord the moment the understanding lays claim to an independence full of dangers. Once the relation of science and metaphysics with "intellectual intuition" is misunderstood, Kant has no difficulty in showing that our science is entirely relative and our metaphysics wholly artificial. Because he strained the independence of the understanding in both cases, because he relieved metaphysics and science of the "intellectual intuition" which gave them their inner weight, science with its relations presents to him only an outer wrapping of form, and metaphysics with its things, an outer wrapping of matter. Is it surprising, then, that the first shows him only frameworks within frameworks, and the second phantoms pursuing phantoms?

He struck our science and metaphysics such rude blows that they have not yet entirely recovered from their shock. Our mind would willingly resign itself to see in science a wholly relative knowledge and in metaphysics an empty speculation. It seems to us even today that Kantian criticism applies to all metaphysics and to all science. In reality it applies especially to the philosophy of the ancients, as well as to the form—still ancient—that the moderns have given most often to their thought. It is valid against a metaphysics which claims to give us a *unique* and ready-made system of things, against a science which would be a *unique* system of relations, finally against a science and a metaphysics which present themselves with the architectural simplicity of the Platonic theory of Ideas, or of a Greek temple. If metaphysics claims to be made up of concepts we possessed prior to it, if it consists in an ingenious arrangement of pre-existing ideas which we utilize like the materials of construction for a building, in short, if it is something other than the constant dilation of our mind, the constantly renewed effort to go beyond our actual ideas and perhaps our simple logic as well, it is too evident that it becomes artificial like all works of pure understanding. And if science is wholly the work of analysis or of conceptual representation, if experience is only to serve as the verification of "clear ideas," if instead of starting from multiple and varied intuitions inserted into the movement proper to each reality but not always fitting into one another, it claims to be an immense mathematics, a single system of relations which imprisons the totality of the real in a mesh prepared for it, it becomes a knowledge purely relative to the human understanding.

A close reading of the *Critique of Pure Reason* will show that for Kant this kind of *universal mathematics* is science, and this barely modified Platonism, metaphysics. To tell the truth, the dream of a universal mathematics is itself only a survival of Platonism. Universal mathematics is what the world of Ideas becomes when one assumes that the Idea consists in a relation or a law, and no longer in a thing. Kant took for a reality this dream of certain modern philosophers: much more, he thought that all scientific knowledge was only a detached fragment, or rather a projecting stone of universal mathematics. The main task of the *Critique,* therefore, was to lay the foundations of this mathematics, that is, to determine what the intelligence should be and what should be the object in order that an unbroken mathematics might bind them together. And it follows that if all possible experience is thus assured of admittance into the rigid and already constituted framework of our understanding (unless we assume a pre-established harmony), our understanding itself organizes nature and finds itself reflected in it as in a mirror. Whence the possibility of science, which owes all its effectiveness to its relativity,—and the impossibility of metaphysics, since the latter will find nothing more to do than to parody, on the phantoms of things, the work of conceptual arrangement which science pursues seriously on relations. In short, the *whole* Critique of Pure Reason *leads to establishing the fact that Platonism, illegitimate if Ideas are things, becomes legitimate if ideas are relations, and that the ready-made idea, once thus brought down from heaven to earth, is indeed as Plato wished, the common basis of thought and nature. But the whole* Critique of Pure Reason *rests also upon the postulate that our thought is incapable of anything but Platonizing,* that is, of pouring the whole of possible experience into pre-existing moulds.

That is the whole question. If scientific knowledge is indeed what Kant insisted it was, there is a simple science pre-formed and even preformulated in nature, as Aristotle believed: from this logic immanent in things the great discoveries only illuminate point by point the line traced in advance, as, on a festival night, a string of bulbs flick on, one by one, to give the outline of a monument. And if metaphysical knowledge is indeed what Kant intended, it is reduced to the equal possibility of two opposed attitudes of mind toward all the great problems; its manifestations are so many arbitrary choices, always ephemeral, between two solutions virtually formulated from all eternity: it lives and dies from antinomies. But the truth is that neither does the science of modern times present this unilinear simplicity, nor the metaphysics of the moderns these irreducible oppositions.

Modern science is neither one nor simple. It rests, I readily agree, upon ideas one ultimately finds clear; but these ideas, when they are profound, become progressively clear by the use made of them; they owe then the best part of their luminosity to the light cast back upon them, through reflection, by the facts and applications to which they have led, the clarity of a concept being little else, accordingly, than the assurance, once it is acquired, of manipulating it to advantage. At the start, more than one of them must have appeared obscure, difficult to reconcile with the ideas already accepted by science, and bordering on the absurd. That is to say that science does not proceed by the regular nesting of concepts predestined to fit neatly inside one another. Profound and fruitful ideas are so many points of contact with currents of reality which do not necessarily converge on a same point. It is true that the concepts in which they lodge always manage somehow or other, in rounding off their corners by reciprocal friction, to makeshift among themselves.

On the other hand, the metaphysics of the moderns is not made of solutions so radical that they can lead to irreducible oppositions. This would no doubt be so if there were no means of accepting at the same time and in the same field the thesis and antithesis of the antinomies. But to philosophize consists precisely in placing oneself, by an effort of intuition, inside this concrete reality on which from the outside the *Critique* takes the two opposing views, thesis and antithesis. I shall never imagine how black and white intermingle if I have not seen grey, but I have no difficulty in understanding, once I have seen grey, how one can envisage it from the double viewpoints of black and white. Doctrines which have a basis of intuition escape Kantian criticism to the exact extent that they are intuitive; and these doctrines are the whole of metaphysics, provided one does not take the metaphysics congealed and dead in *theses,* but living in *philosophers*. To be sure, these divergences are striking between the schools, that is to say, in short, between the groups of disciples formed around certain of the great masters. But would one find them as clear-cut between the masters themselves? Something here dominates the diversity of systems, something, I repeat, simple and definite like a sounding of which one feels that it has more or less reached the bottom of a same ocean, even though it brings each time to the surface very different materials. It is on these materials that disciples normally work: in that is the role of analysis. And the master, in so far as he formulates, develops, translates into abstract ideas what he brings, is already, as it were, his own disciple. But the simple act which has set analysis in motion and which hides behind analysis, emanates from a faculty quite different from that of analysing. This is by very definition intuition.

Let it be said, in conclusion, that there is nothing mysterious about this faculty. Whoever has worked successfully at literary composition well knows that when the subject has been studied at great length, all the documents gathered together, all notes taken, something more is necessary to get down to the work of composition itself: an effort, often painful, immediately to place oneself in the very heart of the subject and to seek as deeply as possible an impulsion which, as soon as found, carries one forward of itself. This impulsion, once received, sets the mind off on a road where it finds both the information it had gathered and other details as well; it develops, analyzes itself in terms whose enumeration follows on without limit; the farther one goes the more is disclosed about it; never will one manage to say everything: and yet, if one turns around suddenly to seize the impulsion felt, it slips away; for it was not a thing but an urge to movement, and although indefinitely extensible, it is simplicity itself. Metaphysical intuition seems to be something of the same kind. What in this case matches the notes and documents of the literary composition, is the collection of observations and experiences gathered by positive science and above all by a reflection of the mind on the mind. For one does not obtain from reality an intuition, that is to say, a spiritual harmony with its innermost quality if one has not gained its confidence by a long comradeship with its superficial manifestations. And it is not a question simply of assimilating the outstanding facts; it is necessary to accumulate and fuse such an enormous mass of them that one may be assured, in this fusion, of neutralizing by one another all the preconceived and premature ideas observers may have deposited unknowingly in their observations. Only thus does the raw material of the known facts emerge. Even in the simple and privileged case which served us as an example, even for the direct contact of the self with the self, the definitive effort of distinct intuition would be impossible for anyone who had not gathered and collated a very great number of psychological analyses. The masters of modern philosophy have been men who had assimilated all the material of the science of their time. And the partial eclipse of metaphysics since the last half century has been caused more than anything else by the extraordinary difficulty the philosopher experiences today in making contact with a science already much too scattered. But metaphysical intuition, although one can achieve it only by means of material knowledge, is an entirely different thing from the summary or synthesis of this knowledge. It is as distinct from it as the motor impulsion is distinct from the path traced by the moving object, as the tension of the spring is distinct from the visible movements in the clock. In this sense, metaphysics has nothing in common with a generalization of experience, and yet it could be defined as the whole of experience (*l'expérience intégrale*).

TIME IN THE HISTORY OF WESTERN PHILOSOPHY[1]

Now, if we try to characterize more precisely our natural attitude toward Becoming, this is what we find. Becoming is infinitely varied. That which goes from yellow to green is not like that which goes from green to blue: they are different *qualitative* movements. That which goes from flower to fruit is not like that which goes from larva to nymph and from nymph to perfect insect: they are different *evolutionary* movements. The action of eating or of drinking is not like the action of fighting: they are different *extensive* movements. And these three kinds of movement themselves—qualitative, evolutionary, extensive—differ profoundly. The trick of our perception, like that of our intelligence, like that of our language, consists in extracting from these profoundly different becomings the single representation of becoming *in general,* undefined becoming, a mere abstraction which by itself says nothing and of which, indeed, it is very rarely that we think. To this idea, always the same, and always obscure or unconscious, we then join, in each particular case, one or several clear images that represent *states* and which serve to distinguish all becomings from each other. It

[1] From: *Creative Evolution,* Henri Bergson, pp. 330-385. The Modern Library, Random House, New York, 1944.

is this composition of a specified and definite state with change general and undefined that we substitute for the specific change. An infinite multiplicity of becomings variously colored, so to speak, passes before our eyes: we manage so that we see only differences of color, that is to say, differences of state, beneath which there is supposed to flow, hidden from our view, a becoming always and everywhere the same, invariably colorless.

Suppose we wish to portray on a screen a living picture, such as the marching past of a regiment. There is one way in which it might first occur to us to do it. That would be to cut out jointed figures representing the soldiers, to give to each of them the movement of marching, a movement varying from individual to individual although common to the human species, and to throw the whole on the screen. We should need to spend on this little game an enormous amount of work, and even then we should obtain but a very poor result: how could it, at its best, reproduce the suppleness and variety of life? Now, there is another way of proceeding, more easy and at the same time more effective. It is to take a series of snapshots of the passing regiment and to throw these instantaneous views on the screen, so that they replace each other very rapidly. This is what the cinematograph does. With photographs, each of which represents the regiment in a fixed attitude, it reconstitutes the mobility of the regiment marching. It is true that if we had to do with photographs alone, however much we might look at them, we should never see them animated: with immobility set beside immobility, even endlessly, we could never make movement. In order that the pictures may be animated, there must be movement somewhere. The movement does indeed exist here; it is in the apparatus. It is because the film of the cinematograph unrolls, bringing in turn the different photographs of the scene to continue each other, that each actor of the scene recovers his mobility; he strings all his successive attitudes on the invisible movement of the film. The process then consists in extracting from all the movements peculiar to all the figures an impersonal movement abstract and simple, *movement in general,* so to speak: we put this into the apparatus, and we reconstitute the individuality of each particular movement by combining this nameless movement with the personal attitudes. Such is the contrivance of the cinematograph. And such is also that of our knowledge. Instead of attaching ourselves to the inner becoming of things, we place ourselves outside them in order to recompose their becoming artificially. We take snapshots, as it were, of the passing reality, and, as these are characteristic of the reality, we have only to string them on a becoming, abstract, uniform and invisible, situated at the back of the apparatus of knowledge, in order to imitate what there is that is characteristic in this becoming itself. Perception, intellection, language so proceed in general. Whether we would think becoming, or express it, or even perceive it, we hardly do anything else than set going a kind of cinematograph inside us. We may therefore sum up what we have been saying in the conclusion that the *mechanism of our ordinary knowledge is of a cinematographical kind.*

Of the altogether practical character of this operation there is no possible doubt. Each of our acts aims at a certain insertion of our will into the reality. There is, between our body and other bodies, an arrangement like that of the pieces of glass that compose a kaleidoscopic picture. Our activity goes from an arrangement to a rearrangement, each time no doubt giving the kaleidoscope a new shake, but not interesting itself in the shake, and seeing only the new picture. Our knowledge of the operation of nature must be exactly symmetrical, therefore, with the interest we take in our own operation. In this sense we may say, if we are not abusing this kind of illustration, that *the cinematographical character of our knowledge of things is due to the kaleidoscopic character of our adaptation to them*.

The cinematographical method is therefore the only practical method, since it consists in making the general character of knowledge form itself on that of action, while expecting that the detail of each act should depend in its turn on that of knowledge. In order that action may always be enlightened, intelligence must always be present in it; but intelligence, in order thus to accompany the progress of activity and ensure its direction, must begin by adopting its rhythm. Action is discontinuous, like every pulsation of life; discontinuous, therefore, is knowledge. The mechanism of the faculty of knowing has been constructed on this plan. Essentially practical, can it be of use, such as it is, for speculation? Let us try with it to follow reality in its windings, and see what will happen.

I take of the continuity of a particular becoming a series of views, which I connect together by "becoming in general." But of course I cannot stop there. What is not determinable is not representable: of "becoming in general" I have only a verbal knowledge. As the letter *x* designates a certain unknown quantity, whatever it may be, so my "becoming in general," always the same, symbolizes here a certain transition of which I have taken some snapshots; of the transition itself it teaches me nothing. Let me then concentrate myself wholly on the transition, and, between any two snapshots, endeavor to realize what is going on. As I apply the same method, I obtain the same result; a third view merely slips in between the two others. I may begin again as often as I will, I may set views alongside of views for ever, I shall obtain nothing else. The application of the cinematographical method therefore leads to a perpetual recommencement, during which the mind, never able to satisfy itself and never finding where to rest, persuades itself, no doubt, that it imitates by its instability the very movement of the real. But though, by straining itself to the point of giddiness, it may end by giving itself the illusion of mobility, its operation has not advanced it a step, since it remains as far as ever from its goal. In order to advance with the moving reality, you must replace yourself within it. Install yourself within change, and you will grasp at once both change itself and the successive stages in which *it might* at any instant be immobilized. But with these successive states, perceived from without as real and no longer as potential immobilities, you will never reconstitute movement. Call them *qualities, forms, positions,* or *intentions,* as the case may be, multiply the number of them as you will, let the interval between two consecutive states be infinitely small: before the intervening movement you will always experience the disappointment of the child who tries by clapping his hands together to crush the smoke. The movement slips through the interval, because every attempt to reconstitute change out of states implies the absurd proposition, that movement is made of immobilities.

Philosophy perceived this as soon as it opened its eyes. The arguments of Zeno of Elea, although formulated with a very different intention, have no other meaning.

Take the flying arrow. At every moment, says Zeno, it is motionless, for it cannot have time to move, that is, to occupy at least two successive positions, unless at least two moments are allowed it. At a given moment, therefore, it is at rest at a given point. Motionless in each point of its course, it is motionless during all the time that it is moving.

Yes, if we suppose that the arrow can ever *be* in a point of its course. Yes again, if the arrow, which is moving, ever coincides with a position, which is motionless. But the arrow never *is* in any point of its course. The most we can say is that it might be there, in this sense, that it passes there and might stop there. It is true that if it did stop there, it would be at rest there, and at this point it is no longer movement that we should have to do with. The truth is that if the arrow leaves the point A to fall down at the point B, its movement AB is as simple, as indecomposable, in so far as it is movement, as the tension of the bow that shoots it. As the shrapnel, bursting before it falls to the ground, covers the explosive zone with an indivisible danger, so the arrow which goes from A to B displays with a single stroke, although over a certain extent of duration, its indivisible mobility. Suppose an elastic stretched from A to B, could you divide its extension? The course of the arrow is this very extension; it is equally simple and equally undivided. It is a single and unique bound. You fix a point C in the interval passed, and say that at a certain moment the arrow was in C. If it had been there, it would have been stopped there, and you would no longer have had a flight from A to B, but *two* flights, one from A to C and the other from C to B, with an interval of rest. A single movement is entirely, by the hypothesis, a movement between two stops; if there are intermediate stops, it is no longer a single movement. At bottom, the illusion arises from this, that the movement, *once effected,* has laid along its course a motionless trajectory on which we can count as many immobilities as we will. From this we conclude that the movement, *whilst being effected,* lays at each instant beneath it a position with which it coincides. We do not see that the trajectory is created in one stroke, although a certain time is required for it; and that though we can divide at will the trajectory once created, we cannot divide its creation, which is an act in progress and not a thing. To suppose that the moving body *is* at a point of its course is to cut the course in two by a snip of the scissors at this point, and to substitute two trajectories for the single trajectory which we were first considering. It is to distinguish two successive acts where, by the hypothesis, there is only one. In short, it is to attribute to the course itself of the arrow everything that can be said of the interval that the arrow has traversed, that is to say, to admit *a priori* the absurdity that movement coincides with immobility.

We shall not dwell here on the three other arguments of Zeno. We have examined them elsewhere. It is enough to point out that they all consist in applying the movement to the line traversed, and supposing that what is true of the line is true of the movement. The line, for example, may be divided into as many parts as we wish, of any length that we wish, and it is always the same line. From this we conclude that we have the right to suppose the movement articulated as we wish, and that it is always the same movement. We thus obtain a series of absurdities that all express the same fundamental absurdity. But the possibility of applying the movement *to* the line traversed exists only for an observer who, keeping outside the movement and seeing at every instant the possibility of a stop, tries to reconstruct the real movement with these possible immobilities. The absurdity vanishes as soon as we adopt by thought the continuity of the real movement, a continuity of which every one of us is conscious whenever he lifts an arm or advances a step. We feel then indeed that the line passed over between two stops is described with a single indivisible stroke, and that we seek in vain to practice on the movement, which traces the line, divisions corresponding, each to each, with the divisions arbitrarily chosen of the line once it has been traced. The line traversed by the moving body lends itself to any kind of division, because it has no internal organization. But all movement is articulated inwardly. It is either an indivisible bound (which may occupy, nevertheless, a very long duration) or a series of indivisible bounds. Take the articulations of this movement into account, or give up speculating on its nature.

When Achilles pursues the tortoise, each of his steps must be treated as indivisible, and so must each step of the tortoise. After a certain number of steps, Achilles will have overtaken the tortoise. There is nothing more simple. If you insist on dividing the two motions further, distinguish both on the one side and on the other, in the course of Achilles and in that of the tortoise, the *submultiples* of the steps of each of them; but respect the natural articulations of the two courses. As long as you respect them, no difficulty will arise, because you will follow the indications of experience. But Zeno's device is to reconstruct the movement of Achilles according to a law arbitrarily chosen. Achilles with a first step is supposed to arrive at the point where the tortoise was, with a second step at the point which it has moved to while he was making the first, and so on. In this case, Achilles would always have a new step to take. But obviously, to overtake the tortoise, he goes about it in quite another way. The movement considered by Zeno would only be the equivalent of the movement of Achilles if we could treat the movement as we treat the interval passed through, decomposable and recomposable at will. Once you subscribe to this first absurdity, all the others follow.[2]

Nothing would be easier, now, than to extend Zeno's argument to qualitative becoming and to evolutionary becoming. We should find the same contradictions in these. That the child can become a youth, ripen to maturity and decline to old age, we understand when we consider that vital evolution is here the reality itself. Infancy, adolescence, maturity, old age, are mere views of the mind, *possible stops* imagined by us, from without, along the continuity of a progress. On the contrary, let childhood, adolescence, maturity and old age be given as integral parts of the evolution, they become *real stops,* and we can no longer conceive how evolution is possible, for rests placed beside rests will never be equivalent to a movement. How, with what is made, can we reconstitute what is being made? How, for instance, from childhood once posited as a *thing,* shall we pass to adolescence, when, by the hypothesis, childhood only is given? If we look at it closely, we shall see that our habitual manner of speaking, which is fashioned after our habitual manner of thinking, leads us to actual logical deadlocks—deadlocks to which we allow ourselves to be led without anxiety, because we feel confusedly that we can always get out of them if we like: all that we have to do, in fact, is to give up the cinematographical habits of our intellect. When we say "The child becomes a man," let us take care not to fathom too deeply the literal meaning of the expression, or we shall find that, when we posit the subject "child," the attribute "man" does not yet apply to it, and that, when we express the

[2] That is, we do not consider the sophism of Zeno refuted by the fact that the geometrical progression $a\ (1 + \frac{1}{n} + \frac{1}{n^2} + \frac{1}{n^3} + \ldots$, etc.)—in which a designates the initial distance between Achilles and the tortoise, and n the relation of their respective velocities—has a finite sum if n is greater than 1. On this point we may refer to the arguments of F. Evellin, which we regard as conclusive (see Evellin, *Infini et quantité,* Paris, 1880, pp. 63-97; cf. *Revue philosophique,* vol. xi., 1881, pp. 564-568). The truth is that mathematics, as we have tried to show in a former work, deals and can deal only with lengths. It has therefore had to seek devices, first, to transfer to the movement, which is not a length, the divisibility of the line passed over, and then to reconcile with experience the idea (contrary to experience and full of absurdities) of a movement that is a length, that is, of a movement *placed upon* its trajectory and arbitrarily decomposable like it.

attribute "man," it applies no more to the subject "child." The reality, which is the *transition* from childhood to manhood, has slipped between our fingers. We have only the imaginary stops "child" and "man," and we are very near to saying that one of these stops *is* the other, just as the arrow of Zeno *is*, according to that philosopher, at all the points of the course. The truth is that if language here were molded on reality, we should not say "The child becomes the man," but "There is becomng from the child to the man." In the first proposition, "becomes" is a verb of indeterminate meaning, intended to mask the absurdity into which we fall when we attribute the state "man" to the subject "child." It behaves in much the same way as the movement, always the same, of the cinematographical film, a movement hidden in the apparatus and whose function it is to superpose the successive pictures on one another in order to imitate the movement of the real object. In the second proposition, "becoming" is a subject. It comes to the front. It is the reality itself; childhood and manhood are then only possible stops, mere views of the mind; we now have to do with the objective movement itself, and no longer with its cinematographical imitation. But the first manner of expression is alone conformable to our habits of language. We must, in order to adopt the second, escape from the cinematographical mechanism of thought.

We must make complete abstraction of this mechanism, if we wish to get rid at one stroke of the theoretical absurdities that the question of movement raises. All is obscure, all is contradictory when we try, with states, to build up a transition. The obscurity is cleared up, the contradiction vanishes, as soon as we place ourselves along the transition, in order to distinguish states in it by making cross cuts therein in thought. The reason is that there is *more* in the transition than the series of states, that is to say, the possible cuts—*more* in the movement than the series of positions, that is to say, the possible stops. Only, the first way of looking at things is conformable to the processes of the human mind; the second requires, on the contrary, that we reverse the bent of our intellectual habits. No wonder, then, if philosophy at first recoiled before such an effort. The Greeks trusted to nature, trusted the natural propensity of the mind, trusted language above all, in so far as it naturally externalizes thought. Rather than lay blame on the attitude of thought and language toward the course of things, they preferred to pronounce the course of things itself to be wrong.

Such, indeed, was the sentence passed by the philosophers of the Eleatic school. And they passed it without any reservation whatever. As becoming shocks the habits of thought and fits ill into the molds of language, they declared it unreal. In spatial movement and in change in general they saw only pure illusion. This conclusion could be softened down without changing the premises, by saying that the reality changes, but that it *ought not* to change. Experience confronts us with becoming: that is *sensible* reality. But the *intelligible* reality, that which *ought* to be, is more real still, and that reality does not change. Beneath the qualitative becoming, beneath the evolutionary becoming, beneath the extensive becoming, the mind must seek that which defies change, the definable quality, the form or essence, the end. Such was the fundamental principle of the philosophy which developed throughout the classic age, the philosophy of Forms, or, to use a term more akin to the Greek, the philosophy of Ideas.

The word εἶδος, which we translate here by "Idea," has, in fact, this threefold meaning. It denotes (1) the quality, (2) the form or essence, (3) the end or *design* (in the sense of *intention*) of the act being performed, that is to say, at bottom, the *design* (in the sense of *drawing*) of the act supposed accomplished. *These three aspects are those of the adjective, substantive and verb, and correspond to the three essential categories of language.* After the explanations we have given above, we might, and perhaps we ought to, translate εἶδος by "view" or rather by "moment." For εἶδος is the stable view taken of the instability of things: the *quality,* which is a moment of becoming; the *form,* which is a moment of evolution; the *essence,* which is the mean form above and below which the other forms are arranged as alterations of the mean; finally, the intention or *mental design* which presides over the action being accomplished, and which is nothing else, we said, than the *material design,* traced out and contemplated beforehand, of the action accomplished. To reduce things to Ideas is therefore to resolve becoming into its principal moments, each of these being, moreover, by the hypothesis, screened from the laws of time and, as it were, plucked out of eternity. That is to say that we end in the philosophy of Ideas when we apply the cinematographical mechanism of the intellect to the analysis of the real.

But, when we put immutable Ideas at the base of the moving reality, a whole physics, a whole cosmology, a whole theology follows necessarily. We must insist on the point. Not that we mean to summarize in a few pages a philosophy so complex and so comprehensive as that of the Greeks. But, since we have described the cinematographical mechanism of the intellect, it is important that we should show to what idea of reality the play of this mechanism leads. It is the very idea, we believe, that we find in the ancient philosophy. The main lines of the doctrine that was developed from Plato to Plotinus, passing through Aristotle (and even, in a certain measure, through the Stoics), have nothing accidental, nothing contingent, nothing that must be regarded as a philosopher's fancy. They indicate the vision that a systematic intellect obtains of the universal becoming when regarding it by means of snapshots, taken at intervals, of its flowing. So that, even today, we shall philosophize in the manner of the Greeks, we shall rediscover, without needing to know them, such and such of their general conclusions, in the exact proportion that we trust in the cinematographical instinct of our thought.

We said there is *more* in a movement than in the successive positions attributed to the moving object, *more* in a becoming than in the forms passed through in turn, *more* in the evolution of form than the forms assumed one after another. Philosophy can therefore derive terms of the second kind from those of the first, but not the first from the second: from the first terms speculation must take its start. But the intellect reverses the order of the two groups; and, on this point, ancient philosophy proceeds as the intellect does. It installs itself in the immutable, it posits only Ideas. Yet becoming exists: it is a fact. How, then, having posited immutability alone, shall we make change come forth from it? Not by the addition of anything, for, by the hypothesis, there exists nothing positive outside Ideas. It must therefore be by a diminution. So at the base of ancient philosophy lies necessarily this postulate: that there is more in the motionless than in the moving, and that we pass from immutability to becoming by way of diminution or attenuation.

It is therefore something negative, or zero at most, that must be added to Ideas to obtain change. In that consists the Platonic "non-being," the Aristotelian "matter"—a metaphysical zero which, joined to the Idea, like the arithmetical zero to unity, multiplies it in space and time. By it the motionless and simple Idea is refracted into a movement spread out indefinitely. In right, there ought to be nothing but immutable Ideas, immutably fitted to each other. In fact, matter comes to add to them its void, and thereby lets loose the universal becoming. It is an elusive nothing, that creeps between the Ideas and creates endless agitation, eternal disquiet, like a suspicion insinuated between two loving hearts. Degrade the immutable Ideas: you obtain, by that alone, the perpetual flux of things. The Ideas or Forms are the whole of intelligible reality, that is to say, of truth, in that they represent, all together, the theoretical equilibrium of Being. As to sensible reality, it is a perpetual oscillation from one side to the other of this point of equilibrium.

Hence, throughout the whole philosophy of Ideas there is a certain conception of duration, as also of the relation of time to eternity. He who installs himself in becoming sees in duration the very life of things, the fundamental reality. The Forms, which the mind isolates and stores up in concepts, are then only snapshots of the changing reality. They are moments gathered along the course of time; and, just because we have cut the thread that binds them to time, they no longer endure. They tend to withdraw into their own definition, that is to say, into the artificial reconstruction and symbolical expression which is their intellectual equivalent. They enter into eternity, if you will; but what is eternal in them is just what is unreal. On the contrary, if we treat becoming by the cinematographical method, the Forms are no longer snapshots taken of the change, they are its constitutive elements, they represent all that is Positive in Becoming. Eternity no longer hovers over time, as an abstraction: it underlies time, as a reality. Such is exactly, on this point, the attitude of the philosophy of Forms or Ideas. It establishes between eternity and time the same relation as between a piece of gold and the small change—change so small that payment goes on forever without the debt being paid off. The debt could be paid at once with the piece of gold. It is this that Plato expresses in his magnificent language when he says that God, unable to make the world eternal, gave it Time, "a moving image of eternity." [3]

Hence also arises a certain conception of extension, which is at the base of the philosophy of Ideas, although it has not been so explicitly brought out. Let us imagine a mind placed alongside becoming, and adopting its movement. Each successive state, each quality, each form, in short, will be seen by it as a mere cut made by thought in the universal becoming. It will be found that form is essentially extended, inseparable as it is from the extensity of the becoming which has materialized it in the course of its flow. Every form thus occupies space, as it occupies time. But the philosophy of Ideas follows the inverse direction. It starts from the Form; it sees in the Form the very essence of reality. It does not take Form as a snapshot of becoming; it posits Forms in the eternal; of this motionless eternity, then, duration and becoming are supposed to be only the degradation. Form thus posited, independent of time, is then no longer what is found in a perception; it is a *concept*. And, as a reality of the conceptual order occupies no more of extension than it does of duration, the Forms must be stationed outside space as well as above time. Space and time have therefore necessarily, in ancient philosophy, the same origin and the same value. The same diminution of being is expressed both by extension in space and detention in time. Both of these are but the distance between what is and what ought to be. From the standpoint of ancient philosophy, space and time can be nothing but the field that an incomplete reality, or rather a reality that has gone astray from itself, needs in order to run in quest of itself. Only it must be admitted that the field is created as the hunting progresses, and that the hunting in some way deposits the field beneath it. Move an imaginary pendulum, a mere mathematical point, from its position of equilibrium: a perpetual oscillation is started, along which points are placed next to points, and moments succeed moments. The space and time which thus arise have no more "positivity" than the movement itself. They represent the remoteness of the position artificially given to the pendulum from its normal position, *what it lacks* in order to regain its natural stability. Bring it back to its normal posi-

[3] Plato, *Timaeus,* 37 D.

tion: space, time and motion shrink to a mathematical point. Just so, human reasonings are drawn out into an endless chain, but are at once swallowed up in the truth seized by intuition, for their extension in space and time is only the distance, so to speak, between thought and truth.[4] So of extension and duration in relation to pure Forms or Ideas. The sensible forms are before us, ever about to recover their ideality, ever prevented by the matter they bear in them, that is to say, by their inner void, by the interval between what they are and what they ought to be. They are forever on the point of recovering themselves, forever occupied in losing themselves. An inflexible law condemns them, like the rock of Sisyphus, to fall back when they are almost touching the summit, and this law, which has projected them into space and time, is nothing other than the very constancy of their original insufficiency. The alternations of generation and decay, the evolutions ever beginning over and over again, the infinite repetition of the cycles of celestial spheres—this all represents merely a certain fundamental deficit, in which materiality consists. Fill up this deficit: at once you suppress space and time, that is to say, the endlessly renewed oscillations around a stable equilibrium always aimed at, never reached. Things re-enter into each other. What was extended in space is contracted into pure Form. And past, present and future shrink into a single moment, which is eternity.

This amounts to saying that physics is but logic spoiled. In this proposition the whole philosophy of Ideas is summarized. And in it also is the hidden principle of the philosophy that is innate in our understanding. If immutability is more than becoming, form is more than change, and it is by a veritable fall that the logical system of Ideas, rationally subordinated and co-ordinated among themselves, is scattered into a physical series of objects and events accidentally placed one after another. The generative idea of a poem is developed in thousands of imaginations which are materialized in phrases that spread themselves out in words. And the more we descend from the motionless idea, wound on itself, to the words that unwind it, the more room is left for contingency and choice. Other metaphors, expressed by other words, might have arisen; an image is called up by an image, a word by a word. All these words run now one after another, seeking in vain, by themselves, to give back the simplicity of the generative idea. Our ear only hears the words: it therefore perceives only accidents. But our mind, by successive bounds, leaps from the words to the images, from the images to the original idea, and so gets back, from the perception of words—accidents called up by accidents—to the conception of the Idea that posits its own being. So the philosopher proceeds, confronted with the universe. Experience makes to pass be-

[4] We have tried to bring out what is true and what is false in this idea, so far as spatiality is concerned (see Chapter III [of *Creative Evolution*]). It seems to us radically false as regards *duration*.

fore his eyes phenomena which run, they also, one behind another in an accidental order determined by circumstances of time and place. This physical order—a degeneration of the logical order—is nothing else but the fall of the logical into space and time. But the philosopher, ascending again from the percept to the concept, sees condensed into the logical all the positive reality that the physical possesses. His intellect, doing away with the materiality that lessens being, grasps being itself in the immutable system of Ideas. Thus Science is obtained, which appears to us, complete and ready-made, as soon as we put back our intellect into its true place, correcting the deviation that separated it from the intelligible. Science is not, then, a human construction. It is prior to our intellect, independent of it, veritably the generator of Things.

And indeed, if we hold the Forms to be simply snapshots taken by the mind of the continuity of becoming, they must be relative to the mind that thinks them, they can have no independent existence. At most we might say that each of these Ideas is an *ideal*. But it is in the opposite hypothesis that we are placing ourselves. Ideas must then exist by themselves. Ancient philosophy could not escape this conclusion. Plato formulated it, and in vain did Aristotle strive to avoid it. Since movement arises from the degradation of the immutable, there could be no movement, consequently no sensible world, if there were not, somewhere, immutability realized Ideas. So, having begun by refusing to Ideas an independent existence, and finding himself nevertheless unable to deprive them of it, Aristotle pressed them into each other, rolled them up into a ball, and set above the physical world a Form that was thus found to be the Form of Forms, the Idea of Ideas, or, to use his own words, the Thought of Thought. Such is the God of Aristotle—necessarily immutable and apart from what is happening in the world, since he is only the synthesis of all concepts in a single concept. It is true that no one of the manifold concepts could exist apart, such as it is in the divine unity: in vain should we look for the ideas of Plato within the God of Aristotle. But if only we imagine the God of Aristotle in a sort of refraction of himself, or simply inclining toward the world, at once the Platonic Ideas are seen to pour themselves out of him, as if they were involved in the unity of his essence: so rays stream out from the sun, which nevertheless did not contain them. It is probably this *possibility of an outpouring* of Platonic Ideas from the Aristotelian God that is meant, in the philosophy of Aristotle, by the active intellect, the νοῦς that has been called ποιητικός—that is, by what is essential and yet unconscious in human intelligence. The νοῦς ποιητικός is Science entire, posited all at once, which the conscious, discursive intellect is condemned to reconstruct with difficulty, bit by bit. There is then within us, or rather behind us, a possible vision of God, as the Alexandrians said, a vision always virtual, never actually realized by the conscious intellect. In this intuition we should see God expand in

Ideas. This it is that "does everything," [5] playing in relation to the discursive intellect, which moves in time, the same rôle as the motionless Mover himself plays in relation to the movement of the heavens and the course of things.

There is, then, immanent in the philosophy of Ideas, a particular conception of causality, which it is important to bring into full light, because it is that which each of us will reach when, in order to ascend to the origin of things, he follows to the end the natural movement of the intellect. True, the ancient philosophers never formulated it explicitly. They confined themselves to drawing the consequences of it, and, in general, they have marked but points of view of it rather than presented it itself. Sometimes, indeed, they speak of an *attraction,* sometimes of an *impulsion* exercised by the prime mover on the whole of the world. Both views are found in Aristotle, who shows us in the movement of the universe an aspiration of things toward the divine perfection, and consequently an ascent toward God, while he describes it elsewhere as the effect of a contact of God with the first sphere and as descending, consequently, from God to things. The Alexandrians, we think, do no more than follow this double indication when they speak of *procession* and *conversion.* Everything is derived from the first principle, and everything aspires to return to it. But these two conceptions of the divine causality can only be identified together if we bring them, both the one and the other, back to a third, which we hold to be fundamental, and which alone will enable us to understand, not only why, in what sense, things move in space and time, but also why there is space and time, why there is movement, why there are things.

This conception, which more and more shows through the reasonings of the Greek philosophers as we go from Plato to Plotinus, we may formulate thus: *The affirmation of a reality implies the simultaneous affirmation of all the degrees of reality intermediate between it and nothing.* The principle is evident in the case of number: we cannot affirm the number 10 without thereby affirming the existence of the numbers 9, 8, 7, . . . , etc.—in short, of the whole interval between 10 and zero. But here our mind passes naturally from the sphere of quantity to that of quality. It seems to us that, a certain perfection being given, the whole continuity of degradations is given also between this perfection, on the one hand, and the nought, on the other hand, that we think we conceive. Let us then posit the God of Aristotle, thought of thought—that is, thought *making a circle,* transforming itself from subject to object and from object to subject by an instantaneous, or rather an eternal, circular process: as, on the other hand, the nought appears to posit itself, and as, the two extremities

[5] Aristotle, *De anima,* 430 a 14 *καὶ ἔστιν ὁ μὲν τοιοῦτος νοῦς τῷ πάντα γίνεσθαι, ὁ δὲ ῷτ πάντα ποιεῖν, ὡς ἕξις τὶς, οἷον τὸ φῶς. τρόπον γάρ τίνα καὶ τὸ φῶς ποιεῖ τὰ δυνάμει ὄντα χρώματα ἐνεργείᾳ χρώματα.*

being given, the interval between them is equally given, it follows that all the descending degrees of being, from the divine perfection down to the "absolute nothing," are realized automatically, so to speak, when we have posited God.

Let us then run through this interval from top to bottom. First of all, the slightest diminution of the first principle will be enough to precipitate Being into space and time; but duration and extension, which represent this first diminution, will be as near as possible to the divine inextension and eternity. We must therefore picture to ourselves this first degradation of the divine principle as a sphere turning on itself, imitating, by the perpetuity of its circular movement, the eternity of the circle of the divine thought; creating, moreover, its own place, and thereby place in general,[6] since it includes without being included and moves without stirring from the spot; creating also its own duration, and thereby duration in general, since its movement is the measure of all motion.[7] Then, by degrees, we shall see the perfection decrease, more and more, down to our sublunary world, in which the cycle of birth, growth and decay imitates and mars the original circle for the last time. So understood, the causal relation between God and the world is seen as an attraction when regarded from below, as an impulsion or a contact when regarded from above, since the first heaven, with its circular movement, is an imitation of God and all imitation is the reception of a form. Therefore, we perceive God as efficient cause or as final cause, according to the point of view. And yet neither of these two relations is the ultimate causal relation. The true relation is that which is found between the two members of an equation, when the first member is a single term and the second a sum of an endless number of terms. It is, we may say, the relation of the gold piece to the small change, if we suppose the change to offer itself automatically as soon as the gold piece is presented. Only thus can we understand why Aristotle has demonstrated the necessity of a first motionless mover, not by founding it on the assertion that the movement of things must have had a beginning, but, on the contrary, by affirming that this movement could not have begun and can never come to an end. If movement exists, or in other words, if the small change is being counted, the gold piece is to be found somewhere. And if the counting goes on forever, having never begun, the single term that is eminently equivalent to it must be eternal. A perpetuity of mobility is possible only if it is backed by an eternity of immutability, which it unwinds in a chain without beginning or end.

Such is the last word of the Greek philosophy. We have not at-

[6] *De caelo*, ii. 287 a 12 τῆς ἐσχάτης περιφορᾶς οὔτε κενόν ἐστιν ἔξωθεν οὔτε τόπος. *Phys*. iv. 212 a 34 τὸ δὲ πᾶν ἔστι μὲν ὡς κινήσεται ἔστι δ'ὡς οὔ. ὡς μὲν γὰρ ὅλον, ἅμα τὸν τόπον οὐ μεταβάλλει. κύκλῳ δὲ κινήσεται, τῶν μορίων γὰρ οὗτος ὁ τόπος.

[7] *De caelo*, i. 279 a 12 οὐδὲ χρόνος ἐστὶν ἔξω τοῦ οὐρανοῦ. *Phys*. viii. 251 b 27 ὁ χρόνος πάθος τι κινήσεως.

tempted to reconstruct it *a priori.* It has manifold origins. It is connected by many invisible threads to the soul of ancient Greece. Vain, therefore, the effort to deduce it from a simple principle.[8] But if everything that has come from poetry, religion, social life and a still rudimentary physics and biology be removed from it, if we take away all the light material that may have been used in the construction of the stately building, a solid framework remains, and this framework marks out the main lines of a metaphysic which is, we believe, the natural metaphysic of the human intellect. We come to a philosophy of this kind, indeed, whenever we follow to the end the cinematographical tendency of perception and thought. Our perception and thought begin by substituting for the continuity of evolutionary change a series of unchangeable forms which are, turn by turn, "caught on the wing," like the rings at a merry-go-round, which the children unhook with their little stick as they are passing. Now, how can the forms be passing, and on what "stick" are they strung? As the stable forms have been obtained by extracting from change everything that is definite, there is nothing left to characterize the instability on which the forms are laid, but a negative attribute, which must be indetermination itself. Such is the first proceeding of our thought: it dissociates each change into two elements—the one stable, definable for each particular case, to wit, the Form; the other indefinable and always the same, Change in general. And such, also, is the essential operation of language. Forms are all that it is capable of expressing. It is reduced to taking as understood or is limited to *suggesting* a mobility which, just because it is always unexpressed, is thought to remain in all cases the same.—Then comes in a philosophy that holds the dissociation thus effected by thought and language to be legitimate. What can it do, except objectify the distinction with more force, push it to its extreme consequences, reduce it into a system? It will therefore construct the real, on the one hand, with definite Forms or immutable elements, and, on the other, with a principle of mobility which, being the negation of the form, will, by the hypothesis, escape all defintion and be the purely indeterminate. The more it directs its attention to the forms delineated by thought and expressed by language, the more it will see them rise above the sensible and become subtilized into pure concepts, capable of entering one within the other, and even of being at last massed together into a single concept, the synthesis of all reality, the achievement of all perfection. The more, on the contrary, it descends toward the invisible source of the universal mobility, the more it will feel this mobility sink beneath it and at the same time become void, vanish into what it will call the "non-being." Finally, it will have on the one hand the system of ideas, logically co-ordinated together or concentrated into one only, on the other a quasi-nought, the Platonic

[8] Especially have we left almost entirely on one side those admirable but somewhat fugitive intuitions that Plotinus was later to seize, to study and to fix.

"non-being" or the Aristotelian "matter."—But, having cut your cloth, you must sew it. With supra-sensible Ideas and an infra-sensible non-being, you now have to reconstruct the sensible world. You can do so only if you postulate a kind of metaphysical necessity in virtue of which the confronting of this All with this Zero *is equivalent* to the affirmation of all the degrees of reality that measure the interval between them—just as an undivided number, when regarded as a difference between itself and zero, is revealed as a certain sum of units, and with its own affirmation affirms all the lower numbers. That is the natural postulate. It is that also that we perceive as the base of the Greek philosophy. In order then to explain the specific characters of each of these degrees of intermediate reality, nothing more is necessary than to measure the distance that separates it from the integral reality. Each lower degree consists in a diminution of the higher, and the *sensible* newness that we perceive in it is resolved, from the point of view of the *intelligible,* into a new quantity of negation which is superadded to it. The smallest possible quantity of negation, that which is found already in the highest forms of sensible reality, and consequently *a fortiori* in the lower forms, is that which is expressed by the most general attributes of sensible reality, extension and duration. By increasing degradations we will obtain attributes more and more special. Here the philosopher's fancy will have free scope, for it is by an arbitrary decree, or at least a debatable one, that a particular aspect of the sensible world will be equated with a particular diminution of being. We shall not necessarily end, as Aristotle did, in a world consisting of concentric spheres turning on themselves. But we shall be led to an analogous cosmology—I mean, to a construction whose pieces, though all different, will have none the less the same relations between them. And this cosmology will be ruled by the same principle. The physical will be defined by the logical. Beneath the changing phenomena will appear to us, by transparence, a closed system of concepts subordinated to and co-ordinated with each other. Science, understood as the system of concepts, will be more real than the sensible reality. It will be prior to human knowledge, which is only able to spell it letter by letter; prior also to things, which awkwardly try to imitate it. It would only have to be diverted an instant from itself in order to step out of its eternity and thereby coincide with all this knowledge and all these things. Its immutability is therefore, indeed, the cause of the universal becoming.

Such was the point of view of ancient philosophy in regard to change and duration. That modern philosophy has repeatedly, but especially in its beginnings, had the wish to depart from it, seems to us unquestionable. But an irresistible attraction brings the intellect back to its natural movement, and the metaphysic of the moderns to the general conclusions of the Greek metaphysic. We must try to make this point clear, in order to show by what invisible threads our mechanistic philosophy remains bound to the ancient philosophy of Ideas, and how also it responds to the requirements, above all practical, of our understanding.

Modern, like ancient, science proceeds according to the cinematographical method. It cannot do otherwise; all science is subject to this law. For it is of the essence of science to handle *signs,* which it substitutes for the objects themselves. These signs undoubtedly differ from those of language by their greater precision and their higher efficacy; they are none the less tied down to the general condition of the sign, which is to denote a fixed aspect of the reality under an arrested form. In order to think movement, a constantly renewed effort of the mind is necessary. Signs are made to dispense us with this effort by substituting, for the moving continuity of things, an artificial reconstruction which is its equivalent in practice and has the advantage of being easily handled. But let us leave aside the means and consider only the end. What is the essential object of science? It is to enlarge our influence over things. Science may be speculative in its form, disinterested in its immediate ends: in other words we may give it as long a credit as it wants. But, however long the day of reckoning may be put off, some time or other the payment must be made. It is always then, in short, practical utility that science has in view. Even when it launches into theory, it is bound to adapt its behavior to the general form of practice. However high it may rise, it must be ready to fall back into the field of action, and at once to get on its feet. This would not be possible for it, if its rhythm differed absolutely from that of action itself. Now action, we have said, proceeds by leaps. To act is to re-adapt oneself. To know, that is to say, to foresee in order to act, is then to go from situation to situation, from arrangement to rearrangement. Science may consider rearrangements that come closer and closer to each other; it may thus increase the number of moments that it isolates, but it always isolates moments. As to what happens in the interval between the moments, science is no more concerned with that than are our common intelligence, our senses and our language: it does not bear on the interval, but only on the extremities. So the cinematographical method forces itself upon our science, as it did already on that of the ancients.

Wherein, then, is the difference between the two sciences? We indicated it when we said that the ancients reduced the physical order to the vital order, that is to say, laws to genera, while the moderns try to resolve genera into laws. But we have to look at it in another aspect, which, moreover, is only a transposition, of the first. Wherein consists the difference of attitude of the two sciences toward change? We may formulate it by saying that *ancient science thinks it knows its object sufficiently when it has noted of it some privileged moments, whereas modern science considers the object at any moment whatever.*

The forms or ideas of Plato or of Aristotle correspond to privileged or salient moments in the history of things—those, in general, that have been fixed by language. They are supposed, like the childhood or the old age of a living being, to characterize a period of which they express the quintessence, all the rest of this period being filled by the passage, of no interest in itself, from one form to another form. Take, for instance, a falling body. It was thought that we got near enough to the fact when we characterized it as a whole: it was a movement *downward;* it was the tendency toward a *center;* it was the *natural* movement of a body which, separated from the earth to which it belonged, was now going to find its place again. They noted, then, the final term or culminating point (τέλος, ἀκμή) and set it up as the essential moment: this moment, that language has retained in order to express the whole of the fact, sufficed also for science to characterize it. In the physics of Aristotle, it is by the concepts "high" and "low," spontaneous displacement and forced displacement, own place and strange place, that the movement of a body shot into space or falling freely is defined. But Galileo thought there was no essential moment, no privileged instant. To study the falling body is to consider it at it matters not what moment in its course. The true science of gravity is that which will determine, for any moment of time whatever, the position of the body in space. For this, indeed, signs far more precise than those of language are required.

We may say, then, that our physics differs from that of the ancients chiefly in the indefinite breaking up of time. For the ancients, time comprised as many undivided periods as our natural perception and our language cut out in it successive facts, each presenting a kind of individuality. For that reason, each of these facts admits, in their view, of only a *total* definition or description. If, in describing it, we are led to distinguish phases in it, we have several facts instead of a single one, several undivided periods instead of a single period; but time is always supposed to be divided into determinate periods, and the mode of division to be forced on the mind by apparent crises of the real, comparable to that of puberty, by the apparent release of a new form.—For a Kepler, or a Galileo, on the contrary, time is not divided objectively in one way or another by the matter that fills it. It has no natural articulations. We can, we ought to, divide it as we please. All moments count. None of them has the right to set itself up as a moment that represents or dominates the others. And, consequently, we know a change only when we are able to determine what it is about at any one of its moments.

The difference is profound. In fact, in a certain aspect it is radical. But, from the point of view from which we are regarding it, it is a difference of degree rather than of kind. The human mind has passed from the first kind of knowledge to the second through gradual perfecting, simply by seeking a higher precision. There is the same relation between these two sciences as between the noting of the phases of a movement by the eye and the much more complete recording of these phases by instantaneous photography. It is the same cinematographical mechanism in both cases, but it reaches a precision in the second that it cannot have in the first. Of the gallop of a horse our eye perceives chiefly a characteristic, essential or rather schematic attitude, a form that appears to radiate over a whole period and so fill up a time of gallop. It is this attitude that sculpture has fixed on the frieze of the Parthenon. But instantaneous photography isolates any moment; it puts them all in the same rank, and thus the gallop of a horse spreads out for it into as many successive attitudes as it wishes, instead of massing itself into a single attitude, which is supposed to flash out in a privileged moment and to illuminate a whole period.

From this original difference flow all the others. A science that considers, one after the other, undivided periods of duration, sees nothing but phases succeeding phases, forms replacing forms; it is content with a *qualitative* description of objects, which it likens to organized beings. But when we seek to know what happens within one of these periods, at any moment of time, we are aiming at something entirely different. The changes which are produced from one moment to another are no longer, by the hypothesis, changes of quality; they are *quantitative* variations, it may be of the phenomenon itself, it may be of its elementary parts. We were right then to say that modern science is distinguishable from the ancient in that it applies to magnitudes and proposes first and foremost to measure them. The ancients did indeed try experiments, and on the other hand Kepler tried no experiment, in the proper sense of the word, in order to discover a law which is the very type of scientific knowledge as we understand it. What distinguishes modern science is not that it is experimental, but that it experiments and, more generally, works only with a view to measure.

For that reason it is right, again, to say that ancient science applied to *concepts,* while modern science seeks *laws*—constant relations between variable magnitudes. The concept of circularity was sufficient to Aristotle to define the movement of the heavenly bodies. But, even with the more accurate concept of elliptical form, Kepler did not think he had accounted for the movement of planets. He had to get a law, that is to say, a constant relation between the quantitative variations of two or several elements of the planetary movement.

Yet these are only consequences—differences that follow from the fundamental difference. It did happen to the ancients accidentally to experiment with a view to measuring, as also to discover a law expressing a constant relation between magnitudes. The principle of Archimedes is a true experimental law. It takes into account three variable magnitudes: the volume of a body, the density of the liquid in which the body is immersed, the vertical pressure that is being exerted. And it states indeed that one of these three terms is a function of the other two.

The essential, original difference must therefore be sought elsewhere. It is the same that we noticed first. The science of the ancients is static. Either it considers in block the change that it studies, or, if it divides the change into periods, it makes of each of these periods a block in its turn: which amounts to saying that it takes no account of time. But modern science has been built up around the discoveries of Galileo and of Kepler, which immediately furnished it with a model. Now, what do the laws of Kepler say? They lay down a relation between the areas described by the heliocentric radius-vector of a planet and the *time* employed in describing them, a relation between the longer axis of the orbit and the *time* taken up by the course. And what was the principle discovered by Galileo? A law which connected the space traversed by a falling body with the *time* occupied by the fall. Furthermore, in what did the first of the great transformations of geometry in modern times consist, if not in introducing—in a veiled form, it is true—time and movement even in the consideration of figures? For the ancients, geometry was a purely static science. Figures were given to it at once, completely finished, like the Platonic Ideas. But the essence of the Cartesian geometry (although Descartes did not give it this form) was to regard every plane curve as described by the movement of a point on a movable straight line which is displaced, parallel to itself, along the axis of the abscissae—the displacement of the movable straight line being supposed to be uniform and the abscissa thus becoming representative of the time. The curve is then defined if we can state the relation connecting the space traversed on the movable straight line to the time employed in traversing it, that is, if we are able to indicate the position of the movable point, on the straight line which it traverses, at any moment whatever of its course. This relation is just what we call the equation of the curve. To substitute an equation for a figure consists, therefore, in seeing the actual position of the moving points in the tracing of the curve at any moment whatever, instead of regarding this tracing all at once, gathered up in the unique moment when the curve has reached its finished state.

Such, then, was the directing idea of the reform by which both the science of nature and mathematics, which serves as its instrument, were renewed. Modern science is the daughter of astronomy; it has come down from heaven to earth along the inclined plane of Galileo, for it is through Galileo that Newton and his successors are connected with Kepler. Now, how did the astronomical problem present itself to Kepler? The question was, knowing the respective positions of the planets at a given moment, how to calculate their positions at any other moment. So the same question presented itself, henceforth, for every material system. Each material point became a rudimentary planet, and the main question, the ideal problem whose solution would yield the key to all the others was, the positions of these elements at a particular moment being given, how to determine their relative positions at any moment. No doubt the problem cannot be put in these precise terms except in very simple cases, for a schematized reality; for we never know the respective positions of the real elements of matter, supposing there are real elements; and, even if we knew them at a given moment, the calculation of their positions at another moment would generally require a mathematical effort surpassing human powers. But it is enough for us to know that these elements might be known, that their present positions might be noted, and that a superhuman intellect might, by submitting these data to mathematical operations, determine the positions of the elements at any other moment of time. This conviction is at the bottom of the questions we put to ourselves on the subject of nature, and of the methods we employ to solve them. That is why every law in static form seems to us as a provisional instalment or as a particular view of a dynamic law which alone would give us whole and definitive knowledge.

Let us conclude, then, that our science is not only distinguished from ancient science in this, that it seeks laws, nor even in this, that its laws set forth relations between magnitudes: we must add that the magnitude to which we wish to be able to relate all others is time, and that *modern science must be defined pre-eminently by its aspiration to take time as an independent variable.* But with what time has it to do?

We have said before, and we cannot repeat too often, that the science of matter proceeds like ordinary knowledge. It perfects this knowledge, increases its precision and its scope, but it works in the same direction and puts the same mechanism into play. If, therefore, ordinary knowledge, by reason of the cinematographical mechanism to which it is subjected, forbears to follow becoming in so far as becoming is moving, the science of matter renounces it equally. No doubt, it distinguishes as great a number of moments as we wish in the interval of time it considers. However small the intervals may be at which it stops, it authorizes us to divide them again if necessary. In contrast with ancient science, which stopped at certain so-called essential moments, it is occupied indifferently with any moment whatever. But it always considers moments, always virtual stopping-places, always, in short, immobilities. Which amounts to saying that real time, regarded as a flux, or, in other words, as the very mobility of being, escapes the hold of scientific knowledge. We have already tried to establish this point in a former work. We alluded to it again in the first chapter of this book. But it is necessary to revert to it once more, in order to clear up misunderstandings.

When positive science speaks of time, what it refers to is the movement of a certain mobile T on its trajectory. This movement has been chosen by it as representative of time, and it is, by definition, uniform. Let us call T1, T2, T3, . . . etc., points which divide the trajectory of the mobile into equal parts from its origin T0. We shall say that 1, 2, 3, . . . units of time have flowed past, when the mobile is at the points T1, T2, T3, . . . of the line it traverses. Accordingly, to consider the state of the universe at the end of a certain time *t,* is to examine where it will be when T is at the point T*t* of its course. But of the *flux* itself of time, still less of its effect on consciousness, there is here no question; for there enter into the calculation only the points T1, T2, T3, . . . taken on the flux, never the flux itself. We may narrow the time considered as much as we will, that is, break up at will the interval between two consecutive divisions Tn and Tn + 1; but it is always with points, and with points only, that we are dealing. What we retain of the movement of the mobile T are positions taken on its trajectory. What we retain of all the other points of the universe are their positions on their respective trajectories. To each *virtual stop* of the moving body T at the points of division T1, T2, T3, . . . we make correspond a *virtual stop* of all the other mobiles at the points where they are passing. And when we say that a movement or any other change has occupied a time *t,* we mean by it that we have noted a number T of correspondences of this kind. We have therefore counted simultaneities; we have not concerned ourselves with the flux that goes from one to another. The proof of this is that I can, at discretion, vary the rapidity of the flux of the universe in regard to a consciousness that is independent of it and that would perceive the variation by the quite qualitative *feeling* that it would have of it: whatever the variation had been, since the movement of T would participate in this variation, I should have nothing to change in my equations nor in the numbers that figure in them.

Let us go further. Suppose that the rapidity of the flux becomes infinite. Imagine, as we said in the first pages of this book, that the trajectory of the mobile T is given at once, and that the whole history, past, present and future, of the material universe is spread out instantaneously in space. The same mathematical correspondences will subsist between the moments of the history of the world unfolded like a fan, so to speak, and the divisions T1, T2, T3, . . . of the line which will be called, by definition, "the course of time." In the eyes of science nothing will have changed. But if, time thus spreading itself out in space and succession becoming juxtaposition, science has nothing to change in what it tells us, we must conclude that, in what it tells us, it takes account neither of *succession* in what of it is specific nor of *time* in what there is in it that is fluent. It has no sign to express what strikes our consciousness in succession and duration. It no more applies to becoming, so far as that is moving, than the bridges thrown here and there across the stream follow the water that flows under their arches.

Yet succession exists; I am conscious of it; it is a fact. When a physical process is going on before my eyes, my perception and my inclination have nothing to do with accelerating or retarding it. What is important to the physicist is the *number* of units of duration the process fills; he does not concern himself about the units themselves and that is why the successive states of the world might be spread out all at once in space without his having to change anything in his science or to cease talking about time. But for us, conscious beings, it is the units that matter, for we do not count extremities of intervals, we feel and live the intervals themselves. Now, we are conscious of these intervals as of *definite* intervals. Let me come back again to the sugar in my glass of water:[9] why must I wait for it to melt? While the duration of the phenomenon is *relative* for the physicist, since it is reduced to a certain number of units of time and the units themselves are indifferent, this duration is an *absolute* for my consciousness, for it coincides with a certain degree of impatience which is rigorously determined. Whence comes this determination? What is it that obliges me to wait, and to wait for a certain length of physical duration which is forced upon me, over which I have no power? If succession, in so far as distinct from mere juxtaposition, has no real efficacy, if time is not a kind of force, why does the universe unfold its successive states with a velocity which, in regard to my consciousness, is a veritable absolute? Why with this particular velocity rather than any other? Why not with an infinite velocity? Why, in other words, is not everything given at once, as on the film of the cinematograph? The more I consider this point, the more it seems to me that, if the future is bound to *succeed* the present instead of being given alongside of it, it is because the future is not altogether determined at the present moment, and that if the time taken up by this succession is something other than a number, if it has for the consciousness that is installed in it absolute value and reality, it is because there is unceasingly being created in it, not indeed in any such artificially isolated system as a glass of sugared water, but in the concrete whole of which every such system forms part, something unforeseeable and new. This duration may not be the fact of matter itself, but that of the life which reascends the course of matter; the two movements are none the less mutually dependent upon each other. *The duration of the universe must therefore be one with the latitude of creation which can find place in it.*

When a child plays at reconstructing a picture by putting together the separate pieces in a puzzle game, the more he practices, the more and more quickly he succeeds. The reconstruction was, moreover, instantaneous, the child found it ready-made, when he opened the box on leaving the shop. The operation, therefore, does not require a definite time, and indeed, theoretically, it does not require any time. That is because the result is given. It is because the picture is already created, and because to obtain it requires only a work of recomposing and rearranging—a work that can be supposed going faster and faster, and even infinitely fast, up to the point of being instantaneous. But, to

[9] See [Creative Evolution], page 12.

the artist who creates a picture by drawing it from the depths of his soul, time is no longer an accessory; it is not an interval that may be lengthened or shortened without the content being altered. The duration of his work is part and parcel of his work. To contract or to dilate it would be to modify both the psychical evolution that fills it and the invention which is its goal. The time taken up by the invention is one with the invention itself. It is the progress of a thought which is changing in the degree and measure that it is taking form. It is a vital process, something like the ripening of an idea.

The painter is before his canvas, the colors are on the palette, the model is sitting—all this we see, and also we know the painter's style: do we foresee what will appear on the canvas? We possess the elements of the problem; we know in an abstract way, how it will be solved, for the portrait will surely resemble the model and will surely resemble also the artist; but the concrete solution brings with it that unforeseeable nothing which is everything in a work of art. And it is this nothing that takes time. Nought as matter, it creates itself as form. The sprouting and flowering of this form are stretched out on an unshrinkable duration, which is one with their essence. So of the works of nature. Their novelty arises from an internal impetus which is progress or succession, which confers on succession a peculiar virtue or which owes to succession the whole of its virtue—which, at any rate, makes succession, or *continuity of interpenetration* in time, irreducible to a mere instantaneous juxtaposition in space. This is why the idea of reading in a present state of the material universe the future of living forms, and of unfolding now their history yet to come, involves a veritable absurdity. But this absurdity is difficult to bring out, because our memory is accustomed to place alongside of each other, in an ideal space, the terms it perceives in turn, because it always represents *past* succession in the form of juxtaposition. It is able to do so, indeed, just because the past belongs to that which is already invented, to the dead, and no longer to creation and to life. Then, as the succession to come will end by being a succession past, we persuade ourselves that the duration to come admits of the same treatment as past duration, that it is, even now, unrollable, that the future is there, rolled up, already painted on the canvas. An illusion, no doubt, but an illusion that is natural, ineradicable, and that will last as long as the human mind!

Time is invention or it is nothing at all. But of time-invention physics can take no account, restricted as it is to the cinematographical method. It is limited to counting simultaneities between the events that make up this time and the positions of the mobile T on its trajectory. It detaches these events from the whole, which at every moment puts on a new form and which communicates to them something of its novelty. It considers them in the abstract, such as they would be outside of the living whole, that is to say, in a time unrolled in space. It retains only the events or systems of events that can be thus isolated without being made to undergo too profound a deformation, because only these lend themselves to the application of its method. Our physics dates from the day when it was known how to isolate such systems. To sum up, *while modern physics is distinguished from ancient physics by the fact that it considers any moment of time whatever, it rests altogether on a substitution of time-length for time-invention.*

It seems then that, parallel to this physics, a second kind of knowledge ought to have grown up, which could have retained what physics allowed to escape. On the flux itself of duration science neither would nor could lay hold, bound as it was to the cinematographical method. This second kind of knowledge would have set the cinematographical method aside. It would have called upon the mind to renounce its most cherished habits. It is within becoming that it would have transported us by an effort of sympathy. We should no longer be asking where a moving body will be, what shape a system will take, through what state a change will pass at a given moment: the moments of time, which are only arrests of our attention, would no longer exist; it is the flow of time, it is the very flux of the real that we should be trying to follow. The first kind of knowledge has the advantage of enabling us to foresee the future and of making us in some measure masters of events; in return, it retains of the moving reality only eventual immobilities, that is to say, views taken of it by our mind. It symbolizes the real and transposes it into the human rather than expresses it. The other knowledge, if it is possible, is practically useless, it will not extend our empire over nature, it will even go against certain natural aspirations of the intellect; but, if it succeeds, it is reality itself that it will hold in a firm and final embrace. Not only may we thus complete the intellect and its knowledge of matter by accustoming it to install itself within the moving, but by developing also another faculty, complementary to the intellect, we may open a perspective on the other half of the real. For, as soon as we are confronted with true duration, we see that it means creation, and that if that which is being unmade endures, it can only be because it is inseparably bound to what is making itself. Thus will appear the necessity of a continual growth of the universe, I should say of a *life* of the real. And thus will be seen in a new light the life which we find on the surface of our planet, a life directed the same way as that of the universe, and inverse of materiality. To intellect, in short, there will be added intuition.

The more we reflect on it, the more we shall find that this conception of metaphysics is that which modern science suggests.

For the ancients, indeed, time is theoretically negligible, because the duration of a thing only manifests the degradation of its essence: it is with this motionless essence that science has to deal. Change being only the effort of a form toward its own realization, the realization is all that it concerns us to know. No doubt the realization is never complete: it is this that ancient philosophy expresses by saying that we do not perceive form without matter. But if we consider the changing object at a certain essential moment, at its apogee, we may say that there it just touches its intelligible form. This intelligible form, this ideal and, so to speak, limiting form, our science seizes upon. And possessing in this the gold-piece, it holds eminently the small money which we call becoming or change. This change is less than being. The knowledge that would take it for object, supposing such knowledge were possible, would be less than science.

But, for a science that places all the moments of time in the same rank, that admits no essential moment, no culminating point, no apogee, change is no longer a diminution of essence, duration is not a dilution of eternity. The flux of time is the reality itself, and the things which we study are the things which flow. It is true that of this flowing reality we are limited to taking instantaneous views. But, just because of this, scientific knowledge must appeal to another knowledge to complete it. While the ancient conception of scientific knowledge ended in making time a degradation, and change the diminution of a form given from all eternity—on the contrary, by following the new conception to the end, we should come to see in time a progressive growth of the absolute, and in the evolution of things a continual invention of forms ever new.

It is true that it would be to break with the metaphysics of the ancients. They saw only one way of knowing definitely. Their science consisted in a scattered and fragmentary metaphysics, their metaphysics in a concentrated and systematic science. Their science and metaphysics were, at most, two species of one and the same genus. In our hypothesis, on the contrary, science and metaphysics are two opposed although complementary ways of knowing, the first retaining only moments, that is to say, that which does not endure, the second bearing on duration itself. Now, it was natural to hesitate between so novel a conception of metaphysics and the traditional conception. The temptation must have been strong to repeat with the new science what had been tried on the old, to suppose our scientific knowledge of nature completed at once, to unify it entirely, and to give to this unification, as the Greeks had already done, the name of metaphysics. So, beside the new way that philosophy might have prepared, the old remained open, that indeed which physics trod. And, as physics retained of time only what could as well be spread out all at once in space, the metaphysics that chose the same direction had necessarily to proceed as if time created and annihilated nothing, as if duration had no efficacy. Bound, like the physics of the moderns and the metaphysics of the ancients, to the cinematographical method, it ended with the conclusion, implicitly admitted at the start and immanent in the method itself: *All is given.*

That metaphysics hesitated at first between the two paths seems to us unquestionable. The indecision is visible in Cartesianism. On the one hand, Descartes affirms universal mechanism: from this point of view movement would be relative,[10] and, as time has just as much reality as movement, it would follow that past, present and future are given from all eternity. But, on the other hand (and that is why the philosopher has not gone to these extreme consequences), Descartes believes in the free will of man. He superposes on the determinism of physical phenomena the indeterminism of human actions, and, consequently, on time-length a time in which there is invention, creation, true succession. This duration he supports on a God who is unceasingly renewing the creative act, and who, being thus tangent to time and becoming, sustains them, communicates to them necessarily something of his absolute reality. When he places himself at this second point of view, Descartes speaks of movement, even spatial, as of an absolute.[11]

He therefore entered both roads one after the other, having resolved to follow neither of them to the end. The first would have led him to the denial of free will in man and of real will in God. It was the suppression of all efficient duration, the likening of the universe to a thing *given,* which a superhuman intelligence would embrace at once in a moment or in eternity. In following the second, on the contrary, he would have been led to all the consequences which the intuition of true duration implies. Creation would have appeared not simply as *continued,* but also as *continuous.* The universe, regarded as a whole, would really evolve. The future would no longer be determinable by the present; at most we might say that, once realized, it can be found again in its antecedents, as the sounds of a new language can be expressed with the letters of an old alphabet if we agree to enlarge the value of the letters and to attribute to them, retroactively, sounds which no combination of the old sounds could have produced beforehand. Finally, the mechanistic explanation might have remained universal in this, that it can indeed be extended to as many systems as we choose to cut out in the continuity of the universe; but mechanism would then have become a *method* rather than a *doctrine.* It would have expressed the fact that science must proceed after the cinematographical manner, that the function of science is to scan the rhythm of the flow of things and not to fit itself into that flow.—Such were the two opposite conceptions of metaphysics which were offered to philosophy.

It chose the first. The reason of this choice is undoubtedly the mind's tendency to follow the cinematographical method, a method so natural to our intellect, and so well adjusted also to the requirements of our science, that we must feel doubly sure of its speculative impotence to renounce it in metaphysics. But ancient philosophy also influenced the choice. Artists forever admirable, the Greeks created a type of suprasensible truth, as of sensible beauty, whose attraction is hard

[10] Descartes, *Principes,* ii. § 29.

[11] Descartes, *Principes,* ii. §§ 36 ff.

to resist. As soon as we incline to make metaphysics a systematization of science, we glide in the direction of Plato and of Aristotle. And, once in the zone of attraction in which the Greek philosophers moved, we are drawn along in their orbit.

Such was the case with Leibniz, as also with Spinoza. We are not blind to the treasures of originality their doctrines contain. Spinoza and Leibniz have poured into them the whole content of their souls, rich with the inventions of their genius and the acquisitions of modern thought. And there are in each of them, especially in Spinoza, flashes of intuition that break through the system. But if we leave out of the two doctrines what breathes life into them, if we retain the skeleton only, we have before us the very picture of Platonism and Aristotelianism seen through Cartesian mechanism. They present to us a systematization of the new physics, constructed on the model of the ancient metaphysics.

What, indeed, could the unification of physics be? The inspiring idea of that science was to isolate, within the universe, systems of material points such that, the position of each of these points being known at a given moment, we could then calculate it for any moment whatever. As, moreover, the systems thus defined were the only ones on which the new science had hold, and as it could not be known beforehand whether a system satisfied or did not satisfy the desired condition, it was useful to proceed always and everywhere *as if* the condition was realized. There was in this a methodological rule, a very natural rule—so natural, indeed, that it was not even necessary to formulate it. For simple common sense tells us that when we are possessed of an effective instrument of research, and are ignorant of the limits of its applicability, we should act as if its applicability were unlimited; there will always be time to abate it. But the temptation must have been great for the philosopher to hypostatize this hope, or rather this impetus, of the new science, and to convert a general rule of method into a fundamental law of things. So he transported himself at once to the limit; he supposed physics to have become complete and to embrace the whole of the sensible world. The universe became a system of points, the position of which was rigorously determined at each instant by relation to the preceding instant and theoretically calculable for any moment whatever. The result, in short, was universal mechanism. But it was not enough to formulate this mechanism; what was required was to found it, to give the reason for it and prove its necessity. And the essential affirmation of mechanism being that of a reciprocal mathematical dependence of all the points of the universe, as also of all the moments of the universe, the reason of mechanism had to be discovered in the unity of a principle into which could be contracted all that is juxtaposed in space and successive in time. Hence, the whole of the real was supposed to be given at once. The reciprocal determination of the juxtaposed appearances in space was explained by the indivisibility of true being, and the inflexible determinism of successive phenomena in time simply expressed that the whole of being is given in the eternal.

The new philosophy was going, then, to be a recommencement, or rather a transposition, of the old. The ancient philosophy had taken each of the *concepts* into which a becoming is concentrated or which mark its apogee: it supposed them all known, and gathered them up into a single concept, form of forms, idea of ideas, like the God of Aristotle. The new philosophy was going to take each of the *laws* which condition a becoming in relation to others and which are as the permanent substrata of phenomena: it would suppose them all known, and would gather them up into a unity which also would express them eminently, but which, like the God of Aristotle and for the same reasons, must remain immutably shut up in itself.

True, this return to the ancient philosophy was not without great difficulties. When a Plato, an Aristotle, or a Plotinus melt all the concepts of their science into a single one, in so doing they embrace the whole of the real, for concepts are supposed to represent the things themselves, and to possess at least as much positive content. But a law, in general, expresses only a relation, and physical laws in particular express only *quantitative* relations between concrete things. So that if a modern philosopher works with the laws of the new science as the Greek philosopher did with the concepts of the ancient science, if he makes all the conclusions of a physics supposed omniscient converge on a single point, he neglects what is concrete in the phenomena—the qualities perceived, the perceptions themselves. His synthesis comprises, it seems, only a fraction of reality. In fact, the first result of the new science was to cut the real into two halves, quantity and quality, the former being credited to the account of *bodies* and the latter to the account of *souls*. The ancients had raised no such barriers either between quality and quantity or between soul and body. For them, the mathematical concepts were concepts like the others, related to the others and fitting quite naturally into the hierarchy of the Ideas. Neither was the body then defined by geometrical extension, nor the soul by consciousness. If the ρυχή of Aristotle, the entelechy of a living body, is less spiritual than our "soul," it is because his σῶμα, already impregnated with the Idea, is less corporeal than our "body." The scission was not yet irremediable between the two terms. It has become so, and thence a metaphysic that aims at an abstract unity must resign itself either to comprehend in its synthesis only one half of the real, or to take advantage of the absolute heterogeneity of the two halves in order to consider one as a translation of the other. Different phrases will express different things if they belong to the same language, that is to say, if there is a certain relationship of sound between them. But if they belong to two different languages, they might, just because of their radical diversity of sound, express the same thing. So of quality and quantity, of soul and body. It is for having cut all connection between the two terms that philosophers have been led to establish between them a rigorous parallelism, of which the ancients had not dreamed, to regard them as translations and not as inversions of each other; in short, to posit a fundamental identity as a substratum to their duality. The synthesis to which they rose thus became capable of embracing everything. A divine mechanism made the phenomena of thought to correspond to those of extension, each to each, qualities to quantities, souls to bodies.

It is this parallelism that we find both in Leibniz and in Spinoza—in different forms, it is true, because of the unequal importance which they attach to extension. With Spinoza, the two terms Thought and Extension are placed, in principle at least, in the same rank. They are, therefore, two translations of one and the same original, or, as Spinoza says, two attributes of one and the same substance, which we must call God. And these two translations, as also an infinity of others into languages which we know not, are called up and even forced into existence by the original, just as the essence of the circle is translated automatically, so to speak, both by a figure and by an equation. For Leibniz, on the contrary, extension is indeed still a translation, but it is thought that is the original, and thought might dispense with translation, the translation being made only for us. In positing God, we necessarily posit also all the possible views of God, that is to say, the monads. But we can always imagine that a view has been taken from a point of view, and it is natural for an imperfect mind like ours to class views, qualitatively different, according to the order and position of points of view, qualitatively identical, from which the views might have been taken. In reality the points of view do not exist, for there are only views, each given in an indivisible block and representing in its own way the whole of reality, which is God. But we need to express the plurality of the views, that are *unlike* each other, by the multiplicity of the points of view that are *exterior* to each other; and we also need to symbolize the more or less close relationship between the views by the relative situation of the points of view to one another, their nearness or their distance, that is to say, by a magnitude. That is what Leibniz means when he says that space is the order of coexistents, that the perception of extension is a confused perception (that is to say, a perception relative to an imperfect mind), and that nothing exists but monads, expressing thereby that the real Whole has no parts, but is repeated to infinity, each time integrally (though diversely) within itself, and that all these repetitions are complementary to each other. In just the same way, the visible relief of an object is equivalent to the whole set of stereoscopic views taken of it from all points, so that, instead of seeing in the relief a juxtaposition of solid parts, we might quite as well look upon it as made of the *reciprocal complemantarity* of these whole views, each given in block, each indivisible, each different from all the others and yet representative of the same thing. The Whole, that is to say, God, is this very relief for Leibniz, and the monads are these complementary plane views; for that reason he defines God as "the substance that has no point of view," or, again, as "the universal harmony," that is to say, the reciprocal complementarity of monads. In short, Leibniz differs from Spinoza in this, that he looks upon the universal mechanism as an aspect which reality takes for us, whereas, Spinoza makes of it an aspect which reality takes for itself.

It is true that, after having concentrated in God the whole of the real, it became difficult for them to pass from God to things, from eternity to time. The difficulty was even much greater for these philosophers than an Aristotle or a Plotinus. The God of Aristotle, indeed, had been obtained by the compression and reciprocal compenetration of the Ideas that represent, in their finished state or in their culminating point, the changing things of the world. He was, therefore, transcendent to the world, and the duration of things was juxtaposed to His eternity, of which it was only a weakening. But in the principle to which we are led by the consideration of universal mechanism, and which must serve as its substratum, it is not concepts or *things,* but laws or *relations* that are condensed. Now, a relation does not exist separately. A law connects changing terms and is immanent in what it governs. The principle in which all these relations are ultimately summoned up, and which is the basis of the unity of nature, cannot, therefore, be transcendent to sensible reality; it is immanent in it, and we must suppose that it is at once both in and out of time, gathered up in the unity of its substance and yet condemned to wind it off in an endless chain. Rather than formulate so appalling a contradiction, the philosophers were necessarily led to sacrifice the weaker of the two terms, and to regard the temporal aspect of things as a mere illusion. Leibniz says so in explicit terms, for he makes of time, as of space, a confused perception. While the multiplicity of his monads expresses only the diversity of views taken of the whole, the history of an isolated monad seems to be hardly anything else than the manifold views that it can take of its own substance: so that time would consist in all the points of view that each monad can assume toward itself, as space consists in all the points of view that all monads can assume toward God. But the thought of Spinoza is much less clear, and this philosopher seems to have sought to establish, between eternity and that which has duration, the same difference as Aristotle made between essence and accidents: a most difficult undertaking, for the *υλη* of Aristotle was no longer there to measure the distance and explain the passage from the essential to the accidental, Descartes having eliminated it forever. However that may be, the deeper we go into the Spinozistic conception of the "inadequate," as related to the "adequate," the more we feel ourselves moving in the direction of Aristotelianism—just as the Leibnizian monads, in proportion as they mark themselves out the more clearly, tend to approximate to the Intelligibles of Plotinus.[12] The natural trend of these two philosophies brings them back to the conclusions of the ancient philosophy.

To sum up, the resemblances of this new metaphysic to that of the ancients arise from the fact that both suppose ready-made—the former above the sensible, the latter within the sensible—a science one and complete, with which any reality that the sensible may contain is believed to coincide. *For both, reality as well as truth are integrally given in eternity*. Both are opposed to the idea of a reality that creates itself gradually, that is, at bottom, to an absolute duration.

Now, it might easily be shown that the conclusions of this metaphysic, springing from science, have rebounded upon science itself, as it were, by ricochet. They penetrate the whole of our so-called empiricism. Physics and chemistry study only inert matter; biology, when it treats the living being physically and chemically, considers only the inert side of the living: hence the mechanistic explanations, in spite of their development, include only a small part of the real. To suppose *a priori* that the whole of the real is resolvable into elements of this kind, or at least that mechanism can give a complete translation of what happens in the world, is to pronounce for a certain metaphysic—the very metaphysic of which Spinoza and Leibniz have laid down the principles and drawn the consequences. Certainly, the psychophysiologist who affirms the exact equivalence of the cerebral and the psychical state, who imagines the possibility, for some superhuman intellect, of reading in the brain what is going on in consciousness, believes himself very far from the metaphysicians of the seventeenth century, and very near to experience. Yet experience pure and simple tells us nothing of the kind. It shows us the interdependence of the mental and the physical, the necessity of a certain cerebral substratum for the psychical state—nothing more. From the fact that two things are mutually dependent, it does not follow that they are equivalent. Because a certain screw is necessary to a certain machine, because the machine works when the screw is there and stops when the screw is taken away, we do not say that the screw is the equivalent of the machine. For correspondence to be equivalence, it would be necessary that to any part of the machine a definite part of the screw should correspond—as in a literal translation in which each chapter renders a chapter, each sentence a sentence, each word a word. Now, the relation of the brain to consciousness seems to be entirely different. Not only does the hypothesis of an equivalence between the psychical state and the cerebral state imply a downright absurdity, as we have

[12] In a course of lectures on Plotinus, given at the Collège de France in 1897-1898, we tried to bring out these resemblances. They are numerous and impressive. The analogy is continued even in the formulae employed on each side.

tried to prove in a former essay,[13] but the facts, examined without prejudice, certainly seem to indicate that the relation of the psychical to the physical is just that of the machine to the screw. To speak of an equivalence between the two is simply to curtail, and make almost unintelligible, the Spinozistic or Leibnizian metaphysic. It is to accept this philosophy, such as it is, on the side of Extension, but to mutilate it on the side of Thought. With Spinoza, with Leibniz, we suppose the unifying synthesis of the phenomena of matter achieved, and everything in matter explained mechanically. But, for the conscious facts, we no longer push the synthesis to the end. We stop half-way. We suppose consciousness to be coextensive with a certain part of nature and not with all of it. We are thus led, sometimes to an "epiphenomenalism" that associates consciousness with certain particular vibrations and puts it here and there in the world in a sporadic state, and sometimes to a "monism" that scatters consciousness into as many tiny grains as there are atoms; but, in either case, it is to an incomplete Spinozism or to an incomplete Leibnizianism that we come back. Between this conception of nature and Cartesianism we find, moreover, intermediate historical stages. The medical philosophers of the eighteenth century, with their cramped Cartesianism, have had a great part in the genesis of the "epiphenomenalism" and "monism" of the present day.

[13] "Le Paralogisme psycho-physiologique" (*Revue de métaphysique et de morale*, Nov. 1904, pp. 895-908). Cf. *Matière et mémoire*, Paris, 1896, chap. i.

Gabriel Marcel

ON THE ONTOLOGICAL MYSTERY[1]

The title of this essay is likely to annoy the philosopher as much as to startle the layman, since philosophers are inclined to leave mystery either to the theologians or else to the vulgarisers, whether of mysticism or of occultism, such as Maeterlinck. Moreover, the term *ontological,* which has only the vaguest meaning for the layman, has become discredited in the eyes of Idealist philosophers; while the term *mystery* is reserved by those thinkers who are imbued with the ideas of Scholasticism for the revealed mysteries of religion.

Thus my terminology is clearly open to criticism from all sides. But I can find no other which is adequate to the body of ideas which I intend to put forward and on which my whole outlook is based. Readers of my *Journal Métaphysique* will see that they represent the term of the whole spiritual and philosophical evolution which I have described in that book.

Rather than to begin with abstract definitions and dialectical arguments which may be discouraging at the outset, I should like to start with a sort of global and intuitive characterisation of the man in whom the sense of the ontological—the sense of being—is lacking, or, to speak more correctly, of the man who has lost the awareness of this sense. Generally speaking, modern man is in this condition; if ontological demands worry him at all, it is only dully, as an obscure impulse. Indeed I wonder if a psychoanalytical method, deeper and more discerning than any that has been evolved until now, would not

[1] From: *The Philosophy of Existence,* Gabriel Marcel, Ch. 1. The Philosophical Library, Inc., New York, 1949. By permission.

reveal the morbid effects of the repression of this sense and of the ignoring of this need.

The characteristic feature of our age seems to me to be what might be called the misplacement of the idea of function, taking function in its current sense which includes both the vital and the social functions.

The individual tends to appear both to himself and to others as an agglomeration of functions. As a result of deep historical causes, which can as yet be understood only in part, he has been led to see himself more and more as a mere assemblage of functions, the hierarchical interrelation of which seems to him questionable or at least subject to conflicting interpretations.

To take the vital functions first. It is hardly necessary to point out the role which historical materialism on the one hand, and Freudian doctrines on the other, have played in restricting the concept of man.

Then there are the social functions—those of the consumer, the producer, the citizen, etc.

Between these two there is, in theory, room for the psychological functions as well; but it is easy to see how these will tend to be interpreted in relation either to the social or the vital functions, so that their independence will be threatened and their specific character put in doubt. In this sense, Comte, served by his total incomprehension of psychical reality, displayed an almost prophetic instinct when he excluded psychology from his classification of sciences.

So far we are still dealing only with abstractions, but nothing is easier than to find concrete illustrations in this field.

Travelling on the Underground, I often wonder with a kind of dread what can be the inward reality of the life of this or that man employed on the railway—the man who opens the doors, for instance, or the one who punches the tickets. Surely everything both within him and outside him conspires to identify this man with his functions—meaning not only with his functions as worker, as trade union member or as voter, but with his vital functions as well. The rather horrible expression 'time table' perfectly describes his life. So many hours for each function. Sleep too is a function which must be discharged so that the other functions may be exercised in their turn. The same with pleasure, with relaxation; it is logical that the weekly allowance of recreation should be determined by an expert on hygiene; recreation is a psycho-organic function which must not be neglected any more than, for instance, the function of sex. We need go no further; this sketch is sufficient to suggest the emergence of a kind of vital schedule; the details will vary with the country, the climate, the profession, etc., but what matters is that there is a schedule.

It is true that certain disorderly elements—sickness, accidents of every sort—will break in on the smooth working of the system. It is therefore natural that the individual should be overhauled at regular intervals like a watch (this is often done in America). The hospital plays the part of the inspection bench or the repair shop. And it is from this same standpoint of function that such essential problems as birth control will be examined.

As for death, it becomes, objectively and functionally, the scrapping of what has ceased to be of use and must be written off as total loss.

I need hardly insist on the stifling impression of sadness produced by this functionalised world. It is sufficient to recall the dreary image of the retired official, or those urban Sundays when the passers-by look like people who have retired from life. In such a world, there is something mocking and sinister even in the tolerance awarded to the man who has retired from his work.

But besides the sadness felt by the onlooker, there is the dull, intolerable unease of the actor himself who is reduced to living as though he were in fact submerged by his functions. This uneasiness is enough to show that there is in all this some appalling mistake, some ghastly misinterpretation, implanted in defenceless minds by an increasingly inhuman social order and an equally inhuman philosophy (for if the philosophy has prepared the way for the order, the order has also shaped the philosophy).

I have written on another occasion that, provided it is taken in its metaphysical and not its physical sense, the distinction between the *full* and the *empty* seems to me more fundamental than that between the *one* and the *many*. This is particularly applicable to the case in point. Life in a world centred on function is liable to despair because in reality this world is *empty,* it rings hollow; and if it resists this temptation it is only to the extent that there come into play from within it and in its favour certain hidden forces which are beyond its power to conceive or to recognise.

It should be noted that this world is, on the one hand, riddled with problems and, on the other, determined to allow no room for mystery. I shall come back to this distinction between problem and mystery which I believe to be fundamental. For the moment I shall only point out that to eliminate or to try to eliminate mystery is (in this functionalist world) to bring into play in the face of events which break in on the course of existence—such as birth, love and death—that psychological and pseudo-scientific category of the 'purely natural' which deserves a study to itself. In reality, this is nothing more than the remains of a degraded rationalism from whose standpoint cause explains effect and accounts for it exhaustively. There exist in such a world, nevertheless, an infinity of problems, since the causes are not known to us in detail and thus leave room for unlimited research. And in addition to these theoretical puzzles there are innumerable technical problems, bound up with the difficulty of knowing how the various functions, once they have been inventoried and labelled, can be made to work together without doing one another harm. These theoretical and technical questions are interdependent, for the theoretical problems arise out of the different techniques while the technical problems cannot be solved without a measure of pre-established theoretical knowledge.

In such a world the ontological need, the need of being, is exhausted in exact proportion to the breaking up of personality on the one hand and, on the other, to the triumph of the category of the 'purely natural' and the consequent atrophy of the faculty of *wonder*.

But to come at last to the ontological need itself; can we not approach it directly and attempt to define it? In reality this can only be done to a limited extent. For reasons which I shall develop later, I suspect that the characteristic of this need is that it can never be wholly clear to itself.

To try to describe it without distorting it we shall have to say something like this:

Being is—or should be—necessary. It is impossible that everything should be reduced to a play of successive appearances which are inconsistent with each other ('inconsistent' is essential), or, in the words of Shakespeare, to 'a tale told by an idiot'. I aspire to participate in this being, in this reality—and perhaps this aspiration is already a degree of participation, however rudimentary.

Such a need, it may be noted, is to be found at the heart of the most inveterate pessimism. Pessimism has no meaning unless it signifies: it would surely be well if there were being, but there is no being, and I, who observe this fact, am therefore nothing.

As for defining the word 'being', let us admit that it is extremely difficult. I would merely suggest this method of approach: being is what withstands—or what would withstand—an exhaustive analysis bearing on the data of experience and aiming to reduce them step by step to elements increasingly devoid of intrinsic or significant value. (An analysis of this kind is attempted in the theoretical works of Freud.)

When the pessimist Besme says in *La Ville* that *nothing is,* he means precisely this, that there is no experience that withstands this analytical test. And it is always towards death regarded as the manifestation, the proof of this ultimate nothingness that the kind of inverted apologetic which arises out of absolute pessimism will inevitably gravitate.

A philosophy which refuses to endorse the ontological need is, nevertheless, possible; indeed, generally speaking, contemporary thought tends towards this abstention. But at this point a distinction must be made between two different attitudes which are sometimes confused: one which consists in a systematic reserve (it is that of agnosticism in all its forms), and the other, bolder and more coherent, which regards the ontological need as the expression of an outworn body of dogma liquidated once and for all by the Idealist critique.

The former appears to me to be purely negative: it is merely the expression of an intellectual policy of 'not raising the question'.

The latter, on the contrary, claims to be based on a positive theory of thought. This is not the place for a detailed critical study of this philosophy. I shall only note that it seems to me to tend towards an unconscious relativism, or else towards a monism which ignores the personal in all its form, ignores the tragic and denies the transcendent, seeking to reduce it to its caricatural expressions which distort its essential character. I shall also point out that, just because this philosophy continually stresses the activity of verification, it ends by ignoring *presence*—that inward realisation of presence through love which infinitely transcends all possible verification because it exists in an immediacy beyond all conceivable mediation. This will be clearer to some extent from what follows.

Thus I believe for my part that the ontological need cannot be silenced by an arbitrary dictatorial act which mutilates the life of the spirit at its roots. It remains true, nevertheless, that such an act is possible, and the conditions of our life are such that we can well believe that we are carrying it out; this must never be forgotten.

These preliminary reflections on the ontological need are sufficient to bring out its indeterminate character and to reveal a fundamental paradox. To formulate this need is to raise a host of questions: Is there such a thing as being? What is it? etc. Yet immediately an abyss opens under my feet: I who ask these questions about being, how can I be sure that I exist?

Yet surely I, who formulate this *problem,* should be able to remain *outside* it—*before* or *beyond* it? Clearly this is not so. The more I consider it the more I find that this problem tends inevitably to invade the proscenium from which it is excluded in theory: it is only by means of a fiction that Idealism in its traditional form seeks to maintain on the margin of being the consciousness which asserts it or denies it.

So I am inevitably forced to ask: Who am I—I who question being? How am I qualified to begin this investigation? If I do not exist, how can I succeed in it? And if I do exist, how can I be sure of this fact?

Contrary to the opinion which suggests itself at this point, I believe that on this plane the *cogito* cannot help us at all. Whatever Descartes may have thought of it himself, the only certainty with which it provides us concerns only the epistemological subject as organ of objective cognition. As I have written elewhere, the *cogito* merely guards the threshold of objective validity, and that is strictly all; this is proved by the indeterminate character of the *I*. The *I am* is, to my mind, a global statement which it is impossible to break down into its component parts.

There remains a possible objection; it might be said: Either the being designated in the question 'What am I?' concerns the subject of cognition, and in this case we are on the plane of the *cogito;* or else that which you call the ontological need is merely the extreme point (or perhaps only the fallacious transposition) of a need which is, in reality, vital and with which the metaphysician is not concerned.

But is it not a mistake arbitrarily to divide the question, *Who am I?* from the ontological 'problem' taken as a whole? The truth is that neither of the two can be dealt with separately, but that when they are taken together, they cancel one another out *as problems.*

It should be added that the Cartesian position is inseparable from a form of dualism which I, for my part, would unhesitatingly reject. To raise the ontological problem is to raise the question of being as a whole and of oneself seen as a totality.

But should we not ask ourselves if we must not reject this dissociation between the intellectual and the vital, with its resultant over- or under-estimation of the one or the other? Doubtless it is legitimate to establish certain distinctions within the unity of the being who thinks and who endeavours to *think himself;* but it is only beyond such distinctions that the ontological problem can arise and it must relate to that being seen in his all-comprehensive unity.

To sum up our reflections at this point, we find that we are dealing with an urge towards an affirmation—yet an affirmation which it seems impossible to make, since it is not until it has been made that I can regard myself as qualified to make it.

It should be noted that this difficulty never arises at a time when I am actually faced with a problem to be solved. In such a case I work on the data, but everything leads me to believe that I need not take into account the *I* who is at work—it is a factor which is presupposed and nothing more.

Here, on the contrary, what I would call the ontological status of the investigator assumes a decisive importance. Yet so long as I am concerned with thought itself I seem to follow an endless regression. But by the very fact of recognising it as endless I transcend it in a certain way: I see that this process takes place within an affirmation of being—an affirmation which I *am* rather than an affirmation which I *utter:* by uttering it I break it, I divide it, I am on the point of betraying it.

It might be said, by way of an approximation, that my inquiry into being presupposes an affirmation in regard to which I am, in a sense, passive, *and of which I am the stage rather than the subject.* But this is only at the extreme limit of thought, a limit which I cannot reach without falling into contradiction. I am therefore led to assume or to recognise a form of participation which has the reality of a subject; this participation cannot be, by definition, an *object* of thought; it cannot serve as a solution—it appears beyond the realm of problems: it is meta-problematical.

Conversely, it will be seen that, if the meta-problematical can be asserted at all, it must be conceived as transcending the opposition between the subject who asserts the existence of being, on the one hand, and being *as asserted by that subject,* on the other, and as underlying it in a given sense. To postulate the meta-problematical is to postulate the primacy of being over knowledge (not of being as *asserted,* but of being as *asserting itself*); it is to recognise that knowledge is, as it were, environed by being, that it is interior to it in a certain sense—a sense perhaps analogous to that which Paul Claudel tried to define in his *Art Poètique*. From this standpoint, contrary to what epistemology seeks vainly to establish, there exists well and truly a mystery of cognition; knowledge is contingent on a participation in being for which no epistemology can account because it continually presupposes it.

At this point we can begin to define the distinction between mystery and problem. A mystery is a problem which encroaches upon its own data, invading them, as it were, and thereby transcending itself as a simple problem. A set of examples will help us to grasp the content of this definition.

It is evident that there exists a mystery of the union of the body and the soul. The indivisible unity always inadequately expressed by such phrases as *I have a body, I make use of my body, I feel my body,* etc., can be neither analysed nor reconstituted out of precedent elements. It is not only data, I would say that it is the basis of data, in the sense of being my own presence to myself, a presence of which the act of self-consciousness is, in the last analysis, only an inadequate symbol.

It will be seen at once that there is no hope of establishing an exact frontier between problem and mystery. For in reflecting on a mystery we tend inevitably to degrade it to the level of a problem. This is particularly clear in the case of the problem of evil.

In reflecting upon evil, I tend, almost inevitably, to regard it as a disorder which I view from outside and of which I seek to discover the causes or the secret aims. Why is it that the 'mechanism' functions so defectively? Or is the defect merely apparent and due to a real defect of my vision? In this case the defect is in myself, yet it remains objective in relation to my thought, which discovers it and observes it. But evil which is only stated or observed is no longer evil which is suffered: in fact, it ceases to be evil. In reality, I can only grasp it as evil in the measure in which it *touches* me—that is to say, in the measure in which I am *involved,* as one is involved in a law-suit. Being 'involved' is the fundamental fact; I cannot leave it out of account except by an unjustifiable fiction, for in doing so, I proceed as though I were God, and a God who is an onlooker at that.

This brings out how the distinction between what is *in me* and what is only *before me* can break down. This distinction falls under the blow of a certain kind of thought: thought at one remove.

But it is, of course, in love that the obliteration of this frontier can best be seen. It might perhaps even be shown that the domain of the meta-problematical coincides with that of love, and that love is the only starting point for the understanding of such mysteries as that of body and soul, which, in some manner, is its expression.

Actually, it is inevitable that, in being brought to bear on love, thought which has not thought itself—unreflected reflection—should tend to dissolve its meta-problematical character and interpret it in terms of abstract concepts, such as the will to live, the will to power, the *libido,* etc. On the other hand, since the domain of the problematical is that of the objectively valid, it will be extremely difficult—if not impossible—to refute these interpretations without changing to a new ground: a ground on which, to tell the truth, they lose their meaning. Yet I have the assurance, the certainty—and it envelops me like a protective cloak—that for as much as I really love I must not be concerned with these attempts at devaluation.

It will be asked: What is the criterion of true love? It must be answered that there is no criteriology except in the order of the objective and the problematical; but we can already see at a distance the eminent ontological value to be assigned to fidelity.

Let us take another illustration, more immediate and more particular, which may shed some light on the distinction between problem and mystery.

Say that I have made an encounter which has left a deep and lasting trace on all my life. It may happen to anyone to experience the deep spiritual significance of such a meeting—yet this is something which philosophers have commonly ignored or disdained, doubtless because it effects only the particular person as person—it cannot be universalised, it does not concern rational being in general.

It is clear that such a meeting raises, if you will, a problem; but it is equally clear that the solution of this problem will always fall short of the only question that matters. Suppose that I am told, for instance: 'The reason you have met this person in this place is that you both like the same kind of scenery, or that you both need the same kind of treatment for your health'—the explanation means nothing. Crowds of people who apparently share my tastes were in the Engadine or in Florence at the time I was there; and there are always numbers of patients suffering from the same disease as myself at the health resort I frequent. But neither this supposed identity of tastes nor this common affliction has brought us together in any real sense; it has nothing to do with that intimate and unique affinity with which we are dealing. At the same time, it would be transgression of this valid reasoning to treat this affinity as if it were itself the cause and to say: 'It is precisely this which has determined our meeting.'

Hence I am in the presence of a mystery. That is to say, of a reality rooted in what is beyond the domain of the problematical properly so called. Shall we avoid the difficulty by saying that it was after all nothing but a coincidence, a lucky chance? But the whole of me immediately protests against this empty formula, this vain negation of what I apprehend with the deepest of my being. Once again we are brought back to our first definition of a mystery as a problem which encroaches upon its own data: I who inquire into the meaning and the possibility of this meeting, I cannot place myself outside it or before it; I am engaged in this encounter, I depend upon it, I am inside it in a certain sense, it envelops me and it comprehends me—even if it is not comprehended by me. Thus it is only by a kind of betrayal or denial that I can say: 'After all, it might not have happened, I would still have been what I was, and what I am to-day.' Nor must it be said: I have been changed by it as by an outward cause. No, it has developed me from within, it has acted in me as an inward principle.

But this is very difficult to grasp without distortion. I shall be inevitably tempted to react against this sense of the inwardness of the encounter, tempted by my probity itself, by what from a certain standpoint I must judge to be the best—or at least the safest—of myself.

There is a danger that these explanations may strengthen in the minds of my readers a preliminary objection which must be stated at once.

It will be said: The meta-problematical of which you speak is after all a content of thought; how then should we not ask ourselves what is its mode of existence? What assures us of its existence at all? Is it not itself problematical in the highest degree?

My answer is categorical: To think, or, rather, to assert, the meta-problematical is to assert it as indubitably real, as a thing of which I cannot doubt without falling into contradiction. We are in a sphere where it is no longer possible to dissociate the idea itself from the certainty or the degree of certainty which pertains to it. Because this idea *is* certainty, it *is* the assurance of itself; it is, in this sense, something other and something more than an idea. As for the term *content of thought* which figured in the objection, it is deceptive in the highest degree. For content is, when all is said and done, derived from experience; whereas it is only by a way of liberation and detachment from experience that we can possibly rise to the level of the meta-problematical and of mystery. This liberation must be *real;* this detachment must be *real;* they must not be an abstraction, that is to say a fiction recognised as such.

And this at last brings us to recollection, for it is in recollection and in this alone that this detachment is accomplished. I am convinced, for my part, that no ontology—that is to say, no apprehension of ontological mystery in whatever degree—is possible except to a being who is capable of recollecting himself, and of thus proving that he is not a living creature pure and simple, a creature, that is to say, which is at the mercy of its life and without a hold upon it.

It should be noted that recollection, which has received little enough attention from pure philosophers, is very difficult to define—if only because it transcends the dualism of being and action or, more correctly, because it reconciles in itself these two aspects of the antinomy. The word means what it says—the act whereby I re-collect myself as a unity; but this hold, this grasp upon myself, is also relaxation and abandon. *Abandon to . . . relaxation in the presence of . . .*—yet there is no noun for these prepositions to govern. The way stops at the threshold.

Here, as in every other sphere, problems will be raised, and it is the psychologist who will raise them. All that must be noted is that the psychologist is no more in a position to shed light on the metaphysical bearing of recollection than on the noetic value of knowledge.

It is within recollection that I take up my position—or, rather, I become capable of taking up my position—in regard to my life; I withdraw from it in a certain way, but not as the pure subject of cognition; *in this withdrawal I carry with me that which I am and which perhaps my life is not.* This brings out the gap between my being and my life. I am not my life; and if I can judge my life—a fact I cannot deny without falling into a radical scepticism which is nothing other than despair—it is only on condition that I encounter myself within recollection beyond all possible judgment and, I would add, beyond all representation. Recollection is doubtless what is least spectacular in the soul; it does not consist in looking at something, it is an inward hold, an inward reflection, and it might be asked in passing whether it should not be seen as the ontological basis of memory—that principle of effective and non-representational unity on which the possibility of remembrance rests. The double meaning of 'recollection' in English is revealing.

It may be asked: is not recollection identical with that dialectical moment of the turning to oneself (*retour sur soi*) or else with the *fuer sich sein* which is the central theme of German Idealism?

I do not think so. To withdraw into oneself is not to be for oneself nor to mirror oneself in the intelligible unity of subject and object. On the contrary. I would say that here we come up against the paradox of that actual mystery whereby the I into which I withdraw ceases, for as much, to belong to itself. 'You are not your own'—this great saying of St. Paul assumes in this connection its full concrete and ontological significance; it is the nearest approach to the reality for which we are groping. It will be asked: is not this reality an object of intuition? Is not that which you term 'recollection' the same as what others have termed 'intuition'?

But this again seems to me to call for the utmost prudence. If intuition can be mentioned in this content at all, it is not an intuition which is, or can be, given as such.

The more an intuition is central and basic in the being whom it illuminates, the less it is capable of turning back and apprehending itself.

Moreover, if we reflect on what an intuitive knowledge of being could possibly be, we see that it could never figure in a collection, a procession of simple experiences or *Erlebnisse,* which all have this characteristic that they can be at times absorbed and at others isolated and, as it were, uncovered. Hence, any effort to remember such an intuition, to represent it to oneself, is inevitably fruitless. From this point of view, to be told of an intuitive knowledge of being is like being invited to play on a soundless piano. Such an intuition cannot be brought out into the light of day, for the simple reason that we do not possess it.

We are here at the most difficult point of our whole discussion. Rather than to speak of intuition in this context, we should say that we are dealing with an assurance which underlies the entire development of thought, even of discursive thought; it can therefore be approached only by a second reflection—a reflection whereby I ask myself how and from what starting point I was able to proceed in my initial reflection, which itself postulated the ontological, but without knowing it. This second reflection is recollection in the measure in which recollection can be self-conscious.

It is indeed annoying to have to use such abstract language in a matter which is not one of dialectics *ad usum philosophorum,* but of what is the most vital and, I would add, the most dramatic moment in the rhythm of consciousness seeking to be conscious of itself.

It is this dramatic aspect which must now be brought out.

Let us recall what we said earlier on: that the ontological need, the need of being, can deny itself. In a different context we said that being and life do not coincide; my life, and by reflection all life, may appear to me as for ever inadequate to something which I carry within me, which in a sense I am, but which reality rejects and excludes. Despair is possible in any form, at any moment and to any degree, and this betrayal may seem to be counselled, if not forced upon us, by the very structure of the world we live in. The deathly aspect of this world may, from a given standpoint, be regarded as a ceaseless incitement to denial and to suicide. It could even be said in this sense that the fact that suicide is always possible is the essential starting point of any genuine metaphysical thought.

It may be surprising to find in the course of this calm and abstract reasoning such verbal star turns—words so emotionally charged—as 'suicide' and 'betrayal.' They are not a concession to sensationalism. I am convinced that it is in drama and through drama that metaphysical thought grasps and defines itself *in concreto*. Two years ago, in a lecture on the 'Problem of Christian Philosophy' which he delivered at Louvain, M. Jacques Maritain said: 'There is nothing easier for a philosophy than to become tragic, it has only to let itself go to its human weight.' The allusion was doubtless to the speculation of a Heidegger. I believe, on the contrary, that the natural trend of philosophy leads it into a sphere where it seems that tragedy has simply vanished—evaporated at the touch of abstract thought. This is borne out by the work of many contemporary Idealists. Because they ignore the person, offering it up to I know not what ideal truth, to what principle of pure inwardness, they are unable to grasp those tragic factors of human existence to which I have alluded above; they banish them, together with illness and everything akin to it, to I know not what disreputable suburb of thought outside the ken of any philosopher worthy of the name. But, as I have stressed earlier on, this attitude is intimately bound up with the rejection of the ontological need; indeed, it is the same thing.

If I have stressed despair, betrayal and suicide, it is because these are the most manifest expressions of the will to negation as applied to being.

Let us take despair. I have in mind the act by which one despairs of reality as a whole, as one might despair of a person. This appears to be the result, or the immediate translation into other terms, of a kind of balance sheet. Inasmuch as I am able to evaluate the world of reality (and, when all is said and done, what I am unable to evaluate is for me as if it were not) I can find nothing in it that withstands that process of dissolution at the heart of things which I have discovered and traced. I believe that at the root of despair there is always this affirmation: 'There is nothing in the realm of reality to which I can give credit—no security, no guarantee.' It is a statement of complete insolvency.

As against this, hope is what implies credit. Contrary to what was thought by Spinoza, who seems to me to have confused two quite distinct notions, fear is correlated to desire and not to hope, whereas what is negatively correlated to hope is the act which consists in putting things at their worst—an act which is strikingly illustrated by what is known as defeatism, and which is ever in danger of being degraded into the desire of the worst. Hope consists in asserting that there is at the heart of being, beyond all data, beyond all inventories and all calculations, a mysterious principle which is in connivance with me, which cannot but will that which I will, if what I will deserves to be willed and is, in fact, willed by the whole of my being.

We have now come to the centre of what I have called the ontological mystery, and the simplest illustrations will be the best. To hope against all hope that a person whom I love will recover from a disease which is said to be incurable is to say: It is impossible that I should be alone in willing this cure; it is impossible that reality in its inward depth should be hostile or so much as indifferent to what I assert is in itself a good. It is quite useless to tell me of discouraging *cases* or *examples:* beyond all experience, all probability, all statistics, I assert that a given order shall be re-established, that reality *is* on my side in willing it to be so. I do not wish: I assert; such is the prophetic tone of true hope.

No doubt I shall be told: 'In the immense majority of cases this is an illusion.' But it is of the essence of hope to exclude the consideration of cases; moreover, it can be shown that there exists an ascending dialectic of hope, whereby hope rises to a plane which transcends the level of all possible empirical disproof—the plane of salvation as opposed to that of success in whatever form.

It remains true, nevertheless, that the correlation of hope and despair subsists until the end; they seem to me inseparable. I mean that while the structure of the world we live in permits—and may even seem to counsel—absolute despair, yet it is only such a world that can give rise to an unconquerable hope. If only for this reason, we cannot be sufficiently thankful to the great pessimists in the history of thought; they have carried through an inward experience which needed to be made and of which the radical possibility no apologetics should disguise; they have prepared our minds to understand that despair can be what it was for Nietzsche (though on an infra-ontological level and in a domain fraught with mortal dangers) the springboard to the loftiest affirmation.

At the same time, it remains certain that, for as much as hope is a mystery, its mystery can be ignored or converted into a problem. Hope is then regarded as a desire which wraps itself up in illusory judgments to distort an objective reality which it is interested in disguising from itself. What happens in this case is what we have already observed in connection with encounter and with love; it is because mystery can—and, in a sense, logically must—be degraded into a problem that an interpretation such as that of Spinoza, with all the confusion it implies, had to be put forward sooner or later. It is important and must be stressed that this attitude has nothing against it so long as our standpoint is on the hither-side of the realm of the ontological. Just as long as my attitude towards reality is that of someone who is not involved in it, but who judges it his duty to draw up its minutes as exactly as possible (and this is by definition the attitude of the scientist), I am justified in maintaining in regard to it a sort of principle of mistrust, which in theory is unlimited in its application; such is the legitimate standpoint of the workman in the laboratory, who must in no way prejudge the result of his analysis, and who can all the better envisage *the worst,* because at this level the very notion of worst is empty of meaning. But an investigation of this sort, which is just like that of an accountant going through the books, takes place on the hither-side of the order of mystery, an order in which the problem encroaches upon its own data.

It would indeed be a profound illusion to believe that I can still maintain this same attitude when I undertake an inquiry, say, into the value of life; it would be a paralogism to suppose that I can pursue such an inquiry as though my own life were not at issue.

Hence, between hope—the reality of hope in the heart of the one whom it inhabits—and the judgment brought to bear upon it by a mind chained to objectivity there exists the same barrier as that which separates a pure mystery from a pure problem.

This brings us to a nodal point of our subject, where certain intimate connections can be traced.

The world of the problematical is the world of fear and desire, which are inseparable; at the same time, it is that world of the functional—

or of what can be functionalised—which was defined at the beginning of this essay; finally, it is the kingdom of technics of whatever sort. Every technique serves, or can be made to serve, some desire or some fear; conversely, every desire as every fear tends to invent its appropriate technique. From this standpoint, despair consists in the recognition of the ultimate inefficacy of all technics, joined to the inability or the refusal to change over to a new ground—a ground where all technics are seen to be incompatible with the fundamental nature of being, which itself escapes our grasp (in so far as our grasp is limited to the world of objects and to this alone). It is for this reason that we seem nowadays to have entered upon the very era of despair; we have not ceased to believe in technics, that is to envisage reality as a complex of problems; yet at the same time the failure of technics *as a whole* is as discernible to us as its *partial* triumphs. To the question: what can man achieve? we continue to reply: He can achieve as much as his technics; yet we are obliged to admit that these technics are unable *to save man himself,* and even that they are apt to conclude the most sinister alliance with the enemy he bears within him.

I have said that man is *at the mercy of his technics.* This must be understood to mean that he is increasingly incapable of controlling his technics, or rather of *controlling his own control.* This control of his own control, which is nothing else than the expression on the plane of active life of what I have called thought at one remove, cannot find its centre or its support anywhere except in recollection.

It will be objected that even those whose faith in technics is strongest are bound to admit that there exist enormous realms which are outside man's control. But what matters is the spirit in which this admission is made. We have to recognise that we have no control over meteorological conditions, but the question is: do we consider it desirable and just that we should have such control? The more the sense of the ontological tends to disappear, the more unlimited become the claims of the mind which has lost it to a kind of cosmic governance, because it is less and less capable of examining its own credentials to the exercise of such dominion.

It must be added that the more the disproportion grows between the claims of the technical intelligence on the one hand, and the persisting fragility and precariousness of what remains its material substratum on the other, the more acute becomes the constant danger of despair which threatens this intelligence. From this standpoint there is truly an intimate dialectical correlation between the optimism of technical progress and the philosophy of despair which seems inevitably to emerge from it—it is needless to insist on the examples offered by the world of to-day.

It will perhaps be said: This optimism of technical progress is animated by great hope. How is hope in this sense to be reconciled with the ontological interpretation of hope?

I believe it must be answered that, *speaking metaphysically, the only genuine hope is hope in what does not depend on ourselves,* hope springing from humility and not from pride. This brings us to the consideration of another aspect of the mystery—a mystery which, in the last analysis, is one and unique—on which I am endeavouring to throw some light.

The metaphysical problem of pride—*hubris*—which was perceived by the Greeks and which has been one of the essential themes of Christian theology, seems to me to have been almost completely ignored by modern philosophers other than theologians. It has become a domain reserved for the moralist. Yet from my own standpoint it is an essential—if not the vital—question. It is sufficient to recall Spinoza's definition of *superbia* in his *Ethics* (III, def. XXVIII) to see how far he was from grasping the problem: 'Pride is an exaggeratedly good opinion of ourselves which arises from self-love.' In reality, this is a definition of vanity. As for pride, it consists in drawing one's strength solely from oneself. The proud man is cut off from a certain form of communion with his fellow men, which pride, acting as a principle of destruction, tends to break down. Indeed, this destructiveness can be equally well directed against the self; pride is in no way incompatible with self-hate; this is what Spinoza does not seem to have perceived.

An important objection may be raised at the point we have now reached.

It will perhaps be said: Is not that which you are justifying ontologically in reality a kind of moral quietism which is satisfied by passive acceptance, resignation and inert hope? But what, then, becomes of man as man, as active being? Are we to condemn action itself inasmuch as it implies a self-confidence which is akin to pride? Can it be that action itself is a kind of degradation?

This objection implies a series of misunderstandings.

To begin with, the idea of inert hope seems to me a contradiction in terms. Hope is not a kind of listless waiting; it underpins action or it runs before it, but it becomes degraded and lost once the action is spent. Hope seems to me, as it were, the prolongation into the unknown of an activity which is central—that is to say, rooted in being. Hence it has affinities, not with desire, but with the will. The will implies the same refusal to calculate possibilities, or at any rate it suspends this calculation. Could not hope therefore be defined as the will when it is made to bear on what does not depend on itself?

The experimental proof of this connection is that it is the most active saints who carry hope to its highest degree; this would be inconceivable if hope were simply an inactive state of the soul. The mistake so often made here comes from a stoical representation of the will as a stiffening of the soul, whereas it is on the contrary relaxation and creation.

The term 'creation', which occurs here for the first time, is, nevertheless, decisive. Where there is creation there can be no degradation, and to the extent that technics are creative, or imply creativity, they are not degrading in any way. Degradation begins at the point where creativeness falls into self-imitation and self-hypnotism, stiffening and falling back on itself. This may, indeed, bring out the origin of the confusion which I denounced in the context of recollection.

Great is the temptation to confuse two distinct movements of the soul, whose opposition is blurred by the use of spacial metaphors. The stiffening, the contraction, the falling back on the self which are inseparable from pride, and which are indeed its symbol, must not be confused with the humble withdrawal which befits recollection and whereby I renew my contact with the ontological basis of my being.

There is every reason to think that such withdrawal in recollection is a presupposition of aesthetic creativity itself. Artistic creation, like scientific research, excludes the act of self-centring and self-hypnotism which is, ontologically speaking, pure negation.

It may perhaps seem that my thesis comes so near to that of Bergson as to coincide with it, but I do not think that this is the case. The terms almost invariably used by Bergson suggest that for him the essential character of creativity lay in its inventiveness, in its spontaneous innovation. But I wonder if by limiting our attention to this aspect of creation we do not lose sight of its ultimate significance, which is its deep-rootedness in being. It is at this point that I would bring in the notion of *creative fidelity;* it is a notion which is the more difficult to grasp and, above all, to define conceptually, because of its underlying and unfathomable paradox, and because it is at the very centre of the realm of the meta-problematical.

It is important to note that the idea of fidelity seems difficult to maintain in the context of Bergsonian metaphysics, because it will tend to be interpreted as a routine, as an observance in the pejorative sense of the word, as an arbitrary safeguard *against* the power of renewal which is the spirit itself.

I am inclined to think that there is something in this neglect of the values of fidelity which deeply vitiates the notion of static religion as it is put forward in *Les Deux Sources de la Morale et de la Religion.* It may perhaps be useful to devote some thought to creative fidelity in order to elucidate this point.

Faithfulness is, in reality, the exact opposite of inert conformism. It is the active recognition of something permanent, not formally, after the manner of a law, but ontologically; in this sense, it refers invariably to a presence, or to something which can be maintained within us and before us as a presence, but which, *ipso facto,* can be just as well ignored, forgotten and obliterated; and this reminds us of that menace of betrayal which, to my mind, overshadows our whole world.

It may perhaps be objected that we commonly speak of fidelity to a principle. But it remains to be seen if this is not an arbitrary transposition of the notion of fidelity. A principle, in so far as it is a mere abstract affirmation, can make no demands upon me because it owes the whole of its reality to the act whereby I sanction it or proclaim it. Fidelity to a principle as a principle is idolatry in the etymological sense of the word; it might be a sacred duty for me to deny a principle from which life has withdrawn and which I know that I no longer accept, for by continuing to conform my actions to it, it is myself—myself as presence—that I betray.

So little is fidelity akin to the inertia of conformism that it implies an active and continuous struggle against the forces of interior dissipation, as also against the sclerosis of habit. I may be told: This is nevertheless no more than a sort of active conservation which is the opposite of creation. We must, I think, go much further into the nature of fidelity and of presence before we can reply to this point.

If presence were merely an *idea* in us whose characteristic was that it was nothing more than itself, then indeed the most we could hope would be to maintain this idea in us or before us, as one keeps a photograph on a mantelpiece or in a cupboard. But it is of the nature of presence as presence to be uncircumscribed; and this takes us once again beyond the frontier of the problematical. Presence is mystery in the exact measure in which it is presence. Now fidelity is the active perpetuation of presence, the renewal of its benefits—of its virtue which consists in a mysterious incitement to create. Here again we may be helped by the consideration of aesthetic creativeness; for if artistic creation is conceivable, it can only be on condition that the world is present to the artist in a certain way—present to his heart and to his mind, present to his very being.

Thus if creative fidelity is conceivable, it is because fidelity is ontological in its principle, because it prolongs presence which itself corresponds to a certain kind of hold which being has upon us; because it multiplies and deepens the effect of this presence almost unfathomably in our lives. This seems to me to have almost inexhaustible consequences, if only for the relationships between the living and the dead.

I must insist once again: A presence to which we are faithful is not at all the same thing as the carefully preserved effigy of an object which has vanished; an effigy is, when all is said and done, nothing but a likeness; metaphysically it is *less* than the object, it is a diminution of the object. Whereas presence, on the contrary, is *more* than the object, it exceeds the object on every side. We are here at the opening of a vista at whose term death will appear as the *test of presence.* This is an essential point and we must consider it carefully.

It will no doubt be said: What a strange way of defining death! Death *is* a phenomenon definable in biological terms; it *is not* a test.

It must be answered: It is what it signifies and, moreover, what it signifies to a being who rises to the highest spiritual level to which it is possible for us to attain. It is evident that if I read in the newspaper of the death of Mr. So-and-so, who is for me nothing but a name, this event *is* for me nothing more than the subject of an announcement. But it is quite another thing in the case of a being who has been granted to me as a presence. In this case, everything depends on me, on my inward attitude of maintaining this presence which could be debased into an effigy.

It will be objected: This is nothing more than a description in recondite and unnecessarily metaphysical terms of a common psychological fact. It is evident that it depends upon us in a certain measure to enable the dead to survive in our memory, but this existence is no more than subjective.

I believe that the truth is altogether different and infinitely more mysterious. In saying, 'It depends upon us that the dead should live on in our memory', we are still thinking of the idea in terms of a diminution or an effigy. We admit that the object has disappeared, but that there remains a likeness which it is in our power to keep, as a daily woman 'keeps' a flat or a set of furniture. It is all too evident that this manner of keeping can have no ontological value whatsoever. But it is altogether different in the case where fidelity is creative in the sense which I have tried to define. A presence is a reality; it is a kind of influx; it depends upon us to be permeable to this influx, but not, to tell the truth, to call it forth. Creative fidelity consists in maintaining ourselves actively in a permeable state; and there is a mysterious interchange between this free act and the gift granted in response to it.

An objection which is the converse of the preceding one may be expected at this point. I will be told: 'All right. You have now ceased to decorate a psychological platitude with metaphysical ornaments, but only to make a gratuitous assertion which is unproved and which is beyond all possible experimental proof; this was inevitable as soon as you replaced the ambiguous and neutral term "presence" by the much more compromising term "influx".'

To reply to this objection, we must refer again to what I have already said of mystery and of recollection. Indeed, it is only on the metaproblematical level that the notion of influx can possibly be accepted. If it were taken in its objective sense, as an accretion of strength, we would indeed be faced with a thesis, not of metaphysics, but of physics, which would be open to every possible objection. When I say that a being is granted to me as a presence or as a being (it comes to the same, for he is not a being for me unless he is a presence), this means that I am unable to treat him as if he were merely placed in front of me; between him and me there arises a relationship which, in a sense, surpasses my awareness of him; he is not only before me, he is also within me—or, rather, these categories are transcended, they have no longer any meaning. The word influx conveys, though in a manner which is far too physical and spacial, the kind of interior accretion, of accretion from within, which comes into being as soon as presence is effective. Great and almost invincible is the temptation to think that such effective presence can be only that of an object; but if we believed this we would fall back to the level of the problematical and remain on the hither-side of mystery; and against this belief fidelity raises up its voice: 'Even if I cannot see you, if I cannot touch you, I feel that you are with me; it would be a denial of you not to be assured of this.' *With* me: note the metaphysical value of this word, so rarely recognised by philosophers, which corresponds neither to a relationship of inherence or immanence nor to a relationship of exteriority. It is of the essence of genuine *coesse*—I must use the Latin word—that is to say, of genuine intimacy, to lend itself to the decomposition to which it is subjected by critical thought; but we already know that there exists another kind of thought, a thought which bears upon that thought itself, and is related to a bottled up yet efficacious underlying intuition, of which it suffers the attraction.

It must be added (and this brings us to the verge of another sphere) that the value of such intimacy, particularly in regard to the relation between the living and the dead, will be the higher and the more assured the more this intimacy is grounded in the realm of total spiritual availability (*disponibilité*)—that is to say, of pure charity; and I shall note in passing that an ascending dialectic of creative fidelity corresponds to the dialectic of hope to which I have already referred.

The notion of availability is no less important for our subject than that of presence, with which it is bound up.

It is an undeniable fact, though it is hard to describe in intelligible terms, that there are some people who reveal themselves as 'present'—that is to say, at our disposal—when we are in pain or in need to confide in someone, while there are other people who do not give us this feeling, however great is their goodwill. It should be noted at once that the distinction between presence and absence is not at all the same as that between attention and distraction. The most attentive and the most conscientious listener may give me the impression of not being present; he gives me nothing, he cannot make room for me in himself, whatever the material favours which he is prepared to grant me. The truth is that there is a way of listening which is a way of giving, and another way of listening which is a way of refusing, of refusing *oneself;* the material gift, the visible action, do not necessarily witness to presence. We must not speak of proof in this connection; the word would be out of place. Presence is something which reveals itself immediately and unmistakably in a look, a smile, an intonation or a handshake.

It will perhaps make it clearer if I say that the person who is at my disposal is the one who is capable of being with me with the whole of himself when I am in need; while the one who is not at my disposal seems merely to offer me a temporary loan raised on his resources.

For the one I am a presence; for the other I am an object. Presence involves a reciprocity which is excluded from any relation of subject to object or of subject to subject-object. A concrete analysis of unavailability (*indisponibilité*) is no less necessary for our purpose than that of betrayal, denial or despair.

Unavailability is invariably rooted in some measure of alienation. Say, for instance, that I am told of some misfortune with which I am asked to sympathise: I understand what I am told; I admit in theory that the sufferers deserve my sympathy; I see that it is a case where it would be logical and just for me to respond with sympathy; I even offer my sympathy, but only with my mind; because, when all is said and done, I am obliged to admit that I feel absolutely nothing. Indeed, I am sorry that this should be so; the contradiction between the indifference which I feel in fact and the sympathy which I know I ought to feel is humiliating and annoying; it diminishes me in my own eyes. But it is no use; what remains in me is the rather embarrassing awareness that, after all, these are people I do not know—if one had to be touched by every human misfortune life would not be possible, it would indeed be too short. The moment I think: After all, this is only a case, No. 75,627, it is no good, I can feel nothing.

But the characteristic of the soul which is present and at the disposal of others is that it cannot think in terms of *cases;* in its eyes there are *no cases at all.*

And yet it is clear that the normal development of a human being implies an increasingly precise and, as it were, automatic division between what concerns him and what does not, between things for which he is responsible and those for which he is not. Each one of us becomes the centre of a sort of mental space arranged in concentric zones of decreasing interest and participation. It is as though each one of us secreted a kind of shell which gradually hardened and imprisoned him; and this sclerosis is bound up with the hardening of the categories in accordance with which we conceive and evaluate the world.

Fortunately, it can happen to anyone to make an encounter which breaks down the framework of this egocentric topography; I know by my own experience how, from a stranger met by chance, there may come an irresistible appeal which overturns the habitual perspectives just as a gust of wind might tumble down the panels of a stage set—what had seemed near becomes infinitely remote and what had seemed distant seems to be close. Such cracks are repaired almost at once. But it is an experience which leaves us with a bitter taste, an impression of sadness and almost of anguish; yet I think it is beneficial, for it shows us as in a flash all that is contingent and—yes—artificial in the crystallised pattern of our personal system.

But it is, above all, the sanctity realised in certain beings which reveals to us that what we call the normal order is, from a higher point of view, from the standpoint of a soul rooted in ontological mystery, merely the subversion of an order which is its opposite. In this connection, the study of sanctity with all its concrete attributes seems to me to offer an immense speculative value; indeed, I am not far from saying that it is the true introduction to ontology.

Once again a comparison with the soul which is not at the disposal of others will throw light on our subject.

To be incapable of presence is to be in some manner not only occupied but encumbered with one's own self. I have said in some manner; the immediate object of the preoccupation may be one of any number; I may be preoccupied with my health, my fortune, or even with *my inward perfection.* This shows that to be occupied with oneself is not so much to be occupied with *a particular object* as to be occupied in *a particular manner.* It must be noted that the contrary of this state is not a state of emptiness or indifference. The real contrast is rather between the being who is opaque and the being who is transparent. But this inward opacity remains to be analysed. I believe that it consists in a kind of obduracy or fixation; and I wonder if, by generalising and adapting certain psychoanalytical data, we would not find that it is the fixation in a given zone or in a given key of a certain disquiet which, in itself, is something quite different. But what is remarkable is that the disquiet persists within this fixation and gives it that character of constriction which I mentioned in connection wth the degradation of the will. There is every reason to believe that this indefinite disquiet should be identified with the anguish of temporality and with that aspiration of man not towards, but *by* death, which is at the heart of pessimism.

Pessimism is rooted in the same soil as the inability to be at the disposal of others. If the latter grows in us as we grow old, it is only too often because, as we draw near to what we regard as the term of our life, anxiety grows in us almost to the point of choking us; to protect itself, it sets up an increasingly heavy, exacting and, I would add, vulnerable mechanism of self-defence. The capacity to hope diminishes in proportion as the soul becomes increasingly chained to its experience and to the categories which arise from it, and as it is given over more completely and more desperately to the world of the problematical.

Here at last can be brought together the various motifs and thematic elements which I have had to bring out one by one. In contrast to the captive soul we have described, the soul which is at the disposal of others is consecrated and inwardly dedicated; it is protected against suicide and despair, which are interrelated and alike, because it knows that it is not its own, and that the most legitimate use it can make of its freedom is precisely to recognise that it does not belong to itself; this recognition is the starting point of its activity and creativeness.

The difficulties of a philosophy of this sort must not be disguised. It is inevitably faced by a disquietening alternative: Either it will try to solve these difficulties—to give all the answers; in that case it will fall into the excesses of a dogmatism which ignores its vital principles and, I would add, into those of a sacrilegious theodicy, or else it will allow these difficulties to subsist, labelling them as mysteries.

Between these two I believe that there exists a middle way—a narrow, difficult and dangerous path which I have tried to discover. But, like Karl Jaspers in his *Philosophy of Existence,* I can only proceed in this kind of country by calling out to other travellers. If, as it occasionally happened, certain minds respond—not the generality, but this being and that other—then there is a way. But, as I believe Plato perceived with incomparable clarity, it is a way which is undiscoverable except through love, to which alone it is visible, and this brings us to what is perhaps the deepest characteristic of that realm of the metaproblematical of which I have tried to explore certain regions.

A serious objection remains to be mentioned. It will perhaps be said: All that you have said implies an unformulated reference to the data of Christianity and can only be understood in the light of these data. Thus we understand what you mean by presence if we think of the Eucharist and what you mean by creative fidelity if we think of the Church. But what can be the value of such a philosophy for those who are a-Christian—for those who ignore Christianity or who do not accept it? I would answer: it is quite possible that the existence of the fundamental Christian data may be necessary *in fact* to enable the mind to conceive some of the notions which I have attempted to analyse; but these notions cannot be said to depend on the data of Christianity, and *they do not presuppose it.* On the other hand, should I be told that the intellect must leave out of account anything which is not a universal data of thinking as such, I would say that this claim is exaggerated and in the last analysis, illusory. Now, as at any other time, the philosopher is placed in a given historical situation from which he is most unlikely to abstract himself completely; he would deceive himself if he thought that he could create a complete void both within and around himself. Now this historical situation implies as one of its essential data the existence of the Christian fact—quite independently of whether the Christian religion is accepted and its fundamental assertions are regarded as true or false. What appears to me evident is that we cannot reason to-day as though there were not behind us centuries of Christianity, just as, in the domain of the theory of knowledge, we cannot pretend that there have not been centuries of positive science. But neither the existence of Christianity nor that of positive science plays in this connection more than the role of a fertilising principle. It favours the development of certain ideas which we might not have conceived without it. This development may take place in what I would call para-Christian zones; for myself, I have experienced it more than twenty years before I had the remotest thought of becoming a Catholic.

Speaking more particularly to Catholics, I should like to note that from my own standpoint the distinction between the natural and the supernatural must be rigorously maintained. It will perhaps be objected that there is a danger that the word 'mystery' might confuse this very issue.

I would reply that there is no question of confusing those mysteries which are enveloped in human experience as such with those mysteries which are revealed, such as the Incarnation or Redemption, and to which no effort of thought bearing on experience can enable us to attain.

It will be asked: why then do you use the same word for two such distinct notions? But I would point out that no revelation is, after all, conceivable unless it is addressed to a being who is *involved—committed*—in the sense which I have tried to define—that is to say, to a being who participates in a reality which is non-problematical and which provides him with his foundation as subject. Supernatural life *must,* when all is said and done, find a hold in the natural—which is not to say that it is the flowering of the natural. On the contrary it seems to me that any study of the notion of *created Nature,* which is fundamental for the Christian, leads to the conclusion that there is in the depth of Nature, as of reason which is governed by it, a fundamental principle of inadequacy to itself which is, as it were, a restless anticipation of a different order.

To sum up my position on this difficult and important point, I would say that the recognition of the ontological mystery, in which I perceive as it were the central redoubt of metaphysics, is, no doubt, only possible through a sort of radiation which proceeds from revelation itself and which is perfectly well able to affect souls who are strangers to all positive religion of whatever kind; that this recognition, which takes place through certain higher modes of human experience, in no way involves the adherence to any given religion; but it enables those who have attained to it to perceive the possibility of a revelation in a way which is not open to those who have never ventured beyond the frontiers of the realm of the problematical and who have therefore never reached the point from which the mystery of being can be seen and recognised. Thus, a philosophy of this sort is carried by an irresistible movement towards the light which it perceives from afar and of which it suffers the secret attraction.

Jean-Paul Sartre

MATERIALISM AND REVOLUTION[1] *

The revolutionary myth

Young people of today are uneasy. They no longer recognize their right to be young. It is as though youth were not an age of life, but a class phenomenon, an unduly prolonged childhood, a spell of irresponsibility accorded to the children of the well-to-do. The workers go without transition from adolescence to manhood. And it really does look as though our age, which is in the process of eliminating the various European bourgeoisies, is also eliminating that abstract and metaphysical period of which people have always said, "It will have its fling." Most of my former students have married early because they felt ashamed of their youth and of the leisure that was once the fashion.

They have become fathers before they have finished their studies. They still receive money from their families at the end of each month, but it is not enough. They have to give lessons or do translations or odd jobs. They are part-time workers. In one way, they are like kept women and, in another, like "home-workers". They no longer take the time, as we did at their age, to play about with ideas before adopting one set in particular. They are fathers and citizens, they vote, they must

[1] From: *Literary and Philosophical Essays,* Jean-Paul Sartre, Ch. 13. Copyright 1955 by Criterion Books, Inc., and Rider and Co., London. By permission of the publishers.

* As I have been unfairly reproached with not quoting Marx in this article, I should like to point out that my criticisms are not directed against him, but against the Marxist scholasticism of 1949. Or, if you prefer, against Marx *through* Neo-Stalinist Marxism.

commit themselves. This is probably not a bad thing. It is fitting, after all, that they be asked to choose immediately for or against man, for or against the masses. But if they choose the first side, their difficulties begin, because they are persuaded that they must strip themselves of their subjectivity. If they consider doing this, it is for reasons which remain subjective, as they are still inside. They take counsel with *themselves* before plunging *themselves* into the water and, as a result, the more seriously they contemplate abandoning subjectivity, the greater the importance it assumes in their eyes. And they realize, with annoyance, that their notion of objectivity is still subjective. Thus they go round and round, unable to choose sides, and if they do come to a decision, they jump in with their eyes shut, out of weariness or impatience.

However, that is not the end of it. They are now told to choose between materialism and idealism; they are told that there is nothing in between and that it must be one or the other. Now, to most of them, the principles of materialism seem philosophically false; they are unable to understand how matter could give rise to the *idea* of matter. Nevertheless, they protest that they utterly reject idealism. They know that it acts as a myth for the propertied classes and that it is not a rigorous philosophy but a rather vague kind of thinking whose function is to mask reality or to absorb it into the idea. "It doesn't matter," they are told. "Since you are not materialists, you will be idealists in spite of yourselves, and if you rebel against the quibbling of the professors, you will find yourselves the victims of a more subtle and all the more dangerous illusion."

Thus, they are hounded even in their thoughts, which are poisoned at the source, and they are condemned to serve unwillingly a philosophy they detest or to adopt out of discipline a doctrine in which they are unable to believe. They have lost the carefree quality characteristic of their age without acquiring the certainty of maturity. They are no longer at leisure and yet they cannot commit themselves. They remain at the threshold of communism without daring either to enter or to go away. They are not guilty; it is not their fault if the very people who at present invoke the dialectic wish to force them to choose between two opposites and reject, with the contemptuous name of "Third Party", the synthesis which embraces them. Since they are deeply sincere and hope for the coming of a socialist regime, since they are prepared to serve the Revolution with all their might, the only way to help them is to ask oneself, as they do, whether materialism and the myth of objectivity are really required by the cause of the Revolution and if there is not a discrepancy between the revolutionary's action and his ideology. I shall therefore turn back to materialism and attempt to re-examine it.

It seems as though its first step is to deny the existence of God and transcendent finality; the second, to reduce the action of mind to that of matter; the third, to eliminate subjectivity by reducing the world, and man in it, to a system of objects linked together by universal relationships. I conclude in all good faith that it is a metaphysical doctrine and that materialists are metaphysicians. But they immediately stop me. I am wrong. There is nothing they loathe so much as metaphysics; it is not even certain that philosophy finds a favour in their eyes. Dialectical materialism is, according to M. Naville, "the expression of a progressive discovery of the world's interactions, a discovery which is in no way passive but which implies the activity of the discoverer, seeker and struggler". According to M. Garaudy, dialectical materialism's first step is to deny the existence of any legitimate knowledge apart from scientific knowledge. And for Madame Angrand, one cannot be a materialist without first rejecting all *a priori* speculation.

This invective against metaphysics is an old acquaintance. It goes back to the writings of the positivists of the last century. But the positivists, who were more logical, refused to take a stand as to the existence of God because they considered all possible conjecture on the subject to be unverifiable, and they abandoned, once and for all, all speculation on the relation between body and mind because they thought that we could not know anything about it. It is indeed obvious that the atheism of M. Naville or Madame Angrand is not "the expression of a progressive discovery". It is a clear and *a priori* stand on a problem which infinitely transcends our experience. This is also my own stand, but I did not consider myself to be any the less a metaphysician in refusing existence to God than Leibnitz was in granting it to Him. And by what miracle is the materialist, who accuses idealists of indulging in metaphysics when they reduce matter to mind, absolved from the same charge when he reduces mind to matter? Experience does not decide in favour of his doctrine—nor, for that matter, does it decide in favour of the opposing one either. Experience is confined to displaying the close connection between the physiological and the psychological, and this connection is subject to a thousand different kinds of interpretation. When the materialist claims to be *certain* of his principles, his assurance can come only from intuition or *a priori* reasoning, that is, from the very speculation he condemns. I now realize that materialism is a metaphysics hiding behind positivism; but it is a self-destructive metaphysics, for by undermining metaphysics out of principle, it deprives its own statements of any foundation.

It thereby also destroys the positivism under which it takes cover. It was out of modesty that Comte's disciples reduced human knowledge to mere scientific knowledge alone. They confined reason within the narrow limits of our experience because it was there only that reason proved to be effective. The success of science was for them a fact, but it was a *human* fact. From the point of view of man, and for man, it is true that science succeeds. They took good care not to ask themselves whether the universe *in itself* supported and guaranteed scientific rationalism, for the very good reason that they would have had to depart from themselves and from mankind in order to compare the universe as it *is* with the picture of it we get from science, and to assume God's point of view on man and the world. The materialist, however, is not so shy. He leaves behind him science and subjectivity and the human and substitutes himself for God, Whom he denies, in order to contemplate the spectacle of the universe. He calmly writes, "The materialist conception of the world means simply the conception of nature as it is, without anything foreign added." [2]

What is involved in this surprising text is the elimination of human subjectivity, that "addition foreign to nature". The materialist thinks that by denying his subjectivity he has made it disappear. But the trick is easy to expose. *In order* to eliminate subjectivity, the materialist declares that he is an *object,* that is, the subject matter of science. But once he has eliminated subjectivity in favour of the object, instead of seeing himself as a thing among other things, buffeted about by the physical universe, he makes of himself an *objective beholder* and claims to contemplate nature as it is, in the absolute.

There is a play on the word objectivity, which sometimes means the passive quality of the object beheld and, at other times, the absolute value of a beholder stripped of subjective weaknesses. Thus, having transcended all subjectivity and identified himself with pure objective truth, the materialist travels about in a world of objects inhabited by human objects. And when he returns from his journey, he communicates what he has seen: "Everything that is rational is real," he tells us, and "everything that is real is rational." Where does he get this rationalistic optimism? We can understand a Kantian's making statements about nature since, according to him, reason constitutes experience. But the materialist does not admit that the world is the product of our constituent activity. Quite the contrary. In his eyes it is we who are the product of the universe. How then could we know that the real is rational, since we have not created it and since we reflect only a tiny part of it from day to day? The success of science may, at the most, lead us to think that this rationality is *probable,* but it may be a matter of a local, statistical rationality. It may be valid for a certain order of size and might collapse beyond or under this limit.

Materialism makes a certainty of what appears to us to be a rash induction, or, if you prefer, a postulate. For materialism, there is no doubt. Reason is within man and outside man. And the leading materialist magazine calmly calls itself *"Thought* (*La Pensée*), the organ of modern rationalism". However, by a dialectical reversal which might have been foreseen, materialist rationalism "passes" into irrationalism and destroys itself. If the psychological fact is rigorously conditioned by the biological, and the biological fact is, in turn, conditioned by the

[2] Marx and Engels; *Complete Works;* Ludwig Fuerbach, Volume XIV, p. 651, Russian edition. I quote this passage in order to show the use made of it *today.* I plan to show elsewhere that Marx had a much deeper and richer conception of objectivity.

physical state of the world, I quite see how the human mind can express the universe as an effect can express its cause, but not in the way a thought expresses its object. How could a captive reason, governed from without and manoeuvred by a series of blind causes, still be reason? How could I believe in the principles of my deductions if it were only the external event which has set them down within me and if, as Hegel says, "reason is a bone"? What stroke of chance enables the raw products of circumstances to constitute the keys to Nature as well? Moreover, observe the way in which Lenin speaks of our consciousness: "It is only the reflection of being, in the best of cases an approximately exact reflection." But who is to decide whether the present case, that is, materialism, is "the best of cases"? We would have to be within and without at the same time in order to make a comparison. And as there is no possibility of that, according to the very terms of our statement, we have no criterion for the reflection's validity, except internal and subjective criteria: its conformity with other reflections, its clarity, its distinctness and its permanence. Idealistic criteria, in short. Moreover, they determine only a truth *for man,* and this truth not being constructed like those offered by the Kantians, but experienced, will never be more than a faith without foundation, a mere matter of habit.

When materialism dogmatically asserts that the universe produces thought, it immediately passes into idealist scepticism. It lays down the inalienable rights of Reason with one hand and takes them away with the other. It destroys positivism with a dogmatic rationalism. It destroys both of them with the metaphysical affirmation that man is a material object, and it destroys this affirmation by the radical negation of all metaphysics. It sets science against metaphysics and, unknowingly, metaphysics against science. All that remains is ruins. Therefore, can I be a materialist?

It may be objected that I have understood nothing of the matter, that I have confused the naïve materialism of Helvetius and Holbach with *dialectical* materialism. There is, I am told, a dialectical movement within nature whereby opposites which clash are suddenly surmounted and reunited in a new synthesis; and this new product "passes" in turn into its opposite and then blends with it in another synthesis. I immediately recognize the characteristic movement of the Hegelian dialectic, which is based entirely on the dynamism of Ideas. I recall how, in Hegel's philosophy, one Idea leads to another, how every Idea produces its opposite. I know that the impulse behind this immense movement is the attraction exerted by the future on the present, and by the whole, even when it does not exist, on its parts. This is as true of the partial syntheses as of the absolute Totality which finally becomes Mind.

The principle of this Dialectic is, thus, that a whole governs its parts, that an idea tends of itself to complete and to enrich itself, that the forward movement of consciousness is not linear, like that which proceeds from cause to effect, but synthetic and multi-dimensional, since every idea retains within itself and assimilates to itself the totality of antecedent ideas, that the structure of the concept is not the simple juxtaposition of invariable elements which might, if necessary, combine with other elements to produce other combinations, but rather an organization whose unity is such that its secondary structures cannot be considered apart from the whole without becoming "abstract" and losing their essential character.

One can readily accept this dialectic in the realm of ideas. Ideas are naturally synthetic. It appears, however, that Hegel has inverted it and that it is, in reality, characteristic of matter. And if you ask what *kind* of matter, you will be told that there is only one kind and that it is the matter of which scientists talk. Now the fact is that matter is characterized by its inertia. This means that it is incapable of producing anything by itself. It is a vehicle of movements and of energy, and it always receives these movements and this energy from without. It borrows them and relinquishes them. The mainspring of all dialectics is the idea of totality. In it, phenomena are never isolated appearances. When they occur together, it is always within the high unity of a whole, and they are bound together by inner relationships, that is, the presence of one modifies the other in its inner nature. But the universe of science is quantitative, and quantity is the very opposite of the dialectical unit. A sum is a unit only in appearance. Actually, the elements which compose it maintain only relations of contiguity and simultaneity; they are there together, and that is all. A numerical unit is in no way influenced by the co-presence of another unit; it remains inert and separated within the number it helps to form. And this state of things is indeed necessary in order for us to be able to count; for were two phenomena to occur in intimate union and modify one another reciprocally, we should be unable to decide whether we were dealing with two separate terms or with only one. Thus, as scientific matter represents, in a way, the realization of quantity, science is, by reason of its inmost concerns, its principles and its methods, the opposite of dialectics.

When science speaks of forces that are applied to a point of matter, its first concern is to assert their independence; each one acts as though it were alone. When science studies the attraction exerted by bodies upon one another, it is careful to define the attraction as a strictly external relationship, that is to reduce it to modifications in the direction and speed of their movements. Science does occasionally employ the word "synthesis", for example, in regard to chemical combinations. But it never does so in the Hegelian sense; the particles forming a combination retain their properties. If an atom of oxygen combines with atoms of sulphur and hydrogen to form water, it retains its identity. Neither water nor acid is a real whole which changes and governs its composing elements, but simply a passive resultant, a *state*. The entire effort of biology is aimed at reducing the so-called living syntheses to physico-chemical processes. And when M. Naville, who is a materialist, feels the need to construct a scientific psychology, he turns to "behaviourism" which regards human conduct as a sum of conditioned reflexes. Nowhere in the universe of science do we encounter an organic totality. The instrument of the scientist is analysis. His aim is to reduce the complex to the simple, and the recomposition which he afterwards effects is only a counterproof, whereas the dialectician, on principle, considers these complexes as irreducible.

Of course Engels claims that "the natural sciences . . . have proved that, in the last analysis, Nature proceeds dialectically, that it does not move in an eternally identical circle that perpetually repeats itself, but that it has a real history". In support of his thesis, he cites the example of Darwin: "Darwin inflicted a severe blow to the metaphysical conception of Nature by demonstrating that the entire organic world . . . is the product of a process of development that has been going on for millions of years." [3] But, first of all, it is obvious that the notion of *natural history* is absurd. History cannot be characterized by change nor by the pure and simple action of the past. It is defined by the deliberate resumption of the past by the present; only human history is possible. Besides, if Darwin has shown that the species derive from one another, his attempt at explanation is of a mechanical and not dialectical order. He accounts for individual differences by the theory of small variations, and he regards each of these variations as the result not of a "process of development", but of mechanical chance. In a group of individuals of the same species, it is statistically impossible that there not be some who are superior in weight, strength or some particular detail. As to the struggle for existence, it cannot *produce* a new synthesis through the fusion of opposites; it has strictly negative effects, since it *eliminates* definitively the weaker elements. In order to understand it, all we need do is compare its results with the really dialectical ideal of the class struggle. In the latter case, the proletariat will absorb the bourgeoisie within the unity of a classless society. In the struggle for existence, the strong simply cause the weak to disappear. Finally, the chance advantage *does not develop:* it remains inert and is transmitted unchanged by heredity; it is a *state,* and it is not this state which will be modified by an inner dynamism to produce a higher degree of organization. Another chance variation will simply be joined to it from without, and the process of elimination will recur mechanically. Are we to conclude that Engels is irresponsible or dishonest? In order to prove that Nature has a history, he uses a scientific hypothesis that is explicitly meant to reduce all natural history to mechanical series.

Is Engels more responsible when speaking of physics? "In physics," he tells us, "every change is a transition from quantity to quality, from the quantity of movement—of any form whatever—inherent in the body or communicated to the body. Thus, the temperature of water in

[3] Engels.

the liquid state is, at first, unimportant, but if you increase or diminish the temperature of the water, there comes a moment when its state of cohesion is modified and the water is transformed, in one case into vapour and in another into ice." But he is tricking us; it is all done with mirrors. The fact is that scientific investigation is not in the least concerned with demonstrating the transition from quantity to quality; it starts from the perceptible quality, which is regarded as an illusory and subjective appearance, in order to find behind it the quantity which is regarded as the truth of the universe. Engels naïvely regards temperature as if it were, as a matter of *primary* data, a pure quantity. But actually it appears first as a quality; it is the state of discomfort or of contentment which causes us to button up our coats or else to take them off. The scientist has reduced this perceptible quality to a quantity in agreeing to substitute the measurement of cubic expansions of a liquid for the vague information of our senses. The transformation of water into steam is for him an equally quantitative phenomenon or, if you prefer, it exists for him only as quantity. He defines steam in terms of pressure or of some kinetic theory which reduces it to a certain quantitative state (position, speed) of its molecules. We must therefore choose. Either we remain within the domain of perceptible quality, in which case steam is a quality and so is temperature; we are not being scientific; we witness the action of one quality on another. Or else we regard temperature as a quantity. But then the transition from the liquid to the gaseous state is scientifically defined as a quantitative change, that is, by a measurable pressure exerted on a piston or by measurable relationships among molecules. For the scientist, quantity gives rise to quantity; laws are quantitative formulas and science possesses no symbol for the expression of quality as such. What Engels claims to present as a scientific procedure is the pure and simple movement of his mind which passes from the universe of science to that of naïve realism and back again to the scientific world and the world of pure sensation. And besides, even if we were to allow him this, does this intellectual coming-and-going in the least resemble a dialectical process? Where does he see a progression? Let us concede that the change of temperature, regarded as quantitative, produces a qualitative transformation of water; water is changed into vapour. What then? It will exert a pressure on an escape-valve and raise it; it will shoot up into the air, grow cold and become water again. Where is the progression? I see a cycle. To be sure, the water is no longer contained in the recipient, but is outside, on the grass and the earth, in the form of dew. But in the name of what metaphysics can this change of place be regarded as a progress? [4]

[4] Let no one hope to get out of the difficulty at this point by talking of intensive quantities. Bergson long ago demonstrated the confusion and error of this myth of intensive quantity which was the undoing of the psychophysicists. Temperature, as we feel it, is a quality. It is not warmer today than it was yesterday, but

It will perhaps be objected that certain modern theories—like that of Einstein—are synthetic. We know that in his system there are no longer any isolated elements; each reality is defined in relation to the universe. There is considerable matter for discussion here. I shall confine myself to observing that there is no question of a synthesis, for the relations which can be established among the various structures of a synthesis are *internal* and *qualitative,* whereas the relations which, in Einstein's theory, enable us to define a position or a mass remain *quantitative* and *external.* Moreover, the question lies elsewhere. Whether the scientist be Newton, Archimedes, Laplace or Einstein, he studies not the concrete totality, but the general and abstract conditions of the universe. Not the *particular* event which catches and absorbs into itself light, heat and life and which we call the "glistening of the sun through leaves on a summer's day", but light in general, heat phenomena, the general conditions of life. There is never any question of examining *this particular* refraction through *this particular* piece of glass which has its history and which, from a certain point of view, is regarded as the concrete synthesis of the universe, but the conditions of possibility of refraction *in general.* Science is made up of *concepts,* in the Hegelian sense of the term. Dialectics, on the other hand, is essentially the play of notions. We know that for Hegel the notion organizes and fuses concepts together in the organic and living unity of concrete reality. The Earth, the Renaissance, Colonization in the eighteenth Century, Nazism, are objects of *notions;* being, light and energy are abstract concepts. Dialectical enrichment lies in the transition from the abstract to the concrete, that is, from elementary concepts to notions of greater and greater richness. The movement of the dialectic is thus the reverse of that of science.

"It is true," a Communist intellectual admitted to me, "that science and dialectics pull in opposite directions. But that is because science expresses the bourgeois point of view, which is an analytical one. Our dialectic is, on the other hand, the very thought of the proletariat." That is all very well—even though Soviet science does not seem to differ much in its methods from that of the bourgeois countries—but why, in that case, do the Communists borrow arguments and proofs from science in order to support their materialism? I agree that the basic spirit of science is materialist. But on the other hand it is presented to us as being analytic and bourgeois. The positions are thereby reversed, and I distinctly see two classes struggling. One, the bourgeoisie, is materialist; its method of thinking is analysis, and its ideology is science. The

---

warm in a different way. And, conversely, the *degree,* measured according to cubic expansion is a pure and simple quantity, to which there remains attached, in the mind of the layman, a vague idea of perceptible quality. And modern physics, far from retaining this ambiguous notion, reduces heat to certain atomic *movements.* What becomes of intensity? And what are the intensities of a sound or a light, if not mathematical relationships?

other, the proletariat, is idealist; its method of thinking is synthesis, and its ideology is dialectic. And as there is a struggle between the classes, the ideologies should be incompatible. But this is not the case. It seems that the dialectic is the crown of science and makes full use of its results. It seems that the bourgeoisie, availing itself of analysis and then reducing the higher to the lower, is idealist, whereas the proletariat—which thinks synthetically and is guided by the revolutionary idea—even when affirming the irreducibility of a synthesis to its elements, is materialist. What are we to make of this?

Let us come back to science which, whether bourgeois or not, has at least proved itself. We know what science teaches us about matter. A material object is animated from without, is conditioned by the total state of the world, is subject to forces which always come from elsewhere, is composed of elements that unite, though without interpenetrating, and that remain foreign to it. It is exterior to itself. Its most obvious properties are statistical; they are merely the resultant of the movements of the molecules composing it. Nature, as Hegel so profoundly remarked, is externality. How are we to find room in this externality for the dialectic, which is a movement of absolute interiorization? Is it not obvious that, according to the very idea of synthesis, life cannot be reduced to matter and human consciousness cannot be reduced to life? There is the same discrepancy between modern science, which is the object of materialist love and faith, and the dialectic which the materialists claim to be their instrument and method, as we observed earlier between their positivism and their metaphysics; the one destroys the other. Thus, they will sometimes tell you, and with the same imperturbability, that life is only a complex chain of physicochemical phenomena and, at other times, that it is an irreducible moment in the dialectic of nature. Or rather, they dishonestly try to think both ways at the same time.

One feels throughout their confused discourse that they have invented the slippery and contradictory notion of reducible irreducibles. M. Garaudy is satisfied with this. But when we hear him speak, we are struck with his wavering; at one moment he affirms, in the abstract, that mechanical determinism has had its day and that it must be replaced by the dialectic and, at another, when he tries to explain a concrete situation, he reverts to causal relationships, which are linear and presuppose the absolute externality of the cause in relation to its effect. It is this notion of *cause,* perhaps, which best indicates the great intellectual confusion into which the materialists have fallen. When I challenged M. Naville to define within the framework of the dialectic this famous causality which he is so fond of employing, he seemed troubled and remained silent. How well I understand him! I would even say that the idea of cause remains suspended between scientific relationships and dialectical syntheses. Since materialism is, as we have seen, an *explanatory* metaphysics (it tries to *explain* certain social phenomena in terms of others, the psychological in terms of the biological, the biological in terms of physico-chemical laws), it employs on principle the scheme of causality.

But as materialism sees in science the explanation of the universe, it turns to science and observes with surprise that the causal link is not scientific. Where is the cause in Joule's law or Mariotte's law or in Archimedes' principle or in Carnot's? Science generally establishes functional relationships between phenomena and selects the independent variable that suits its purpose. It is, moreover, strictly impossible to express the qualitative relationship of causality in mathematical language. Most physical laws simply take the form of functions of the type $y = f(x)$. Some set up numerical constants, and others give us phases of irreversible phenomena, but without our being able to tell whether one of these phases is a *cause* of the following one. (Can one say that nuclear dissolution in mitosis is a *cause* of the segmentation of the protoplasmic filament?) Thus, materialist causality remains suspended in air. The reason is that its origin lies in the metaphysical intention of reducing mind to matter and explaining the psychological by the physical. Disappointed because science offers *too little* to bolster his causal explanations, the materialist reverts to the dialectic. But the dialectic contains *too much;* the causal link is linear and the cause remains external to its effect. In addition, the effect never contains more than the cause; if it did, this residue would, according to the perspectives of causal explanation, remain unexplained. Dialectical progress is, on the contrary, cumulative; at each new stage, it turns back to the ensemble of positions transcended and embraces them all. And the transition from one state to another is always a process of enrichment. The synthesis always contains *more* than the united thesis and antithesis. Thus, the materialist cause can neither draw its support from science nor hang on to dialectic; it remains a vulgar and practical notion, the sign of materialism's constant effort to bend one towards the other and to join by force two mutually exclusive methods; it is the very type of the false synthesis and the use of it is dishonest.

This is nowhere more evident than in the Marxists' efforts to study "superstructures". For them, these are, in a sense, the "reflections" of the mode of production. "If," writes Stalin, "under a regime of slavery we encounter certain ideas and social theories, certain opinions and political institutions, while under feudalism we find others, and under Capitalism still others, this is not to be explained by 'nature' or by the 'properties' of ideas, theories, opinions and political institutions themselves, but by the different conditions of the material life of society at different periods of social development. The state of society and the conditions of its material existence are what determine its ideas, theories, political opinions and political institutions." [5]

[5] Stalin, *Dialectical Materialism and Historical Materialism.*

The use of the term "reflection" and the verb "determine", as well as the general tone of this passage are sufficiently revealing. We are on deterministic ground; the superstructure is completely supported and conditioned by the social situation of which it is the reflection; the relationship of the mode of production to the political institution is that of cause to effect. Thus, we have the case of the simple-minded thinker who regarded Spinoza's philosophy as a direct reflection of the Dutch wheat trade. But at the same time, for the very purposes of Marxist propaganda, ideologies must be, to a certain extent, self-sufficient and be able to act in turn upon the social situation that conditions them. That means, in short, a certain autonomy in relation to the substructures. As a result, the Marxists fall back on the dialectic and make of the superstructure a synthesis that does, to be sure, proceed from conditions of production and of material existence, but whose nature and laws of development have a real "independence". In the same pamphlet, Stalin writes, "New social ideas and theories arise only when the development of the material existence of society confronts society with new tasks. . . . If new social theories and ideas arise, they do so because they are necessary to society, because without their organizing, mobilizing and transforming action, the solution of urgent problems entailed by the development of the material existence of society is *impossible.*"[6]

In this text, as is apparent, necessity has assumed a completely different aspect; an idea arises because it is necessary to the carrying out of a new task. This means that the task, even before it is carried out, *calls forth* the idea which "will facilitate" its being carried out. The idea is postulated and worked by a vacuum which it then fills. The word "evoked" is actually the one which Stalin uses a few lines later. This action of the future, this necessity which is one with finality, this organizing, mobilizing and transforming power of the idea very clearly leads us back to the terrain of the Hegelian dialectic. But how can I believe in both of Stalin's affirmations at once? Is the idea "determined by the state of society" or "evoked by the new tasks to be carried out"? Am I to think, as he does, that "society's mental life is a reflection of objective reality, a *reflection of* being", that is a derived and borrowed reality which has no *being* of its own, something analogous to the "lecta" of the Stoics? Or, on the contrary, am I to declare, with Lenin, that "ideas become living realities when they live in the consciousness of the masses"? Which am I to accept, a causal and linear relationship implying the inertia of the effect, of the reflection, or a dialectical and synthetic relationship which would imply that the last synthesis turns back to the partial syntheses which have produced it in order to embrace them and absorb them into itself, and, consequently, that the mental life, although proceeding from the material conditions of society, turns back

[6] My italics.—J.-P.S.

to them and completely absorbs them? The materialists are unable to decide: they waver between one and the other. They assert abstractly the existence of dialectic progression, but their concrete studies are limited, for the most part, to Taine's explanations in terms of environmental determinism and the historical moment.[7]

That is not all. What exactly is this concept of *matter* that the dialecticians employ? If they borrow it from science, the poorer concept will fuse with other concepts in order to arrive at a concrete notion, the richer one. This notion will finally include within it, as one of its structures, the concept of matter, but far from being explained by it, the contrary will occur: the notion will explain the concept. In this case, one can start with matter as the emptier of the abstractions. One can also start from Being, as Hegel does. The difference is not very great, though the Hegelian point of departure, being more abstract, is the happier choice. But if we must really *invert* the Hegelian dialectic and "stand it on its feet again" it must be admitted that matter, chosen as a point of departure for the dialectical movement, does not appear to the Marxists to be the poorer concept, but the richer notion. It is identified with the whole universe; it is the unity of all phenomena; life, thoughts and individuals are merely its modes. It is, in short, the great Spinozist totality.

But if this be the case and if Marxist matter be the exact counterpart of Hegelian spirit, we arrive at the following paradoxical result: that Marxism, in order to stand the dialectic on its feet again, has set the richer notion at the point of departure. And certainly for Hegel the spirit exists from the start, but as a virtuality, as a summons; the dialectic is one with its history. For the Marxists, on the other hand, it is all of matter, as act, that is given in the first place, and the dialectic, whether applied to the history of species or to the evolution of human societies, is merely the retracing of the partial development of one of the modes of this reality. But then if the dialectic is not the very generating of the world, if it is not an act of progressive enriching, it is nothing at all. In obligingly dismissing the dialectic, Marxism has given it its death-blow. "Save me from my friends," one thinks. You may wonder how this could have passed unnoticed. Because our materialists have dishonestly constructed a slippery and contradictory concept of "matter". At times it is the poorest of abstractions and at others the richest of concrete totalities, depending on their needs. They jump from one to the other and mask one with the other. And when they are finally cornered and can no longer escape, they declare that materialism is a method, an intellectual orientation. If you pushed them a bit further, they would say it is a style of living. They are not far wrong in this, and I, for my part, certainly regard it as one of the forms of the conventional mentality and of flight from one's own self.

[7] Only they define the environment more precisely in terms of the material conditions of existence.

But if materialism is a *human attitude,* with all the subjective, contradictory and emotional aspects involved in such an attitude, it ought not to be presented as a rigorous philosophy, as the doctrine of objectivity. I have witnessed conversions to materialism; one enters into materialism as into a religion. I should define it as the subjectivity of those who are ashamed of their subjectivity. It is, of course, also the irritation of those who suffer physically and who are familiar with the reality of hunger, illness, manual work and everything that can sap a man's strength. It is, in a word, a doctrine of the first impulse. Now, the first impulse is perfectly legitimate, particularly when it expresses the spontaneous reaction of an oppressed person—but that does not mean that it is the correct impulse. It always contains an element of truth, but goes beyond it. To affirm the crushing reality of the material world in opposition to idealism is not necessarily to be a materialist. We will return to this.

Furthermore, how did the dialectic retain its necessity in its fall from heaven to earth? Hegelian consciousness has no need to set up the dialectical *hypothesis:* it is not a pure, objective witness observing the generating of ideas from without; it is itself dialectical; it is self-generating in accordance with the laws of synthetic progression. There is no need for it to *assume* necessity in relationships; it *is* this necessity; it experiences this necessity. And its certainty does not come from some evidence that is more or less open to criticism, but from the progressive identification of the dialectic of consciousness with the consciousness of the dialectic. If, on the other hand, the dialectic represents the way in which the material world develops, if consciousness, far from wholly identifying itself with the whole dialectic, is but a "reflection of being", a partial product, a moment of synthetic progress, if, instead of taking part in its own generation from within, it is invaded from the outside by feelings and ideologies which have their roots elsewhere and if it is influenced by them without producing them, it is merely a link in a chain whose beginning and end are very far apart. And what can it say with *certainty* about the chain, unless it be the whole chain? The dialectic deposits a few effects in it and pursues its way.

On considering these effects, one may conclude that they bear witness to the probable existence of a synthetic mode of progression. Or else one may form conjectures on the consideration of exterior phenomena. In any case, one must be content with regarding the dialectic as a working hypothesis, as a method to be tried, a method which is justified if proved successful. How is it that the materialists regard this method of research as a structure of the universe and that some of them declare that "the reciprocal relationships and conditioning of phenomena, established by the dialectical method, constitute the necessary laws of matter in motion" [8] since the natural sciences proceed in a spirit

[8] Stalin, *Ibid.,* p. 13.

contrary to this and use rigorously opposite methods, since the science of history is only in its primary stages? It is obviously because in transferring the dialectic from one world to the other they did not want to forgo the advantages it had enjoyed in the first world. They retained its necessity and certainty, while removing the means they had of checking them. They wished, thus, to give matter the mode of synthetic development which belongs only to the idea and they borrowed from the reflection of the idea in itself a kind of certainty which has no place in the world's experience. But matter itself thereby becomes an idea; it nominally retains its denseness, inertia and exteriority, but it presents, in addition, a perfect translucency—since one can decide, with complete certainty and on principle, about its internal processes—it is a synthesis, it progresses through constant enrichment.

Let us make no mistake; there is no simultaneous transcendence of materialism and idealism here;[9] denseness and transparency, exteriority and interiority, inertia and synthetic progression are simply juxtaposed in the spurious unity of "dialectical materialism". Matter has remained that which is revealed to us by science. There has been no combination of opposites, for lack of a new concept which might establish them within itself, something which is not exactly matter nor exactly idea. Their opposition cannot be surmounted by surreptitiously attributing the qualities of one of these opposites to the other. Actually, it must be admitted that materialism, in claiming to be dialectical, slides into idealism.

Just as the Marxists claim to be positivists and destroy their positivism through the use they implicitly make of metaphysics, just as they proclaim their rationalism and destroy it by their conception of the origin of thought, so, at the very moment they posit it, they deny their basic principle, materialism, by a furtive recourse to idealism.[10]

[9] Although Marx sometimes claimed there was. In 1844 he wrote that the antinomy between idealism and materialism would have to be transcended, and Henri Lefebvre, commenting on his thinking, states in *Matérialisme Dialectique* (pp. 53, 54), "Historical materialism, which is clearly expressed in *Deutsche Ideologie,* attains the unity of idealism and materialism foreshadowed and announced in the Manuscripts of 1844." But then why does M. Garaudy, another spokesman for Marxism, write in *Les Lettres Francaises,* "Sartre rejects materialism and claims, nevertheless, to avoid idealism. That is where the futility of that impossible 'third party' reveals itself . . ." How confused these people are!

[10] It may be objected that I have not spoken of the common source of all transformations in the universe, which is energy, and that I have taken up my position on the ground of mechanism in order to appraise dynamic materialism. My reply is that energy is not a directly perceived reality, but a concept fashioned in order to account for certain phenomena, that scientists are familiar with it through its effects rather than through its nature, and that at the most they know, as Poincaré said, that "something remains". Besides, the little we can state about energy is in rigorous opposition to the demands of dialectical materialism. Its total quantity is conserved, it is transmitted in discrete quantities, it undergoes a constant reduction. This last principle, in particular, is incompatible with the demands of a dialectic which claims to be enriched with each step. And let us not forget, more-

This confusion is reflected in the materialist's attitude towards his own doctrine; he claims to be *certain* of his principles, but he asserts more than he is able to prove. "The materialist *grants* . . .", says Stalin. But why does he grant it? Why grant that God does not exist, that mind is a reflection of matter, that the world's development proceeds through the conflict of opposite forces, that there is an objective truth, that there are no unknowable things in the world, but only things that are still unknown? We are not told why. But if it is true that "new ideas and social theories called forth by the new tasks imposed by the development of society's material existence spring up, become the heritage of the masses which they mobilize and organize against society's decadent forces, thus promoting the overthrowing of these forces which hinder the development of society's material existence", it seems clear that these ideas are adopted by the proletariat because they account for its present situation and needs, because they are the most efficient instrument in its struggle against the bourgeoisie. "The failure of the Utopians, including the populists, anarchists, and revolutionary socialists, can be explained, among other ways," says Stalin in the forementioned work, "by the fact that they do not recognize the major role of material conditions in the development of society. Fallen into idealism, they base their practical activity, not on the needs of the development of material existence in society, but independently and in defiance of these needs, on 'ideal levels' and 'universal projects' detached from the real life of society.

"The strength and vitality of Marxism-Leninism lies in the fact that it bases its practical activity on precisely those needs of the development of the material existence of society without ever detaching itself from the real life of society." Though materialism may be the best instrument for action, its truth is of a pragmatic kind. It is true for the working class, because it is good for it, and since social progress is to be brought about by the working class, it is truer than idealism, which served the interests of the bourgeoisie for a while when it was a rising class, and which today can only obstruct the development of the material existence of society. But when the proletariat will finally have absorbed the bourgeoisie and brought about the classless society, new tasks will make their appearance, tasks which will "give rise to" new ideas and social theories.

Materialism will have had its day, since it is the mode of thought of the working class and the working class will no longer exist. Regarded objectively as an expression of class needs and tasks, material-

over, that a body always receives its energy from without (even intra-atomic energy is so received); it is within the framework of the general principle of inertia that we are able to study the problem of equivalence of energy. To make energy the vehicle of the dialectic would be to transform it by violence into *idea*.

ism becomes an *opinion,* that is, a mobilizing, transforming and organizing force whose objective reality is measured in terms of its power of action. And this opinion which claims to be certitude carries within it its own destruction, for it is obliged, in the very name of its principles, to regard itself as an objective fact, as a reflection of being, as an object of science, and, at the same time, it destroys the science which should analyse and establish it—at least as an opinion. The circle is obvious, and the whole system remains suspended in air, perpetually floating between being and nothingness.

The Stalinist extricates himself through faith. If he "grants" materialism, it is because he wants to act and to change the world. When one is engaged in so vast an enterprise, one hasn't the time to be too particular about the choice of principles justifying it. He believes in Marx, Lenin and Stalin, he admits of the principle of authority, and, finally, he retains the blind and tranquil faith in the certitude of Marxism. This conviction will influence his general attitude towards all ideas proposed to him. Scrutinize closely one of his doctrines or one of his concrete assertions and he will say that he has no time to waste, that the situation is urgent, that he has to act, to attend to first things first and to work for the revolution. Later on we will have the leisure to challenge principles —or rather they will challenge themselves. But for the moment, we have to reject all argument, because it is liable to have a weakening effect. That is quite all right, but when it's his turn to attack and to criticize bourgeois thinking or a particular intellectual position that he judges to be reactionary, he then claims to possess the truth.

The same principles which he just told you could not be disputed at the time suddenly became patent facts. They pass from the level of useful opinions to that of truths. "The Trotskyists," you say to him, "are wrong, but they are not, as you claim, police informers. You *know perfectly well* they are not." "On the contrary," he will reply, "I know perfectly well that they are. What they really think is a matter of indifference to me. Subjectivity does not exist. But *objectively* they play into the hands of the bourgeoisie. They *behave* like provocateurs and informers, because playing into the hands of the police and deliberately assisting it come to the same thing." You reply that it does not come to the same thing, and that in all *objectivity,* the behaviour of the Trotskyist and that of the policeman are not alike. He retorts that one is as harmful as the other and that the effect of both is to hinder the advancement of the working class. And if you insist, if you demonstrate to him that there are several ways of hindering this advancement and that they are not equivalent, even in their results, he replies proudly that these distinctions, even if true, do not interest him. We are in a period of struggle; the situation is simple and the positions clearly defined. Why be over-subtle? The militant Communist must not encumber himself with so many nuances. So we are back to the useful. Thus, the proposition, "the Trotskyist is an informer," wavers perpetually between the state of useful opinion and that of objective truth.[11]

Nothing demonstrates this ambiguity in the Marxist notion of truth better than the ambivalence of the Communist attitude towards the scientist. The Communists claim to derive from him; they exploit his discoveries and make his thinking the only kind of valid knowledge. But their mistrust of him remains guarded. In so far as they lean on the rigorously scientific idea of *objectivity,* they have need of his critical spirit, his love of research and challenging, his lucidity, which rejects the principle of authority and refers constantly to experience or rational proof. But in so far as they are believers and science challenges all beliefs, they are suspicious of these virtues. If the scientist brings his scientific qualifications with him into the Party, if he claims the right to examine principles, he becomes an "intellectual"; his dangerous freedom of thought which is an expression of his relative material independence, is countered by the faith of the militant worker who, because of his very situation, *needs* to believe in his leaders' orders.[12]

This, then, is the materialism they want me to choose, a monster, an elusive Proteus, a large, vague, contradictory semblance. I am asked to choose, this very day, in all intellectual freedom, in all lucidity, and that which I am to choose freely and lucidly and with all my wits about me is a doctrine that destroys thought. I know that man has no salvation other than the liberation of the working class; I know this *before* being a materialist and from a plain inspection of the facts. I know that our intellectual interest lies with the proletariat. Is that a reason for me to demand of my thinking, which has led me to this point, that it destroy itself? Is that a reason for me to force it henceforth to abandon its criteria, to think in contradictions, to be torn between incompatible theses, to lose even the clear consciousness of itself, to launch forth blindly in a giddy flight that leads to faith? "Fall to thy knees and thou shalt believe," says Pascal. The materialist's effort is very closely akin to this.

Now, if it were only a matter of my falling to my knees, and if by this sacrifice I could assure man's happiness, I ought certainly to agree to it. But what is involved is everyone's relinquishing the right to free criticism, the right to facts, the right to truth. I am told that this will all be restored to us later, but what proof is there of this? How am I to believe in a promise made in the name of mutually destructive principles? I know only one thing, that my mind has to relinquish its independence this very day. Have I fallen into the inacceptable dilemma of

[11] This is a résumé of conversations about Trotskyism that I have had time and again with Communist intellectuals, and not the least important of them. They always follow the pattern I have just indicated.

[12] As can be seen in the Lysenko case, the scientist who recently provided Marxist politics with a groundwork by guaranteeing the truth of materialism, has to submit, in his research, to the demands of this politics. It is a vicious circle.

betraying the proletariat in order to serve truth or betraying truth in the name of the proletariat?

If I consider the materialist faith, not in its content but in its history, as a social phenomenon, I clearly see that it is not a caprice of intellectuals nor a simple error on the part of philosophers. As far back as I go, I find it bound up with the revolutionary attitude. The first man who made a deliberate attempt to rid men of their fears and bonds, the first man who tried to abolish slavery within his domain, Epicurus, was a materialist. The materialism of the great philosophers, like that of the "intellectual societies", contributed not a little to the preparation of the French Revolution; finally, the Communists, in defence of their thesis, readily made use of an argument which bears a strange resemblance to that which the Catholic employs in the defence of his faith. "If materialism were erroneous," they say, "how do you explain the fact that it is responsible for the unity of the working class, that it has enabled it to be led into battle and that during the last fifty years it has brought us, in spite of the most violent repression, this succession of victories?" This argument, which is scholastic, and which offers an *a posteriori* proof in terms of success, is far from insignificant.

It is a fact that materialism is now the philosophy of the proletariat precisely in so far as the proletariat is revolutionary. This austere, false doctrine is the bearer of the purest and most ardent hopes; this theory which constitutes a radical denial of man's freedom has become the most radical instrument of his liberation. That means that its content is suited to "mobilizing and organizing" revolutionary forces and, also, that there is a deep relationship between the *situation* of an oppressed class and the materialist *expression* of this situation. But we cannot conclude from this that materialism is a philosophy, and still less that it is *the* truth.

In so far as it permits of coherent action, in so far as it expresses a concrete situation, in so far as millions of men find in it hope and the image of their condition, materialism certainly must contain some truth. But that in no way means that it is wholly true as doctrine. The truths contained in it can be shrouded and drowned in error; it is possible that in order to attend to first things first, and to get back to these truths, revolutionary thinking has sketched out a rapid and temporary structure, what dressmakers call a basted garment. In that case, materialism offers much more than is required by the revolutionary. It also offers a good deal less, for this hasty and forced joining of elements of truth prevents them from organizing spontaneously among themselves and from attaining true unity. Materialism is indisputably the *only myth* that suits revolutionary requirements.

The politician goes no further; the myth is useful and so he adopts it. But if his undertaking is a long-range affair, it is not a myth that he needs but the *Truth*. It is the philosopher's business to make the truths contained in materialism hang together and to build, little by little, a philosophy which suits the needs of the revolution as exactly as the myth does. And the best way of spotting these truths within the error in which they are steeped is to determine these requirements on the basis of a careful examination of the revolutionary attitude, to reconstruct, in each case, the path by which they have led to the demand for a materialist representation of the universe, and to see whether they have not, each time, been deflected and diverted from their primary meaning. If they are freed from the myth which crushes them and which hides them from themselves, perhaps they may plot the main lines of a coherent philosophy which will be superior to materialism in being a *true* description of nature and of human relationships.

2. *The philosophy of revolution*

The game of the Nazis and their collaborators was to blur ideas. The Pétain regime called itself a Revolution, and things reached such a point of absurdity that one day the following headline appeared in the *Gerbe:* "The motto of the National Revolution is—*hold fast.*" It is fitting, then, that we bear in mind a few basic truths. In order to avoid any presuppositions, we shall adopt the *a posteriori* definition of revolution given by a historian, A. Mathiez. In his opinion, revolution takes place when a change in institutions is accompanied by a profound modification in the property system.

We shall call revolutionary the party or the person in the party whose acts intentionally prepare such a revolution. The first observation to be made is that not anyone can become a revolutionary. The existence of a strong and organized party whose object is revolution can, to be sure, exert its attraction upon individuals or groups of any origin, but the organization of this party can belong only to people of a certain social condition. In other words, the revolutionary is *in a situation.* It is obvious that he is to be found only among the oppressed, but it does not suffice to be oppressed to choose to be a revolutionary. The Jews can be classed with the oppressed—and the same holds true for racial minorities in certain countries—but many of them are oppressed within the bourgeoisie and, as they share the privileges of the class which oppresses them, they are unable, without contradiction, to work for the destruction of these privileges.

In the same way, we cannot call the feudal colonial nationalists or the American Negroes revolutionaries, though their interests may coincide with those of the party which is working for the revolution. They are not completely integrated into society. The former ask for the *return* to an earlier state of things; they want to *regain* their supremacy and to cut the bonds which attach them to the colonizing society. What the American Negroes and the bourgeois Jews want is an equality of rights which in no way implies a change of structure in the property system. They wish simply to share the privileges of their oppressors, that is, they really want a more complete integration.

The situation of the revolutionary is such that he cannot share in these privileges in any way whatever. The only way he can get what he wants is by the destruction of the class that oppresses him. This means that the oppression is not, like that of the Jews or the American Negroes, a secondary and, as it were, lateral characteristic of the social regime under consideration, but that it is, on the contrary, a constituent one. The revolutionary is, thus, both an oppressed person and the keystone of the society which oppresses him. In other words it is as an oppressed person that he is indispensable to this society. That is, the revolutionary belongs to those who *work* for the dominant class.

The revolutionary is necessarily a worker and one of the oppressed, and it is as a worker that he is oppressed. This double character of producer and oppressed person is sufficient to define the revolutionary's situation, but not the revolutionary himself. The silk-weavers of Lyons and the workers of June, 1848, were not revolutionaries, but rioters; they were fighting for particular improvements and not for a radical transformation of their existence. That means that they were hemmed in by their situation and that they accepted it as a whole. They accepted being hirelings, working at machines of which they were not the owners; they recognized the rights of the propertied class; they were obedient to its morality. They were simply demanding an increase of salary within a state of things which they had neither transcended nor even recognized.

The revolutionary, on the other hand, is defined by his *going beyond* the situation in which he is placed. And because he does go beyond it towards a radically new situation, he can grasp it in its synthetic wholeness, or, if you like, he makes it exist for himself as totality. Thus it is by means of this thrust toward the future and from the point of view of the future that he *realizes* it. Instead of appearing to him, as it does to a resigned victim, as a definitive and *a priori* structure, it is for him only a moment of the universe. Since he wants to change it, he must consider it immediately from a historical point of view and he must consider himself an historical agent.

Thus, from the very beginning, as a result of this projection of the self into the future, he escapes from the society that crushes him and turns back towards it in order to understand it. He sees a human history which is one with man's destiny and of which the change he wishes to bring about is, if not the end, at least an essential stage. He sees history as progress, since he judges the state toward which he wishes to lead us to be better than that in which we are at present. At the same time, he sees human relationships from the point of view of work, since work is his lot. Now, work is, among other things, a direct link between man and the universe, man's hold on Nature and, at the same time, a primary kind of relation between men.

It is, therefore, an essential attitude of human reality which, within the unity of a self-same project, both "exists" and causes his relation with nature and his relation with others to exist in their mutual dependence. And in so far as he demands his liberation *as* a worker, he knows perfectly well that it cannot be brought about by a simple integration of himself with the privileged class. What he hopes for, quite to the contrary, is that the relationships of solidarity which he maintains with other workers will become the very model of human relationships. He hopes, therefore, for the liberation of the entire oppressed class; unlike the lonely rebel, the revolutionary understands himself only in his relationships of solidarity with his class.

Thus, because he becomes conscious of the social structure upon which he depends, the revolutionary demands a philosophy which considers his situation, and, as his action has meaning only if it brings man's fate into question, this philosophy must be total, that is, it must produce a total explanation of the human condition. And since he himself is, as a worker, an essential structural unit of society and the link between man and Nature, he has no need of a philosophy which does not express, primarily and essentially, the original relation of man to the world, which is precisely the co-ordinated action of one upon the other.

Finally, since this philosophy is born of a historical enterprise and must represent for him who requires it a certain mode of historicizing which he has chosen, it must necessarily present the course of history as being oriented or as being, at least, capable of being oriented. And as it is born of action and reconsiders, so as to clarify it, the action which necessitated it, this philosophy is not a contemplation of the world, but ought, itself, to be an action. We must understand that this philosophy does not come to tack itself on to the revolutionary effort, but that it is indistinguishable from this effort; it is embodied in the original plan of the worker who joins the revolutionary party, and is implicit in his revolutionary attitude, for any plan for changing the world is inseparable from a certain understanding which reveals the world from the viewpoint of the change one wishes to bring about in it.

The task of the philosopher of revolution will therefore consist in indicating, and elaborating upon, the great, guiding themes of the revolutionary point of view. And this philosophical effort is in itself an act, for it cannot elucidate these themes without taking its place within the very movement which begets them, namely, the revolutionary movement. It is an act also because once the philosophy is made clear it makes the militant revolutionary more conscious of his destiny, of his place in the world, and of his ends.

Thus revolutionary thinking is a *thinking within a situation;* it is the thinking of the oppressed in so far as they rebel together against oppression; it cannot be reconstructed from the outside; you can come to know it, once it has been developed, by reproducing within yourself the revolutionary movement and by considering it on the basis of the situation from which it arises. It should be noted that the thinking of philosophers of the ruling class also constitutes action. Nizan has clearly demonstrated this in his *Chiens de Garde* (*Watch Dogs*). It aims at defending, conserving and repelling. But its inferiority to revolutionary thinking is due to the fact that the philosophy of oppression tries to conceal its pragmatic character; as it is aimed not at changing the world, but at maintaining it, it claims to *contemplate* the world as it *is*. It regards society and nature from the viewpoint of pure knowledge, without admitting to itself that this attitude tends to perpetuate the present state of the universe by implying that the universe can be known rather than changed and that if one actually does want to change it, one must first know it.

The theory of the primacy of knowledge, unlike any philosophy of work which grasps the object through the action that modifies it by using it, exerts a negative and inhibiting influence by conferring a pure and static essence upon the object. But the theory contains within itself a negation of the action it involves, since it affirms the primacy of knowledge and rejects all pragmatic conceptions of truth. The superiority of revolutionary thinking consists in its first proclaiming its active nature; it is conscious of being an act, and if it presents itself as a total comprehension of the universe, it does so because the oppressed worker's scheme is a total point of view toward the entire universe. But as the revolutionary needs to distinguish between the true and the false, this indissoluble unity of thought and action calls for a new and systematic theory of truth. The pragmatic conception of truth will not do, for it is subjectivist idealism, pure and simple.

That is why the materialist myth was invented. It has the advantage of reducing thought to nothing more than one of the forms of universal energy and of stripping it of its wan will-o'-the-wisp look. In addition, it presents thought, in each particular case, as one objective mode of conduct among others, that is, as occasioned by the state of the world and turning back upon that state in order to modify it. But we saw earlier that the idea of a conditioned thinking is self-destructive; I shall presently show that the same holds true for the idea of a determined action. It is not a question of inventing a cosmogonic myth which will present thinking-action in symbolic form, but of abandoning all myths and reverting to the real revolutionary necessity, which is to unite action with truth and thought with realism.

What is needed is, in a word, a philosophical theory which shows that human reality is action and that action upon the universe is identical with the understanding of that universe as it is, or, in other words, that action is the unmasking of reality, and, *at the same time,* a modification of that reality.[13] As we have seen, the myth of materialism

[13] This is what Marx, in his "theses on Feuerbach" calls "practical materialism". But why "materialism"?

is, in addition, the representation in image form and within the unity of a cosmology and of historical movement, of the relation of man to matter. The representation, therefore, of the relation between men, and, in short, of all the revolutionary themes. We must revert to the skeletal structure of the revolutionary attitude and examine it in detail so as to see whether it does not call for something other than a mythical representation, or if, on the contrary, they call for the groundwork of a rigorous philosophy.

Any member of the ruling class is a man of divine right. Born into a class of leaders, he is convinced from childhood that he is born *to* command and, in a certain sense, this is true, since his parents, who do command, have brought him into the world to carry on after them. A certain social function, into which he will slip as soon as he is of age, the metaphysical reality, as it were, of his person, awaits him. Thus, in his own eyes, he is a person, an *a priori* synthesis of legal right and of fact. Awaited by his peers, destined to relieve them at the appointed time, he exists because he *has the right* to exist.

This sacred character which the bourgeois has for his fellow and which manifests itself in ceremonies of *recognition* (the greeting, the formal announcement, the ritual visit, etc.) is what is called human dignity. The ideology of the ruling class is completely permeated with this idea of dignity. And when men are said to be "the lords of creation", this expression is to be taken in its strongest sense; they are its monarchs by divine right; the world is made for them; their existence is the absolute and perfectly satisfying value to the mind which gives its meaning to the universe. That is the original meaning of all philosophical systems which affirm the primacy of the subject over the object and the composition of Nature through the activity of thought. It is self-evident that man, under these conditions is a supra-natural being; what we call Nature is the sum-total of that which exists without having the right to do so.

For the sacrosanct, the oppressed classes are part of Nature. They are not to command. In other societies perhaps, the fact of a slave's being born within the *domus* also conferred a sacred character upon him, that of being born *to* serve, that of being the man of divine duty in relation to the man of divine right. But the same cannot be said in the case of the proletariat. The worker's son, born in an outlying working-class district, living among the crowd, has no direct contact with the propertied élite; he has no personal duty save those that are defined by law. It is not even forbidden him, should he possess that mysterious grace we call merit, to gain access, under certain circumstances and with certain reservations, to the upper class. His son or grandson will become a man of divine right. Thus, he is only a living being, the best organized of the animals. Everyone has felt the contempt implicit in the term "native", used to designate the inhabitants of a colonized country.

The banker, the manufacturer, even the professor in the home country, are not natives of any country; they are not natives at all. The oppressed person, on the other hand, feels himself to be a native; each single event in his life repeats to him that he has not the right to exist. His parents have not brought him into the world for any particular purpose, but rather by chance, *for no reason;* at best, because they liked children or because they were open to a certain kind of propaganda, or because they wanted to enjoy the advantages accorded to large families. No special function awaits him and, if he has been apprenticed, it was not done so as to prepare him to exercise the priesthood of a profession, but only to enable him to continue the unjustifiable existence he has been leading since his birth. He will work in order to live, and to say that the ownership of the fruits of his labour are stolen from him is an understatement. Even the meaning of his work is stolen from him, since he does not have a feeling of solidarity with the society for which he produces.

Whether he be a fitter or an unskilled labourer, he knows perfectly well that he is not irreplaceable; the worker is actually characterized by interchangeability. The doctor's or jurist's work is appreciated for its quality, the "good" worker's only for its quantity. He becomes conscious of himself through the circumstances of his situation as a member of a zoological species, the human species. So long as he remains on this level, his condition will seem natural to him; he will go on with his life as he began it, with sudden rebellions, if the oppression makes itself more severely felt, but these will be merely sporadic. The revolutionary goes beyond this situation because he wishes to change it, and considers it from the point of view of this will to change.

It should be observed, first of all, that he wishes to change the situation for his whole class and not for himself; if he were thinking only of himself, he could, as a matter of fact, leave the realm of the species and embrace the values of the ruling class. It stands to reason, then, that he would accept *a priori* the sacronsanct character of the men of divine right for the mere purpose of benefiting by it in turn. But as he cannot dream of claiming this divine right for his *entire class,* since the origin of this right lies in the very oppression that he wishes to destroy, his first step will be to contest the rights of the ruling class.

Men of divine right do not exist in his eyes. He has not approached them, but he senses that they lead the same existence as he does, an existence that is equally vague and unjustifiable. Unlike the oppressors, he does not seek to exclude the members of the other class from the community of men. But he wishes, first of all, to strip them of that magical aspect which makes them formidable in the eyes of those they override. By a spontaneous impulse he also denies the values they originally set up.

If it were true that their Good had an *a priori* existence, then the essence of revolution would be polluted; to set oneself up against the oppressors would mean setting oneself up against Good in general.

But he does not dream of replacing this Good with another *a priori* Good, for he is not at a constructive stage. He wants only to free himself of all the values and rules of conduct that the ruling class has invented, because these values and rules act only as checks to his behaviour and, by their very nature, aim at prolonging the *status quo*. And since he wants to change the organization of society, he must first reject the idea that it was established by Providence. Only if he considers it as a fact can he hope to replace it with another fact that suits him better. At the same time, revolutionary thinking is humanistic.

The declaration that "we too are men" is at the bottom of any revolution. And the revolutionary means by this that his oppressors are men. Certainly he will do violence to them, he will try to break their yoke, but if he must destroy some of their lives, he will always try to reduce this destruction to a minimum, because he needs technicians and experts. Thus, in spite of everything, the bloodiest of revolutions involves coalition.

It is, above all, an absorption and an assimilation of the oppressing class by the oppressed. Unlike the turncoat or the persecuted minority which wishes to raise itself to the level of the privileged and to be identified with them, the revolutionary wishes, by denying the validity of their privileges, to bring them down to his level. And as the constant feeling of his own contingent nature inclines him to recognize himself as an unjustifiable fact, he regards the men of divine right as simple facts like himself. Thus, the revolutionary is not a man who demands rights, but rather a man who destroys the very idea of rights, which he regards as a product of force and custom. His humanism is not based on human dignity, but, on the contrary, denies man any particular dignity.

The unity into which he wants to merge himself and his fellows is not that of the human kingdom, but of the human species. There is a human species, a contingent and unjustifiable phenomenon; the circumstances of its development have brought about a state in which there is a kind of lack of inner balance; the revolutionary's task is to help it to achieve a more rational balance beyond its present state. Just as the species has taken possession of the man of divine right and absorbed him, so Nature takes possession of man and absorbs him. Man is a fact of nature and humanity one species among others.

Only in this way can the revolutionary think of being able to escape the hoaxes of the privileged class. The man who identifies himself with the natural can never again be taken in by an appeal to an *a priori* ethics. Materialism seems at this point to offer its aid; it is the epic of the factual. The links established throughout the materialistic world are probably necessary, but necessity appears within an original contingency. If the universe exists, its development and the succession of its states can be regulated by laws. But it is not *necessary* that the universe exist, nor is it necessary that being, in general, exist, and the contingency of the universe is communicated through all the links, even the most rigorous, to each particular fact. Each state, governed from without by the preceding one, can be modified, if one acts upon its causes. And the new state is neither more nor *less natural* than the preceding one—if we mean thereby that it is not based upon rights and that its necessity is merely relative.

At the same time, since the imprisonment of man in the world is involved, materialism has the advantage of offering a crude myth about the origin of the species whereby the more complex forms of life proceed from the simpler ones. The question is not one of merely replacing the end with the cause in each individual case, but of presenting a stereotyped image of a world in which ends are everywhere substituted for causes. It is apparent, even in the attitude of the first and most naïf of the great materialists, that materialism has always had this function.

Epicurus recognizes the possibility of an infinite number of equally valid explanations that might account no less precisely for phenomena, but he challenges us to find one which will liberate man more completely from his fears. And Man's basic fear especially when he suffers is less the fear of death or of the existence of a harsh God, but simply rather that the state of things from which he suffers might have been produced and may be maintained for transcendental and unknowable ends.

In this case, any effort to modify it would be vain and wrong. A subtle discouragement would insinuate itself into his judgments and prevent his hoping for or even conceiving of any improvement. Epicurus reduced death to a fact by removing the moral aspect it acquired from the fiction of seats of judgment in the nether world. He did not do away with ghosts but regarded them as strictly physical phenomena. He did not dare do away with the gods, but reduced them to a mere divine *species,* unrelated to us; he removed their power of self-creation and showed that they were the products of the play of atoms, just as we were.

But, once again, is the materialistic myth, which may have been useful and encouraging, really necessary? The revolutionary's conscience demands that the privileges of the oppressor class be unjustifiable, that the primordial contingency he finds in himself also be a constituent part of his oppressor's very existence, that the system of values set up by his masters, the purpose of which is to confer *de jure* existence upon *de facto* advantages, may be transcended towards an organization of the world which does not yet exist and which will exclude, both in law and in fact, all privileges. But his attitude toward the *natural* is obviously ambivalent. In a way, he plunges into Nature, dragging his masters with him.

But, on the other hand, he proclaims that he wants to substitute a rational adjustment of human relationships for what has been produced blindly by Nature. The Marxist expression for designating the society of the future is *antiphysis.* This means that Marxists want to set up a human order whose laws will constitute the negation of natural laws. And we are probably to understand by this that this order will be produced only by obeying the prescriptions of Nature. But the fact is that this order must *be conceived* within a Nature that denies it; the fact is that in the anti-Natural society the conception of law will precede the establishment of law, whereas, at present, law, according to materialism, conditions our conception of it.

In short, transition to antiphysis means the replacement of the society of laws by the community of ends. And there is no doubt that the revolutionary distrusts values and refuses to recognize that he is trying to achieve a better organization of the human community. He fears that a return to values, even by an indirect path, may open the door to further chicanery. But on the other hand, the mere fact that he is ready to sacrifice his life to an order, the coming of which he never expects to see, implies that this future order, which justifies all his acts but which he will not enjoy, acts as a value for him. What is a value if not the call of something which does not yet exist? [14]

In order to account for these various requirements, a revolutionary philosophy ought to set aside the materialistic myth and endeavour to show: (1) That man is unjustifiable, that his existence is contingent, in that neither he nor any Providence has produced it; (2) That, as a result of this, any collective order established by men can be transcended towards other orders; (3) That the system of values current in a society reflects the structure of that society and tends to preserve it; (4) That it can thus always be transcended toward other systems which are not yet clearly perceived since the society of which they are the expression does not yet exist—but which are adumbrated and are, in a word, invented by the very effort of the members of society to transcend it.

The oppressed person lives out his original contingency, and revolutionary philosophy must reckon with this. But in living out his contingency he accepts the *de facto* existence of his oppressors and the absolute value of the ideologies they have produced. He becomes a revolutionary only through a movement of transcendence which challenges these rights and this ideology. The revolutionary philosopher has, above all, to explain the possibility of this movement of transcendence. It is obvious that its source is not to be found in the individual's purely natural and material existence, since the individual turns back on this existence to judge it from the viewpoint of the future.

This possibility of *rising above* a situation in order to get a perspective on it (a perspective which is not pure knowledge, but an indissoluble linking of understanding and action) is precisely that which we call freedom. No materialism of any kind can ever explain it. A series of causes

[14] This ambiguity appears again in the Communist's judgments of his adversaries. For materialism ought actually to forbid his making judgments. A bourgeois is only the product of a rigorous necessity. But the climate of *l'Humanité* (the French Communist newspaper) is one of moral indignation.

and effects may very well impel me to a gesture or to behaviour which itself will be an effect and which will modify the state of the world; it cannot make me look back at my situation in order to grasp it in its totality.

In short, it cannot account for revolutionary class consciousness. Dialectical materialism undoubtedly exists in order to explain and justify this transcendence toward the future. But it endeavours to ascribe freedom to things, not to man—which is absurd. A state of the world will never be able to produce class consciousness. And the Marxists are so well aware of this that they rely upon militants—that is, upon a conscious and concerted action—in order to activate the masses and awaken this consciousness within them.

That is all very well, but where do these same militants derive their understanding of the situation? Must they not have detached themselves at some time or other to get perspective? In order to avoid the revolutionary's being duped by his former masters, he should be shown that established values are simply given facts. But if they are given, and, consequently, capable of being transcended, this is not because they are values, but because they are established. And in order that there be no self-deception on his part, he must be given the means of understanding that the end he is pursuing—whether he call it anti-physis, classless society or the liberation of man—is also a value and that, if this value cannot be transcended, the reason is simply that it has not been realized.

Moreover, this is what Marx foresaw when he talked of something beyond Communism, and what Trotsky meant when he spoke of the permanent revolution. Revolutionary man claims to be a contingent being, unjustifiable but free, wholly plunged into a society which oppresses him, but capable of transcending that society through his efforts to change it. Idealism deceives him in that it binds him with rights and values that are already given; it conceals from him his power to blaze his own path. But materialism, by robbing him of his freedom, also deceives him. Revolutionary philosophy should be a philosophy of transcendence.

But the revolutionary himself mistrusts freedom—and that prior to any use of sophistry. And he is right. There have always been prophets to tell him he was free, and each time it was in order to fool him. Stoical freedom, Christian freedom, Bergsonian freedom, in hiding his chains from him, have only reinforced them. All of these can be reduced to a certain *inner* freedom that man could retain in any situation. This inner freedom is a pure idealist hoax; care is taken never to present it as the necessary condition of the *act*. It is really pure enjoyment of itself. If Epictetus, in chains, does not rebel, it is because he feels free, because he enjoys his freedom.

On that basis, one state is as good as another, the slave's situation is as good as the master's; why should anyone want to change it? This freedom is fundamentally reducible to a more or less clear affirmation of the autonomy of thought. But in conferring independence upon thought, this affirmation separates it from the situation—since truth is universal, one can think truth under any conditions. It also separates thought from action; since we are responsible only for intention, the act, in being realized, undergoes the pressure of the world's real forces which deform it and render it unrecognizable to its very author.

What remain for the slave are abstract thoughts and empty intentions, under the name of metaphysical freedom. And, meanwhile, his master's orders and the necessity of living have involved him in crude and concrete actions, and oblige him to think in concrete terms, about matter and instruments. In fact, the liberating element for the oppressed person is work. In this sense it is work that is revolutionary to begin with. To be sure, it is *ordered* and has, at first, the appearance of the worker's enslavement. It is not likely that the worker would have chosen to do *this* work under *these* conditions and within *this* length of time for *these* wages, had it not been forced upon him.

The employer, more rigorous than the master of ancient times, goes so far as to determine in advance the worker's gestures and behaviour. He breaks down the worker's act into its component parts, takes certain of them away from him, and has them performed by other workers, reduces the worker's conscious and synthetic activity to a mere sum of constantly repeated gestures. Thus, by putting the worker's conduct on the same footing as property, the master tends to reduce the worker to the state of a mere thing.

Madame de Staël, in the account of her trip to Russia at the beginning of the nineteenth century, cites a striking example of this: "Each of the twenty musicians (in an orchestra of Russian serfs) played one single note each time it recurred. Each of these men bears the name of the note he is supposed to execute. People say, as they pass by, 'There's Mr. Narishkine's "g", "e" or his "d".' " The individual is limited to a constant characteristic which defines him as atomic weight or melting temperature.

Modern Taylorism does the same thing. The worker becomes the man of a single operation which he repeats a hundred times a day; he is a mere object, and to tell a shoe-stitcher or the Ford employee who places the needles on the speedometers that they retain, within the action in which they are engaged, an inner freedom of thought, would be childish or hateful. But at the same time, work offers the beginning of concrete liberation, even in extreme cases, because it is, first of all, the negation of the accidental and capricious order that is the master's. The victim at work no longer worries about pleasing the master, he escapes from the world of politeness, ceremony, psychology and the dance; he does not have to guess what goes on in the boss's head, he is no longer at the mercy of someone's humour. His work is imposed upon him to begin with, of course, and its end product is finally stolen from him.

But within these two limits, his work bestows mastery over things upon him; the worker sees himself as a possibility of infinitely varying the form of a material object by acting upon it in conformance to certain universal rules. In other words, the determinism of matter gives him his first picture of his freedom. A worker is not a determinist in the way the scientist is; he does not make of determinism an explicitly formulated postulation. He lives it in his gestures, in the movement of the arm striking a rivet or pounding a crowbar. He is so thoroughly permeated with it that when the desired effect is not produced he tries to find out what hidden cause has prevented its realization, never conceiving of any waywardness or sudden and accidental break in the natural order. And since it is deep within his slavery, at the very moment at which the master's sweet pleasure transforms him into a thing that action, by bestowing upon him sovereignty over objects and a specialist's autonomy over which the master has no power liberates him, the idea of liberation is linked in his mind with that of determinism.

He does not learn of his freedom by a reflective movement back upon himself, but rather transcends his enslaved state by his action on phenomena which, through the very rigour of their connection, reflect the image of a concrete freedom, the power to modify these phenomena. And since the adumbration of his concrete freedom makes its appearance to him in the connecting-links of determinism, it is not surprising that he aims to replace the relationship of man to man, which seems to him that of a tyrannical freedom to a humiliated obedience, with that of man to thing and, finally—since the man who reigns over things is, in turn, and from another point of view a thing—by that of thing to thing.

Thus determinism, in so far as it is opposed to the psychology of civility, seems to him a kind of purifying thinking, a catharsis. And if he turns back to consider himself as a determined thing, he thereby liberates himself from his master's deadly freedom, for he sweeps them along into determinism's links, considering them, in turn, as things by explaining their commands in terms of their situation, instincts and history, that is, by plunging them into the universe. If all men are things, there are no more slaves, there are only slaves *de facto*.

Like Samson, who accepted burial under the ruins of the temple provided that the Philistines perished with him, the slave frees himself by doing away with his own and his master's freedom and by submerging himself with them in matter. The liberated society of which he conceives is, from that point on, a reversal of the Kantian community of ends; it is not based on the mutual recognition of freedoms. But since the liberating relationship is the relationship between man and things, that is what will form the basic structure of this society.

It is only a question of destroying the oppressive relationship between men so that the slave's will and that of the master's, which exhaust themselves in struggling against one another, can be turned back wholly upon things. The liberated society will be a harmonious enterprise of exploitation of the world. Since it is produced by the absorption of the privileged classes and is defined by work, that is by action upon matter, and since it is in itself subject to deterministic laws, the wheel comes full circle, the world is closed.

The revolutionary, in contradistinction to the rebel, actually wants an *order*. And since the spiritual orders proposed to him are always to one degree or another the sham images of the society that oppresses him, he will choose material order, that is the order of efficiency in which he figures both as cause and effect. Here, too, materialism offers him its services. This myth offers the most precise image of a society in which freedoms are alienated. Auguste Comte defined it as the doctrine which tries to explain the upper in terms of the lower. The words "upper" and "lower" are obviously not to be understood here in their moral sense, but as designating more or less complicated forms of organization.

Now, the worker is considered as an inferior by those whom he nourishes and protects, and the oppressor class originally considers itself as the superior class. Because its internal structures are finer and more complex, it is this class which produces the ideologies, culture and value systems. The upper layers of society tend to explain the lower in terms of the upper, whether by seeing in it a degradation of the superior or by thinking that it exists *in order* to serve the needs of the superior.

This kind of finalist explanation naturally attains the level of a principle of interpretation of the universe. The explanation "from below", that is in terms of economic, technical and, finally, biological conditioning is, in an inverse sense, the one adopted by the oppressed individual because it makes of him the supporting element of the entire society. If the superior is only an emanation from the inferior, then the "exquisite class" is merely an epiphenomenon. Should the oppressed refuse to cater to it, it will sicken and die; by itself it is nothing.

One has merely to widen this view, which is correct, and to make of it a general explanatory principle, and you have the beginning of materialism. And the materialist explanation of the universe, the explanation, that is, of the biological in terms of the physico-chemical and of thought by matter, becomes, in its turn, a justification of the revolutionary attitude; though an organized myth, the explanation makes what had been the victim's spontaneous impulse to rebellion against his oppressor into the universal mode of existence and of reality.

Here, too, materialism offers the revolutionary more than he asks for. For the revolutionary does not insist upon being a thing, but upon mastering things. It is true that in his work he has acquired a just appreciation of freedom. The freedom reflected for him by his action upon things is far removed from the Stoic's abstract freedom of thought. It becomes manifest within a particular situation into which the worker has been cast by the accident of his birth and through his master's whim or interest.

It makes its appearance within an undertaking which he has not originated of his own free will and which he will not terminate; it is not to be distinguished from his very commitment within this undertaking; but if, within his slavery, he becomes conscious of his freedom, it is because he gauges the efficacy of his concrete action. He does not have the pure idea of an autonomy which he does not enjoy, but he does know his power which is proportionate to his action. What he notices while engaged in this same action is that he transcends the present material state through a precise plan of arranging it in one fashion or another, and that, as this project is identical with the management of means directed toward ends, he really does succeed in arranging it as he had wished.

If he discovers the relation between cause and effect, it is not in submitting to it, but in the very act which transcends the material state (the adhesion of the coal to the walls of the mine, etc.) towards a certain end which illuminates and defines this state from within the future. Thus the relation of cause to effect is revealed in and through the efficacy of an act which is both plan and realization. It is, indeed, the tractability and, at the same time, the resistance of the universe which reflects for him the steadiness of causal series and the image of his freedom, but that is because his freedom is indistinguishable from the use of causal series toward an end which establishes this very freedom. Without the illumination bestowed upon it by this end the present situation could contain neither a causal relationship, nor the relationship of means to end, or rather, it would contain an indistinct and infinite number of means and ends, effects and causes, just as without the generating act of the mathematician who traces a figure in relating a series of chosen points according to a certain law, geometric space would contain an undifferentiated infinity of circles, ellipses, triangles and polygons.

Thus, in the realm of work, determinism does not reveal freedom in so far as it is an abstract natural law, but in so far as a human project carves out and illuminates a certain partial determinism within the infinite interaction of phenomena. And in this determinism, which proves itself simply through the efficacy of human action—as Archimedes' principle was already in use and understood by shipbuilders long before Archimedes had given it conceptual form—the relation of cause to effect is indistinguishable from that of means to end.

The organic unity of the worker's plan consists in the simultaneous emergence of an end which did not originally exist in the universe and which is manifested through the organization of means adopted to obtain it (for the end is no more than the synthetic unity of all the means manipulated for producing it) and the under layer which underlies these means and reveals itself, in turn, through their very organization. It is the relation of cause to effect; like Archimedes' principle, it constitutes both support and content for the shipbuilder's technique. In this sense, we may say that the atom was created by the atomic bomb, which was inconceivable except in the light of the Anglo-American plan for winning the war.

Thus freedom is to be discovered only in the act, and is one with the act; it forms the basis of the relations and interrelations that constitute the act's internal structures. It never derives pleasure from itself, but reveals itself in and through its results. It is not an inner virtue which permits us to detach ourselves from very pressing situations, because, for man, there is no inside and no outside. But it is, on the contrary, the power to commit one's self in present action and to build a future; it generates a future which enables us to understand and to change the present.

Thus the worker really learns of his freedom through things; but precisely because he does learn of it through things, he is anything but a thing. And it is here that materialism deceives him and becomes, in spite of itself, an instrument in the hands of the oppressors. For if the worker discovers his freedom in his work, which is conceived as a primary relationship between man and material objects, in his relationship with his oppressor-master he thinks of himself as an object; it is the master who, in reducing him, through Taylorism or another process, to a mere sum of ever-identical operations, transforms him into a passive object, the mere support of constant properties.

Materialism, in decomposing man into behaviour patterns rigorously modelled upon Taylorist operations,[15] is playing into the master's hands. It is the master who sees the slave as a machine. By considering himself a mere natural product, as a "native", the slave sees himself through his master's eyes. He thinks of himself as an Other, and with the thoughts of the Other. The materialist revolutionary's conception harmonizes with that of his oppressors. And it may be objected that materialism ends by catching the master and transforming him into an object, like the slave.

But the master knows nothing of this and cares less; he lives within his ideologies, his rights, his culture. It is only to the slave's subjectivity that he appears an object. Instead of straining ourselves, by concealing his real freedom, to show him that the master is an object, it is, then, infinitely more valid and useful to let the slave discover his freedom to change the world, and, consequently, his own state, from his work. And if it be true that materialism, as explanation of the upper in terms of the lower, is a convenient image of the present social structures, it is then only all the more obvious that it is merely a myth in the Platonic sense of the word. For the revolutionary has no use for a symbolic expression of the present situation; he wants a kind of thinking that will enable him to forge the future. Now the materialist myth loses all meaning in a classless society in which neither uppers nor lowers will exist.

But, say the Marxists, if you teach man that he *is* free, you betray

[15] Behaviourism is the philosophy of Taylorism.

him; for he no longer needs to *become* free; can you conceive of a man free from birth who demands to be liberated? To this I reply that if man is not originally free, but determined once and for all, we cannot even conceive what his liberation might be. Some may say, "We will release human nature from its determining constraints." These people are fools.

What indeed can the nature of a man be, apart from that which he concretely is in his present existence? How can a Marxist believe in a *real* human nature, concealed, only, by oppressive circumstances? Other people claim to bring about the happiness of the species. But what is a happiness which is not *felt* and *experienced?* Happiness is, in its essence, subjectivity. How could it exist in the kingdom of objectivity? The only result one can really hope to attain in the hypothesis of universal determinism and from the point of view of objectivity is simply a more rational organization of society. But what value can an organization of this kind retain if it is not experienced as such by a free subjectivity and transcended toward new ends? No opposition really exists between these two necessities of action, namely that the agent be free and that the world in which he acts be determined. For these two things are not both necessary from the same point of view or in relation to the same realities.

Freedom is a structure of human action and appears only in commitment; determinism is the law of the world. And the act only calls for partial linkages and local constants. Similarly, it is not true that a free man cannot hope to be liberated. For he is not free and bound in respect to the same things. His freedom is like the illumination of the situation into which he is cast. But other people's freedoms can render his situation unbearable, drive him to rebellion or to death.

If a slave's freedom is manifest in his work it is nonetheless true that this work is imposed, nullifying and destructive, that he is cheated of its products, that he is isolated by it, excluded from a society which exploits him and in which he does not share, applied as he is against matter by a *vis a tergo*. It is true that he is merely a link in a chain of which he knows neither the beginning nor the end; it is true that the master's look, his ideology and his orders tend to refuse him any existence other than the material one.

It is precisely in becoming revolutionaries, that is, in organizing with other members of their class to reject the tyranny of their masters, that slaves best manifest their freedom. Oppression leaves them no choice other than resignation or revolution. But in both cases they manifest their freedom to choose. And, finally, no matter what end is allotted to the revolutionary, he transcends it and sees in it only a stage. If he is looking for security or a better material organization of society, it is in order that they may serve as his point of departure.

This is how the Marxists themselves replied when reactionaries, speaking about a minor demand concerning wages, talked of the "sordid materialism of the masses". They gave one to understand that behind these material demands there was the affirmation of a humanism, that these workers were not only demanding a few more *sous,* but that their demand was a kind of concrete symbol of their demand to be men. Men; that is, freedoms in possession of their own destinies.[16] This remark holds true for the revolutionary's final purpose.

Class-consciousness demands a new humanism, above and beyond the rational organization of the community, it is an alienated freedom which has taken freedom as its end. Socialism is merely the means which will allow for the realization of the reign of freedom; a materialistic socialism is contradictory, therefore, because socialism establishes humanism as its end, a humanism which materialism renders inconceivable.

One characteristic of idealism which the revolutionary particularly loathes is the tendency to represent changes in the world as controlled by ideas, or better still, as changes in ideas. Death, unemployment, strike-suppression, poverty and hunger are not ideas. They are everyday realities that are experienced in horror. They certainly have significancies, but they retain above all an underlayer of irrational opaqueness.

The First World War was not, as Chevalier said it was, "Descartes against Kant"; it was the inexpiable deaths of twelve million young men. The revolutionary, crushed beneath reality, refuses to let it sneak away. He knows that the revolution will not be a mere consumption of ideas, but that it will cost blood, sweat and human lives. He is in a position to know that things are solid and sometimes insuperable obstacles and that the best laid plan encounters resistances which are often responsible for its failure. He knows that action is not a felicitous combination of thoughts, but a whole man's efforts against the obstinate impenetrability of the universe. He knows that when one has deciphered the meanings in things that there remains an unassimilable residue, the otherness, the irrationality, the opaqueness of the real, and that it is this residue which in the end stifles and crushes.

Unlike the idealist whose slack thinking he denounces, he wants to think hard. Or rather, against the adversity of objects he wishes to set up not the idea, but action which comes down, finally, to effort, exhausting fatigue and sleeplessness. Here again materialism seems to offer him the most satisfying expression of his demand, since it affirms the predominance of impenetrable matter over the idea. For materialism, all is fact and conflict of forces, action. Thought itself becomes a real phenomenon in a measurable world; it is produced by matter and consumes energy. The famous predominance of the object has to be conceived in terms of realism.

But is this interpretation so deeply satisfying? Does it not overstep

[16] That is what Marx explains admirably in *Political Economy and Philosophy.*

its purpose and defraud the need which generated it? If it is true that nothing gives less of an impression of effort than the generation of ideas by other ideas, the effort fades away just as entirely as if we regard the universe as the balance of various forces. Nothing gives less of an impression of effort than a force applied to a physical point; it accomplishes the work of which it is capable—neither more nor less—and is transformed mechanically into kinetic or caloric energy.

Nowhere, and in no instance, does nature itself give us the impression of resistance overcome, of rebellion and submission, of lassitude. This applied force is always all that it is capable of being, and no more. And forces in opposition produce resultants according to the calm laws of mechanics. In order to account for reality as a resistance to be overcome by work, this resistance must be experienced by a subjectivity that seeks to subdue it. Nature conceived as pure objectivity is the opposite of the idea. But precisely because of this, it becomes transformed into idea; it is the pure idea of objectivity. The *real* vanishes.

For the real is that which is impermeable to subjectivity; it is the piece of sugar whose melting I wait for, as Bergson says, or, if you prefer, it is the subject's obligation to experience a similar waiting. It is the human design or scheme, it is my thirst which decides that it "takes a long time" to melt. When considered apart from a human situation, it melts neither slowly nor fast, but within a time which is dependent upon its nature, its thickness and the amount of water in which it is soaking.

It is human subjectivity which discovers the *adversity* of the real in and through the scheme it conceives to get beyond it toward the future. In order for a hill to be easy or hard to ascend, one must have planned to climb it to its summit. Both idealism and materialism cause the real to disappear in like manner, the one because it eliminates the object, the other because it eliminates subjectivity.

In order for reality to be revealed, it is necessary for a man to struggle against it. The revolutionary's realism, in a word, necessitates the existence of the world and of subjectivity; better still, it calls for such a correlation of one with the other that neither a subjectivity outside the world nor a world which would not be illuminated by an effort on the part of the subjectivity can be conceived of.[17] The maximum of reality, the maximum of resistance, will be obtained if we suppose that man is, by definition, within-a-situation-in-the-world and that he comes to learn the stubbornness of reality in defining himself in relation to it.

Let us take note, moreover, of the fact that an over-narrow adhesion to universal determinism runs the risk of eliminating all of reality's *resistance*. I received the proof of this in a conversation with M. Garaudy and two of his friends. I asked them if the stakes were really down when Stalin signed the Russo-German pact and when the French communists decided to take part in the de Gaulle government; I asked if, in both

[17] It is, once again, Marx's point of view in 1844, that is until the unfortunate meeting with Engels.

cases, the people responsible had not *taken their chances* with the rather anguished feeling of their responsibilities. For it seems to me that freedom is principally characterized by the fact that you are never sure of winning with it and that the consequences of our acts are probable, only. But M. Garaudy interrupted me; for him the stakes are down in advance; there exists a science of history and the interlinking of facts is rigorous, and so we bet on a sure thing. He was carried so far away in his zeal that he ended by saying excitedly to me: "And what does Stalin's intelligence matter? I don't care a rap for it!" I might add that, under the severe glances of his friends, he blushed, lowered his eyes and added, with a rather devout look, "Besides, Stalin is very intelligent."

Thus, in contradiction to revolutionary realism which asserts that the least little result is attained with difficulty and amidst the greatest uncertainties, the materialist myth leads certain minds to a profound reassurance as to the outcome of their efforts. It is impossible, they think, for them to fail. History is a science, its consequences are already inscribed, we have only to decipher them. This attitude is quite patently a flight. The revolutionary has overthrown the myths of the bourgeoisie, and the working class has undertaken, through a thousand vicissitudes, victories and defeats, to forge its own destiny in freedom and in anguish.

But our Garaudys are afraid. What they seek in communism is not liberation, but a re-enforcement of discipline; there is nothing they fear so much as freedom; if they have renounced the *a priori* values of the class from which they come, it is in order to find *a priori* elements in scientific knowledge and paths already marked out in history. There are no risks and no anxiety; everything is sure and certain; the results are guaranteed. Reality immediately vanishes and history is merely an idea that develops.

M. Garaudy feels sheltered within this idea. Some communist intellectuals to whom I reported this conversation shrugged their shoulders. "Garaudy is a scientist," they told me with contempt, "he is a bourgeois Protestant who, for purposes of personal edification, has replaced the finger of God with historical materialism." I agree. I admit, also, that M. Garaudy did not seem to me to be a shining light, but after all, he writes a great deal and the communists do not disown him. And it is not by chance that most of the scientists have joined hands with the Communist Party and that this party, so hard on heresies, does not condemn them.

We must, at this point, repeat the following: the revolutionary, if he wishes to act, cannot regard historical events as the result of lawless contingencies; but he by no means demands that this path be cleared in advance; he wishes to clear it himself. Certain partial series, constancies and structural laws within determined social forms are what he needs in order to see ahead. If you give him more, everything fades away into ideas and history no longer has to be *made,* but rather to be *read,* day by day; the real becomes a dream.

We were called upon to choose between materialism and idealism, we were told that we would be unable to find a middle way between these two doctrines. Without preconceived ideas, we have allowed revolutionary demands to speak for themselves and we have seen that they trace, of themselves, the features of an odd sort of philosophy that dismisses idealism and materialism unsuited. The revolutionary act seemed to us, at first, the free act *par excellence*. Not free in an anarchist and individualist way at all; if that were true, the revolutionary, by the very nature of his situation, could only claim, with a greater or lesser degree of explicitness, the rights of the "exquisite class", that is, his integration with the upper social layers.

But as he demands, within the oppressed class and for the entire oppressed class, a more rational social status, his freedom resides in the act by which he demands the liberation of his whole class and, more generally, of all men. It springs from a recognition of other freedoms and it demands recognition on their part. Thus, from the beginning, it places itself on the level of solidarity. And the revolutionary act contains within itself the premises of a philosophy of freedom, or, rather, by its very existence it creates this philosophy.

But since, at the same time, the revolutionary discovers himself through and in his free designs, as an oppressed person within an oppressed class, his original position requires that we explain the nature of oppression. That means, once again, that men are free—for oppression of matter by matter cannot exist, but only the composition of forces—and that a certain relationship between freedoms can exist, so that one does not recognize the other and acts upon it from without to transform it into an *object.* And conversely, just as oppressed freedom wants to free itself by force, so the revolutionary attitude demands a theory of violence as an answer to oppression. Here too, materialistic terms are no more adequate to the explanation of violence than idealist ones are. Idealism, which is a philosophy of digestion and assimilation, does not even conceive of the absolute and insurmountable pluralism of freedoms marshalled against one another; idealism is a sort of monism. But materialism is also monistic; there is no "conflict of opposites" within material unity. There are not really even any opposites; hot and cold are simply different degrees on the thermometric scale; you pass progressively from light to darkness; two equal forces in opposite directions cancel one another and simply produce a state of equilibrium. The idea of a conflict of opposites constitutes a projection of human relationships upon material relationships.

A revolutionary philosophy ought to account for the plurality of freedoms and show how each one can be an object for the other while being, at the same time, a freedom for itself. Only this double character of freedom and objectivity can explain the complex notions of oppression, conflict, failure and violence. For one never oppresses anything but a freedom, but one cannot oppress it if it lends itself in some way to this oppression, if, that is, it presents the appearance of a thing to the Other. The revolutionary movement and its plan—which is to make society pass through the violence of one state in which liberties are alienated to another state based on their mutual recognition—is to be understood in these terms.

Similarly, the revolutionary who *lives through* oppression bodily and in each of his gestures in no way wishes to underestimate the yoke imposed upon him nor to tolerate idealist criticism's dispelling this oppression in ideas. At the same time, he contests the rights of the privileged class and thereby destroys the general idea of rights. But it would be erroneous to believe, with the materialist, that he does this in order to replace them with the plain and simple fact. For facts can only generate facts, and not the representation of facts; the present generates another present, not the future.

Thus the revolutionary act demands that we transcend, in the unity of a synthesis, opposition—which can account for a society's disintegration, but not the *construction* of a new society—and idealism, which confers a legal existence upon facts. It calls for a new philosophy, with a different view of man's relations with the world. If the revolution should be possible, man ought to possess the contingent quality of the fact and be different, nevertheless, from the fact in his practical ability to transcend the present, to disengage himself from his situation.

This disengagement is in no way comparable to the negative movement through which the Stoic tries to take refuge in himself; it is by projecting himself ahead, in committing himself in ventures of one kind or another, that the revolutionary transcends the present; and since he is a man, doing a man's work, this power of disengagement must really be attributed to *all human activity*. The slightest human gesture can be understood in terms of the future; even the reactionary faces the future, since he is concerned with preparing a future that will be identical with the past.

The tactician's absolute realism demands that man be plunged into reality, menaced with concrete dangers, victim of a concrete oppression from which he will deliver himself through equally concrete acts. Blood, sweat, sorrow and death are not ideas; the rock that crushes and the bullet that kills are not ideas. But in order that objects may reveal what Bachelard rightly calls their "co-efficient of adversity", the light of a plan or illuminating scheme, be it only the very simple and crude one of living, is necessary.

It is not true, then, that man is outside Nature and the world, as the idealist has it, or that he is only up to his ankles in it, baulking like a bather having a dip while her head is in the clouds. He is completely in Nature's clutches, and at any moment Nature can crush him and annihilate him, body and soul. He is in her clutches from the very beginning: for him being born really means "coming into the world" in a situation not of his choice, with *this particular* body, *this* family, and *this* race, perhaps.

But if he happens to plan, as Marx expressly states, to "change the world", it means that he is, to begin with, a being for whom *the world* exists in its totality, as a piece of phosphorus or lead, which is a *part* of the world and ridden by forces to which it uncomprehendingly submits, will never be. This means that man transcends the world toward a future state from which he can contemplate it. It is in changing the world that we can come to know it. Neither the detached consciousness that would soar over the universe without being able to get a standpoint on it, nor the material object which reflects a condition without understanding it can ever "grasp" the totality of existence in a synthesis, even a purely conceptual one.

Only a man situated in the universe and completely crushed by the forces of Nature and transcending them completely through his design to master them can do this. It is the elucidation of the new ideas of "situation" and of "being-in-the-world" that revolutionary behaviour specifically calls for. And if he escapes the jungle of rights and duties into which the idealist tries to mislead him, it should not be only to fall into the gorges rigorously marked out by the materialist. Intelligent Marxists admit of a certain contingent element in history, of course, but only to say that if socialism fails, humanity will sink into barbarism.

If constructive forces are to triumph, historical determinism assigns them only one path. But there are many possible varieties of barbarism and socialism, and perhaps even a barbarous socialism. What the revolutionary demands is the possibility for man to invent his own law. This is the basis of his humanism and of his socialism. He does not, deep within himself, think—at least so long as he is not being tricked—that socialism waits for him around history's bend, like a bandit with a cudgel, concealed somewhere in the woods.

The revolutionary considers that he *builds* socialism, and since he has shaken off and overthrown all legal rights, he recognizes its existence only in so far as the revolutionary class invents, wills and builds it. And, in this sense, this slow, stern conquest of socialism is none other than the affirmation of human freedom in and through history. And precisely because man is free, the triumph of socialism is not at all certain. It does not lie at the end of the road, like a boundary-mark; it is *the* scheme formulated by humanity. It will be what men make it; it is the outcome of the soberness with which the revolutionary envisages his action. He feels responsible not only for the coming of a socialist republic in general, but for the particular character of this socialism as well.

Thus the philosophy of revolution, transcending both idealist thinking which is bourgeois and the myth of materialism which suited the oppressed masses for a while, claims to be the philosophy of *man* in the general sense. And this is quite natural; if it is true it will indeed be universal. The ambiguity of materialism lies in its claim to be a class ideology at one time and the expression of an absolute truth at another.

But the revolutionary, in his very choice of revolution, takes a privileged position; he, unlike the militants of the bourgeois parties, fights not for the conservation of a class but for the elimination of classes; he does not divide society into men of divine right on the one hand, and natives or "Untermenchsen" on the other, but calls for the unification of ethnic groups and classes, the unity, in short, of *all men.* He does not allow himself to be humbugged by the rights and duties lodged *a priori* in an intelligible heaven, but, in the very act of rebellion against them, posits human freedom, metaphysical and entire.

His cause is, thus, essentially, man's cause and his philosophy ought to express the *truth* about man. But, you will say, if his philosophy is universal, or true for all men, isn't it, as a matter of fact, beyond parties and classes? Don't we revert to rootless, a-political, and a-social idealism? My reply is as follows: the meaning of this philosophy is open, at first, to revolutionaries only, that is to men in the *situation of oppressed persons,* and it has need of them in order to become manifest to the world. But it is true that this ought to be the philosophy of all men, in so far as a bourgeois oppressor is the victim of his own oppression. For in order to maintain his authority over the oppressed classes, he is obliged to pay with his own person and to become entangled in the maze of rights and values of his own invention.

If the revolutionary retains the materialist myth, the young bourgeois can come to the revolution only upon the perception of social injustices; he comes to it through personal generosity, which is always suspect, for the source of generosity can be exhausted, and his swallowing of the materialism his reasoning power rejects and which does not express his personal situation constitutes an additional test.

But once the philosopher of revolution makes his point of view clear, the bourgeois who formulated a criticism of the ideology of his class, who has recognized his own contingent quality and his freedom, who has come to understand that this freedom can be asserted only by the *recognition* bestowed upon it by other freedoms, will discover that in so far as he wants to strip the middle class of its mystifying trappings and assert himself as a man among men. At this point revolutionary humanism does not seem to be the philosophy of an oppressed class, but the truth itself, humiliated, masked, oppressed by men whose interests lie in flight from it, and it becomes evident for all men of good will that truth is the revolutionary thing. Not the abstract Truth of idealism, but concrete truth, willed, created, maintained and conquered through social struggle by men who work at the liberation of man.

It may be objected that since the only existing revolutionaries are Marxists who give their allegiance to materialism, this analysis of revolutionary needs is abstract. It is true that the Communist Party is the only revolutionary party. And it is true that the party's doctrine is materialism. But I have not attempted to describe the Marxists' *beliefs,* but rather to bring out the implications of their *actions*. And the frequenting of communists has taught me that nothing is more variable, abstract and subjective than what is called their Marxism. What could be more at variance with M. Garaudy's naïve and stubborn scientism than M. Hervé's philosophy? You may say that this is the reflection of a difference in intelligence, and this is true.

But above all, it indicates the respective degrees of belief in the materialist myth. It is not by chance that Marxist thinking is passing through a crisis today and that it has resigned itself to adopting people like Garaudy for spokesmen. It is due to the fact that the communists are caught between the obsolesence of the materialist myth and the fear of creating division, or hesitation at least, in their ranks through the adoption of a new ideology. The best of them are silent; the silence is filled in with the chatter of imbeciles. "After all," the leaders probably think, "what does ideology matter? Our old materialism has proved itself and will surely lead us to victory. Ours is not a struggle of ideas; it is a political and social struggle between men." They are probably right in so far as the present, or even the near future, is concerned. But what kind of men are they forming? You cannot, with impunity, form generations of men by imbuing them with successful, but false, ideas. What will happen if materialism stifles the revolutionary design to death one day?

Albert Camus

THOUGHT AT THE MERIDIAN[1]

Rebellion and murder

Far from this source of life, however, Europe and the revolution are being shaken to the core by a spectacular convulsion. During the last century, man cast off the fetters of religion. Hardly was he free, however, when he created new and utterly intolerable chains. Virtue dies but is born again, more exacting than ever. It preaches an ear-splitting sermon on charity to all comers and a kind of love for the future which makes a mockery of contemporary humanism. When it has reached this point of stability, it can only wreak havoc. A day arrives when it becomes bitter, immediately adopts police methods, and, for the salvation of mankind, assumes the ignoble aspect of an inquisition. At the climax of contemporary tragedy, we therefore become intimates of crime. The sources of life and of creation seem exhausted. Fear paralyzes a Europe peopled with phantoms and machines. Between two holocausts, scaffolds are installed in underground caverns where humanist executioners celebrate their new cult in silence. What cry would ever trouble them? The poets themselves, confronted with the murder of their fellow men, proudly declare that their hands are clean. The whole world absentmindedly turns its back on these crimes; the victims have reached the extremity of their disgrace: they are a bore. In ancient times the blood of murder at least produced a religious horror and in this way sanctified the value of life. The real condemnation of the period we live in is, on the contrary, that it leads us to think that it is not

[1] From: *The Rebel,* Albert Camus, Part 5. Alfred A. Knopf, Inc., New York, 1956. Reprinted by permission of the publisher.

bloodthirsty enough. Blood is no longer visible; it does not bespatter the faces of our pharisees visibly enough. This is the extreme of nihilism; blind and savage murder becomes an oasis, and the imbecile criminal seems positively refreshing in comparison with our highly intelligent executioners.

Having believed for a long time that it could fight against God with all humanity as its ally, the European mind then perceived that it must also, if it did not want to die, fight against men. The rebels who, united against death, wanted to construct, on the foundation of the human species, a savage immortality are terrified at the prospect of being obliged to kill in their turn. Nevertheless, if they retreat they must accept death; if they advance they must accept murder. Rebellion, cut off from its origins and cynically travestied, oscillates, on all levels, between sacrifice and murder. The form of justice that it advocated and that it hoped was impartial has turned out to be summary. The kingdom of grace has been conquered, but the kingdom of justice is crumbling too. Europe is dying of this disappointing realization. Rebellion pleaded for the innocence of mankind, and now it has hardened its heart against its own culpability. Hardly does it start off in search of totality when it receives as its portion the most desperate sensations of solitude. It wanted to enter into communion with mankind and now it has no other hope but to assemble, one by one, throughout the years, the solitary men who fight their way toward unity.

Must we therefore renounce every kind of rebellion, whether we accept, with all its injustices, a society that outlives its usefulness, or whether we decide, cynically, to serve, against the interest of man, the inexorable advance of history? After all, if the logic of our reflection should lead to a cowardly conformism it would have to be accepted as certain families sometimes accept inevitable dishonor. If it must also justify all the varieties of attempts against man, and even his systematic destruction, it would be necessary to consent to this suicide. The desire for justice would finally realize its ambition: the disappearance of a world of tradesmen and police.

But are we still living in a rebellious world? Has not rebellion become, on the contrary, the excuse of a new variety of tyrant? Can the "We are" contained in the movement of rebellion, without shame and without subterfuge, be reconciled with murder? In assigning oppression a limit within which begins the dignity common to all men, rebellion defined a primary value. It put in the first rank of its frame of reference an obvious complicity among men, a common texture, the solidarity of chains, a communication between human being and human being which makes men both similar and united. In this way, it compelled the mind to take a first step in defiance of an absurd world. By this progress it rendered still more acute the problem that it must now solve in regard to murder. On the level of the absurd, in fact, murder would only give rise to logical contradictions; on the level of rebellion it is mental laceration. For it is now a question of deciding if it is possible to kill someone whose resemblance to ourselves we have at last recognized and whose identity we have just sanctified. When we have only just conquered solitude, must we then re-establish it definitively by legitimizing the act that isolates everything? To force solitude on a man who has just come to understand that he is not alone, is that not the definitive crime against man?

Logically, one should reply that murder and rebellion are contradictory. If a single master should, in fact, be killed, the rebel in a certain way is no longer justified in using the term *community of men* from which he derived his justification. If this world has no higher meaning, if man is only responsible to man, it suffices for a man to remove one single human being from the society of the living to automatically exclude himself from it. When Cain kills Abel, he flees to the desert. And if murderers are legion, then this legion lives in the desert and in that other kind of solitude called promiscuity.

From the moment that he strikes, the rebel cuts the world in two. He rebelled in the name of the identity of man with man and he sacrifices this identity by consecrating the difference in blood. His only existence, in the midst of suffering and oppression, was contained in this identity. The same movement, which intended to affirm him, thus brings an end to his existence. He can claim that some, or even almost all, are with him. But if one single human being is missing in the irreplaceable world of fraternity, then this world is immediately depopulated. If we are not, then I am not and this explains the infinite sadness of Kaliayev and the silence of Saint-Just. The rebels, who have decided to gain their ends through violence and murder, have in vain replaced, in order to preserve the hope of existing, "We are" by the "We shall be." When the murderer and the victim have disappeared, the community will provide its own justification without them. The exception having lasted its appointed time, the rule will once more become possible. On the level of history, as in individual life, murder is thus a desperate exception or it is nothing. The disturbance that it brings to the order of things offers no hope of a future; it is an exception and therefore it can be neither utilitarian nor systematic as the purely historical attitude would have it. It is the limit that can be reached but once, after which one must die. The rebel has only one way of reconciling himself with his act of murder if he allows himself to be led into performing it: to accept his own death and sacrifice. He kills and dies so that it shall be clear that murder is impossible. He demonstrates that, in reality, he prefers the "We are" to the "We shall be." The calm happiness of Kaliayev in his prison, the serenity of Saint-Just when he walks toward the scaffold, are explained in their turn. Beyond that farthest frontier, contradiction and nihilism begin.

Nihilistic murder

Irrational crime and rational crime, in fact, both equally betray the value brought to light by the movement of rebellion. Let us first consider the former. He who denies everything and assumes the authority to kill—Sade, the homicidal dandy, the pitiless Unique, Karamazov, the zealous supporters of the unleashed bandit—lay claim to nothing short of total freedom and the unlimited display of human pride. Nihilism confounds creator and created in the same blind fury. Suppressing every principle of hope, it rejects the idea of any limit, and in blind indignation, which no longer is even aware of its reasons, ends with the conclusion that it is a matter of indifference to kill when the victim is already condemned to death.

But its reasons—the mutual recognition of a common destiny and the communication of men between themselves—are always valid. Rebellion proclaimed them and undertook to serve them. In the same way it defined, in contradiction to nihilism, a rule of conduct that has no need to await the end of history to explain its actions and which is, nevertheless, not formal. Contrary to Jacobin morality, it made allowances for everything that escapes from rules and laws. It opened the way to a morality which, far from obeying abstract principles, discovers them only in the heat of battle and in the incessant movement of contradiction. Nothing justifies the assertion that these principles have existed externally; it is of no use to declare that they will one day exist. But they do exist, in the very period in which we exist. With us, and throughout all history, they deny servitude, falsehood, and terror.

There is, in fact, nothing in common between a master and a slave; it it is impossible to speak and communicate with a person who has been reduced to servitude. Instead of the implicit and untrammeled dialogue through which we come to recognize our similarity and consecrate our destiny, servitude gives sway to the most terrible of silences. If injustice is bad for the rebel, it is not because it contradicts an eternal idea of justice, but because it perpetuates the silent hostility that separates the oppressor from the oppressed. It kills the small part of existence that can be realized on this earth through the mutual understanding of men. In the same way, since the man who lies shuts himself off from other men, falsehood is therefore proscribed and, on a slightly lower level, murder and violence, which impose definitive silence. The mutual understanding and communication discovered by rebellion can survive only in the free exchange of conversation. Every ambiguity, every misunderstanding, leads to death; clear language and simple words are the only salvation from this death.[2] The climax of every tragedy lies in the deafness of its heroes. Plato is right and not Moses and Nietzsche. Dia-

[2] It is worth noting that the language peculiar to totalitarian doctrines is always a scholastic or administrative language.

logue on the level of mankind is less costly than the gospel preached by totalitarian regimes in the form of a monologue dictated from the top of a lonely mountain. On the stage as in reality, the monologue precedes death. Every rebel, solely by the movement that sets him in opposition to the oppressor, therefore pleads for life, undertakes to struggle against servitude, falsehood, and terror, and affirms, in a flash, that these three afflictions are the cause of silence between men, that they obscure them from one another and prevent them from rediscovering themselves in the only value that can save them from nihilism—the long complicity of men at grips with their destiny.

In a flash—but that is time enough to say, provisionally, that the most extreme form of freedom, the freedom to kill, is not compatible with the sense of rebellion. Rebellion is in no way the demand for total freedom. On the contrary, rebellion puts total freedom up for trial. It specifically attacks the unlimited power that authorizes a superior to violate the forbidden frontier. Far from demanding general independence, the rebel wants it to be recognized that freedom has its limits everywhere that a human being is to be found—the limit being precisely that human being's power to rebel. The most profound reason for rebellious intransigence is to be found here. The more aware rebellion is of demanding a just limit, the more inflexible it becomes. The rebel undoubtedly demands a certain degree of freedom for himself; but in no case, if he is consistent, does he demand the right to destroy the existence and the freedom of others. He humiliates no one. The freedom he claims, he claims for all; the freedom he refuses, he forbids everyone to enjoy. He is not only the slave against the master, but also man against the world of master and slave. Therefore, thanks to rebellion, there is something more in history than the relation between mastery and servitude. Unlimited power is not the only law. It is in the name of another value that the rebel affirms the impossibility of total freedom while he claims for himself the relative freedom necessary to recognize this impossibility. Every human freedom, at its very roots, is therefore relative. Absolute freedom, which is the freedom to kill, is the only one which does not claim, at the same time as itself, the things that limit and obliterate it. Thus it cuts itself off from its roots and—abstract and malevolent shade—wanders haphazardly until such time as it imagines that it has found substance in some ideology.

It is then possible to say that rebellion, when it develops into destruction, is illogical. Claiming the unity of the human condition, it is a force of life, not of death. Its most profound logic is not the logic of destruction; it is the logic of creation. Its movement, in order to remain authentic, must never abandon any of the terms of the contradiction that sustains it. It must be faithful to the *yes* that it contains as well as to the *no* that nihilistic interpretations isolate in rebellion. The logic of the rebel is to want to serve justice so as not to add to the injustice of the human condition, to insist on plain language so as not to increase the universal falsehood, and to wager, in spite of human misery, for happiness. Nihilistic passion, adding to falsehood and injustice, destroys in its fury its original demands and thus deprives rebellion of its most cogent reasons. It kills in the fond conviction that this world is dedicated to death. The consequence of rebellion, on the contrary, is to refuse to legitimize murder because rebellion, in principle, is a protest against death.

But if man were capable of introducing unity into the world entirely on his own, if he could establish the reign, by his own decree, of sincerity, innocence, and justice, he would be God Himself. Equally, if he could accomplish all this, there would be no more reasons for rebellion. If rebellion exists, it is because falsehood, injustice, and violence are part of the rebel's condition. He cannot, therefore, absolutely claim not to kill or lie without renouncing his rebellion and accepting, once and for all, evil and murder. But no more can he agree to kill and lie, since the inverse reasoning which would justify murder and violence would also destroy the reasons for his insurrection. Thus the rebel can never find peace. He knows what is good and, despite himself, does evil. The value that supports him is never given to him once and for all; he must fight to uphold it, unceasingly. Again the existence he achieves collapses if rebellion does not support it. In any case, if he is not always able not to kill, either directly or indirectly, he can put his conviction and passion to work at diminishing the chances of murder around him. His only virtue will lie in never yielding to the impulse to allow himself to be engulfed in the shadows that surround him and in obstinately dragging the chains of evil, with which he is bound, toward the light of good. If he finally kills himself, he will accept death. Faithful to his origins, the rebel demonstrates by sacrifice that his real freedom is not freedom from murder but freedom from his own death. At the same time, he achieves honor in metaphysical terms. Thus Kaliayev climbs the gallows and visibly designates to all his fellow men the exact limit where man's honor begins and ends.

Historical murder

Rebellion also deploys itself in history, which demands not only exemplary choices, but also efficacious attitudes. Rational murder runs the risk of finding itself justified by history. The contradiction of rebellion, then, is reflected in an apparently insoluble contradiction, of which the two counterparts in politics are on the one hand the opposition between violence and non-violence, and on the other hand the opposition between justice and freedom. Let us try to define them in the terms of their paradox.

The positive value contained in the initial movement of rebellion supposes the renunciation of violence committed on principle. It consequently entails the impossibility of stabilizing a revolution. Rebellion is, incessantly, prey to this contradiction. On the level of history it becomes even more insoluble. If I renounce the project of making human identity respected, I abdicate in favor of oppression, I renounce rebellion and fall back on an attitude of nihilistic consent. Then nihilism becomes conservative. If I insist that human identity should be recognized as existing, then I engage in an action which, to succeed, supposes a cynical attitude toward violence and denies this identity and rebellion itself. To extend the contradiction still farther, if the unity of the world cannot come from on high, man must construct it on his own level, in history. History without a value to transfigure it, is controlled by the law of expediency. Historical materialism, determinism, violence, negation of every form of freedom which does not coincide with expediency and the world of courage and of silence, are the highly legitimate consequences of a pure philosophy of history. In the world today, only a philosophy of eternity could justify non-violence. To absolute worship of history it would make the objection of the creation of history and of the historical situation it would ask whence it had sprung. Finally, it would put the responsibility for justice in God's hands, thus consecrating injustice. Equally, its answers in their turn, would insist on faith. The objection will be raised of evil, and of the paradox of an all-powerful and malevolent, or benevolent and sterile, God. The choice will remain open between grace and history, God or the sword.

What, then, should be the attitude of the rebel? He cannot turn away from the world and from history without denying the very principle of his rebellion, nor can he choose eternal life without resigning himself, in one sense, to evil. If, for example, he is not a Christian, he should go to the bitter end. But to the bitter end means to choose history absolutely and with it murder, if murder is essential to history: to accept the justification of murder is again to deny his origins. If the rebel makes no choice, he chooses the silence and slavery of others. If, in a moment of despair, he declares that he opts both against God and against history, he is the witness of pure freedom; in other words, of nothing. In our period of history and in the impossible condition in which he finds himself, of being unable to affirm a superior motive that does not have its limits in evil, his apparent dilemma is silence or murder—in either case, a surrender.

And it is the same again with justice and freedom. These two demands are already to be found at the beginning of the movement of rebellion and are to be found again in the first impetus of revolution. The history of revolutions demonstrates, however, that they almost always conflict as though their mutual demands were irreconcilable. Absolute freedom is the right of the strongest to dominate. Therefore it prolongs the conflicts that profit by injustice. Absolute justice is achieved by the suppression of all contradiction: therefore it destroys freedom.[3] The revolution to achieve justice, through freedom, ends by aligning them against each other. Thus there exists in every revolution, once the class that dominated up to then has been liquidated, a stage in which it gives birth, itself, to a movement of rebellion which indicates its limits and announces its chances of failure. The revolution, first of all, proposes to satisfy the spirit of rebellion which has given rise to it; then it is compelled to deny it, the better to affirm itself. There is, it would seem, an ineradicable opposition between the movement of rebellion and the attainments of revolution.

But these contradictions only exist in the absolute. They suppose a world and a method of thought without meditation. There is, in fact, no conciliation possible between a god who is totally separated from history and a history purged of all transcendence. Their representatives on earth are, indeed, the yogi and the commissar. But the difference between these two types of men is not, as has been stated, the difference between ineffectual purity and expediency. The former chooses only the ineffectiveness of abstention and the second the ineffectiveness of destruction. Because both reject the conciliatory value that rebellion, on the contrary, reveals, they offer us only two kinds of impotence, both equally removed from reality, that of good and that of evil.

If, in fact, to ignore history comes to the same as denying reality, it is still alienating oneself from reality to consider history as a completely self-sufficient absolute. The revolution of the twentieth century believes that it can avoid nihilism and remain faithful to true rebellion, by replacing God by history. In reality, it fortifies the former and betrays the latter. History in its pure form furnishes no value by itself. Therefore one must live by the principles of immediate expediency and keep silent or tell lies. Systematic violence, or imposed silence, calculation or concerted falsehood become the inevitable rule. Purely historical thought is therefore nihilistic: it whole-heartedly accepts the evil of history and in this way is opposed to rebellion. It is useless for it to affirm, in compensation, the absolute rationality of history, for historical reason will never be fulfilled and will never have its full meaning or value until the end of history. In the meanwhile, it is necessary to act, and to act without a moral rule in order that the definitive rule should one day be realized. Cynicism as a political attitude is only logical as a function of absolutist thought; in other words, absolute nihilism on the one hand, absolute rationalism on the other.[4] As for the consequences, there is no

[3] In his *Entretiens sur le bon usage de la liberté* (*Conversations on the Good Use of Freedom*), Jean Grenier lays the foundation for an argument that can be summed up thus: absolute freedom is the destruction of all value; absolute value suppresses all freedom. Likewise Palante: "If there is a single and universal truth, freedom has no reason for existing."

[4] We see again, and this cannot be said too often, that absolute rationalism is not rationalism. The difference between the two is the same as the difference between cynicism and realism. The first drives the second beyond the limits that

difference between the two attitudes. From the moment that they are accepted, the earth becomes a desert.

In reality, the purely historical absolute is not even conceivable. Jaspers's thought, for example, in its essentials, underlines the impossibility of man's grasping totality, since he lives in the midst of this totality. History, as an entirety, could exist only in the eyes of an observer outside it and outside the world. History only exists, in the final analysis, for God. Thus it is impossible to act according to plans embracing the totality of universal history. Any historical enterprise can therefore only be a more or less reasonable or justifiable adventure. It is primarily a risk. In so far as it is a risk it cannot be used to justify any excess or any ruthless and absolutist position.

If, on the other hand, rebellion could found a philosophy it would be a philosophy of limits, of calculated ignorance, and of risk. He who does not know everything cannot kill everything. The rebel, far from making an absolute of history, rejects and disputes it, in the name of a concept that he has of his own nature. He refuses his condition, and his condition to a large extent is historical. Injustice, the transience of time, death—all are manifest in history. In spurning them, history itself is spurned. Most certainly the rebel does not deny the history that surrounds him; it is in terms of this that he attempts to affirm himself. But confronted with it, he feels like the artist confronted with reality; he spurns it without escaping from it. He has never succeeded in creating an absolute history. Even though he can participate, by the force of events, in the crime of history, he cannot necessarily legitimate it. Rational crime not only cannot be admitted on the level of rebellion, but also signifies the death of rebellion. To make this evidence more convincing, rational crime exercises itself, in the first place, on rebels whose insurrection contests a history that is henceforth deified.

The mystification peculiar to the mind which claims to be revolutionary today sums up and increases bourgeois mystification. It contrives, by the promise of absolute justice, the acceptance of perpetual injustice, of unlimited compromise, and of indignity. Rebellion itself only aspires to the relative and can only promise an assured dignity coupled with relative justice. It supposes a limit at which the community of man is established. Its universe is the universe of relative values. Instead of saying, with Hegel and Marx, that all is necessary, it only repeats that all is possible and that, at a certain point on the farthest frontier, it is worth making the supreme sacrifice for the sake of the possible. Between God and history, the yogi and the commissar, it opens a difficult path where contradictions may exist and thrive. Let us consider the two contradictions given as an example in this way.

A revolutionary action which wishes to be coherent in terms of its

---

give it meaning and legitimacy. More brutal, it is finally less efficacious. It is violence opposed to force.

origins should be embodied in an active consent to the relative. It would express fidelity to the human condition. Uncompromising as to its means, it would accept an approximation as far as its ends are concerned and, so that the approximation should become more and more accurately defined, it would allow absolute freedom of speech. Thus it would preserve the common existence that justifies its insurrection. In particular, it would preserve as an absolute law the permanent possibility of self-expression. This defines a particular line of conduct in regard to justice and freedom. There is no justice in society without natural or civil rights as its basis. There are no rights without expression of those rights. If the rights are expressed without hesitation it is more than probable that, sooner or later, the justice they postulate will come to the world. To conquer existence, we must start from the small amount of existence we find in ourselves and not deny it from the very beginning. To silence the law until justice is established is to silence it forever since it will have no more occasion to speak if justice reigns forever. Once more, we thus confide justice into the keeping of those who alone have the ability to make themselves heard—those in power. For centuries, justice and existence as dispensed by those in power have been considered a favor. To kill freedom in order to establish the reign of justice comes to the same as resuscitating the idea of grace without divine intercession and of restoring by a mystifying reaction the mystic body in its basest elements. Even when justice is not realized, freedom preserves the power to protest and guarantees human communication. Justice in a silent world, justice enslaved and mute, destroys mutual complicity and finally can no longer be justice. The revolution of the twentieth century has arbitrarily separated, for over-ambitious ends of conquest, two inseparable ideas. Absolute freedom mocks at justice. Absolute justice denies freedom. To be fruitful, the two ideas must find their limits in each other. No man considers that his condition is free if it is not at the same time just, nor just unless it is free. Freedom, precisely, cannot even be imagined without the power of saying clearly what is just and what is unjust, of claiming all existence in the name of a small part of existence which refuses to die. Finally there is a justice, though a very different kind of justice, in restoring freedom, which is the only imperishable value of history. Men are never really willing to die except for the sake of freedom: therefore they do not believe in dying completely.

The same reasoning can be applied to violence. Absolute non-violence is the negative basis of slavery and its acts of violence; systematic violence positively destroys the living community and the existence we receive from it. To be fruitful, these two ideas must establish final limits. In history, considered as an absolute, violence finds itself legitimized; as a relative risk, it is the cause of a rupture in communication. It must therefore preserve, for the rebel, its provisional character of effraction and must always be bound, if it cannot be avoided, to a personal responsibility and to an immediate risk. Systematic violence is part of the order of things; in a certain sense, this is consolatory. *Führerprinzip* or historical Reason, whatever order may establish it, it reigns over the universe of things, not the universe of men. Just as the rebel considers murder as the limit that he must, if he is so inclined, consecrate by his own death, so violence can only be an extreme limit which combats another form of violence, as, for example, in the case of an insurrection. If an excess of injustice renders the latter inevitable, the rebel rejects violence in advance, in the service of a doctrine or a reason of State. Every historical crisis, for example, terminates in institutions. If we have no control over the crisis itself, which is pure hazard, we do have control over the institutions, since we can define them, choose the ones for which we will fight, and thus bend our efforts toward their establishment. Authentic arts of rebellion will only consent to take up arms for institutions that limit violence, not for those which codify it. A revolution is not worth dying for unless it assures the immediate suppression of the death penalty; not worth going to prison for unless it refuses in advance to pass sentence without fixed terms. If rebel violence employs itself in the establishment of these institutions, announcing its aims as often as it can, it is the only way in which it can be really provisional. When the end is absolute, historically speaking, and when it is believed certain of realization, it is possible to go so far as to sacrifice others. When it is not, only oneself can be sacrificed, in the hazards of a struggle for the common dignity of man. Does the end justify the means? That is possible. But what will justify the end? To that question, which historical thought leaves pending, rebellion replies: the means.

What does such an attitude signify in politics? And, first of all, is it efficacious? We must answer without hesitation that it is the only attitude that is efficacious today. There are two sorts of efficacity: that of typhoons and that of sap. Historical absolutism is not efficacious, it is efficient; it has seized and kept power. Once it is in possession of power, it destroys the only creative reality. Uncompromising and limited action, springing from rebellion, upholds this reality and only tries to extend it farther and farther. It is not said that this action cannot conquer. It is said that it runs the risk of not conquering and of dying. But either revolution will take this risk or it will confess that it is only the undertaking of a new set of masters, punishable by the same scorn. A revolution that is separated from honor betrays its origins that belong to the reign of honor. Its choice, in any case, is limited to material expediency and final annihilation, or to risks and hence to creation. The revolutionaries of the past went ahead as fast as they could and their optimism was complete. But today the revolutionary spirit has grown in knowledge and clear-sightedness; it has behind it a hundred and fifty years of experience. Moreover, the revolution has lost its illusions of being a public holiday. It is, entirely on its own, a prodigious and calculated enterprise, which embraces the entire universe. It knows, even though it does not always say so, that it will be world-wide or that it will not be at all. Its chances are balanced against the risk of a universal war, which, even in the event of victory, will only present it with an Empire of ruins. It can remain faithful to its nihilism, and incarnate in the charnel houses the ultimate reason of history. Then it will be necessary to renounce everything except the silent music that will again transfigure the terrestrial hell. But the revolutionary spirit in Europe can also, for the first and last time, reflect upon its principles, ask itself what the deviation is which leads it into terror and into war, and rediscover with the reasons for its rebellion, its faith in itself.

Moderation and excess

The errors of contemporary revolution are first of all explained by the ignorance or systematic misconception of that limit which seems inseparable from human nature and which rebellion reveals. Nihilist thought, because it neglects this frontier, ends by precipitating itself into a uniformly accelerated movement. Nothing any longer checks it in its course and it reaches the point of justifying total destruction or unlimited conquest. We now know, at the end of this long inquiry into rebellion and nihilism, that rebellion with no other limits but historical expediency signifies unlimited slavery. To escape this fate, the revolutionary mind, if it wants to remain alive, must therefore return again to the sources of rebellion and draw its inspiration from the only system of thought which is faithful to its origins: thought that recognizes limits. If the limit discovered by rebellion transfigures everything, if every thought, every action that goes beyond a certain point negates itself, there is, in fact, a measure by which to judge events and men. In history, as in psychology, rebellion is an irregular pendulum, which swings in an erratic arc because it is looking for its most perfect and profound rhythm. But its irregularity is not total: it functions around a pivot. Rebellion, at the same time that it suggests a nature common to all men, brings to light the measure and the limit which are the very principle of this nature.

Every reflection today, whether nihilist or positivist, gives birth, sometimes without knowing it, to standards that science itself confirms. The quantum theory, relativity, the uncertainty of interrelationships, define a world that has no definable reality except on the scale of average greatness, which is our own. The ideologies which guide our world were born in the time of absolute scientific discoveries. Our real knowledge, on the other hand, only justifies a system of thought based on relative discoveries. "Intelligence," says Lazare Bickel, "is our faculty for not developing what we think to the very end, so that we can still believe in reality." Approximative thought is the only creator of reality.[5]

The very forces of matter, in their blind advance, impose their own limits. That is why it is useless to want to reverse the advance of technology. The age of the spinning-wheel is over and the dream of a civilization of artisans is vain. The machine is bad only in the way that it is now employed. Its benefits must be accepted even if its ravages are rejected. The truck, driven day and night, does not humiliate its driver, who knows it inside out and treats it with affection and efficiency. The real and inhuman excess lies in the division of labor. But by dint of this excess, a day comes when a machine capable of a hundred operations, operated by one man, creates one sole object. This man, on a different scale, will have partially rediscovered the power of creation which he possessed in the days of the artisan. The anonymous producer then more nearly approaches the creator. It is not certain, naturally, that industrial excess will immediately embark on this path. But it already demonstrates, by the way it functions, the necessity for moderation and gives rise to reflections on the proper way to organize this moderation. Either this value of limitation will be realized, or contemporary excesses will only find their principle and peace in universal destruction.

This law of moderation equally well extends to all the contradictions of rebellious thought. The real is not entirely rational, nor is the rational entirely real. As we have seen in regard to surrealism, the desire for unity not only demands that everything should be rational. It also wishes that the irrational should not be sacrificed. One cannot say that nothing has any meaning, because in doing so one affirms a value sanctified by an opinion; nor that everything has a meaning, because the word everything has no meaning for us. The irrational imposes limits on the rational, which, in its turn, gives it its moderation. Something has a meaning, finally, which we must obtain from meaninglessness. In the same way, it cannot be said that existence takes place only on the level of essence. Where could one perceive essence except on the level of existence and evolution? But nor can it be said that being is only existence. Something that is always in the process of development could not exist—there must be a beginning. Being can only prove itself in development, and development is nothing without being. The world is not in a condition of pure stability; nor is it only movement. It is both movement and stability. The historical dialectic, for example, is not in continuous pursuit of an unknown value. It revolves around the limit, which is its prime value. Heraclitus, the discoverer of the constant change of things, nevertheless set a limit to this perpetual process. This

[5] Science today betrays its origins and denies its own acquisitions in allowing itself to be put to the service of State terrorism and the desire for power. Its punishment and its degradation lie in only being able to produce, in an abstract world, the means of destruction and enslavement. But when the limit is reached, science will perhaps serve the individual rebellion. This terrible necessity will mark the decisive turning-point.

limit was symbolized by Nemesis, the goddess of moderation and the implacable enemy of the immoderate. A process of thought which wanted to take into account the contemporary contradictions of rebellion should seek its inspiration from this goddess.

As for the moral contradictions, they too begin to become soluble in the light of this conciliatory value. Virtue cannot separate itself from reality without becoming a principle of evil. Nor can it identify itself completely with reality without denying itself. The moral value brought to light by rebellion, finally, is no farther above life and history than history and life are above it. In actual truth, it assumes no reality in history until man gives his life for it or dedicates himself entirely to it. Jacobin and bourgeois civilization presumes that values are above history, and its formal virtues then lay the foundation of a repugnant form of mystification. The revolution of the twentieth century decrees that values are intermingled with the movement of history and that their historical foundations justify a new form of mystification. Moderation, confronted with this irregularity, teaches us that at least one part of realism is necessary to every ethic: pure and unadulterated virtue is homicidal. And one part of ethics is necessary to all realism: cynicism is homicidal. That is why humanitarian cant has no more basis than cynical provocation. Finally, man is not entirely to blame; it was not he who started history; nor is he entirely innocent, since he continues it. Those who go beyond this limit and affirm his total innocence end in the insanity of definitive culpability. Rebellion, on the contrary, sets us on the path of calculated culpability. Its sole but invincible hope is incarnated, in the final analysis, in innocent murderers.

At this limit, the "We are" paradoxically defines a new form of individualism. "We are" in terms of history, and history must reckon with this "We are," which must in its turn keep its place in history. I have need of others who have need of me and of each other. Every collective action, every form of society, supposes a discipline, and the individual, without this discipline, is only a stranger, bowed down under the weight of an inimical collectivity. But society and discipline lose their direction if they deny the "We are." I alone, in one sense, support the common dignity that I cannot allow either myself or others to debase. This individualism is in no sense pleasure; it is perpetual struggle, and, sometimes, unparalleled joy when it reaches the heights of proud compassion.

Thought at the meridian

As for knowing if such an attitude can find political expression in the contemporary world, it is easy to evoke—and this is only an example—what is traditionally called revolutionary trade-unionism. Cannot it be said that even this trade-unionism is ineffectual? The answer is simple: it is this movement alone that, in one century, is responsible for the enormously improved condition of the workers from the sixteen-hour day to the forty-hour week. The ideological Empire has turned socialism back on its tracks and destroyed the greater part of the conquests of trade-unionism. It is because trade-unionism started from a concrete basis, the basis of professional employment (which is to the economic order what the commune is to the political order), the living cell on which the organism builds itself, while the Caesarian revolution starts from doctrine and forcibly introduces reality into it. Trade-unionism, like the commune, is the negation, to the benefit of reality, of bureaucratic and abstract centralism.[6] The revolution of the twentieth century, on the contrary, claims to base itself on economics, but is primarily political and ideological. It cannot, by its very function, avoid terror and violence done to the real. Despite its pretensions, it begins in the absolute and attempts to mold reality. Rebellion, inversely, relies on reality to assist it in its perpetual struggle for truth. The former tries to realize itself from top to bottom, the latter from bottom to top. Far from being a form of romanticism, rebellion, on the contrary, takes the part of true realism. If it wants a revolution, it wants it on behalf of life, not in defiance of it. That is why it relies primarily on the most concrete realities—on occupation, on the village, where the living heart of things and of men is to be found. Politics, to satisfy the demands of rebellion, must submit to the eternal verities. Finally, when it causes history to advance and alleviates the sufferings of mankind, it does so without terror, if not without violence, and in the most dissimilar political conditions.[7]

But this example goes farther than it seems. On the very day when the Caesarian revolution triumphed over the syndicalist and libertarian spirit, revolutionary thought lost, in itself, a counterpoise of which it cannot, without decaying, deprive itself. This counterpoise, this spirit which takes the measure of life, is the same that animates the long tradition that can be called solitary thought, in which, since the time of the Greeks, nature has always been weighed against evolution. The history of the First International, when German Socialism ceaselessly fought against the libertarian thought of the French, the Spanish, and the Italians, is the history of the struggle of German ideology against the Mediterranean mind.[8] The commune against the State, concrete society

[6] Tolain, the future Communard, wrote: "Human beings emancipate themselves only on the basis of natural groups."

[7] Scandinavian societies today, to give only one example, demonstrate how artificial and destructive are purely political opposites. The most fruitful form of trade-unionism is reconciled with constitutional monarchy and achieves an approximation of a just society. The first preoccupation of the historical and natural State has been, on the contrary, to crush forever the professional nucleus and communal autonomy.

[8] See Marx's letter to Engels (July 20, 1870) hoping for the victory of Prussia over France: "The preponderance of the German proletariat over the French proletariat would be at the same time the preponderance of our theory over Proudhon's.

against absolutist society, deliberate freedom against rational tyranny, finally altruistic individualism against the colonization of the masses, are, then, the contradictions that express once again the endless opposition of moderation to excess which has animated the history of the Occident since the time of the ancient world. The profound conflict of this century is perhaps not so much between the German ideologies of history and Christian political concepts, which in a certain way are accomplices, as between German dreams and Mediterranean traditions, between the violence of eternal adolescence and virile strength, between nostalgia, rendered more acute by knowledge and by books and courage reinforced and enlightened by the experience of life—in other words, between history and nature. But German ideology, in this sense, has come into an inheritance. It consummates twenty centuries of abortive struggle against nature, first in the name of a historic god and then of a deified history. Christianity, no doubt, was only able to conquer its catholicity by assimilating as much as it could of Greek thought. But when the Church dissipated its Mediterranean heritage, it placed the emphasis on history to the detriment of nature, caused the Gothic to triumph over the romance, and, destroying a limit in itself, has made increasing claims to temporal power and historical dynamism. When nature ceases to be an object of contemplation and admiration, it can then be nothing more than material for an action that aims at transforming it. These tendencies—and not the concepts of mediation, which would have comprised the real strength of Christianity—are triumphing in modern times, to the detriment of Christianity itself, by an inevitable turn of events. That God should, in fact, be expelled from this historical universe and German ideology be born where action is no longer a process of perfection but pure conquest, is an expression of tyranny.

But historical absolutism, despite its triumphs, has never ceased to come into collision with an irrepressible demand of human nature, of which the Mediterranean, where intelligence is intimately related to the blinding light of the sun, guards the secret. Rebellious thought, that of the commune or of revolutionary trade-unionism, has not ceased to deny this demand in the presence of bourgeois nihilism as well as of Caesarian socialism. Authoritarian thought, by means of three wars and thanks to the physical destruction of a revolutionary elite, has succeeded in submerging this libertarian tradition. But this barren victory is only provisional; the battle still continues. Europe has never been free of this struggle between darkness and light. It has only degraded itself by deserting the struggle and eclipsing day by night. The destruction of this equilibrium is today bearing its bitterest fruits. Deprived of our means of mediation, exiled from natural beauty, we are once again in the world of the Old Testament, crushed between a cruel Pharaoh and an implacable heaven.

In the common condition of misery, the eternal demand is heard again; nature once more takes up the fight against history. Naturally, it is not a question of despising anything, or of exalting one civilization at the expense of another, but of simply saying that it is a thought which the world today cannot do without for very much longer. There is, undoubtedly, in the Russian people something to inspire Europe with the potency of sacrifice, and in America a necessary power of construction. But the youth of the world always find themselves standing on the same shore. Thrown into the unworthy melting-pot of Europe, deprived of beauty and friendship, we Mediterraneans, the proudest of races, live always by the same light. In the depths of the European night, solar thought, the civilization facing two ways awaits its dawn. But it already illuminates the paths of real mastery.

Real mastery consists in refuting the prejudices of the time, initially the deepest and most malignant of them, which would reduce man, after his deliverance from excess, to a barren wisdom. It is very true that excess can be a form of sanctity when it is paid for by the madness of Nietzsche. But is this intoxication of the soul which is exhibited on the scene of our culture always the madness of excess, the folly of attempting the impossible, of which the brand can never be removed from him who has, once at least, abandoned himself to it? Has Prometheus ever had this fanatical or accusing aspect? No, our civilization survives in the complacency of cowardly or malignant minds—a sacrifice to the vanity of aging adolescents. Lucifer also has died with God, and from his ashes has arisen a spiteful demon who does not even understand the object of his venture. In 1950, excess is always a comfort, and sometimes a career. Moderation, on the one hand, is nothing but pure tension. It smiles, no doubt, and our Convulsionists, dedicated to elaborate apocalypses, despise it. But its smile shines brightly at the climax of an interminable effort: it is in itself a supplementary source of strength. Why do these petty-minded Europeans who show us an avaricious face, if they no longer have the strength to smile, claim that their desperate convulsions are examples of superiority?

The real madness of excess dies or creates its own moderation. It does not cause the death of others in order to create an alibi for itself. In its most extreme manifestations, it finds its limit, on which, like Kaliayev, it sacrifices itself if necessary. Moderation is not the opposite of rebellion. Rebellion in itself is moderation, and it demands, defends, and re-creates it throughout history and its eternal disturbances. The very origin of this value guarantees us that it can only be partially destroyed. Moderation, born of rebellion, can only live by rebellion. It is a perpetual conflict, continually created and mastered by the intelligence. It does not triumph either in the impossible or in the abyss. It finds its equilibrium through them. Whatever we may do, excess will always keep its place in the heart of man, in the place where solitude is found. We all carry within us our places of exile, our crimes and our ravages. But our task is not to unleash them on the world; it is to fight them in ourselves and in others. Rebellion, the secular will not to surrender of which Barrès speaks, is still today at the basis of the struggle. Origin of form, source of real life, it keeps us always erect in the savage, formless movement of history.

Beyond nihilism

There does exist for man, therefore, a way of acting and of thinking which is possible on the level of moderation to which he belongs. Every undertaking that is more ambitious than this proves to be contradictory. The absolute is not attained nor, above all, created through history. Politics is not religion, or if it is, then it is nothing but the Inquisition. How would society define an absolute? Perhaps everyone is looking for this absolute on behalf of all. But society and politics only have the responsibility of arranging everyone's affairs so that each will have the leisure and the freedom to pursue this common search. History can then no longer be presented as an object of worship. It is only an opportunity that must be rendered fruitful by a vigilant rebellion.

"Obsession with the harvest and indifference to history," writes René Char admirably, "are the two extremities of my bow." If the duration of history is not synonymous with the duration of the harvest, then history, in effect, is no more than a fleeting and cruel shadow in which man has no more part. He who dedicates himself to this history dedicates himself to nothing and, in his turn, is nothing. But he who dedicates himself to the duration of his life, to the house he builds, to the dignity of mankind, dedicates himself to the earth and reaps from it the harvest that sows its seed and sustains the world again and again. Finally, it is those who know how to rebel, at the appropriate moment, against history who really advance its interests. To rebel against it supposes an interminable tension and the agonized serenity of which René Char also speaks. But the true life is present in the heart of this dichotomy. Life is this dichotomy itself, the mind soaring over volcanoes of light, the madness of justice, the extenuating intransigence of moderation. The words that reverberate for us at the confines of this long adventure of rebellion are not formulas for optimism, for which we have no possible use in the extremities of our unhappiness, but words of courage and intelligence which, on the shores of the eternal seas, even have the qualities of virtue.

No possible form of wisdom today can claim to give more. Rebellion indefatigably confronts evil, from which it can only derive a new impetus. Man can master in himself everything that should be mastered. He should rectify in creation everything that can be rectified. And after he has done so, children will still die unjustly even in a perfect society. Even by his greatest effort man can only propose to diminish arithmetically the sufferings of the world. But the injustice and the suffering of the world will remain and, no matter how limited they are, they will not cease to be an outrage. Dimitri Karamazov's cry of "Why?" will continue to resound; art and rebellion will die only with the last man.

There is an evil, undoubtedly, which men accumulate in their frantic desire for unity. But yet another evil lies at the roots of this inordinate movement. Confronted with this evil, confronted with death, man from the very depths of his soul cries out for justice. Historical Christianity has only replied to this protest against evil by the annunciation of the kingdom and then of eternal life, which demands faith. But suffering exhausts hope and faith and then is left alone and unexplained. The toiling masses, worn out with suffering and death, are masses without God. Our place is henceforth at their side, far from teachers, old or new. Historical Christianity postpones to a point beyond the span of history the cure of evil and murder, which are nevertheless experienced within the span of history. Contemporary materialism also believes that it can answer all questions. But, as a slave to history, it increases the domain of historic murder and at the same time leaves it without any justification, except in the future—which again demands faith. In both cases one must wait, and meanwhile the innocent continue to die. For twenty centuries the sum total of evil has not diminished in the world. No paradise, whether divine or revolutionary, has been realized. An injustice remains inextricably bound to all suffering, even the most deserved in the eyes of men. The long silence of Prometheus before the powers that overwhelmed him still cries out in protest. But Prometheus, meanwhile, has seen men rail and turn against him. Crushed between human evil and destiny, between terror and the arbitrary, all that remains to him is his power to rebel in order to save from murder him who can still be saved, without surrendering to the arrogance of blasphemy.

Then we understand that rebellion cannot exist without a strange form of love. Those who find no rest in God or in history are condemned to live for those who, like themselves, cannot live: in fact, for the humiliated. The most pure form of the movement of rebellion is thus crowned with the heart-rending cry of Karamazov: if all are not saved, what good is the salvation of one only? Thus Catholic prisoners, in the prison cells of Spain, refuse communion today because the priests of the regime have made it obligatory in certain prisons. These lonely witnesses to the crucifixion of innocence also refuse salvation if it must be paid for by injustice and oppression. This insane generosity is the generosity of rebellion, which unhesitatingly gives the strength of its love and without a moment's delay refuses injustice. Its merit lies in making no calculations, distributing everything it possesses to life and to living men. It is thus that it is prodigal in its gifts to men to come. Real generosity toward the future lies in giving all to the present.

Rebellion proves in this way that it is the very movement of life and that it cannot be denied without renouncing life. Its purest outburst, on each occasion, gives birth to existence. Thus it is love and fecundity or it is nothing at all. Revolution without honor, calculated revolution which, in preferring an abstract concept of man to a man of flesh and blood, denies existence as many times as is necessary, puts resentment in the place of love. Immediately rebellion, forgetful of its generous origins, allows itself to be contaminated by resentment; it denies life, dashes toward destruction, and raises up the grimacing cohorts of petty rebels, embryo slaves all of them, who end by offering themselves for sale, today, in all the marketplaces of Europe, to no matter what form of servitude. It is no longer either revolution or rebellion but rancor, malice, and tyranny. Then, when revolution in the name of power and of history becomes a murderous and immoderate mechanism, a new rebellion is consecrated in the name of moderation and of life. We are at that extremity now. At the end of this tunnel of darkness, however, there is inevitably a light, which we already divine, and for which we only have to fight to ensure its coming. All of us, among the ruins, are preparing a renaissance beyond the limits of nihilism. But few of us know it.

Already, in fact, rebellion, without claiming to solve everything, can at least confront its problems. From this moment high noon is borne away on the fast-moving stream of history. Around the devouring flames, shadows writhe in mortal combat for an instant of time and then as suddenly disappear, and the blind, fingering their eyelids, cry out that this is history. The men of Europe, abandoned to the shadows, have turned their backs upon the fixed and radiant point of the present. They forget the present for the future, the fate of humanity for the delusion of power, the misery of the slums for the mirage of the eternal city, ordinary justice for an empty promised land. They despair of personal freedom and dream of a strange freedom of the species; reject solitary death and give the name of immortality to a vast collective agony. They no longer believe in the things that exist in the world and in living man; the secret of Europe is that it no longer loves life. Its blind men entertain the puerile belief that to love one single day of life amounts to justifying whole centuries of oppression. That is why they wanted to efface joy from the world and to postpone it until a much later date. Impatience with limits, the rejection of their double life, despair at being a man, have finally driven them to inhuman excesses. Denying the real grandeur of life, they have had to stake all on their own excellence. For want of something better to do, they deified themselves and their misfortunes began; these gods have had their eyes put out. Kaliayev, and his brothers throughout the entire world, refuse, on the contrary, to be deified in that they refuse the unlimited power to inflict death. They choose, and give us as an example the only original rule of life today: to learn to live and to die, and, in order to be a man, to refuse to be a god.

At this meridian of thought, the rebel thus rejects divinity in order to share in the struggles and destiny of all men. We shall choose Ithaca, the faithful land, frugal and audacious thought, lucid action, and the generosity of the man who understands. In the light, the earth remains our first and our last love. Our brothers are breathing under the same sky as we; justice is a living thing. Now is born that strange joy which helps one live and die, and which we shall never again postpone to a later time. On the sorrowing earth it is the unresting thorn, the bitter brew, the harsh wind off the sea, the old and the new dawn. With this joy, through long struggle, we shall remake the soul of our time, and a Europe which will exclude nothing. Not even that phantom Nietzsche, who for twelve years after his downfall was continually invoked by the West as the blasted image of its loftiest knowledge and its nihilism; nor the prophet of justice without mercy who lies, by mistake, in the unbelievers' plot at Highgate Cemetery; nor the deified mummy of the man of action in his glass coffin; nor any part of what the intelligence and energy of Europe have ceaselessly furnished to the pride of a contemptible period. All may indeed live again, side by side with the martyrs of 1905, but on condition that it is understood that they correct one another, and that a limit, under the sun, shall curb them all. Each tells the other that he is not God; this is the end of romanticism. At this moment, when each of us must fit an arrow to his bow and enter the lists anew, to reconquer, within history and in spite of it, that which he owns already, the thin yield of his fields, the brief love of this earth, at this moment when at last a man is born, it is time to forsake our age and its adolescent furies. The bow bends; the wood complains. At the moment of supreme tension, there will leap into flight an unswerving arrow, a shaft that is inflexible and free.

ABOUT THE EDITORS

HENRY AIKEN was born in Portland, Oregon, and after attending Reed College in Oregon, received his M.A. degree from Stanford and his Ph.D. from Harvard. At present a Professor of Philosophy at Harvard, he has edited a number of books including *Humes' Moral and Political Philosophy, Humes' Dialogues Concerning Natural Religion,* and *The Age of Ideology,* for which he wrote the long introduction.

WILLIAM C. BARRETT was born in New York City, attended C.C.N.Y., and received both his M.A. and Ph.D. from Columbia. At present a Professor of Philosophy at New York University, he has taught at the University of Illinois, Brown University, the University of California, and served as an Instructor for the Naval Air Forces. Professor Barrett is the author of *What Is Existentialism?, Irrational Man,* and the co-editor (with D. T. Suzuki) of *Zen Buddhism.*